Marcel Breuer, Architect

THE CAREER AND THE BUILDINGS

Isabelle Hyman

Marcel Breuer, Architect
THE CAREER AND THE BUILDINGS

HARRY N. ABRAMS, INC., PUBLISHERS

EDITOR
Diana Murphy
DESIGNER
Henk van Assen
PHOTO EDITOR
John K. Crowley

Library of Congress Cataloging-in-Publication Data

Hyman, Isabelle.
    Marcel Breuer, architect: the career and the buildings / Isabelle Hyman.
                p. cm.
    Includes bibliographical references and index.
    ISBN 0-8109-4265-8
    1. Breuer, Marcel, 1902- 2. Architects–United States–Biography.
    3. Modern movement (Architecture)–United States. I. Breuer, Marcel, 1902- II. Title.

NA737.B68 H97 2001
720'.92–dc21
[B]
                                          2001022593

Printed and bound in Hong Kong
10 9 8 7 6 5 4 3 2 1

Harry N. Abrams, Inc.
100 Fifth Avenue
New York, N.Y. 10011
www.abramsbooks.com

Front endsheet:
Breuer photographed by László Moholy-Nagy. 1925
Back endsheet:
Breuer in 1975

PART I
A PROFESSIONAL LIFE

PART II
WORKS (BUILT AND NOT BUILT)

Preface and Acknowledgments

IN 1966, MARCEL BREUER (1902–1981)—an efficient and methodical man who kept everything—donated a large number of his papers and office drawings to Syracuse University "for the students and faculty of the School of Architecture and for researchers and scholars interested in architectural history."[1] He gave Syracuse an additional eighty-one tubes of architectural drawings in 1973. Housed in the Department of Special Collections, Syracuse University Library, this material was barely touched for historical research until shortly before Breuer's death, when Christopher Wilk used it for his *Marcel Breuer: Furniture and Interiors*, published in 1981 in conjunction with an exhibition of the same name at the Museum of Modern Art.[2] Another large donation of Breuer material (including 300 tubes of drawings and 25 transfiles of papers) went to Syracuse in 1987 from the architectural firm of Gatje, Papachristou, Smith, the successor to Marcel Breuer Associates (as the Breuer office, formerly Marcel Breuer and Associates, was known from Breuer's retirement in 1976 until 1987).

Saint John's Abbey Church, Collegeville, Minnesota. 1958–61. Balcony

In 1987, Constance L. Breuer gave to the Archives of American Art, Smithsonian Institution, Washington, D.C., through its regional office in New York City, much of her husband's remaining material, including correspondence, a large file of photographs, and tapes of interviews that she had initiated with friends and colleagues after his death. To the Breuer Papers at the Syracuse University Library, Mrs. Breuer in 1995 and 1999 added dozens of sheets of freehand architectural sketches by Breuer in ink, crayon, and pencil that were not previously known or studied, along with hundreds of original working drawings for much of Breuer's furniture and interior design from 1928 to 1937. The donation made in 1999 also included unpublished drawings for house projects from 1929 and 1930, and correspondence concerning the Deutsche Werkbund contribution to the international exhibition held in Paris in 1930 and sponsored by the Société des artistes décoratifs français. In 1995, Hamilton P. Smith, one of the partners in Marcel Breuer and Associates and later a principal in Gatje, Papachristou, Smith, gave Syracuse University his design presentation books and architectural drawings relating to the buildings and projects that he had participated in during his years in the Breuer office.

The foundation for all Breuer research is now this vast assemblage of drawings, sketches (many still unidentified), plans, correspondence, publications, photographs, job records, contracts, project books, and documents that went to Syracuse and Washington from 1966 to 1999. Source material for Breuer and his work is also in Breuer files at the Bauhaus-Archiv, Berlin, and with the Walter and Ise Gropius documents there; in the Prints and Drawings Collection, with the F. R. S. Yorke material and catalogued independently, at the Royal Institute of British Architects, London; at Harvard University among the Walter Gropius Papers in the Houghton Library, in Gropius's architectural archive in the Busch-Reisinger Museum, and in the papers of the Graduate School of Design in the Harvard University Archives; at the American Institute of Architects, Washington D.C.; and at the Museum of Modern Art, New York. Individual institutional archives at a number of Breuer buildings contain correspondence, internal memorandums, renderings, models, and printed and photographic material not duplicated in Breuer office files in Syracuse and Washington: New York University, New York; Whitney Museum of American Art and, with respect to the Whitney, Landmarks Preservation Commission Records, New York; Saint John's Abbey, Collegeville, Minnesota; Priory of the Annunciation, Bismarck, North Dakota; Cleveland Museum of Art, Cleveland, Ohio; Grosse Pointe Public Library, Grosse Pointe, Michigan; Bureau of Reclamation, Grand Coulee Project Office, Grand Coulee, Washington. Relating to Breuer's design for a memorial to Franklin Delano Roosevelt, there are documents in the archives of the Commission of Fine Arts and in the files of the National Capital Planning Commission, Washington, D.C. Material pertaining to Breuer can be found in the municipal archives of cities where he worked, such as Boston, and in individual collections in the United States and Canada, such as in the papers of Herbert Bayer, Naum Gabo, Douglas Haskell, Lewis Mumford, and Constantino Nivola, to cite only a few.

In 1990, there appeared the first systematic, scholarly study of Breuer's earlier architecture and his process of design—Joachim Driller's "Marcel Breuer: Das architektonische Frühwerk bis 1950"—a dissertation based on a meticulous critical examination and analysis of the drawings and documents deposited in Syracuse and Washington through the end of the 1980s, on interviews, and on additional archival material, including drawings from the English partnership projects of Breuer & Yorke now at the RIBA and published by Driller for the first time.[3] Driller also consulted a collection of drawings of the Doldertal apartment houses in the private collection of architect Alfred Roth in Zürich and unpublished Breuer correspondence in the Sigfried Giedion archives in Zürich. Driller followed this in 1998 with his more specialized and equally invaluable study of the full corpus of Breuer's residential work: *Marcel Breuer: Die Wohnhäuser, 1923–1973*, translated as *Breuer Houses* in 2000.[4]

In his long, rich life, Breuer (who was known as Lajkó) had partners, associates, friends, clients, colleagues, draftsmen employed in his offices, and students all over the world. Many still have vivid memories of knowing him and working with him; relatives and descendants of others no doubt are in possession of letters, notes, and perhaps sketches and other mementos. With the abundance of sources and documents now available for research, there will be future books on the work of Marcel Breuer and they will, inevitably, close the gaps. One of the principal gaps—the subject of Breuer and architectural structure—is beyond the reach of this book and calls for a specialized technological study. Indeed, in the case of many Breuer buildings, most saliently the hyperbolic paraboloid of St. Francis de Sales Church in Muskegon, Michigan, the structure is the architecture.

The nature and extent of the source material dictated the format of this book because of the new information it provided about the course of Breuer's career as architect as well as about the works. The outline of that career is familiar; Breuer himself set it down for biographical encyclopedia entries, exhibition catalogues, press releases, and interviews, accompanied by lists of selected examples of his work. The works increased in number, of course, as the decades went by, but they never were compiled into a comprehensive record. And although Breuer's professional history was often recapitulated, it remained little more than the original outline. I therefore divided the text so that in Part I, "A Professional Life," a narrative account of Breuer's architectural career is given, and in Part II, "Works," his buildings (built and not built) are documented, summarized, and arranged according to the type of commission.

During the years I carried out my research I was given assistance at many institutions by many people. In general I have used the titles and affiliations of those who helped me as they existed at the time. Grateful acknowledgment is here made:

To the John Simon Guggenheim Memorial Foundation; the Graham Foundation for Advanced Studies in the Fine Arts; the New York University Research Challenge Fund; and the National Endowment for the Humanities for a travel grant from the Division of Fellowships and Seminars.

To Constance L. Breuer for her permission to use the Marcel Breuer Papers at the Archives of American Art, Smithsonian Institution; for making available unpublished photographs, taped interviews, architectural sketches, and other source material; and for responding to many requests for information.

To two brilliant and irreplaceable scholars of modern architecture missed and mourned by friends and colleagues—Reyner Banham and Richard Pommer—whose support for the validity of a book on Breuer's architecture accounted for my decision to go forward in a new field.

To architect Robert F. Gatje, the friend from whom I first learned of the collection of Breuer material in Syracuse and Washington and who encouraged me to undertake this book. His "total recall" of events and people relevant to his years as associate and partner of Breuer, his willingness to impart and share information, and his own book, *Marcel Breuer: A Memoir*, were essential to this project.[5]

To architects Herbert Beckhard, Tician Papachristou, and Hamilton P. Smith—partners of Breuer along with Robert Gatje—for interviews filled with information about Breuer and the office and about the many architectural projects on which they each worked and to which they made their own design contributions. I am further indebted to Tician Papachristou for his book *Marcel Breuer: New Buildings and Projects*, which I consulted often.[6]

To architect Mario Jossa, partner in the Paris office of MBA (successor to the Breuer firm), who answered my requests for information, and to architect Beat Jordi, formerly in the Breuer office in New York and now practicing in Bern, who gave up working time to accompany me through the convent in Baldegg and kept me informed about Breuer material in European exhibitions.

To Rufus and Leslie Stillman, clients and close friends of Breuer from 1950 until his death, for their hospitality in Litchfield, Connecticut. They made it possible for me to visit the three residences that Breuer built for them in Litchfield in 1950, 1965, and 1973, and they mapped out the sites of the Breuer buildings in and near Litchfield and Torrington that owed their existence to the Stillmans' admiration of Breuer's work. I am further indebted to Rufus Stillman for his own writings on Breuer's architecture and for making available records pertaining to the construction of his houses as well as his correspondence with Breuer.

To David H. Stam, former director of the Syracuse University Library, and the staff at the library and at the Department of Special Collections, especially Kathleen Manwaring, Mark F. Weimer, Carolyn A. Davis, Barbara Ann Opar, Peter Verheyen, David Boda, and their assistants. The help given at Syracuse University Library to researchers and visiting scholars is celebrated among those who use its resources. It was my good fortune there to become the "charge" of Kathleen Manwaring, archives and manuscripts supervisor, whom I think of as chief angel in research heaven and who must be singled out for her exceptional assistance and for her professional and personal hospitality.

To the director, Richard J. Wattenmaker, and the generous, efficient staff at the Archives of American Art, Smithsonian Institution, Washington, D.C., and to former Regional Directors William McNaught and Stephen Polcari. For assistance in the New York office, I am grateful to David Derringer, Nancy Malloy, and the late Dominic Madormo. In Washington, I am greatly indebted to Judith E. Throm, Jean Fitzgerald, Wendy Hurlock, and photographer Lee D. Ewing.

To Magdalena Droste, formerly at the Bauhaus-Archiv Museum für Gestaltung, Berlin; to the staff there, especially Barbara Stolle and Hildegard Bremer; and to Sabine Hartmann, director of the photo archive, for the hospitality of the institution and for their generosity with Bauhaus photographic and archival material.

To Mrs. Winthrop Sargeant for permission to quote from the manuscript draft of the unpublished profile of Breuer written for the New Yorker by her late husband.

To Mrs. Joella Bayer for sending, through Mrs. Breuer, photographs and copies of letters between Breuer and Herbert Bayer.

I also thank Tony Wrenn, American Institute of Architects, Washington, D.C.; Sue A. Kohler, Commission of Fine Arts, Washington, D.C.; Maria L. LaNeve, National Capital Planning Commission, Washington, D.C.; Emilie Norris, Busch-Reisinger Museum, Harvard University; Harvard University Archives and the Houghton Library at Harvard for permission to consult and to quote from their collections; Gerald M. McCue, former dean of the Harvard Graduate School of Design; Mary Daniels, Special Collections librarian, Harvard Graduate School of Design; Nancy M. Cricco and the staff at the New York University Archives; Mathilda McQuaid, Museum of Modern Art, New York; Margaret McMahon, Landmarks Preservation Commission, New York; and the staff of the Prints and Drawings Collection in the RIBA Library in London.

Many of Lajkó's friends, associates, clients, and colleagues in addition to those already mentioned responded to requests for information and for interviews. First and foremost, I am indebted to the late Leonard Currie for material about the Cambridge years and the Gropius-Breuer partnership projects. For sending material and for conversations about Breuer, I am indebted to William W. Landsberg, Harry Seidler, and the late George S. Lewis. I am grateful also to Edward Larrabee Barnes, Jay Fleishman, Robert Geddes, Philip Johnson, Laurie Maurer, Stanley Maurer, Richard Meier, I. M. Pei, Carlton Rochell, Gabriel Sedlis, Carl Stein, Amy Weisser, and Adam Yarinsky.

At Vassar College, where as an undergraduate I watched the construction of the first modern building on campus— Breuer's Ferry Cooperative Dormitory—I was given special help by President Frances D. Fergusson, Professors Nicholas Adams and Elizabeth Daniels, and alumnus Adam Clem. For answering inquiries about specific Breuer works, I thank Dr. Robert Crease of the State University of New York, Stonybrook, for information about Brookhaven; Efrom Fader for information about the Torin factory in Van Nuys, California; Mrs. Jerome Apt, Jr., for information about the Frank House; and New York City Parks Commissioner Henry J. Stern for his help with the Central Park Stables Competition project.

I am grateful to the current and, in some cases, original owners of Breuer houses in this country and in Europe who offered a cordial welcome and overlooked the intrusion on their privacy: Sandra Bishop Ebner; Mr. and Mrs. John Horgan; Mr. and Mrs. Roger Ketron; Walter Rogers and Leslie Lawson; Mr. and Mrs. Jacques Lennon; Professor and Mrs. Marion Levy; the late Dr. William Staehelin and Mrs. Staehelin; Mr. and Mrs. Rufus Stillman; and Mr. and Mrs. Harry Thompson. Institutional hospitality was equally generous, and I am indebted to the sisters at the Priory of the Annunciation in Bismarck, North Dakota; the sisters at the

Convent of Divine Providence, Baldegg, Switzerland; the brothers and lay administrators at Saint John's Abbey, Collegeville, Minnesota, especially Brother Frank Kacmarcik; the staff at the Cleveland Museum of Art; at the church of St. Francis de Sales in Muskegon, Michigan, Reverend H. Louis Stasek; the staff at Grosse Pointe Public Library, Grosse Pointe, Michigan; at Pirelli Armstrong Tire Corporation, New Haven, Connecticut, the public-relations office; at the Bureau of Reclamation, Grand Coulee Project, Grand Coulee, Washington, Craig Sprankle, chief public-affairs officer, and Judy Quill, photo archivist.

I am grateful to Ralph Lieberman for photographs of Breuer buildings made at my request; to Richard Rutkowski and the Division des services généraux at UNESCO, Paris, for permission to photograph; to Stephen W. Feingold for advice regarding the publication of copyrighted material; and to Renate Franciscono, Matthew Johnson, and, especially, Alice Krinsky for assistance with German translation. Thanks are due to Whitney S. Stoddard, professor emeritus at Williams College, for sharing his deep knowledge of Breuer's work; to the students in my graduate seminar on Breuer at Williams, where I was visiting professor in the fall 1991 semester; to Sarah Allaback, Mosette Broderick, Elaine Lustig Cohen, Eugene J. Johnson, Carol Herselle Krinsky, Sarah Bradford Landau, Irving Lavin, James D. Morgan, Irene Pavitt, Robert Rosenblum, Irving Sandler, Lucy Freeman Sandler, Edward Sullivan, Franklin Toker, and Valerie Vago-Laurer. At Harry N. Abrams, Inc., I am grateful to John K. Crowley, Director, Photo and Permissions Department, and especially to Diana Murphy, Senior Editor, for her extraordinary help and guidance.

Finally, I come to The One Person Without Whom. To my husband, Jerome E. Hyman, for his unfailing goodness and wise counsel I am more grateful than I ever can say.

1   *Interiors*, October 1966, 12.

2   Christopher Wilk, *Marcel Breuer: Furniture and Interiors* (New York: Museum of Modern Art, 1981).

3   Joachim Driller, "Marcel Breuer: Das architektonische Frühwerk bis 1950" (Phil. diss., Albert-Ludwigs-Universität, Freiburg, 1990).

4   Joachim Driller, *Marcel Breuer: Die Wohnhäuser, 1923–1973* (Stuttgart: Deutsche Verlags-Anstalt, 1998), and *Breuer Houses*, trans. Mark Cole and Jeremy Verrinder (London: Phaidon Press, 2000).

5   Robert F. Gatje, *Marcel Breuer: A Memoir* (New York: Monacelli Press, 2000).

6   Tician Papachristou, *Marcel Breuer: New Buildings and Projects, 1960–70* (New York: Praeger, 1970).

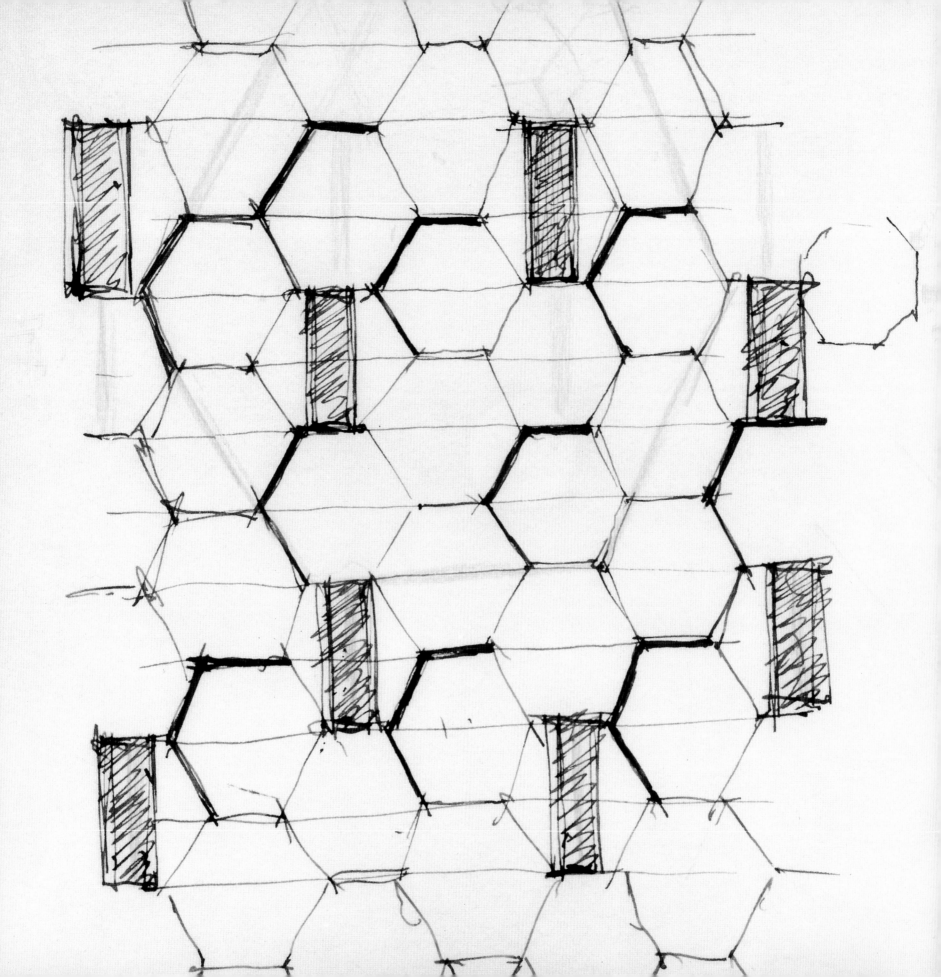

Introduction

De Bijenkorf Department Store,
Rotterdam, the Netherlands.
1955–57. Sketch

IN THE ALMOST SIX DECADES OF A PROFESSIONAL LIFE arrested toward the end only by illness, Marcel Breuer never stopped working. As an architect, he designed and built close to 150 structures on four continents; more than 100 others had been designed, but not built. This does not take into account his furniture, interiors (offices, showrooms, stores, and residences), and industrial designs. In his lifetime, he was heaped with architectural honors and awards, named one of the "form-givers" of the twentieth century, and described as a "monumental figure among modern architects."[1] During his ten years (1937–47) on the faculty in the Department of Architecture of the Graduate School of Design at Harvard, he was an effective and greatly admired teacher.[2] Works by his students became significant monuments of twentieth-century building, as did many of his own. Nevertheless, in the later part of his career and in the years soon after his death, his architecture—both by itself and in its identification as Bauhaus-generated modernism (even though Breuer had long since forged an independent identity and worked hard to dissociate himself from Bauhaus design and the architecture of Walter Gropius)—was subjected to stinging criticism that had begun in the 1960s while his practice was still at full tide. And notwithstanding that he designed few pieces of mass-marketed furniture after 1936,[3] an obituary carried the opinion of the design curator at the Museum of Modern Art (who was hardly alone in thinking this) that "Mr. Breuer will be better remembered for his furniture designs than for his architecture."[4]

Breuer's transgression was to have mastered two skills instead of one. But because his achievement within the sweep of his long career in architecture was uneven in quality, in contrast to the consistent brilliance of the furniture design and its universal approbation, he was assailed by vitiating comparisons with himself. His architecture, it was said, "never lived up to" his furniture.[5] Even his collaboration with other architects, in a profession where such arrangements are often necessary or required, were regarded with suspicion: "As an architect [Breuer] so often appears in collaboration—with F. R. S. Yorke, with Walter Gropius, with [Pier Luigi] Nervi and [Bernard] Zehrfuss—that one can't decide whether his personal contribution amounts to more than honest craftsmanship. [However], nobody can question [his] achievement as a furniture designer," wrote Alan Bowness in a review of Breuer's *Sun and Shadow*.[6] Yet had Breuer not designed furniture, had he produced only the buildings that compose half a century of his work with and without collaboration, he still would have been remembered by posterity—reward for any artist—without having had to be even "better remembered," as predicted in the obituary, for his chairs.

Any consideration of Breuer's career, and of the furniture/architecture issue, must not fail to take into account that Breuer's four years (1920–24) at the Bauhaus in Weimar represented his entire professional education. It was not until after he graduated and the school moved to Dessau (where he became master of the furniture workshop) that there was an architecture department and official instruction in architecture, although some relevant technical courses had been offered in Weimar. He drew well, and during his lifetime made hundreds of freehand architectural sketches and a few measured drawings, but he was never trained in architectural drafting. As for construction and materials, let alone architectural design, he was almost wholly self-taught. His letters reveal that his most profound disappointment with the Bauhaus was the absence of practical experience and an education in architecture. A few students, such as Farkas Molnár, came to the Bauhaus as trained architects from technical institutions. Breuer was the only one who "came in without architecture, went through the Bauhaus, and emerged as an architect without any training."

Although Breuer's original ambition to become a painter or a sculptor was displaced by his discovery of a talent for designing and crafting furniture, he began to direct himself toward architecture within two years of his arrival in Weimar, probably because of the example of Gropius. Breuer, who had known nothing of building, became engaged with Gropius's projects for architecture and urbanism. He developed an interest in working out the structure and design of buildings at the same time that he was working out his modern reformulations of furniture. He began to nurture the idea of a professional future for himself as an architect because in Weimar he perceived that it was possible for a painter or a sculptor, or for the furniture craftsman he had become, to design and construct buildings without undergoing years of training in Germany's Technische Hochschulen, as others had done, without acquiring refined drafting skills and a knowledge of Classicism: "We have no time to be Greeks" was a Bauhaus slogan.[7] Those buildings would be based on modern principles of design and construction that called for standardized types and could be transferred from one medium to another. By 1923, Breuer's experiments in furniture design and his contemporaneous architectural projects had become strongly tied to idioms of modern architecture—pure forms of geometry, interlocking flat-roofed cubes—and to the architectonic attributes of painting and sculpture of the modern movement. Neither then nor later did he deny, or see any reason to deny, his dependence on the kinship of furniture and building design. To the contrary, he used it as an operating strategy throughout his career and he taught it in the classroom: "The Planning of Regions, Towns, Streets, Buildings, and Furniture: Common Elements of Approach" was the title of one in a series of lectures he planned for a design course at Harvard in 1943. Even thirty years later, in a retrospective German-language interview with a television reporter, Breuer described a systematic course of development that went from the study of small elements to larger ones ("von kleineren Teilen zu grösseren Teilen"): "I studied smaller units such as chairs and other furniture. Then I concentrated on individual parts of buildings, such as window construction, doors, flooring, lighting and similar details. I went from furniture to private houses . . . and studying small houses led me to larger buildings."[8]

It is sometimes forgotten, because of the nature and duration of his association with Gropius, that Breuer belonged not to the generation of the founders of modernism, but to the first generation that followed them—"the youngest of the Bauhaus rebels," he was called.[9] He inherited but did not invent the expression of his earliest architecture, which traces its provenance to Gropius, Johannes Itten, Le Corbusier, Constructivism, and de Stijl. Almost twenty years younger than Gropius, Breuer was only nine years old when Gropius in 1911 established the canon of modern industrial architecture with the Fagus Shoe Last Factory in Alfeld. By 1976, on the occasion of his receiving the Grande Médaille d'or from France's Académie d'architecture, Breuer was called "the last living landmark of the Bauhaus international school of architecture"; when he died five years later, he was eulogized as "the last modernist."[10]

Assessments of Breuer's place in the history of modern architecture have ranged widely, with some of the New Theorist criticism of his buildings and designs—beginning with the "bringing down" of modernism in the 1960s[11]—so harsh that it is difficult to avoid a defensive tone in attempting to take a just measure of his accomplishment. As early as 1938, there was Henry-Russell Hitchcock's claim that Breuer's first constructed building, the Harnischmacher House (1932) in Wiesbaden, immediately ranked "as one of the finest modern houses in the world."[12] Reyner Banham described Breuer from the time of his emigration to the United States (1937) to the commission for the UNESCO complex in Paris (1952) as being "almost the favorite [architect] of the progressive establishment."[13] This is borne out by his selection (remembered today by museum insider Peter Blake as less a selection than a process of elimination)[14] in 1948 as architect of the prestigious exhibition house in the garden of the Museum of Modern Art, the first modern house seen by masses of people (more than

70,000). In 1949, Blake's monograph *Marcel Breuer: Architect and Designer* was published by the museum as the catalogue for the house exhibition, with a text and comprehensive illustrations that, together with the 1947 issue of *Nuestra arquitectura* dedicated to Breuer's work, for the first time documented the scope of his contribution to modernism.[15] Reviewing Blake's book, Frederick Gutheim referred to "the great power [Breuer] exerts today, especially over the imaginations of the younger men in architecture."[16] That view is supported by two invitations Breuer received in 1954: Pietro Belluschi asked him to join the architecture faculty at MIT, and Robert McLaughlin, director of the School of Architecture at Princeton University, offered Breuer an appointment as "Professor of Architecture with tenure—our highest faculty rank," proposing that he move his office to Princeton: "The University feels that it is important for members of the School of Architecture to practice."[17] "Our reasons for wanting you here," he went on, "and for our carefully considered feeling of rightness about your being here . . . are many—although really quite simple and clear. We greatly admire your work, and we know how ably you pass on your understanding of architecture to the younger men." When he turned down both proposals, Breuer cited "the very heavy obligations" of his practice.[18] Reflecting on that practice when examining directions in architecture in the United States at midcentury, Hitchcock wrote that "if there be a 'school,' it would be that of Gropius. . . . But the actual work of the Gropiusites, so to call them, derives in fact more from the practice of his former pupil and partner Breuer than from his own."[19]

All through the 1950s, as one of the profession's most respected practitioners, Breuer was in great demand in the United States and in Europe. "Second to Mies, he had the most illustrious and patronized career as a practicing architect in America," observed Frederick Koeper when surveying American architecture of the 1950s.[20] In that period, he built not only his renowned single-family residences but also a diversity of structures that ranged from a department store in Rotterdam (of its north-facing annex Lewis Mumford wrote that "the architect Marcel Breuer has produced one of the best office-building facades I have seen anywhere"[21]) to the United States Embassy in The Hague, the first portions of a vast Benedictine abbey in Minnesota, and, with Nervi and Zehrfuss, the UNESCO complex in Paris. Breuer's only partly facetious view on this was that "a house presents so many problems that the man who can design one successfully can build anything."[22]

The decade ended with the completion of his first New York City structures: the library, classroom, and administration buildings on the Bronx campus of Hunter College. Ada Louise Huxtable described them in 1963 as "novel, daring, and unlike anything the city has built before or since"[23] and in 1966 as buildings that "broke the negative mold" of mediocrity in public architecture.[24] In the mid-1960s, however, as modernism—particularly Bauhaus modernism—along with its founders, true believers, and disciples, was becoming increasingly anathematized, at the second biennial Modern Architecture Symposium (MAS), held at Columbia University in 1964 (its theme was "The Decade 1929–1939"), the acerbic Sibyl Moholy-Nagy opined that "people like Breuer and Mendelsohn and others absolutely collapsed in their architectural imagination once they were no longer on native ground"[25] and that "America looked the other way when Gropius and Breuer built those astonishingly ugly little houses."[26] Also in 1964, as critical theory began its ascent, Breuer and Serge Chermayeff were classified in a lecture given in Cambridge, England, by architect John Meunier (a disciple of Colin Rowe) as "great second-raters" who never reached the "pinnacle" because they "lacked a strong and explicit formal/theoretical position."[27]

Breuer's architecture was caustically dismissed at the Modern Architecture Symposium also by Vincent Scully, who, ignoring the purposeful antimonumentalism of Bauhaus design, saw Breuer as the "victim" of a Bauhaus education.[28] Scully did not mean an education in architecture because, as noted, there had not been much of one at the Bauhaus. He referred to the "pictorial" education that Breuer had received at the school, claiming that as an architect he worked pictorially—with weightless planes, transparency, asymmetry, and nonmonumentality. He described Breuer as an architect whose talent was limited to a "small-scale graphic sensibility" that "made it impossible for him to build a monumental building" and whose work had more in common with that of Paul Klee than that of Le Corbusier. Comparing Breuer's campanile at Saint John's Abbey with Le Corbusier's High Court at Chandigarh, he saw in Breuer's work only small-scale relationships connected to graphic design and furniture design in contrast to the heroic proportions and autonomous structural forces expressed by Le Corbusier. These "deficiencies" Scully attributed to "Bauhaus methods."

The question of scale has always been central to the criticism of Breuer's architecture. Weaknesses in the larger projects have been inevitably linked to the furniture, to "an incomplete transformation of this inheritance from furniture design into architectural scale," as it was expressed by William H. Jordy.[29] The question of scale has also accounted for the major concentration on Breuer as a house architect while the big commissions and multibuilding complexes are less respected. Yet in 1966, Breuer and his partner Hamilton P. Smith produced one of New York City's most esteemed and, indeed, monumental buildings with the Whitney Museum of American Art. In 1960, his vast IBM Research Center (with Robert Gatje) at La Gaude, near Nice, was designed with the weight and density that give Egyptian architecture its great power, and it was sited against the region's rocky peaks (*baous*) in a manner reminiscent of that of the Middle Kingdom mortuary temples at Deir el-Bahari. Breuer had a deep interest in the monumental architecture of Egypt and its formal constructs—the ramps, the battered walls of the pylons, the flat-topped inclines of the low-lying mastabas, the trapezoidal masses of heavy stone, and the serial repetition of individual elements, all of which found their way into his work. It is understandable that in 1964 he would agree to write a short preface entitled "The Contemporary Aspect of Pharaonic Architecture" for Jean Louis de Cenival's book on the architecture of Egypt.[30] Interviewed in France in 1974 and speaking of the great sculptural possibilities of reinforced concrete, Breuer used as an example his colossally scaled power plant at the Grand Coulee Dam, with, as he described them, "dimensions truly Egyptian."[31]

Throughout the 1960s, the Breuer office was busier and more productive than it ever had been, even surviving a serious and highly publicized New York urbanistic and design polemic generated by an ill-advised project to erect a fifty-five-story tower above Grand Central Terminal. ("Hitler's revenge" the project was called by Sibyl Moholy-Nagy, as she excoriated Breuer and the Bauhaus for what she took to be the consequences of exiled German functionalist ideology.[32]) It was a decade in which Breuer, who had become a master of concrete technology, was commissioned to carry out challenging projects of both small and large (often very large) scale for private, corporate, governmental, and institutional patrons all over the world, patrons who valued the famed efficiency of his operation and for whom his particular brand of modernism was far from dead. (Mumford had sounded the death knell in 1960 when he declared the recently completed UNESCO complex a "museum of the antiquities of modern art and architecture."[33]) Breuer's built work in this period included the not widely known power plant and forebay dam at Grand Coulee, Washington (with Smith); the hyperbolic paraboloid church of St. Francis de Sales in Muskegon, Michigan (with Herbert Beckhard); and two towns in France (with Gatje): one a ski resort in Flaine, near Chamonix, and the other a low-income satellite-city development near Bayonne. But two decades later and within five years after Breuer's death, in an architectural climate where the precepts he had upheld all his professional life had been challenged and effectively repudiated by architects, theorists, critics, and historians of revisionist persuasion, the Whitney Museum, for example, was threatened with visual, if not actual physical, extinction by Michael Graves's designs (1985–88) for the museum's expansion. In those years of the eclipse of Breuer's reputation in the wake of postmodernism, architects such as Hugh Newell Jacobsen, referring to Breuer's committed noncontextualism, could describe the Whitney as "basically outrageous" ("those dear little row houses on either side of the museum have a much greater sense of humanity") and Breuer as "arrogant in assuming that history was bad, history was out, and modern architecture was absolutely correct."[34]

Also in the mid-1980s, identified as he was with the Bauhaus-based modernist canon that he and Gropius had taught at Harvard, Breuer had to take the heat, even posthumously, not only for his own buildings but also for the prevailing censorious view of the "Bauhaus/Harvard ethos," for the "failure of the Bauhaus legacy" in America as it was codified by such critics as Klaus Herdeg, an architect and a professor at Columbia University.[35] The Graduate School of Design at Harvard was now regarded as the place that had given architects the equivalent of Bauhaus training after the Bauhaus proper ceased to exist. The Museum of Modern Art, in its approbation of the buildings of GSD graduates, was considered an instrument of Bauhaus propaganda. Gropius and Breuer as teachers were held responsible for what Herdeg regarded as the ugly modernist buildings designed by their students (as well as themselves) that "deformed" American architecture and were "injurious" to their physical context. Breuer as architect was censured by Herdeg for espousing noncontextualism, for adopting a stultifying programmatic functionalism, for lacking wit and humor, for not being Le Corbusier, and, inevitably, for having produced buildings (specifically his Museum of Modern Art exhibition house) whose elements only "pose as the architectural idea itself while in reality they assume . . . the importance of furniture . . . no more than accessories to the architectural idea."[36]

Herdeg compared Breuer's MoMA house with Le Corbusier's Errazuris House (1930) because both were organized beneath the so-called butterfly-roof (which Breuer, tellingly, also called "the inverted Colonial"[37]). He was hardly wrong in pointing out the superior spatial and formal integration and coherence of the Le Corbusier house, in contrast to a disunity in the Breuer design that came from an emphasis on its programmatic function, on the "diagram" that determined the allotments of space and defined the formal envelope. "Poetic allusions" in Le Corbusier's design transcended mere functionalism, Herdeg claimed.[38] Conscious poetic allusion was certainly the last thing on Breuer's mind; from his Bauhaus days through the end of his career, he was committed to a *sachlich* architecture determined more than anything else by the expression of use. The work of Breuer and his Harvard students was now to be measured by standards relating to signification, allusion, intellectualism, formalism, and similar historically based elements that he had labored for decades to purge from architecture.

Regardless, during the half century when European modernism evolved into what became the prevailing architectural idiom worldwide, Breuer's individual manner appealed to enough discerning and important clients to generate a huge and influential body of work. For a relatively small practitioner (he and his partners employed no more than about fifty draftsmen at the height of their activity[39]), his architectural output was prodigious and diverse, although much of it, in out-of-the-way places, is sought out chiefly by enthusiasts. Indeed, Breuer was convinced that a lot of his work, often his best work, suffered from a lack of "visibility" and critical attention because of its distance from cultural centers. Referring to Saint John's Abbey and to the church of St. Francis de Sales, he said that the abbey is "way out in Minnesota, and Muskegon is not the center of the world. If [the buildings] were in New York, or Paris, or Washington or somewhere in a more frequented place, the attention would be much greater."[40]

Attention to his buildings in New York, however, would not always be complimentary, and the city played a more critical role in Breuer's career than he might have predicted. The Whitney Museum was subjected to intense scrutiny, of course, when it was completed in 1966, controversial in design—"one of the boldest forms devised in this century," claims Douglas Davis in *The Museum Transformed*[41]—and in the interpretation of its relation to its site. But it was more admired than abhorred and led to Breuer's commissions for a new wing at the Cleveland Museum of Art, the Atlanta Central Library, and the (ultimately rejected) design for a memorial to Franklin Delano Roosevelt in Washington, D.C. Twenty years later, however, defending the Whitney against Graves's "encroachment" was a discomfort for many New York City supporters of Breuer, not because the building had become an icon of the modernist-postmodernist debate, but because Breuer had himself attempted to obliterate an earlier civic masterpiece by topping it with a massive new building. "Pelion on Ossa" was only one of many disparaging descriptions of his design for 175 Park Avenue—towering above, in the first plan, and then replacing, in the second one, the Beaux-Arts facade of Grand Central Terminal. Breuer weathered the storm, but it marked a turning point in his career. If it was the exhibition house of 1949 at the Museum of Modern Art that can be said to have first put Breuer's architecture in the favorable opinion of the general public, it was his Grand Central tower project of 1968 that began to reverse that opinion.

Generally speaking, Breuer's architecture, especially his work after the mid-1950s, has been passed over in art-historical studies, a reflection of the view that "after the war his work lost its sense of direction."[42] While it was published widely in the professional press, trade journals, consumer magazines, illustrated books with limited or controlled texts, and sometimes in surveys of modern architecture, it was given little in the way of serious critical attention other than in theses, dissertations, and exhibition catalogues when the partnership projects with Gropius were being discussed.[43] An important exception was the exploration of Breuer's earlier work by Jordy, published in 1972, that hinged on his analysis of the Ferry Cooperative Dormitory at Vassar College, a building that Jordy held in high regard but identified, nevertheless, with Breuer's furniture.[44] This followed Jordy's 1969 essay about the influence of Gropius, Mies, and Breuer, as former teachers at the Bauhaus, on architecture and design in the United States.[45] Before Jordy, only Blake's *Marcel Breuer: Architect and Designer* (1949) and Giulio Carlo Argan's *Marcel Breuer: Disegno industriale e architettura* (1957)—both slim volumes and now long outdated—and Whitney S. Stoddard's *Adventure in Architecture: Building the New Saint John's* (1958) provided any significant interpretive examination of Breuer as architect.[46] The situation was finally rectified in 1990 with Joachim Driller's "Marcel Breuer: Das architektonische Frühwerk bis 1950," an exhaustive study of the work up to 1950, and with his *Marcel Breuer: Die Wohnhäuser* (1998), which accounts for the residential work through 1973—both of which have permanently reshaped the discussion of Breuer's architecture.[47]

The early architecture of Breuer—roughly defined as the work of 1922 to 1952—and the residential architecture are one thing; the full Breuer career is another. He practiced through the mid-1970s and designed so many buildings overall that his productivity was a surprise even to followers and longtime friends and colleagues: "Although I thought I was pretty well aware of what you have been doing [in the past decade] I was unprepared for the amount of work," wrote Richard Stein to Breuer in 1970, after he had seen Tician Papachristou's *Marcel Breuer: New Buildings and Projects, 1960–70*.[48] And in 1963, after looking through *Marcel Breuer: Buildings and Projects, 1921–1961*, the earlier survey volume edited by Cranston Jones, Gropius had written to him that "many of your buildings were still unknown to me."[49] With such an abundant output, Breuer can indeed be faulted for too often reverting to formulaic devices recycled and reinvented from his own work and from proto-types of European modernism ("All my life I have been wonder-ing how somebody can be a genius from morning to evening," he once wrote[50]). Still, he remained committed, bold, and experimental through his final years of practice. The same can-not be said of many of Breuer's colleagues who had been at the top of the modernist hierarchy in the mid-twentieth century.

The buildings that Breuer designed and built during an era of exceptional architectural activity the world over are not only of a quantity but also of a diversity of structure, material, form, and purpose he could not have imagined at the outset of his life as a professional architect. To present a history of that pro-fessional life and a survey of that body of work seemed an undertaking appropriate to commemorate the centenary, in 2002, of his birth and to mark the passing of the century whose culture and physical environment Breuer helped shape.

List of Abbreviations

AAA	Marcel Breuer Papers, Archives of American Art, Smithsonian Institution, Washington, D.C.
AIA	American Institute of Architects
BHA	Bauhaus-Archiv, Berlin
BRM	Busch-Reisinger Museum, Harvard University, Cambridge, Mass.
CLB	Constance L. Breuer
GSD	Graduate School of Design, Harvard University, Cambridge, Mass.
HL	Walter Gropius Papers (Breuer Letters): bMS Ger 208 (518), (519), and (1826), Houghton Library, Harvard University, Cambridge, Mass. Publication by permission of the Houghton Library
HUA	Harvard University Archives, Cambridge, Mass. Publication courtesy of the Harvard University Archives
HUAL	Frances Loeb Library, Graduate School of Design, Harvard University, Cambridge, Mass.
HUL	Harvard University Library, Cambridge, Mass.
IGD/E	Ise Gropius Diaries, English translation, Microfilm 2393, AAA
MoMA	Museum of Modern Art, New York
RIBA	Royal Institute of British Architects, London
SUL	Marcel Breuer Papers, Department of Special Collections, Syracuse University Library, Syracuse, New York. Numbers are those of the boxes containing Breuer material

Much of the Breuer correspondence is duplicated in several places. Citations in the notes refer to the location at which the letter was consulted by the author. Letters not written in English appear in translation.

1 *Time*, July 2, 1956, 51; see also Cranston Jones, ed., *Form Givers at Mid-Century* [exhibition catalogue] (New York, 1959), 36–39.

2 Breuer joined the faculty at Harvard in the academic year 1937–38 as research associate; on January 1, 1939, he was named associate professor of architecture, an appointment that was renewed until he resigned at the end of 1947. During 1946 and 1947 he was on leave of absence and did not return to teaching.

3 This is in contrast to the unique pieces—residential and institutional furniture such as tables, chairs, desks, and built-in cabinets, and church furniture such as altars, lecterns, and fonts—made for individual clients throughout his career. For the best accounts of Breuer's furniture, see Christopher Wilk, *Marcel Breuer: Furniture and Interiors* (New York: Museum of Modern Art, 1981), and Magdalena Droste and Manfred Ludewig, *Marcel Breuer Design* (Cologne: Taschen, 1992).

4 "Although Mr. Breuer might not have agreed, [Stewart] Johnson said he believes Mr. Breuer will be better remembered for his furniture designs than for his architecture" (Sarah Booth Conroy, "Marcel Breuer Obituary," *Washington Post*, July 3, 1981, B12). Conroy also quotes Christopher Wilk, who along with Johnson worked for three years with Breuer preparing the 1981 exhibition of his furniture at the Museum of Modern Art: "He had rather talk about his latest building than his furniture of 56 odd years ago."

5 Anonymous reviewer of the proposal for this book.

6 Marcel Breuer, *Marcel Breuer: Sun and Shadow: The Philosophy of an Architect*, ed. Peter Blake (New York: Dodd, Mead, 1955); Alan Bowness, "Line-Men and Mass-Men," *New Statesman and Nation*, July 28, 1956, 113. F. R. S. Yorke quickly came to Breuer's defense against this "unfair assessment," writing that "Breuer's own very personal approach towards building has been consistent through all his collaborations, and his associates have left him unscathed . . . he has had more influence on them than they on him" (Letter to the Editor, *New Statesman and Nation*, August 11, 1956, 162).

7 Winthrop Sargeant, "Profile of Marcel Breuer" (manuscript draft prepared for the *New Yorker*, ca. 1971–72).

8 Marcel Breuer, interview with Istvan Gardes, n.d. ["im jahre 1972 oder 1973"], transcript, Speeches and Writings, AAA.

9 Clipping, review of *Marcel Breuer: Buildings and Projects, 1921–1961*, edited by Cranston Jones, *Times* (London), n.d. [ca. 1963], AAA.

10 *Newsweek*, August 17, 1981, 70.

11 Charles A. Jencks, *Post-Modernism: The New Classicism in Art and Architecture* (New York: Rizzoli, 1987), 11–29.

12 Henry-Russell Hitchcock, "Marcel Breuer and the American Tradition in Architecture" [essay and exhibition catalogue, Harvard University, Graduate School of Design, June–September 1938] (GSD, Cambridge, Mass., 1938, mimeographed), 11, HUAL. Hitchcock's view of the status of the Harnischmacher House in relation to that of other modern houses of the period is challenged by Joachim Driller, *Breuer Houses*, trans. Mark Cole and Jeremy Verrinder (London: Phaidon Press, 2000), esp. 22–34.

13 Reyner Banham, *Age of the Masters: A Personal View of Modern Architecture*, rev. ed. (Tonbridge: Whitefriars Press, 1975), 26.

14 Peter Blake, *No Place Like Utopia: Modern Architecture and the Company We Kept* (New York: Knopf, 1993), 138.

15 Peter Blake, *Marcel Breuer: Architect and Designer* (New York: Museum of Modern Art, 1949); *Nuestra arquitectura* [special double issue], September–November 1947.

16 Frederick Gutheim, review of *Marcel Breuer: Architect and Designer*, by Peter Blake, *Architectural Record*, September 1949, 28. Gutheim, furthermore, saw Breuer "essentially as an artist rather than a theorist." In a memorial tribute, architect Ulrich Franzen said that "among the Bauhaus teachers at Harvard, Breuer was the artist" (*Journal of the American Institute of Architects*, August 1981, 11).

17 Robert McLaughlin to Breuer, January 21, 1954, Correspondence, AAA. In 1950, William Wurster, then dean of the School of Architecture at the University of California, Berkeley, felt Breuer out about relocating his practice and teaching at Berkeley: "I would request a full Professorship for you if you would think of coming" (Wurster to Breuer, November 22, 1950, Correspondence, AAA).

18 Breuer to Belluschi, April 7, 1954.

19 Henry-Russell Hitchcock, Introduction to *Built in USA: Post-war Architecture*, ed. Henry-Russell Hitchcock and Arthur Drexler (New York: Museum of Modern Art, 1952), 15.

20 Frederick Koeper, *American Architecture*, vol. 2, *1860–1976* (Cambridge, Mass.: MIT Press, 1990), 394.

21 Lewis Mumford, "A Walk Through Rotterdam," in *The Highway and the City* (New York: Harcourt, Brace & World, 1963), 39. Breuer supposedly was Mumford's choice when in 1954 Phyllis Bronfman Lambert was considering the "leading practitioners of international modernism" to select the architect for the Seagram Building (Witold Rybczynski, *Looking Around: A Journey Through Architecture* [New York: Viking Penguin, 1993], 194). I am grateful to Robert Gatje for bringing this information to my attention.

22 Quoted in *Time*, October 22, 1956, 90–91, in an article on the Starkey House in Duluth, Minnesota.

23 Ada Louise Huxtable, "Building's Case History," *New York Times*, August 9, 1963.

24 Ada Louise Huxtable, "Building a Third-Class City," *New York Times*, January 30, 1966.

25 Quoted in "Modern Architecture Symposium (MAS 1964): The Decade 1929–1939," *Journal of the Society of Architectural Historians* 24 (1965): 80.

26 Sibyl Moholy-Nagy, "The Diaspora," in "Modern Architecture Symposium (MAS 1964): The Decade 1929–1939," *Journal of the Society of Architectural Historians* 24 (1965): 25.

27 John Meunier, review of *The Decorated Diagram*, by Klaus Herdig, *Journal of Architectural Education* 38 (1985 [1986]): 31.

28 Vincent Scully, Jr., "Doldrums in the Suburbs," in "Modern Architecture Symposium (MAS 1964): The Decade 1929–1939," *Journal of the Society of Architectural Historians* 24 (1965): 40.

29 William H. Jordy, "The Domestication of Modern: Marcel Breuer's Ferry Cooperative Dormitory at Vassar College," in *American Buildings and Their Architects: The Impact of European Modernism in the Mid-Twentieth Century* (Garden City, N.Y.: Doubleday, 1972), 215. By deconstructing Breuer's method of composition in the early architecture, Joachim Driller, too, compares Ferry House with the furniture and concludes that Breuer's architectural works are often furniture on a larger scale and that his process of architectural design is based on the same principles as that of furniture design ("Marcel Breuer: Das architektonische Frühwerk bis 1950" [Phil. diss., Albert-Ludwigs-Universität, Freiburg, 1990], 22). Comparisons of Breuer's furniture and architecture appear throughout the critical literature, most saliently by Scully, Jordy, and Driller, preceded by Giulio Carlo Argan, who observed that "not only does Breuer's phase of furniture construction precede his phase of house construction, but all his later architecture is marked by that earlier experience" (*Marcel Breuer: Disegno industriale e architettura* [Milan: Görlich, 1957], 68). The subject was perceptively explored in Adam Eli Clem, "The City in Miniature: From Chair to Building in the Work of Marcel Breuer" (art history thesis, Vassar College, 1993), which is worthy of attention.

30 Jean Louis de Cenival, *Living Architecture: Egyptian* (New York: Grosset & Dunlap, 1964), 3–5. Breuer was still thinking about the architecture of Egypt in 1977. Responding to a question about the pyramids, he said: "The pyramids, however, are neither architecture nor sculpture. They are a symbol, a form. But I have gone into them and the going in was completely different from the form—unlike churches and other buildings where the exterior form has a lot to do with the interior space" (Marcel Breuer, interview with Shirley Reiff Howarth, November 21, 1977, in "Marcel Breuer: On Religious Architecture," *Art Journal* 38 [1979]: 260).

31 Marcel Breuer, interview for *Les Archives du XXième siècle*, March 30 and 31, 1974, 15, Speeches and Writings, AAA. Other historical architecture Breuer admired was the sober unadorned mass of the Escorial in Spain, the buildings on the Acropolis in Athens, and the dark-and-light-striped architecture of Tuscany and Umbria (particularly the cathedral of Orvieto). Hamilton Smith, in conversation with the author, recalled that in 1972 Breuer had insisted on a complicated change of travel plans and hotel reservations so that Smith could visit Orvieto. Interviewing Breuer for his *New Yorker* article, Sargeant quoted him as saying, "I think that the Escorial is one of the world's great buildings, and this is not exactly a new idea but I like the Acropolis in Athens. When I saw it for the first time I was fed up with the Classical Greek style of architecture that you have to learn in school. But I was astonished. The massive grace of the buildings, and how they are laid out on granite rock, you have to learn this old architecture, not to imitate it, but to be stimulated" ("Profile of Marcel Breuer").

32 Sibyl Moholy-Nagy, "Hitler's Revenge," *Art in America*, September–October 1968, 42–43.

33 Lewis Mumford, "Unesco House: Out, Damned Cliché!" in *Highway and City*, 70.

34 Barbaralee Diamonstein, "Interview with Hugh Jacobsen" [1982–84], in *Architecture Now II* (New York: Rizzoli, 1985), 134.

35 Klaus Herdeg, *The Decorated Diagram: Harvard Architecture and the Failure of the Bauhaus Legacy* (Cambridge, Mass.: MIT Press, 1983).

36 Ibid., 5.

37 Inscription in Breuer's handwriting on his sketch for a house in the 1940s, similar to his Museum of Modern Art exhibition house, Sketches, SUL, CLB Donation, 1995.

38 Herdeg, *Decorated Diagram*, 10.

39 Robert Gatje, conversation with author.

40 Breuer, interview with Howarth, 260.

41 Douglas Davis, *The Museum Transformed: Design and Culture in the Post-Pompidou Age* (New York: Abbeville Press, 1990), 24.

42 Anna Rowland, *Bauhaus Source Book* (London: Quantum Books, 1997), 77.

43 For example, Winfried Nerdinger, *Walter Gropius: The Architect Walter Gropius. Drawings, Prints and Photographs from Busch-Reisinger Museum, Harvard University Art Museums, Cambridge, Mass., and from Bauhaus-Archiv Berlin* [exhibition catalogue] (Berlin: Mann Verlag, 1985).

44 Jordy, "Domestication of Modern," 165–219; see also Driller, "Marcel Breuer"; Scully, "Doldrums in the Suburbs"; Argan, *Marcel Breuer*; and Clem, "City in Miniature."

45 William H. Jordy, "The Aftermath of the Bauhaus in America: Gropius, Mies, and Breuer," in *The Intellectual Migration: Europe and America, 1930–1960*, ed. Donald Fleming and Bernard Bailyn (Cambridge, Mass.: Harvard University Press, 1969), 485–543.

46 Whitney S. Stoddard, *Adventure in Architecture: Building the New Saint John's* (New York: Longmans, Green, 1958).

47 Joachim Driller, *Marcel Breuer: Die Wohnhäuser, 1923–1973* (Stuttgart: Deutsche Verlags-Anstalt, 1998), and *Breuer Houses*.

48 Richard G. Stein to Breuer, November 20, 1970, Correspondence, AAA; Tician Papachristou, *Marcel Breuer: New Buildings and Projects, 1960–70* (New York: Praeger, 1970).

49 Walter Gropius to Breuer, January 13, 1963, Correspondence, AAA; Cranston Jones, ed., *Marcel Breuer: Buildings and Projects, 1921–1961* (New York: Praeger, 1962).

50 Breuer to Jacques Koerfer, November 6, 1963, SUL 80.

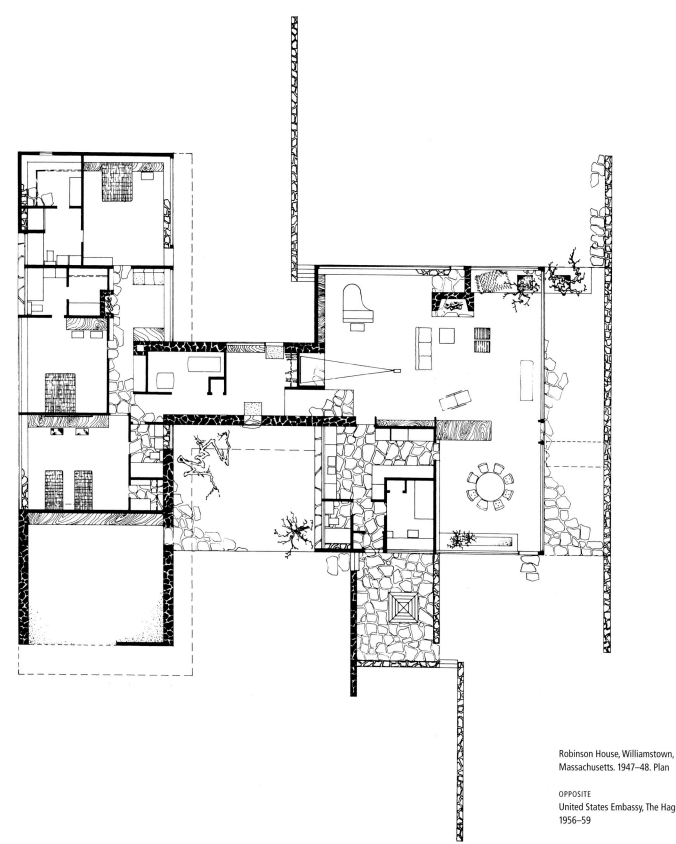

Robinson House, Williamstown,
Massachusetts. 1947–48. Plan

OPPOSITE
United States Embassy, The Hague.
1956–59

Untitled. Watercolor, signed "Lajkó M. 1922"

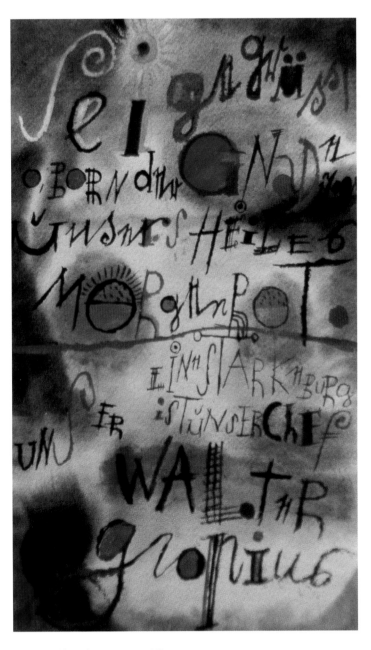

Birthday card for Walter Gropius. ca. 1923

Armchair. Oak and fabric. 1922

Dressing table with mirror. Tubular steel, wood, and glass. 1925–26

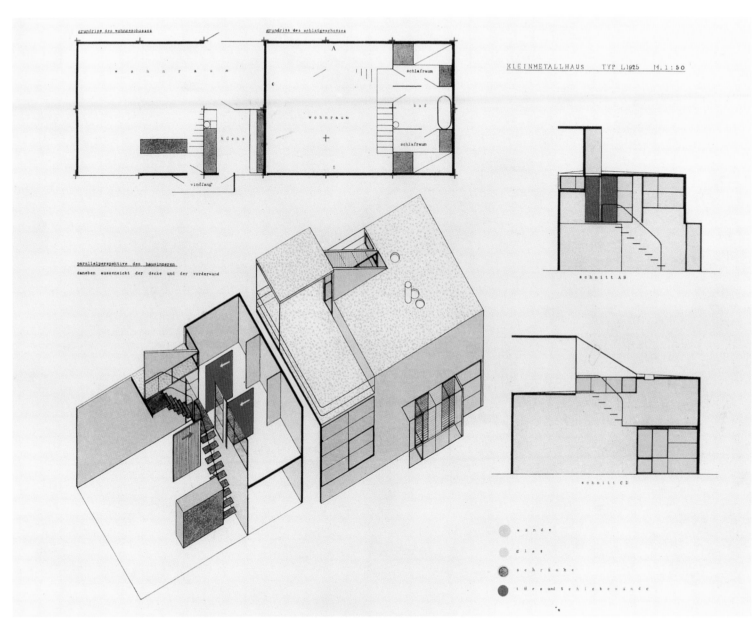

Small Metal House (Kleinmetallhaus), 1925 Type. 1925 (not built)

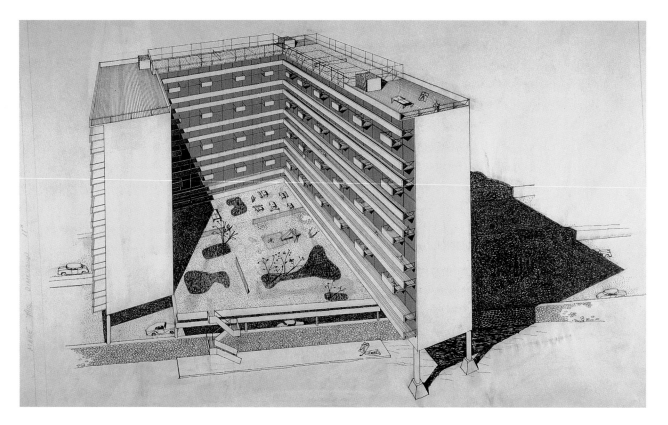

Apartment House, New York. 1946 (not built)

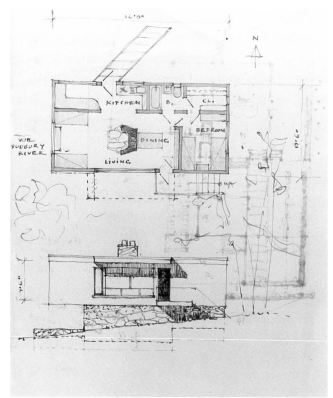

Chamberlain Cottage, Wayland, Massachusetts. ca. 1940.
Preliminary sketch of plan and elevation

Robinson House, Williamstown, Massachusetts. 1947–48

Caesar Cottage, Lakeville, Connecticut. 1952. Model

De Bijenkorf Department Store, Rotterdam, the Netherlands. 1955–57. Construction field office

Edgar Stillman, Jr., Cottage, Wellfleet, Massachusetts. 1953–54

Gagarin House I, Litchfield, Connecticut. 1956–57

OPPOSITE
UNESCO Headquarters, Paris. 1955–58. Secretariat

Hooper House II, Baltimore, Maryland. 1957–59

OPPOSITE
Staehelin House, Feldmeilen, Switzerland. 1957–58

Saint John's Abbey Church, Collegeville, Minnesota. 1958–61. Campanile

PART 1
A PROFESSIONAL LIFE

1. Weimar and Dessau:
The Bauhaus Years, 1920–28

"SOMEONE SHOWED ME A LITTLE BROCHURE from the Weimar Bauhaus with the emblem 'Return of the Craftsman' and with a woodcut of Lyonel Feininger,"[1] was the way Marcel Breuer remembered the day in Vienna in 1920 when, discouraged and dispirited—"the six or eight weeks I spent in Vienna were perhaps the unhappiest of my life," he later would recall[2]—he had been handed a copy of the *Programm des Staatlichen Bauhauses in Weimar* (1919) with Feininger's famous woodcut of a cathedral on the cover accompanying Walter Gropius's "incantatory" words.[3] For the eighteen-year-old Breuer, it was the moment of truth; he had been looking for a revolution in art without knowing where to find it, and, by chance, in the form of the four-page flyer aimed at recruiting new students for the Bauhaus, it found him instead.[4] "I decided immediately to go to Weimar," he said, arriving after the term had begun at the new experimental art school that would determine the course of his life and career. Possibly he brought with him a portfolio of drawings and paintings—Breuer at that point wanted to be a painter or a sculptor—although it was not until 1921 that prospective Bauhaus students were required to provide samples of their work when applying for admission.[5] Recalling himself at that moment, Breuer later said that he had arrived at the Bauhaus "a veritable innocent." Before 1920, he had no awareness of the Bauhaus, its prehistory, or the institutions and issues behind its founding.[6] Indeed, he could barely speak German.

Self-Portrait.
Oil on canvas. ca. 1917

The Breuer children. ca. 1907. Lajkó is at the center

Only two months before he discovered the Bauhaus program, Breuer had gone to Vienna with a scholarship to the Akademie der bildenden Kunst from his native Pecs in Hungary. He had expected to be trained in design and materials at the Akademie and, equally important to him, to be shown the practical applications of art: "I began to look for a relation between the practical and spiritual things in life." But even though he knew little about art-school curricula, and next to nothing about contemporary avant-garde developments in painting and sculpture, he was taken aback by the conservative methods he encountered at the Akademie and the limitations he perceived in its traditional Classical instruction. Years afterward, he described his experience there: "I walked into the Academy and walked out again. I saw it wasn't for me. In my provincial Hungarian city I had had the impression that Vienna was full of charm, and that the Academy was full of great talents. Instead I found poverty, dirty and infected hotels, and the Academy a meeting place of indifferent students and professors." [7]

At home in Pecs, Breuer had painted, sketched, and modeled in wax; at school, he had excelled at mechanical drawing and mathematics. In his book about Breuer's furniture and interiors, Christopher Wilk described the bourgeois household of the Breuer family, where cultural pursuits were encouraged and the arts and art journals held a respected place. [8] Two oil paintings made in Pecs around 1917 by the adolescent Breuer survive, predictably an introspective self-portrait and a landscape. [9] They reflect some awareness of Cézanne or Braque or even Wassily Kandinsky before 1910. Breuer may have seen illustrations of their work or that of derivative Hungarian painters in national and international journals. His memories of this period in Pecs were of having been cut off from any kind of broad culture, a feeling of dissociation. "During 1918 to 1920," he said, "we were occupied by the Serbs and the Yugoslavs and were completely isolated. Consequently I had no knowledge of modern art." [10] Between 1915 and 1925, Hungarian avant-garde art and related social ideologies could be found in activist journals, such as *A Tett* (The Deed) and *MA* (Today), and in galleries in Budapest, such as MA Gallery. [11] There is no indication that Breuer was aware of them while living in Pecs. He was exposed to vanguard Hungarian art and international progressive movements in literature, politics, and art only after leaving Hungary for Vienna immediately upon graduating from secondary school. [12]

At the time of Breuer's brief residence there in 1920, Vienna was a sanctuary for left-leaning Hungarian artists and political exiles after the failure of the Hungarian Communist revolution in 1919. [13] Fifty years later, he recalled that "in the cafés of Vienna I met some Hungarian refugees, young intellectuals and artists not very gifted but good talkers." Emigré journals and organized cultural activities reflected the interest that new experimental art held for such Hungarians. There was, for example, the MA group's famous "Russian evening" of November 20, 1920, when art-history student and journalist Konstantin Umansky gave his illustrated lecture on the work of Kandinsky, Kazimir Malevich, Aleksandr Rodchenko, Varvara Stepanova, Nadezhda Udal'tsova, Vladimir Tatlin, and others. It was an event that S. A. Mansbach suggests may have been one of the first presentations of Russian avant-garde art

Landscape. Oil on canvas. ca. 1917

in Western Europe after the war.[14] Awakened to Russian and other modern art by 1920, Breuer—who, in any event, had left Vienna a month before the "Russian evening"— remembered that "during my short stay in Vienna I studied with great interest art journals in the cafés, but these publications of contemporary art were very rare."

His first contact with important modern buildings also would have been in Vienna, with its radically plain turn-of-the-century architecture, particularly Adolf Loos's flat-roofed cubiform structures and the white stucco, windowless surfaces of Josef Maria Olbrich's conspicuous Secession Building. Some of the private residences designed by Loos around 1912 were still startling in 1920 not only for their unrelieved cubic severity but also for their unexpected profiles. Deep in Breuer's memory bank would be stored the stepped-back trilevel mass

of Loos's Scheu House, which, tilted ninety degrees, found expression first in the overhanging cantilevers of the Elberfeld hospital project Breuer designed in 1928–29 with Gustav Hassenpflug, and again almost a half century later in the granite-faced projections of the Whitney Museum facade and the terraced profile of its concrete elevation. To gain some practical experience during his Vienna sojourn, Breuer worked briefly as a self-described "volunteer designer" for an architect-cabinetmaker named Bolek, but nothing much came of it.

Gropius's claim in his Bauhaus Manifesto that "there is no essential difference between the artist and the craftsman" is what appealed to Breuer above all.[15] A radical art-school curriculum with the potential for practical results, a teaching faculty of notable painters and sculptors whose work was abstract and untraditional, and a program that encouraged the application of good design to marketable products corresponded precisely to his ambitions. When he dropped everything and moved to Weimar, he became, according to Bauhaus historian Frank Whitford, one of the "students whom the school suited ... successful from the moment they entered. What distinguished them from the malcontents was above all their willingness to acquire craft skills and to collaborate with others."[16] Although Whitford reports that most of the students were older than average because they had fought in the First World War (some still wearing tattered uniforms), Breuer was an exception. Born on May 21, 1902, he had not been old enough for military service during the war nor had his education been interrupted by it.[17]

BAUHAUS-WEIMAR, 1920–24

Breuer arrived in Weimar in the school's second and still-chaotic year as one of the 143 students matriculated in the academic year 1920–21. As a result of this accidental good timing, he belonged forever after to the elite corps of "early Bauhaus." Gropius was even then fiercely striving to organize operational procedures and to establish the state-supported school politically in Weimar. Money and equipment were in short supply, especially for the much-touted workshops, and the faculty was not in place. Many of the educational strategies and methods on which Gropius based his vision of a utopian society engendered by art and administered by correctly trained artist-craftsmen were far from being carried out.[18]

Although Breuer liked to suggest otherwise, a substantial number of his papers, drawings, documents, and original work from his Bauhaus years survived.[19] At his request in 1938, his former wife, Martha Erps Breuer, then living in South America, sent 415 photographs and 40 drawings of his work in her possession to the Museum of Modern Art for selection for its Bauhaus exhibition, held in 1938–39.[20] For the same exhibition, Breuer asked Herbert Bayer, in Germany, to search for additional material that he had left behind in Berlin.[21] A complete and accurate account of the curriculum that Breuer followed during his four years in Weimar and of the range of his

activities while a student there, and later as a master in Dessau, is not possible to reconstruct. Across the distance of decades, Breuer himself recalled events with some inconsistency.[22] But what is certain is that after his late arrival in Weimar, he became Johannes Itten's student in the Preliminary Course, which had become obligatory for all students in the fall semester of 1920 and on which all further design studies at the school depended.[23] He followed this with artisan craft training in the carpentry workshop, which had begun operating even without being fully equipped. Gropius served as the shop's nominal Master of Form and Josef Zachmann as Master of Craft, but Itten was principally in charge. Since the craft workshops were intrinsic to the pedagogic ideals on which Gropius had founded the Bauhaus— "The school is the servant of the workshop"[24]—implementing those shops was of paramount importance to him. Recalling his goals in 1949 in a letter to Peter Blake, Gropius wrote:

What I found was there did not exist as in earlier periods men who were trained in both design and execution. There was no carpenter who could not only make a chair but invent and design it simultaneously. There was an absolute separation between invention and design on the one side and execution on the other. This led me to give the student two teachers simultaneously, one for design [Master of Form] and one for the craft [Master of Craft].[25]

All histories of the early years of the Bauhaus trace the rocky road Gropius traveled in seeking to establish this, the heart of his program, and the conflicting attitudes on the part of his faculty toward it and toward one another because of it.

Soon after Gropius had invited Itten to become a member of the faculty in 1919, he accepted Itten's proposal for a Preliminary Course to be required of students before they could progress to workshop training. Essentially Expressionistic in direction, the course was described for the first time in 1921 in the statutes of the Bauhaus as "elementary instruction in form, in conjunction with studies of materials (in the experimental craft workshop[26])." It has been described by Bauhaus students and historians and by Itten himself.[27] Fifty years later, Breuer remembered it as a course that consisted "of

The Raising of the Cross. Woodcut, signed "M. Breuer, Weimar 1920"

Self-Portrait (?). Woodcut. Weimar, ca. 1921

doing rhythmic movements, designing in rhyme, reinterpreting the Old Masters of art, studying the textures of materials, and expressing our different feelings in a direct manner," a course that "changed visual education."[28] Breuer also described Itten:

He was a dynamic man who dominated his students, a brilliant man but with very important deficiencies. He was a kind of magician, a catalyst, but a convincing artist. His influence during the first three years of the Bauhaus was very powerful. As far as I was concerned I didn't feel myself much in accord with Itten, even though he impressed me, perhaps because I sensed something artificial about his character.

The artifice that Breuer referred to is simply one more interpretation of the complex, cultish personality of the strange and charismatic artist-teacher and Mazdaznan mystic[29] who simultaneously fascinated and repelled contemporaries at the Bauhaus with his appearance, bizarre habits of dress, and rituals of behavior.[30] One senses from Breuer's recollections, however, that he nonetheless appreciated and benefited from

the undisputed brilliance of Itten's instruction. This is important for Breuer's development because it was in the carpentry shop that he made his first significant designs, and Itten played the most important instructional role in that shop until he resigned from the Bauhaus in 1923. His influence on his shop students must have been "powerful," as Breuer described that influence on the Bauhaus in general. It was the impact on the eighteen-year-old Breuer of the combination of Gropius and Itten in the first years of the carpentry workshop that launched him as a designer into the mainstream of modern art.

Within weeks of his arrival at the school, Breuer was fully engaged with the Bauhaus process and became richly productive, his creative powers at last set free. Spongelike, he soaked up everything current, not only the content of the course work and the manual exercises in design but also the forms, colors, and textures of abstraction and Expressionism no longer new to twentieth-century art but new to him. Two woodcuts—a preferred Expressionist medium—survive from Breuer's first Bauhaus year. One, probably based on an Old Master (Rubens?)

prototype depicting the Raising of the Cross and signed "M. Breuer, Weimar 1920," was probably made for Itten's course, in which an important class exercise was the analysis and reformulation of historical works of art. With its barbed lines, angular cuts, and charged atmosphere, it is a dramatic departure from Breuer's tranquil "post-Impressionist" paintings of two or three years earlier and an unmistakable reflection of his response to the presence on the Bauhaus staff of Gerhard Marcks and Feininger and their medievalizing, Germanic printmaking modes.[31] The other woodcut, signed but not dated (around 1921) and also in vivid contrast to Breuer's earlier self-portrait in oil, is a highly Expressionistic abstract head, possibly a self-portrait, its clarity wiped away by a broad pattern of savage cuts and slashes. It resembles similar exercises by fellow students and, like the first, was probably an assignment for Itten's class.

First Interest in Architecture

As a rule, the story of Breuer at the Bauhaus has been the story of his furniture designs and the carpentry workshop. An equally salient factor for his future, however, was his close contact with Gropius and his awareness of Gropius's architecture. For Breuer, whose desire for a radical education in art and its practical application was answered by the unique institution at which he found himself, Gropius, as the institution's dynamic leader and at the same time a practicing architect, became a guiding force. By 1922, Oskar Schlemmer, who had joined the Bauhaus faculty in the winter of 1920–21, would note in his diary in a tone of some disdain that Breuer had voluntarily, but certainly at a price, renounced painting, for which he had a talent, and had become a cabinetmaker instead.[32] In 1938, Henry-Russell Hitchcock, reviewing an exhibition at Harvard of Breuer's work, observed that a nonarchitectural abstract watercolor, executed in 1922 and "frankly in the tradition of Klee" (see p. 25), was "probably finer than the earliest furniture projects and room designs."[33] Breuer's Ittenesque birthday card for Gropius, made around 1923 (see p. 25), and paintings and poster designs he executed in a Constructivist idiom in 1923 and 1926 reveal a painter completely self-assured in color and composition. Reflecting late in life on a suggestion by an acquaintance that if he had devoted himself to painting he would have become one of the greats, Breuer remarked:

But it isn't so. To be a painter you have to be a genius or you are nothing. Take Picasso, for example. He processes everything into art. That takes enormous self-confidence and Picasso has plenty of that. I like to do something more normal. A painter does something and then sells it; an architect sells it first and then does it. This sets up pressures. Picasso manages everything without such pressures. He has an incredibly rich process, which rests on itself. While I think I am also experimental, I am so only when somebody puts pressure on me.[34]

The assessment of Breuer's talent as a painter by an artist of the significance of Schlemmer, and by others, is not to be taken lightly. As a Bauhaus student his concentration first on carpentry and furniture design and almost simultaneously on architecture at the expense of painting and sculpture can be explained by the effect that Gropius had on Breuer's vision of his future.[35] The Gropius magic to which Breuer as well as everyone else felt compellingly drawn has been described by Gropius's biographer Reginald R. Isaacs and by Andrew Saint, who accounts for Gropius's "lifelong charisma" and for those aspects of his presence and magnetic personality that "unfailingly impressed" all those who met him, worked with him, and knew him.[36] Looking back fifty years, Breuer recalled that Gropius also "had a great interest in young people; it was one of his most profound traits. . . . And another of his characteristics was the recognition of quality in others." Breuer, for his part, possessed the facility for getting along well with people older than himself—mentors, clients, and friends—and gaining their confidence. At the Bauhaus, for example, Kandinsky, who became a great friend and patron, was thirty-six years older than Breuer; Paul Klee, twenty-two; Gropius, nineteen; and Josef Albers and Schlemmer, fourteen. For Gropius, Breuer would become a favorite apprentice whom he would eventually invite to join the Bauhaus faculty ("I dared to make him a Professor at my school at the age of 23"[37]) and who in time would become his close friend and partner. Despite periods of estrangement, and even after the serious rupture brought about by a bitter quarrel at Harvard in 1941 that severely strained the bonds of friendship,[38] Gropius and Breuer sustained a congenial relationship for half a century. Equally consequential for Breuer, although difficult if not impossible for him to acknowledge, was the impact of some of Gropius's early work on his own. The distinctive contour of Gropius's redesign of the existing Machine Hall in the Cologne Werkbund exhibition of 1914 (derived from the Berlin Bahnhof Friedrichstrasse shed) was borrowed by Breuer for his gymnasium building (1954–56) at Litchfield High School; the triangular shards at the base of Gropius's Kapp Putsch Memorial (1921–22) found their way into Breuer's design for a Franklin Delano Roosevelt memorial (1966); and Gropius's use of modular archetypes as standardized interchangeable planning elements was crucial to Breuer's design strategy throughout his career.

Breuer said that he had enrolled in the Bauhaus carpentry workshop rather than in any of the other craft shops because he considered himself manually clumsy and wished to improve his dexterity and because he simply wanted to learn how to build things.[39] While these were important factors, equally significant was the special attention Gropius gave to the carpentry workshop beginning in 1921, which meant that Breuer was brought together with him in a closer professional relationship than that of simply director and student. Gropius, moreover, embodied the Bauhaus ideals that had the greatest appeal for Breuer, with his genius for simultaneously theorizing about, creating, and teaching art—and earning something of a living from it as well with a private architectural practice transferred with state permission from Berlin to Weimar.[40] From the beginning, as a condition of his appointment as director of the Weimar Art Academy (soon to become the Bauhaus), Gropius had insisted on the right to carry out building commissions, to pursue an architectural career.[41] Most important was Gropius's employment (with salary) of Bauhaus apprentices, including Breuer, to assist with the private architectural commissions that came into the Weimar office,[42] even though in time "whispered complaints about Gropius's use of publicly subsidized Bauhaus students in his private architectural office began to be heard," according to Elaine Hochman.[43]

In a fortunate coincidence, at the time of Breuer's arrival at the school Gropius and Adolf Meyer, his assistant-collaborator in the Berlin-Weimar practice, were engaged with two architectural enterprises in which the Bauhaus was to be involved. One was the design and construction of a residence in the Steglitz section of Berlin for Adolf Sommerfeld, a lumber dealer, building contractor, and Bauhaus patron.[44] For the decoration and furnishings of the villa and for the construction of a subsidiary service structure on the property, Gropius drew on Bauhaus talent; Breuer was included because the first of the new skills he had discovered as apprentice in the carpentry workshop was that of furniture design and construction. Crafting furniture had appealed to Breuer's practical side and to his design side, and the earliest objects to survive from his first year in the workshop are chairs. With little experience, but with his discernible gift for designing furniture, the nineteen-year-old Breuer became affiliated with the Bauhaus-Sommerfeld team, which included Gropius and Meyer, Joost Schmidt, Albers, and Alfréd Forbàt. He produced in 1921 a five-legged cherrywood tea table and cubiform cherrywood and leather chairs for the house, his first opportunity to display his skill. Along with his peculiar arcuated "African Chair" of the same year, they are the first works by Breuer to enter the history of modern design.[45]

More far-reaching than the Sommerfeld House in its impact on Breuer's future in architecture was another building enterprise on the drawing board in Gropius's office. For the Bauhaus community, Gropius envisioned the construction of a cooperative residential colony (*Siedlung*) of modular houses of mixed size and height—for masters, instructors, and students—arranged in clusters on a sloping site in the eastern part of Weimar.[46] He had acquired a four-acre property in 1920, but the establishment of a new settlement there was protested by residents on the adjoining street, am Horn, so the land was put to temporary use as a kitchen garden to supply produce for the Bauhaus. In 1922, Gropius commissioned Forbàt, a trained architect and one of the assistants in his private practice (also a Pecs native, five years older than Breuer[47]) to design some houses for the *Siedlung*. To others at the Bauhaus, Gropius assigned the smaller residences. Breuer was

TOP
Gymnasium, Litchfield High School,
Litchfield, Connecticut. 1954–56

BOTTOM LEFT
Walter Gropius. Machine Hall (redesign),
Werkbund Exhibition, Cologne. 1914

BOTTOM RIGHT
Railroad station shed, Friedrichstrasse, Berlin

asked to plan one of the single-family house types; in his Type 3, a rectangular living room rose above the flat roof of an L-shaped house body that wrapped around two of its sides. Designs for the Bauhaussiedlung project, including Breuer's, were exhibited at the school in June 1922.

Despite the serious planning for it, a fully constructed *Siedlung* was impossible. Not only were the neighbors against it, but Gropius was also stopped, Richard Pommer has pointed out, by local officials who "attacked the flat roofs as unsuitable for the landscape."[48] As a compromise, Gropius decided that the site plan, drawings, and models relating to the full project would be prominently displayed as part of the exhibition to be held at the school from August 15 to September 30, 1923. Planning was begun in 1922 for this historic exhibition, which was to be one of the earliest public demonstrations of student work.[49] When Breuer claimed that 1922 marked the beginning of his serious interest in architectural design, he was thinking of these events. Moreover, it was in the autumn of 1922 that the first exhibition of abstract Russian art was held in the Galerie van Diemen in Berlin. There Breuer saw the Constructivist experiment expressed in objects and images (paintings, constructions, posters, pottery, and architectural designs)[50] that were to have a profound effect on his painting, his furniture, and his early architectural designs.

Architecture at the Bauhaus

Under pressure from those students for whom architecture was a dominant interest, Gropius agreed that as the showpiece for the 1923 exhibition one full-scale exemplar of a completely furnished single-family *Siedlung* house would be erected on a plot of land adjoining the Bauhaus garden on am Horn. In the winter of 1922, a design by painter and Bauhaus faculty member Georg Muche, based on one of the original plans by Forbàt (who was prevented by illness from participating in the project), was selected. Construction of the resulting "Experimental Haus am Horn" was overseen by the Gropius architectural office and supervised by Adolf Meyer.[51] The cornerstone was laid on April 11, 1923; coinciding as it did with Germany's ruinous inflation of 1923, the construction had to be subvented by Sommerfeld. For the living room and one of the bed-

rooms, Breuer designed free-standing and built-in furniture that was produced in the Bauhaus carpentry shop. The rug for the Breuer living room was designed and executed by Martha Erps, a student in the weaving workshop whom Breuer married in 1926 (and divorced in 1934).[52] From Magdalena Droste's history of Breuer's furniture, we know that the woman's dressing table he crafted for the Haus am Horn bedroom qualified him as journeyman in June 1923.[53] Breuer and the other apprentices and journeymen employed on the project were paid at current subcontractor rates.[54] As significant for Breuer as the opportunity to display his work in a widely publicized exhibition with important international artists and critics among the 15,000 or 20,000 (both figures are recorded) visitors was the on-site laboratory for modernist building practices that the construction of the Haus am Horn provided. It marked the beginning of his lifelong interest in experimental prefabrication technologies and new industrial materials.[55]

The flat roof, clear shapes, and white smooth-surfaced concrete slabs of the Haus am Horn displaced the aesthetic of the peak-roofed Sommerfeld House and its expressive wood textures and dark hues. Important for their impact on future house designs by Breuer were a clerestory window in the central tower that lighted the interior and a layout that provided a separate entrance from the children's room directly to an outside terrace.

In 1925, the plan and isometric drawing of Breuer's Single-Family Dwelling Type 3 appeared in *Ein Versuchshaus des Bauhauses*, third in the series of books planned and edited by Gropius and László Moholy-Nagy.[56] Devoted exclusively to the Haus am Horn, *Ein Versuchshaus des Bauhauses* announced on its title page that the house had been designed by Muche and the Department of Architecture (Architekturabteilung) of the Bauhaus, a misleading description since one of the serious and well-known problems at the school was its lack of an architecture department. Breuer's increasing desire to become an architect was thwarted by this paradox of the early Bauhaus experiment: despite Gropius's own technical training and his ideas about the primacy of architecture as an art, the Bauhaus was, in the words of Saint, "primarily an arts-and-crafts school in which during Gropius's time the architectural strain ran thin. No true architectural course was taught there for the first eight years of its existence, 1919–27."[57] As early as 1921, Schlemmer criticized the school and Gropius for this deficiency. Without architecture, he claimed, the Bauhaus was not distinguishable from an applied-arts school. His diary entry reads: "At the Bauhaus there are no classes in architecture and no student can hope to become an architect, rather he cannot from this background. The Bauhaus is nevertheless believed to represent architectural leadership. This naturally becomes the fault of Gropius; he is the only architect at the Bauhaus and he has no time to give instruction."[58]

One impediment to establishing an architecture department was the contradiction between Gropius's high-minded commitment to a "unity of the visual arts under architecture" and his belief that "on-site work with actual building materials and structures" took precedence over classroom instruction in architectural techniques and design.[59] According to Marcel Franciscono, "Except for a few technical courses, architecture in the [Bauhaus] Weimar period was taught to selected students largely in Gropius's own office, whose activities were to an extent coordinated with the work of the shops."[60] Because the school could not afford an actual building plot—Gropius's ideal modus operandi for architectural experimentation—it was his conviction that "only an architect's office could provide the necessary practical experience for a qualified journeyman."[61] He believed, too, that architecture should not be emphasized at the early stages of education, but should be "the pinnacle of design development."[62] "I have had my own very definite ideas for a long time, very different from the existing ways, as to how architecture is to be taught," he wrote to his mother in 1918 just before founding the school.[63]

Although it may not have been a substitute for systematic training, some architectural experience at the Bauhaus was available if the student-apprentice was strongly motivated. For one thing, the most powerful of the commitments driving the school's program, at least at the time of its founding in an atmosphere of German postwar regeneration, was to the social responsibility of art and design. Even if only on a doctrinal level, this led students to an engagement with building, particularly with housing, in their crusade to remake the world

in the aftermath of the war. But their engagement was in fact more than merely doctrinal. Adolf Meyer gave technical architectural instruction on a part-time basis from 1919 to 1922, and Gropius himself, at least in 1920, taught a course in architectural geometry.[64] Until 1922, regular lectures were given by Paul Klopfer, director of the local school of building trades, the Weimar Baugewerkschule, where masons, plumbers, and carpenters learned their skills and received some instruction in building and engineering theory and practice.[65] Gropius and Klopfer agreed that Bauhaus and Baugewerkschule students could attend courses at the respective schools. Even before Breuer's arrival at the school, in 1919 and 1920 constructive and projective drawing were taught by adjunct "Baumeister" Ernst Schumann.[66] The class schedule for the winter semester of 1921–22 indicates that mechanical drawing was offered on Wednesdays for three hours to "Group II" and for two hours to "Group I."[67] It was at this period that Breuer, responding instinctively to the Bauhaus emphasis on versatility, was discovering his talent for the design and structure of furniture and, simultaneously, his interest in architecture. Speaking of Bauhaus students, Whitford says, "They could paint, take photographs, design furniture, turn pots and sculpt. Herbert Bayer and Marcel Breuer could design buildings as well."[68]

The "architectural strain at the Bauhaus" may indeed have been "thin," at least pedagogically speaking, but the exhibition in 1923 signified the ideological commitment of the school to architecture. "The spirit of architecture hovers over the exhibition," wrote Walter Pasarge in his review of the event in Das Kunstblatt. "The actual heart is the international architecture exhibition," he went on to say, "while the show of free art [painting and sculpture] in the Landesmuseum is only marginal."[69] The "heart" he refers to was the display in the school's main building of drawings and models, plans and photographs of international contemporary architecture—by J. J. P. Oud, Willem Dudok, and Le Corbusier, among others—and of the Bauhaussiedlung project, gathered and arranged by Gropius to illustrate that a new modern architecture had developed throughout Europe and in Russia.[70]

The excitement that Gropius generated among visitors, critics and reviewers, and, above all, his students with this exhibition subverted its effect to some extent, since it underscored the absence of a structured architecture curriculum at the school. Still, it was the exhibition of 1923 and its planning sessions of 1922 that set Breuer on the path toward architecture as a career. Apprenticing in carpentry and learning how to construct things, as Breuer did in Weimar, was the way craftsmen became architects in the centuries before architecture evolved into a distinct profession with schools, guilds, and apprenticeships within the practice. In an undated (probably around 1947) and unedited draft of handwritten notes to accompany the publication of photographs of his works, Breuer described his Rietveldian chair of 1922 (see p. 26) in the language of architecture: "One simple cross section is used in an elementary simple way for the whole structure. Cantilevered parts."[71]

Breuer was defensive about his lack of technical architectural training. "I see myself as a man who developed everything by *doing* it and not by books or theories," he said when he was seventy years old. "My attention was always directed towards doing things, observing and asking questions, towards human experience, discussions, facts."[72]

Breuer and the Bauhaus Faculty

Breuer's furniture and architecture designs reflected not only the modernist abstractions of Gerrit Rietveld and de Stijl but also the appointment to the Bauhaus faculty of Kandinsky, Klee, and Moholy-Nagy, each to become a friend and/or teacher of Breuer.[73] Negotiations were begun in 1922 by Gropius for a faculty position for Moholy-Nagy, who, like other Constructivist artists, devised pictorial equivalents of architectonic form. Bauhaus histories now generally agree that Moholy's dynamic impact as a teacher (he took over the Preliminary Course after Itten left in March 1923 and he headed the metal workshop) and perception of art as a counterpart to technology and science finally liberated the Bauhaus from its Arts and Crafts origins and from Itten's romantic Expressionism, "transforming" it into an institution for art that could be identified with industrialized techno-Constructivism. In 1975, Breuer, in a moving speech, accepted a posthumous award from a Hungarian organization for his compatriot and friend Moholy, "a man with a mile-wide smile showing not 32 but at least 64 teeth."[74] He recalled (inaccurately) that he and Moholy had not collaborated on any creative work,[75] but "among other horizons we shared a common vision in technology as a natural force in the service of a more human surrounding and philosophy." "Of all the artists I knew," Breuer continued, "Moholy was nearest to our world. He died [in 1946] much too young, although he would now be eighty-one, which in itself is difficult to imagine."

Breuer's experiments beginning in 1923 with building designs and urban planning directed to social reform were focused on Germany's postwar problems: the need for affordable housing, improved living conditions for low-income families, multifamily dwellings, prefabrication, and institutions such as hospitals and sanatoriums. Soon he and Muche would initiate special studies of tall buildings as a way to house many families.[76] He explored questions about architectural structure and on this subject delivered a lecture, "Form Funktion," in one of the Bauhaus evenings that were among the events connected to the exhibition. It was admired by Gropius and published in 1924 in the special Bauhaus number of the periodical *Junge Menschen*.[77]

When in 1974 Breuer enumerated the principal architectural "researches" that he had carried out in Weimar on his own, his list included housing for the population in general, economy of construction, prefabrication, and a "habitational system" in which all spaces could be used for varied functions, not for a single purpose—one room, for example, that could serve as well for sleeping as for working and socializing. "I tried in that period," Breuer also said, espousing modernist housing principles, "to analyze the function of windows: ventilation, light, sun, view of the landscape, the physical and visual connection between interior and exterior space."

Around 1976, in response to a biographical questionnaire[78] that asked about "teachers who especially influenced your work," Breuer named two: a high-school "teacher of Descriptive Geometry, Prof. J. Kiss" and Paul Klee. His answer furnished an insight into the student Breuer, drawn early to geometry, and his steps toward architecture. From Kiss he learned all the mechanical drawing he used during his lifetime as an architect.[79] Klee, in Breuer's view "the sage of the Bauhaus," began teaching there in the winter of 1921, soon after Breuer's matriculation. Descriptions of his courses and his instructional notebooks make clear that the material he taught was almost exclusively theoretical and conceptual. His courses were not in painting per se but in the pictorial equivalents of structure, of architectonic form, and of the creative process that led to the making of form and the definition of three-dimensional space.[80] At the Klee Symposium held at the Museum of Modern Art in 1950, Breuer described first the vision he had had as a nineteen-year-old of Klee from his paintings before meeting him, then the reality, and finally his memory of Klee in the classroom: "During one of his lecture illustrations on the blackboard he drew an arrow pointing to the right, wrote over it 'Movement,' then another one pointing towards the left with the caption 'Counter Movement.' It took the audience some time to discover that with the second arrow he changed the crayon into his left hand and wrote 'Counter Movement' from right to left."[81]

In addition to the impact of Klee and Itten, Breuer's work at the Weimar Bauhaus reflected the controversial but catalytic presence of Dutch painter and critic Theo van Doesburg. Although never a teacher at the Bauhaus, the polemical van Doesburg became an important agent of change there and was recognized as such by members of the faculty, including Schlemmer and Feininger, if not by Gropius.[82] In lecture-seminars given in Weimar in 1921 and 1922 (not attended by Breuer),[83] van Doesburg, who also designed two model houses while he was there,[84] expounded the tenets of de Stijl-Constructivism as they related to the architectonics of three-dimensional construction. He has been credited with starting the process, later finished by Moholy-Nagy, of transforming the Bauhaus from a school with an Expressionistic ideology dedicated to handcrafting skills into an institution based on machine technology and industrially produced objects.[85] "I have radically turned everything upside down in Weimar," wrote van Doesburg triumphantly to poet Anthony Kok.[86] Gropius commented on this in 1949 when going over the draft of Blake's book about Breuer: "The preliminary course of the Bauhaus curriculum (Itten and Albers) and the subsequent

experiences in the workshop had more to do with Breuer's finding himself as a creative artist than any other influence, including the 'Stijl,'" an influence that Gropius regarded as "entirely out of proportion to the facts" and "understandable wishful thinking on the part of Nelly van Doesburg." Regarding Breuer, Gropius wrote that "his preoccupation has always been structural and I don't remember him to have been under anyone's spell for long. His outstanding quality was his completely unbiased mind and the independence and boldness with which he attacked technical and aesthetic problems."[87]

Breuer, too, would deny any conscious impact on his work from de Stijl or from van Doesburg: "I met him two or three times. We did not speak more than two words each time, because I was not interested in his activities or in his art." When the interviewer pressed Breuer on this point, claiming that "Theo van Doesburg said that you were one of those he had 'led to order and discipline,'" and then asked, "What did he mean by that phrase?" Breuer replied defensively: "That is his position. Among the numerous influences that affected a young man of twenty it is difficult for me to decide which directed me towards order and towards discipline. But I do not believe that Doesburg was one of these influences." When asked what he had thought of the de Stijl movement and if he had been influenced by it, he answered, predictably, that he knew it "in '23 or '24" and "had great respect for the works of Mondrian, Oud, and Rietveld. If there was an influence I am sure I was not conscious of it." The influence of Rietveld on Breuer's furniture is in fact pronounced, particularly in the years around 1922 and 1923,[88] even though Breuer displayed a command of "order and discipline" from the start, or at least immediately following the one or two "eccentric" chairs of 1921 that represented his earliest work and were reflections of the Expressionist character of Itten's Preliminary Course. But de Stijl-inspired effects, such as Doesburgian (and Mondrian-esque) arrangements of mullions on large fields of fenestration, were used by Breuer throughout his career, in buildings of all types—institutions such as the UNESCO Headquarters (1955–58) in Paris, commercial buildings like the Cleveland Trust tower (1969–71), and private residences such as Geller House II (1968–69) on Long Island.

Gropius's reluctance to join architectural practice to theory,[89] and an escalating interest on the part of students like Breuer who were hoping to become architects and were stimulated by activity in Gropius's architectural office "within sight of the students," led to the formation in April 1924 of an independent architectural study group.[90] (It was only one of a number of student rebellions in the early years.[91]) Breuer and Muche were its "driving forces," according to Bauhaus archivist Hans Wingler, who also credits Breuer with having made "the strongest and most independent achievements of the group."[92] In a letter written to Gropius in 1948 that referred to this period, Breuer mentioned "my own little palace revolution of 1924 requesting that an architecture department be established in the Bauhaus."[93] Gropius attempted to appease the dissatisfied students by initiating an experimental architecture workshop in his office with the assistance of Adolf Meyer and Ernst Neufert,[94] but it was not expansive enough and the Breuer-Muche collaborative supplanted it.

A published document from the Staatsarchiv Weimar—unsigned but believed to have been composed by Breuer, Muche, and Farkas Molnár (also one of the founders of the study group) and dated April 2, 1924[95]—is a brief, forceful statement of their aims: to see an architecture department established that would take on architectural commissions from "outside" and finance itself (with a percentage to the Bauhaus) through building contracts, that would sponsor design projects based on new ideas and on the investigation of contemporary living problems, and that would be made up of the three members who founded it and Emil Lange, an engineer and architect and the Bauhaus business manager. Responding to a question put to him fifty years later about his "activities as an architect from the time of his entrance to the Bauhaus in 1920" and his "studies and projects alone or with Georg Muche," Breuer gave an answer that was puzzling but consistent with his later efforts to emphasize his independence: "My special studies of architecture at the Bauhaus between 1922 and 1928 were made alone. With Muche I often had conversations as with an interested friend, but he never participated in my work nor I in his."

The failure of the architectural study group to prevail on Gropius to establish a real department of architecture at the Bauhaus ("a vain effort," Breuer recalled) resulted in a moment of crisis for Breuer and drove him, in frustration, away from Weimar to Paris in late September 1924. "I was demoralized like many others at the Bauhaus," he recalled, "and decided to leave Germany, where, in any case, I did not wish to spend my whole life." (Understandably, Breuer was often believed to be German. On this subject, he expressed himself definitively [as was necessary in 1948 America] in response to an article in the *Tucson Daily Citizen*: "I was pleased to see the article your paper carried about my Tucson visit . . . however, I am not a German expatriate but, unimportant as it sounds, originally a Hungarian, and somehow I am quite happy about this fact, which I consider always as specially good luck, not being a German."[96]) He had just graduated and was restless ("I wanted to know more of the world"), his search for practical architectural experience not having been successful in the school, which, in any case, "had become for me too narrow and too academic." In 1924, Lange resigned from the Bauhaus, and Muche left for travel in the United States. Breuer's departure for Paris coincided, moreover, with the deterioration of state financial and political support for the Bauhaus by both the Weimar government and the newly elected rightist Thuringian government, which placed the future of the school in jeopardy. On December 26, 1924, three months after Breuer left for Paris, Gropius announced that the Weimar Bauhaus would close in March 1925 when staff contracts expired.

First Architectural Projects

"Projects are the proper activity of youth; and when modern architecture was young and its exponents were young as well, projects properly played a great part in its development," wrote Henry-Russell Hitchcock in 1938, reviewing the Harvard exhibition of Breuer's work—mostly unexecuted projects.[97] There were few years between 1923 and 1932 (his first executed building) when Breuer did not design architectural projects that were rendered in some format: ground plan, model, axonometric drawing, perspective sketch. Building was more interesting to him than any other pursuit, and his commitment to architecture was unwavering even in the most discouraging circumstances. Just before he was given the Harnischmacher House commission in 1932, Breuer wrote to Ise Gropius from Madrid: "A marvelous time is 'our time,' an interesting time, an awful time! Should I continue for another nine years to make architectural plans without ever seeing them carried out? Then painting makes more sense. If only it were not so boring. For half an hour, OK, but forever or a day is too much!"[98]

Before Breuer's departure for Paris, and before the invention in 1925 of the earliest version of the radical tubular-steel-and-canvas armchair ("Wassily") that would establish his first fame, he designed in 1923 a facade for "skipped-level apartments," published as "Breuer's first architectural design."[99] With openings for windows and air vents arranged as black rectangles on a white plane in syncopated rhythms and varied dimensions, the visual effect is decidedly nonarchitectural and suggests instead a flat, diagrammatic painting, even a design for fabric or a rug. Continuing to experiment with multifamily dwellings during 1923, he also designed a seven-story, seven-bay terraced duplex apartment slab that he submitted in 1924 to a housing-design competition sponsored by the Berlin architectural periodical *Die Bauwelt*. Speaking of Breuer and the idea of a vertical slab for housing, Wingler says that this "beginner who had no practical experience whatsoever had created an entirely new type of building which years later became commonly accepted as an integral component of modern apartment architecture."[100] The format probably originated in the tall-house experiments that Breuer undertook with Muche in their study group, but it can also be read as a crossover between Breuer's designs for architecture and for furniture. Since it was realized only in the dimensions of a scale model, it corresponded to a number of his contemporaneous pieces of wood furniture—for

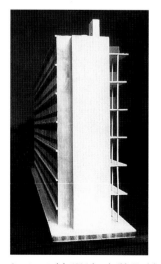

Apartment slab. 1924 (not built). Model

example, the large wall unit in the "woman's bedroom" of the Haus am Horn and similar independent cabinets of 1922 to 1924—and the continuous terraces are equivalents of bookcase shelves with vertical dividers.[101] Breuer gave serious thought, sociological as well as architectural, to the matter of the tall building. In 1930, he set down his ideas in an article for *Die Form*, journal of the Deutsche Werkbund,[102] where at the same time he called attention to current thinking in advanced circles about freeing women from the servitude of domestic work to pursue an independent professional existence and the effect of this notion on architectural planning.[103]

PARIS, 1924

In September 1924, speaking little French, Breuer made his way to the Latin Quarter and a hotel in rue Cujas. More important, with photographs of his work, he visited Léonce Rosenberg's Galerie de l'effort moderne on the Right Bank. Rosenberg sent Breuer to various centers of the Parisian avant-garde to meet artists and editors of art journals: "I met Ozenfant and Le Corbusier, Zervos, Léger, Braque and Mondrian, Delaunay and Mme. Delaunay, and some younger architects and painters whose names I no longer remember." He found design work for a few weeks at the studio of Pierre Chareau, who had been trained as an architect and in 1931 would build the Maison de Verre on rue Saint-Guillaume, one of the most innovative modernist structures in France, but who in 1924 and 1925 was chiefly a cabinetmaker and designer of custom-made furniture and interiors.[104] "To earn my daily bread and wine I have a job with an architect until 6:30 every evening," Breuer wrote to a Bauhaus colleague.[105] His presence in Paris coincided with the period preceding the opening in April 1925 of the Exposition internationale des arts décoratifs et industriels modernes, for which Chareau designed one of the twenty-five rooms (the bureau-bibliothèque) in the showpiece French Embassy and the dining room of the Indochinese pavilion. Even with the political exclusion of Germany, the most significant overall modernist contribution to the exposition was still that of architecture, notably

Breuer seated in his tubular-steel-and-canvas "Wassily" armchair. 1928

al training and experience, Ise Gropius recorded in her diary on July 12, 1925, that Breuer "told us that he had had an offer from Corbusier at one time to join his office, but that he was not entirely satisfied with Corbusier's design approach which he found too formalistic."[107] It was a letter from Gropius "with a new perspective" that sent him back to Germany to take charge of the carpentry workshop at the Bauhaus. When the school was reestablished in Dessau,[108] with a new group of buildings and new housing for the masters, Breuer became one of five Weimar students (Albers, Bayer, Breuer, Hinnerk Scheper, and Joost Schmidt) elevated to the status of "young master."[109] "Of all the younger masters he is the most cultured and has the broadest base," was the opinion of Ise Gropius.[110] Within two years of his appointment, however, Breuer considered resigning because, as Ise wrote, he was "feeling hampered in his personal development and wanted to work in a wider field of activity."[111] Both Walter and Ise Gropius regarded this as "a very serious problem since Breuer is the most important personality among the young masters. The question whether he will really leave remains open for the time being."[112]

BAUHAUS-DESSAU, 1925–28

Konstantin Melnikov's Soviet pavilion (awarded first prize for design) and the prefabricated Pavillon de l'Esprit Nouveau by Le Corbusier and Amédée Ozenfant. Breuer could not have seen much of the Pavillon de l'Esprit Nouveau, for although it had been designed in 1924 it was not completed before July 1925 and until then was hidden behind a tall fence in the garden of the Grand Palais.[106] But in and near Paris, Le Corbusier's Atelier Ozenfant and Maisons La Roche-Jeanneret and Ker-Ka-Re (Villa Besnus) had been completed, and Breuer knew his designs for the Ville Contemporaine and its Immeubles-Villas from their display in the Bauhaus exhibition in 1923.

It might have been possible for Breuer to make a place for himself in the art world of mid-1920s Paris, as he was inclined to do. Although no reference to this appears in Breuer material, and unlikely as it seems considering his lack of architectur-

In reply to a 1955 letter from Herbert Read requesting biographical information, Breuer reported that "I studied in the Bauhaus 1920–24. In 1924 I took over the direction of the furniture department there, and when the Bauhaus moved to Dessau in 1925, I combined my work as the director of the furniture department with teaching at the Bauhaus and with architectural work."[113] This inclusion of "architectural work" in Breuer's account of his Dessau years, especially since it was in those years that he developed his tubular-steel furniture and instituted an independent entrepreneurial program for its production,[114] indicates the sustained importance that architecture held in his vision of a professional life. He recalled 1925 and 1926 as the years in which he concentrated on the joint question of prefabrication and the small single-family house. His design for a "small metal house" that survives in an axonometric drawing showing an interior-exterior elevation and ground plan is an experiment in the application of industrial building methods and materials to small-scale residential architecture (see p. 27). In the 1940s, writing about himself at this time, Breuer said that "his first architectural projects, in 1923, for low-cost apartment houses guided him towards prefabrication, first in steel, like the 'small metal house.' A two-story row house that could function as an independent dwelling or as one unit in a series, the 'small metal house' uses a standardized insulated light panel system on a modular steel frame." The skeleton, also light, and the inset wall and window units could be erected in two or three weeks. Contrasting this with traditional masonry architecture, Breuer loftily claimed: "Instead of the pyramid, the Eiffel tower."[115] Hitchcock recognized in Breuer's metal-house design some relation to the small-dwelling projects of Le Corbusier, but he wrote that "essentially this first architectural study is wholly original, independent and markedly superior to the general level of the time in technical ingenuity and distinction of proportions."[116] Its novelty is borne out by Gilbert Herbert's observation that before 1926 there were no German metal houses.[117] With this all-metal prefabricated project, which Breuer called "my first industrial design,"[118] he confronted modern architecture's crucial issues: prefabrication and mass-production, advanced technology, industrial materials, and standardized parts.

In the 1925 edition of his *Internationale Architektur*, the earliest of the Bauhaus books, Gropius published Breuer's apartment-house model of 1923.[119] As most of the volume consisted of photographs of modern architecture assembled originally for the Bauhaus exhibition of 1923, the young Breuer was placed in the company of the inner circle of architects of the pan-European modern movement—including Peter Behrens, Hendrik Berlage, Le Corbusier and Pierre Jeanneret, Erich Mendelsohn, and Gropius himself—"a selection of the best modern architectural work," as the publisher's advertisement claimed. In the 1927 edition, Gropius added Breuer's "small metal house."[120]

Breuer and the Gropiuses at the Bauhaus

From the start, Walter and Ise Gropius, impressed by Breuer's intelligence ("intellectually Breuer is the most superior in spite of his 23 years"), abilities as craftsman and designer ("in Weimar [he was] already a brilliant designer"), and steady character ("he has proved himself very capable"), encouraged and promoted his career both as architect and as designer of furniture and interiors.[121] The friendship that developed between Breuer and Gropius within a short time of Breuer's arrival in Weimar, despite the generational difference and the director-student gap, was deepened after Gropius's marriage, in October 1923, when Breuer and Ise Gropius, five years older, became close friends. No documents are more revealing of Breuer's ideas, wit, and feelings in these early years than the letters he exchanged with Ise (Pia) and that she saved for four decades. In 1971, thanking her for copies she sent him, Breuer remembered "those hopeless and *auch* personally terrible years. . . . I cannot grasp how you managed to guard [the letters] that long from country to country."[122] With Breuer, Ise was simultaneously maternal and flirtatious, the letters between them frequently but discreetly referring to his romantic adventures. At one point, she told him that "the inexhaustible unused motherly feelings in me are at your service. . . . As a young man one needs a female mentor, you know, and I find it is better that it is me."[123] Throughout the years that the three of them spent together in Weimar and Dessau and on vacations, both Ise and Walter continued to hold Breuer in high esteem in spite of his

Breuer at the Bauhaus, Dessau. Second half of the 1920s

involvement from time to time in irritating but transient institutional crises, so much so that in 1925, well before the post-Gropian destiny of the Bauhaus could have been envisioned, Ise wrote in her diary that Breuer "is certainly the sharpest thinker among the Bauhausler and G[ropius] draws him in whenever possible to try to educate him into becoming his successor."[124] A few months later, she reiterated that idea: "In spite of his youth he is really the only one who understands what it means to run this Bauhaus."[125]

Dessau and Stuttgart

Approval for the Bauhaus by the Dessau Municipal Council was voted on March 24, 1925. Awaiting the installation of the legitimate Department of Architecture in the new school, Gropius opened an office for private practice in Dessau, as he had done in Weimar. Once again, students and former students worked there as apprentices and draftsmen—"design work" was given to Molnár, Schmidt, and Breuer.[126] Working drawings for the new Bauhaus building, arguably Gropius's greatest work, were completed in June 1925, and construction began in September at the same time as the houses for the Bauhaus masters. Pressing Gropius once again to give them practical architectural experience, Breuer and Muche asked to participate in designing both projects, a request denied by Gropius. Surely reflecting her husband's views, Ise wrote that the proposal lacked feasibility: "Muche . . . had no schooling as an architect [and] Breuer . . . already a brilliant designer had had no actual building experience at all. Since the success of the whole enterprise in Dessau depended on the utmost speed in execution before hostile groups in the city organized themselves to interfere, a collaboration between Gropius, Muche and Breuer would have delayed everything considerably."[127]

Classes began on October 14, 1925, in temporary spaces; the topping-out ceremony took place on March 20, 1926; by September, classrooms and workshops were in use, and on December 4 the new building was officially inaugurated. The entire Dessau enterprise invigorated Breuer and reinforced his attachment to Gropius in spite of his thwarted efforts to practice architecture.[128]

By this time, Breuer's furniture had "become identified as the furniture of the modern movement."[129] The canteen and auditorium of the Dessau Bauhaus and the houses of some of the masters—Kandinsky's, for one—were furnished with his designs. On the subject of metal furniture and modern space planning, Breuer would write:

Today . . . we change our lives more rapidly than in the past. It is natural that our environment must undergo corresponding changes. This leads us to installations, rooms, buildings, all or most of whose components can be converted, moved, and recombined. The furnishings, and even the walls of the rooms, are no longer massive, monumental, apparently rooted to the spot, or literally bricked in. Rather they are airily perforated and, as it were, outlined in space; they obstruct neither movement nor the view across the room.[130]

Lecturing in Delft in 1931, Breuer elaborated his ideas about interior design and brought in the notion of a modern home that was "more comfortable in a biological sense."[131] In 1927, he had remodeled an apartment for the Berlin theater producer Erwin Piscator in which he installed, in light-filled free-flowing spaces, tubular-steel furniture and cabinetry of wood, glass, and metal. Wilk writes about this project that the extensive use of gymnasium equipment in Piscator's bedroom was "typical of the 1920s obsession with health and physical fitness."[132]

Much of the interior-design work commissioned to Breuer in the Dessau period came his way through Gropius, who also used Breuer's metal furniture in the two houses he designed for the Deutsche Werkbund's 1927 Stuttgart Weissenhof-siedlung. Mies van der Rohe, as the *Siedlung*'s artistic director, had invited Breuer to participate in the housing experiment as furniture designer for one of three houses by Dutch architect Mart Stam, but it is unclear if there had ever been a role in the Stuttgart enterprise for Breuer as architect, or if he had even sought one.[133] Despite the six or seven projects he had designed and the four years spent in quest of architectural experience, Breuer in 1927 was still five years away from executing his first building. He would have had no standing in the eyes of the selection committee.

Plans for the Weissenhof settlement were announced in 1925. According to a memorandum of February 1927, Breuer expressed several times to the directorate his interest in participating, but the memo does not indicate in what capacity.[134] His appeals resulted at least in a recommendation that he be invited to produce building designs for the auxiliary temporary exhibitions that were to be installed at sites separate from the *Siedlung*—an international exhibition of modern architecture with plans and models (Internationale Plan- und Modellausstellung Neuer Baukunst) and an experiments exhibition that featured materials and construction techniques.[135] For the latter, he was asked to design metal furniture and a metal house that the Deutsche Kupferinstitut (German Copper Institute) wanted to construct, but the commission did not materialize.

The Weissenhofsiedlung and its accompanying activities and exhibitions, both creative and technological, must have been Breuer's richest and most instructive experience after the Bauhaus exhibition of 1923 in terms of his future as an architect. Experiments in Stuttgart with materials, color, construction technology, and, most important, prefabrication became critical lessons once he was established as a practicing architect and designer of private residences. Villas he built in England during his partnership with F. R. S. Yorke, for example, reflected aspects of Hans Sharoun's houses for the Weissenhofsiedlung. And in the United States, the single-family row houses Gropius and Breuer designed for Aluminum City (1941), a defense-housing project in New Kensington, Pennsylvania, owed as much to Oud's five two-story houses in Stuttgart as they did to Bauhaus typeform precedents. Breuer's Harnischmacher House (1932) could not have come into being without his having confronted the work of Le Corbusier, not only in Paris and its environs but also in Stuttgart.

Last Years at the Bauhaus

Gropius finally made good on his intention to establish a department of architecture as part of the Dessau curriculum. Pressure from the mayor of Dessau for Bauhausler participation in Gropius's housing settlement planned and executed in 1926–28 for the nearby town of Törten led Ise Gropius to restate that "the Bauhaus has no architectural office yet which would be the basis for such an undertaking," and "the introduction of an architecture class at the Bauhaus which could independently take on commissions without having to rely on the Gropius office is a great necessity."[136] On April 1, 1927, Swiss architect Hannes Meyer became head of the new department, first having had, as he said, "interesting talks with Gropius as well as with Kandinsky, Moholy, Schlemmer, and Breuer." Meyer's politics (Marxist) and philosophy of architecture ("objective and anti-aesthetic") made his appointment, and his subsequent replacement of Gropius as director of the Bauhaus, highly complex, a situation brilliantly dissected by Saint.[137] In December 1926, Gropius had invited Meyer to join the faculty and establish the department. On the same day that she recorded Meyer's acceptance in her diary, Ise Gropius noted that there had been a discussion with Breuer: "He proposes to take over the practical implementation of the work done in the new building workshop of Hannes Meyer. His ambition grows almost alarmingly, and G[ropius] had to decline this plan since it cannot be assumed that Meyer will want to give away the practical side of his job, and also because Breuer is too young and inexperienced."[138]

The department fell into place, but the personal and political crises that had plagued the institution from its beginnings—many described in Schlemmer's letters to his wife—multiplied during 1926 and 1927.[139] In 1927, he wrote: "May revolution at the Bauhaus . . . against the egotistic masters and the lazy students . . . Kandinsky angry, Gropius in a fix. Likewise a Breuer crisis."[140] The "crisis" Schlemmer refers to was a conflict between Breuer and the Bauhaus regarding the independent manufacturing company (Standard-Möbel) that Breuer founded in 1926 and 1927 for the production of his tubular-steel furniture.[141] "A very unpleasant event with Breuer," recorded Ise Gropius. "He has made a deal about his metal chairs with a Berlin friend without telling anybody and that will now lead to great difficulties in the negotiations of Dr. Konig in Dresden about a Bauhaus GmbH. Dr. Konig . . . has written a very outspoken letter to Breuer about this."[142] By the end of 1927, Breuer had decided to resign; by January 1928,

Gropius, fed up with criticisms of the school and with accusations against him about excessive fees for the Törten project, had had enough. In mid-January, Schlemmer wrote to his wife: "This is meant for you in strictest confidence: Breuer and Bayer have formally resigned. I very nearly did likewise, but caution and patience prevailed."[143] A month later, he called it "this turning point in the stormy history of the Bauhaus" and told his friend Otto Meyer that "Moholy is leaving; likewise less directly in connection with Gropius' departure, Breuer."[144]

The press of work for private clients is one reason that Breuer gave for his resignation, but he had ideological conflicts as well. He was disinclined to follow Hannes Meyer's direction toward increased technology at the expense of aesthetics and to go along with what Moholy-Nagy described as "trade specialization in the workshops," whereby application and specialized vocational training were emphasized.[145] "Breuer, for example," writes Gillian Naylor, "did not wish to be restricted to furniture design, and resented having to rely on the wall-painting workshop for the spatial organization of interiors, which, he believed, he could, and should, do himself."[146] Functioning already as the "total architect" he later would become, Breuer wanted to be responsible for all the details of his projects. The conflicts engendered by his position were recorded by Ise Gropius. In December 1926, she wrote in her diary: "In the evening assembly of all Bauhaus members Breuer gave the main report and directed the discussion. He proposed that it should be made possible for the individual Bauhaus member to see a whole project through from A–Z, instead of being confined to only a small part in it. He stated that a kind of specialist's point of view was increasing in the school which he considered to be a dangerous trend." In April, she added:

Breuer says that he doesn't like the atmosphere any longer and that he would prefer to work alone in the future. His ambition prohibits him from tolerating the slightest bit of subordination, which cannot be altogether avoided when working in the large, communal team effort of the Bauhaus. The mood of the students is also partly critical of him. For G[ropius] a great loss, but Breuer's attitude of late has become so difficult that there is apparently no other way out.[147]

But by November, Breuer had reinstated himself in her good opinion even though he expressed another disappointment with the new direction of the school:

Breuer spoke his mind about something in the Bauhaus that does not seem too productive in his opinion—the overemphasis on political and social topics that is fostered by Hannes Meyer. He has talked with Meyer about this and Meyer had admitted some mistakes. It disturbs the . . . laboratory-like spirit in the workshops when topics are dealt with that belong in the field of political economics . . . the school is, after all, not planning to establish a new world order. Breuer substantiates his opinions always so well it is a pleasure to listen to him.[148]

The "official" reason for Breuer's departure, as reported in the *Frankfurter Zeitung* of March 17, 1928, was that "in order for his work to get ahead he must be able to experiment on a large scale. He hopes to find a better chance for close connections with industry when he is working as a freelancer."[149] Again, much of the uproar had to do with Breuer's insistence on independent licensing and manufacturing contracts for the production of his steel furniture, which he did not regard as Bauhaus objects, "any more than a Klee painting is a Bauhaus object."[150] On a personal level, Breuer's decision was influenced also by Martha Erps Breuer's plan, formulated in the winter of 1928, to visit her brother in Brazil for a year. (Erps and Breuer had married on August 14, 1926.) During that time, reported Ise Gropius, "Breuer will establish a base for himself in Berlin. He wants to leave as soon as possible; Albers could take over his workshop." "It is such a pity," she went on, "that Breuer, who is so superior to Meyer in his thinking and in many ways much more mature, is still so young that he cannot be proposed as successor to G. His stamina, also physically, is not yet strong enough, otherwise he would be the right leader."[151]

"So the farewell party for Gropius is over . . . a dance, wild shouting. Everyone screaming and yelling," Schlemmer wrote to his wife.[152] Bauhaus parties had been famous—for the jazz band, the dancing, and especially the costumes (Gropius once came dressed as Le Corbusier[153])—and this one apparently was no exception. On March 26, 1928, Gropius and Ise left Dessau to resettle in Berlin, where Gropius would again establish his private practice and where a few months later Breuer would join them, but first they and their friend Renee Sommerfeld embarked for a visit to the United States. Breuer had hoped to accompany them, but could not afford the trip.[154] The Gropiuses went to some lengths to raise enough money for his travel expenses, without success—"I had written to Dr. Bett of Bett, Simon & Co. to ask him whether he would support a trip to America for Breuer," wrote Ise—so Breuer reluctantly had to give up the plan.[155] In Berlin, he would continue experimenting with designs for metal furniture, but he wanted first and foremost to open a studio and establish himself as an independent architect.

It was, however, during the winter of 1928 that Gropius had been discussing a design for a residence in Mainz with Paul Harnischmacher, an enlightened industrialist who was the director of a successful company that manufactured wax and shoe polish. Harnischmacher had first seen Gropius about this house almost a year earlier: "Harnischmacher from Mainz here. Gave G. the commission to design his house according to his own discretion," wrote Ise Gropius.[156] Breuer was to design the interior.[157] The house project did not materialize, but Harnischmacher's office in Mainz and apartment in Wiesbaden were remodeled and furnished by Breuer in 1928 and 1929 at Gropius's suggestion.[158] Breuer sustained the connection to Harnischmacher, with whom he got along well; three years later, when the client finally decided to build an independent villa in Wiesbaden, he wrote to Breuer, then traveling in Spain, asking him to be his architect. It was the opportunity that Breuer had been waiting for. Returning to Germany, he lived in Wiesbaden for nine months while the house was under construction. He also became a lifelong friend of Harnischmacher, for whom he designed a second house in 1953 to replace the 1932 villa, which was destroyed in the Second World War. In gratitude for the Breuer houses he loved, Harnischmacher bequeathed to his friend and architect a painting by Klee. Breuer learned of this tribute through a note from Marianne Harnischmacher after the death of her husband on August 19, 1957.[159]

In the summer of 1928, Breuer left Dessau for "emancipated, civilized" Berlin, as William L. Shirer recalled the Berlin of the Weimar Republic.[160] One of his memories of this decisive passage was summoned up almost half a century later when, in December 1974, Breuer responded to an inquiry from a New York art dealer regarding the history and provenance of a watercolor by Kandinsky: "The date is 1927," he wrote. "I left the Bauhaus—where I served as a member of the faculty—in the summer of 1928. My Bauhaus friends assembled an album as my farewell gift. One sheet in this album was the watercolor from Wassily Kandinsky. He was a close friend in spite of some thirty-six years of age difference."[161]

BAUHAUS EPILOGUE

On October 4, 1960, Breuer received a letter from Hans Wingler, at that time director of the Bauhaus-Archiv in Darmstadt, informing him that he had been nominated to the Kuratorium (to become an "Overseer") of the Bauhaus-Archiv in the company of, among others, Albers, Bayer, Sigfried Giedion, Gropius, Ludwig Grote, Ludwig Hilbersheimer, Itten, Mies van der Rohe, and Muche. A week later, Breuer responded that he was happy to accept the nomination.[162] But in 1968, at the time of a Bauhaus exhibition in Paris in which plans and photographs of Breuer's UNESCO Headquarters and Whitney Museum of American Art were displayed, in a letter to the Bauhaus representative in the United States, he added: "I did not receive an invitation to the Bauhaus exhibition opening, nor a catalog, nor any other information about the exhibition and the material I sent there. As you can imagine, I cannot help but have some bitter feelings about this."[163] It was not the only time that Breuer was to feel embittered about the Bauhaus. When in 1948 a photograph of the Harnischmacher House prepared for a MoMA traveling exhibition of Breuer's work was labeled "an independent expression for one who was trained at the Bauhaus," Gropius wrote to Breuer, saying that he considered this "a slap against the Bauhaus and just the opposite of the truth, as the tendency and achievement of the Bauhaus you and I know has certainly been to fight any rigid narrow approach and to leave the door open to independent personalities."[164] But in his letter of response, Breuer wrote that he saw nothing wrong with the description of the Harnischmacher House because "the architectural expression of the Bauhaus is usually identified with the *Gropius* architecture of 1920–28."[165]

As crucial as Breuer knew the Bauhaus had been to his formation as an artist, he would be ambivalent about it, and about the significance of his various roles there, for the rest of his life. It was an ambivalence engendered and sustained by the complex nature of his friendship with Gropius and by his resentment of the continuing association of his architecture with the work of Gropius because of their Bauhaus and partnership past, without due recognition of his independent accomplishments. It was tied to Breuer's vexation at having been held back as an architecture professional because of Gropius's views about methods for the training of architects. It was linked also to Breuer's ambiguous, and occasionally devalued, position as a Hungarian national in the ethnocentric culture of Germany after the First World War. It reflected his discomfort with the praise of his Bauhaus furniture at the expense of his post-Bauhaus architecture. And, some might argue, his limitations as well as his strengths as an architect can be traced directly to the school. Free of the doctrines and norms of traditional training, he was able to work pragmatically and creatively during his professional lifetime. But he could not break away—or at least not definitively away—from the modernist and Constructivist framework of the early Bauhaus, which had had such a potent impact on him during his initial development as an architect in 1922 and 1923. Nor could he dispute that his work, more than that of any other Bauhausler, would come to most perfectly exemplify the Bauhaus founding ideal of the interaction of arts and crafts to create a unified work of architecture.

Besides, it was at the Bauhaus-Archiv Museum in Berlin that in 1975 Marcel Breuer's work, both the furniture and the architecture, was exhibited in Germany—for the first time.

1   It was Hungarian architect Alfréd (Fred) Forbàt who told Breuer about the Bauhaus, according to Christopher Wilk, *Marcel Breuer: Furniture and Interiors* (New York: Museum of Modern Art, 1981), 16. Also see n. 47.

2   Marcel Breuer, interview for *Les Archives du XXième siècle*, March 30 and 31, 1974, transcript, Speeches and Writings, AAA. Unless otherwise indicated, statements by Breuer (author's translation) quoted in this chapter are taken from the transcription of this interview.

3   Gropius's tone is so described in Gillian Naylor, *The Bauhaus Reassessed* (New York: Dutton, 1985), 54.

4   The recruitment flyer included not only the program of study, but also the manifesto of the founding of the school. Descriptions of courses and requirements for study are found in many accounts of the early Bauhaus, especially Hans M. Wingler, *Bauhaus* (Cambridge, Mass.: MIT Press, 1986); see also Marcel Franciscono, *Walter Gropius and the Creation of the Bauhaus in Weimar* (Urbana: University of Illinois Press, 1971); Naylor, *Bauhaus Reassessed*; and Eva Forgács, *The Bauhaus Idea and Bauhaus Politics*, trans. John Batki (Budapest: Central European University Press, 1995).

5   For admission requirements set down in the 1919 program and those that appeared in the 1921 pamphlet, *The Statutes of the Staatliche Bauhaus in Weimar* ("The following must be furnished as a basis for admission: Original work [drawings, painting, sculpture, craftwork, designs, photography, etc.]"), see Wingler, *Bauhaus*, 33, 44. Herbert Bayer remembered that in 1921, "[Gropius] was in his office / at the van de velde bauhaus building in weimar / when I first met him, / presenting my work / to become a student at the bauhaus" ("Homage to Gropius," in *Bauhaus and Bauhaus People*, ed. Eckhard Neumann [New York: Van Nostrand Reinhold, 1970], 131).

6   On the ideological and historical background of the founding of the Bauhaus, see, especially, Naylor, *Bauhaus Reassessed*; Franciscono, *Creation of the Bauhaus*; Forgács, *Bauhaus Idea*; and Elaine S. Hochman, *Bauhaus: Crucible of Modernism* (New York: Fromm International, 1997).

7   Quoted, in part, in Peter Blake, *Marcel Breuer: Architect and Designer* (New York: Museum of Modern Art, 1949), 8, and Biderman, Tolk & Associates, "Marcel Breuer: A Narrative Biography," public-relations release, n.d., AAA.

8   Wilk, *Furniture and Interiors*, 15.

9   These paintings are in the possession of Constance L. Breuer, and I am grateful to her for permitting me to reproduce them.

10 Breuer is referring to the effort to carve up Hungary into independent ethnic nations after the end of the First World War. Independence movements generated by Czechs, Slavs, Serbs, and Romanians took over parts of the country.

11 S. A. Mansbach, "Confrontation and Accommodation in the Hungarian Avant-Garde," *Art Journal* 49 (1990): 9–20, esp. n. 1; John Kish, *The Hungarian Avant-Garde, 1914–1933* [exhibition catalogue] (Storrs: William Benton Museum of Art, University of Connecticut, 1987); Charles Dautrey and Jean-Claude Guerlain, eds., *L'Activisme hongrois* (Montrouge: Goutal-Darly, 1977). See also Gábor Andrási, Gábor Pataki, György Szücs, and András Zwickl, *The History of Hungarian Art in the Twentieth Century*, trans. Johm Bátki (Budapest: Corvina Books, 1999).

12 Blake, *Marcel Breuer*, Acknowledgments, 8. In general, Breuer was reluctant to discuss his life in much detail, but with Blake he was willing "to talk for many hours on subjects of which there was little record outside his own memory."

13 Control of Hungary was the objective of a nationalist revolutionary group led by Béla Kun that in March 1919 succeeded in taking control of the government for 133 days. When his revolution failed, Kun fled to Vienna. Artists, writers, and

intellectuals philosophically allied to the revolutionaries were in danger of becoming victims of the reprisals that followed the uprising, and in 1919 refugee groups migrated to Moscow, Berlin, and Vienna.

14 Mansbach, "Confrontation and Accommodation," 12, n. 21; see also Oliver A. I. Bottar, "From the Avant-Garde to 'Proletarian Art,'" *Art Journal* 52 (1993): 34, n. 6, and Christina Lodder, *Russian Constructivism* (New Haven, Conn.: Yale University Press, 1983), 235.

15 Quoted in Wingler, *Bauhaus*, 31.

16 Frank Whitford, *Bauhaus* (London: Thames and Hudson, 1986), 69.

17 Wilk points to an inconsistency in the record regarding the day of the month of Breuer's birth, May 21 or 22 (*Furniture and Interiors*, 15, n. 1). However, there is a Hungarian document among Breuer's papers recording that he was born Marcell Lajos Breuer on May 21, 1902, to Franciska Kann, age thirty, who had been born in Budapest, and Jakab Breuer, age thirty-five, a dental technician, who had been born in Györ ("data from Marcel Breuer's birth certificate: #459. Notation from the Bureau of Birth Registry in District II," AAA). Breuer (the youngest of three children) was born at home, 4 Irgalmasok Boulevard.

18 Franciscono, *Creation of the Bauhaus*, 175. In a speech delivered on October 13, 1920, Gropius described the "chaotic" life of the Bauhaus. For one account of the problems at the school during this first period of organization, see Whitford, *Bauhaus*, 41–46.

19 On October 11, 1966, Breuer replied to a letter from Harvard, where a special exhibition—"Bauhaus: A Teaching Idea"—was being organized: "It is unfortunate that I cannot be of very much help. . . . All my Bauhaus documents and drawings, etc. were destroyed or lost" (Correspondence, AAA).

20 To Herbert Bayer, who was installing the exhibition, Breuer wrote: "I am sending you today 415 photographs and 40 drawings which I just received from Martha. Please be very careful of this material" (Breuer to Bayer, October 6, 1938, SUL 5).

21 Herbert Bayer to Breuer, May 10, 1938, Correspondence, AAA.

22 "According to his own account," Wilk writes, "Breuer arrived too late in the term to join the introductory course. He looked into several different courses and settled on the carpentry or woodworking workshop where he finally received the 'practical' training he had sought in Vienna" (*Furniture and Interiors*, 20). This memoir does not quite accord with the facts of Bauhaus history or with other recollections by Breuer. In 1974 he said, "I arrived at the Bauhaus six weeks late and I began as a student in Johannes Itten's Preliminary Course." Itten's own memory can be summoned up: "Breuer, Scheper, Schmidt, Stozl, Bayer, [Anni] Albers were students during the second and third vorkurs" ("How the Tremendous Influence of the Bauhaus Began," in *Bauhaus and Bauhaus People*, ed. Neumann, 21). The carpentry shop (as distinct from the woodcarving shop) was, furthermore, the last of the workshops to be installed, as Franciscono reports that February 7, 1921, is the earliest notice of its operation (*Creation of the Bauhaus*, 161). And the 1921 statutes of the Bauhaus, published in January of that year, state that apprentices could join a workshop only after the successful completion of a six-month probationary period in the Preliminary Course (Wingler, *Bauhaus*, 45).

23 Franciscono, *Creation of the Bauhaus*, 174.

24 This often-quoted dictum is from Gropius's essay "Idee und Aufbau des staatlichen Bauhauses" (1923).

25 Walter Gropius to Peter Blake, March 28, 1949, SUL 52.

26 Wingler, *Bauhaus*, 44. For a description of the course in a pamphlet produced for an exhibition of the work of Bauhaus students in April and May 1922, see ibid., 54.

27 Johannes Itten, *Design and Form: The Basic Course at the Bauhaus*, trans. John Maass (New York: Reinhold, 1964).

28 Breuer, interview for *Les Archives du XXième siècle* and quoted in William H. Jordy, "The Aftermath of the Bauhaus in America: Gropius, Mies, and Breuer," in *The Intellectual Migration: Europe and America, 1930–1960*, ed. Donald Fleming and Bernard Bailyn (Cambridge, Mass.: Harvard University Press, 1969), 506.

29 For the interconnections of calisthenics, nutrition, learning, dress, and art resulting from Itten's commitment to Mazdaznan (based on an ancient Persian religion with physical and mental disciplines similar to yoga), see Paul Citroen, "Mazdaznan at the Bauhaus," in *Bauhaus and Bauhaus People*, ed. Neumann, 45. Citroen was a student at the Bauhaus and a disciple of Itten.

30 According to Felix Klee, "He looked like a priest to me, with his red-violet, high-buttoned uniform, his bald, shaven crown, and his gold-rimmed glasses. From the very first I was fascinated by his personality" ("My Memories of the Weimar Bauhaus," in *Bauhaus and Bauhaus People*, ed. Neumann, 38). For descriptions of Itten by Bauhaus contemporaries, see also Whitford, *Bauhaus*, 52–54, and Naylor, *Bauhaus Reassessed*, 75–82.

31 Feininger and Marcks were Gropius's earliest appointments to the Bauhaus. Principally a sculptor and a designer of ceramics and porcelain for manufacture, Marcks became Master of Form in the pottery workshop. At the same time, however, he designed many woodcuts that were printed in the printing workshop headed by Feininger.

32 Oskar Schlemmer, diary entry, October 25, 1922, in *The Letters and Diaries of Oskar Schlemmer*, ed. Tut Schlemmer, trans. Krishna Winston (Evanston, Ill.: Northwestern University Press, 1990), 130.

33 Henry-Russell Hitchcock, "Marcel Breuer and the American Tradition in Architecture" [essay and exhibition catalogue, Harvard University, Graduate School of Design, June–September 1938] (GSD, Cambridge, Mass., 1938, mimeographed), 6, HUAL.

34 Quoted in Winthrop Sargeant, "Profile of Marcel Breuer" (manuscript draft, prepared for the *New Yorker*, ca. 1971–72).

35 If indeed he had a vision. In an interview with William H. Jordy in the 1960s, Breuer said, "The Bauhaus was starting from zero . . . the Bauhaus student was no professional. When I came to the Bauhaus I had no idea what I would become. In those conditions [a "destroyed society . . . uncertainty everywhere. . . . Germany had lost the war . . . inflation was terrible"] you didn't think about what you would become. The Bauhaus student was nobody" (quoted in "Aftermath of the Bauhaus in America," 506).

36 Reginald R. Isaacs, *Gropius: An Illustrated Biography of the Creator of the Bauhaus* (Boston: Little, Brown, 1991); Andrew Saint, "The Battle of the Bauhaus," in *The Image of the Architect* (New Haven, Conn.: Yale University Press, 1983), 115.

37 Walter Gropius to "Sehr geehrter Herr Redaktur" [editors of Hungarian newspapers], October 31, 1934, Correspondence, AAA.

38 See pp. 108–11 in this volume.

39 Constance L. Breuer, conversation with author.

40 Isaacs, *Gropius*, 72.

41 Hochman, *Bauhaus*, 42, 186.

42 Isaacs, *Gropius*, 72, n. 37; see also 321, n. 120.

43 Hochman, *Bauhaus*, 141.

44 Winfried Nerdinger, *Walter Gropius: The Architect Walter Gropius: Drawings, Prints, and Photographs from Busch-Reisinger Museum, Harvard University Art Museums, Cambridge/Mass., and from Bauhaus-Archiv Berlin* [exhibition catalogue] (Berlin: Mann Verlag, 1985), 44. December 18, 1920, was the date of the topping-out ceremony.

45 For illustrations and discussion of the style of these pieces, see Wilk, *Furniture and Interiors*, 22–23; Magdalena Droste, "Marcel Breuer's Furniture," in Magdalena Droste and Manfred Ludewig, *Marcel Breuer Design* (Cologne: Taschen, 1992), 9–10; and Naylor, *Bauhaus Reassessed*, 105. It may be that Breuer designed the so-called African Chair with the Sommerfeld House in mind—its idiosyncratic nature suggests there may have been a "program" behind it—and that it was rejected. Although Blake allied the chair with "the then current interest in primitive Negro art" and with Hungarian peasant furniture (*Marcel Breuer*, 16), if looked at with the woodcut announcing the Sommerfeld topping-out (Franciscono, *Creation of the Bauhaus*, 45) and particularly with the patterned geometries of Joost Schmidt's carvings on the beams, entrance door, and hall, the chair seems less peculiar and possibly part of a coordinated design effort. Naylor says that "with its folk-art, totem-like quality [it] might have been inspired by Itten's teaching" (*Bauhaus Reassessed*, 105). The sketch of the vestibule and staircase of the Sommerfeld House, "drawn in Gropius's private architectural studio by the architect Carl Fieger according to directions given by Gropius and Meyer" (Wingler, *Bauhaus*, 239), depicts high-backed, pointed-arched arm chairs that are consistent with the contours of Breuer's design.
   In 1963, Breuer received a letter from a woman in California who wrote that "at an auction in 1933 in Berlin my parents were able to buy and preserve the furniture you had designed for the Adolf Sommerfeld House in Berlin" and that it was still in her mother's possession. Breuer responded that he was "surprised to learn that it is still in existence" (Correspondence, AAA).

46 The history of this settlement is in Nerdinger, *Walter Gropius*, 58–60, and Christine Kutschke, "Bauhausbauten der Dessauer Zeit" (diss., Hochschule für Architektur und Bauwessen, Weimar, 1981).

47 On Hungarians at the Bauhaus, see the section "Bauhaus," in *Wechsel Wirkungen: Ungarische Avantgarde in der Weimarer Republik*, ed. Hubertus Gassner [exhibition catalogue, Neue Galerie, Kassel, and Museum Bochum] (Marburg: Jonas Verlag, 1986), specifically, on Breuer, Hubertus Gassner, "Zwischen den Stühlen sitzend sich im Kreise drehen: Marcel Breuer und Gyula Pap als Bauhaus-Gestalter," 312–38, and Otto Mezei, "Ungarische Architekten am Bauhaus," 339–87, esp. 341–42, 361.

48 Richard Pommer, "The Flat Roof: A Modernist Controversy in Germany," *Art Journal* 43 (1983): 163, n. 36.

49 For the background of this project, see Nerdinger, *Walter Gropius*, 60; for the significance of the exhibition, see Forgács, *Bauhaus Idea*, chap. 10.

50 "From the Catalogue of the 'first Exhibition of Russian Art,' Van Diemen Gallery, Berlin (1922)," in *The Tradition of Constructivism*, ed. Stephen Bann (New York: Viking, 1974), 70.

51 Wingler, *Bauhaus*, 66–67; Nerdinger, *Walter Gropius*, 16–18, 58–60.

52 In 1919, about one-quarter of the 150 students at the Bauhaus were women (Isaacs, *Gropius*, 75).

53 Droste, "Marcel Breuer's Furniture," 11. Following traditional guild categories, a Bauhaus student could move from apprentice to journeyman and from journeyman to junior master by passing examinations. After three years of workshop activities, the Bauhaus student took the journeyman's exam and an exam in design in front of the faculty before receiving the diploma (Isaacs, *Gropius*, 70). According to Whitford, "Gropius' private practice frequently sub-contracted to the workshops the furniture and fittings of houses that the director had been commissioned to design" (*Bauhaus*, 69).

54 Whitford, *Bauhaus*, 69. The kitchen of Haus am Horn, designed by Benita Otte and Ernest Gebhard, received much acclaim and has mistakenly been attributed to Breuer. For example, Bauhausler Heinrich Konig has noted, "Today when we see the kitchen equipment of this experimental house designed by Marcel Breuer" ("The Bauhaus—Yesterday and Today," in *Bauhaus and Bauhaus People*, ed. Neumann, 121). This attribution is repeated in many accounts of the Bauhaus.

55 Wingler, *Bauhaus*, 385. For some of the materials (such as "Tortoleum" tiles for insulation), see Muche's own description of the house in ibid., 66–67, and Naylor, *Bauhaus Reassessed*, 115. On construction methods in this period, including the Jurko construction (concrete blocks) used at Haus am Horn, see Nerdinger, *Walter Gropius*, 16, n. 75.

56 Walter Gropius and László Moholy-Nagy, eds., *Ein Versuchshaus des Bauhauses*, Bauhausbücher 3 (Munich: Langen, 1925); Wingler, *Bauhaus*, 130, 446.

57 Saint, "Battle of the Bauhaus," 117.

58 Oskar Schlemmer, diary entry, June 23, 1921, in *Letters and Diaries*, ed. Schlemmer, 109. Recent reassessments of the Bauhaus take the view that " architecture played a key role in Bauhaus research design from the very beginning" (review of *Bauhaus 1919–1933: Da Kandinsky a Klee, da Gropius a Mies van der Rohe*, ed. Marco De Michelis and Agnes Kohlmeyer, *Journal of the Society of Architectural Historians* 57 [1998]: 68), but this is not the same as offering technical instruction in architecture.

59 Isaacs, *Gropius*, 66.

60 Franciscono, *Creation of the Bauhaus*, 140–41.

61 Ibid., 141.

62 Quoted in Isaacs, *Gropius*, 57.

63 Quoted in ibid., 92.

64 Ibid.

65 Ibid.

66 Franciscono, *Creation of the Bauhaus*, 163, n. 33; see also *Das frühe Bauhaus und Johannes Itten* [exhibition catalogue] (Weimar: Hatje, 1994), 510.

67 Wingler, *Bauhaus*, 53.

68 Whitford, *Bauhaus*, 70.

69 Quoted in Wingler, *Bauhaus*, 67.

70 Whitford, *Bauhaus*, 145.

71 Marcel Breuer, notes, n.d. [ca. 1947], "Autobiography," SUL 39.

72 Quoted in Sargeant, "Profile of Marcel Breuer."

73 On Breuer's furniture in relation to influences from the dominant artistic movements of the period, see Wilk, *Furniture and Interiors*, 23–34. An important observation about Klee is made by Franciscono: "His lessons were conceived in terms closely analogous to those of architecture," wherein "painting itself was understood as a construction built up or put together from repeatable, more or less geometric—in effect modular—units in ways generally comparable to the way architecture is put together" (*Creation of the Bauhaus*, 242, n. 1).

74 Marcel Breuer, speech, November 19, 1975, Speeches and Writings, AAA.

75 Breuer and Moholy had collaborated on an exhibition booth for the Architectural Press at the London Building Exhibition of 1936 (*Architects' Journal*, September 17, 1936, 382).

76 Isaacs, *Gropius*, 115.

77 Marcel Breuer, "Form Funktion," *Junge Menschen: Monatshefte für Politik, Kunst, Literatur und Leben*, November 1924, 191, reprinted as "On the Reorganization of the Bauhaus," in *Marcel Breuer: Buildings and Projects, 1921–1961*, ed. Cranston Jones (New York: Praeger, 1962), 261–62.

78 *Contemporary Architects* (London: St. James Press, [1976]), AAA.

79 Sargeant, "Profile of Marcel Breuer."

80 See, for example, Jürg Spiller, ed., *Paul Klee: The Thinking Eye: The Notebooks of Paul Klee*, trans. Ralph Manheim (New York: Wittenborn, 1961), and Franciscono, *Creation of the Bauhaus*, esp. 212–13, 242.

81 Marcel Breuer, speech at Klee Symposium, MoMA, February 2, 1950, Speeches and Writings, AAA.

82 In a letter to Peter Blake, Gropius refers to a manuscript by Breuer for a Bauhaus discussion about the 1923 exhibition: "On the first page he gives a very accurate reason why we refused the Doesburg approach. It couldn't have been better said" (Gropius to Blake, February 7, 1949, Breuer file, MoMA).

83 Andor Weininger kept a list of those who signed up for the "styl-kursus in Weimar durch Theo van Doesburg" from March to July 1922, on Wednesdays from 7:00 to 9:00 p.m. Breuer's name does not appear. The list is in *Andor Weininger: Vom Bauhaus zur Konzeptuellen Kunst* [exhibition catalogue, Kunstverein für die Rheinlande und Westfalen] (Stuttgart: Cantz, 1990). On van Doesburg at the Bauhaus, see Forgács, *Bauhaus Idea*, 65–70.

84 Naylor, *Bauhaus Reassessed*, 95.

85 All histories of the Bauhaus account for this change of direction. See, for example, Whitford, *Bauhaus*, 116–21.

86 Theo van Doesburg to Antony Kok, January 7, 1921, quoted in *de Stijl, cat. 81, Stedelijk Museum Amsterdam 6.7.'51–25.9.'51* [exhibition catalogue] (Amsterdam: Stedelijk Museum, [1951]), 100.

87 Walter Gropius to Peter Blake, January 10, 1949, Breuer file, MoMA.

88 Wilk, *Furniture and Interiors*, 23–34.

89 High expectations for the importance of architecture at the Bauhaus were kept alive by the symbol of the organization of study accompanying Gropius's essay "Idee und Aufbau des staatlichen Bauhauses" (1923)—a series of circles with *Bau* at the core (Wingler, *Bauhaus*, 52).

90 Isaacs, *Gropius*, 115.

91 "Today much trouble in the Bauhaus; these people deserve to be spanked" and "We face an inner crisis of great tension. Tonight is a student assembly" were representative observations by Gropius (Walter Gropius to Ise Gropius, March 12, 1924, 39, IGD/E: Correspondence Ise Gropius and Walter Gropius, 1931–68).

92 Wingler, *Bauhaus*, 388.

93 Breuer to Walter Gropius, November 4, 1948, Correspondence, AAA.

94 Isaacs, *Gropius*, 115.

95 Reprinted in Mezei, "Ungarische Architekten am Bauhaus," 361.

96 Breuer to George Rosenberg, March 9, 1948, SUL 21.

97 Hitchcock, "Marcel Breuer and the American Tradition," 4.

98 Breuer to Ise Gropius, March 16, 1932, Walter Gropius Papers (Breuer Letters), HL.

99 Jones, ed., *Marcel Breuer*, 233, fig. 10.

100 Wingler, *Bauhaus*, 388; see also Ronald Wiedenhoeft, *Berlin's Housing Revolution: German Reform in the 1920s* (Ann Arbor, Mich.: UMI Research Press, 1985). A coexistent drawing by Muche, also prophetic, called for a fifteen-story dwelling, but it differed in character and materials from Breuer's and was not shaped as a narrow slab.

101 Wilk, *Furniture and Interiors*, figs. 12, 17, 19.

102 Marcel Breuer, "Beiträge zur Frage des Hochhauses," *Die Form* 5 (1930): 113–17, in *"Die Form": Stimme des deutschen Werkbundes, 1925–1934*, ed. Felix Schwarz and Frank Gloor (Gütersloh: Mohn, 1969), 163–67. The three projects Breuer used as examples were the Spandau-Haselhorst *Siedlung*, Elberfeld hospital, and Fuld factory.

103 Social questions about the role of women, domestic work, house and kitchen design, communal facilities, and the like had been important at the Bauhaus (Wiedenhoeft, *Berlin's Housing Revolution*, 170).

104 In the Architects' Qualification Register he submitted to the New York City Housing Authority on October 21, 1949, under the section headed "Experience prior to independent practice," Breuer stated: "Designer with Pierre Chareau, Paris, 1924" (SUL 51). On Chareau's work and career, see Marc Vellay and Kenneth Frampton, *Pierre Chareau: Architect and Craftsman, 1883–1950* (New York: Rizzoli, 1985).

105 Quoted in Droste, "Marcel Breuer's Furniture," 13.

106 Tim Benton, "Urbanism," in *Le Corbusier: Architect of the Century* [exhibition catalogue] (London: Arts Council of Great Britain, 1987), 212.

107 IGD/E, July 12, 1925, 54–55.

108 For political background relating to the termination of the Bauhaus enterprise in Weimar and its next phase, in Dessau, see Hochman, *Bauhaus*, chaps. 10, 12.

109 There was to be a sixth, Grete Stolzl for the weaving workshop, but she did not take over the shop until 1927 when Muche resigned.

110 IGD/E, February 16, 1928, 290.

111 IGD/E, November 27, 1926, 166–67.

112 Ibid.

113 Breuer to Herbert Read, August 9, 1955, Correspondence, AAA.

114 Breuer continues in his letter to Read: "Later on these designs and the production of the tubular chairs and tables were taken over by Thonet Industries, a concern with factories in most countries of Europe and America. I acted for a number of years as their design consultant in connection with the production."

115 Marcel Breuer, "Das Kleinmetallhaus Typ 1926," *Offset-Buch und Werbekunst* 7 (1926): 372.

116 Hitchcock, "Marcel Breuer and the American Tradition," 8.

117 Gilbert Herbert, *The Dream of the Factory-Made House: Walter Gropius and Konrad Wachsmann* (Cambridge, Mass.: MIT Press, 1986), 106. Ise Gropius recorded in her diary that there was a question about Breuer's priority with regard to the idea of a steel house: "Breuer suspects that Muche plots against him," and "G[ropius] . . . heard him [Paulick] say that Breuer had stolen the idea of the metal house from his son [architect Richard Paulick] and Muche" (IGD/E, May 12, 1926, 143).

118 Breuer to Herbert Read, August 9, 1955.

119 Walter Gropius, *Internationale Architektur: Auswahl der besten neuzeitlichen Architektur-werke* (Munich: Langen, 1925), 90.

120 Walter Gropius, *Internationale Architektur: Auswahl der besten neuzeitlichen Architektur-werke*, 2d ed. (Munich: Langen, 1927), 90, 91. The small metal house was also published in Breuer, "Kleinmetallhaus," 371.

121 IGD/E, May 21, 1925, 39; April (no day) 1925, 80–81; May 21, 1925, 39.

122 Breuer to Ise Gropius, March 15, 1971, HL.

123 Ise Gropius to Breuer, May 20, 1935, Correspondence, AAA.

124 IGD/E, July 12, 1925, 54–55.

125 IGD/E, February 13, 1926, 113.

126 Isaacs, *Gropius*, 120.

127 IGD/E, April 1925, for insertion on p. 34 of the diary.

128 For Gropius's forty-second birthday, Breuer had composed a handwritten greeting in the jokey mode of Bauhaus birthday celebrations with double meanings and hyperbole: "Süsser Schatz! / Grosser Baumensch! / Unerreich-

barer Zeugungslied der werdenden Kultur!/. . . im zeichen des grossen G⋆ mögest Du BLUHEN!" (Sweet treasure! / great man of building! / unrivaled procreator of a new culture! /. . . in the symbol of the big G⋆ may you flourish!) (Breuer to Gropius, May 18, 1925, BHA).

129 Richard Pommer and Christian F. Otto, *Weissenhof 1927 and the Modern Movement in Architecture* (Chicago: University of Chicago Press, 1991), 127.

130 Marcel Breuer, "Metallmöbel und moderne Räumlichkeit," *Das neue Frankfurt*, January 2, 1928, ill., quoted in Karin Kirsch, *The Weissenhofsiedlung: Experimental Housing for the Deutscher Werkbund, Stuttgart, 1927* (New York: Rizzoli, 1989), 126.

131 Marcel Breuer, "Das Innere des Hauses," *Die Bauwelt*, May 7, 1931, 615–16, quoted in Wilk, *Furniture and Interiors*, 185–86.

132 Wilk, *Furniture and Interiors*, 64; see also Naylor, *Bauhaus Reassessed*, 148–52.

133 Pommer and Otto, *Weissenhof 1927*, 209, n. 82.

134 Ibid.

135 Ibid.

136 IGD/E, April 26, 1926, 134.

137 Saint, "Battle of the Bauhaus," 123–27.

138 IGD/E, February 10, 1927, 193.

139 Oskar Schlemmer to Tut Schlemmer, in *Letters and Diaries*, ed. Schlemmer, 195, 208.

140 Oskar Schlemmer to Tut Schlemmer, May (no day) 1927, in ibid., 204–5.

141 Droste, "Marcel Breuer's Furniture," 117. A page in the 1927 catalogue has the "preis-liste für Metall-Möbel System Marcel Breuer." See also Wilk, *Furniture and Interiors*, 52–53.

142 IGD/E, March 24, 1927, 203–4.

143 Oskar Schlemmer to Tut Schlemmer, January 14, 1928, in *Letters and Diaries*, ed. Schlemmer, 219.

144 Oskar Schlemmer to Otto Meyer, February 27, 1928, in ibid., 228.

145 Quoted in Naylor, *Bauhaus Reassessed*, 166.

146 Ibid.

147 IGD/E, December 16, 1926, 175; April 6, 1927, 207.

148 IGD/E, November 13, 1927, 254.

149 Quoted in Wingler, *Bauhaus*, 137.

150 Wilk, *Furniture and Interiors*, 40.

151 IGD/E, February 5, 1928, 285.

152 Oskar Schlemmer to Tut Schlemmer, March 26, 1928, in *Letters and Diaries*, ed. Schlemmer, 230.

153 Farkas Molnár, cited in Forgács, *Bauhaus Idea*, 92, n. 23.

154 Isaacs, *Gropius*, 143.

155 IGD/E, March 3, 1928, 297.

156 IGD/E, May 20, 1927, 218.

157 IGD/E, March 3, 1928, 296.

158 Dozens of unpublished working drawings and floor plans, still folded in their original office binders, for the custom-designed furniture, free-standing and built-in, and for the arrangement of the spaces for this job, were added to SUL in 1999.

159 Marianne Harnischmacher to Breuer, on the reverse of a printed notice of thanks for messages of sympathy, September 1957, SUL 152. The Harnischmachers were grateful to Breuer for his many acts of friendship. Depressed after the end of the Second World War, Paul Harnishmacher wrote to Breuer that "it is deeply moving that our friendship has been maintained over the course of so many years and that it should be you who extends a helping hand to us when those who belong to the nation to which my wife and I once belonged have been the origin of so many evils in the past several years. The fact that in spite of all this your helpful gift was still possible gives us some hope in our distress" (Harnishmacher to Breuer, October 28, 1946, Correspondence, AAA).

160 William L. Shirer, *Berlin Diary* (New York: Knopf, 1942), 13.

161 Breuer to Paul McGriel, Bernard Danenberg Galleries, December 20, 1974, Correspondence, AAA.

162 Breuer to Hans Wingler, October 12, 1960, Correspondence, AAA.

163 Breuer to Charlotte Wiedler, February 12, 1969, Correspondence, AAA.

164 Walter Gropius to Breuer, October 11, 1948, Correspondence, AAA.

165 Breuer to Walter Gropius, November 4, 1948, Correspondence, AAA. Emphasis added.

2. Berlin, Zürich, and Budapest:
The Nomadic Years, 1928–35

Von der Heydt apartment,
Berlin. 1929–30. Interior design
and furniture by Breuer

WITH PRINTED CARDS AND LETTERHEAD reading "Marcel Breuer Architekt," in the summer of 1928 Breuer set himself up in a studio apartment in Berlin at 121C Potsdamerstrasse, a few doors from Walter Gropius's combined home and reactivated architectural office at 121A. In the seven years that would elapse between his departure from Dessau—the end of his official connection to the Bauhaus—and his emigration to London in 1935, he practiced architecture in Germany, Switzerland, and Hungary alongside degree holders from the technical institutes. He entered (usually collaboratively) the same important competitions as Gropius and other traditionally trained and well-established architects, and for some projects he won prizes and commendations—a ranking of third out of ten for his Fuld factory (1929) in Frankfurt and a first prize for the buildings for the Spring Trade Fair (1934) in Budapest. Despite his foreign nationality he became a member of the Bund Deutscher Architekten (BDA), Germany's leading professional group of architects, thanks to Gropius, who had been elected director in 1927.[1] He joined the newly founded Congrès international d'architecture moderne (CIAM), dedicated to social, economic, and political reforms through housing and city planning, and he attended its historic first meeting in La Sarraz, Switzerland, in 1928. The theme of CIAM's congress in Frankfurt in 1929 was "Die Wohnung für das existenzminimum" (the low-cost dwelling); an important feature of this meeting for Breuer, because of his interest in prefabrication and metal houses, was the exhibition there of Le Corbusier's Maisons Loucheur project (1928–29)—dry-assembly, semidetached steel houses.[2]

In 1930, Breuer may have encouraged László Moholy-Nagy—or Moholy perhaps thought of it on his own—to promote him for one of the more exotic modernist architectural ventures then floating on international currents. On his behalf, Moholy wrote to Hilla Rebay soon after she made known the intentions of Solomon Guggenheim to enlarge his collection of nonobjective art and to found a museum for the collection in New York City: "Breuer, who I think is the most talented architect of our time, has even decided to dream about the museum that is to be built in the USA."[3] While his architectural activity in these years was discouragingly confined to "dreams," such as designing a museum in New York, or to competition projects and exhibition structures, Breuer was occupied by carrying out for a number of clients the remodeling and reorganizing of house and apartment interiors and, in this connection, the custom designing of furniture. Few architectural projects could be realized, in any event, as Germany was enveloped in the Great Depression, which slowed every kind of building activity and left more than 90 percent of architects without work by 1932.[4] Breuer lamented to Ise Gropius about "the internal poison of unrealized ideas" in a letter from Budapest;[5] earlier to Gropius, he had written with some bitterness about how "our times are really hostile towards [architects]."[6] Breuer built only two works in the seven years between Dessau and London: a house for Paul and Marianne Harnischmacher in Wiesbaden in 1932 and, in collaboration with Alfred and Emil Roth, the Doldertal apartment buildings in Zürich first planned in 1932 and constructed in 1935–36. They were, however, works that would put him on the map of interwar European modernism.

BERLIN, 1928–31

If Breuer's greater ambitions were stifled, his creativity was not. In Berlin in 1928 (possibly earlier, in Dessau), he produced the final version of his original 1925 classic, the "Wassily" club armchair, and he designed the universally successful cantilevered tubular-steel-and-cane side chair and armchair (B 32, 34), now identified as the "Breuer Chair." The chronology and

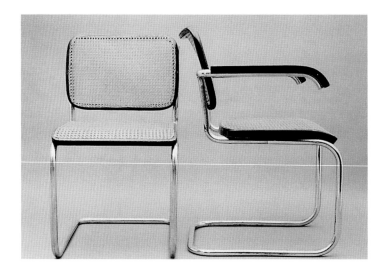

Breuer side chair (B 32) and armchair (B 34). Tubular steel, wood, and cane. 1928

attribution of the invention of a cantilevered tubular-steel chair became the bases of a dispute between Breuer and Dutch architect-designer Mart Stam, each of whom claimed the priority.[7]

Collaboration was essential for carrying out the entries in the large-scale competition projects that defined much of Germany's vision of a partnership between social welfare and architecture. Intricate technical reports, mathematical calculations, and rationalized economic analyses, together with drafting skills and model making, were required of architects involved in designing housing projects and devising city-planning strategies. The exhaustive calculations demanded of competitors for the Spandau-Haselhorst housing project of 1928 are described in detail by Ronald Wiedenhoeft in his study of housing in Berlin in the 1920s.[8] Training in this and similar exercises during the period of his Berlin practice gave Breuer the foundation for comparable undertakings in his American housing experiments, notably his prodigious but unsuccessful effort to capture the commission for Stuyvesant Town in New York in 1943 and 1944. It also contributed to the respect he would earn for business acumen and for the efficiency of his architectural practice.

Gustav Hassenpflug had been Breuer's furniture design student in the carpentry workshop in the Dessau Bauhaus from 1926 to 1928 and became his draftsman and collaborator in Berlin. Five years younger than Breuer, journeyman carpenter and son of a master carpenter, Hassenpflug in his third and fourth semesters at the Bauhaus took courses in the new Department of Architecture, begun in 1927 under Hannes Meyer, where he developed his architectural skills. He had a special interest in the uses of architecture for the benefits of health and physical therapy (hospitals and medical clinics). In 1928, he joined Breuer in Berlin while still affiliated with the Bauhaus as a student. He worked with him until 1931, principally as draftsman for Breuer's many commissions for residential interiors and professional offices (room layouts and working drawings for the custom-designed furniture), from which they earned some money, and for unexecuted house projects and housing competitions, from which they earned little or none. With Hassenpflug's assistance between 1929 and 1931, Breuer submitted competition projects for housing in Spandau-Haselhorst (1928), a hospital in Elberfeld (1928–29), a factory complex in Frankfurt (1929), and a theater in Kharkov, Soviet Union (1930–31). They produced designs for weekend houses and standardized independent single-family dwellings during 1929 and 1930, for projects destined for an international exhibition in Paris in 1930, and for the Deutsche Bauausstellung, held in Berlin in 1931, which included their well-known House for a Sportsman.[9] After 1931, Hassenpflug left Berlin for Moscow, where he worked until 1934 as an architect and urbanist with a group organized by Ernst May, former municipal architect of Frankfurt, to plan new cities in Siberia.[10] In a letter to Ise Gropius, Breuer reported that "Hassenpflug writes that he too is doing only projects in Russia—that's nothing new for him."[11]

The most important as well as the most exacting of the projects in this period was the government competition for 4,000 workers' housing units at Spandau-Haselhorst.[12] The scale of the project and the style in which Breuer's design was drafted represented a marked change from what he had been doing. Instead of his small, elegant individual or row-house dwellings, or the restrained mid-rise multifamily slab of 1923–24, he now fashioned an immense run of tall buildings that stretched behind a similar series of lower ones, evoking the well-known disturbing image of Ludwig Hilbersheimer's dehumanized urban-housing scheme (1924).[13] Breuer's efforts in these years became the subject of an article on tall buildings

that he wrote and illustrated with his projects for Spandau-Haselhorst, Elberfeld, and Frankfurt.[14] Adapting the rationale behind Spandau-Haselhorst for notions about housing in general, he wrote about family needs, household work, gardening, and communal facilities in the context of an architectural program that was guided by new social and domestic issues of modern life. They were ideas he held fast to and transferred to his work during his early years in the United States, when housing and suburban living became the most important concerns in the building field.

Not just residential, but for the first time commercial, industrial, institutional, recreational, and urbanistic projects were designed by Breuer in his Berlin studio. He proposed, for example, innovative circulation patterns for the rebuilding and modern reformulating of Berlin's Potsdamer Platz in 1928, demonstrating an early use of a cloverleaf crossover for vehicular traffic. His project for the 1,100-bed hospital in Elberfeld, like that for the housing in Spandau-Haselhorst, belonged to a new species of architectural gigantism that emerged in response to the enormity of the reformist social agenda for reconstructing post–First World War Germany. Along with drawings, a large and elaborate model of the hospital was made in his studio and photographed by Martha Erps Breuer. Perhaps the unrealizability of such an ambitious project emboldened Breuer and Hassenpflug to stretch the limits, for this institutional building was more elaborate in its proposed structure and design than anything Breuer alone or collaboratively had done before. Set on sloping terrain, it was an ensemble of structures of six to twelve stories with deeply stepped masses that allowed south-facing patient rooms to be fronted by continuous terraces.

Of much the same magnitude was the entry he submitted for the international competition sponsored by the Soviet government in 1930 for a 4,000-seat Ukrainian state theater–opera house in Kharkov. Won by Aleksandr and Victor Vesnin and ultimately unrealized, the Kharkov theater competition drew projects from many prominent architects, including Gropius. Breuer, assisted by Hassenpflug,[15] proposed a technologically complex interactive auditorium-stage environment with a novel arrangement of seats laid out in single front-to-

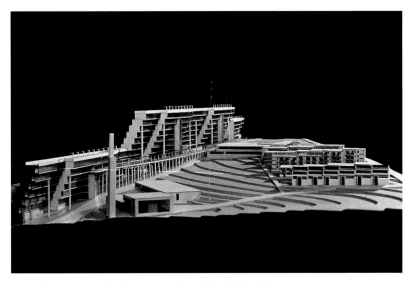

Hospital for 1,100 Beds, Elberfeld, Germany. 1928–29 (not built). Model

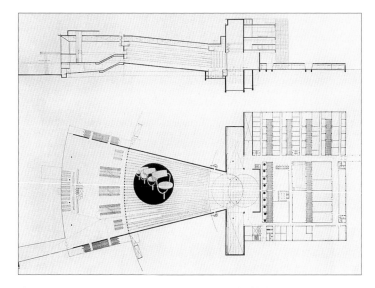

Ukrainian State Theater, Kharkov, Soviet Union. 1930–31 (not built). Plan and section

rear rows conforming to the wedge-shaped body of the auditorium. Theater had been a dynamic feature of Bauhaus life, and while Breuer did not design an auditorium before this one, he had designed the seats for the Bauhaus theater and had ideas about stage technology and theater space. His metal furniture had played its own role in modernist theater beyond Bauhaus auditorium seating. In 1929, Moholy-Nagy designed a revolutionary stage set for a production of Jacques Offenbach's *Tales of Hoffman* at the Berlin Krolloper, described in an essay by Hans Curjel: "For the first time in theater history, steel furniture was used on stage which Moholy's Bauhaus colleague Marcel Breuer had designed and which was considered a most daring innovation."[16]

In Breuer's design for the theater in Kharkov, performance space and audience space would be unified, and within the one building a variety of communal events—artistic, political, and athletic—could be accommodated. Called on later in his career to design theaters and auditoriums, Breuer would reuse one or another of the features he first proposed for the Kharkov theater, which, like his other early experiments, became a repository of readaptable compositional devices.[17]

Two important international exhibitions, one in Paris in 1930 and the other in Berlin in 1931, would showcase the applicability of German design to a modern life predicated on machines, technology, and science and would "demonstrate in competition with all nations, that our [Germany's] creative

energy is unimpaired."[18] Sponsored by the Société des artistes décoratifs français, the Paris exhibition was held at the Grand Palais from May to July 1930. The Deutsche Werkbund, responsible for Germany's contribution to the French exhibition (it was the first invitation to Germany to exhibit in Paris since before the First World War), turned the responsibility over to Gropius, who selected Breuer as one member of his team; Herbert Bayer and Moholy-Nagy were the others. Each was assigned space for his own display.[19] Housing concepts were at the heart of the exhibition, as was the display of German industrial-design products—furniture and appliances, architectural models, photography, textiles, even jewelry—intended for mass-production to enhance "une vie nouvelle." Bayer designed the catalogue, posters, and much of the installation of standardized products; Moholy was in charge of lighting fixtures and a photo exhibition of Germany; Breuer produced a model apartment—living area, study, dressing room, bathroom, kitchen—that would be suitable for a residential hotel (*Wohnhotel*) and, with Hassenpflug, an architectural model of the eleven-story building itself. Communal facilities—swimming pool and gymnasium, café and dance floor, reading room—for a residential building of that type were designed by Gropius and fitted out with Breuer's furniture. The French press lauded the entire "section allemande" for its "lightness," regarded as an intrinsic aspect of modern design in contrast to the heaviness, solemnity, and clutter of past traditions. German officials in Paris who had been nervous about the "radical" character of their country's contribution to the exhibition and uncertain about its reception by the French, with their great tradition of refined craftsmanship, were relieved by the positive reaction. Novel furniture designs, such as revolving cupboards and a movable writing desk made by Breuer for his model apartment, were praised by the reviewers for their beautiful detail and finish. The triumph of the German enterprise resulted, consequently, in "belated recognition" for the Bauhaus.[20]

"The success of the exhibit is due in no small measure to Marcel Breuer," wrote Sigfried Giedion, "as in his [model apartment] the public are able to obtain a very direct sensation of reality."[21] Breuer published a report on the exhibition in which he explained that space for communal facilities was needed in high-rise buildings because economic changes and changes in living patterns necessitated smaller individual living units.[22] Social life for apartment dwellers was, therefore, more easily pursued outside the residential units. According to Giedion, the emphasis on communal activities and centralized services for the inhabitants of apartment complexes like that designed by Breuer represented the "manifesto of a new form of living."[23] But in a perceptive account of the social significance of the project that goes to the political heart of the modernist dilemma, David Anderson observed:

This mode of living would be suitable for only a limited segment of society, and least of all for those who needed housing the most—the working class. Breuer's Wohnhotel apartment and Gropius's communal facilities might be suitable for single people who desired mobility, but how they could serve the needs of working people with children is difficult to imagine. In short, this type of life was created for the "new man" of modern civilization who did not in fact exist in any significant numbers, if at all.[24]

Similar to the Paris exhibition in that it took as its theme modern living, the Deutsche Bauausstellung was installed at the Berlin fairgrounds from May through August 1931. According to Christopher Wilk, Breuer was invited to participate only a few weeks before the opening by Mies van der Rohe, who was the director and who had originally not included him.[25] For this event, Breuer formulated one of his most accomplished early designs, the so-called House for a Sportsman (Haus für eines Sportsmann). Furnished model interiors and drawings of plan and elevation were exhibited. It was one of two works he produced for this exhibition (the other was a small [70-square-meter, or 753-square-foot] model apartment, furnished). Intended as a combined fitness club and residence for a teacher of gymnastics, the house had an outdoor workout terrace sheltered by an extended overhang. Although in a later article Breuer claimed for the house "new methods of construction,"[26] at least in structure and format the house could not have existed without Mies's German pavilion, designed for the Barcelona International Exposition of 1929. Breuer's own words—"As the roof is carried on slender steel supports, therefore there is complete freedom as far as the walls of the house are concerned"[27]—are by themselves a description of Mies's system. A glamorous and privileged setting for leisure activity, the House for a Sportsman must certainly have been one of the projects at the Bauausstellung that led to a protest demonstration by a group of left-wing architectural students. They staged a counter-exhibition in empty factory buildings in a working-class section of Berlin, dramatizing the discrepancy between the models and plans being shown at the Bauausstellung and the actual living conditions of the working class.[28]

From his Berlin studio, Breuer continued to carry out interior work, both residential and commercial, that he had begun for private clients while still in Dessau. For the well-known psychologist Kurt Lewin (a relative of Adolf Sommerfeld), he designed the interiors of a large residence in Zehlendorf in 1930 and 1931—a particularly interesting commission since the house had been built for Lewin by Peter Behrens, and "after difficulties with Behrens Kurt Lewin commissioned the young Marcel Breuer to complete the interior design," reports Tilmann Buddensieg.[29] In 1972, the Heinersdorff House, in the Berlin suburb of Lichterfelde, by then the property of the Aquinata nursing sisters, was destroyed to make room for a new hospital.[30] The house had been designed by architect Walter Wurzbach for glassworks industrialist Gottfried Heinersdorff in 1928 and 1929 and decorated by Breuer—on the recommendation of Josef Albers—with gray, black, and white glass mosaics and many pieces of newly designed furniture.[31] Breuer's commission for the Heinersdorff House decoration had been forgotten, and thus the destruction of the house took with it the only remaining example of his early work in Berlin and one of the rare specimens of his glass art.[32]

A few potential clients seeking to hire Breuer for the design and construction of private villas, not merely for the decorating or remodeling of an interior, turned up at his office in these years. There was a project for a Schneider Residence in Wiesbaden of 1929—a partially elevated concrete-frame house with a projecting balcony and an exterior spiral stair, which survives in the form of photographs of a model. Breuer included two of the photos in the exhibition of his work at Harvard in 1938. This project was later confused in the literature, in photo labels, and by Breuer himself with a house project of 1930—the Melder House in Maehrisch-Ostrau, Czechoslovakia—known from archival photographs of a facade drawing. Several previously unknown projects for villas and weekend houses designed in 1929 and 1930 came to light in 1999 among the drawings from Breuer's Berlin studio donated to Syracuse in that year. They include a drawing for a "Haus M" that corresponds to the Melder House facade design, settling the issue of the Schneider/Melder conflation. And, inspired by American industry's mass-production methods, Breuer imagined an assembly-line process in the industrial complex of factory buildings that he designed for the H. Fuld Telephone and Telegraph Company competition in 1929 in Frankfurt. Henry Ford's books were known and read in Bauhaus circles—by Ise Gropius, for example, in 1924.[33]

In his work of 1928 to 1931, Breuer was concerned primarily with rationalizing function, economizing on the cost of construction, experimenting with new materials, and offering efficiency and social and personal benefits to his clients. But there is an air of futuristic unreality about those projects that are heavily dependent on mechanical devices, such as the Kharkov theater and the Fuld factory, or those of gigantic size and structural complexity, such as Elberfeld hospital. Breuer had not yet constructed a building: unlike Mies, he had not grown up among artisans and builders; he was dependent on trained draftsmen for the visualization of his designs; and his experience with structure at the Bauhaus had been limited almost exclusively to the design, manufacture, and installation of his furniture. Breuer's "architecture" of 1928 to 1931, especially the institutional projects, belonged in the realm of fantasy rather than reality. It was still a paper architecture that never had to be tested through construction.

TRAVEL, 1931–32

Marketing his furniture, carrying out commissions for interior designs and remodelings, entering competitions, and lecturing and writing kept Breuer busy. But the future, professionally and politically, was inauspicious. In 1931, therefore, he left Berlin, "mainly to get away from the mid-European Depression," he wrote many years later. "He installed his office in his car and went on a trip to Spain and North Africa, and later to Greece, with rather indefinite aims" is a much-quoted bit of Breuer autobiography.[34] Living apart from his wife, he traveled, often in the company of Herbert Bayer, to Spain, North Africa, Greece, Switzerland, Italy, and the Balkans (visiting his brother in Yugoslavia). A famously bad driver, he reported to Ise Gropius, with whom he continued his amicable epistolary relationship, that "no one passed me between Berlin and Barcelona."[35] Ise forwarded mail to stops in Zürich, Locarno, Marseille, and Barcelona, and occasionally helped with details concerning the office he had left behind in Berlin. In 1931, Breuer also visited the Netherlands, where in Delft he delivered the lecture about house interiors already cited, which was published in the May issue of *Die Bauwelt*.[36]

Before Christmas, Breuer was in Spain, hoping, impracticably it would seem, to find architectural work in Madrid and asking Ise: "What's happening in Germany? Hitler? I can't get any German newspapers."[37] En route to Spain, he had driven through Toulon and visited Le Corbusier's Villa de Mandrot in Le Pradet, reporting to Ise that "since I saw Corbusier's Mandrot House my conscience is at rest once and for all: the house leaks not only from above but from all sides—the window panes are cracking, poor Mandrot is in despair."[38] Despite Breuer's complaints about its condition, the de Mandrot villa was to have significant formal and material consequences, first recognized by William H. Jordy, for Breuer's future architecture: the incorporation of Constructivist fragmentation; independent wall planes that meet to form an enclosed box instead of the continuous enclosure of a stretched skin that creates a *prisme pur*; a masonry platform support instead of pilotis; and rugged native stone rendered in modern geometries.[39] In the same letter, Breuer told Ise that "the Noailles house is trash [ist ein Schmarzen]," referring to Robert Mallet-Stevens's sprawling and incoherent villa (1924–33) at Hyères built for the vicomte de Noailles. By Christmas, Breuer was in Morocco, first in Fez and then in Tetuan, and to Ise on Christmas Eve he wrote, "Thank you very much for your letter—I would like to answer cheerfully but I am afraid I won't succeed."[40]

Much of the time, he was bored and aimless, uncertain about what the next day would bring and thinking of lost opportunities in Germany during his absence. Introspectively, on the back of a letter to Bayer, Breuer sketched a map of Europe marked with the cities that represented his personal developmental journey from Pecs to Tetuan. During the winter of 1932, he asked Ise for news about the status of the Kharkov theater competition and for advice, only partly in jest, about his future: "What does [Gropius] think, should I come back or aim everything at remaining here forever?"[41] Living in Spain was pleasurable, but it made him nostalgic for the old days in Weimar: "The beautiful talented Spaniards, great friends, have no soul! Suddenly the forgotten and repudiated concepts of the very earliest Bauhaus come back to me here—when it was inward, intellectual, emotional, human." He paid attention to the historical architecture of Spain, and on March 16, 1932, wrote to Ise that "the day before yesterday I visited Toledo . . . result headache and by yesterday everything already forgotten. The Cathedral of Pecs is more beautiful than the Cathedral of Toledo . . . the Escorial is different."[42] He was undecided where his travels would take him, but planned to return to Berlin in May or June when he would "perhaps rent a studio à la Xanti [Alexander Schawinsky] and live on my misery."[43]

BACK TO BERLIN, ZURICH, BUDAPEST, 1932–35

What sent Breuer back to Germany in 1932—to live and work in a studio apartment at 63 Sachsistrasse in the Wilmersdorf section of Berlin, to reside part-time in Wiesbaden, and soon to have a temporary auxiliary office in Zürich at 66 Seefeldstrasse—was the opportunity he had been hoping would come his way. In a matter-of-fact tone forty years later, Breuer said tersely about himself that "he returned at the call of one of his former clients,"[44] but his letter of June 12, 1932, to Ise captures his true feelings: "Thank you from the bottom of my heart for your letter. I would already have told you the great news—that Harnischmacher is building—if I didn't know that you would get it directly from Herbert [Bayer]. You can imagine how happy I am. I really believed that it would never happen. So for the moment I feel like a pig in clover here."[45] Ten years after turning his attention to architecture, but as yet with no built work, Breuer finally was commissioned to build a spacious villa for Paul Harnischmacher, Gropius's client for whom he had carried out interior remodeling and furniture design for an apartment in Wiesbaden and an office in Mainz in 1928 and 1929.

Putting into effect ideas about residential architecture that he had assimilated for a decade, Breuer made a stunning debut with the Harnischmacher House (1932) in Wiesbaden. More Breuer's Garches than his Poissy, its debt to Le Corbusier's villas—at least in terms of its exterior appearance—is obvious and respectful. The Harnischmacher House earned a place in the canon of European modern residential architecture of the period. Destroyed in the last days of the Second World War, it had only a brief existence. When in 1947 Breuer's American client Preston Robinson of Williamstown, Massachusetts, was preparing to travel to Europe, Breuer suggested that he might like to meet Harnischmacher: "The gentleman for whom I built my first house is Paul Harnischmacher, Wilhelmshohe 5–7, Wiesbaden. The house is now destroyed, but as far as I know Mr. and Mrs. Harnischmacher have created some sort of a provisional shelter at the same address."[46] The "provisional shelter" was a new house, not by Breuer, built soon after the

Harnischmacher House I, Wiesbaden, Germany. 1932

Breuer during construction of Harnischmacher House I

end of the war near the foundations of the destroyed residence. But in 1952, Breuer designed a second house for the Harnischmachers on the site of their interim home.

The Harnischmacher House was oriented to the garden side on the south and west of the hill into which it was nested. A terraced construction of almost Mannerist complexity, it was composed of stepped levels with shifts of direction and complex rhythms of open and closed elements, with ribbon windows and a projecting dining room–porch terrace surmounted by an open balcony that was protected by a wall of opaque glass. Beneath this terrace, which faced south, was originally a boccie court that was later closed in by the clients. Cantilevers, a pair of suspended stairs with slender tubular railings, nautical details such as stretched cables, and varied materials, including bush-hammered concrete, forecast the future of Breuer's residential designs.

The Harnischmacher commission launched Breuer's architectural career. It may have been the most dramatic, but it was hardly the only, benefit of the generosity and patronage of Gropius. Throughout the post-Dessau period, with limited substantial employment despite his success in competitions and exhibitions, Breuer was consistently helped by both Walter and Ise. Typical of Gropius's support was the postscript he added to a letter from Ise in Berlin to Breuer in Budapest: "I have propagandized strongly for you here among the aluminum people and have written an article with photos of the chairs for the metal factories."[47] In response to a request from Breuer, who was trying to establish a practice in Budapest in the autumn of 1934, Gropius drafted a letter to editors "of important newspapers" in Hungary. He wrote of his having championed at the Bauhaus such Hungarian architects as Farkas Molnár and Alfréd Forbàt: "Now Marcel Breuer, one of the most talented of young architects, has recently settled down in Budapest. I feel as an objective observer that this is so important for your city that I would like to take the liberty of asking you to inform your readers who might not know of the professional importance of Breuer [who] . . . in the peak years of his development has returned to his homeland."[48]

When the Gropius office was too busy to take on new architectural commissions, the overflow was often directed to Breuer. In the summer of 1933, therefore, Gropius tried to get for Breuer the commission for a modest private house that was too small to bother with. To lawyer Albin Wolf of Burgkunstadt, the potential client, Gropius wrote:

After a rough comparison between the maximum funds available to you for construction and your spatial requirements, I am of the opinion that the problem posed by you could only be solved if a presently unemployed competent architect were to occupy himself exclusively with this building and, with the utmost economy and without consideration for his own profit, were to undertake all aspects of the commission himself. With the apparatus under my direction, the expenses would be too great relative to the smallness of the object. I would like to suggest, therefore, that you turn the execution of your building over to the architect Marcel Breuer, BDA . . .

whom I can recommend as extremely competent, reliable, and artistically in my own line. He was my collaborator and a teacher at the Bauhaus, which I directed, and has been independent now for several years. Like many others today, he now has very little work because of the economic situation and would for this reason be prepared to undertake the difficult task of completing the building within the narrow range of the specified amount. We are dealing here with a stroke of luck, which I urgently recommend you to take advantage of.[49]

Even though Breuer took up the lead, proposing to Wolf a working arrangement and suggesting that he inspect the Harnischmacher House to get an idea of his work,[50] the project dissolved.

Sigfried Giedion, historian and secretary general of CIAM, was a friend of Gropius who appreciated Breuer's talents. He was a founder, in 1931, with Werner Moser and Rudolf Graver, of the Wohnbedarf shops, where modern furniture and design were promoted and where Breuer's metal furniture was featured. Giedion asked Breuer to design the Zürich shop and its branch in Basel in 1932 (in 1956, Breuer would renovate the Zürich store). Of this work, Breuer wrote in the third person that "at the period of the Harnischmacher house his other works were mainly industrial design and store arrangements,"[51] referring to Wohnbedarf and Matzinger in Switzerland and to the S. S. Kettenladen shops in Berlin, the last regarded by Henry-Russell Hitchcock as "peculiarly satisfactory as examples of standardized [modern] shop fronts."[52] More to the point, however, was Giedion's idealistic project to build and privately finance a group of small modern apartment houses in the Zürich suburb of Doldertal, where he resided, and in 1933 to offer this commission to Breuer in collaboration with the Swiss architects Alfred and Emil Roth, who were cousins. The resistance to modern buildings in a conservative Swiss suburb was potent, and serious debate in the building department in Zürich as well as uncertainty about the extent of Giedion's financial commitment to the project led to delays.

On April 27, 1934, while in Zürich, Breuer delivered a lecture to the Swiss Werkbund on the theory of the "New Architecture." Entitled "Wo Stehen Wir?" (Where Do We Stand?), the text had been published in English by 1935, and was eventually followed by reprints in Italian, Spanish, and

Hungarian and by excerpts in German.[53] It was Breuer's personal interpretation of Gropius's ideas about the unity of art and technology, and a statement of Breuer's belief that the dominant impulse of the modern movement was "clarity," meaning the "definite expression of the purpose of a building and a sincere expression of its structure." Republished in English by Peter Blake as an appendix to *Marcel Breuer: Architect and Designer*, "Where Do We Stand?" remained one of Breuer's most thoughtful statements on the ideology and functionalist approach of modern architecture in its relation to modern life.[54] Many of the ideas expressed in that essay represented the foundation of his philosophy of architecture as it was later developed more fully in his book *Sun and Shadow*.[55] Breuer had begun to lecture and write on art theory while still a student at the Weimar Bauhaus; as early as 1923, illustrations of his furniture, graphic art, and painting were published; by 1925, he had published independent articles and texts of his lectures. Although his earliest articles were about furniture and the Bauhaus furniture workshop, he was also concerned with theories of design, with ideas about form, function, and the nature of modern dwelling spaces. When he began to direct his attention to architecture, his writings took up architectural matters almost exclusively, but throughout his career he would deviate little from the philosophy he set down so confidently and emphatically in "Where Do We Stand?"

By December 1933, Breuer was working principally out of an office in Budapest, where he was in joint practice with Farkas Molnár and Jozsef Fischer, trying to make some money with architecture and commuting to Zürich while the Doldertal project hung fire. The Zürich building department refused permission for the Doldertal design, and Breuer in frustration lamented to Ise that "our Doldertal project has been crushed; we have to begin all over. . . . No contract concluded for a long time, very disturbing."[56] (Her response from Berlin on December 20, 1933, included the observation that "the racial and genealogical frenzy is continuing and is leading to the most peculiar manifestations."[57])

Breuer wrote to Gropius from Zürich on January 17, 1934, that "I am trying to maintain my residence in [Nazi] Berlin but the success is questionable."[58] Architectural prospects in

Hungary were as dismal as in Germany, and Breuer grumbled to Ise that Hungarians claimed that they were poor, but money certainly seemed to be around: "Somewhere behind the bushes there are clients lurking, all of whom have no money but still build quite beautiful houses for themselves."[59] A few days later, he complained further that "in Hungary and Yugoslavia I am not getting anywhere with the chairs; here no one thinks of paying in advance, and not even afterwards."[60] The Hungarian partners had arranged a lecture by Gropius in connection with a meeting in Budapest of the Comité international pour la résolution du problème de l'architecture contemporaine (CIRPAC)[61] and an accompanying exhibition sponsored by the Engineer's Circle. The visit took place in February 1934 at a moment when Breuer had to be in Zürich, so Molnár and the Fischers were the hosts. Gropius's lecture was delivered to a standing-room-only audience at the Technische Hochschule. Ise described the social atmosphere of their visit as being in "a steel furniture ghetto"; she wanted to "get out and meet people *not* interested in modern architecture."[62] By April, Breuer wrote that "in any case my Hungarian hopes are pretty much destroyed. You would understand this if you could see how our work here on the Spring Trade Fair is progressing."[63] With Fischer and Molnár, he had entered a competition for a temporary installation at the Spring Trade Fair in Budapest; fairs were and still are an opportunity to offer radical new ideas in architecture to a wide public. The design—a dynamic ensemble of ramps, towers, and pavilions sited in a park around an existing exhibition hall—was awarded first prize, but was only partially executed.

In April 1934, the Zürich building department authorities finally approved a revised version of the plans for the Doldertal apartments. Construction began a year later on the pair of buildings that are generally considered to be the epitome of Swiss *neue Sachlichkeit* and were to be Breuer's only experience with constructed multifamily architecture before he emigrated to the United States. The social context in which the Doldertal project took shape, however, was at a far remove from the economies posited in the 1920s for multifamily dwellings to house the low-income displaced populations of postwar Europe. Still, Breuer was able to see some of his theories about adaptability of function and open-plan design put into practice in the Zürich buildings. His contributions at Doldertal, together with his work for the Harnischmachers, would confirm that his persistence in pursuing architecture and the high opinion of his talent by those who believed in him were justified. A fully assimilated functional modernism, a mastery of steel-and-concrete structure, and a creative approach to materials pointed to an architectural personality destined to make a major impact on the future of twentieth-century building. But conditions on the Continent in 1932 to 1935 made that future precarious. The Bauhaus in Dessau, directed by Mies van der Rohe, was terminated by the city government in 1932 and, following a brief afterlife in Berlin, was closed down there in April 1933 soon after Hitler came to power and the new regime took over.

By October 1934, Walter and Ise Gropius had left Germany for London, and Breuer would follow within a year.

1 Magdalena Droste claims that "despite having Gropius as a referee, [Breuer] was refused membership [in] the German Architects' Association on the grounds that he could demonstrate no practical architectural experience" ("Marcel Breuer's Furniture," in Magdalena Droste and Manfred Ludewig, *Marcel Breuer Design* [Cologne: Taschen, 1992], 21). However, a 1933 letter reminding Breuer that he was in arrears for dues payment since 1931 is proof of his BDA membership (chairman of the Brandenberg region of the BDA to "Herrn Architekten BDA" and Marcel Breuer, November 18, 1933, SUL 7).

2 Le Corbusier, *The Athens Charter*, trans. Anthony Eardley, with a new foreword by Josep Lluis Sert (New York: Grossman, 1973). The founders of CIAM were Sert, Le Corbusier, Gropius, and Sigfried Giedion. See also Tim Benton, "Six Houses" and "Urbanism," in *Le Corbusier: Architect of the Century* [exhibition catalogue] (London: Arts Council of Great Britain, 1987), 46, n. 16, 205–6.

3 Quoted in Joan M. Lukach, *Hilla Rebay: In Search of the Spirit in Art* (New York: Braziller, 1983), 77.

4 Gilbert Herbert, *The Dream of the Factory-Made House: Walter Gropius and Konrad Wachsmann* (Cambridge, Mass.: MIT Press, 1986), 140, n. 56.

5 Breuer to Ise Gropius, March 11, 1934, Walter Gropius Papers (Breuer Letters), HL.

6 Breuer to Walter Gropius, May 18, 1933, Walter Gropius Papers (Breuer Letters), HL.

7 For a discussion of the problem, see Christopher Wilk, *Marcel Breuer: Furniture and Interiors* (New York: Museum of Modern Art, 1981), 70–71. Breuer designed the interior of one of the three houses by Stam built for the Weissenhofsiedlung in 1927.

8 Ronald Wiedenhoeft, *Berlin's Housing Revolution: German Reform in the 1920s* (Ann Arbor, Mich.: UMI Research Press, 1985), 165–70; see also Winfried Nerdinger, *Walter Gropius: The Architect Walter Gropius: Drawings, Prints, and Photographs from Busch-Reisinger Museum, Harvard University Art Museums, Cambridge/Mass., and from Bauhaus-Archiv Berlin* [exhibition catalogue] (Berlin: Mann Verlag, 1985), 116–18.

9 Of the hundreds of original drawings from Breuer's Berlin practice recently added to SUL, more than 300 carry Hassenpflug's signature as draftsman.

10   Barbara Miller Lane, *Architecture and Politics in Germany, 1918–1945* (Cambridge, Mass.: Harvard University Press, 1968, 1985), 103. As of 1968, Hassenpflug was professor at the Munich Technische Hochschule (265, n. 79).

11   Breuer to Ise Gropius, January 27, 1932, Walter Gropius Papers (Breuer Letters), HL.

12   Wiedenhoeft, *Berlin's Housing Revolution*, 165–18; Nerdinger, *Walter Gropius*, 116–18.

13   Richard Pommer, "'More a Necropolis than a Metropolis': Ludwig Hilbersheimer's Highrise City and Modern City Planning," in Richard Pommer, David Spaeth, and Kevin Harrington, *In the Shadow of Mies* (Chicago: Art Institute of Chicago, in association with Rizzoli, 1988), 16–53.

14   Marcel Breuer, "Beiträge zur Frage des Hochhauses," *Die Form* 5 (1930): 113–17, in *"Die Form": Stimme des deutschen Werkbundes, 1925–1934*, ed. Felix Schwarz and Frank Gloor (Gütersloh: Mohn, 1969), 163–67.

15   The name Momontoff appears along with that of Hassenpflug in some of the literature on this project.

16   Hans Curjel, "Moholy-Nagy and the Theater," *Du* 24 (1964): 11–15, excerpted in *Moholy-Nagy*, ed. Richard Kostelanetz (New York: Praeger, 1970), 95.

17   Even though the Kharkov design became the prototype for Breuer's future theater-auditorium projects, a photograph of the side elevation found in his office files carries a note on the verso, probably written in the 1960s: "Mr. B. does not identify this off hand" (Photographs, AAA).

18   Statement made at a Werkbund meeting in Württemberg in 1926 when the 1931 international exhibition in Germany was first planned, quoted in Karin Kirsch, *The Weissenhofsiedlung: Experimental Housing for the Deutscher Werkbund, Stuttgart, 1927* (New York: Rizzoli, 1989), 33.

19   For more on this exhibition, see Sigfried Giedion, *Walter Gropius: Work and Teamwork* (New York: Reinhold, 1954), 49–52, and Arthur A. Cohen, *Herbert Bayer: The Complete Work* (Cambridge, Mass.: MIT Press, 1984), 288–95.

20   Giedion, *Walter Gropius*, 52.

21   Ibid., 51.

22   Marcel Breuer, "Die Werkbundausstellung in Paris 1930," *Zentralblatt der Bauverwaltung*, July 9, 1930, 477.

23   Giedion, *Walter Gropius*, 51.

24   David Christian Anderson, *Architecture as a Means for Social Change in Germany, 1918–1933* (Ann Arbor, Mich.: University Microfilms, 1973), 114.

25   Wilk, *Furniture and Interiors*, 99.

26   Marcel Breuer, "Architecture and Material," in *Circle: International Survey of Constructive Art*, ed. J. L. Martin, Ben Nicholson, and N. Gabo (London: Faber and Faber, 1937), 195.

27   Ibid.

28   Anderson, *Architecture as a Means for Social Change*, 169, n. 305.

29   Tilmann Buddensieg, "Introduction: Aesthetic Opposition and International Style," in *Berlin, 1900–1933: Architecture and Design* (Berlin: Mann Verlag, 1987), 30.

30   Annemarie Richter, "Ein Wohnhaus, eingerichtet von Marcel Breuer," *Die Bauwelt*, August 21, 1981, 1380–81.

31   Illustrated in Droste and Ludwig, *Marcel Breuer Design*, 84. Drawings for the furniture and for the layouts of the interior of the Heinersdorff House were added to SUL in 1999.

32   According to Peter Blake, who published an illustration of the mosaic entrance foyer of the Heinersdorff House in *Marcel Breuer: Architect and Designer* ([New York: Museum of Modern Art, 1949], 37, fig. 63), "Breuer today intensely dislikes this small job" (31). The job also included a multilens window that, as described and illustrated by Blake and attributed to Breuer and Hassenpflug, "repeated the outside image in a series of circular frames, each formed by a concavity ground into the large sheet of plate glass" (31, 37, fig. 62).

33   IGD/E, Ise Gropius to Walter Gropius, March 1924, 37–38.

34   Marcel Breuer, "Autobiography," SUL 39.

35   Breuer to Ise Gropius, November 20, 1931, Walter Gropius Papers (Breuer Letters), HL.

36   Marcel Breuer, "Das Innere des Hauses," *Die Bauwelt*, May 7, 1931, 615–16.

37   Breuer to Ise Gropius, December 16, 1931, Walter Gropius Papers (Breuer Letters), HL.

38   Breuer to Ise Gropius, November 20, 1931. The lament of Hélène de Mandrot is well known, as is Le Corbusier's letter scolding her for complaining (Benton, "Six Houses," 47).

39   William H. Jordy, "The Domestication of Modern: Marcel Breuer's Ferry Cooperative Dormitory at Vassar College," in *American Buildings and Their Architects: The Impact of European Modernism in the Mid-Twentieth Century* (Garden City, N.Y.: Doubleday, 1972), 206–10.

40   Breuer to Ise Gropius, December 24, 1931, Walter Gropius Papers (Breuer Letters), HL.

41   Breuer to Ise Gropius, winter 1932, Walter Gropius Papers (Breuer Letters), HL.

42   Breuer to Ise Gropius, March 16, 1932, Walter Gropius Papers (Breuer Letters), HL.

43   Breuer to Ise Gropius, February 22, 1932, Walter Gropius Papers (Breuer Letters), HL. Schawinsky was a Bauhaus student with a special talent for stage design and theatrical performance, and one of Oskar Schlemmer's principal collaborators.

44   Breuer, "Autobiography," SUL 39.

45   Breuer to Ise Gropius, June 12, 1932, Walter Gropius Papers (Breuer Letters), HL.

46   Breuer to Preston Robinson, February 17, 1947, SUL 17.

47   Walter Gropius to Breuer, December 20, 1933, Walter Gropius Papers (Breuer Letters), HL. First prize at an international competition in Paris for aluminum furniture was an important accomplishment for Breuer in 1933. Judged by two committees—one an international group of aluminum manufacturers, and the other composed of Gropius, Le Corbusier, and Giedion—the award was given for his "split-bar, two-spring system for chairs," wrote Breuer, who correctly designated himself as the "inventor of the first springing aluminum furniture" (November 17, 1935, SUL 3, 50).

48   Walter Gropius to "Sehr geehrter Herr Redaktur," October 31, 1934, Correspondence, AAA.

49   Walter Gropius to Albin Wolf, August 31, 1933, Correspondence, AAA.

50   Breuer to Albin Wolf, September 10, 1933, Correspondence, AAA.

51   Breuer, "Autobiography," SUL 39.

52   Henry-Russell Hitchcock, "Marcel Breuer and the American Tradition in Architecture" [essay and exhibition catalogue, Harvard University, Graduate School of Design, June–September 1938] (GSD, Cambridge, Mass., 1938, mimeographed), 12, HUAL.

53   Marcel Breuer, "Where Do We Stand?" *Architectural Review*, April 1935, 133–36; *Casabella*, March 1935, 2–7; *Nuestra arquitectura* [special issue], September 1947; excerpts in *Werk*, December 1935, 426–27; Hungarian translation, typescript, SUL 10.

54   Blake, *Marcel Breuer*, 119–22.

55   Marcel Breuer, *Marcel Breuer: Sun and Shadow: The Philosophy of an Architect*, ed. Peter Blake (New York: Dodd, Mead, 1955).

56   Breuer to Ise Gropius, December 16, 1933, Walter Gropius Papers (Breuer Letters), HL.

57   Ise Gropius to Breuer, December 20, 1933, Correspondence, AAA.

58   Breuer to Walter Gropius, January 17, 1934, Correspondence, AAA.

59   Breuer to Ise Gropius, December 16, 1933.

60   Breuer to Ise Gropius, December 28, 1933, Walter Gropius Papers (Breuer Letters), HL.

61   CIRPAC was a task force whose mission was to develop themes for CIAM congresses.

62   Ise Gropius to Breuer, February 19, 1934, Correspondence, AAA.

63   Breuer to Ise Gropius, April 6, 1935, Walter Gropius Papers (Breuer Letters), HL.

3. London:
The Emigré Years, 1935–37

Garden City of the Future.
1936. Model

"BIRDS OF PASSAGE," "BAUHAUS REFUGEE," "foreign architect," "refugee from the Continent," and similar phrases were used to describe Breuer, Gropius, and other architects and designers who in the mid-1930s found themselves in an England where modernism—in contrast to its more vigorous history in Germany, the Netherlands, France, and the Soviet Union—had only just begun to exist. Henry-Russell Hitchcock noted that England had been "barely represented" in the "International Exhibition of Modern Architecture," held at the Museum of Modern Art in 1932, but, by 1933, had come to world attention through a single monument—Lubetkin & Tecton's streamlined Penguin Pond at Regent's Park Zoo in London.[1]

The émigrés were welcomed in England by the handful of pioneers who were already practitioners in the modern movement, although, as G. E. Kidder Smith observed, those vanguardists "blazed lonely trails."[2] English advocates of modernism were heartened by the presence of Gropius and Breuer and the other Continentals, who seemed to promise strengthened support for the fragile foundations of modernist building and could enhance its practice with fresh ideas about design, structure, and materials. In the end, however, it was, as Anthony Jackson, writing about modern English architecture, perceived, their *presence* that proved to be more important than their work, to which the English were largely indifferent.[3]

Gropius arrived in London on October 19, 1934, from Germany by way of Rome and Zürich in a politically complex journey.[4] He was given a residence and respectful professional responsibility by the sympathetic and benevolent Jack Pritchard, founder (in 1931) and head of the English modern industrial-design firm he named Isokon (from "isometric unit construction") Control Company. Pritchard invited Walter and Ise Gropius to live in one of the studio apartments in Lawn Road Flats in Hampstead and appointed Gropius as design consultant to Isokon. Pritchard also helped Gropius form a partnership with the established English architect Maxwell Fry in 1936 so that he could practice architecture along with the consulting and design work he was carrying out for Isokon.

White, flat-roofed, taut-surfaced Lawn Road Flats was a small apartment block privately sponsored by Pritchard (as Sigfried Giedion had sponsored the Doldertal apartment houses); it was based on the idea of the one- and two-room "minimum" flat as most suited to the pared-down and transient character of modern life. Designed for Pritchard by architect Wells Coates as a three-story terraced block abutted by a taller stair tower, along the lines of Continental modernist housing, the building had just been completed in 1934.[5] All its apartments were reached from an open corridor, and some had independent balconies. Housekeeping and food services were available for tenants. Isokon was located in the flats, and Pritchard and his family lived there, as did a number of distinguished artists and writers, both native and émigré, comfortable among the artists and intellectuals who gave Hampstead its special character. In an undated letter to Breuer written soon after the Gropiuses' arrival, Ise said that "our landlord is Mr. Pritchard, a still young very pleasant man who is full of energy and wants to revolutionize the English world." She went on: "Our flat has become very attractive and we are finally living as we have always advised and built for others. A large room with a sleeping alcove, an anteroom, kitchen, dressing room and bath. And above all, no fiendish gas fireplace but central heating."[6]

Both Ise and Walter Gropius encouraged Breuer to leave the Continent and resettle in London, as they had done. They used their influence to smooth a path for him—making contacts and speaking to authoritative people on his behalf; arranging for the publication of his designs and for the translation, editing, and publication of his writings in English journals; and setting up business connections for the manufacture of his aluminum furniture. When eventually Breuer did follow them to London, Gropius saw to it that Pritchard employed him as a furniture designer. It was for Isokon that Breuer developed his laminated bent-plywood furniture. The plywood long chair of 1936 became a classic of modern furniture.[7]

Breuer had visited England at least once before, in 1932,[8] but now he vacillated for months about emigrating. His conflicts and irresolutions are recorded in the letters exchanged from late 1934 through May 1935 with Ise Gropius and with his prospective English partner, architect F. R. S. Yorke. Overriding all other concerns was his uncertainty about finding architectural work in England, and he told Yorke that he envied the opportunities that, he believed, Gropius would have there.[9] To Ise, Breuer wrote in April 1935 that "I envy you very much over there, especially because you know English. Since the middle of February I haven't been able to take lessons because I am always somewhere else and always for an indefinite time."[10]

It was clear that there would be no future in Germany for Breuer following the rise to power of Adolf Hitler in 1933. He was a Hungarian national, born Jewish (although in Dessau in 1926, in accordance with a statutory provision, he had filed a declaration withdrawing from the religion),[11] and from the point of view of the Nazi government, he was a "Bolshevist" Bauhausler even if he was no longer at the Bauhaus. The house that he had designed for Paul and Marianne Harnischmacher might have led to a fast-growing career for its architect in an undisturbed Germany. But politics and the Great Depression brought even the small-scale revolution in architecture in Germany to a halt and forced Breuer, in the absence of work, to spend too much time "bumming around," as he described it ("ich habe zu viel gebummelt in den letzen jahren"),[12] and struggling to establish an independent architectural practice in places other than Germany—in the face of tremendous obstacles.

From Budapest, Breuer wrote to Ise Gropius in London on Christmas Day 1934: "Your letter sounds as if it comes from a fairyland. I am especially glad that you seem to judge your stay in England as being more permanent, and that Pius views his professional prospects favorably."[13] By this time, Breuer already had a proposal from Yorke (whom he had not yet met) for a joint practice. It was mandatory for émigré architects who wanted to work to enter a partnership with established English architects; RIBA regulations, "hastily devised" at that period to cope with the influx of foreign architects, permitted them to be employers, but not employees.[14] Breuer responded immediately and positively to Yorke, but to Ise Gropius he elaborated:

I would like to work with him provided that we have something to do. Judging from what you wrote that seems possible. I don't want to go to England without having something half-concrete to do there . . . to give up [what I am doing now] for something uncertain. If I were to go to England I would do it with the intention of staying there forever, or at least for 15 years, without the feeling that after a questionable experiment I would have to regretfully return to Hungary. . . . [A]t any rate your descriptions of the possibilities there excite me a whole lot. All in all I'm not preoccupied with earning a living here—I'm living cheaply and for the moment without cares and will surely be able to stay above water. Here I have Molnár and Fischer. For them the design, the work itself, isn't important except insofar as it provides material for advertisements, for propaganda, to get patronage . . . it has to be modern only because after all that's our metier. Now I am working on the competition for the Spring Fair—I enjoy it. When the translations of my articles are finished please send them to me right away—I've promised them to America. Albers is doing well there, he sounded very content. He said he felt as though he were back in the old Bauhaus—everything young, fresh, unspoiled, and interesting.[15]

The England of 1935 provided few reasons for similar optimism from the alien Breuer, who wished to design and build modern structures in a country still unreceptive to modernism and who hardly knew the language: "I already see myself under your protective wing, Pia, wrapped in proper English silence. . . . That language!"[16] But by January 1935, he had come to a decision, for Ise Gropius wrote that

I've heard you've said yes to Yorke. He is 28 and we have no judgement of his artistic work, but he's certainly an especially nice guy who you would like very much. He began studying architecture in a small English town, found the eternal drawing of columns so boring and dumb that he decided to go into the Navy when he saw a Bauhaus book and Corbusier's book [*Vers une architecture*]. He turned his attention to that and a while ago brought out his own book about international modern architecture [*The Modern House*]. They live in a fantastic little apartment, invited God and the world to a cocktail party at 6:30 in the afternoon and there was a very nice mood to it.[17]

In the same letter, Ise told Breuer of Pritchard's interest in producing his wooden chairs because of an affiliation he had with a lumber firm: "He wants to know your price to use the patent so write us your conditions. There is a certain difficulty here with steel furniture as long as so few people have central heating."

Yorke was to be an ideal partner for Breuer.[18] One of the founders in 1933 of the Modern Architectural Research (MARS) Group—the English branch of the Congrès international d'architecture moderne (CIAM)—and assistant editor of *Architects' Journal*, he identified himself in his practice and in his writing with England's young progressive architects. Jeremy Gould, in his study of English houses of this period, claims that Yorke "had as much knowledge of the Modern Movement as any architect in England,"[19] although Breuer undeniably was far ahead of him in talent and experience. The son of an architect, he studied architecture at the University of Birmingham and became interested in materials and structure and in town planning. In 1934, he published his well-researched book *The Modern House*, an important illustrated compendium of information about materials, structural systems, plans, details, architects, and theories of international modernism.[20] By the time Breuer joined him, Yorke had also become well acquainted with strategies for dealing with local building authorities and with the routines and practical procedures for seeing a project through construction, a valuable contribution to the partnership he was about to undertake with an expatriate.

Despite continued encouraging letters from Ise Gropius, a pattern later repeated when Breuer was indecisive about following Gropius to the United States, Breuer's uncertainties revived during the spring of 1935 and were compounded by a general pessimism about the future of the modern movement. When "Wo Stehen Wir?" (edited by Ise) was published by architectural writer Morton Shand in English as "Where Do We Stand?" Breuer wrote to Ise that "I received the *Architectural Review* with my article. In my present mood I would rename it 'Where Do We Come to a Halt?' or 'Monkey Dead, Den Closed' or 'Building and Whoring, a New Unity.'"[21] "So things are going for you as they are everywhere in the world—one step forward, two steps backward—it's a lousy situation," she replied.[22] The Harnischmacher House was published three months later, also in *Architectural Review*, with a brief text written and translated into English by Ise.[23] In London, with efficiency and goodwill and through her continual correspondence with Breuer, Ise took care of all matters concerning the English publication of his material.

At the same time, Yorke, in the process of preparing a new book on modern flats, wrote to Breuer: "I hear from Frau Gropius it is not your intention to come to England at present. This in many ways I regret, but I understand your feelings in the matter and should not like to invite you to join me here and then find there is no work for you to do. I will keep you informed of developments and hope to meet you at some later date."[24] But the tenor of Breuer's letters shifted once again, and on May 20 Ise wrote, "It is terrific Lajkó that you are really thinking of picking up knowledge of the English language."[25] By summer, Breuer had decided to make a month-long visit to England[26] and at that point began to take the necessary steps for permanently relocating and for obtaining permission to work, by drafting a letter of application for residence as an alien.

He was helped by several English friends, particularly E. J. (Bobby) Carter of the RIBA, who reported to Breuer on July 31 that he had talked with "the Secretary" (Undersecretary of State, Aliens Department, Home Office, Whitehall) about Breuer's application and that "he says that if you present yourself chiefly as a furniture designer there should be no difficulty at all."[27] Two weeks later, on August 13, Breuer paid a personal call to the secretary to discuss his resettlement; back in Zürich on August 29, he filed his official request for

permission to reside in England. He included a brief autobiography in which he (reluctantly) emphasized his furniture designs and their industrial production, as Carter had advised him to do, but he defined himself primarily as "architect by profession," as "independent architect in Berlin from 1928 to 1931," and as head of the "department of interior-architecture" at the Bauhaus in Dessau from 1925 to 1928. He added that he had been assured (by Carter) that his work "would be advantageous to the development of the English architectural-industry" and that "I have the intention of settling down in London this October, where I wish to open an atelier with Mr. F. R. S. Yorke RIBA for architecture and furniture-designing, and also for experiments with industrial models with the expenses and income of this atelier divided equally between Mr. Yorke and myself."[28] With his application, Breuer submitted supporting letters from H. de C. Hastings, the editor of the Architectural Press; well-connected arts patron Lady Peter Norton, whom Breuer and Herbert Bayer had met while skiing in the Tyrol a few years earlier; and others.[29] A letter from Herbert Read ("inveterate spokesman for the New"[30]) that had arrived too late to be included with the first group of references was forwarded on September 14.

"We are very much looking forward to your coming," Ise wrote to Breuer after his plans finally were in place. Pritchard invited Breuer to stay at Lawn Road Flats, and Ise wrote to say that "a room here in Lawn Road Flats stands ready. I haven't definitely taken it in case you want to find something cheaper."[31] She also told him that she was glad he had given up the idea of bringing a car, "when I think how you would put your life on the line every minute here with this traffic and left-side driving." Breuer transferred a bank account from Berlin to London/Switzerland in July while he was still at work in Zürich on the Doldertal apartment houses.[32] By September 18, he was able to write to Yorke about the Zürich buildings that "everything is progressing nicely and I hope [they] will be finished by the beginning of December."[33] During November and December, his furniture and household effects were moved from Budapest to London, and before he settled into 4 Tregunter Road, the house and office he shared with Yorke, he lived for a time at 15 Lawn Road Flats.[34]

Breuer in London. 1936

In London on November 19, 1935, Breuer and Yorke met to talk about a format for their partnership. Breuer made notes of the conversation ("Mit Yorke. Besprechung am 19.Nov.35"),[35] which ranged from commonplace details of everyday life in their shared office-residence, such as the gas meter, hot water, telephone extensions, and garage (he sketched a ground plan arranging the space), to conditions for their partnership agreement. Two years later, in a similar simple handwritten draft, Breuer would set down the terms for his partnership with Gropius in the United States.

The essential points of the agreement were that Breuer and Yorke would enter into partnership for architectural work; revenues and expenditures would be shared equally; the partners would maintain a joint office that would handle all their building commissions; drafts, sketches, publications, and exhibitions would be signed with the names of both partners; each project would be directed by one of the partners, whose name would appear first and who would decide about matters on which the partners might disagree; and, in cases where the leadership was not determined by the client or by other means, the partners would take turns directing projects. Their contract was to be valid for one year and could be termi-

nated within a half year's notice unless the partners agreed otherwise. The scope of the partnership would not include Yorke's activities at the Architectural Press or Breuer's projects for the furniture industry or for his publications, unless they pertained to works produced by the partnership. Breuer sent a copy of his draft of the agreement to Gropius for comments.

The partnership was known as Breuer & Yorke. The order of the names reflected the principals' understanding that precedence generally was to be given to Breuer for design credit, and there appears never to have been an argument about this arrangement or about design responsibility during the two years the association existed. As in all Breuer's partnerships, the extent of his contribution has to be deduced from analyses of documents and office drawings, the visual evidence of the works, the memory of associates, and conjecture. The process is problematic because he did not do his own drawings; in the Gropius-Breuer partnership it is especially so because neither one of them drew, although Breuer sketched continually. Breuer & Yorke (Yorke "did not consider himself a brilliant draughtsman," according to Alan Powers)[36] employed a secretary and one principal draftsman: T. R. (Randall) Evans, a young New Zealand architect who admired Breuer's work and would later recall him as "a beautiful and economic detailer, particularly in timber."[37]

In the summer of 1935, even before the partnership agreement was worked out and before Breuer received his emigration papers, he and Yorke began to work together. Yorke had a potential house client in Wimbledon for whom sketches were made, but the project fell through; Breuer remodeled a house in Clifton, near Bristol, for its owner, Crofton Gane. Gane, interested in craftsmanship and design, was the head of a family-run furniture company in Bristol. Since 1824, P. E. Gane had manufactured and sold traditional furniture ("When we began to sell furniture George IV was on the throne"[38]) until Crofton Gane changed its direction toward modern design. Using new materials (a wall of white-painted corrugated asbestos sheeting in the dining room), reorganizing the space, and filling the Bristol house with furniture and cabinetry he designed especially for it, Breuer transformed the traditional rooms into an elegant and efficient twentieth-century interior—bright, transparent, and uncluttered. The furniture, casually but artfully placed, was of light-colored woods, aluminum, and black glass. Many of its features became Breuer trademarks in later residential buildings—the cantilevered stair, for example, reappearing in the United States in the Hagerty House (1938) and the Ferry Cooperative Dormitory (1950) at Vassar College. In 1964, Gane wrote to Breuer: "Your work in this house in 1936 is considered of such permanent value that about a score of students . . . come term by term to examine it and there is no question both from the close interest manifested and by the judgements of their leaders that I am the happy possessor of so much that is of permanent value." [39]

In London, Breuer became part of the art and design avant-garde as a member of MARS and of Circle, a professional group of like-minded artists and architects,[40] and he led an urbane social life. Henry Moore and Naum Gabo were among his friends, and he recommended their work to clients whose apartments and houses he was remodeling. (Writing to Yorke from the United States in the early 1940s, Breuer would inquire about Pritchard, Fry, the Tecton people, Shand, J. M. Richards, Ben and Christopher Nicholson, Carter, and others.) Finding enough remunerative work, however, was not a simple matter. For the six months from January through June 1937, for example, Yorke's profit from the partnership was only £160 and Breuer's, £161.[41] Architecture commissions were scarce, and Breuer was known in England less for his architecture than for the prestige of his Bauhaus affiliation, for his connection to Gropius and to Isokon, and for his furniture and interiors. He was interviewed on July 10, 1935, by the "Scientific Correspondent" of the *Manchester Guardian* and was asked mostly about his metal furniture. Anticipating Breuer's arrival, Fry wrote to him in Zürich inquiring if he would join with six "architect-designers" to design new furniture for exhibit and sale at Heal & Sons on Tottenham Court Road, saying that "the exhibition will be well advertised and may be quite important if we can produce good designs."[42] A fee of 40 guineas was offered to each designer; alert to any opportunity in the British design world, Breuer replied that he would be "very pleased to take part in the suggested exhibition."[43] By March 1936, the "Seven Architects Exhibition" of

furniture had opened at Heal's; some visitors recognized Breuer as an architect, too—an alert manufacturer of a Swedish fiberboard product called Treetex wrote: "I know you have designed some houses with flat roofs [still a novel feature] . . . and Treetex is ideally efficient under bitumen and asphalt for flat roof propositions either big and small." [44]

Even an opportunity to design airplane seats was not uninteresting to Breuer in the winter of 1936. John Duncan Miller, director of a decoration and design firm on Lower Grosvenor Place, proposed that "if the idea of making the seats for aeroplanes that we talked about on Monday really interests you, we are going down to the aerodrome on Saturday and we would very much like you to come too. You could then see the various problems and decide whether you would like to try them." [45] Dimensions of the airplane cabin were taken, and sections of metal tube were sent to Breuer for experiment—he was to be paid a royalty of 5 percent on the selling price of the seats. Among Breuer's papers is the draft of a contract, but the project was never realized.[46]

The most salient aspect of Breuer's professional life in England was the partnership with Yorke, even though most of his time and energy had to be spent on designs for the new modern furniture division of Isokon and on problems connected with the licensing and manufacturing of his earlier furniture, still a major source of revenue. Commissions carried out by Breuer while in the partnership were principally for interior remodelings. But the built works and unexecuted

Isokon chaise longue. Bent plywood and fabric. 1936

architectural projects, while few in number, came for late-arriving Breuer at a moment of great readiness.[47]

Before the appearance of the "Bauhaus refugees," modern architecture in England had developed within two or three years. It evolved from a few simple geometric single-family houses built around 1930 by young architects Amyas Connell, Basil Ward, and Colin Lucas (the last of whom designed the first reinforced-concrete house in England, the preferred material for modern buildings) and culminated in the Penguin Pond of 1933 by the partnership of Lubetkin & Tecton, formed only one year earlier. ("Modern architecture for animals, as humans were not interested," Jean-Louis Cohen drolly observed about the pond and England.[48]) Between 1933 and 1938, there appeared what Anthony Jackson has described as "a succession of outstanding buildings," including the high-rise apartment blocks known as Highpoint I (1934–35) and II (1938), London's most advanced examples of modern apartment-house planning, also designed and built by Lubetkin & Tecton.[49] In 1936, Breuer had the opportunity to design and decorate a spacious Highpoint flat for Dorothea Ventris—a cultivated and enthusiastic supporter of modern art—and her son Michael Ventris, later to become the celebrated cryptographer who, with John Chadwick, deciphered the Mycenaean script known as Linear B.[50] For Ventris and her son, Breuer created one of the most urbane interiors of his career, a perfect specimen of the sophisticated total design he was producing in the 1930s.[51] The furnishings included his Isokon plywood furniture of organic shape, tubular-steel-and-cane chairs, wall-hung cabinets, and lighting fixtures.

The high quality of Highpoint and buildings like it validated the seriousness and commitment of the British architectural experiment in these years. That movement was promoted and reinforced by a sympathetic architectural press, notably Architects' Journal and Architectural Review, the most important and influential of the professional journals. In the pages of Architectural Review, modern architecture was given attention and visibility with superb photography accompanying articles by enlightened critics, historians, and architects: Morton Shand (called by David Dunster "the amateur guru of

the modern movement in Great Britain"[52]), Coates, Serge Chermayeff, Bertold Lubetkin, Richards, and Yorke.

The brief but inspired spurt of activity that produced a number of exceptional buildings in the 1930s was given exposure and institutional approbation in New York in the winter of 1937 at MoMA, where the director of the Department of Architecture and Design was Philip Johnson. The catalogue for "Modern Architecture in England" was prepared by Hitchcock, who had high praise for the English accomplishment and said of it that "for quantity of sound modern building and quality, too, the English school is ahead of the American."[53]

Breuer lived and worked in England from 1935 to 1937 on the assumption that it was to be his permanent residence, but he never felt fully at home there or fully occupied. Occasionally, he broke through his natural reserve to express this unhappiness and frustration to close friends, such as gallery owner Marian Willard. Replying from New York in late 1936 to a recent letter, she asked Breuer: "Why are you so discouraged? . . . Life is hard, yes, and it can make you bitter, but that doesn't help any."[54] (Breuer, we recall, remembered those years as "hopeless and *auch* personally terrible" in a letter to Ise Gropius.[55])

The two years in London nevertheless proved to be an important interval in his development as an architect. In a letter of 1942, Breuer referred to the "large scale model which I designed during my partnership with F. R. S. Yorke in London in 1936, named the Garden City of the Future. It is a utopian and schematic suggestion for the rebuilding of a city center."[56] Evans remembered that "the project was ninety percent Breuer," according to Powers in his study of Yorke's career.[57] The model of Garden City of the Future (often called Civic Center after one of its sections) was probably the most significant formalist invention of Breuer's career, furnishing him with architectural capital to spend for the rest of his life. It consolidated his experiences with architecture since 1922 and—in terms of city planning, housing, structure, and materials—prepared him for large urban projects, such as the resort town Flaine and a satellite city for working-class families near Bayonne, both in France. It was, moreover, an opportunity to

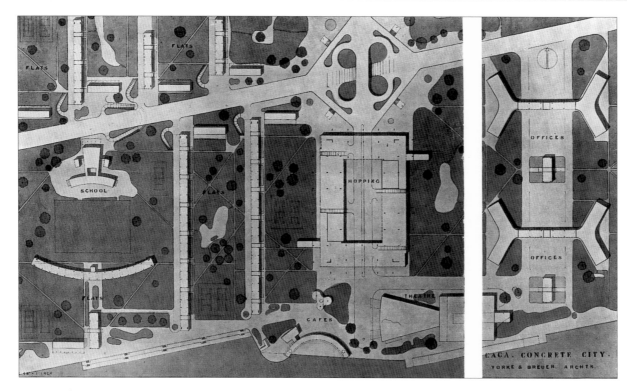

Garden City of the Future. Plan

explore the potential of concrete in ways that Breuer had not yet had the opportunity to do. Twenty-five years later, he acknowledged its importance when writing to Cranston Jones, who was preparing the introduction to a book on Breuer's work. Jones asked for themes to be covered by the illustrations, to which Breuer answered: "Preoccupation with structure and its implications on form. . . . Civic Center of Future is turning point, and in connection with concrete develops toward more plastic form."[58]

Designing Garden City of the Future gave Breuer the opportunity to crystallize ideas about city planning that he had been incubating since 1923. In an interview about the project, he expressed admiration for Robert Moses's Jones Beach, imagining that type of waterside playground for the working classes as "an integral part of the city of the future."[59] He admired, too, the city of Bath, in his view the best example of town planning in the history of urbanism. He thought highly of its street of houses constructed to seem like one building sited on a hill to the south of town and of the entire project accomplished through private enterprise. That the houses in Bath were largely standardized also recommended

them to Breuer. Espousing the Gropian-Bauhaus theory and practice of standardized typeforms on which he was bred, he pointed out that modern housing schemes leaned more and more toward standardization, and he predicted (incorrectly, as it turned out) that the economic and utilitarian advantages of such planning would gradually break down objections to the enforced uniformity of the patterns.

Architects and planners have been reinventing the ideal city since Leon Battista Alberti in the fifteenth century in the hope of improving urban aesthetics and the way people live. For Breuer, Garden City of the Future was the occasion to bring together the ideals he shared with the post–First World War social utopians, and the expression he gave those ideals in his experimental architectural projects, which, until London, had been disjunctive: apartment houses, hospitals, small single-family residences, row houses, low-cost housing, fairgrounds, theaters, traffic and pedestrian patterns, and so forth. Now he could integrate them within a coherent city plan. The fundamental structural component for the project was the reinforced concrete that determined many of the forms. Indeed, the project was sponsored by the British

Cement and Concrete Association and was exhibited at the "Ideal Home" exhibition in 1936; in his letters, Yorke sometimes referred to it as Concrete City.[60] As the material blessed by the modern movement, concrete was employed to its full creative advantage in Garden City, with shapes—especially the Y-shaped buildings—and densities that from then on would define the sculptural character of Breuer's work. It may be that the Y-shaped format first entered Breuer's consciousness by way of the Expressionistic projects of Hans Poelzig in 1920s Germany. As Breuer was living and working in Berlin in 1929, he would have known Poelzig's design for a competition of that year for a library addition to the Reichstag. Its concave-sided Y-design was derived from Poelzig's entry in the well-known competition of 1921 and 1922 for a tall office building near the Friedrichstrasse station in Berlin.

While Garden City of the Future was a visionary concept not intended for construction, an equally important example of early Breuer was a built work. The Gane Pavilion was a temporary exhibition structure made for the Royal Agricultural Show in Bristol in July 1936 to display modern furniture manufactured by P. E. Gane. But when the personnage from the royal court who came to arrange flowers for the official opening by the king looked at the installed display, she asked, "When will the furnishings arrive?"[61] The show, washed out by rain, was a dismal failure, and none of the few visitors to the Gane Pavilion ordered any furniture.[62] Architecturally, however, the building occupies a special place in Breuer's career as an illustration of the harmonizing of irregular shapes; of the creative combination of stone, glass, and wood; and of the use of traditional materials in modern format. Asked in 1958 to name the buildings of which he was most proud, Breuer chose the UNESCO Headquarters and the Gane Pavilion.[63]

Architectural work undertaken by Breuer & Yorke—built and projected—covered a diversity of building types. The partners entered a competition in 1937 for an urban elementary school. Their project accorded with new ideas about progressive education and public works and about the advantages to society from the modern design of schools. An open-plan building with a light, airy courtyard, it reflected the phi-losophy of an open and free (that is, progressive) education, sharing programmatic features and ideas about education with Gropius's executed design for Impington Village College, considered his most successful architectural undertaking in England.[64] Modern school plans were innovations in England of the 1930s.[65] In contrast to the situation in Germany, modern architecture in England evolved during a period of comparative economic stability, so building types were not determined primarily by sociological considerations.[66] Department stores and factories, and houses and apartments for the middle class, took precedence over low-cost housing for workers and even over schools.

If Garden City of the Future was the fount of much of Breuer's later work in commercial, institutional, and multi-family structures, the Gane Pavilion advanced his growth as a designer of single-family residences. Several of the best modern houses in England of the 1930s, on a par with those by Lubetkin & Tecton, and Erich Mendelsohn and Chermayeff, were the work of Breuer & Yorke. Houses of 1936 and 1937 at Angmering-on-Sea in Sussex, at Lee-on-Solent in Hampshire, and at Eton were published together in *Architectural Review* with Yorke's name appearing ahead of Breuer's.[67] Since much of the design and the detailing in the buildings is clearly Breuer's, the terms of the partnership agreement suggest that Yorke brought in the clients and assumed most of the responsibility for construction. This is consistent with the credit sequence in the publication of the Gane Pavilion in *Architectural Review*, where Breuer's name appears first, since his connection to Crofton Gane's furniture business brought about the commission for the exhibition building.[68]

The Macnabb House in Angmering near Littlehampton was a six-bedroom house of painted brick and reinforced concrete. Its T-shape was a functional construct determined by the site and the client's wish for a view of the sea from as many rooms as possible. Thus the rooms were arranged on the upper tier of a long stem raised on oval pilotis above a continuous lawn. Before working with Breuer at Angmering, Yorke had used structural wall systems rather than columns for support.[69] Although the T-shape may have been a response to exigencies of need and place, Breuer found it a

Gane's Pavilion, Bristol, England. 1936

Macnabb House, Angmering-on-Sea, Sussex, England. 1937. View of the curved balcony

useful configuration and would call on it often in the future—the elevated bedroom wing of his Ferry Cooperative Dormitory (1950) at Vassar being one of the most successful lineal descendants. The ground floor at Angmering housed a small entrance hall, kitchen, maid's quarters, and garage, while above in the family wing were a dining room (with built-in furniture and a dumbwaiter connecting it with the kitchen below), living room, and terrace, all designed as one continuous space. The upper living room–dining room terrace—protected from the wind by a glazed screen, shaded by a striped awning, and joined to ground level by an external stair, as at the Harnischmacher House—was formed as a grand, swinging curve. It constituted the most remarkable formal aspect of the design, its voluptuous S-shape a dramatic contrast to the rectilinearity of the rest of the house. Even though the initial design was modified due to the resistance of local building authorities to modern architecture, the completed Macnabb House—with its red-and-white striped awnings, white walls, high-gloss metallic-gray paint on the woodwork, and floors of polished cork tiles—must have seemed a wild foreign creature in 1936 Sussex.

The curving shape, rare but not unknown in Breuer's architectural designs before his move to England (a 1929 project for a single-family dwelling [Wohnhaus I], for example), was used with assertive vigor not only in Angmering but in Bristol and in Garden City of the Future. It turns up, too, in the sinuous contours of his contemporaneous laminated-plywood furniture designed for Isokon. It was a positive response to the Expressionistic effect and sculptural nature of curved forms in English modernism, especially in the work of Lubetkin and Chermayeff.[70]

At the same time that the Sussex house was in construction, Breuer & Yorke were building another villa of concrete and steel, named by its owners Shangri-La, in Hampshire, at Lee-on-Solent. The plan of this house was Yorke's, replicating at the client's request Yorke's design for a residence (Torilla) at Nast Hyde, Hatfield, Hertfordshire, built a year earlier, in 1935, before he and Breuer formed their partnership (but with additions by Yorke and Breuer in 1936).[71] In general, though, the plan and elevation are less integrated and more complex than those of Breuer's previous residential designs. Having first learned about architecture when it was based on economy, in his later career Breuer often carried out his most ingenious residential designs when he was under budgetary restraints. When the programs were complex and the requirements luxurious, his houses could get out of control. The size and appointments of Lee-on-Solent prepared Breuer for the difficulties of the large and luxurious Frank House in Pittsburgh, which he and Gropius undertook as partners in 1939.

Less uncompromising and more expressive and picturesque than that on the Continent, modern architecture in England in the 1930s was consistent with characteristics of English architecture that were present since the Middle Ages. To the rigorous format of German and Dutch prototypes, the English added expansive curves, oblique joinings, and color, as at Lee-on-Solent, which imparted to even their modern buildings a distinctive national identity.

Twin houses on adjoining sites for masters at Eton College, Willowbrook, Buckinghamshire—to be built at a cost of no more than £2,500 each, including built-in furniture—were a Breuer & Yorke project for which economy was important. Evans recalls that "Breuer played little part in the design,"[72] and the buildings were completed in 1938 after he had left England. (Yorke informed him later that "unfortunately the occupants have used entirely the wrong sort of curtains."[73]) Still, the two-story brick cuboids, with steel angles above the window openings to support the brick walls,[74] were to have an impact on future designs by Breuer. On the ground floor, a small canopied porch led to an entrance hall with stair, and on the south front a terrace was covered with a wood-frame pergola, features that Breuer would use again a few years later in Lincoln, Massachusetts, and that he had employed at the Gane Pavilion. Distinctive also at Eton College was the living-room window that gave onto the terrace: in contrast to the other standard casements, it reached floor level and became a sliding glass wall.

Breuer's English work, overall, was typical of his versatility. For several clients who admired the Bauhaus and its products, he remodeled and/or decorated commercial and residential interiors;[75] he installed a theater in a remodeled building for the London Theatre Studio; he designed a modern-art gallery on Cork Street for Lady Peter Norton and a bar-club (Isobar) on the ground floor at Lawn Road Flats for the tenants. He designed temporary exhibition booths at trade fairs and a studio for the display of high fashion for women (Motley's Fashion Studio).

One of Breuer's last projects before leaving London on his uncertain journey to the New World was the design of a small ski-resort hotel, "for sportsmen, not for the fashionable,"[76] in Ober-Gurgl in the Austrian Tyrol, where he and his friends often skied. Breuer worked out final plans for the design in the United States in 1937. But the plans were rejected by the Austrian authorities, and even if they had been revised once again the project was to have no future because the scheduled construction for March 1938 would have coincided with the Anschluss. Referring to the old Hotel Edelweiss & Gurgl, where Breuer regularly stayed, Xanti Schawinsky wrote on March 19, 1938, that "at your hotel in Ober-Gurgl a Nazi flag will soon be flying."[77] "Hitler was quicker and the client, Hans Falkner, had to leave his country [because he was an] Anglophile and consequently anti-German," Breuer explained when writing about his hotel project to Edgar Kaufmann, Jr., a few years later.[78] Ober-Gurgl was the subject of one of the earliest American publications of Breuer's architectural work, having been requested for the September 1938 issue of Architectural Record by its editor, James Marston Fitch.

The inaccessibility of Ober-Gurgl dictated the use of wood (light in weight) and stone (available at the site) instead of steel, concrete, and plate glass, which were expensive and difficult to transport. From that exigency came a new structural system. "The appearance of the building is not governed alone by formal use of stone and wood but by the constructive use of the two materials," Breuer wrote.[79] The potential of that system was realized not in Austria but in American houses of the 1930s designed by Breuer while in partnership with Gropius, when he amalgamated the Ober-Gurgl construction strategy into his adaptation of New England wood framing.

He described that strategy in a letter to Yorke about the Chamberlain Cottage (1940–41) in Wayland, Massachusetts: "The parapet wall is made of three layers of cross-wise boarding, a kind of home-made plywood affair, or a reinforced concrete in wood, if you want to call it that. The traditional American frame construction is considered in this, as in most of my others, as having truss-like walls, which can be cantilevered or built over large openings without beams. Very similar to reinforced concrete walls."[80] And of the Weizenblatt House (1940–41) in Asheville, North Carolina, he wrote that "I gave Konrad [Wachsmann] a model photo of a ski hotel in Ober-Gurgl showing the same principle of construction."[81]

Breuer's two years in London brought him refuge and personal safety from Hitlerism. Well-illustrated and well-written appraisals of his pre-England work, of his interiors, and of Breuer & Yorke buildings appeared in Architectural Review and Architects' Journal and helped keep him visible internationally. But he and other progressive designers were swimming against a tide of aesthetic conservatism, becoming, as Jackson puts it, "part of another struggle for recognition that they had already come through in the previous decade."[82] Eager and ready for vigorous architectural activity, and accustomed to the theoretical and practical complexities of iconoclastic Continental modernism, Breuer found the England of 1935 to 1937 professionally unfulfilling. But, unexpectedly, his life was to be changed by visits made with discretion and some secrecy to Gropius in London by three Americans. First, in July 1936, came MoMA director Alfred Barr at the request of Joseph Hudnut, dean of the School of Architecture at Harvard. Barr was followed soon after by Hudnut himself and, in October, by James B. Conant, president of Harvard. Their mission—ultimately successful—was to explore the possibility of an appointment for Gropius at Harvard.[83] Gropius left England in March 1937 after a farewell dinner presided over by H. G. Wells. In the catalogue to the MoMA exhibition "Modern Architecture in England," published in February 1937, Hitchcock wrote: "It is the privilege of this catalogue to announce that Gropius has accepted the position of Nelson Robinson, Jr., Professor of Architecture at Harvard."[84]

Walter and Ise Gropius worked hard on Breuer's behalf in Cambridge, as they had done in London, before he finally decided to emigrate, and they encouraged him to follow them to the United States, as they had encouraged him to move to England. Throughout the years of their friendship, most of the correspondence between Breuer and the Gropiuses was carried out by Ise and Lajkó, with brief postscripts added by Walter. But a month after his arrival in Cambridge, Walter himself wrote a rare four-page letter to Breuer that could hardly contain his joy:

Dear Lajkó, It's wonderful here. Don't tell the English, but we are both heavenly happy to have escaped from the land of fog and emotional nightmare. Air clear as glass, lots of sun, and blue Roman skies. All around an unspoiled, untamed landscape, most of which has not been degraded into parks and in which one doesn't always feel like a trespasser. In addition, fine wooden houses in the Colonial style, painted white, which will delight you as much as they do me. In their simplicity, functionality, and uniformity they are completely in our line. The inviting appearance of these houses mirrors the incredible hospitality of this country, which probably stems from old pioneer times.[85]

Breuer made a trial visit in the summer of 1937 and a month after he arrived, on August 31, wrote to Yorke: "Before I left, everybody told me 'you will stay in America.' I am afraid it will happen indeed. You know I was always anxious to get more interesting jobs in London than we actually had. Now Gropius suggested that I go in partnership with him and that seems to be a promising step in that direction. I see in the U.S.A. a lot of possibilities for this partnership."[86]

The partnership of Breuer & Yorke was fiscally terminated as of June 30, 1937. Small payments were made by Breuer through August 1939, when he sent Yorke the final $50 (half the income tax for 1936/37) of his obligation to their contract. Correspondence between the two architects on this inevitably touchy matter was conducted in tones of civility and friendship. Before he left England in July 1937, Breuer made an agreement with Isokon regarding licensing and royalty arrangements for his furniture designs. He was to receive, furthermore, a fee of £100 a year to serve as Isokon's adviser, "substantially on the same terms as Gropius acted as adviser,

an appointment to last for one year certain and thereafter so long as both parties agree."[87]

The contrast between the static character of modern architecture in England and the vitality he perceived for its future in America inspired Breuer to emigrate. Once again, it was not a simple decision; but this time he could anticipate that in the United States his personal financial balance might finally shift so that he could arrange his priorities in the way he had hoped for more than a decade. With a partnership in private enterprise with Gropius, and a potential salaried position on the Harvard faculty in the Department of Architecture, he might become both a practicing architect and a teacher of architecture with an interest in furniture design, rather than the reverse. "What the two of you write looks as favorable for me as I could possibly imagine," he wrote to Ise and Walter on June 15, 1937. "I would be quite satisfied with $5,000 a year to start with [at Harvard], and later even more of course with $8,000 in case it goes that far. But the main thing for me would always be our joint private office. . . . So we'll be earning something yet from architecture, I would never have believed it."[88]

After he was established in the New World, Breuer continued to receive requests from English journalists and editors to publish his American work, and he maintained professional and personal friendships with his English colleagues of the 1930s. With the hindsight of two decades, an English reviewer writing in the London *Times* in the late 1950s about Breuer's *Sun and Shadow* referred to Breuer as the "youngest of the Bauhaus rebels" and, more to the point, as "the architect we let go."[89] In 1954, when Yorke was collecting material for a reprint of his book *The New Small House*, he requested information from Breuer on houses he wanted to include: Breuer's first house (1947–48) in New Canaan, Connecticut, and the houses for Stillman (1950–51), Clark (1950–51), and Pack (1951). In 1970, Pritchard wrote to Breuer after receiving a copy of Tician Papachristou's *Marcel Breuer: New Buildings and Projects*: "We were talking of you last week and deploring the [unimaginative? (illegible)] English of before the war and how we should have had some of the splendid work of yours here."[90]

On May 21, 1937, Breuer celebrated his thirty-fifth birthday in London. That evening, he received a cable from "Pius/Pia" from Cambridge, Massachusetts: "Cheers, Lajkó. 35 is a good number for a promising new partnership."[91]

1   Henry-Russell Hitchcock and Catherine K. Bauer, *Modern Architecture in England* [exhibition catalogue] (New York: Museum of Modern Art, 1937), 25.

2   G. E. Kidder Smith, *The New Architecture of Europe* (Cleveland: World, 1961), 35.

3   Anthony Jackson, "The Politics of Architecture: English Architecture, 1929–1951," *Journal of the Society of Architectural Historians* 24 (1965): 97–107; see also Anthony Jackson, *The Politics of Architecture: A History of Modern Architecture in Britain* (London: Architectural Press, 1970).

4   For an account of the circumstances of Gropius's departure from the Continent and arrival in England, see Reginald R. Isaacs, *Gropius: An Illustrated Biography of the Creator of the Bauhaus* (Boston: Little, Brown, 1991), 182–87. On the origin of the invitation to Gropius to emigrate to London—a visit in May 1934 when the RIBA sponsored an exhibition of his work and he lectured about the Bauhaus— see Leslie Humm Cormier, *Walter Gropius, Emigré Architect: Works and Refuge, England and America in the 30's* (Ann Arbor, Mich.: University Micofilms, 1986), 21.

5   For more on the Lawn Road Flats, see *Architectural Review*, February 1934, 41, and Charlotte Benton, "The 'Minimum' Flat," in *Thirties: British Art and Design before the War* [exhibition catalogue] (London: Arts Council of Great Britain, 1979), 267–68.

6   Ise Gropius to Breuer, n.d. [probably winter 1934], Correspondence, AAA.

7   On Breuer's Isokon furniture, see Christopher Wilk, *Marcel Breuer: Furniture and Interiors* (New York: Museum of Modern Art, 1981), 126–46.

8   Marcel Breuer, "Autobiography," SUL 39.

9   Wilk, *Furniture and Interiors*, 126.

10   Breuer to Ise Gropius, April 6, 1935, Walter Gropius Papers (Breuer Letters), HL.

11   Documents of official withdrawal, signed by the Anhaltisches Landesrabbinat, Dessau, June 17, 1926, SUL 10. Breuer's withdrawal from Judaism was made possible by a 1920 statute ("Gemass 6 des Gesetzes über den Austritt aus Religionsgesellschaften"). The documents were noted for the first time in Wilk, *Furniture and Interiors*, 187, n. 2.

12   Breuer to Ise Gropius, December 25, 1934, Walter Gropius Papers (Breuer Letters), HL.

13   Ibid.

14   Alan Powers, *In the Line of Development: FRS Yorke, E Rosenberg and CS Mardall to YRM, 1930–1992* [exhibition catalogue] (London: RIBA Heinz Gallery, 1992), 16; Jeremy Gould, *Modern Houses in Britain, 1919–1939* (London: Society of Architectural Historians of Great Britain, 1977), 30, n. 45.

15   Breuer to Ise Gropius, December 25, 1934.

16   Breuer to Ise Gropius, May 22, 1935, Walter Gropius Papers (Breuer Letters), HL.

17   Ise Gropius to Breuer, January 19, 1935, Correspondence, AAA.

18   For the partnership with Breuer, see Powers, *In the Line of Development*, esp. 16–22, and Phyllida Mills, "F. R. S. Yorke: The English Tradition" (third-year diss., Cambridge University, 1988), 15–20, esp. bibliography for Yorke's publications.

19   Gould, *Modern Houses in Britain*, 19.

20   F. R. S. Yorke, *The Modern House* (London: Architectural Press, 1934). The book had many editions.

21   Breuer to Ise Gropius, April 6, 1935, Walter Gropius Papers (Breuer Letters), HL; Marcel Breuer, "Where Do We Stand?" *Architectural Review*, April 1935, 133–36. For publications of the lecture, see Hannah B. Muller, Bibliography, in Peter Blake, *Marcel Breuer: Architect and Designer* (New York: Museum of Modern Art, 1949), 123.

22   Ise Gropius to Breuer, April 10, 1935, Correspondence, AAA.

23   Ise Gropius, "A House at Wiesbaden," *Architectural Review*, July 1935, 13–14.

24   F. R. S. Yorke to Breuer, April 11, 1935, SUL 10.

25   Ise Gropius to Breuer, May 20, 1935, Correspondence, AAA.

26 As he was already a designer of some note, Breuer was interviewed on July 10 by the "Scientific Correspondent" of the *Manchester Guardian* about his visit to England ("Aluminum for Furniture: Inventor's Experiments. From Our Scientific Correspondent," *Manchester Guardian*, July 11, 1935, 6).

27 E. J. Carter to Breuer, July 31, 1935, SUL 10.

28 Breuer to Undersecretary of State, August 29, 1935, SUL 10.

29 Lady Peter Norton to Breuer, October 16, 1935, Correspondence, AAA. The dynamic and influential Noel E. Norton, known as Peter—whose husband, Clifford, was a career diplomat and, in 1938, the last British ambassador to Poland—went personally on Breuer's behalf to the Home Office. She had a strong interest in modern art and opened a gallery designed by Breuer on Cork Street in London.

30 William Feaver, "Art at the Time," in *Thirties*, 33.

31 Ise Gropius to Breuer, n.d., Correspondence, AAA. On rents, building costs, services, and tenants of Lawn Road Flats, see Benton, "'Minimum Flat,'" 267.

32 Breuer's bank records from this period are in SUL 53. He kept all the bills—for string and nails as well as for the larger items—relating to his settling into Tregunter Street.

33 Breuer to F. R. S. Yorke, September 18, 1935, SUL 10.

34 In response to an invitation from Jack Pritchard in 1955 to celebrate Lawn Road Flats' twenty-first birthday, Breuer wrote from New York: "It is good to know that Lawn Road Flats will have a birthday, just like any other human being. I always liked that girl and I think she is getting younger from year to year. . . . [L]et me send off this note as a birthday card . . . and if it sounds a bit nostalgic it is only because it reminds me that already 19 years have passed since I lived with her" (Breuer to Pritchard, March 24, 1955, Correspondence, AAA).

35 Marcel Breuer, notes of conversation with Yorke, November 19, 1935, SUL 53.

36 Powers, *In the Line of Development*, 10.

37 Quoted in Mills, "F. R. S. Yorke," 18.

38 H. W., *A Swan Sings, Being a Memoir of the House of Gane* (London: The Shenval Press, 1954), 3.

39 Crofton Gane to Breuer, May 26, 1964, Correspondence, AAA. They corresponded until Gane's death in 1967.

40 J. L. Martin, Ben Nicholson, and N. Gabo, eds., *Circle: International Survey of Constructive Art* (London: Faber and Faber, 1937).

41 Correspondence and accounts germane to the financial aspects of the partnership are in SUL 8.

42 Maxwell Fry to Breuer, October 3, 1935, SUL 10.

43 Breuer to Maxwell Fry, handwritten draft of reply, n.d., SUL 10.

44 [Signature illegible] to Breuer, April 23, 1936, SUL 14.

45 Duncan Miller to Breuer, January 22, 1936, SUL 14.

46 Draft of contract, March 1936, SUL 14.

47 Several are preserved in the Prints and Drawings Collection, RIBA.

48 Jean-Louis Cohen, lecture in art history course, Institute of Fine Arts, New York University, February 26, 1997.

49 Jackson, "Politics of Architecture," 97.

50 Isabelle Hyman, "The Marcel Breuer Papers and Michael Ventris: A Biographical Note," *Syracuse University Library Associates Courier* 24 (1989): 3–12.

51 Wilk, *Furniture and Interiors*, 142–45.

52 David Dunster, *Key Buildings of the Twentieth Century*, vol. 1, *Houses, 1900–1944* (New York: Rizzoli, 1984), 50.

53 Hitchcock and Bauer, *Modern Architecture in England*, 39.

54 Marian Willard to Breuer, December 4, 1936, Correspondence, AAA.

55 Breuer to Ise Gropius, March 15, 1971, Walter Gropius Papers (Breuer Letters), HL.

56 Breuer to Marian Becker, October 8, 1942, SUL 15.

57 Quoted in Powers, *In the Line of Development*, 18.

58 Cranston Jones, ed., *Marcel Breuer: Buildings and Projects, 1921–1961* (New York: Praeger, 1962); Breuer to Cranston Jones, January 13, 1961, Correspondence, AAA.

59 Marcel Breuer, interview for Carl Warton, "What Cities of Future Will Look Like," *Boston Herald*, December 31, 1939.

60 F. R. S. Yorke to Breuer, May 17, 1938, SUL 8.

61 Breuer to Robert Allan Jacobs, November 11, 1958, Correspondence, AAA.

62 *Bristol Weekend*, July 17, 1963.

63 Breuer to Cranston Jones, January 13, 1961.

64 Leslie Humm Cormier, "Walter Gropius, Emigré Architect: The Persistence of Typeforms," *Arris: Journal of the Southeast Chapter of the Society of Architectural Historians* 4 (1993): 27–31.

65 Ibid., 27–29. Although it concentrates on a later period, Andrew Saint, *Towards a Social Architecture: The Role of School-Building in Post-War England* (New Haven, Conn.: Yale University Press, 1987), contains numerous observations relevant to this subject.

66 Hitchcock and Bauer, *Modern Architecture in England*, 31.

67 "Houses 1, 2, 3," *Architectural Review*, January 1939, 29–35.

68 "Exhibition House at Bristol," *Architectural Review*, August 1936, 69–70.

69 Gould, *Modern Houses in Britain*, 19.

70 On this subject, see Hitchcock and Bauer, *Modern Architecture in England*, 37.

71 Mills, "F. R. S. Yorke," 32.

72 Quoted in Powers, *In the Line of Development*, 19.

73 F. R. S. Yorke to Breuer, February 7, 1938, SUL 8.

74 That these supports were made not of steel, but of reinforced concrete, also appears in the records. The author is unable to verify which is correct.

75 Hyman, "Marcel Breuer Papers and Michael Ventris."

76 Marcel Breuer, memorandum on Ober-Gurgl, August 12, 1938, prepared for the project's forthcoming publication in *Architectural Record*, September 1938, SUL 18.

77 Alexander Schawinsky to Breuer, March 19, 1938, Correspondence, AAA.

78 Breuer to Edgar Kaufmann, Jr., January 31, 1941, SUL 5.

79 Breuer, memorandum on Ober-Gurgl, August 12, 1938.

80 Breuer to F. R. S. Yorke, March 8, 1943, SUL 45.

81 Breuer to H. Herrey, February 19, 1945, SUL 18.

82 Jackson, "Politics of Architecture," 103.

83 Alfred Barr, in "Modern Architecture Symposium (MAS 1964): The Decade 1929–1939," *Journal of the Society of Architectural Historians* 24 (1965): 93; see also Jill Pearlman, "Joseph Hudnut's Other Modernism at the 'Harvard Bauhaus,'" *Journal of the Society of Architectural Historians* 56 (1997): 463.

84 Hitchcock and Bauer, *Modern Architecture in England*, 39.

85 Walter Gropius to Breuer, April 17, 1937, Walter Gropius Papers (Breuer Letters), HL.

86 Breuer to F. R. S. Yorke, August 31, 1937, SUL 8.

87 Breuer to Jack Pritchard, July 20, 1937, SUL 50.

88 Breuer to Walter and Ise Gropius, June 15, 1937, Walter Gropius Papers (Breuer Letters), HL.

89 Clipping, review of Sun and Shadow, by Marcel Breuer, *Times* (London), n.d. [late 1950s], Correspondence, AAA.

90 Jack Pritchard to Breuer, November 6, 1970, Correspondence, AAA; Tician Papachristou, *Marcel Breuer: New Buildings and Projects, 1960–70* (New York: Praeger, 1970).

91 Walter and Ise Gropius to Breuer, May 21, 1937, Correspondence, AAA.

4. Cambridge:
The Harvard Years, 1937–46

LEAVING BEHIND HIM THE MORIBUND PRESENT and uncertain future of modernist architecture in England, Breuer made an immediate adjustment to the United States, his creative potential finally unleashed. The years of frustration, involuntary exile, and lack of continual work—years when he feared that he was "becoming completely rusty as an architect"[1]—were expunged by his elated response to America. "Creative energies long suppressed, concealed, starved and deformed by England are creeping forth to American life," he wrote to Ise Gropius as he prepared to leave Europe.[2] Less than two months later from Massachusetts, he wrote to Crofton Gane that "I see a lot of possibilities for me in this country so I have decided to remain here."[3] Learning of Breuer's decision, Jack Pritchard told him that "when you went I half believed you would not come back. . . . Had you stayed here you would have developed a good practice within two or three years, but all your old friends would be in America."[4]

Breuer House, Lincoln, Massachusetts.
1939. Living room

ARRIVAL IN THE UNITED STATES, 1937

Gropius and Breuer came to America in a second wave of interwar immigrant architects, preceded by Richard Neutra and Rudolph Schindler, Erich Mendelsohn and William Lescaze. But instead of coming at considerable risk, as their predecessors had, to sit at the feet of Frank Lloyd Wright or to venture into private practice, Gropius and Breuer were sheltered and sustained by their powerful institutional affiliations—the immense combined prestige of Harvard, the Museum of Modern Art, and the Bauhaus.

Breuer had not thought of teaching when first considering a move to the United States, nor did he ever imagine a position at Harvard alongside Gropius. The idea came entirely from Walter and Ise, who took the steps to make it happen. Their incentives were to sustain a congenial friendship without an ocean in between and to give a deserving Breuer the best chance at architecture he yet had had. But they also saw it, prudently, as security against the uncertainties of beginning a time-consuming new practice in a new country. Breuer was willing, but tentative: "If our collaboration could somehow be brought about in such a way that I could exist over there and get going on some work, I would come at any time. . . . I would be happy to participate in classes at Harvard and very actively, if it doesn't force me to brew up a systematic course of instruction which I feel I have little bent for."[5] In a study of the prevailing character of the Graduate School of Design under Dean Joseph Hudnut, Jill Pearlman convincingly argues against a widely held idea that Gropius's campaign to bring Breuer (and Josef Albers) to Harvard was "the first step in transforming the GSD into an American Bauhaus."[6]

Uncertainty continued to shadow Breuer's decision in the spring and summer of 1937 to resettle. "I am now overwhelmed by the American campaign," he wrote to Ise Gropius on May 28.[7] There was the matter of his commitment to the partnership with F. R. S. Yorke: Breuer believed that even a summer visit to the Gropiuses in Massachusetts would fan rumors already circulating in London about a permanent departure, and any change "probably would be accompanied by Yorke's silent disapproval." There was the question of a "contract still floating in the distance" for the production of his aluminum furniture, and there was a delay on the American side in the confirmation of a position at Harvard. After her ebullient birthday telegram to Breuer in May, Ise had misgivings: "It is not that your prospects are worse, but it is just moving slowly. Walter is in New York with Hudnut on your behalf today, and hopes to resolve the matter once and for all."[8] Still, the principal motivation to emigrate remained firm in Breuer's mind: the irresistible opportunity for "a 100% partnership with Pius," for which Breuer "would have to scrape together about 500 to 1,000 pounds . . . and I have a 90% hope that I can get it together." It was the prospect of "really attacking something proper together with Pius" that gave him the determination to break with the Old World.

The first letters to Breuer from Gropius in America had been filled with exciting expectations about a practice:

I have informed Hudnut about our plans [for an architectural partnership]. He will sympathetically support them, and we are already considering with him what steps could be undertaken to give you financial security at the beginning. I have told him that your presence here would be of great importance to the students. Perhaps you would agree to participate in some way in the instruction. Then, at least at the start, it would be financially easier for you.[9]

Even before Gropius arrived at Harvard, Hudnut had written to Albert Mayer in New York that "it is my intention to make Mr. Gropius's academic burden light so that he can devote a considerable part of his time to professional work: that was, in fact, one of my important reasons for bringing him here."[10] Gropius told Breuer that Hudnut had arranged for the most advanced students to "take part in the work of the practice. In this he is also thinking of reducing costs for me."[11] And, with rising enthusiasm, he wrote: "Harvard looks good. . . . Dean Hudnut is a splendid fellow. I have already plunged in among the students and find that they are at least bright and lively. Something can be done here, and often the primitive naiveté gives me more hope than English common sense." He went on: "Hudnut has arranged two commissions for me which look promising . . . an art center . . . and a large auditorium at

Connecticut College for Women. . . . [W]ith these two things you and I could open fire."

For himself, or for discussion with Gropius, Breuer drafted conditions for such a partnership, based in part on his experience with Yorke: each partner would contribute capital, inventory, and commissions already in hand; limits would be placed on withdrawals from the firm's account; the firm's bank account would be jointly signed by Gropius and Breuer, but (for convenience) one of the partners could be represented by the secretary; and income and payments would be on a 50-50 basis, except for royalties from academic lectures and articles and for income from licensed works completed before the formation of the partnership. Later licenses would belong to the firm; all works would be signed jointly and published as Walter Gropius and Marcel Breuer, and the firm would be designated by that name; the administration of individual commissions would be alternatively handled by one partner or the other; and the agreement could be terminated for any reason with six months' notice from either partner.[12]

Breuer sailed from Southampton in late July 1937 and disembarked on August 2 in New York City. The Gropiuses had hoped to meet him—"I'm for greeting you at the pier with shouts and then going without delay to Duke Ellington," wrote Ise [13]—but instead he was welcomed by Wallace K. Harrison, who had known Gropius in Berlin in 1931 and to whom Breuer had been introduced in London by their mutual friend Marian Willard. After a few days in the city, he joined Walter and Ise at their rented house on Buzzards Bay in Massachusetts to spend August and the first days of September. From that house, one week after he arrived, he wrote to Hans Falkner that "here at the seaside with the Gropiuses I am having a magnificent time; America has above all taken me by pleasant surprise."[14] So pleasant was the surprise that at the end of the first month he told Yorke that he would stay: "The U.S.A. generally attracts me very much. . . . If you have no objections in principle against our separation would you please suggest how we could settle our current affairs. . . . I am sorry I could not fill this letter with only a good description of the beautiful bathing here, the Colonial style and the skyscrapers."[15]

RCA Building, Rockefeller Center, New York, photographed by Breuer. 1937

The skyscrapers of Manhattan made as astonishing an impact on Breuer as on most new arrivals, and he told Yorke that seeing New York City for the first time was "one of the greatest impressions of my life."[16] Especially impressed by the perfect metaphor of American technology and dynamism—the seventy stories of the new RCA Building in Rockefeller Center—Breuer photographed the building in the Futurist mode of Fritz Lang's film *Metropolis* (1926) and immediately sent a print to *Architects' Journal* in London. It was published in the December 9, 1937, issue with a caption that read: "An illustration of two necessities in skyscraper design: a new sense of scale and a robust faith in the effective life of a steel frame. A photograph of the Rockefeller Centre, New York, taken on a recent visit by Marcel Breuer, who has just accepted an appointment at Harvard."[17]

Harvard had become an essential, even if unexpected, factor in Breuer's decision to emigrate, since teaching would provide his only certain income. The strongest magnet, however, remained the potential for designing buildings and for manufacturing and marketing his furniture, so that on arrival he wrote to an executive at R. H. Macy & Company whom he had met at Isokon requesting an introduction to "influential aluminum or plywood people": "I am now in the States to initiate the manufacturing of my new plywood and aluminum furniture on the basis of mass production."[18] In the nine years since his departure from the Bauhaus, Breuer had become well known in modernist circles in Europe as a prize-winning designer of furniture and interiors; his invention of tubular-steel furniture was one of the most significant achievements in the history of modern design. Possibilities for industrial design promised by the New York World's Fair of 1939 had been of great interest to him while still in Europe. He wrote to Gropius describing a Marcel Breuer–Herbert Bayer project for the fair conceived in the spring of 1937 in Berlin and London: "It could become the most wonderful creative work coming from the midst of our thirsting minds—like eunuchs who suddenly get balls, we would get right down to it."[19]

Breuer and Bayer's World's Fair project was to be based on a major theme of the fair—"the man of the future"—and would represent "the modern movement in art, architecture and the cultural fields (films, theatre, advertising, town planning and regional planning)."[20] It would display "the achievements of people who work independently in seemingly unconnected spheres of activity"—art, technology, and commerce—to create a "new world picture [neues Weltbild]" out of the "spiritual and material tendencies that stir man's imagination." A draft by Breuer entitled "The Blue Horizon, An Exhibition of Modern Thought [Horizont, Ausstellung des modernes Gedankens]" listed personalities as diverse as Alfred Barr, Le Corbusier, Albert Einstein, Carola Giedion-Weicker, James Joyce, Alexander Schawinsky, and H. G. Wells. Bayer sketched a cosmological diagram with Mensch at the center and Wissenschaften in an outer ring, the two connected by "spheres of activity." Far-fetched and hopelessly abstract, the proposal was introduced by Breuer, seeking financial support, to executives at Time and Fortune, publications he believed represented "the most culturally directed press in the United States."

In its original format, the Breuer-Bayer World's Fair project reached a dead end, but it was reformulated to become the exhibition portion of the Gropius-Breuer interior of the Pennsylvania State Pavilion (1939) at the fair. Satisfied with the design of the exhibition and its installation in the pavilion interior, Breuer was bitter and defensive about the nonmodern, traditional appearance of the outside—a version of Philadelphia's historic Independence Hall—about which he, Gropius, and Bayer had no say. To Aladar Olgyay he wrote in early 1939 that "we are doing the Pennsylvania State Pavilion inside; if you should happen to see this pavilion, be assured we have nothing to do with the outside."[21] Breuer's early enthusiasm about the fair vanished with the event itself. As it was taking shape, from Cambridge he wrote to a friend on Christmas Eve 1938 that "I do not like to miss this opportunity of telling you that the last time I was in New York at the World's Fair it frankly seemed to be quite a mess."[22] (Organizers of the contemporaneous San Francisco World's Fair—the Golden Gate International Exhibition—were insistent about including furniture by Breuer. Thirteen pieces, which were to be offered for sale as well as displayed, were shipped to San Francisco from Isokon on December 15, 1938.[23])

Breuer also contributed photographs, models, and drawings of his work to the exhibition "Bauhaus 1919–1928," held at the Museum of Modern Art in 1938–39. Supervised by Gropius, who edited the catalogue with Ise and Bayer, the now-historic exhibition was assembled and installed by Bayer in the underground concourse of Rockefeller Center while the new museum building by Philip Goodwin and Edward Durrell Stone was under construction.[24] The idea for such an exhibition had come, interestingly, from Hudnut, who submitted a proposal in the winter of 1937 to the museum's Committee on Architecture and Industrial Art.[25] Correspondence between Breuer and Bayer during the planning stages, and between Breuer and Ise Gropius at the time of the organization of the catalogue, reveal some sensitivities. To Bayer, Breuer wrote: "You say in your letter that you never received anything from me, but I must say that you have never asked for anything." Bayer replied: "You are quite right that I did not ask you officially to send material for the exhibition, but I didn't think it would be necessary."[26] Breuer's furniture was given ample display; he would have liked more of his post-Dessau apartment interiors and architectural work to have been included.

BREUER AND THE GRADUATE SCHOOL OF DESIGN AT HARVARD, 1938–47

Breuer's first response to Cambridge, Massachusetts—"I like it here more than I thought I would"—is recorded in a letter to Harrison, thanking him for his help in New York.[27] Hudnut hoped to make Breuer's appointment to the Graduate School of Design official by the beginning of the academic year 1937–38, but it was delayed for several months because the university administration insisted that funds for his salary be found outside Harvard. He had not, after all, been part of the original plan when the university recruited Gropius for a lifetime appointment. Gropius continued to press for Breuer's appointment—"We have a strong student following which strengthens our position with the administration," he told Breuer—and by the end of September, Hudnut was feeling optimistic.[28] While waiting for a final decision, Breuer returned to Europe for six weeks to wind up his affairs in London, Budapest, and Zürich. He arrived back in the United States on January 1, 1938, to begin a new life, for his research and teaching post had been confirmed at Harvard. His spoken and written English still needed polish, but the circumstances recall other stories of émigré bold-spiritedness—the telegrams exchanged by Anni Albers and Philip Johnson, for example, regarding a teaching position at Black Mountain College: "Josef does not speak English," she wired. "Come anyway" was Johnson's reply.[29] After one semester in Cambridge, Breuer wrote to Yorke that "I like teaching at Harvard very much, more than I expected."[30] It seems that he liked everything about the United States more than he expected, although Gropius reported in a letter to Albers at Black Mountain that Breuer "had been disappointed by the cultural level in the United States."[31]

The salary for Breuer as Research Associate in Design was secured by Hudnut through a Carnegie Corporation grant. Responding to an inquiry from Meyer Schapiro, his friend and former colleague at Columbia University, about the problem of establishing displaced European scholars, Hudnut advised that in "appealing to foundations for help of this kind I am most successful when I am able to offer some prospect of a permanent position in the future."[32] This he certainly did for Breuer, who on January 1, 1939, was promoted to Associate Professor of Architecture, an appointment that was annually renewed through the academic year 1946–47, when he left Harvard and Cambridge for independent practice in New York City.

The project that would define his Research Associateship of 1937–38 had been devised in London and refined in consultation with Gropius and Hudnut in Cambridge. Its goal was to reorganize "along modern lines" instruction in the Department of Architecture by taking into account industrial processes and new materials as they related to architectural design. According to Hudnut, "The great weakness in the education of architects in this country has been its purely representative character. Students make designs on paper without having any real consciousness of space composition or of the materials which they are indicating on their drawings."[33] Thus as part of their architectural training—"a training which is no longer purely theoretical," Hudnut reported to the Carnegie Corporation on November 1, 1937—Harvard students would now become familiar with products, materials, and equipment used in modern industry and would confer with industrial technicians.

Breuer at first collaborated with Gropius in teaching the advanced design studio (Architecture 4d) for the master's degree; with Walter F. Bogner, he developed a prearchitectural undergraduate program (Architectural Sciences) at Harvard College taught by the Faculty of the Graduate School of Design together with the Faculty of Arts and Sciences that would introduce shop work and building techniques. Hudnut was careful to explain that it was not to give the students skill in various crafts (Harvard was not becoming a trade school), but to allow them to learn how industry could influence building and design. Breuer's Carnegie Corporation grant project involved establishing a "sample room" with a changing collection of industrial products and materials that students would examine and that would link architects and manufacturers, a European idea based on prototypes such as the test tent at the Weissenhofsiedlung in Stuttgart in 1927. The Faculty of

Design had been instituted as a separate faculty at Harvard in 1936, uniting the formerly independent Schools of Architecture, Landscape Architecture, and City Planning as three departments in the newly constituted Graduate School of Design. Before Hudnut directed it toward modernism with a new curriculum, the architecture program at Harvard, as at most American schools, had been modeled on that at the Ecole des Beaux-Arts in Paris.[34] Hudnut had moved from Columbia to Harvard in 1935 as Professor of Architecture and became dean of the new faculty (serving until his retirement in 1953) and chairman of the Department of Architecture. He had written, a few months before Gropius came to Harvard, that "we are, naturally, very much excited by our good fortune in having [Gropius] here: perhaps we are beginning a new era in American architecture. . . . Perhaps I should even say in American design."[35] Hudnut had written the preface for the English-language edition of Gropius's *New Architecture and the Bauhaus*.[36] Inquiring about Gropius's impact on enrollment at the GSD after a year, *Architectural Forum* requested comparative figures: seventy students were enrolled in 1936 and ninety-five in 1937.[37]

In February 1938, Hudnut resigned the department chairmanship (and Gropius took over), saying that "it is felt that the Dean of the School will be better qualified to direct the general administration of the School as a whole if he is not at the same time identified with a particular department in the School."[38] It was a situation that could not have been foreseen when Gropius was appointed as chairman, but power struggles would erupt between Hudnut and Gropius in the 1940s, and conflicts would develop between students and faculty regarding the direction of the GSD's program and curriculum.[39] Housing design, the nature of modernism, and the social responsibility of architecture became disputed issues. In 1941, GSD students published a manifesto documenting their intellectual unrest and their desire to repudiate European modernism's *neue Sachlichkeit* and "the skeptical teaching of Gropius" in favor of "the organic approach" of Frank Lloyd Wright. Their training in modern architecture was, they claimed, complacent, uncommitted to the social organization of contemporary society, and not fundamentally different from

a Beaux-Arts curriculum. About Ludwig Mies van der Rohe the students wrote: "This great architect is an example of a man with absolute disregard for the conception of the architect as a social entity. He is mainly interested in types of building depending upon a particular financial and intellectual elite."[40]

When Gropius and Breuer began to teach at Harvard, however, it made for a transforming moment in American architecture. For a student such as George S. Lewis (future executive director of the New York chapter of the American Institute of Architects), who was familiar with the modern architecture of Europe, "it was awe-inspiring to see Gropius and Breuer" at Harvard.[41] When William W. Landsberg, one of the few students at Carnegie Tech, as he remembered it, to be genuinely interested in modern architecture, saw in a newspaper report that Gropius was joining the faculty at Harvard, he applied for admission and arrived there in the fall of 1938.[42] Leonard Currie and other self-described "future-oriented" students regarded Breuer as an "international guru of modern design who was going to bring us the message and hopefully the formula of how to do it."[43] Edward Larrabee Barnes remembered Gropius's first lecture at Harvard. Anticipating "something revolutionary," Barnes heard instead a diplomatic talk about New England design and white clapboard houses that avoided offending the old guard and tactfully constructed—at least with words—a bridge linking traditional New England architecture and modern structures.[44] Barnes also recalled first meeting Breuer in his Cambridge apartment at 19 Everett Street—a reception hall and two rooms for $38 a month[45]—and finding there "a whole new world" in the metal furniture, mirrors, walls of bright color, and carefully arranged objects "floating in some sort of white space, the whole seating level lowered—totally different from the kind of Aalto Swedish-Finnish modern or Frank Lloyd Wright or anything else I had ever seen." This impression of a Breuer interior is corroborated by Harry Seidler, who attended Harvard a little later, in 1945, and who writes of Breuer's "almost lyrically romantic spatial aesthetic."[46]

During the first Gropius-Breuer years, biannual seminars in design were held at the GSD by Albers, and lectures were given by Neutra, by Alvar Aalto in November 1938 in connection with an exhibition of his work, and by Bayer in 1939. During the winter of 1938–39, Sigfried Giedion gave the Charles Eliot Norton lectures that would later be published as *Space, Time, and Architecture*.[47] The presence of Gropius, Breuer, Albers, Neutra, Giedion, Bayer, and other visitors from the inner circles of modernism gave the GSD a distinctive European avant-garde cast. In October 1943—in the midst of the Second World War and at a moment when models of Mies's Tugendhat House and of Gropius's Dessau Bauhaus were on display in the school's exhibition hall on loan from the Museum of Modern Art—Hudnut responded to alumni reaction to his "Notes on Modern Architecture," published in the June issue of the *Harvard Alumni Bulletin*. In a letter to the editor, he wrote:

I feel I ought to give your readers some assurances in respect to the intentions of the Faculty of Design. Let me say, therefore, that (1) it is NOT our intention to make Robinson Hall a center of foreign Kultur, (2) we are NOT conspiring to corrupt the taste of innocent graduate students, and (3) NEVER NEVER will we take part in any effort to eradicate charm, hospitality, warmth, privacy, womanhood, or beauty from the American home.[48]

Although jaunty in tone, Hudnut's words reflected not only the alarm felt by older alumni with regard to modern architecture, but the serious assaults on foreign, particularly German, refugee designers and on International Style architecture by influential members of the architecture and planning worlds—Robert Moses, for one—that were appearing in the American press.[49] Irving Sandler points out that "Barr and the Museum [of Modern Art] came under continual criticism for favoring foreign artists and neglecting Americans," causing Barr to spend "considerable time and energy refuting it."[50]

Exhibition of Breuer's Work at Harvard, June 1938

Hudnut worked hard to help Breuer professionally and to enhance Harvard with any prestige that might accrue from increased public awareness of his achievements. When an article about the Department of Architecture appeared in *Time*, Hudnut wrote to the editor, bringing to his attention "one sentence which appears to be somewhat misleading. You refer to

Professor Marcel Breuer, who has recently accepted an appointment on our Faculty, as an 'industrial designer.' Mr. Breuer is a distinguished architect who is widely known both in Europe and America as a skillful and original designer of buildings."[51] At the same time, he wrote to Henry-Russell Hitchcock, then the reigning critic-scholar of modern architecture, asking if he would be willing "to write a descriptive and critical article" about Breuer's work.[52] "I feel that the work of Mr. Breuer has not received sufficient recognition in this country. I should like very much to have his work reviewed by someone who would give it a sympathetic interpretation and naturally there is no one who could do this quite so well as you," continued Hudnut. He was referring to an exhibition of Breuer's work planned for June 1938 as the principal feature of the GSD's annual commencement exhibition: "My idea is . . . to bring the attention of a greater number of people to the work of a man who we think is among the important men in modern architecture."

That Hitchcock's catalogue essay was commissioned by Hudnut for a fee has probably not been known. A disclaimer from Hudnut ("with the distinct understanding that you are free to express whatever critical judgements you wish") was answered with a scruple by Hitchcock: "I suggest the payment be considered for 'work in preparation for the exhibition' or some such thing rather than strictly for the article."[53] "I admire very much Breuer's work and have the highest estimate of his potentialities as an architect. I also like him personally very well. So of course I am only too delighted to write an article about him," he went on to say. Hitchcock had already written the catalogue essay for the exhibition "Modern Architecture in England," in which illustrations of two works by Breuer were included. There he commended Breuer's transformation of traditional rough stone into a modern idiom at the Gane Pavilion and, speaking of America, said that "[we have not] yet had the honor of harboring foreign refugees as important historically as Gropius and Mendelsohn, or as promising as Breuer."[54] Hitchcock could accept Hudnut's invitation for a paid essay with a clear conscience.

Hitchcock's "Marcel Breuer and the American Tradition in Architecture" was the first historically informed assessment of

Breuer's architecture. Especially significant was the title because it made clear that Breuer the architect, not the designer of furniture and interiors, was the Breuer to take into account. Hitchcock—who knew as authoritatively as anyone the subtle differences among national modernist schools—claimed that Breuer's work, despite his ten years in Germany, "was definitely not of the school of Gropius."[55] He compared the Harnischmacher House with the villas of Le Corbusier—"it is the urbanity of the design, somewhat rare perhaps in German modern architecture, which is so striking"—and allied the architecture of Breuer with developments in France and Holland. He praised Breuer's rapid assimilation of wood-frame construction and his application of modern design to American structural techniques. Hitchcock had hoped for more material on Breuer's English work, particularly "the two English houses" at Angmering and Lee-on-Solent and the London Theatre Studio, and suspected that Breuer "did not want them in."[56] Famous for painstaking thoroughness, Hitchcock fretted that he "had to slide over the English period as neatly as I could and I hope readers will not notice too much the omissions, which glare at me." To represent his English work, Breuer did include, along with some interiors, photographs of the Gane Pavilion, of the London Theatre Studio stage, and of the Garden City of the Future model. He had, in fact, requested from England photographs of all the buildings that Hitchcock wanted. But when the two villas (one of them, at Lee-on-Solent, primarily Yorke's design) had been published originally, they had been credited to Yorke ahead of Breuer because the commissions had come through Yorke. In the end, they were not illustrated in the Harvard show and clearly were withheld by Breuer.

On June 24, 1938, Hudnut wrote to Breuer that "I should like to tell you how greatly pleased I am with the Exhibition. . . . We are obliged to you for all the work you did."[57] On display were ninety-seven items from 1923 to 1938—models, photographs of models, plans, sections, elevations, and photographs of buildings and interiors. An article about the exhibition and Breuer's career appeared in the August 1, 1938, issue of *Time*. Proud of the coverage, he sent a copy of the magazine to Gane, calling it "an important criticism of my work."[58]

Breuer was pleased not only to have been given such a retrospective display, but also to have had the participation of Hitchcock, whom he called "the most progressive architectural critic in America."[59]

Breuer as Teacher

By his own admission, Breuer enjoyed teaching. "The architectural department of the University develops very well and it is a pleasure to work there," he reported to friends in England within two years.[60] Barnes remembered that despite his difficulties with English in the beginning, Breuer was "an absolutely wonderful" teacher and design critic. Recalling in 1980 the Harvard of 1939, Landis Gores wrote of the "subtly stimulating and ever thought-provoking influence Breuer cast across the whole school."[61] Johnson, in an interview with John W. Cook and Heinrich Klotz, said, "Breuer was my teacher, and I learned more from him than from Gropius."[62] Currie remembered that as a teacher, Breuer was "much the best on a basis of one-on-one with the student at the drafting board." The students, recalled Landsberg, "knew that Breuer was a person you could talk to, there was something about his bearing and character. We wanted to be like him and do what he did—he was a role model. He solved problems so directly, they always came out clean and sure, the inevitable thing, why didn't everybody think of it?"

To his students, Breuer would not speak about the aesthetics of architecture, Barnes recalled, as though he disapproved of making aesthetic judgments; more important was whether something worked and could be built, how the elements of architecture could be connected to one another: "If he had a column and two beams, or two beams and a column, the size of the column was not the important thing but the clarity of the connection." Barnes and others remember Breuer first asking, "Why *not* to do it?" when looking at a proposal in which traditional design modes were displaced; then he would direct the student to the matter of *how* to do it. "The question 'Why not to do it?' had a lot of meaning," Lewis recalled. "If you're not sure of something, do it and see how it works, he used to tell us." Seidler was another student in those years who revered both Gropius and Breuer, but who especially admired Breuer's approach. Speaking of both men, he said: "It was Breuer who was the architectural taste-setter of that time. He combined two diverse, normally irreconcilable tendencies, an almost lyrically romantic spatial aesthetic with disarmingly simple, uncanny 'Gordian knot' type of solutions to planning and structural problems."[63] Currie's memories of Breuer giving an "individual crit" are of someone who "drew some and talked some. He generally encouraged innovative or unorthodox designs, but tended to push gently towards simplification—simplification of plan, of structure, of overall form." "Gropius's 'crits,'" in contrast, "were not graphic but almost completely verbal," according to Currie. "He looked, and questioned, and suggested some better approaches, verbally describing a building wing in plan . . . occasionally he would pick up a pencil and scratch one line while talking, and then drop the pencil as if it were hot." Speaking of Gropius in contrast to Breuer, Landsberg recalled that "he played a different role—high priest. He showed up only once in a while. He understood what turn architecture had to take, he told it right, and he sold us on it: technology shapes your architecture; you have to deal with the world as it is and make things of beauty out of what the machine can do." In tribute to Breuer's impact on the Graduate School of Design and its students, in the fall 1995 issue of GSD News a special section was dedicated to him.[64]

The approach of Breuer to teaching, which "must have been a matter of policy although it probably came very naturally," Lewis recalled,

was not to tell people how to design, not like Mies in Chicago having everybody do corners of buildings in exactly the right way. There was no style—we knew about Bauhaus buildings but there was none of that at all; Breuer simply left it all to us but he had a marvelous way—I think it was actually intuitive—of seeing what we were trying to do. And he could somehow break the log jam without telling you how, and that's not easy.

For design courses (studios) students were assigned long problems and short sketches. The time allowed for a long problem could be six weeks, followed by faculty appraisal through jury meetings ("jury") and criticisms ("crit"), where students defended their problems after they had been judged. "Three times a week, usually in the afternoon," recalled Lewis,

"the design critic [a member of the faculty] would go from drawing board to drawing board, and sometimes others would gather round and watch." "In the faculty at Harvard in those days there was a very strong sense of collaborative effort," I. M. Pei remembered. "Breuer would be invited in by Gropius on a jury and vice versa; there would be a lot of cross-fertilization. Breuer was a favorite juror among the students."[65] Seidler recalled 1945, the year before Breuer left Harvard, when "it was all very homogenized and everybody knew everybody else and everybody listened to everyone else. The marvelous thing was that when Breuer gave a criticism to someone, everybody stood around the desk in a great semi-circle and listened to him, and one learned from that as much as from anything else."[66] (Yet it was in one of those "homogenized" juries—on May 23, 1941, at 4:15 P.M., as a memo by Gropius meticulously documents—that a serious quarrel erupted between Breuer and Gropius, triggered by a trivial incident, that severed their partnership and altered their friendship.) Collaboration was encouraged among students as well as faculty, and some of the most nostalgic alumni memories are about joint theses and team undertakings to solve complex, often urbanistic, problems.

Breuer's assignments were set down in straightforward pragmatic terms, typical of the way he thought about programs when designing buildings. The problem of a four-bedroom residence required that "two of the bedrooms and one bathroom be designed and located in a way that they can be used separately, connected with the rest of the house mainly by the entrance hall." Characteristic long problems in 1939 and 1940 (not assigned by Breuer) in Architecture 2b called for plans, section, and model of a boarding-school gymnasium; a country riding school; and housing for graduate students.[67] Coming out of the intense engagement with housing in 1920s and 1930s Germany, Gropius and Breuer were fortunate that housing design in the curriculum was strongly supported by Hudnut.[68] During 1938, an exhibition of modern housing circulated by the United States Housing Authority was shown at the GSD. Martin Wagner joined the faculty as Assistant Professor of Regional Planning in 1938. From the end of the First World War until he retired "for political reasons" in 1933, he had headed the Building Department in Berlin, directing the city's vast expansion of public housing and instituting brilliant housing reforms. In the academic year 1944–45, Breuer and Wagner jointly taught a course, collaborating on an urbanistic project for the town of Sudbury, Massachusetts. Breuer taught "Architectural Design and Building Construction" and "Architectural Design and Professional Practice" in various faculty combinations with Gropius, Jean Georges Peter, Henry Atherton Frost, Bogner, George Holmes Perkins, Hugh Stubbins, and Wagner that exemplified the team-taught method favored by Gropius.

Architectural education strategies at Harvard established by Hudnut and carried out by Gropius and Breuer were disavowed in the 1970s and 1980s by postmodern theorists and critics as well as architects, most markedly Klaus Herdeg. Works discredited by Herdeg (for "nondiscourse between plan and appearance") were not only by Breuer, compared with Le Corbusier, but by some of the most distinguished alumni of the GSD whose training there had produced, in Herdeg's view, "a distrust of history and theory" and a "hard nosed pragmatism at the expense of intellectually speculative and architecturally contextual investigations."[69] The "Bauhaus legacy" had become anathema, the rational and functional architecture it engendered pronounced a cultural and aesthetic failure. Important documentary sources for Herdeg's repudiation of the GSD's curriculum and method were the assignments given to the students in Gropius's master's studios, copies of some of which survived in the archives of the GSD.[70] Problems and sketches assigned by Breuer were not known to Herdeg because they were not with the papers at Harvard, but at Syracuse.

Breuer outlined a prospectus for a lecture series for undergraduates, "Components of Design," to be given once a week by members of the GSD faculty and the dean.[71] It is not clear if the program was ever realized, but the document is an important record of Breuer's philosophy of education with regard to modern architecture and its practice, even though designed for undergraduates:

Aim of Pedagogy: our approach (emphasis on the method of thinking); *Function and Form*: modern life and the social system—their expression in form; *Representation and Form, I* (Historic), change in the ethics of form; *Representation and Form, II* (Present Day); *Construction and Form*: Materials

suggest constructions. Constructions suggest forms. Forms suggest new constructions; *Problems of Decor, Textures and Colors, Symmetry*: some means of aesthetics; *The Planning of Regions, Towns, Streets, Buildings, and Furniture*: common elements of approach; *The Jungle and the Cube*: Relation between nature and construction, outside and inside; *Scale; Composition and Necessity*: how about art?; *Story of a House; Industrial Influences; Professional Problems*: planner-architect-engineer-designer; *Urgent Problems I*: housing, slum clearance; *Urgent Problems II*: traffic; *Urgent Problems III*: regional reconstruction; *Genesis of a Project I and II*: history, analysis, criticism—of, for example, [illegible] city development; *Painting, Sculpture, Architecture I and II*: stimulation and disturbances; space.

Breuer remained on the faculty at Harvard until 1947, teaching regularly (until 1946) during the academic year and in some summer sessions. Against the background of the developing war in Europe, he wrote with some guilt to old friends like Gane in devastated Bristol: "I imagine how England's war has affected you and I really am ashamed under these conditions to write you how well and satisfied I am here,"[72] "where life is still peaceful and worth living."[73] In June 1939, he had moved into the house he built for himself in Lincoln, Massachusetts; on March 30, 1940, he and Constance Crocker Leighton were married. In 1941, he and Gropius dissolved their architectural partnership, and each went on to practice separately; in 1944, he became a naturalized American citizen. In June 1944, Hudnut recommended, as usual, Breuer's reappointment as Associate Professor of Architecture for three years.

The war naturally affected enrollment at the GSD. In 1943, Hudnut reported that "this year has been a critical one for the School. Our enrollment which began at 51 ended with less than 40."[74] But everything changed when

the end of the war brought a flood of new students to the School of Design for the academic year 1945–46. We have had to deny admission to several hundred well-qualified candidates. By far the largest number of veterans entered the Department of Architecture as candidates for the degree of B. Arch. To take care of this work we have been obliged to add to our facilities and increase our staff by the appointment of several new instructors.[75]

Currie (later to become Dean of Architecture at Virginia Polytechnic Institute) and Charles Burchard were appointed assistant professors in July 1946; the enrollment in the Department of Architecture was 138, and of this group 66 were war veterans.

PARTNERSHIP WITH WALTER GROPIUS, 1937–41

Accurately described by Currie as "an association of two independent architects" rather than a partnership, the joint practice of Gropius and Breuer was encouraged by Harvard:

We make it our policy in the GSD to permit all instructors to practice their profession, whether it be architecture, landscape architecture, or city planning. It is understood informally that the responsibility of the instructor to the School has priority over his responsibility to his clients. Most of our instructors in architectural design maintain offices as architects or are associated with architectural firms.

Although these words were written by Hudnut in 1951,[76] they correspond to the views he held at the beginning of his deanship fifteen years earlier, and they made it possible for Gropius and Breuer to form their partnership and build buildings in the United States, for the example of their work was understood by Hudnut to be part of their teaching.

Their office was installed at 1430 Massachusetts Avenue as Walter Gropius and Marcel Breuer, Associated Architects, with letterhead designed by Bayer. Commissions began to come into the office almost immediately—John Hagerty wrote to Gropius about a house as early as October 1937, and the Hagerty House, under construction by the following spring, was to be Breuer's first American building. In the summer of 1938, he wrote to Alfred Roth in Zürich that "I myself have a lot of work and I like it very much in America."[77] Two months later, he reported to J. L. Martin in London that "I am going to construct a house in Palm Springs [Margolius House]. Another house in Lincoln, Mass. in which Gropius lives is just finished, and the third one in Cohasset, Massachusetts on the seashore is very near completion."[78] And his letter to Dorothea Ventris a few weeks later sounded a similar note: "I am quite happy here in America. I am rushed with work, which has its difficulties, but which gives a promising outlook for the future."[79] In June 1938, though, Gropius and Breuer had learned that the design they had been invited to submit to the well-publicized competition for an art center at Wheaton College, sponsored by the Museum of Modern Art and

Architectural Forum, had taken only second prize. They had invested in their design high hopes not only for the future of modern architecture on American college campuses but also for their own careers. In a number of letters, Breuer was to describe the result as "depressing." Writing to Carl Maas, associate editor at House Beautiful, Breuer said, "I was very depressed by the result of the competition, indeed; but we have to face that kind of thing if we go into competitions— and I think we will do it again and again."[80] A year later, in a letter to J. M. Richards about the publication in Architectural Review of Gropius and Breuer's work in the United States, Breuer wrote that "if you intend to publish the material as a complete representation of our architectural work in America, I think the Wheaton competition project should be included, as I regard it as the most important part of our work here."[81]

Gropius and Breuer were among fifty architects invited to submit designs in a competition for a new campus for Goucher College in Towson, Maryland, in the spring of 1938. On July 11, 1938, Gropius wrote that "the pressure of other work makes it necessary for Mr. Breuer and myself to withdraw from the list of architects taking part in the competition for Goucher." In his study of modernism and architectural competitions, James Kornwulf suggests that the second place that Gropius and Breuer had just received in the Wheaton College competition, and the conservative composition of the Goucher competition jury, discouraged Gropius about the prospects for modern architecture at American colleges.[82] On July 20, 1938, a bulletin was issued to all Goucher competitors announcing that Gropius and Breuer had decided to withdraw.

Illustrating the variety of potential projects that passed through the office in these months are five sheets of drawings sent by Breuer in October 1938 to Frederick R. Pleasants for the remodeling of some of the gallery interiors in Harvard's Peabody Museum—display cases "made organic with the system of the window walls," as Breuer described them—for a fee of $100.[83] The Peabody had to raise money to see the project through, and there is no record of the execution of this work.

By March 1939, Breuer could tell Raymond McGrath that the "private practice develops rapidly";[84] a little earlier he had written to Yorke that "I am rushed with work, which forces me

Hagerty House, Cohasset, Massachusetts. 1938

The Breuers at home in Lincoln, Massachusetts

to maintain quite an American tempo in everything I do";[85] and in August, he wrote again to Yorke, saying that "I am a little too busy for my capacity."[86] Best of all was the American fairy tale of Breuer's own house. "The newest excitement," he told Dorothea Ventris, "is the opportunity to build a house for myself in Lincoln, about twenty minutes from Cambridge, in any way I like, without having to pay for it."[87]

Helen O. Storrow (Mrs. James J. Storrow), a Boston aristocrat and enlightened philanthropist supportive of modern art and architecture, made it possible for four members of the Harvard faculty—Gropius, Breuer, and Bogner from the GSD, and sociologist James Ford—to build and live in modern houses on lots bordering an apple orchard on a large property she owned in Lincoln (it became known as the Woods End Road colony), about a mile from Thoreau's Walden. Just before leaving England for the United States, Breuer had been given by his friend Frieda Napier (Mrs. Ian Napier) a letter of introduction to Storrow. "Please do your best to get in touch with her. . . . [S]end this letter the moment you arrive," he was advised. "She is one of the most worthwhile people to know in America . . . and interested in everything that is progressive and creative."[88] Clearly, Napier's judgment was correct. Storrow bore the full cost of building and landscaping the houses on Woods End Road (which came to $11,364 for Breuer's house); her tenants then leased their houses (with an option to purchase) at an annual rent of 10 percent of that cost. The Gropius House was completed in December 1938; in 1939, the Ford House, also designed by the Gropius-Breuer partnership, was finished; the Bogner House, designed by Bogner, of course, was built during 1939; Breuer entered into an agreement with a contractor on February 21, 1939, and he moved into his house in June. The Woods End Road colony was like a miniature *Siedlung*, an unconscious re-creation of European housing exhibitions wherein a tract of land was developed with modern houses by modern architects. Such a construct was perhaps realizable in the United States at that time only in the climate created by Hudnut, Gropius, and Breuer at Harvard.

Breuer's house in Lincoln, like his apartment in Cambridge, had an impact on his students almost as significant as that of the instruction in his studios. Invitations for a Sunday-afternoon visit to their new houses at Lincoln were issued by Gropius and Breuer two or three weeks after courses began in 1939. For Seidler, it was "a world-shattering experience to see in the flesh those houses. I knew every corner [of Breuer's house] from the plan [it had been published in *Architectural Forum*], but to see it in three dimensions left a permanent, lasting impact on me."[89] The new modern houses in Lincoln generated considerable interest, and not only local; an article in the *Christian Science Monitor* was illustrated with photographs of models made by students at the GSD of the Lincoln houses and the Hagerty House in Cohasset, Massachusetts, the latter having been completed in December 1938 at the same time as the Gropius House.[90] By March 1940, Turpin Bannister, Professor of Architecture at Rensselaer Polytechnic Institute, was requesting permission to bring fifteen students to Lincoln to see these examples "of outstanding modern work."[91]

The war in Europe continued to be close to the surface of Breuer's life, and it was painful for him to think about his English friends. To Richards he wrote that "I am afraid the war has killed many of your plans and I imagine also influences your professional and personal life. Under these circumstances it seems to me nearly ridiculous to send you new photographs of the Hagerty house. However, I will do it to complete the set of photographs you already have."[92] By 1944, photographs of the Hagerty Cottage were included in an exhibition—"The New Architecture in the United States"—prepared for the Office of War Information by the Museum of Modern Art and sent to Egypt, where it opened in March at the Grand Palais in Cairo.[93] And the museum selected the Ford House (and the Chamberlain Cottage of 1941; see p. 28) to be represented in the architecture section of MoMA's fifteenth-anniversary show in May 1944.

With its four rooms plus kitchen and bath, Breuer's house in Lincoln was, as he characterized it, a small house for a bachelor, but for visitors the impression of expansive space was unforgettable. This expansiveness was achieved through ingenious devices, such as splitting the levels (movement was down to the dining room and up to the bedrooms from the high-ceilinged, two-story living room) and opening walls to the full width of the room. One bedroom was an open mezzanine at the upper end of the tall living room, curtained for privacy. Recalling the house, Pei described it "as a small house but it had a huge space. It had a remarkable three-dimensional flow of space that moved up level by level, space that moved vertically as well as horizontally in contrast to the 'two-dimensional' space of Mies, for example, that moved only horizontally." The ground plan was shaped as a trapezoid, and the fireplace wall as a curve; paired colonettes supported the cantilever of the roof, which was a sunscreen for the south-facing window of the living room; the exterior wood siding ran vertically, relating the house to traditions in American wood-frame architecture. On the interior, the plywood ceiling was painted white to contrast with the natural wood of the walls and the stone fireplace. Breuer rarely wasted an idea, and in the Lincoln house he crystallized notions about form and space in (partially) prefabricated low-cost residential structures that, beginning with his small metal house of 1925, he had been pondering for almost two decades. For the metal house, he had specified a standardized, insulated light panel system on a modular-steel frame; in Lincoln, adopting the American predisposition for wood construction, he substituted prefabricated plywood for the metal panels of Europe.

Breuer admired traditional New England wood architecture, as Gropius had predicted he would, singling out for special appreciation the buildings of Rhode Island.[94] His European experience with woodworking, cabinetry, and furniture construction, and his familiarity with the properties of the material, made for an easy and creative adaption to the wood technology of American building. White clapboard and white-painted shingles on New England houses, churches, and town halls bore a kinship to the white-gray stucco wall, which had been a basic modernist device in Europe. The sincere enthusiasm of both Gropius and Breuer for vernacular American architecture, and their adoption of some indigenous modes of construction and expression—the balloon frame and tongue-and-groove siding, for example—accounted for the notion, now debated, of their having established a "new regionalism," as it was termed by Giedion when writing about the buildings

designed by Gropius in America.[95] It had been anticipated by Hitchcock in 1938 when he described Breuer's appreciation of the "real American tradition of the seventeenth and eighteenth centuries," his "respect for regional traditions," and "his interest in using existing American constructive methods as potentially modern devices."[96] An artificial concept at best, the idea of a "new regionalism" in the modern architecture of 1930s New England has been generally repudiated from an ideological as well as a technological point of view. In *The Details of American Architecture*, Edwin R. Ford points out that while the early New England houses by Gropius and Breuer incorporated aspects of American construction, particularly the wood platform frame (which the author says they found to be "an inspired vernacular creation"), their "new regionalism" was only partly true.[97] "The Gropius house contains so much steel that it is almost a skeletal frame building," he observes. And in contrast to European steel-skeleton modernism, where the structure and the skin were clearly distinguished, the Gropius House, he claims, is a hybrid in which "a structural element may be wood or steel, wall or frame, or plane, or column, depending on its location and its role in the building." Joachim Driller, in his analysis of the completed Gropius House and of earlier phases of its design, has convincingly demonstrated that its style is not related to American precedents but to Gropius's earlier architecture in Germany and England from 1923 to 1936.[98] Moreover, looking deeper into the matter of a "new regionalism" from a political point of view, Driller proposed that Gropius and Breuer probably found it expedient during the war years to promote the idea of something newly invented, Americanized, to dissociate as far as possible their modern New England houses from German prototypes.[99] Nevertheless, the lightness and efficiency of American wood-frame construction appealed to the practical nature of both architects, particularly to Breuer, who in Europe had built with steel and masonry. (Had his Tyrolean ski lodge been realized, it would have been a wood-and-stone building.) But once he began to build in the United States, he came to rely heavily on the integrated structural system of wood-frame construction above a masonry base, formed of lightweight

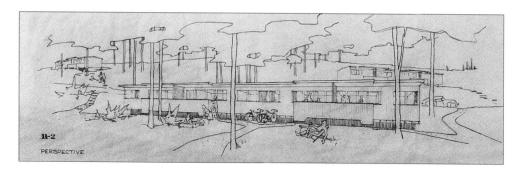

Yankee Portables. 1942 (not built). Perspective sketch

milled lumber cut to standard dimensions and fastened with nails, reducing the time, energy, and cost associated with constructing a house.[100]

Years later, writing his brief "professional autobiography" in the third person, Breuer said: "In the nine years spent at Harvard in teaching and in the reorganization of the architectural school, he continued to study the living qualities of the house, of space, of different materials old and new ones. He spent a good part of his energies also in the study of American building and production technics, of the light frame house, and of prefabrication."[101]

The question of conferring authorship and assigning individual credit in the Gropius-Breuer partnership projects was addressed by scholars in the 1980s and 1990s, notably Winfried Nerdinger, Leslie Cormier, and Driller.[102] Thirty years earlier, in an undergraduate honors thesis, David H. Wright had considered the "artistic facet" of Gropius's architecture.[103] Handwritten notes added to some of its pages indicate that the thesis was discussed with Gropius after it was submitted, and his remarks then were recorded—for example, "Gropius says that Breuer did no work on this house [Ford House]" and "Gropius told me on 9-29-50 that [Maxwell] Fry did not work on the Levy house, that he did it entirely himself, with a German draftsman."[104]

It is now well known that Gropius, although trained to make architectural drawings, did not like to draw. Breuer, an artist, made very good freehand architectural sketches often perfectly scaled, but, not trained as a draftsman, he made few finished drawings. Since others did the drawings for both Gropius and Breuer, attribution hinges less on graphic evidence than on the memories of draftsmen in the office, corre-

spondence, notes made directly on the drawing sheets, and critical stylistic scrutiny of the work. Documentary evidence from the Breuer archives has added information about the nature of the collaboration. Furthermore, personal recollections that provide insight into the design process in the Gropius-Breuer office and at the same time reveal the difficulty of sorting out individual hands have come from architects Currie, who worked for more than a year on the Frank House, and Landsberg. About the Frank House, for example, Currie remembered:

I did many of the working drawings, including details. This job was primarily Walter Gropius's. As the designer of the firm, Breuer made many of the design decisions [about the Frank House] but not with a free hand. Many plan decisions had been agreed upon and fixed between Frank and Gropius both of whom exerted a strong restraining influence [on Breuer]. It was on the Frank job that I recall most discussion between Gropius and Breuer, always in German. At one point Gropius and Breuer seemed to be discussing how they might relieve the "boxiness" of the design. One of Breuer's suggestions was to let the stair tower bulge out with a gently curved stair. They evidently agreed on this; Breuer made a sketch of the change; one of us in the drafting room then drew it up, and it was approved by Mr. Frank.

Currie also remembered the Hagerty House as "Lajkó's first architectural commission in the United States. Actually Grope was approached by John Hagerty after the latter was impressed by Grope's lecture—but Grope turned the job over to Lajkó." Currie recalled, too, that Breuer found Gropius's house in Lincoln "heavy and plodding and [he] kept away from it. At a few crucial moments he stepped in and gave the design some verve." The south facade overhang was Breuer's work, Currie recalled. Through analyzing drawings in the Gropius archive, Driller came to the same conclusion.[105]

There was a very small drafting room in the joint office, "just four draftsmen and a chief draftsman. Breuer would sketch a detail and give it to the draftsman who would hard-line it," Landsberg recalled. "We saw very little of Gropius; it was all Breuer in the drafting room. Breuer was what in a bigger firm would be known as the Chief of Design. As far as the drafting room staff was concerned, Breuer was the person we dealt with." As for the Frank job, Landsberg corroborated Currie's recollections when he said that in the partnership Breuer did most of the designing "except maybe the Frank House," although "Breuer controlled the final look of the house." Scholars of modern architecture such as Richard Pommer speak of "Gropius (in the Breuer phase)."[106] As soon as the partnership had been formed, Breuer plunged in and, with still limited ability to speak English, dealt with draftsmen, clients, contractors, and manufacturers. He was confronted by new conventions, discovering, for example, that American houses needed to accommodate screened windows and doors. He handled most of the correspondence and visited the construction sites.

By 1940, activity in the office began to taper off, as it did elsewhere, due to the increasing concentration on defense activity; by 1941, Breuer would write to Gane that "private building has practically ceased, and the whole building trade is more and more engaged in government work."[107] Built work and unexecuted projects designed during the partnership years were the Gropius House, Lincoln, Massachusetts; Hagerty House, Cohasset, Massachusetts; Wheaton College Arts Center, Norton, Massachusetts (competition); Margolius House, Palm Springs, California; Fischer House, New Hope, Pennsylvania; Festival Theater, College of William and Mary, Williamsburg, Virginia (competition); Breuer House, Lincoln, Massachusetts; Ford House, Lincoln, Massachusetts; Lake Eden Campus, Black Mountain College, Black Mountain, North Carolina; interior of the Pennsylvania State Pavilion, New York World's Fair; Chamberlain Cottage, Wayland, Massachusetts; Weizenblatt House, Asheville, North Carolina; Aluminum City, New Kensington, Pennsylvania; Frank House, Pittsburgh, Pennsylvania; and Abele House, Framingham, Massachusetts.

The partnership lasted for four years (1937–41). In the spring of 1941, Breuer, usually cool under pressure, was intensely stressed. Aluminum City, a defense-housing job in New Kensington, was going forward under extremely difficult conditions; he had financial problems, having written a year earlier to Pritchard that "I have been in pretty bad shape in regard to money until now, and I hope I am now on the slow path of recovery;"[108] seven months later, he told Gane that there was "not much work in my private office."[109] He was not optimistic about the practice. "Due to the situation of the world just now, there is not much chance for architecture in the near future," he had written in January.[110] An example of Breuer's restlessness was his application in February 1941 to the American Institute of Architects for an Edward Langley Scholarship, "beginning as soon as possible."[111] His project was to research and plan air-raid shelters and "air raid-proof regions." He wrote: "I believe defense against air attack is as much a part of realistic regional planning and housing as the walling-in of settlements and towns was in former times. Just as the walls of the old fortifications fundamentally influenced the layout of towns and even individual buildings, planning against modern attack by air will fundamentally influence the form of our communities." At the same time, probably with the idea of generating new work, Breuer and Gropius were collecting photographs, plans, and details in the hope of publishing a book about their American buildings. Writing to Yorke for advice, Breuer explained that "I thought to introduce it with a comparison of an architect's problems in America and those in Europe, looking at it from the various angles of the architect, of the client, of the student of architecture and of the critic. . . . It is very difficult to imagine how such an idea sounds now to you over there. Then it is difficult to have a complete picture of England in this war."[112]

The breakup with Gropius occurred in the afternoon of May 23, 1941, brought about by a petty event. Gropius, late for a jury, kept everyone waiting; when Breuer snapped at him, Gropius responded imperiously and humiliated Breuer, who, "deeply offended," went to his office and dictated a letter on GSD letterhead, with a copy to Hudnut:

Dear Pius, during our jury meeting of today, you handled the school business in a manner which I feel is below the level of the University and which I personally am not willing to accept. I strongly feel that you mis-used your authority and am deeply offended. The incident in itself can be settled privately,— (I am arranging this at the same time), and you may be certain that I wouldn't have brought it up officially if I didn't feel that its background constitutes a serious problem for the atmosphere of our school and faculty. I am sending a copy of this letter to Dean Hudnut.[113]

Probably immediately afterward, he wrote to Gropius at home, and not on letterhead, to terminate the partnership:

I am now convinced that our partnership is objectively and personally possible no longer. As to the reasons, we each certainly have our own ideas, which I feel it would not help to analyze. I suggest that our office close with the first of August, when the New Kensington Housing job and the Abele job will be completed. Please let me know if you agree to this date or have any other suggestions. I also suggest that commissions we may receive before the closing of our common office be handled privately, according to which of us brought it in. This in effect would mean that our partnership ceases immediately, and that our collaboration is concerned only with the two jobs now in progress.

Gropius was stunned, and two days later he replied: "This is to tell you that I accept your suggestions regarding the dissolving of our partnership. Nothing more can be said after your two amazing letters of May 23." He then composed a memorandum, setting down the date and time of the "collision" and the facts as he interpreted them. In July, he wrote about the incident to Bayer, saying that Breuer was "too deeply in love with himself, and the 'kleinmeister complex' against the former Bauhaus Director has brought him to commit betrayal towards me. Also he doesn't need me anymore since he has had enough personal success now."[114]

Breuer and Gropius made an agreement regarding credits for their joint work, and it is referred to in a letter written in the summer of 1941 by Breuer to Sprinza Weizenblatt: "I am not certain whether I mentioned to you that my partnership with Mr. Gropius ceases August 1, 1941. We agreed to let your house be known as my personal work in exchange for another building of ours which is to be regarded as Gropius's own work. This is of significance only in connection with possible publications where your house should go under my name only."[115]

Neither Breuer nor Gropius was ever completely absent from any of their partnership projects. Breuer had a major role in the design concept and the execution of every project that came into the office, and no work proceeded without consultation on some level—administrative or design—with Gropius. Before the severance of the partnership, at least the public stance of the partners was expressed in a letter to the editor of *House & Garden* about the Breuer House and the Hagerty House, "both of which were designed by Gropius and Breuer. As we are in partnership we are constantly collaborating and sign all of our work with both of our names . . . both of these houses are designed by the two of us."[116] Probably for reasons of diplomacy, Breuer never referred to his participation in the design process of the Gropius House; the design concept of the Breuer, Hagerty, Fischer, and Weizenblatt Houses and the Chamberlain Cottage was mostly, if not entirely, his, as it was for the unexecuted Margolius House. On the perspective sketches for the Margolius House, the words "Margolius Residence Breuer" are penciled in the lower- or upper-right-hand corner. According to his correspondence with Gropius, in some way Breuer "collaborated" on the Ford and Abele projects—the two works usually attributed exclusively to Gropius. The commission from the Chamberlains came to Breuer because the clients had seen and very much liked his house in Lincoln, and he duplicated several of its features for them. Edwin Ford linked these two houses typologically and structurally: a T-shape formed by two volumes—a platform frame box with load-bearing walls intersected by a frame and curtain-wall structure, both constructed of wood. Using as illustrations Aalto's Villa Mairea and Mies's Hubbe House project— masonry load-bearing volumes intersected by steel-frame skeletal constructs—Ford analogized the Breuer House and the Chamberlain Cottage to structures being built in Europe at the time.[117] But it is also the case that the Chamberlain and Weizenblatt homes were built according to the wood-trussing structural system invented by Breuer in 1937 for his ski hotel in Ober-Gurgl. The Margoliuses wrote to Breuer directly and asked him to design their California house. The designs for the Festival Theater at the College of William and Mary, the Wheaton College Arts Center, the Pennsylvania State Pavilion

Walter Gropius and Marcel Breuer. Aluminum City Terrace, New Kensington, Pennsylvania. 1941–42. Site plan

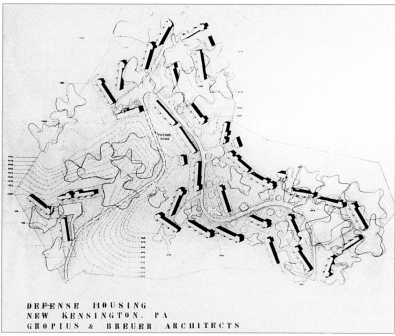

Margolius House, Palm Springs, California. 1938–39 (not built). Perspective sketch

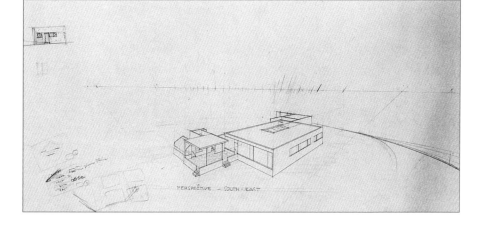

at the New York World's Fair, Black Mountain College, and Aluminum City in New Kensington were more Breuer than Gropius.[118] In 1944, the Ford House and Chamberlain Cottage were selected as "two of the fifty (or less) outstanding examples of American architecture of the past decade which will be shown in the architecture section of the Museum of Modern Art's Anniversary Exhibition."[119]

Aluminum City, the defense-housing project erected in New Kensington, Pennsylvania, was the last of the partnership projects and an example of the government's effort to revamp its housing program for defense workers by commissioning architects outside the Public Building Administration (PBA). For Breuer, it was the first opportunity to realize theories and on-paper-only experiments in low-cost housing and city planning for the working class that had occupied architects in Europe since the end of the First World War. Corresponding with the Federal Works Agency (FWA) of the United States Housing Authority about a potential defense-housing project for Cambridge, Massachusetts, Breuer wrote: "Mr. Gropius and I are intensely interested in housing. We also feel particularly competent in this field and have long regarded housing

and the research work involved as our main architectural passion."[120] For the efficient Breuer, who never threw away a good idea just as he never wasted time or money, New Kensington was a valuable design experience. He made use of it throughout his career, as he had made use of previous theoretical experiments with housing for the New Kensington project. The slatted sunscreens were used in works as varied as small single-family houses and the large UNESCO complex; New Kensington became the prototype for the row houses of Fairview Heights in Ithaca, New York; for the members' housing at the Institute for Advanced Study in Princeton, New Jersey; and for the Ecumenical Institute at Saint John's Abbey in Collegeville, Minnesota.

The former partners addressed the still-sensitive and complicated subject of authorship credits in an exchange of letters in 1948,[121] after the publication of the Breuer issues of *Nuestra arquitectura* in September and November 1947 and at the time of a traveling MoMA exhibition of Breuer's work—his first major exhibition in the United States and more comprehensive, naturally, than the one held at Harvard ten years earlier. Gropius was provoked to complain, albeit in a civilized tone, about the labeling of photographs of the partnership works. When Breuer sent 123 photos to Eduardo Catalano for selection for *Nuestra arquitectura*, he wrote: "As to my various partnerships, I selected only those works or those details of a work which I can truly and fully call my own design. Just the same, naturally, the name of the collaborating partner should always be mentioned."[122] After going back and forth on the issue with Gropius, Breuer's last statement assigned the works with what he called Gropius's "active participation" as the Gropius, Ford, and Frank Houses; the Pennsylvania State Pavilion; and the Community Building in Aluminum City. He continued, "My own contribution to our partnership: the Breuer, Chamberlain, Hagerty and Fischer houses; Aluminum City except for the Community Building; Wheaton, Black Mountain." He unaccountably failed to mention the Weizenblatt and Margolius Houses, which were uncontestably his; in previous correspondence, he had referred to "collaboration" on the Ford and Abele Houses. Gropius in his response did not quite agree, claiming a contribution to the Hagerty House, Aluminum City beyond the Community Building, the Pennsylvania State Pavilion exhibit, and the Abele House, not mentioned by Breuer in his list. Yet, while stylistic and structural signatures in the partnership works can be isolated for each architect,[123] in an overall sense the Gropius-Breuer architecture built between 1937 and 1941 denotes, without conspicuous dissimilarities, both the "comprehensive work in design and sociology which we [did] for German society as a whole," as Gropius described his mission,[124] and the consentient ideology of form, function, and structure out of which the partnership was born.

Not long after their quarrel, Breuer and Gropius patched things up personally, if not professionally. "Gropius," Landsberg recalled, "was very big-hearted—he was a big man. He could have a falling out with Breuer—Breuer could get riled—and yet he would still push for him. Gropius could forgive impolite words and offended feelings." Lewis remembered that "they laughed about the incident and never were heard to have said a bad thing about each other." Indeed, the exhibition "The Architectural Work of Walter Gropius and Marcel Breuer Planned and Executed in This Country" opened in the winter of 1942 at the American School of Design ("The New Bauhaus") in Chicago, directed by László Moholy-Nagy. And it was probably Gropius who was responsible for the selection of Breuer in 1952 as the American member of the international architectural partnership for the building of the UNESCO Headquarters in Paris, one of his most important commissions. Their friendship lasted until Gropius's death in 1969, but some of the warmth had gone out and the strong connection had been weakened.

The dissolution of an enterprise that had been born in Europe before each partner had experienced his American life was probably a relief to both. Breuer had known Gropius for twenty-one years by 1941, and they were no longer disciple and mentor, colleagues in the modernist experiment, or émigré associates in a design enterprise in London. Gropius, busy with fulfilling academic responsibilities, writing, and sustaining his immense reputation, could not give the practice as much attention as Breuer, over whom he had authority as department chair at the GSD. In the day-to-day duties of the practice, Breuer oversaw almost everything—the designing in the drafting room, client correspondence, details of construction—in addition to his teaching. The sharing of credit, much of which Breuer felt belonged to him, created a strain not unprecedented in architectural partnerships. (It had caused the hostile rift between Le Corbusier and Amédée Ozenfant in 1924.) Always independent and self-confident, Breuer had walked away from Gropius's Bauhaus in 1924 and throughout his life resented being cast in the shade of Gropius's celebrity or being thought of as Gropius's "student." As late as 1960, when asked by James Marston Fitch to participate in a roundtable discussion at Columbia University on the Bauhaus ("you, like a number of Gropius' pupils," the invitation read), Breuer responded in a letter, irritable in tone, that "I never considered myself a 'Gropius pupil' with all my sympathy for his personality and aims."[125] Even chronologically, the former partners were no longer in harmony. Gropius had been practicing architecture since 1906; by 1941, the major portion of his designing career was behind him. Breuer, starting late and just beginning to develop momentum, could no longer tolerate the constraints of a satellite partnership role.

POST-PARTNERSHIP WORK, 1941–47

Breuer established his independent practice in the same building in Cambridge where the partnership office had been located. But while the United States was at war between 1941 and 1945, the building industry and building materials were serving the needs of the government almost exclusively, and private work was severely restricted. In the immediate postwar period, if the nature of a commission demanded it or if he had not yet received state licensing, Breuer established agreement-based associations with other architects, such as Serge Chermayeff and Charles Burchard.[126]

Prefabricated Houses, 1941–42

Breuer's refusal to be daunted by the critical attacks on Aluminum City, which deemed it a failure, kept him occupied after 1941 inventing new systems of prefabrication, such as the Plas-2-Point House and Yankee Portables, in response to current demands for prefabricated wartime defense housing and in anticipation of a prodigious postwar need for houses. In 1941, he devised a far-reaching system for sliding glass windows (and walls) that he would develop into a technical mainstay in his design repertoire. At the same time, he was experimenting with materials, many of them war-born—such as molded plastic, plastic-bonded plywoods, and molded plywoods—to be used in new buildings. In 1942, he and Bayer played with the idea of setting up a laboratory for plastic design. But in the end, nothing came of his considerable efforts to put his prefabrication projects into production. By 1944, he was disillusioned about the future of prefabrication and responded to an inquiry about the subject with some pessimism: "The post-war prefabricated industry has, so far as I know, not yet found its real scope. I am afraid prices won't be lower than other houses built in the usual way, and I doubt very much that they will be better. This statement includes my own Plas-2-Point House, which is not yet in production."[127]

The design of the Plas-2-Point House—described by Breuer as "radically new"[128]—was developed in Cambridge in 1942 and 1943 and was intended for housing projects composed of single and twin units and blocks of row houses. Prefabricated parts would be assembled in a "jig" shed on the site, and the completed house moved by tractor to its designated location, tipped onto foundation blocks, and anchored in place. After making a list of imaginative names on a sheet that included his small, quick sketch of the concept, he settled on Plas-2-Point. A demountable house secured even on sloping terrain at two points on each of two short (5-foot, 8-inch) foundation blocks, it eliminated grading work and full foundations and basements. It was exceptionally light in weight (the complete two-bedroom unit weighed 2 tons) and consisted of prefabricated roof and floor trusses cantilevered from central girders of plastic-bonded plywood. Standardized and prefabricated plywood panels for floor, wall, ceiling, and roof rested on the girders and cross-trusses. Supporting posts at both ends tied the girders together and carried the roof load. That the structure bears a resemblance to the wings of an airplane of that era is not a coincidence, and, indeed, the text accompanying a sketch of the design in an advertisement for Monsanto Plastics in *Architectural Forum* claimed that Breuer had "pondered the skeleton of a modern bomber." Partition panels and walls were to be non-load-bearing, acting as tension members to give the structure rigidity. A small-scale version of curtain-wall construction, all or part of the exterior could be varied in material according to local climatic needs (insulated panels in the North, screened panels in the South). For Breuer, this kind of flexibility was a goal of good design, and he did all he could to achieve it with varying room sizes, adaptable function, and a pragmatic response to region and climate.

The Monsanto advertisement was noticed by builders all over America, and inquiries came to Breuer from developers and contractors readying themselves in 1944 for postwar prefabrication and in need of designs. The economies of construction of the Plas-2-Point House were appealing (Breuer estimated the complete one-bedroom house with full equipment at $2,400), but, not surprisingly, the design was puzzling: "Is there a tendency for this house to rock when exposed to severe wind pressure?" wrote the head of one construction firm in Illinois, and again, "We are wondering if this design

Plas-2-Point House. 1943 (not built). Notes and preliminary sketch

Plas-2-Point House. Preliminary sketches

would lend itself to exterior treatment that would not be too different from the accepted, conventional small house."[129] Plas-2-Point was a sophisticated version, never seen before, of a peak-roofed bungalow seemingly poised in suspension, made modern by its cantilever, diagonal stair volume, and monopane and ribbon windows. Its unusual, even eccentric, profile and its failure to interest any developers only bears out the observation of Reyner Banham about the modern "factory-made house as *conceived by architects*" as a "doomed concept."[130] The Plas-2-Point House, by itself or in long blocks, looked far too "architectural" for America in the 1940s; within five years, Levittown was to set an aesthetic standard for suburbia. When compared with the elaborately detailed but commonplace appearance of another failed émigré experiment in prefabrication—the Packaged House System for the General Panel Corporation, designed by Konrad Wachsmann and Gropius ("six months to draw a hinge," recalled one of Wachsmann's students)—Breuer's Plas-2-Point was more pragmatic and

less High Architecture, but it was certainly an original, "artistic" design that intimidated American builders.

At about the same time he was developing the Plas-2-Point House, Breuer was at work on another system for minimal prefabricated defense-housing units ("de-mountable and re-erectable") that he hoped to present to the government for approval to produce in quantity. Resembling in shape his Chamberlain Cottage, these one-story bungalow-type structures were, like Plas-2-Point, imaginatively named. Breuer called them Yankee Portables, an expression of his admiration for the Puritan elite, the Yankee gentlemen he encountered at Harvard, and the New England of his first American experience. It also suggested historic Yankee ingenuity, with which he identified his own design endeavors. The naming process was Breuer's way of defining himself as an American and of allying himself with the Yankee traditions of New England, the new home he was happy to find himself in and where he was prepared to spend the rest of his life.

It was important to Breuer to make clear that the prefabrication system (on a foundation of concrete piles with crawl space, and with corrugated asbestos-cement skirting) for Yankee Portables, which he compared with the American and Swedish frame house, did not represent any kind of "counterfeit" housing. He emphasized that with its interior plywood finishes, horizontal sliding windows with screens, and generous built-in closet space, the Yankee Portable was high-quality housing for limited incomes. He took care, he said, "not to lower the standard of defense housing with the excuse of demountability. In other words, I tried to avoid the promotion of eventual slums." [131]

The principal construction feature of Yankee Portables was a flexible wall joint that allowed ample tolerance for prefabricated parts. The tolerance problem, Breuer believed, was the most important consideration for prefabricated construction in low-cost housing because it "replaces the principle of precision." "No nails are used in any of the erection operations. Also the workmen are requested to turn in their saws before starting work." [132] To manufacture Yankee Portables, Breuer made an arrangement with Custance Brothers, long-established building contractors in Lexington, Massachusetts, which had built his house in Lincoln and whose work he respected. Custance Brothers would collaborate with the nearby Lexington Lumber Company, which had mill facilities for producing the light panel prefabricated sections and could handle sizable government contracts. On March 25, 1942, Howard E. Custance sent specifications and ten drawings for one-, two-, and three-bedroom Yankee Portables from Breuer's office to the National Housing Agency in Washington, D.C. Expecting to obtain a priority for the materials, and prepared to handle a volume of up to 500 houses, Custance calculated (on the basis of 100 houses within a 50-mile radius of Boston) the cost per unit at $2,838. [133]

Despite the labor-intensive activity of Breuer and his draftsmen and the enthusiastic cooperation of the builders he enlisted, his plans for single-family prefabricated residences were never put into production. They saw the light only in publications or in exhibitions such as "Shelter in Transit and Transition," mounted in November 1942 at the Cincinnati Modern Art Society. For this exhibition, which emphasized demountable houses and new communities, Breuer submitted illustrations of Yankee Portables and Garden City of the Future (1936). But he never abandoned his fascination with the structural efficiency and cost efficiency of prefabrication in varied materials, and it accounted for his repeated use of precast-concrete units in many of the large institutional structures he designed in the 1960s and 1970s.

Binuclear House and Other Work, 1943–46

If 1942 was the year for his prefabrication experiments, in 1943 Breuer, with the binuclear house that was destined to become the first of his major postwar design successes, formulated a new American house type for a new generation. The opportunity to build an expansive variation on this theme would come with the commission for the Geller House in 1944. The ideas behind it, however, had been expressed by Breuer first in an article in 1943 about a far more modest postwar house for a working-class family, and later in a statement presented at a symposium at the Museum of Modern Art. [134] Returning from war, he said, house dwellers will more than ever value privacy and intimacy. A high standard of living beyond minimum shelter and leisure time spent around the house will become important desiderata. A house with two zones separated and connected by an entrance hall, with patio beyond, would provide (1) spaces (living room, dining room, kitchen) for everyday "dynamic" activities (sports, gardening, entertaining, eating, listening to the radio), and (2) spaces (bedrooms designed as studies) for concentration and privacy (work and sleep). None of the rooms would have party walls; windows and glass walls would allow broad vistas and catch the sun in winter. Between the zones, the patio with flowers and plants would make a pleasing impression on those entering the house. Beyond the living room would be an outdoor porch-terrace for dining and for children's play space. There would also be a place for a car, and a drying yard would be located between kitchen and garage. That houses designed by Breuer (and by Gropius) were never geared to the working classes, despite the sincere intentions of the architects, is painfully borne out by Breuer's program for his binuclears.

Even earlier, in 1940, he had expressed his philosophy about modern architecture and modern life. What he called "the direct approach" was the foundation of his ideas:

[T]he fundamental instinct of the modern movement is the direct approach, which means to face the problems of architecture free from tradition. We have been without continuity or architectural tradition for about 100 years. We are building a new tradition based on the direct approach controlled by the mentality of our generation. There is a new generation behind the new architecture—not a new fashion—to serve new needs of an informal and healthier life.[135]

Two of Breuer's finest unexecuted projects, neither of them private houses, were designed in 1945 while the Geller House was in progress: one for a war memorial in honor of servicemen and -women from Cambridge, Massachusetts, and the other for a nurses' residence at Long Beach Hospital on Long Island. The design of the latter was one of Breuer's best, and its configuration of blocks—one long and narrow, the other squarish and wide, and the two joined by a bridging element—had been in his repertoire since the Schneider House project (1929) and may have been based on Frank Lloyd Wright's H-plan for Unity Temple and its parish house, known in Europe through its publication in 1910.[136] Peter Blake regards Wright's invention as "the prototype of thousands of eminently successful types of modern plan from houses to city halls . . . the plan that every functionalist from Le Corbusier to Marcel Breuer's young American students has found . . . eminently satisfactory."[137]

The design for the war memorial by Breuer and Lawrence Anderson, an architect and professor at MIT (representing the two universities in Cambridge), had to be revised to counteract the high bids for its construction that came in following initial approval by the city council. But the council was unwilling to go forward with the revised project (its radical nontraditionalism was not popular with the citizens), and Cambridge lost what would have been a rare example of modern memorial architecture made of glass and light. It was the first of two unhappy encounters that Breuer would have with a public memorial project—twenty years later and again after much creative effort frustrated by administrative indecision, his

design for a monument to Franklin Delano Roosevelt in Washington, D.C., was rejected.[138]

While carrying out his teaching responsibilities during 1944 and 1945, Breuer rode the mounting wave of American optimism generated by the imminent conclusion of the Second World War by continuing to design small houses to promote ideas about modern living for returning veterans. This work loosened the hold that Harvard had on him. Possibly the most significant event of those years was his meeting in the winter of 1944 with Bert Geller, who wanted a modern house for his family and asked Breuer to design it. Magnificently photographed by Ezra Stoller when it was completed, the Geller House became a centerpiece in American magazines and journals, such as *House & Garden* and *Progressive Architecture*, where it displayed an ideal—indeed, glamorous—

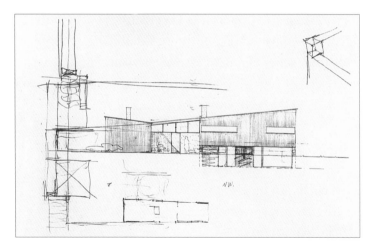

Geller House I, Lawrence, New York. 1945. Sketch

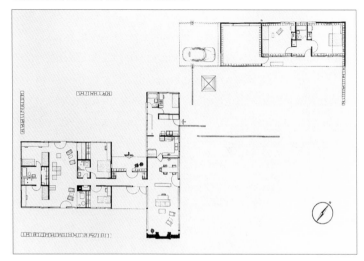

Geller House. Plan

image of upper-middle-class modern life. Its success opened for Breuer a window on the possibilities of independent architectural practice in a postwar America rich with optimism and with fresh cultural and material prospects in a period of disappearing austerity. Change was in the air; in December 1945, Breuer wrote to Moholy-Nagy that "I have quite a bit of work—it is getting interesting."[139]

Soon after designing the Geller House, Breuer was commissioned by Gilbert Tompkins for a house also near the shore on Long Island. Overseeing construction of the Tompkins and Geller Houses at first from his office in Cambridge, Breuer began to think that his future was not to be in Cambridge and in the classroom, but in New York City and its suburbs, where families were waiting for him to realize their hopes for living the good life. It would mean cutting his ties to academia and its emphasis on the theoretical, dedicating himself instead to practice. Looking back, several of Breuer's admirers—Robert Geddes for one—now regard his shift away from theory as crucial to what later would be perceived by critics as a falling off in the quality of his work. "When you look back at the body of work," Geddes said of Breuer in 1991, "you find that the larger projects lack theoretical and conceptual direction. . . . Even when he did studies of cities or housing . . . it was always an object—almost as if he made a city out of furniture."[140]

In New York, on leave of absence from Harvard from July 1, 1946, to July 1, 1947, Breuer made the decision not to return to teaching but to devote himself entirely to independent practice in New York. The decision coincided with the start-up of American building activity (despite the still limited availability of construction materials) after the long interruption of the war. It was a decision that also reached back in Breuer's experience to 1932, when he built the Harnisch-macher House and determined thereafter to make his living as a practicing architect. Had the disintegration of Europe not occurred, in all likelihood he would have succeeded in doing exactly that, and without changing continents.

"Dear Lajkó," wrote Hudnut to Breuer on May 15, 1947, "I will send your resignation as Associate Professor to the President but with the understanding that we will make a place for you in case you wish to come back to us."[141] As things turned out, he did not wish to come back. But framed and displayed on the wall of his New York office was a petition signed by 147 students at the GSD (with a copy to the administration), dated February 9, 1948, nine months after Breuer had resigned from the faculty and shortly after he had returned to give a lecture: "Professor Breuer, We the undersigned, students of the Graduate School of Design, deeply concerned with the existing quality of work in the School, urge you to return to the School as teacher and critic."[142]

Breuer in 1945

1   Breuer to Ise Gropius, June 21, 1937, Walter Gropius Papers (Breuer Letters), HL.

2   Ibid.

3   Breuer to Crofton Gane, September 28, 1937, SUL 30.

4   Jack Pritchard to Breuer, September 14, 1937, SUL 50.

5   Breuer to Walter Gropius April 21, 1937, Walter Gropius Papers (Breuer Letters), HL.

6   Jill Pearlman, "Joseph Hudnut's Other Modernism at the 'Harvard Bauhaus,'" *Journal of the Society of Architectural Historians* 56 (1997): 467. On Hudnut and Gropius, Harvard and the Bauhaus, also see Margret Kentgens-Craig, *The Bauhaus and America: First Contacts 1919–36* (Cambridge, Mass.: MIT Press, 1999), esp. 194–200.

7   Breuer to Ise Gropius, May 28, 1937, Walter Gropius Papers (Breuer Letters), HL.

8   Ise Gropius to Breuer, May 27, 1937, Walter Gropius Papers (Breuer Letters), HL.

9   Walter Gropius to Breuer, April 17, 1937, Walter Gropius Papers (Breuer Letters), HL.

10 Joseph Hudnut to Albert Mayer, February 26, 1937, GSD Papers (Hudnut Correspondence, UAV 322.7, Subseries I), HUA.

11 Gropius to Breuer, April 17, 1937.

12 Breuer, handwritten original draft, in German, of conditions of partnership with Gropius, n.d., AAA.

13 Ise Gropius to Breuer, June 1, 1937, Walter Gropius Papers (Breuer Letters), HL.

14 Breuer to Hans Falkner, August 8, 1937, SUL 5.

15 Breuer to F. R. S. Yorke, August 31, 1937, SUL 8.

16 Breuer to F. R. S. Yorke, December 20, 1938, SUL 8.

17 *Architects' Journal*, December 9, 1937, 942. As a student at the Bauhaus, Breuer had become interested, as had many others, in the amateur craze for photography and over the years had become a creditable photographer. His photograph of the RCA Building was published again, but with an erroneous attribution to Herbert Bayer, in Arthur A. Cohen, *Herbert Bayer: The Complete Work* (Cambridge, Mass.: MIT Press, 1984), 277. Breuer and Bayer arrived in the United States on the same ship; Bayer probably had a print of Breuer's photograph that ended up unidentified among Bayer's papers.

18 Breuer to Joseph P. Kasper, August 24, 1937, SUL 50.

19 Breuer to Gropius, April 21, 1937.

20 Ibid.

21 Breuer to Aladar Olgyay, March 3, 1939, Correspondence, AAA.

22 Breuer to a friend, December 24, 1938, SUL 6. He repeated this view to F. R. S. Yorke a month later, saying that he hoped Yorke would soon come to the United States and see the fair, "also to see an awful mess there" (Breuer to Yorke, January 18, 1939, SUL 8).

23 Isokon folder, SUL 50.

24 Irving Sandler and Amy Newman, Introduction to Alfred Barr, Jr., "Bauhaus 1919–1928: Preface," in *Defining Modern Art: Selected Writings by Alfred Barr, Jr.*, ed. Irving Sandler and Amy Newman (New York: Abrams, 1986), 98; Herbert Bayer, Walter Gropius, and Ise Gropius, eds., *Bauhaus 1919–1928* [exhibition catalogue] (New York: Museum of Modern Art, 1938, 1975).

25 Minutes, "Eighth Meeting of the Committee on Architecture and Industrial Art held Thursday, February 4, 1937 at the Museum of Modern Art at 4 P.M."

26 Breuer-Bayer correspondence, October–November 1939, SUL 5.

27 Breuer to Wallace K. Harrison, October 8, 1937, SUL 10.

28 Walter Gropius to Breuer, September 30, 1937, Walter Gropius Papers (Breuer Letters), HL.

29 Caption for photograph in "Josef Albers: A Retrospective," exhibition at the Solomon R. Guggenheim Museum, New York, 1988; see also Nicholas Fox Weber, "The Artist as Alchemist," in *Josef Albers, a Retrospective* (New York: Guggenheim Museum, 1988), 31.

30 Breuer to F. R. S. Yorke, July 14, 1938, SUL 8.

31 Quoted in Mary Emma Harris, *The Arts at Black Mountain College* (Cambridge, Mass.: MIT Press, 1987), 53.

32 Joseph Hudnut to Meyer Schapiro, December 14, 1938, GSD Papers (Hudnut Correspondence, UAV 322.7, Subseries I), HUA.

33 Joseph Hudnut, "Report of Progress under Grant Made by the Carnegie Corporation November 1, 1937 to Harvard University–Graduate School of Design," GSD Papers (Hudnut Papers, UAV 322.7, Subseries I), HUA.

34 On the Hudnut era at the GSD, see Pearlman, "Joseph Hudnut's Other Modernism."

35 Joseph Hudnut to Frances Pollak, Design Laboratory, New York, January 20, 1937, GSD Papers (Hudnut Correspondence, UAV 322.7, Subseries I), HUA.

36 Walter Gropius, *The New Architecture and the Bauhaus*, trans. Morton Shand (New York: Museum of Modern Art, 1936), with a dust jacket designed by László Moholy-Nagy.

37 Joseph Hudnut to *Architectural Forum*, October 11, 1937, GSD Papers (Hudnut Correspondence, UAV 322.7, Subseries I), HUA.

38 Joseph Hudnut, letter of resignation, February 16, 1938, GSD Papers (Hudnut Correspondence, UAV 322.7, Subseries I), HUA.

39 Richard Wesley, review of *The Decorated Diagram*, by Klaus Herdeg, *Journal of the Society of Architectural Historians* 45 (1986): 311; Richard Plunz, *A History of Housing in New York City: Dwelling Type and Social Change in the American Metropolis* (New York: Columbia University Press, 1990), 259–60, where Plunz says that Hudnut's program at Harvard was "blown away" by Gropius; see also Pearlman, "Joseph Hudnut's Other Modernism."

40 *An Opinion on Architecture* (Cambridge, Mass., 1941), 11.

41 George S. Lewis, conversation with author. All quotations from Lewis in this chapter are from this conversation.

42 William W. Landsberg, conversation with author. All quotations from Landsberg in this chapter are from this conversation.

43 Leonard Currie, correspondence and conversations with author. All quotations from Currie in this chapter are from these letters and conversations.

44 Edward Larrabee Barnes, conversation with author. All quotations from Barnes in this chapter are from this conversation.

45 SUL 10.

46 Quoted in Peter Blake, *Architecture for the New World: The Work of Harry Seidler* (New York: Wittenborn, 1973), 232.

47 Sigfried Giedion, *Space, Time, and Architecture*, 5th ed. (Cambridge, Mass.: Harvard University Press, 1967).

48 Joseph Hudnut, "Notes on Modern Architecture," *Harvard Alumni Bulletin*, June 1938, and Letter to the Editor, *Harvard Alumni Bulletin*, October 13, 1943, GSD Papers (Hudnut Correspondence, UAV 322.7, Subseries I), HUA.

49 "Mr. Moses Dissects the 'Long-Haired Planners,'" in *Architecture Culture, 1943–68*, ed. Joan Ockman, with Edward Eigen (New York: Rizzoli, 1993), 55–63. Gropius is among those Robert Moses denounces in his invective.

50 Irving Sandler, Introduction to *Defining Modern Art*, ed. Sandler and Newman, 15.

51 Joseph Hudnut to Editor, *Time*, April 13, 1938, GSD Papers (Hudnut Correspondence, UAV 322.7, Subseries I), HUA.

52 Joseph Hudnut to Henry-Russell Hitchcock, April 12, 1938, GSD Papers (Hudnut Correspondence, UAV 322.7, Subseries I), HUA.

53 Henry-Russell Hitchcock to Joseph Hudnut, April 14, 1938, GSD Papers (Hudnut Correspondence, UAV 322.7, Subseries I), HUA.

54 Henry-Russell Hitchcock and Catherine K. Bauer, *Modern Architecture in England* [exhibition catalogue] (New York: Museum of Modern Art, 1937), 39.

55 Henry-Russell Hitchcock, "Marcel Breuer and the American Tradition in Architecture" [essay and exhibition catalogue, Harvard University, Graduate School of Design, June–September 1938] (GSD, Cambridge, Mass., 1938, mimeographed), 11, HUAL.

56 Henry-Russell Hitchcock to Joseph Hudnut, June 16, 1938, GSD Papers (Hudnut Correspondence, UAV 322.7, Subseries I), HUA.

57 Joseph Hudnut to Breuer, June 24, 1938, GSD Papers (Hudnut Correspondence, UAV 322.7, Subseries I), HUA. The models and photographs were supplied by Breuer.

58 Breuer to Crofton Gane, October 19, 1938, SUL 30.

59 Ibid.

60 Breuer to Crofton Gane, December 10, 1940, SUL 30.

61 Landis Gores to AIA Awards Program Director, October 8, 1980, Breuer file, AIA Archives, Washington, D.C.

62 Quoted in John W. Cook and Heinrich Klotz, *Conversations with Architects* (New York: Praeger, 1973), 26.

63 Quoted in Blake, *Architecture for the New World*, 232.

64 Edward Larrabee Barnes and Harry Seidler, interviews in "Remembered by Edward Larrabee Barnes and Harry Seidler"; Marcel Breuer, "Tell Me, What Is Modern Architecture?"; and Philip Johnson, "An Artist in Architecture," in "Great Teachers: Marcel Breuer" [special section], *GSD News*, Fall 1995, 26–31, 32, 33.

65 I. M. Pei, conversation with author. All quotations from Pei in this chapter are from this conversation.

66 Harry Seidler, taped interview with Constance L. Breuer, January 2, 1985, transcribed by author, AAA.

67 Some problems and assignments are in the GSD Papers (UAV 322.7.4, Subseries IV), HUA.

68 This is in contrast to Hudnut's views on city planning: "I do not regard city planning as a branch of architecture but rather as a science which is much more closely affiliated withe the social sciences than with the arts of Design" (Joseph Hudnut to Carl Feiss, April 24, 1937, GSD papers [Hudnut Correspondence, UAV 322.7, Subseries I], HUA).

69 Klaus Herdeg, *The Decorated Diagram: Harvard Architecture and the Failure of the Bauhaus Legacy* (Cambridge, Mass.: MIT Press, 1983), 83, 84.

70 Ibid., Appendix. Herdeg found and published three—from 1948, 1949, and 1951—but had none from Breuer's classes.

71 Marcel Breuer, copy of handwritten draft of "Components of Design," in the possession of Constance L. Breuer.

72 Breuer to Crofton Gane, January 11, 1940, SUL 30.

73 Breuer to Crofton Gane, February 7, 1941, SUL 30.

74 Joseph Hudnut, in *Official Register of Harvard University*, July 7, 1947, Report of Departments for 1943–44 (Cambridge, Mass.: By the University, 1947), 222.

75 Ibid.

76 Joseph Hudnut to director of the School of Architecture, University of Manitoba, May 3, 1951, GSD Papers (Hudnut Correspondence, UAV 322.7, Subseries I), HUA.

77 Breuer to Alfred Roth, August 16, 1938, SUL 7

78 Breuer to J. L. Martin, October 3, 1938, SUL 6.

79 Breuer to Dorothea Ventris, November 16, 1938, SUL 8.

80 Breuer to Carl Maas, June 9, 1938, Correspondence, AAA.

81 Breuer to J. M. Richards, August 30, 1939, SUL 18.

82 James D. Kornwolf, "Goucher College Competition," in *Modernism in America, 1937–1941: A Catalogue and Exhibition of Four Architectural Competitions*, ed. James D. Kornwolf (Williamsburg, Va.: College of William and Mary, 1985), 72.

83 SUL 47.

84 Breuer to Raymond McGrath, March 24, 1939, SUL 6.

85 Breuer to Yorke, December 20, 1938.

86 Breuer to F. R. S. Yorke, August 11, 1939, SUL 8.

87 Breuer to Ventris, November 16, 1938.

88 Frieda Napier to Breuer, n.d., Correspondence, AAA.

89 Seidler, interview with Constance L. Breuer, January 2, 1985.

90 "Ultra Modern Houses Make Bid in Staid New England," *Christian Science Monitor*, July 29, 1939.

91 Turpin Bannister to Breuer, March 15, 1940, SUL 6

92 Breuer to J. M. Richards, September 7, 1939, SUL 18.

93 Elizabeth Mock, acting curator in Department of Architecture, MoMA, to Breuer, January 5, 1944, SUL 15.

94 J. Murphy to Breuer, September 14, 1939, SUL 9. About the Hotel Narragansett, he wrote: "You were right, it is simply amazing."

95 Sigfried Giedion, *Walter Gropius: Work and Teamwork* (New York: Reinhold, 1954), 74.

96 Hitchcock, "Marcel Breuer and the American Tradition", 1, 17.

97 Edwin R. Ford, *The Details of American Architecture* (Cambridge, Mass.: MIT Press, 1990), 311.

98 Joachim Driller, *Breuer Houses*, trans. Mark Cole and Jeremy Verrinder (London: Phaidon Press, 2000), 108–11.

99 Joachim Driller, "Bauhaus Architecture New England Style? Remarks on the Gropius House in Lincoln, Mass." (Paper presented at the annual meeting of the Society of Architectural Historians, Seattle, April 1995).

100 Michael Koop, review of *Homes in the Heartland: Balloon Frame Farmhouses of the Upper Midwest, 1850–1920*, by Fred W. Peterson, and *Buying Wood and Building Farms: Marketing Lumber and Farm Building Designs on the Canadian Prairies, 1880 to 1920*, by G. E. Mills, *Journal of the Society of Architectural Historians* 52 (1993): 353.

101 Marcel Breuer, "Autobiography," SUL 39

102 Winfried Nerdinger, *Walter Gropius: The Architect Walter Gropius: Drawings, Prints, and Photographs from Busch-Reisinger Museum, Harvard University Art Museums, Cambridge/Mass., and from Bauhaus-Archiv Berlin* [exhibition catalogue] (Berlin: Mann Verlag, 1985); Leslie Humm Cormier, "Walter Gropius, Emigré Architect: The Persistence of Typeforms" (Ph.D. diss., Brown University, 1986); Joachim Driller, "Marcel Breuer: Das architektonische Frühwerk bis 1950" (Phil. diss., Albert-Ludwigs-Universität, Freiburg, 1990), *Marcel Breuer: Die Wohnhäuser, 1923–1973* (Stuttgart: Deutsche Verlags-Anstalt, 1998), and *Breuer Houses*.

103 David H. Wright, "The Architecture of Walter Gropius" (Thesis for Honors, Harvard College, April 1950).

104 Ibid., 46, 19.

105 Driller, *Breuer Houses*, 112.

106 Richard Pommer, "The Art and Architecture Building at Yale, Once Again," *Burlington Magazine*, December 1972, 858.

107 Breuer to Crofton Gane, November 6, 1941, SUL 5.

108 Breuer to Jack Pritchard, May 22, 1940, SUL 50.

109 Breuer to Crofton Gane, December 10, 1940, SUL 50.

110 Breuer to Charles Newhull, January 5, 1941, SUL 6.

111 Marcel Breuer, application for Edward Langley Scholarship, February 1941, SUL 8.

112 Breuer to F. R. S. Yorke, January 16, 1941, SUL 8.

113 Breuer-Gropius correspondence relating to the quarrel, Walter Gropius Papers, HL.

114 Quoted in Reginald R. Isaacs, *Gropius: An Illustrated Biography of the Creator of the Bauhaus* (London: Little, Brown, 1991), 247.

115 Breuer to Sprinza Weizenblatt, n.d. [summer 1941], SUL 47.

116 Breuer to Arthur McK. Stires, January 26, 1940, SUL 18.

117 Ford, *Details of American Architecture*, 313.

118 See the discussion of individual works in Part II of this book.

119 Elizabeth B. Mock to Breuer, January 15, 1944, SUL 15.

120 Breuer to Federal Works Agency, April 22, 1941, SUL 45.

121 Gropius-Breuer correspondence, October 11–November 4, 1948, folder 77, BHA.

122 Breuer to Eduardo Catalano, June 28, 1947, SUL 39.

123 Nowhere is this carried out more astutely than in the Gropius-Breuer sections in Driller, *Breuer Houses*, esp. 102–43.

124 Quoted in Isaacs, *Gropius*, 180.

125 Breuer to James Marston Fitch, December 30, 1960, Correspondence, AAA.

126 Marcel Breuer, draft of agreement with Charles Burchard to establish Marcel Breuer, Charles Burchard, Architects, Industrial Consultants, October 22, 1945, SUL 41.

127 Breuer to a potential client, December 15, 1944, SUL 47.

128 Breuer to Glenn Bass, November 22, 1944, SUL 47.

129 GBH-Way Homes to Breuer, November 22, 1944, SUL 47.

130 Reyner Banham, review of *The Dream of the Factory-Made House*, by Gilbert Herbert, *Design Book Review* 8 (1986): 18. Emphasis added.

131 Breuer to Howard Myers, *Architectural Forum*, April 13, 1942, SUL 18.

132 Ibid.

133 Howard E. Custance to National Housing Agency, March 25, 1942, SUL 42.

134 Marcel Breuer, "On a Design for a By-Nuclear House," *California Arts & Architecture*, December 1943, 24–25, and "What Is Happening to Modern Architecture?" [statement at MoMA symposium, February 11, 1948], *Museum of Modern Art Bulletin* 15 (1948): 15; *Arts & Architecture*, May 1948, 31; and Peter Blake, *Marcel Breuer: Architect and Designer* (New York: Museum of Modern Art, 1949), 122.

135 Marcel Breuer, "Tell Me, What Is Modern Architecture?" *House & Garden*, April 1940, 47.

136 *Ausgeführte Bauten und Entwürfe von Frank Lloyd Wright*, intro. Frank Lloyd Wright, 2 vols. (Berlin: Wasmuth, 1910). Gropius had a copy at the Bauhaus.

137 Peter Blake, *Frank Lloyd Wright: Architecture and Space* (Baltimore: Penguin, 1960), 50.

138 Breuer received inquiries about other memorial monuments in this period. As chairman of a committee appointed by the mayor of Cambridge, Hudnut asked him in June 1945 if he would be willing to design a memorial to mark the site of the "Washington Elm" at the end of Cambridge Common, where, in July 1775, "under a great elm tree General George Washington took command of the armies of the United Colonies." Breuer said yes, and that it should be designed jointly with Lawrence Anderson. There is no further record regarding the project (Hudnut-Breuer correspondence, June–July 1945, SUL 41).

A Milwaukee group—the Metropolitan Milwaukee War Memorial, Inc.—asked Breuer in July 1945 to design a war memorial. This request particularly pleased him because, as he wrote, "It is refreshing to see the departure from the anachronistic merely-monument-memorial toward a more social solution with useful functions." He sent a telegram with available dates for an interview on August 14, 1945, but there is no record of his having prepared a design (Metropolitan Milwaukee War Memorial-Breuer correspondence, SUL 42).

139 Breuer to László Moholy-Nagy, December 17, 1945, SUL 18.

140 Robert Geddes, conversation with author.

141 Joseph Hudnut to Breuer, May 15, 1947, GSD Papers (Hudnut Correspondence, UAV 322.7, Subseries I), HUA.

142 Original in the possession of Constance L. Breuer.

I have great respect for the local builders in this country, and have as a whole had very good experience with them. I also try to make the work easy for them with exhaustive and very exact drawings.

Marcel Breuer to a client,
February 4, 1949

5. New York:
The Early Postwar Years and the Decisive Decade, 1946–60

I never had the feeling that certain materials were acceptable and others were not.

Marcel Breuer quoted in Paul Heyer,
*Architects on Architecture, New
Directions in America,* 1966

WHEN IN 1949 BREUER COMMENDED the American builders he had been working with for a dozen years, he probably would not have predicted that he would go on to design, and with their help construct, more than 100 buildings in this country, many of them the single-family houses that have a secure place among the examples of America's great residential architecture. Widely published in international architectural journals, Breuer houses projected a reassuring image of postwar material and spiritual recovery and of modern family life.

This productive period had already begun in Cambridge with the end of the Second World War and the planning of the Geller and Tompkins Houses, before Breuer moved to New York City in May 1946 to take up the independent practice of architecture "on a larger scale."[1] The decision to leave Cambridge and the teaching of architecture for private practice in New York was the step that would lead to the changed perception of Breuer from Bauhaus designer and Gropius disciple to major independent international architect whose name was linked with those of the modernist greats.

House in the Museum Garden,
Museum of Modern Art, New York. 1948–49

MARCEL BREUER, ARCHITECT, 438 EAST EIGHTY-EIGHTH STREET AND 113 EAST THIRTY-SEVENTH STREET

In New York, Breuer established an office and family apartment on two remodeled floors in a building owned by photographer Rollie McKenna at 438 East Eighty-eighth Street. Some of "the boys" from Harvard and from the Cambridge office worked as draftsmen: "My present staff is going with me," Breuer wrote to a job applicant.[2] More than one regarded the experience as the equivalent of a new education in architecture.[3] For Harry Seidler, after graduating from the Graduate School of Design and then studying design with Josef Albers at Black Mountain College,

there was only one thing in the whole world I wanted to do and that was to work for Breuer. . . . I simply turned up at 88th Street one day and said I wanted to work there. . . . I'll draw for you, it doesn't matter that you can't pay . . . it was the greatest move I ever made in my life because the following two years or so that I spent there was when I learned my trade. The houses I worked on with Lajkó in those few years are really the basis of what I have done in my own work.[4]

George S. Lewis recalled convivial lunchtime discourse in neighborhood Hungarian restaurants that led to the planning of some of the most notable of those houses—the Museum of Modern Art exhibition house; the Robinson House in Williamstown, Massachusetts (see p. 29); and Breuer's own first house in New Canaan, Connecticut.[5] In August 1947, Eliot Noyes joined Seidler, William Landsberg, and Rolland Thompson as a new associate in an effort by Breuer to add an industrial-design component to the practice. Noyes had worked with Breuer in Cambridge, but became increasingly engaged with industrial design as head of the Department of Industrial Design at the Museum of Modern Art and as design director for Norman Bel Geddes and Company.[6] Thompson, a graduate of the GSD, also had a degree in engineering from MIT. There were frequent shifts in personnel at the office as associates and draftsmen departed for other cities or the pursuit of independent careers (Seidler left in early 1948) or as the work ebbed and flowed and promising new apprentices

appeared. The organizational fabric was held together by administrative secretary Margaret Firmage, whose name democratically appeared on the letterhead along with that of the associates and consultants.

As in Cambridge and in later Breuer offices, the draftsmen at East Eighty-eighth Street turned out large, meticulous drawings of details that had been refined in project after project. Discussing fees with a prospective client in 1949, Breuer said: "When you see the drawings and details which we will supply the builder with, I am sure you will find the fees low in relation to the amount of work involved. I try to make the work easy for [the builders] with exhaustive and very exact drawings, and have found that this makes the work quite a bit more economical."[7] To Father Cloud Meinberg at Saint John's Abbey, he wrote:

You probably noted that my office is going more into special design of the details than probably most other American offices. Where we have experience we feel that the special work is not more expensive than the standard industrial product. It should also be mentioned that before your windows have been detailed, similar or identical windows have been used in some 20 cases and we have the benefit of long time thinking and past experimentation.[8]

Breuer in 1948

Pushing hard to move ahead after his late start in architectural practice and following every lead to opportunities for work, even considering a road-building project in 1946,[9] Breuer had inexhaustible energy and ambition. His practice began to expand and prosper from the acceleration of postwar construction and from the growing number of commissions that came in. He was soon building houses that ranged from $13,000 to $300,000. By March 1947, he could report that "my office, small as it is, is quite busy now and quite promising."[10] After two years in the small space at 438 East Eighty-eighth Street, he moved to a full-fledged atelier at 113 East Thirty-seventh Street in September 1948, with Landsberg as his "chief designer."[11] Key members of the early team in this office, in addition to Noyes, Landsberg, and Thompson—all contributing to the design processes and to the supervision of construction—included Julian Neski, Belva J. Barnes, and Peter Fraser.

Clients usually sought Breuer out after having seen one of his houses. "Each time we look at [our] house we experience the same thrill as when we first saw the Kniffin House," wrote a client during the construction of a residence in 1949. The facade of the Kniffin House (1948) in New Canaan, Connecticut, was articulated by sun louvers, which played an essential role in controlling heat and light at Breuer buildings until air-conditioning became universal (and until his sun-protection devices had disastrous consequences at the UNESCO Headquarters and elsewhere). "Nearly every one of my works is an experiment in sun protection," said Breuer in 1953, thinking back to the researches of his Bauhaus and post-Dessau years that stressed orientation to the sun for light and warmth in a continuing search for amenities in low-cost workers' housing.[12] Taking the sun into account in architectural planning was carried by Breuer to America from Germany. The appreciation of sunlight in northern Europe because of its short supply for much of the year made its control an important goal when laying out houses and apartments. Light-colored surfaces, balconies and roof terraces, photographs taken for journals and newspapers in full summer featuring a *brise-soleil*, awnings, and long shadows—all became "Mediterranean" modernist clichés for buildings of the 1920s and 1930s. But by the 1950s, the clutter of elements needed for sun con-

trol on the wide faces of Breuer's eight-story UNESCO Secretariat, for example, compromised the unity and coherence of the design without solving the problem of excessive heat in the interior spaces and led to sharp criticism, even ridicule, of Breuer. It also led Breuer to begin replacing sun-filtering elements applied to surfaces with deep recessed windows, moving him toward the sculptural chiaroscuro of the later work.

House ground-plan and elevation formats by Breuer, with inventive variations, became typologized. There was the long house, the binuclear house, the in-line house, the T-shaped and H-shaped houses, the two-story cantilevered or "offset" house with extruded porches and terraces—categories that have been usefully redefined and augmented by Joachim Driller in his studies of Breuer's residential architecture.[13] The MoMA exhibition house and the Geller and Robinson Houses

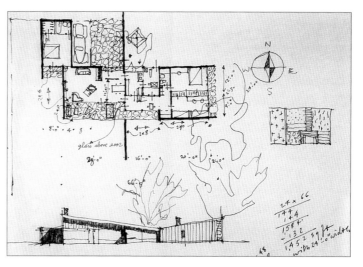

House in the Museum Garden. Sketch

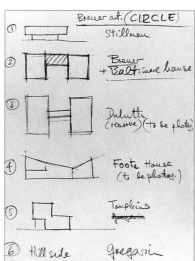

Breuer house types of the 1940s and 1950s

were among the more evolved versions of the binuclear type, which Breuer developed during the mid-1940s in response to calls by magazines, newspapers, and manufacturers for house designs for returning servicemen.

Even before he left Cambridge, Breuer had participated in design competitions such as those sponsored in 1945 by the *Ladies' Home Journal* for a small modern postwar house, and in 1946 by the *Chicago Tribune* "to encourage better home designs, to help launch America's home building revival and to provide more jobs." The design he submitted to the *Ladies' Home Journal* exemplified his 1940s small-house program and was conceived with a quick ink sketch of plan and elevation on the verso of a letter he had received from the associate editor of the magazine.[14] The house was organized with a living zone toward a garden on the south and with service spaces toward the street on the north. Closets were taken out of the bedrooms ("closet doors ruin small bedrooms," Breuer said) and lined the corridor instead. Bedrooms—Breuer preferred to call them bed-living rooms—were planned for two beds and a worktable. Next to the kitchen were a utility room for laundry and heating, a drying yard, and a car shelter, since "everybody hates to open or close a garage door." The 30-foot-long open-plan living space (study, living room, dining area) was subdivided by only a fireplace wall and was expanded to the garden through glass walls protected from the sun by a cantilevered and louvered strip of roof. Sliding windows were horizontal strips. The kitchen was aligned with the (optional) porch for outdoor eating; the porch would have stone parapet walls for seating and a free-standing dividing wall of stone for privacy. As for structure ("of extreme simplicity"), the house could be prefabricated of tongue-and-groove stressed plywood on a 3-foot, 4-inch module, constructed locally of semi-prefabricated parts, or built in traditional frame construction with interior and exterior plywood sheeting. Floor construction would be concrete slab with radiant heating.

Breuer's perception of their needs and wishes was appreciated by most of his clients. He understood what middle-class postwar Americans were seeking in a house because he sought it, too, in his own cost-efficient New Canaan residence, built in 1947–48. "After World War Two most Americans had a

vision of a better life just ahead. At the core of it was owning one's own house," wrote David Halberstam in *The Fifties*.[15] That better life, however, was not urban; it was predicated on the automobile and the highway, and it embraced new American ideals that were reflected in Breuer's designs—informality, outdoor living, family unity, special attention to children. His clients tended to be well-educated professionals in publishing, advertising, the family business, and law who had grown up during the Great Depression and survived the war. Economically and perhaps culturally beyond those who settled in the mass-produced housing of Levittown and other simultaneously developing suburbias, a typical Breuer client was seeking an architect-designed modern house, often on substantial private property and occasionally with costly requirements. The Gellers asked for a large playroom for their children and, adjacent to the garage, a separate suite for guests; the Robinsons had an immense glass-walled living room and a cantilevered canopy above a broad outdoor terrace to frame and expand their spectacular view of the Berkshires. It helped that never had two decades in America been more prosperous than the 1950s and 1960s. So rapidly and successfully did the residential component of his practice develop that by 1955, responding to a suggestion by one of his staff that the office establish "a special cell for houses," Breuer (then in Paris) wrote that "the suggestion went very often through my mind, but I have my doubts that it would work."[16]

Breuer's success as a house architect was helped also by a postwar phenomenon observed by architect Janet Temos, writing about the Robinson House and "the popularization of modernism":

During the enforced building moratorium caused by the war, there seems to have been a shift in American taste in favor of modernism. This trend had begun in the mid-thirties when popular magazines, such as *House & Garden*, and professional journals, most notably *Architectural Forum*, began to feature modern designs in their pages. . . . Most convincingly [a 1935 article in the conservative *Fortune* magazine] concluded with the information that a "modern house may be built for about 30 percent less than a comparable house in a traditional style."[17]

Breuer House—New Canaan I, New Canaan, Connecticut, photographed by Breuer. 1947–48

Citing Witold Rybczynski's *Home: A Short History of an Idea*, Temos points out that modernism, moreover, was seen as "a nationalistic response prompted by the war. Because of Nazi reaction against the style it was cheerfully and nationalistically embraced by discriminating Americans."[18] In the words of Rybczynski, "Its antitotalitarian reputation . . . helped, and it became a 'Free World' style, representing democracy and America."[19] This notion also supports Driller's idea, already mentioned, that Gropius and Breuer emphasized the American "regionalism" aspect of the modern houses they built in New England in the late 1930s and early 1940s in order to deemphasize their German sources.

"When one is one's own client, one can sing one's own song," said architect Berthold Lubetkin.[20] Breuer did precisely that in the first of the two houses he built for himself in New Canaan, Connecticut, combining shape, structure, and material with such originality that the house resembled no other.

Published more than any earlier Breuer house, it became an icon of American postwar suburban modernism. Its connection to Breuer's principles of furniture construction has been recognized. According to Adam Clem:

The double layer of boards running in opposite diagonals is based on the very same construction principle governing the engineering of the laminated Isokon furniture; constant in both idioms is the idea that the form as structure flows from the inner logic of materials and construction, materially and logically contiguous . . . the connection between the New Canaan home and the cantilevered chair [B32] and Isokon units is clear, in that the box of the New Canaan house is self supporting, bound by tension throughout the frame and across the uniform wooden interior.[21]

For Vincent Scully, the house was less architectural than pictorial, an example of what he regarded as Breuer's Bauhaus-based small-scale antimonumentality: "Suspended like a little insect, like a little creature off the ground with all the old sta-

Wellfleet cottage type, Wellfleet, Massachusetts. 1948. Rendering

bilities of architecture overset, now everything is utterly light, held together by wires."[22] Experimental and daring, the house endured several near-disasters during construction, most of which took place while Breuer was in South America.

Another Breuer-family house, a low-budget vacation cottage designed in 1945 and built in Wellfleet, Massachusetts, in 1948, geared to informal living and minimum housekeeping chores, became the model for several versions also built in Wellfleet for friends such as Gyorgy Kepes and Howard Wise.

Museum of Modern Art Exhibition House, 1949

Appearing at the peak of the postwar housing shortage, Breuer's exhibition house (1948–49) in the garden of the Museum of Modern Art corresponded to a moment of high public interest in houses and in museum exhibitions regarding houses. Even in 1945, when, in collaboration with the *Ladies' Home Journal*, MoMA held an exhibition of scale models entitled "Tomorrow's Small House," attendance on one day was twice the average daily museum attendance.[23] The MoMA

house gave Breuer's architecture its first expansive exposure and favorably dissociated him in the public's view from the design aesthetic identified with the Bauhaus. With its warm and familiar "American" wood siding and its expressive silhouette, the house was perceived as a rejection of the austere white blocks of International Style villas, whose interior layout was not configured on the outside, roofs were flat, and skin was stretched tightly over abstract cubic volumes. "Modern architects don't like severity in a house," Breuer said in an interview about the exhibition house. "Perhaps we did once, but we don't anymore."[24]

Peter Blake, then curator of the Department of Architecture and Design at MoMA, remembered the selection of Breuer to design a model house for the museum as seeming "a trifle bizarre at the time," but the trustees, at least on the record, were fully behind it.[25] He was considered a dependable compromise candidate, since Mies van der Rohe, Frank Lloyd Wright, and other Pantheonic architects were found unsuitable for one reason or another. According to a report of May 12, 1948, MoMA trustees had long discussed giving Mr. Breuer an exhibition, not only of his architecture but also of his furniture, which many feel is the best modern furniture now available. . . . The Department [of Architecture and Design] feels that Mr. Breuer's name ranks next to those of Le Corbusier, Wright, and Mies van der Rohe, to whom we have already given exhibitions. Fortunately, Mr. Breuer has spent a great deal of time working on the problem of the small house. We feel that he is therefore better equipped than his more famous colleague, Mr. Frank Lloyd Wright, who is not particularly interested in low cost building.[26]

Indeed, when the proposal of Breuer as designer of a house to be exhibited at the museum was being contemplated, Philip Johnson and trustees Mrs. John D. Rockefeller III, A. Conger Goodyear, and Mrs. E. Bliss Parkinson traveled to Long Island with Breuer to visit the Geller and Tompkins Houses.

In a commitment to high-quality modernist design in residential architecture, the museum in 1948 initiated a program to exhibit built structures, specifically model houses, in order to expose the public to the work of well-known modern architects in a format other than that of photographs, plans, and drawings.[27] It was an East Coast counterpart to the now-famous full-scale Case Study house program, which had originated in 1945 in California with John Entenza's *Arts & Architecture* magazine. Promoting affordable house designs geared to informal living and to prefabricated construction with modern industrial materials, the California experiment was a visionary undertaking that produced a number of superb modern houses, even if it did not result in widespread application in the home-building industry, as had been anticipated.[28]

Breuer's model house was not a low-cost building by the standards of the period. At $27,475 ($21,960 unexpanded) and intended for one acre of land, it was well beyond the reach not only of the average American but even of the middle-income family for which it purportedly was built. Exhibited in its expanded state in the museum's 400-foot-long sculpture garden, the house attracted thousands of visitors who, by paying the 35-cent admission fee, had their first experience with a built modern house and how it "worked." Robert Gatje, Breuer's future associate and partner, was one of them; years later, he claimed that "it just stunned me." Blake's *Marcel Breuer: Architect and Designer* was written and published in connection with the exhibition.[29] The Geller House in Lawrence, New York, and the recently completed Robinson House had been given visibility in the professional and popular press, but as private residences they received comparatively few visitors. (The Geller House was, however, the first modern house seen by Herbert Beckhard, later one of Breuer's associates and partners, and its impression "made me redirect my thinking about my own career and about architecture," he recalled.[30]) Fully equipped and furnished, from dishes and bed linens to a Breuer-designed television-radio-phonograph console, the house in the MoMA garden spoke to the hunger of the American public for consumer goods denied during the war years, for new technological gadgets to improve the quality of life, and for new ways for family life to be comfortable and informal. Breuer-designed furniture, some hung from walls and elevated above the floor, some occupying a minimum of the floor area, increased the sense of roominess and openness.

A generation of American architects was educated about "humanistic" modernism through the impact of Breuer's first postwar houses. With the ensuing versions and transmutations of the exhibition house, and with the new house formats that came out of his office in the later 1940s and the 1950s, he exercised a powerful influence on American residential architecture that is documented in the pages of the leading architectural journals published from 1949 to 1959.[31] The MoMA and Geller Houses were designed with the inverted-peak roof, which expressed in contour Breuer's "zoning" of interior space, and allowed for a second-story bedroom under the upward slope of one wing. The exhibition house had a two-story zone on the west—garage below and bedroom with balcony above, reached by interior and exterior stairs—demonstrating the expansion capabilities of a basically modest one-story house. Important to Breuer and his clients was the potential for house expansion in general. The enframed open carport at the Hanson House (1950), which in a formal sense represented the "other part" of a butterfly bipartite design, for example, was built as a temporary car shelter intended as a future three-bedroom, two-bathroom "addition" to the house. The butterfly-roof format also eliminated gutters and drains at roof edge (a single drain passed from the roof through the center of the house, where inside heating supposedly prevented winter freezing). Technical problems with flat roofs—by 1949 a standard feature of the modern house—motivated Breuer to design a new edging detail that he wanted to patent, made with standard metal coping sections applied on the job without soldering or welding, instead of the two-by-four covered with copper that he had been using and that could not be counted on to keep the edge watertight.[32] But, as it would be with his new frameless sliding window in 1953, he did not succeed in finding a commercial manufacturer or a market for his invention, which he continued to detail on a job-by-job basis.

The house in the museum garden brought Breuer many clients—above all, Rufus and Leslie Stillman, who commissioned a house (of different design) in Litchfield, Connecticut, and were responsible for much of Breuer's success then and later with their influential recommendations to friends and relatives, institutions and businesses.[33] Some clients preferred newly designed models based on the MoMA prototype; others wanted to buy copies of the original plans to build with their own contractor. "Both my son and daughter-in-law not only want a Breuer house but, in particular, the Modern Museum house you are building in Red Bank, New Jersey [Tilley House] and elsewhere. It is assumed that the design and details of the house will be substantially identical to the Modern Museum and Red Bank house," wrote a prospective client.[34]

A significant factor for Breuer's residential practice, moreover, was the government's postwar subsidization of the single-family house. Studied by Richard Plunz, income-tax laws of the period gave homeowners substantial advantages; added to mechanisms for mortgage guarantees that had been established since the New Deal—the Federal Home Loan Bank System in 1932 and the Federal Housing Authority (FHA) loan guarantee programs in 1934—was the Home Loan Guaranty Program of 1944 to help resettle returning veterans.[35]

Multiple-Family Dwellings

As much as single-family houses, multiple-apartment dwellings interested Breuer at this period, although the opportunity to build them would elude him until the 1960s. The signing by President Harry S. Truman on July 15, 1949, of a public-housing bill, directed to the establishment of ambitious slum-clearance programs and to the construction of more than 800,000 public-housing units carrying long-term federal rent subsidies, was one attempt to solve postwar housing problems on a large scale. In response to this new national initiative, and with the hope that it would bring in work, on October 21, 1949, Breuer submitted an Architects' Qualification Roster to the New York City Housing Authority with a "statement about the firm's qualifications for public housing."[36] He reported that he had always "given special attention to housing particularly in its lower cost aspects," that he had carried out "many theoretical projects," and that he specialized in the "humanizing of contemporary design for public housing" by taking into account "the problem of children in relation to housing" and "housing in relation to community planning." He drew attention to his efforts at "structural analysis with special attention to costs" and to his "planning for utilizing solar heat and light."

With this application, Breuer strove to find opportunities to build urban multiple-family dwellings large or small, to put into practice the theoretical housing exercises of his European years, and to follow up the successful experience of the Doldertal apartment houses (1935–36) and the less successful Aluminum City Terrace (1941) in New Kensington, Pennsylvania. As early as 1945, he had discussed a possible partnership venture with his client Bert Geller for an apartment house in Lawrence, New York, recognizing the postwar demand for and scarcity of apartments as a rich opportunity for good modern architecture and for capital investment. From 1943 to 1948, he pursued possibilities for average-income housing projects and for profit-making apartment-house development—ten- to fourteen-story terraced structures that he presciently envisioned at scenic sites in New York City and New Jersey. He tried relentlessly during 1943 and 1944 to replace the accepted design for Stuyvesant Town in New York (thirty-five thirteen-story "towers in the park") with an alternative of his own, the "Stuyvesant Six."[37] (Formed as Y-shaped fifteen-story buildings combined into a hexagonal layout, they were still towers in the park.) In 1945 and 1946, he attempted, unsuccessfully, to interest his friend Edgar Kaufmann, Jr., son of the Pittsburgh department-store magnate and just returned from service in the Second World War, in investing in an apartment-house development on Sutton Place in Manhattan (see p. 28). Breuer had excellent intuition regarding available real-estate parcels in New York at pleasing locations with river views and parks—Sutton Place between Fifty-fourth and Fifty-fifth Streets, Seventy-ninth Street and the Hudson River, Gramercy Park, Washington Square—and in New Jersey at Englewood Cliffs. In the same way that he had prepared his entries in German housing competitions of the 1920s, he made extensive calculations about rentability, footage, and construction costs. To sharpen and verify his conclusions, he consulted Martin Wagner at Harvard. Not until the market-driven development frenzy of the 1960s did Breuer succeed in finding the transactional partners that enterprises of this magnitude required.

South America

Accepting what he described as a combined invitation from the University of Buenos Aires and the government of Colombia, Breuer spent the summer and fall of 1947 in South America while orchestrating and controlling in absentia the activities of his office, where Noyes, Seidler, and Landsberg served as alter egos. The invitation to visit Buenos Aires came from Eduardo Catalano, who had been a student for a master's degree at the GSD and who wanted Breuer to lecture to architecture students at the University of Buenos Aires about housing and urbanism. Even more, he hoped that Breuer would establish and become director of a new school of architecture and planning that would bring about "the end of a dark period for our architectural school."[38] Such a relocation would be "a radical change of life [for me]," Breuer wrote,[39] yet the prospect was taken seriously enough on both sides for the drafting of a contract:[40] Breuer proposed to spend April through November in Argentina for two years. "If after two years we mutually should decide that I should continue my work at the university I would terminate my office in New York." He still would be free to accept architectural commissions, "but the university would be my first job."

Breuer left on July 30, 1947, for Rio de Janeiro, where he would spend three days and then go on to Buenos Aires. He had requested from Charles Burchard at Harvard photostats of theses and other student work to take along for the preparation of a curriculum: "I am especially interested in hospital projects, theater projects and housing projects."[41] Officially, the visit and eight-week course were sponsored and financed by the Facultad de ciencias exactas, físicas y naturales. Catalano warned Breuer about noted architects who had lectured in Buenos Aires with uneven success. "Architects here prefer the European culture rather than the North American one," he said, probably referring to Le Corbusier's entrenched influence in Buenos Aires since 1929, and proposed that "a very interesting theme for a lecture would be the Bauhaus (but perhaps you are tired of talking about it)."[42] Richard Neutra had been a disappointment because "he explained the same things as were in the American magazines."

After working for more than a month with the students in Buenos Aires, Breuer left for Bogotá at the end of September. He had been invited as Consultant on Urbanism by the Colombian government through architects Alvaro Ortega and Gabriel Solano. "At present Solano and myself, among other young architects, are working with the government in the National Buildings Department of the Ministry of Public Works," Ortega told him.[43] Aware that Breuer was to be in Argentina, they hoped that he would come to Colombia for "good advisement" on a housing project and medical center as part of a radical redevelopment plan for Bogotá. In a list of his "major works" submitted to Blake in 1949,[44] Breuer included the planning proposals for Bogotá that he had completed in December 1947. Among them were a hospital city with medical center and 3,800 beds; an 1,100-unit, low-cost housing project with shopping center and schools; food markets with "a smooth floor surface and the least possible number of walls and columns"; and an administration center with government offices and a presidential palace.

Breuer's master plan for Bogotá, begun with optimism and the seeming support of the Ministry of Public Works, never brought him a contract—"a complete lack of government responsibility," Ortega complained.[45] (The project was taken over in 1950 by José Luis Sert and Paul Lester Wiener in collaboration with Le Corbusier.) But while in Buenos Aires, Breuer had designed (without seeing the site) the cloverleaf-shaped Ariston Club, a restaurant and dance club at a recreational beach development in Mar del Plata. A month after he left the city, the building department accepted the drawings, and construction (overseen by Catalano) was begun; by February 1948, the club, with significant departures from the original design, was ready to open. Catalano apologized that the architectural details "are somehow rough, because of the short time," but "all the architectural students have gone to the place to see your work."[46] In a characteristic instance of self-borrowing, the design was a variant of the elevated cloverleaf in Breuer's Garden City of the Future project.

Ten years after his projects in Argentina and Colombia, Breuer, with his associate Herbert Beckhard, undertook another South American venture, this time in Venezuela in collaboration with architect Julio Volante, for a seaside cooperative apartment–beach club complex near Caracas. It was never realized, but on the seeming strength of the backing of the project, Breuer in 1959–60 set up an office in Caracas with Beckhard in charge.

The Practice

Returning to New York from South America in the fall of 1947, Breuer completed his house in New Canaan and other residences that had been overseen in his absence by the staff. Between 1945 and 1956, more than twenty of his houses were built, some of them in America's most conventional bastions of upper-middle-class architectural conservatism—Litchfield, New Canaan, and Orange, Connecticut; Williamstown and Andover, Massachusetts; Duluth, Minnesota; and towns on the North Shore of Long Island—defying regional traditions. Still, at least in New England, Breuer's frame construction, fieldstone walls, independent staircase units, and large fireplaces bore some connection to America's architectural heritage. His contribution to the period's polemical issue of regionalism in modern American residential building, debated on the basis of "organic" or "inorganic" architecture, was

made at a well-known symposium held on February 11, 1948, at the Museum of Modern Art. "What Is Happening to Modern Architecture," organized by Alfred Barr and moderated by Lewis Mumford, continued to haunt Breuer's memory half a century later. Responding in 1948 to Mumford's praise of the architecture of the San Francisco Bay Area, with its friendly relation to nature through its emphasis on indigenous natural materials (exemplified by the houses designed by Breuer's good friend William Wurster), Breuer made his famous riposte: "If 'human' is considered identical with redwood all over the place, or if it is considered identical with imperfection and imprecision, I am against it; also, if it is considered identical with camouflaging architecture with planting, with nature, with romantic subsidies."[47] In the catalogue of a 1995 exhibition about Wurster's houses, Marc Trieb characterizes Breuer's comments as "vicious" and, because of the use of wood siding and stone in his own houses, as "hypocritical."[48] But Breuer's remarks pointed to his impatience with the prolongation of what he called a "controversy which was in order, I am afraid, about twenty-five years ago," at the expense of his current and far more egalitarian commitment to "achievement," to "the contrasting elements of our nature . . . the crystallic quality of an unbroken white, flat slab . . . together with and in contrast to the rough, 'texture-y' quality of natural wood or broken stone."[49]

A stone-clad residence that was the modern addition to an older structure, built by Breuer for the Hooper family of Baltimore in 1949 and 1950, led to two important institutional commissions: the Grosse Pointe Public Library and the Ferry Cooperative Dormitory at Vassar College, sponsored by Edith Ferry Hooper's father, M. Dexter Ferry. The Stillman House (1950) brought Breuer commissions for the first in a series of buildings for the Torrington (later Torin) Manufacturing Company and, equally important, for several schools and juvenile institutions designed as one-story units entered from covered walkways, in and near Litchfield. In the early 1950s, there were still shortages of and priorities for such critical wartime building materials as steel, copper, and aluminum, which affected school, college, and library construction. On September 7, 1951, the Federal Security Agency Office of Education issued *Defense Information Bulletin* 975153: "Education construction as affected by shortages of critical materials," a "con-

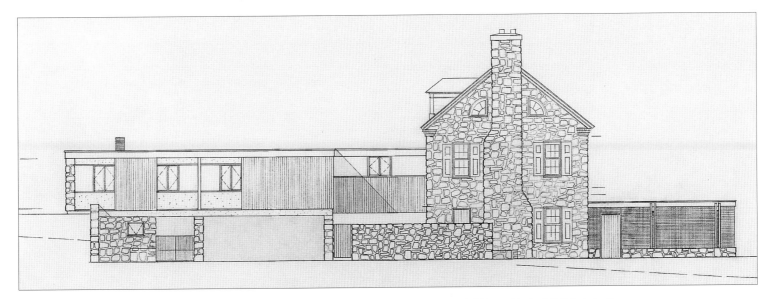

Hooper House I, Baltimore, Maryland. 1949. East elevation

trolled materials plan." A copy of the *Bulletin* is filed with the papers for the construction of the Grosse Pointe Public Library, which indicates that Breuer and his client had to be alert to specifications and priorities of allocated materials: "The current situation will require a cutback, and in many cases, a deferment of plans for construction," the *Bulletin* stated.

During the early 1950s, suburban development offered Breuer opportunities for architecture beyond houses. There were small factories, schools, and, on burgeoning Long Island, the expansion of retail facilities geared to the automobile that led to the construction of a branch of Abraham & Straus, the long-established Brooklyn department store. Breuer was commissioned to design in 1951 and 1952 the exterior of what was described as the "newest, largest and most complete suburban department store in the Northeastern United States,"[50] with 236,000 square feet of space and 9 acres of parking with facilities for 1,200 cars. "Accessibility to shoppers driving their own cars" was one of the new store's biggest selling points. A photograph of Breuer's sketch was published in the *New York Times* on December 28, 1950, where it was referred to as "ultramodern in design."

The Ferry Cooperative Dormitory (1949–50) at Vassar College in Poughkeepsie, New York, the focus of a searching formal analysis of Breuer's architecture by William H. Jordy,[51] was his first opportunity after the early unfulfilled projects for Wheaton College, Black Mountain College, Smith College,

and the College of William and Mary to change the appearance of traditional college campuses in the United States through the medium of modern architecture. (By the time he retired, Breuer had made innovative changes at Vassar College, Sarah Lawrence College, Hunter College, Saint John's University, New York University, University of Mary, Yale University, the University of Massachusetts at Amherst, and the State University of New York at Buffalo.) But it was inevitable that in 1949 a proposal for a modern building on a traditional college campus such as Vassar's would create argument and dispute. President Sarah Gibson Blanding of Vassar reported to Breuer, following a trustees' meeting, that "there was quite some articulate objection to placing on the campus the house you designed."[52] In the end, the dormitory was not sited in the prominent position first envisioned for it, but was removed to the margins of the campus where it was for the most part invisible and unobtrusive. Soon after the completion of the Vassar building, Breuer was asked to design, for another prestigious woman's college—Sarah Lawrence in Bronxville, New York—an art center that included a dance studio, a music department, an exhibition space, and a 500-seat multi-purpose theater.

Varied as they were in purpose and size, the buildings designed and built by Breuer since he had come to the United States soon would be dwarfed by two of the largest commissions he would receive in the five decades of his practice: a

100-year comprehensive plan for the Benedictine abbey of Saint John near Collegeville in central Minnesota, about eighty miles northwest of Minneapolis, and, in collaboration with Pier Luigi Nervi and Bernard Zehrfuss, the complex of UNESCO buildings in Paris. The story of the monastery and the initial phase of its long-range plan for expansion was written by Whitney S. Stoddard.[53] This moment in Breuer's career coincided with the acceleration of architectural activity in the United States following the postwar recovery, with the rebuilding of a destroyed Europe, and with a national and international affirmation of modernism—to such a degree that it was to become doctrinaire as the preferred language of new design. The summer of 1952 was a decisive moment: writing to Hawkins Ferry in Grosse Pointe, while the library was in construction, Breuer announced that "I am facing now an unexpected turn of things: I have just been appointed to be the architect for the new permanent headquarters for Unesco in Paris . . . as you may imagine it is a very important and interesting work, and I am leaving this afternoon for Paris."[54]

To Europe Once Again

The headquarters for UNESCO (see p. 32)—about 500,000 square feet of gross floor area—was Breuer's first large public building and a turning point in his career equal in magnitude to his decision to emigrate to the United States. He saw it as "the symbol of a great idea" destined to be expressed in "the architectural spirit of our time."[55] It united him once again on an architectural project with Gropius, who was chairman of UNESCO's international advisory panel of architects, known as The Five,[56] and allied him with a prestigious project of grand scale in a great capital city that at that time was notably unresponsive to modern architecture. It also returned him to Europe as an architect, launching him on a series of impressive commissions in Germany, France, Switzerland, and, especially, Holland—among them the United States Embassy in The Hague, the large department store De Bijenkorf in Rotterdam (to replace the old store destroyed in the Second World War), and the Van Leer office building in Amstelveen. And it transformed him into a master of concrete construction and technology because the plastic qualities of reinforced concrete suited his natural proclivities toward a sculptural architecture and toward structure as design. It was in the early 1950s that Breuer began to use concrete instead of steel frames for structural purposes, and he had been interested in the potential of the material even earlier. A letter from Breuer in Buenos Aires to Seidler in the New York office in 1947 carried the request for blueprints from engineers Sigman & Farkas "showing details of some of the beamless reinforced concrete structures which they use for apartment houses . . . showing structural details, reinforcing, etc."[57] And it was the moment when Le Corbusier was displacing his purist aesthetic with the plastic, organic effects of rough concrete.

Back in Europe, Breuer also reactivated his pre-American designing past—the bold architectural statements and gestures that had begun with his 1923 project for a mid-rise apartment slab. The De Bijenkorf ("beehive") department store, with its huge street sculpture of architectural scale by Naum Gabo, was comfortably related to prewar European Constructivist art and to Dutch modern architecture; the format of the UNESCO Secretariat was based on the Y-shapes that Breuer had used in Garden City of the Future. Garden City also included a large shopping center, and Breuer had described its stores as "arrayed like the cells of a honeycomb."[58] De Bijenkorf's construction field office (see p. 30) was an elevated network of honeycombs that harmonized with the unified pattern of the facade hexagons, its structure derived from a recreation building that Breuer had imagined in the London prototype. The honeycomb-hexagon was an efficient kind of planning that appealed to Breuer because, as he said, "it allows the greatest amount of space while still adjacent to other space, you can't do this with a circle. Bees, noted for their efficiency, knew this and designed their hives that way." The De Bijenkorf facade, furthermore, was a successful attempt by Breuer to subordinate clearly separated stories in a multistory building to an overall pattern that unified the levels. Features of Breuer's European work, such as the concrete engineering of UNESCO and the hexagons of De Bijenkorf, were, in turn, brought back to refertilize his contemporaneous American projects, accounting for the successful folded-wall construction of Saint John's Abbey Church and for the revised system

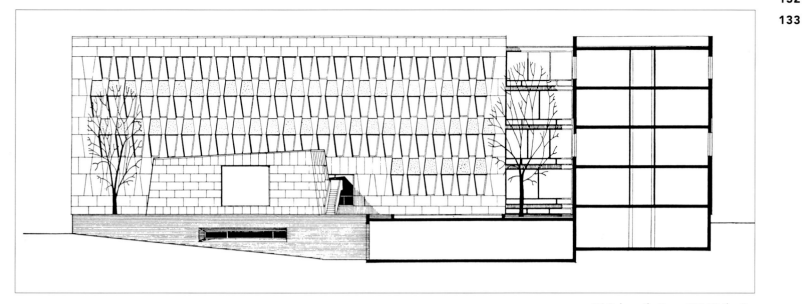

U.S. Embassy, The Hague. 1956–59. Elevation

UNESCO Headquarters, Paris. 1955–58.
Conference Building, folded wall

UNESCO Headquarters, Paris. 1955–58. Secretariat

Breuer (second from left) with associates during
planning of the UNESCO Headquarters, Paris. ca. 1954

Breuer and Gropius in Paris. ca. 1954

of its facade, on which Mondrianesque panels that enframed the stained glass in the original format were transformed into the hexagonal grill of the final design.

Europe also brought him commissions for houses, some—the Staehelin House (1957–58) overlooking the Zürichsee, for example (see p. 34)—of large size at magnificent sites. Perhaps the most dramatic symbol of the return to Europe of architect Breuer was Harnischmacher House II (1954), built in Wiesbaden to replace the original 1932 milestone house, which had been destroyed in the Second World War. It was in a letter from Paul Harnischmacher in 1945 ("the first one I received from occupied countries") that Breuer learned that the original house was gone ("many times I asked myself what happened to the house, my first love"[59]). Writing about the stonework of the new house—designed by Breuer in New York and carried out in Wiesbaden by a local architect— Breuer told Harnischmacher that "our American houses are mostly complete wood structures with a stone or brick veneer ('veneer' is a somewhat misleading American term—it is used for all kinds of facing, even though it is, say 25 or 30 cms. thick)."[60] In what was perhaps a postwar German conciliatory gesture, a civic architectural jury in Wiesbaden awarded a prize to Harnischmacher House II in 1955, and the descriptive language of the award captured those qualities in Breuer villas most valued by his clients: an unpretentious exterior aspect giving on to a series of spaces, open views and terraces, joined to an intimate and secluded garden enclosure.[61] It was to the Harnischmachers that Breuer had written in a jubilant tone in November 1954 that the UNESCO building costs were about $1 million below the estimates: "This is very unusual and good news."[62]

Staehelin House, Feldmeilen, Switzerland. 1957–58

Partners, Marcel Breuer and Associates. 1960s. Left to right: Herbert Beckhard, Robert F. Gatje, Tician Papachristou, and Hamilton P. Smith

MARCEL BREUER AND ASSOCIATES, ARCHITECTS

The prestigious European commissions helped certify Breuer as a leader in the profession in the United States. As the potential of his practice increased, he expanded the office. Beckhard joined in 1952, working for a short period as an unpaid apprentice. He was followed in 1953 by Hamilton Smith and Gatje. Landsberg left in 1954 to open his own office on Long Island, and Breuer hired Murray Emslie to take his place. The organization changed in 1956, when Breuer offered an "associateship" to several of the architects working for him. Not all accepted; Beckhard, Emslie, Gatje, and Smith did, and the firm became known as Marcel Breuer and Associates, Architects, instead of Marcel Breuer, Architect.[63] Breuer remained sole proprietor, but the agreement with his associates stipulated that after ten years they would become partners. In fact, Beckhard, Emslie, and Smith did on January 1, 1964; Gatje followed one year later. In 1967, the partners (except for Emslie, who had withdrawn earlier) became full partners—"equal-equal," said Breuer, who had had a larger share. A new partnership agreement to include Tician Papachristou became effective on January 1, 1974.

Breuer was very protective of his name. The partnership agreement stipulated that if he withdrew because of retirement or disability, or in the event of his death, the firm could be known as The Associates of Marcel Breuer, but if he withdrew voluntarily, all reference to him in the firm name would be eliminated. This was amended later so that if Breuer withdrew and at least two partners remained, they would have the right to use Marcel Breuer and Associates, Architects, for three years. After that, the name could not include any reference to Breuer. Furthermore, if the basic design of a project was completed before he withdrew, Breuer would be identified as one of the architects. If the design was not completed until afterward, one or more of the partners would be identified as architect "in such a way as to avoid attribution of the basic design to Breuer."

Breuer's fastidious attention to the impact of his name on the title of the firm and on the credit for the work reflected the hierarchy of the office. Distinctive contributions by different hands may have been an element in every project, but only one mind and one will directed and controlled the design at every phase and in all its processes. Within that organization, Breuer allowed the contribution of individual associates and partners to be recognized. Smith expressed this approach in a letter in 1972: "[I]t has long been the practice of our office in public announcements to use Mr. Breuer's name and that of the partner who worked with him, in preference to the firm name. We do so in the interest of appearing less impersonal and of better reflecting our manner of working together."[64] The Breuer office culture was misunderstood by David Masello, who, while calling attention to the problem of credit and attribution when creative design was involved, misrepresented the hierarchical organization of the practice when he classified a group of Breuer houses as "Breuer and Beckhard houses."[65] Breuer's associates, later his partners, all made contributions to the designs on which they worked and for which they were credited, but the conceptualization and authorship belonged to, and was understood to have belonged to, Breuer alone.

To a journalist seeking information about office practices, Smith wrote: "In a design-oriented office such as ours, headed as it is by Marcel Breuer, the initiative in establishing the concept remains with the architect [not the client]."[66] An example of Breuer's understanding of his role in relation to the client appears in a letter about an especially difficult job (it ultimately led to arbitration, which was decided in favor of Breuer):

I understand you gave the builder direct instructions to move the garage south window. Though this is not too important a point, I object to it because all instructions to the builder should go through this office as far as the house and my design are concerned. I am afraid we have come to a point where we will have to clarify this matter. It seems to me you ought to make up your mind if you want to build the house yourself or to build it with me. If I am to remain in the picture I must have the responsibility of the architecture and the technical features of the houses. My professional services consist not in taking orders from the client, but to do my best in his interests.[67]

No matter the physical distance of the project from the office, his stance on design control was unwavering: "While it is a pity to lose the opportunity, I am also somewhat relieved: the job was too individual to be so far away," he wrote about a rejected proposal for a California project.[68]

Breuer would sketch a form or a shape, and it was often the responsibility of the project partner to "interpret" that sketch, sometimes in consultation with structural engineers and other technicians, and transform it into a detailed working drawing. When the Koerfer House was in process and a local supervising architect was being sought, Breuer wrote: "The man must have some understanding of my work. The drawings are exact and exhaustive, but still every drawing is open to interpretation."[69]

The benign but tight control that Breuer exercised over his practice, and the cordial disposition of his office (which was often compared with a European atelier), have been documented by his partners, associates, and clients, and by generations of draftsmen and apprentices who worked for him. Scores of letters bear out the image of a self-confident and authoritative Breuer, good at business and management, who ran a practice noted for its lean, nonwasteful cost efficiency. To a potential client on January 31, 1975, the year before he retired, Breuer said that

with all the attention and dedication we give to the architectural nature of our buildings, we are quite close to their cost aspect. While we don't claim to be magicians—especially these unpredictable days—we would like to mention just a few significant cases: NYU campus / 8% below budget; H.U.D. headquarters / 25% below budget; H.E.W. headquarters / 16% below budget. Our cost consciousness is and always has been an integral part of our architectural attitude.[70]

As early as 1949, in a memorandum to the New York City Housing Authority, Breuer had claimed:

The architectural reputation of this office makes possible a special selection of architectural designers and draftsmen. The present staff including the clerical is a tightly knit, unusually productive and reliable organization, which can be rapidly expanded without loss of efficiency. Working drawings, and scheduling of work in this office is studied by many architects and schools, as an example of an economic and effective operation, including supervision of work.[71]

Breuer's practice continued to be studied as a model at least through the 1960s, when it was ranked with the best America offered to the profession. Among his papers is the request for an office visit from a team of Japanese architects traveling through the United States in November 1964 to survey American architecture. Their program included visits to Skidmore, Owings & Merrill to discuss with Gordon Bunschaft "'the design goals of SOM'; to the Seagram Building and Philip Johnson; to Paul Rudolph and Yale; to I. M. Pei in his office to discuss 'the architect and urban design'; to Mies in his office in Chicago; [and] a visit to Marcel Breuer in his office to discuss 'tradition in design.'"[72]

On the matter of the association of the Breuer office with other architects, Breuer wrote to Nervi that

we do this only if the client asks us. Private clients like to have some local architect interested in their project and the U.S. Government likes to associate architects from various locations for political reasons. Otherwise, we like to do our work from the beginning to the end, including construction, etc. in this office by ourselves. The various associations we had and have now with outside architects are based on the principle that the conception of the project, the design and the typical details will be done in this office. The outside office may direct the execution of the project, but in some cases these outside associated offices have also been involved with the preparation of the actual set of complete execution documents—after they have received from us the design and the typical details, also the basic engineering solutions. Generally speaking, our experience with such associations is not bad. On two or three occasions, we had suggestions for associates which we didn't like and we did not accept the job.[73]

A Twentieth-Century "Form-Giver"

The United States Embassy in The Hague was part of a decision made by the State Department in 1954 to "embark on a bold embassy-building program . . . with the stated aim of promoting American prestige abroad and the unstated aim of creating diplomatic monuments to American architectural talent," in the words of Jane C. Loeffler in her study of the government's program.[74] Embassy architects—Edward Larrabee Barnes, Breuer, Gropius, John Johansen, Neutra and Robert Alexander, Eero Saarinen, Sert, Edward Durrell Stone, Hugh Stubbins, John Carl Warnecke, and Harry Weese—represented the core of the modern architecture establishment in the United States in the mid-1950s. (There were, however, notable American architects, members of committees advising the State Department's Foreign Building Operations, who were hostile to the European modernists in the group.[75]) The July 2, 1956, issue of *Time* carried a cover story on Saarinen in which he and twelve other architects, including Breuer (and Wright, Mies, Le Corbusier, Gropius, Neutra, Alvar Aalto, Wallace K. Harrison, Johnson, Skidmore, Owings & Merrill, Stone, and Buckminster Fuller), were named twentieth-century "form-givers." In 1959, the story became a traveling exhibition organized by Cranston Jones for the American Federation of Arts. Breuer's work was represented by the Robinson House, De Bijenkorf, and UNESCO.[76] The exhibition, designed by Kepes, opened on April 23, 1959, at the Corcoran Gallery in Washington, D.C.; the New York preview took place at the Metropolitan Museum of Art on June 8—it would have been the ninetieth birthday of Wright and the date had been set to mark that occasion, but he had died on April 9 and the exhibition became a memorial tribute in his honor.

Members of "the Establishment" were also tapped for the planning of Lincoln Center, one of the most important civic projects to be developed in New York in the mid-1950s. Breuer (along with Aalto, Pietro Belluschi, Sven Markelius, Pei, Henry R. Shepley, Stone, and Skidmore, Owings & Merrill) was recommended by Harrison to be considered as the architect for one of the buildings in the complex and to serve on an advisory design panel. In October 1956, Breuer participated in two weeks of discussions in the office of Harrison & Abramovitz about urban issues raised by the location and design of Lincoln Center. According to the account in *New York 1960* by Robert A. M. Stern, Thomas Mellins, and David Fishman,

some participants advocated creating an introspective place away from the turmoil of the city in the manner of Piazza S. Marco. Other members of the panel, Breuer in particular, accepted the superblock *parti*, but favored a plan that would more fully embrace the city, and he proposed rearranging the buildings around a plaza opening onto Columbus Avenue and Broadway. . . . Breuer subsequently changed his proposal, suggesting an asymmetrical arrangement of buildings around a plaza opening onto 65th street with a broad flight of stairs. . . . Aalto produced a design calling for an internally focused complex punctuated by narrow entryways. Building on this concept, Breuer proposed a narrow continuous building elevated on stilts, with its bottom surface clad in acoustical tile to minimize the intrusion of street noise; the building would define a courtyard opening on to Columbus Avenue.[77]

In her book about Harrison, Victoria Newhouse notes that "led by Breuer, several of the advisory architects expressed their disapproval of the south-north axis's isolation of the plaza, and recommended that the axis be changed to east-west," an orientation that was impossible to achieve because of institutional buildings in its path that could not be torn down.[78] Of these meetings, and issues involved in the choice of architects in 1958, Newhouse remarks that "Breuer, who seemed rigid in his opinions, was generally unpopular."[79]

201 EAST FIFTY-SEVENTH STREET

Breuer was juggling so many challenging projects in the mid-1950s—UNESCO, De Bijenkorf, Saint John's Abbey Church, Hunter College, members' housing at the Institute for Advanced Study in Princeton, the Torin Manufacturing Company in Van Nuys, a large number of houses, and trains and passenger stations for the New York, New Haven, and

Hartford Railroad— that on November 30, 1955, in answer to an inquiry from Giulio Carlo Argan about a possible book project, he wrote that "it would be difficult for me to find the time to assemble the material for a new book. It may serve as my excuse that I am practicing now in three continents and four countries, and have pretty much reached the limit of my own capacities."[80] Argan's inquiry came just as Breuer's profusely illustrated *Sun and Shadow* was published.[81] The book is a visual anthology of Breuer's work, furniture as well as architecture, with statements by Breuer about the nature of architecture that had been recorded in conversations with Blake. Reviews were generally consistent in criticizing the book's peculiar layout (the text is set sideways on the page), suppression of credit to Breuer's collaborators, and pedestrian prose, but the display of his recent architecture, especially the houses, was uniformly welcomed. As always, the furniture ("This stroke of genius which reconciles the opposites of comfort and cold steel," wrote an anonymous reviewer in the London *Times Educational Supplement* of April 5, 1956) was singled out as his greatest contribution to modernism. Argan's own monograph, *Marcel Breuer: Disegno industriale e architettura*, was the result of the award to Breuer in 1955 of the Gran premio internazionale la rinascente compasso d'oro for outstanding industrial design.[82]

By May 1955, employing twelve draftsmen in addition to the associates, Breuer's office was "bursting at the seams," wrote Firmage. To accommodate the needed expansion, at the end of August 1956 Breuer moved the practice from 113 East Thirty-seventh Street to 201 East Fifty-seventh Street.

Saint John's Abbey Church and UNESCO

Breuer's practice in the 1950s was centered around his two major and stylistically cross-referenced projects of the decade—the Saint John's Abbey complex and UNESCO—and by the increasing creative daring of his concrete forms, inspired by Nervi's concrete engineering at UNESCO. He was fully aware of the interdependence of the two works. After he had designed the church at Saint John's Abbey, which in its concrete structure was to be based on the long-span folded-

wall design of UNESCO, he wrote to Abbot Baldwin Dworschak from Paris: "I thought you would be interested to see the enclosed three enlarged snapshots of the Unesco Headquarters under construction . . . the wide spanned structure with the folded end walls and roof system would I believe be of interest to you for the expression they convey. The photos may also help you to visualize our church project."[83]

Early in the evolution of the church design, in the fall of 1953 (working drawings were not begun until January 1957), Hamilton Smith, associate on the project, informed the monastery administration that "Mr. Breuer wants to talk over the structural design of the church with Mr. Nervi while in Paris."[84] Breuer had requested permission from the abbey to allow Nervi to act as consultant with regard to the engineering of the concrete structure of the pleated roof and side walls, a system Breuer used for the interior and exterior of the UNESCO Conference Hall. Although the credit for the engineering brilliance of the concrete work for the Paris building belongs to Nervi, its shape and design are Breuer's. In the spring of 1955, the comprehensive plan for the abbey and a large-scale model of the church, regarded as one of the most significant works of religious architecture in the United States,[85] were displayed for the first time as a museum exhibition at the Walker Art Center in Minneapolis on the occasion of the annual convention of the American Institute of Architects.

It was not only Breuer's work in Europe in the mid-1950s that was structurally and stylistically important for his American projects, but also the experience of Europe itself. Affected in Paris by the pervasive iconic image of the Eiffel Tower—visible from the UNESCO site—in 1956 Breuer revised his design for the campanile of Saint John's, originally conceived in 1954, transforming the closed triangles of the base into wide-curving arcs (see p. 36). A campanile as prominent as Breuer's for Saint John's (and later for the Priory of the Annunciation [1961–63] in Bismarck, North Dakota) emblematized the spiritual as well as the architectural traditions of Catholic Europe, where a monumental campanile would often dominate the silhouette of an ecclesiastical complex. Breuer had been thoroughly briefed about the liturgical and icono-

Saint John's Abbey Church, Collegeville, Minnesota. 1958–61. Campanile

graphic requirements of the Benedictine community, which at every phase required the coordination of the design and the program.

Already accounted for in books and articles about the building of Saint John's was the exceptional harmony between Breuer and the community as well as the continued satisfaction of the community with Breuer as an architect and a person. Most appreciated was "his willingness to learn from us what he felt he needed to know to give us what we wanted," recalled retired Abbot Baldwin Dworschak.[86] Indeed, in no other Breuer buildings was use (and not just function) taken into such careful and precise account as in what he called "our Catholic work," an architecture of community perceived in terms of its symbolism and its purpose in worship and liturgy. From the beginning, the commitment of the abbey was to replace its standard midwestern nineteenth-century Gothic complex with a modern design. After Breuer's plan was submitted to the building committee, its report stated that "[there is] sufficient assurance that responsible Roman authorities do not find Breuer's plan startling, much less alarming."[87]

Breuer thus became one of the leaders in the development of modern Catholic architecture in the United States at its high point in the mid-1950s, a course of events that traced its origins to France and August Perret's reinforced-concrete Notre-Dame (1922–25) at Le Raincy, near Paris.[88] In the summer of 1956, Breuer visited Le Corbusier's recently completed Chapelle Notre-Dame-du-Haut at Ronchamp ("Mediterranean in appearance," he said of it) and, adding support to the Minnesota monastery's affirmation of modernism for its church, reported to the abbot that "I could not detect even a trace of regret that Corbusier was chosen to design the chapel."[89] With an introduction from the abbot at Saint John's, Breuer also visited the historic twelfth-century Benedictine abbey of Maria Laach, south of Cologne, in September 1958.

As impressed as the Benedictine community in Minnesota was with Breuer, he was as strongly impressed by them. In a letter dating from the early stages of the planning process, Breuer wrote:

I can truly state that I have found there the greatest integrity and humanity . . . as a layman it is probably not possible for me to grasp the full depth and scope of their religious thinking, [but] I am convinced that their work and their aims are as profoundly conceived as is humanly possible, and I am personally very much moved by their devotion to a conception of true usefulness and the good of mankind.[90]

The commitment of most of the Saint John's community to architectural modernism was an inspiration to Breuer. In his search for an architect, Abbot Baldwin Dworschak wrote to potential candidates that "we feel that the modern architect with his orientation toward functionalism and honest use of materials is uniquely qualified to produce a Catholic work. In our position it would, we think, be deplorable to build anything less, particularly since our age and our country have thus far produced so little truly significant religious architecture."[91] Responding, Breuer said: "I was especially impressed and moved by your reference to our 'modern architecture.' It is my belief also that the potentialities of this architecture have not been sufficiently recognized up until now, and that generally speaking our religious buildings have not taken full advantage of them."[92] Later, Breuer's English friend and admirer Herbert Read asked for "particulars of the monastery you are building in Minnesota. This is to show the Benedictine monks here in Ampleforth, whose ideas of architecture are derived from [Gothic Revivalist] Giles Gilbert Scott."[93]

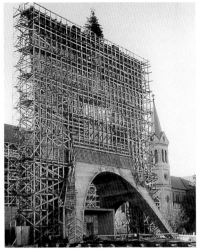

Campanile under construction

Breuer at Saint John's Abbey

Constructing the church at Saint John's was, in some of its aspects, an undertaking reminiscent of the spirit of medieval community architectural enterprises, which had been reflected in Gropius's idea, with its "medieval" resonance, of Bauhaus projects as collaborative craft efforts. According to the Benedictine Rule, in any event, manual labor in Benedictine monasteries has a status equal to that of intellectual work. The monks at Saint John's, therefore, were eager to carry out the physical work whenever possible. This not only led to a spirit of communal enterprise, but was effectively cost efficient since about 20 percent of the labor in the construction of the monastic wing of the monastery complex was undertaken by the monks. Many of them used skills they had already perfected; others learned (as apprentices) new skills while working on the job. In some cases, they were instructed by professional carpenters (who were also farmers from the nearby neighborhoods) who taught them how to lay floors. Wood was cut on monastery land. Along the way, all the workers had to encounter one or another of the new materials used in modern construction, especially concrete.

If the structural materials to which Breuer in his first American phase gave greatest attention were wood and fieldstone, when he returned to Europe his earlier interest in concrete and steel was reanimated. It marked the direction that his architecture would take and set in motion ideas about prefabrication, an interest he could trace back to the experimental methods and materials that had produced Haus am Horn and to the decades when architects had regarded industrially produced, low-cost prefabricated housing as one solution to Germany's most serious social problem after the First World War. To use standardized components fabricated in an assembly-line manner was, at least in theory, a way to build economically. The impetus to revitalize the American building industry through prefabrication immediately following the Second World War withered in the face of opposition from labor unions, building codes that encouraged traditional construction and discouraged standardization, and the public's distrust of the seemingly "temporary" character of prefabricated structures. But the prefabricated construction based on precast concrete that developed in the 1950s and reached an

apogee in the 1960s offered new possibilities to which Breuer was particularly receptive. Standardized elements that were systematic, flexible, and sculptural, and could be efficiently and comparatively inexpensive to produce, lent themselves to additive designs that could be easily expanded or contracted. Breuer adopted the theory and the method wholeheartedly, and while they made possible some of the best work of the late years—the Becton Center at Yale University, for example—they also led to the stultifying and ponderous buildings that signaled the critical eclipse of his reputation.

First Buildings in New York City

In the closing years of the 1950s, Breuer built his first buildings in New York City—on the Bronx campus of Hunter College and on the University Heights campus of New York University. The Hunter College model was shown in the summer and fall of 1957 in "America Builds," an exhibition in Berlin about the American building industry sponsored by the U.S. government and designed by Peter Blake. It was by way of Saint John's Abbey that the Hunter College commission came to Breuer. Arthur Schiller, chief architect for the Board of Higher Education of the City of New York, "knew of our Catholic work," as Breuer said, through the Catholic lay press and friends at Saint John's. At Hunter's library building, Breuer began his exploration of the large-span shells of the hyperbolic paraboloid and the structure-as-design system and fluid spatial properties they suggested. The Hunter job prompted from Breuer a significant comment on context in response to a letter in which his buildings, inserted into their collegiate Gothic surroundings, were praised:

The problem of harmonizing a new building with another architectural style surrounding it comes up again and again. I had to face this situation not only with Hunter College, but in my Embassy Building at The Hague, Holland, and the Unesco building in Paris. As a matter of fact, thoughts in this direction were somewhat more justified in the latter two cases, because the surroundings are truly historical and not, to begin with, an imitation style. My own point of view is that no such thing as "harmonizing" exists, and that everything harmonizes if it is on a certain level. The best example of this is the Piazza San Marco in Venice. It would be difficult to imagine more clashingly varying styles than are represented there, three of them next to each other, and resulting in the most photographed and most visited place in the world. There are certain means of architecture which can be used as connecting bridges between "styles" or "periods." For instance, the material used for the facing of the building, or a general feeling of scale (larger or smaller scale as the case may be) though even these means of architectural expression should not be used to "harmonize" without realizing the inherent danger of falsification of ideas.[94]

The end of the 1950s—Breuer's fabulous decade—also brought its share of problems. One was a serious structural crisis that temporarily threatened the stability of the roof of the church at Saint John's. Another was the basic error he made in failing to realize—as he expanded into the big projects in the years just preceding the universal application of air-conditioning—that in the new, large office buildings of Europe, with their huge expanses of glass and without the protective thermal insulation that came from the thickness of traditional masonry, the theory of heat control through sunscreens, like those used in his houses and small industrial and institutional buildings at a time when expectations of comfort were lower, would not work. He suffered from assaults on this and other issues of design at UNESCO Headquarters by critics of the stature of Lewis Mumford. It was the beginning of a perception that Breuer was more successful with works of small or medium scale than with large-scale structures. Individual clients also had complaints. In April 1964, he heard from Oscar Van Leer in Amstelveen about temperature control in his office building, one of Breuer's most beautiful designs, built eight years earlier:

The immediate purpose of writing this letter is to advise you of the most unsatisfactory ventilation and climatological conditions which exist in our building. For many years we have had nothing but complaints from our personnel, which we hoped would blow over as time went on, but which, on the contrary have become more serious and better founded. . . . We have been consulting . . . for the purpose of determining what would be the simplest and most efficient way to solve our ventilation problems.[95]

Still, the essential Breuer prevailed, confident and inventive, successful and sought after, riding the crest of America's international leadership in architecture. Looking back in 1989 to the selection of Breuer for the great conventual complex he had created for her community in the early 1960s at the Priory of the Annunciation in Bismarck, North Dakota, former Prioress Sister Edane Volk said: "Had we gone to a local architect we would have gotten just another square building." [96]

Van Leer office building, Amstelveen, the Netherlands. 1957–58. Entrance

1   Marcel Breuer, "Autobiography," SUL 39.

2   Breuer to a job applicant, March 25, 1946, Correspondence, AAA.

3   Mrs. A. W. Thompson to Breuer, quoting her son Rolland, ca. February 15, 1947, SUL 41.

4   Harry Seidler, taped interview with Constance L. Breuer, January 2, 1985, transcription by author, AAA.

5   George S. Lewis, conversation with author.

6   Eliot Noyes to Mrs. A. W. Thompson, August 15, 1947, SUL 21.

7   Breuer to Arnold Potter, February 4, 1949, SUL 28.

8   Breuer to Father Cloud Meinberg, January 27, 1955, Correspondence, AAA.

9   Material on road-building project, 1946, SUL 52.

10 Breuer to Eduardo Catalano, March 17, 1947, SUL 39.

11 Marcel Breuer, memorandum on hospital in Ithaca, New York, in September 1948, SUL 152.

12 Marcel Breuer, memorandum, February 10, 1953, UNESCO file, AAA.

13 Joachim Driller, "Marcel Breuer: Das architektonische Frühwerk bis 1950" (Phil. diss., Albert-Ludwigs-Universität, Freiburg, 1990); *Marcel Breuer: Die Wohnhäuser, 1923–1973* (Stuttgart: Deutsche Verlags-Anstalt, 1998); and *Breuer Houses*, trans. Mark Cole and Jeremy Verrinder (London: Phaidon Press, 2000).

14 Richard Pratt to Breuer, December 13, 1944, SUL 51.

15 David Halberstam, *The Fifties* (New York: Villard Books, 1993), 131.

16 Breuer to Margaret Firmage, January 26, 1955, Correspondence, AAA.

17 Janet Temos, "The Preston Robinson House in Williamstown, Massachusetts" (Paper, Williams College Graduate Seminar, 1991).

18 Ibid.; Witold Rybczynski, *Home: A Short History of an Idea* (New York: Penguin, 1987).

19 Rybczynski, *Home*, 202.

20 Quoted in Peter Coe and Malcolm Reading, *Lubetkin and Tecton: Architecture and Social Commitment* (London: Arts Council of Great Britain, 1981), 117.

21 Adam Clem, "The City in Miniature: From Chair to Building in the Work of Marcel Breuer" (art history thesis, Vassar College, 1993).

22 Vincent Scully, "Doldrums in the Suburbs," in Modern Architecture Symposium (MAS 1964): The Decade 1929–1939," *Journal of the Society of Architectural Historians* 24 (1965): 40.

23 Museum of Modern Art, *The Museum of Modern Art Builds a House* [pamphlet announcing the Breuer house] (New York: Museum of Modern Art, ca. 1948), SUL 23.

24 Quoted in "American Gift," *New Yorker*, March 5, 1949, 26.

25 Peter Blake, *No Place Like Utopia: Modern Architecture and the Company We Kept* (New York: Knopf, 1993), 137.

26 Museum of Modern Art, interim report, May 12, 1948, Henry-Russell Hitchcock Archive, Department of Fine Arts, New York University; see also Blake, *No Place Like Utopia*, 136–43.

27 MoMA interim report.

28 Elizabeth A. T. Smith, ed., *Blueprints for Modern Living: History and Legacy of the Case Study Houses* [exhibition catalogue] (Cambridge, Mass.: MIT Press, 1989).

29 Peter Blake, *Marcel Breuer: Architect and Designer* (New York: Museum of Modern Art, 1949).

30 Herbert Beckhard, conversation with author.

31 On the evolution of the formal language of Breuer's residential architecture (as well as that of Richard Neutra, Rudolph Schindler, and Gregory Ain) into an American cultural phenomenon based on commercialism and consumerism and defined as "Good-Life Modernism," see the brilliant study by Mark Jarzombek, "'Good-Life Modernism' and Beyond, the American House in the 1950s and 1960s: A Commentary," *Cornell Journal of Architecture* 4 (1990): 76–93.

32 J. D. Stubbins, Allied Chemical and Dye Corporation, memorandum, "Suggested Roof Edging Detail, Mr. Marcel Breuer, Internationally Famous Architect," to W. L. Bartlett, November 7, 1949, SUL 38.

33 The first contact between the Stillmans and Breuer was a letter from Leslie Stillman to Breuer: "Dear Mr. Breuer, we have been living in Litchfield for three years and now that we are settled in we want very much to buy a piece of property here and build ourselves a house. We own an old farmhouse which we're trying very hard to sell and we have found four acres of land which we're trying very hard to buy. Neither is accomplished yet. We've seen the house you did for the Modern Museum and pictures of your house in New Canaan which we like tremendously. My brother, Harry Caesar, says you have designed other houses in New Canaan and we were wondering if we could possibly make a date to come down and talk with you some Saturday or Sunday and perhaps see your house. Would it be at all convenient the first part of May?" (Leslie Stillman to Breuer, ca. April 1950, SUL 34).

34 Client to Breuer, January 11, 1950, SUL 11.

35 Richard Plunz, *A History of Housing in New York City: Dwelling Type and Social Change in the American Metropolis* (New York: Columbia University Press, 1990), 260.

36 Marcel Breuer, Architect's Qualification Roster, October 21, 1949, SUL 51.

37 Marcel Breuer, "Stuyvesant Six: A Redevelopment Study," *Pencil Points*, June 1944, 68–70, 102, 118.

38 Eduardo Catalano to Breuer, April 23, 1947, SUL 39.

39 Breuer to Eduardo Catalano, March 17, 1947, SUL 39.

40 Contract, SUL 39.

41 Breuer to Charles Burchard, July 22, 1947, SUL 39.

42 Catalano to Breuer, April 23, 1947.

43 Alvaro Ortega to Breuer, May 18, 1947, SUL 39.

44 Marcel Breuer, list of "major works," 1949, SUL 39.

45 Alvaro Ortega to Breuer, June 13, 1948, SUL 39.

46 Eduardo Catalano to Breuer, March 11, 1948, SUL 39.

47 Marcel Breuer, "What Is Happening to Modern Architecture?" *Museum of Modern Art Bulletin* 15 (1948): 15; *Arts & Architecture*, May 1948, 31; and Blake, *Marcel Breuer*, 122.

48 Marc Treib, "William Wilson Wurster: The Feeling of Function," in *An Everyday Modernism: The Houses of William Wurster*, ed. Marc Treib [exhibition catalogue, San Francisco Museum of Modern Art] (Berkeley: University of California Press, 1995), 60.

49 Breuer, "What Is Happening to Modern Architecture?"

50 Abraham & Straus Company, press release, SUL 41.

51 William H. Jordy, "The Domestication of Modern: Marcel Breuer's Ferry Cooperative Dormitory at Vassar College," in *American Buildings and Their Architects: The Impact of European Modernism in the Mid-Twentieth Century* (Garden City, N.Y.: Doubleday, 1972), 165–219.

52 Sarah Gibson Blanding to Breuer, October 24, 1949, SUL 35.

53 Whitney S. Stoddard, *Adventures in Architecture: Building the New Saint John's* (New York: Longmans, Green, 1958).

54 Breuer to Hawkins Ferry, July 14, 1952, SUL 38.

55 Breuer to Walter Gropius, July 9, 1953, UNESCO file, AAA.

56 The Five were Le Corbusier (France), Lucio Costa (Brazil), Gropius (United States), Sven Markelius (Sweden), and Ernesto Rogers (Italy). Eero Saarinen was the consultant to the panel.

57   Breuer to Harry Seidler, August 3, 1947, SUL 39.

58   Clipping, "Designer Here Plans Stores Like Interior of Honeycomb," *Boston* [name obliterated], July 19, 1938, SUL 49.

59   Breuer to Paul Harnischmacher, August 18, 1945, Correspondence, AAA.

60   Breuer to Paul Harnischmacher, August 19, 1953, SUL 152.

61   Award for Harnischmacher House II, 1955, SUL 152.

62   Breuer to Paul and Marianne Harnischmacher, November 17, 1954, SUL 152.

63   Information about the partnership agreements comes from files donated by Constance L. Breuer to SUL in 1994.

64   Hamilton Smith to Walter Everett, American Press Institute, February 9, 1972, SUL 89.

65   David Masello, *Architecture Without Rules: The Houses of Marcel Breuer and Herbert Beckhard* (New York: Norton, 1993); see also Christine Benglia Bevington, review of *Architecture Without Rules*, by David Masello, *Interior Design*, July 1994, 61–63.

66   Hamilton Smith to Robert Finn, *Cleveland Plain Dealer*, May 13, 1969, SUL 93.

67   Breuer to a client, May 24, 1950, SUL 24.

68   Breuer to Huson Jackson, October 5, 1955, Correspondence, AAA.

69   Breuer to T. Szekely, June 16, 1964, SUL 80. ·

70   Breuer to a client, January 31, 1975, Correspondence, AAA.

71   Marcel Breuer, memorandum to New York City Housing Authority, October 21, 1949, SUL 51.

72   Request to visit Breuer office, 1964, Correspondence, AAA.

73   Breuer to Pier Luigi Nervi, June 26, 1967, Zehrfuss folder, UNESCO file, AAA.

74   Jane C. Loeffler, "The Architecture of Diplomacy: Heyday of the United States Embassy-Building Program,1954–1960," *Journal of the Society of Architectural Historians* 49 (1990): 251, 257. This was followed by her important and well-researched book, in which Breuer's embassy building is given more extensive analysis: *The Architecture of Diplomacy: Building America's Embassies* (New York: Princeton Architectural Press, 1998), esp. 212–17.

75   Loeffler, *Architecture of Diplomacy*, 163–85. Ralph Walker, for example, who had been president of the AIA in the early 1950s and had gone on record with essays and letters condemning Gropius, the Bauhaus, and CIAM, detested the embassy that Breuer ultimately built in The Hague, calling it "pure unadulterated and vulgar ugliness" (ibid., 216).

76   "The Maturing Modern," *Time*, July 2, 1956, 50–57; Cranston Jones, ed., *Form Givers at Mid-Century* [exhibition catalogue] (New York, 1959), 36–39.

77   Robert A. M. Stern, Thomas Mellins, and David Fishman, *New York 1960: Architecture and Urbanism Between the Second World War and the Bicentennial* (New York: Monacelli Press, 1995), 681, n. 45.

78   Victoria Newhouse, *Wallace K. Harrison, Architect* (New York: Rizzoli, 1989), 190, 193.

79   Ibid., 193.

80   Breuer to Giulio Carlo Argan, November 30, 1955, Correspondence, AAA.

81   Marcel Breuer, *Marcel Breuer: Sun and Shadow: The Philosophy of an Architect*, ed. Peter Blake (New York: Dodd, Mead, 1955).

82   Giulio Carlo Argan, *Marcel Breuer: Disegno industriale e architettura* (Milan: Görlich, 1957).

83   Breuer to Abbot Baldwin Dworschak, July 30, 1956, SUL 108.

84   Hamilton Smith to Reverend Cloud Meinberg, September 2, 1953, SUL 109.

85   Albert Christ-Janer and Mary Mix Foley, *Modern Church Architecture: A Guide to the Form and Spirit of 20th Century Religious Building* (New York: McGraw-Hill, 1962).

86   Abbot Baldwin Dworschak, conversation with author.

87   "Comments by the Church Committee [for the new building] on Various Comments in Father Cloud's [Meinberg] Report," n.d. [ca. 1956], SUL 105.

88   Christ-Janer and Mix Foley, *Modern Church Architecture*, 4.

89   Breuer to Abbot Baldwin Dworschak, July 30, 1956.

90   Breuer to Margaret H. Kelly, November 15, 1953, SUL 109.

91   Abbot Baldwin Dworschak to Breuer, March 4, 1953, SUL 108.

92   Breuer to Abbot Baldwin Dworschak, March 14, 1953, SUL 108.

93   Herbert Read to Breuer, August 13, 1955, Correspondence, AAA.

94   Breuer to Charles W. Millard, Jr., May 22, 1957, Correspondence, AAA.

95   Oscar Van Leer to Breuer, April 29, 1964, travel file, SUL.

96   Prioress Sister Edane Volk, conversation with author.

I believe the architect can fully express himself as an artist by means of concrete.

Marcel Breuer,
interview with *Schokbeton*,
October 1973

6. New York:
The Later Work, 1960–76

IN THE BOOM YEARS OF THE 1960S, Breuer's practice was active and prosperous. Succeeding beyond his most ambitious hopes, he moved the office from 201 East Fifty-seventh Street to larger quarters at 635 Madison Avenue in June 1965. The previous year, he had opened an office in Paris directed by Robert Gatje to handle the firm's increasing European business. Before a Paris office could be established, Breuer had to jump some legal hurdles so he could belong to France's Ordre des architectes. An architectural diploma was needed, and, from the point of view of the French, he did not have a proper diploma from the Bauhaus; finally, in November 1964, he was admitted.[1] Following the completion of Gatje's tenure in 1966, Mario Jossa took over the direction of the Paris office after an interim administration by Eric Cercler.

Hunter College Library, Bronx, New York. 1957–60.
Hyperbolic paraboloid roof

MODERNISM AFTER MIDCENTURY

In the United States, the federal government commissioned Breuer to design important buildings in Washington, D.C., in the 1960s and 1970s, notably (in collaboration with Nolen-Swinburne) new headquarters for the Department of Housing and Urban Development (HUD, originally Housing and Home Finance Agency) and the Department of Health, Education, and Welfare (HEW, now Health and Human Services). The power plant and forebay dam on the Columbia River at Grand Coulee, Washington, was also a government project, carried out under the auspices of the Bureau of Reclamation of the Department of the Interior. Again for the Department of the Interior, Breuer designed the (unexecuted) Oglala Community High School in Pine Ridge, South Dakota, as part of a government initiative to improve educational facilities for the Native American population of the Pine Ridge Reservation.[2]

The architectural press regarded the commissioning of the HUD building to Breuer as an example of a government effort to improve the quality of federal architecture.[3] In June 1962, President John F. Kennedy had issued to heads of all federal agencies a directive, "Guiding Principles for Federal Architecture," calling for "designs which embody the finest contemporary American architectural thought."[4] Both of Breuer's federal buildings were admired within the profession for their structural innovations and creative technology. HUD, built on a 5.5-acre site in Washington's southwest renewal area, where office and apartment buildings were restricted to a height of eight or ten stories, was one of the first federal buildings to be constructed with precast concrete. Based on a 10-foot module, it was formed of more than 1,500 precast load-bearing window units (each holding the thermal mechanism for heating and cooling) over tapered pilotis spaced along 40-foot centers. Most satisfying to the General Services Administration was its completion for millions of dollars less than the estimate and the appropriations.

For institutional clients, such as the Priory of the Annunciation in Bismarck, North Dakota, and the Whitney Museum of American Art and Cleveland Museum of Art, and for private clients like the Stillmans and the Koerfers who wanted houses, Breuer did some of his best work during this period. It was not the case when it came to corporate projects and real-estate development. The Breuer office had geared itself to respond to the accelerating demand for blockbuster corporate headquarters (advances in construction technology had made 60- to 100-story buildings a matter of course)[5] and for large urban-renewal developments, where housing projects were conceived on the scale of corporate commercial buildings. But while the weighty Expressionist mode that Breuer now favored worked well for churches, museums, height-restricted federal office buildings, and even houses, it was inapposite to the commercial and residential towers he was asked to design.

For his powerfully flexed "Brutalist" concrete structures, which coexisted with the floating, transparent slabs and glass-and-metal curtain-wall boxes that dominated the architectural landscape in the 1960s, Breuer was regarded at the Graduate School of Design as "one of the leaders of the recent massive, sculptural trend in design." Interviewed for the fall 1966 issue of *Connection, Visual Arts at Harvard* on the subject of the interrelation of sculpture with architecture, he was asked: "Do you think that architecture has recently become more sculptural in its own right?" "I think this is a fact, yes," he said.

I think it is the change of the architect's conception of architecture. In the twenties or the thirties the architect wanted to create a completely bodiless space because space was the new invention. And this space was to be as little material as possible. There was a thin structure, a thin skin, transparent, only space; only how many steps you make from one enclosure to another, this is space . . . architecture is something rather abstract, floating and immaterial. After we did some of these spaces, on account of some inner need which you call the development or change of the spirit of the time, mass appealed to us, gravity, solidity, a wall you can lean against and not just a glass wall, which limits your movement. And this change has pushed architecture into what we call a more sculptural concept of architecture. Because architects noticed that with all these ethereal elements they still deal with masses, they still have columns which in a fifty story building on the lower stories are still pretty heavy masses. So consequently the handling of mass is still there. And you don't get away from it, you cannot completely eliminate it.[6]

Breuer was committed to architectural mass and to the concrete that gave it expression, and he had an abiding faith in systems of standardization. This, together with his inveterate respect for a client's budget, led him to make design choices based less on aesthetics than on economy, on what Tician Papachristou remembers as his "European 1920s fear of cost." "It was admirable," Papachristou said, "but it eventually ended up hurting his image at a time when there was a new affluence, and a new 'the-hell-with it' attitude about cost."[7] Cost efficient as prefabricated units of reinforced concrete repeated in series may have been, they tended to produce monotonous corporate boxes or, as his HUD headquarters was described, "too many precast windows on concrete perches."[8] When he used a tower-slab format for housing rather than for offices, the results were more satisfactory because the requisite terraces and balconies gave him greater opportunity to manipulate the rhythms, plasticity, and chiaroscuro of the facades. It was an irony of his career that the slab format, developed for the first time in 1923 by Breuer for economical multiple-family housing, became his creative dead end in its application to the office towers of his late years. But he was in the business of architecture, and he was responsive to the market.

Three important and highly visible projects—cultural, commercial, and commemorative, two in New York and one in Washington, D.C.—generated resonant public response to Breuer during the sixties. When the Whitney Museum of American Art (see p. 173), Breuer's only building in Manhattan, opened to the public on September 27, 1966, it was clear that by "forming the building as a sculpture," as he described it,[9] on a small plot on Manhattan's residential Upper East Side among mostly traditional buildings, he had more than met the challenge to design a distinctive structure. Criticized at first for its assertive appearance and a lack of respect for its neighborhood, the building was nevertheless regarded as a museological success.

Almost simultaneously, Breuer was censured in New York for his willingness to accept a commission to build 175 Park Avenue (Grand Central Tower), a fifty-five-story structure above Grand Central Terminal, whose almost 2 million square feet of valuable air rights were irresistible to commercial devel

Breuer at the Whitney Museum of American Art, New York. 1967

175 Park Avenue (Grand Central Tower), New York. 1967–69 (not built). Rendering

"We think Marcel Breuer really has it licked now."

opers. Breuer tried the design twice. First came a massive high-rise "floating" awkwardly above the terminal's land-marked Beaux-Arts facade in a halfhearted attempt to pre-serve the historic structure below and satisfy the Landmarks Preservation Commission (LPC). When it was rejected by the LPC, he produced a second and more honest version, sup-planting the Beaux-Arts building altogether; it was also reject-ed. When a photograph of Breuer with a rendering of the first solution appeared in the *New York Times* in February 1968, the project was generally greeted with scorn. It was described in the June 29 issue of the *New Yorker* as "an elongated meat cleaver descending on a prune soufflé," and as "Pelion on Ossa" when *Engineering News-Record* reached into Homeric legend to find a metaphor for piling one huge mass on top of another.[10] It soon provoked biting cartoons, such as the one in the *New Yorker* of July 6 showing the terminal on top of the tower with the caption "We think Mr. Breuer really has it licked now."

As it turned out, the rejection of his proposals for 175 Park Avenue, and a United States Supreme Court decision ten years later in favor of the position taken by the LPC, saved Breuer from becoming one of New York's villains of architecture and from being tied forever to Walter Gropius, not for the noble history they shared at the Bauhaus and at Harvard but as designers of two of the city's worst (and adjacent) commercial towers. The Pan Am Building (now Met Life), coauthored by Gropius, Pietro Belluschi, and Emery Roth & Sons, is almost universally regarded today as "the veritable icon of bad sixties architecture."[11] In an article on New York City architecture of the 1960s from the perspective of the 1990s, *New York Times* architecture critic Herbert Muschamp wrote:

Thirty years ago, the cityscape found room for works by Mies van der Rohe, Wallace Harrison, Eero Saarinen, Marcel Breuer, Frank Lloyd Wright, Walter Gropius and Gordon Bunshaft. Not all of their buildings were great; some were terrible. But what they contributed was much more than a handful of potential future landmarks. Even the worst of their projects, like the Pan Am Building, helped create a picture of the city as an open-ended, ongoing project.[12]

In New York's thriving commercial-architecture scene, 175 Park Avenue had received exceptional attention in the press for its appearance and for the urban issues it raised—subway crowding and pedestrian flow on the one hand (the impact of a large new building in the already dense commercial zone of Grand Central Terminal), and architectural preservation on the other. It is well known within the culture of New York urban affairs that, in the words of Philip Johnson, "The fight to stop Breuer from building that 55 story tower over Grand Central was really what put teeth into the Landmarks Commission."[13] The LPC, the first New York landmarks law, and the movement for architectural preservation were born out of the backlash from the demolition in 1962 and 1963 of the great Pennsylvania Station (1910), designed by McKim, Mead, and White, with few efforts to save it. In this context, Breuer's second project for 175 Park Avenue, which would have destroyed the Beaux-Arts facade of Grand Central Terminal, was regarded as yet another "appalling mistake," coming only a few years after the destruction of Pennsylvania Station.

The Pan Am Building understandably stimulated in Breuer the rivalrous ambition to succeed where the Gropius team, even at the time, clearly had failed. There was, furthermore, the prospect of a more than $2 million fee for Breuer and his associates, whose livings, after all, were earned through architecture. The exceptionally important location of the tower would also soothe Breuer's feelings, often expressed, about the remote locations of his best works. But his high standing in the professional community was put in jeopardy because of 175 Park Avenue. Old friends and admirers parted with him on the issue; the American Institute of Architects voted against it; the Municipal Arts Society opposed it. He came out of the polemic still intact only because, in the opinion of most of his peers, "he was a good guy who made a terrible mistake."[14]

The invitation to design a presidential monument in Washington, D.C., in memory of Franklin Delano Roosevelt was, in a national sense, Breuer's most prestigious commission. It followed almost immediately the completion of the Whitney, the renown of having designed a New York City museum not lost on either the FDR Memorial Commission or the artists and critics drawn from the uppermost strata of the country's cultural leadership who were the members of the

Commission of Fine Arts, "arbiters of the nation's taste in public architecture."[15] Contrary to all signs and expectations, however, his proposal failed to win their approval. Members of the commission were alienated by their contradictory perception of, on the one hand, "dated" elements of the design that harked back to early modernism and, on the other, an unwelcome intrusion by the new phenomenon of Pop Art and its Happenings (an image of Roosevelt on a granite surface reproducing the Ben Day dots of a photo enlargement, hidden loudspeakers carrying excerpts from Roosevelt's speeches), although nothing was further from Breuer's mind. It is clear also, from the tone of their discussion recorded in the unpublished minutes of the meetings, that the enormous weight of judging a piece of public art so consequential and already so controversial contributed to their uncertainty. On January 27, 1967, the Commission of Fine Arts issued a press release announcing the failure of the project to meet "the highest standard of artistic achievement." Breuer's proposal was reconsidered two years later and again rejected. People close to him remember this as his greatest professional disappointment.[16]

The decade had begun for Breuer with a trip in the fall of 1961 to Tokyo and Hong Kong by way of San Francisco, where he visited William Wurster, and then on to Karachi and Rawalpindi for meetings with Pakistani architects and authorities about projects for the new capital at Islamabad. The 1960s also began for Breuer with judgments about the UNESCO complex appearing in the critical literature. There were a few favorable reviews, but they were exceptions.[17] Most appraisals within a few years of the completion of the complex were denunciatory ("would that [Le Corbusier] had also done Unesco," wrote G. H. Kidder Smith[18]), and none more than Lewis Mumford's, which served also as an indictment of what he believed modernism had become in the 1950s and 1960s.[19] Calling UNESCO "an instructive failure" and blaming the clients and the program as well as the architects—"The major errors of the United Nations buildings in New York were committed for a second time by the same agency"[20]—he saw in it "all the mistakes of the modern movement assembled in one set of buildings."[21] A basic error in New York, repeated in Paris, was allowing the Secretariat (an office building, the glorification of a bureaucratic idea) instead of the Conference Building, which Mumford admired in purpose and design, to dominate the composition. In Paris, the shape and sweep of the "characterless" but dominant Secretariat concealed the Conference Building and destroyed the coherence of the site.[22] Mumford criticized as modernist clichés the pilotis, the steel-frame-and-glass-wall format, and the sunscreens of the Secretariat; works of art selected to complement the architecture—a Calder mobile (ca. 1935), for example, he regarded as a "dusty period piece."[23] By calling attention to the glass sheathing and what he called the "hothouse mode of construction," Mumford touched a nerve, as Breuer (who had not used huge expanses of glass before UNESCO) was bearing the burden of serious complaints about ineffective heat control despite the sliding panels and the bands of solar glass and *brise-soleil* on the facades that faced the sun. Mumford gave most of the credit for the concrete work and sculptural quality of the Conference Building, "as finely molded as a scallop shell," to Pier Luigi Nervi, "the most imaginative and daring exploiter of the new methods of thin concrete-shell construction."[24] The design of the Conference Building, however—a signature Breuer combination using Nilotic imagery (the mastaba) with a butterfly roof—was criticized by Mumford in almost the same terms that Klaus Herdeg would use ten years later about the angled roof of Breuer's MoMA exhibition house: "the roof sags with a kind of inverted emphasis precisely where the entrance from the street should suggest the opposite movement of elevation."[25] The long expanse of the Secretariat, however, reaffirmed Breuer's belief in the Y-shape as the most efficient design for institutional structures, and he used it often—for HUD, and IBM in La Gaude, France, and Boca Raton, Florida (see p. 176)—because it allowed for a lot of offices and a lot of light and, where the curves meet, a central service core.

Within the critical culture of the 1960s, two of Breuer's most important designs were, therefore, already seen to represent a kind of stale modernism: the Roosevelt memorial, with its Bauhaus origins, and UNESCO, with both the Y-shape of the Secretariat and the trapeze form of the Conference Building in his repertoire since 1936. Other Breuer projects,

too, would eventually come under fire from critics, architectural historians, and younger architects coming of age in the revolutionary decade that was turning its back on modernism. In a business sense, Breuer may have been at the height of his success, but critically and historically he was beginning to recede into the background.

Still, in the 1960s there were many, rather than fewer, clients who valued their association with Breuer and who admired his particular modernist idiom and efficient office operation, clients such as New York University (see p. 175). Pleased by the first constructed phase of a comprehensive plan mapped out for its University Heights campus, NYU felt that Breuer had produced "four distinguished buildings which architecturally speaking are . . . excellent examples of contemporary solutions for American collegiate buildings."[26] The Bard Award for Merit in Urban Architecture, given by the City Club of New York, was presented in 1964 to Breuer's cantilevered Begrisch Hall for New York University. The City Club press release pointed out that "while other universities in the U.S. have recently shown much imagination and courage in commissioning first-rate architecture, the many universities and college-level institutions in New York City have done very little to lead the rest of the community in this field. New York University is one of the very few exceptions to this rule."[27]

An earlier exception had been Breuer's library, classroom, and administrative buildings for Hunter College, admired and commended by Ada Louis Huxtable as a "superior civic-sponsored design." In her article in the *New York Times* generated by the announcement of the HUD commission, she referred to Breuer as "the forgotten man in New York's current civic architecture controversy" and wrote that the government's choice "put the spotlight" on him and on the buildings at Hunter. She lamented that when the City Club had issued a "no award" for excellent design in municipal construction the previous year, the Hunter project had not been submitted to the competition.[28]

A year later, possibly influenced by Huxtable's comments, the City Club gave its award to Begrisch Hall. The building was singled out also by the Concrete Industry Board in admiration of Breuer's skills in exploiting the possibilities of reinforced concrete. From a post-1960s point of view, however, the NYU

Begrisch Hall, New York University, University Heights, New York. 1967–70

buildings and their material suffered a decline in critical opinion and were described by Elliott Willensky and Norval White in the *AIA Guide to New York City* as a "concrete pomposity."[29] In 1977, HUD administrator Lawrence O. Houstoun, Jr., published an evaluation, mostly favorable, of the HUD building after a decade of use, but he noted that "there is nothing big enough and green enough to soften the overall image of concreteness." Moreover, the "exposed aggregate and other concrete interior finishes remain unpopular," he said, and "some see in them an unfinished look."[30]

Sculptor in Concrete

Concrete—reinforced with metal to give it tensile strength along with its normal strength in compression, the grain of the wooden forms in which it was poured creating a permanent bas-relief texture on its otherwise smooth surface—was the material Breuer loved most. "The greatest esthetic design potential in concrete," he said, "is found through interrupting the plane in such a way that sunlight and shadow will enhance its form, while through changing exposure a building will appear differently at various moments of the day."[31] Reinforced concrete had a comparatively late start in the United States, at least among the contractors Breuer worked with in the 1950s. In 1953, when he was designing the third-floor addition to the Abraham & Straus department store in Hempstead, New York, he received a letter from the district engineer in the large company of builders and engineers responsible for the construction, thanking him "for the edifying experience of working with you" and saying that "there was mention of prestressed concrete design at our last meeting, and it must have been obvious that I was completely unfamiliar with the [techniques] involved. Professional publications have been interested [in it] since the war; as to [our company's] experience . . . it is as yet conservative."[32] Papachristou pointed out:

[T]here was always if not a hostility at least an apprehension in the United States about concrete—technically and in terms of its visual popularity. Concrete can invoke the notion of something unfinished and undressed. The postmodernists attacked it right away, and found an audience who had always been nervous about it. Concrete needs to be kept up, and needs not to be relentless, as in the Whitney where it is combined with granite.

Breuer described concrete as a material that is "universal and serves all the basic functions of a building, architecturally as well as structurally. This is in contrast to steel, the potential of which is to provide the building structure to which other materials have to be added."[33] When, in the mid-1950s, Breuer was working out his plans for using reinforced concrete at Saint John's Abbey Church, he wrote to Abbot Baldwin Dworschak:

[S]peaking in rather general terms, three and a half years ago [ca. 1953] most American engineers . . . were rather critical about reinforced concrete structures compared with steel structures. . . . The situation since has changed quite considerably. Due to the Korean War and to steel restrictions, quite a few buildings were re-designed for reinforced concrete. Our engineers are better acquainted with it now than they were four or five years ago. We no longer encounter difficulties when we ask them to consider a reinforced concrete structure; sometimes quite the contrary.[34]

He went on to talk about how reinforced-concrete structure affected costs: "Our concrete is exposed and the structural form, according to experts, is desirable from an acoustical point of view. Thus we eliminate hanging ceilings, plastering of ceilings and walls, and acoustic treatment."

Concrete may have been a workaday material for budget-minded institutions, but Breuer, trained to bring out the best in less expensive materials, was able to elevate it to high levels of expressiveness by exploiting its possibilities for formal invention, dramatic cantilevers, and wide, uninterrupted interior expanses. That concrete parts could be mass-produced also appealed to him because he remained true to his Bauhaus-born belief in prefabrication, adjusting it through the decades to varied materials and changing technologies. By the 1960s, he had become a major prefabrication architect, defining most of his institutional buildings by way of precast-concrete forms. Breuer's partners understood the limitations this imposed, but took an objective view. Hamilton Smith traced the appeal of the single precast units for Breuer to the same source that had given him the inspiration in the 1930s to mold furniture from a single piece of plywood. A sun-shading device may once have been an added element for Breuer in a concrete window-wall panel, but eventually it was united with the panel, which became window and sunscreen and exterior and interior all at once.[35] Papachristou observed that for Breuer, precast units were, above all, the expression of functional demands: "For example, in the window it had to be possible to put in the air-conditioning mechanism, it had to have a certain angle at the top to cast a maximum shadow on the glass, a certain kind of scoring of the surface so that the water wouldn't run down and dirty the glass; the panel had to be shaped so it could be removed without any friction with adjacent vertical surfaces." "We always thought of precast concrete as the material for the ages, and it swept the field and became the standard of the industry for ten or twelve years," said Gatje when speaking about IBM La Gaude. "But it wasn't. It didn't weather well and it had to be maintained, and nobody thinks to maintain it."

Factory-controlled precasting rather than concrete poured at the building site gave Breuer opportunities for creative design—curves and unusual shapes made of angled, faceted members—and for a high degree of surface texturing by exposing the aggregate. Influenced by the work of two brilliant and daring concrete engineers—Robert Maillart, whose constructions and bridges in Switzerland Breuer knew in the 1930s and photographs of whose work he kept among his files, and Pier Luigi Nervi, whose soaring thin shell structures Breuer admired in the 1950s—Breuer felt most able to realize his aesthetic goals as an architect in the 1960s with concrete because it "follows more readily than any other material the imagination of the designer. No material has more potential. [It] allows the architect three dimensions; he can design elevations moving in and out, he can create depth in a facade, he can become master in a new baroque."[36] Working with its density and plasticity, he believed that he could do with the monolithic continuity of concrete what the Egyptians had done with stone. Speaking with Winthrop Sargeant about concrete, Breuer said:

RIGHT
Light metal form for
precast-concrete unit,
Torin factory,
Nivelles, Belgium

FAR RIGHT
Annunciation Priory of the
Sisters of St. Benedict,
Bismarck, North Dakota.
1958–63. Bell tower

I like to use concrete because it has a kind of rugged quality. It is not a sweet material. It is a relief in modern architecture from all that glass and steel. Also concrete can do almost anything in a building. It represents both structure and enclosure and per consequence it expresses structure more directly than any other material. Then, being a homogeneous material, it can make the forces in a building flow, forces for example, between a column and a beam. Flowing forces can be expressed in the exterior of a building, giving it an organic character. I apologize for the word "organic," I know it is a cliché. Folding of great masses of concrete is possible, and hyperbolic paraboloids can be used. On the other hand, I don't dislike glass and steel buildings. There is a certain pleasing effect in the reflections that come from the glass. The only trouble with them is that they have to be cleaned all the time. Concrete doesn't.[37]

For textural contrasts, Breuer liked a bush-hammered surface, achieved when the hard concrete is pounded with an instrument to allow the stones of the aggregate to show. William Landsberg has accounted for Breuer's interest around 1950 in this technique and its results:

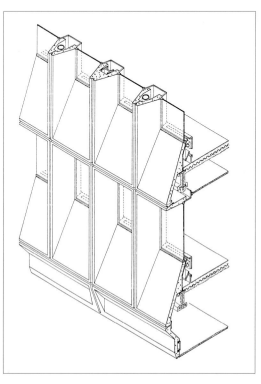

Curtain-wall section,
Armstrong Rubber Company
Headquarters,
West Haven, Connecticut.
1968–70. Isometric drawing

Bush-hammering a concrete wall. 1950s

Bush-hammering was a strange procedure to contractors in this country. Breuer may have been the first to encourage its use. Concrete in those days was seldom if ever exposed in the raw, except in industrial or utilitarian buildings where aesthetics were considered unimportant. It was usually covered with at least a coat of stucco or some other more acceptable finishing material. Breuer chose to make the walls of the entrance steps to the [Grosse Pointe] Library in concrete and use the bush-hammering technique to create a patina of criss-crossed marks that smoothed and refined the surface, exposed the aggregate and rounded the sharp, jagged corners so that the concrete was more acceptable to the touch and the intrinsic aesthetic qualities of concrete were realized. He did a great deal to change the face and look of concrete, as did others such as Le Corbusier and Louis Kahn, but Breuer was in the forefront of this development.[38]

"Concrete exposure is compelling in principal but to me always disappointing in reality," wrote Smith about the interior finish of the American Press Institute.[39] That reality would continue to disappoint as concrete, the hope of modernism in the 1950s and 1960s, proved incompatible with postmodernist opulence of materials and the new taste for architectural glamour and shine. By the 1970s, concrete was all but dead, yet during the 1960s Breuer's architecture—with few exceptions and in a diversity of forms and functions—was most fully realized in terms of concrete.

Breuer found standards of concrete construction higher and results better in Europe, especially in France, than in the United States. Concrete construction defined three of his most far-reaching European assignments in the 1960s, all in France: a satellite city for working-class families near Bayonne; Flaine, a major urban and resort development in the ski country near Chamonix in Haute Savoie (see p. 170); and a research center for IBM in Provence. Almost twenty-five years after his first ski-resort project, Ober-Gurgl, in the Austrian Tyrol, had been aborted, Breuer was asked to design a winter resort. This time it was not a small hotel for twenty guests, but an entire town with five hotels, six condominium apartment buildings, shops, a chapel, and more—the brainchild of Breuer's friend and client Eric Boissonnas. Like Ober-Gurgl, Flaine was in a near-inaccessible site, and ingenious methods for transporting and prefabricating construction materials had to be invented. Since almost all of Flaine is built of precast-concrete parts, a concrete-mixing and -casting facility was installed in a valley below the site; building materials were carried to the town by a specially built aerial tram that eventually was converted to visitor use. Difficult though it was, the job resulted in a successful—financially as well as recreationally—ski town that was also used profitably in summer as a tennis resort. The structural system of the complexes in Flaine, in Bayonne, and for IBM in La Gaude was based on a combination essential to Breuer's architectural language in the 1960s and 1970s: spectacular cantilevers and powerfully sculpted pilotis supporting a series of deeply faceted load-bearing precast-concrete panels that functioned also as sun-protection devices and as chases for ducts and pipes.

Breuer and concrete construction came together with colossal force at the third power plant and forebay dam sited at Grand Coulee against the imposing backdrop of the Columbia River basin. He was not often given an opportunity to build on such a monumental scale. The engineer in Breuer, joined with his love of the big massing shapes that can be produced with poured concrete, conceived a majestic work that bears a remarkable similarity to Fort Peck Dam, Montana, as shown in Margaret Bourke-White's historic photograph, which appeared on the cover of the first issue of *Life*, November 23, 1936, and

Grand Coulee Dam, Grand Coulee, Washington. 1972–75. Detail

which Breuer may have known or consulted. The traditional pylonic format of dams, with their huge, thick-based sloping walls, must have appealed to his fascination with concrete technology and to his innate "Egyptian" manner. A perspective rendering of the interior of the power plant—with its overwhelming size and concrete folded-wall construction, which supports the rails for a beam crane capable of lifting a 275-ton load, and its circular generator covers inserted into the black terrazzo floor—is a vision of both Piranesian imagery and spiritual space.

Speaking of "religious space" or "a religious feeling in space," Breuer, bringing together the power plant with his churches, said that the Grand Coulee plant had that feeling:

It is an enormous empty space carried by monumental concrete walls, folded. Everything is dustless and spotless; there is no daylight, only artificial light, there are no people, only the heads of twelve turbines visible, of which each produces enough electricity to operate the whole city of Denver. Well, all this as expression has very much to do with a religious feeling. . . . Any space which is larger than necessary and higher than necessary and in which the structure and the whole building of the space is visible, as it is in all churches, this kind of space is automatically religious. I think that any large space which is built so that the process of construction is visible on the inside is a religious space. The monks at Saint John's used to say that Breuer is a religious man but he does not know it.[40]

To reach Grand Coulee Dam and the church of St. Francis de Sales requires an effort for nonlocal visitors, and so in accounts of Breuer's architecture these structures tend to be overshadowed by more accessible buildings and more familiar genres. But they, and Breuer's Whitney Museum of American Art and the Education Wing at the Cleveland Museum of Art, hold a significant place in American late modern architecture, a period generally lacking creative vitality.

Urbanism

Breuer was also part of a European initiative in the 1960s and 1970s for urban decentralization that took the form, particularly in France, of constructing new towns within a near radius of a large city. Its purpose, according to Huxtable in her analysis of this urban-planning phenomenon, was to provide needed working-class housing, redistribute the population, and modernize parts of the country.[41] Perceiving it as "the reverse of the American pattern where the rich go to suburbia and the poor are trapped in the inner city," Huxtable pointed to some virtues in the planning, where worker families "have plenty of heat and running water and good bathrooms and open green space, and every serious consideration for all personal needs." Seeing it coincide, however, "with the worst period of architectural design in relation to modernist theory—the housing tower, the monument unrelated to its environment, etc.," she criticized the dehumanized vacant spaces and the vacuous designs of the new towns that have disposed of "the warm enriching animation of [a good] urban environment."

Revisionist thinking about ideologies and goals in modern urban planning, initiated in 1961 by Jane Jacobs and applied critically by Huxtable and many others, would discredit and render obsolete the ideas Breuer expressed in 1973 in an interview about his planning for the satellite city of Bayonne in France. Breuer upheld the utopian idealism of the Bauhaus era, the early Congrès international d'architecture moderne

Water towers, ZUP de Bayonne, France. 1966–73 (not built). Rendering

(CIAM), and the recycling of Le Corbusier's radical urbanist theories of the 1920s without much accommodation to newer ideas.[42] This was in part the consequence of his considerable expenditure of time and thought on the question of large-scale functionalist housing from the 1920s through the 1940s without having an opportunity to build such housing until late in his career, by which time the discourse had radically changed. In Breuer's view, one of the most serious problems in modern town planning was integrating residential and work areas. "It is hard to think that a satisfactory solution to this problem can ever be found in our present social structure," he said, "because so few industries include acceptable living conditions for their employees within their own immediate environment." He advocated planning strategies with tall boxes in open space (Huxtable's "de-humanized vacant spaces") in the center of a big city: people should not leave the inner city for the outskirts, but streets should lead from all directions to an open center. Small and large parks should be laid out within this web of streets: "We followed this approach for the ZUP de Bayonne project. All the tall buildings of the ZUP will be on its periphery; this is the way it should also be in a big modern city. Tall buildings save space and allow for better use of the available land. Low buildings are expensive. The 'saved' land can be used for parks as well as parking which preferably should also be landscaped."

Single-Family Houses

While urban planning, including housing, occupied in theory or practice a significant part of Breuer's international work in these years, he no longer had the time or the inclination to design individual residential architecture. Gatje remembered him saying that house clients liked to deal personally with the architect, whereas corporate clients were willing to deal with the architect's partners and associates. Having only so many hours in a day, and only so many ideas, he now had little time left for houses. He took on a house in an exceptional case or for old clients and friends. "I only do a few—just for the fun of it," Breuer said in an interview quoted in the *New York Times Magazine* of December 15, 1968 ("The Stamp of Breuer"). The near-finale to Breuer's activity as a house architect and, therefore, the end of an era in modern house design had been signaled two years earlier in a letter to Allen Tate in response to Tate's inquiry about a modest retirement house for himself:

The truth of the matter is that despite my liking to build houses, it is simply not possible for me to do it except in very rare cases of large or experimental houses. The reasons are, of course, economical and a drain on my time. . . . On the last house, similar to yours in size, we spent 484 hours. . . . I hope you will forgive me and I hope also that you will believe me when I tell you the above facts of life which are very much against my own feelings.[43]

Breuer was not unhappy to diminish the volume of house commissions, to avoid extensive personal and epistolary interaction with clients, and to eliminate the strains of dealing on a small scale with contractors and idiosyncratic time-consuming programs. He gave the names of talented students and former associates to potential clients inquiring about architect-designed houses. If in the late 1940s and most of the 1950s houses were still the steadiest source of Breuer's income, during the ten years before his retirement he built only seven, each under exceptional circumstances. There were two for the Stillmans and a second for the Gellers and for the Gagarins, since these families were old friends and devoted clients; and there were the Koerfer, Soriano, and Saier Houses (see p. 177), for which an extraordinary site, a major private art collection, and an undeterrable determination on the part of the client had given Breuer enough reason to soften his resolve. After approving the design for his new house, Rufus Stillman wrote to Breuer that "I know you do this for friendship and that makes me very proud."[44] These houses were expensive and spacious (never "showy") and corresponded in character and style, mutatis mutandis, to his large-scale nonresidential work. Dense and weighty, made of concrete and stone, they were dramatic in effect and sculptural in format. With their function architecturally defined by open plans, broad terraces, and cantilevered volumes, they were the culmination of Breuer's residential designs. His unexecuted project for the Van der Wal House (1962–63) in Amsterdam reflected his thinking about the Whitney Museum; Geller House II (1968–69) was formed as a lyrical arched hangar in concrete, indebted to Le Corbusier's 1931 competition design for the Palace of the Soviets and comfortable in the Brutalist environment of the 1960s. Stillman House II (1965), with its rugged concrete structure and deeply pierced masses, its contrasts of open and closed volumes, was a forceful departure from the light wood-frame structure of Stillman House I (1950).

Laboratories, Research Facilities, and Miscellaneous Commissions

At the same time that he was divesting himself of house commissions, Breuer was offered opportunities to design laboratories and research facilities for universities and scientific institutions—Yale, Harvard, and Brookhaven National Laboratory—and for corporate and individual clients, such as IBM and the Sackler brothers (see p. 178), in response to the advancing technological world of the 1960s. One of the jobs in the office in the early 1960s was for (unexecuted) laboratories at Brookhaven; one in the late 1960s was for (unexecuted) laboratories at Harvard, an invitation Breuer received through a reference from a Brookhaven scientist. The Harvard design was based on the Brookhaven prototype of windowless labs borrowing light from windowed offices across the space and through the glass walls of a service corridor. To have had a building at Harvard would have meant a lot to Breuer because of his history at the university, the presence there of Gropius's work, and the centrality of the intended site on the campus. Although the design concept was acceptable at first to the building committee, the strong objection of a distinguished faculty member, followed by others, to the notion of windowless laboratories caused Breuer's proposal to be dropped even after a contract had been signed and drawings and schematic designs had been prepared.[45]

At Yale, the experience was the reverse, and Breuer's muscular Becton Center (1967–70) holds its own as a distinguished addition to the campus's famous array of late modern architecture by establishment stars—Paul Rudolph, Philip Johnson, Robert Venturi, Louis I. Kahn, and Gordon Bunshaft—a fraternity to which Breuer still belonged, his membership reflected in a number of other commissions of the era. He was one in a team of leading architects selected for a government project for Interama, a permanent national center for trade and cultural exhibits in Dade County, Florida, with a bill for the appropriation of funds authorized by both houses of Congress and signed by President Lyndon Johnson. A press release issued on February 23, 1967, carried the following caption beneath a photograph:

Historic collaboration between six of the world's most prominent architects is the Interamerican area at Interama (Interamerican Cultural and Trade Center), the nation's first permanent exposition. Edward Durrell Stone, José Luis Sert, Marcel Breuer, Louis I. Kahn, Robert B. Browne, Architect in Charge, Dr. Irving E. Muskat, Chairman of Interama, Harry M. Weese, and Paul Rudolph. Approval of their designs for the government buildings (U.S. Pavilion by Edward Durrell Stone) was announced today in this meeting at the Overseas Press Club in New York of great architects none of whom have ever before collaborated.[46]

For a number of projects designed (but not executed) in the late 1960s—Interama and the Olgiata Parish Church to name two—Breuer was working in an Expressionistic mode that with postmodernist hindsight could be considered allusionary, calling on referential associations to the massive and severe forms of Mayan and Egyptian stone architecture realized in the "brutalism" of concrete or the austerity of granite. Describing the potential spatial and kinesthetic experience of a visitor to his proposed Roosevelt memorial, Breuer compared it with encountering Greek and Mexican architecture, evoking a nostalgic memory of something lost.[47] These designs were creative releases from and in contrast to his unremarkable office towers of the period—dry, economically driven "trim and tailored" boxes, as 175 Park Avenue was described by Walter McQuade in the July–August 1968 issue of *Architectural Forum*. Thus the Education Wing of the Cleveland Museum of Art was a brilliant success, while the Cleveland Trust Company tower, a version of the second design for 175 Park Avenue, was not. The commission for the Cleveland tower had given Breuer, finally, the chance to build a version of the American skyscraper, not in Manhattan but in the Midwest, fulfilling an ambition nurtured especially by émigré architects of the 1930s. However, conforming as it did to standard-issue late modernist corporate architecture, uninflected, without reference to scale, and with the concrete work at standards unsatisfactory to the Breuer office, it was a lifeless building.

Associationism, conscious or not, also played a role in the aesthetic of the Cleveland Museum wing, inspired by Breuer's known enthusiasm for the striped stonework of the cathedral of Orvieto and by his memories of light-and-dark-patterned brickwork of early modern buildings in Germany. Selected as architect on the basis of his "understanding of a museum's need" demonstrated by the Whitney, Breuer went from the few windows of the Whitney to the windowless addition in Cleveland, slightly larger than its counterpart in New York. Both are bold works that represent a highly individual expression identified not simply as modernist, but as Breuer. Appearing during the last years of the 1960s, they made up for the disappointment of the Roosevelt memorial and the debacle of the Grand Central tower.

The projects that most engaged Breuer's imagination in the 1960s, however, were those in which he was challenged by the combination of engineering and geometry. He experimented with the hyperbolic paraboloid, an outgrowth of concrete technology, and with pylonic back-tilted trapezoidal facades, as in the unexecuted designs for St. Luke's Episcopal Church (1964), Kent School Girl's Chapel (1967; see p. 174), and Olgiata Parish Church (1968–70), and in the constructed bell tower of the Priory of the Annunciation (1961–63) in Bismarck, North Dakota, and, especially, the church of St. Francis de Sales (1964–66) in Muskegon, Michigan (see p. 171). St. Francis de Sales—Breuer's hard-edged version of Le Corbusier's Ronchamp—is his most dramatic building inside and out, where the windowless side walls revolve and, as they rise, twist into the hyperbolic paraboloids that shape the body of the church. The front facade is a trapezoidal banner leaning back against the paraboloids. In his first application of the hyperbolic paraboloid, at the Hunter College library (1957–60), Breuer used it as the building's structural support system (four contiguous inverted umbrellas). Seven years later in Muskegon, the purpose of the hyperbolic paraboloid was formal, not structural, a device for enclosing space. "Sometimes without the building certain possibilities of materials engage my thoughts so that I have them ready when a building is about to be built in these materials. . . . [T]his is what happened in the Muskegon church. It was the concrete enclosure in hyperbolic paraboloids which had been in my mind earlier," he said.[48]

That St. Francis de Sales and Olgiata Parish Church came out of Breuer's imagination at about the same time as 175 Park Avenue only underscores how he was his most daring, most experimental, with the architecture of community—"the Catholic work"—rather than with the architecture of commerce. Beginning with Saint John's Abbey in the 1950s and continuing through the Priory of the Annunciation and the Convent of the Sisters of Divine Providence in Baldegg, Switzerland, in the 1960s and 1970s, with the accord of the Catholic orders for which he was working, he could proffer some of his most independent and experimental ideas and they were for the most part enthusiastically accepted.

It was the model of St. Francis de Sales that Breuer chose when he was elected to the National Institute of Arts and Letters in 1965 for an exhibition honoring new members. In 1965, the American Institute of Architects awarded him its Medal of Honor, and in 1968 its Gold Medal, one of the highest honors of the profession. The University of Virginia elected him Thomas Jefferson Memorial Foundation Professor of Architecture in 1968, and he taught there during the winter semester. Harvard awarded him an honorary degree of Doctor of Arts—given for the first time to an architect—in 1970, and in the same year he received the honorary degree of Doctor from the government of Hungary. In connection with that occasion, an exhibition of Breuer's work opened in the summer of 1970 at the Szepmuveszeti Muzeum in Budapest. Corresponding with Herbert Bayer ten years later, both of them old and ill, Breuer wrote, "Sometimes a bright spot: Pecs wants to build a special Breuer Museum, but: a lot of buts."[49] It never happened.

In the spring of 1965, Breuer's heavy load of work and travel began to take its toll; by August, he was in bed with an inexplicable fever for three weeks, two of them in New York Hospital. When the cornerstone-laying ceremony for HUD took place in October 1966, Breuer was ill and Herbert Beckhard attended in his place. In November, he was hospitalized for a "slight heart attack," his first; by December, as construction of St. Francis de Sales was nearly complete, Breuer wrote to Reverend Louis B. laPres that "it is amazing that this church has actually been built, thanks to your unshaken faith that it would be. I am much better now; I left the hospital, and in a few weeks I will be up and around and healed I expect."[50] But it was not to be, and Breuer's health continued to deteriorate during the next years. In April 1969, he wrote to William Staehelin that "I myself haven't been well in the last weeks and spend most of my time in New Canaan waiting for the sun to come out. Rest and quiet is the doctors' idea, and they include the advice not to get excited—in other words, not to think."[51]

THE "LAST MODERNIST"

The last years of Breuer's practice—from 1970 until his retirement in 1976—coincided with a radical doctrinal and stylistic shift in architecture for the first time in half a century and in which he had little interest. As the modernist initiative of the twentieth century weakened, lost coherence, and gave way to the short-lived, history-based idea of a postmodernism, Breuer's creativity and physical health were waning.[52] The changed world of architecture, with its new discourses and new technologies, was passing him by as he continued "designing Sixties buildings into the Seventies," Udo Kultermann's description of a common occurrence in that period.[53] As new work came into the office, it was easiest for Breuer to slide into the old systems, to give in to the proven efficiency of the standardized small-part accumulations that had served him well, but failed now to add up to something greater than the parts.

An economic downturn in New York in the mid-1970s caused many architectural practices to suffer, but the Breuer office continued to have a fair share of jobs in other places, mainly Europe, and was working at about 60 percent of its capacity. To Staehelin on January 1, 1975, Breuer commented on the economy: "Perhaps with the exception of Switzerland the whole world picture is not too encouraging. I hope it does not affect your office, probably just the opposite. It certainly does affect the architect's noble business, although we are still reasonably occupied."[54] Six months later, with the same theme in mind, he said in a letter to Bayer that "architecture has been dead for the last four to five years, but I lived from the previous years fat and with good luck."[55]

Breuer was beckoned, as were many other American architects in the 1970s, by developing countries whose leaders hoped that a modernist architecture would generate revenues from increasing global tourism and that new public buildings would help align their cultures with twentieth-century advances. Breuer, and later the principals in his successor firm, designed hotels, resorts, and urban complexes to stimulate tourism in locations such as Iran, Afghanistan, and Saudi Arabia. In the early 1960s, he had discussed building projects for the new capital at Islamabad with Pakistani officials. The 6,000-bed capacity of Flaine was an important precedent when, in 1974, Iranian officials were discussing with him the construction of ski resorts. To his credit, Breuer had become aware of the social insensitivity, where modern building in developing countries was concerned, to cultural context and to traditions of vernacular structures.[56] With regard to a potential project for new hotels in Afghanistan, in an interview published in the Kabul Times he said that the buildings should be "in sympathy" with the mud-brick culture of the country: "You don't want to make imitations, what they would build 500 years ago would not be right now. You must express the culture but something entirely new must come out of it. From the architectural point of view, to build correctly in an ancient country something that will satisfy modern demands for comfort is a very special task."[57]

In July 1972, Breuer and Gatje visited Afghanistan at the invitation of the head of the national airline, which, in collaboration with the World Bank, was the primary force behind the country's touristic initiative. The architects were to evaluate a proposal for building hotels in the capital city, Kabul, where there was only an inadequate airport and few hotel rooms. In the Kabul Times interview, Breuer said that "I envision first-class hotels for middle income tourists. Since the average tourist stays less than a week, the hotel in Kabul should certainly be part of the city, not away from it." A contract for consultant's services for two new hotels in Kabul and Bamyam was signed between Breuer and the Government of the Republic of Afghanistan in October 1973 (Walter Brune + Partner, Architects, of Düsseldorf were also named as consultants). Designs were prepared, but the project never went forward in the uncertain political climate of the country. They were, in any event, uninspired works; Breuer, overinvested in precast concrete at the end of his years of active practice, was designing too many self-plagiarizing buildings, bogged down by the aesthetic limitations of planning based on repetitive units.

It was in Kabul that Breuer was hospitalized with the major heart attack that started him on the path leading to his retirement from active practice four years later. Already in

1970, when he had received his honorary degree from Harvard, he had been concerned about participating in the ceremony, about not being able to walk very far in the academic procession.[58] A shortcut was arranged so he could join the procession close to the platform, and he remained seated during most of the formalities. He recovered his strength and continued to work after the heart attack in 1972, but he had to cope with health-related interruptions that forced him to cancel plans and cut back on commitments and travel, commenting that "I have drastically reduced my travelling schedule—my big heart is apparently not big enough."[59] In July 1974, ill and resting in Wellfleet, he wrote to an official of the Luxembourg Bank that

I am trying to recover from the troubles I had after my return in mid-June. As you can imagine, it was not simple for me to give up my work with the Bank, especially under the present conditions. However, I had no choice, and I could not ignore any longer the doctor's advice, which I was forced to do sometimes in the past. (Architecture is like an avalanche, and it is difficult to argue with circumstances and necessities.)[60]

About the same trip, he wrote to a friend in Amsterdam that "after my return from Europe in mid-June I became ill and spent some time in the hospital. . . . I hope to recover fairly soon but not to the degree that I could undertake another trip to Europe in the near future."[61]

Problems connected to Breuer's declining health and the concern of some clients—the Convent of the Sisters in Baldegg, for example—about the extent of his involvement in their work began to appear in 1974. "I appreciate very much your interest in my health," he wrote to a Swiss associate in Lucerne,

but as far as the project for the [new infirmary at the] Baldegg Convent is concerned, please don't worry about it. That up to now no project has been submitted to you is in itself a sign that I have every intention of working on it myself and not submit to you a conception which I am not personally responsible for. The established method of how all our projects have been handled up to now is that I and one of my partners in collaboration are responsible. This letter is to say that while we are trying to reduce my personal responsibilities in the office in consideration of my health, the Infirmary project for the Sisters is still under our established system and I will be involved just as before except in the field work for the project. I hope all this will put your mind at peace.[62]

Correspondence files for the convent project prove that Breuer was as good as his word. He remained fully in control, even of the smallest details such as the color of the walls. He went over the drawings, changing the number of windows and the number of columns for the covered walkway of the cloister. Even after he retired in 1976, his commitment to the convent was a priority: "Let's hope . . . in retiring from the office we have an understanding that I still carry the Baldegg job to the end," he wrote to supervising architect Beat Jordi.[63] Still, the concern at the convent demonstrates why the practice ultimately was not able to survive without Breuer; clients were willing to accept his partners and associates only as long as there was Marcel Breuer at the center. "No designs ever leave my office until I have worked out, or at least supervised, every detail," Breuer said in his interview with Sargeant.[64]

The crucial moment came for Breuer in February 1976, when he was in Paris to receive, from the Académie d'architecture, the Grande Médaille d'or, France's highest award in architecture. He had to interrupt the trip and "rush back to New York because of my health. . . . That incident convinced me that I should do something radical with myself."[65] The "something radical" was his reluctant decision to retire and save his life. On his personal stationery, on March 2, 1976, he wrote to the firm: "It is not easy for me to make this announcement. I have retired from the office as of March 1st 1976. That my health demands serious attention is simply a fact to be faced. Best of luck to the continuing office and to you personally."[66] At almost the same moment, to Mario Jossa in the Paris office, he wrote: "As you already know from Bob [Gatje], the intention here is to continue the New York and Paris offices without any disruption and I enclose my announcement to Eric Boissonnas, Harry Seidler and the New York office staff. Please notify the Paris staff. As this sounds very depressing I should tell you that I feel quite well—if I feel well."[67] Beckhard, Gatje, Papachristou, and Smith sent Breuer a response to his announcement: "Dear Lajkó, We acknowledge your letter telling us of your desire to retire from active participation in the partnership. We do so with a regret which we will not attempt to put into words here."[68]

To Boissonnas, he wrote that "willingly or not I had to face things concerning my health and retired from my office as of March 1st 1976. You can well imagine that it was not an easy decision but I feel and I hope you do that continuity of the Flaine architectural services is already provided for."[69] To his old friend Peter Blake, he explained that "my main trouble is insomnia, and to avoid all possible excitement which would keep me awake I retired from the office. A problem by itself and something to keep you awake."[70] A new partnership agreement was drawn up in 1977, and on March 24, 1978, the name of the partnership was changed from Marcel Breuer and Associates to Marcel Breuer Associates (MBA).

In the years around 1972, Marcel Breuer and Associates had already experienced a slowing down of the high activity and fame it had enjoyed in the 1950s and 1960s, and it recognized a need for more business and greater visibility. The firm engaged a public-relations company to help target opportunities in the most profitable current enterprises—housing (Sun Belt development), corporate building, campus planning. At the same time, close and influential friends of Breuer arranged a retrospective exhibition of his work at the Metropolitan Museum of Art, curated by Arthur Rosenblatt. "For the first time in its 102-year history the Met is giving a one-man architectural show [the first for a living American architect], devoting three central galleries to Breuer's projects," wrote Philip Herrera about the exhibition.[71] It opened on November 30, 1972, and ran through January 14, 1973. (Breuer's own sketches for the layouts of the exhibits are with his papers at Syracuse University.) The exhibition consisted of architectural models, photo murals, full-scale mock-ups, furniture, and tapestries. Highlights from his career were presented through photographs and models, including a replica of the original model of Garden City of the Future made from drawings. There were images of the big projects of the late 1950s and the 1960s, including Saint John's Abbey, the UNESCO complex, the Whitney Museum, and Flaine. Structure and technology were emphasized: there were large plywood models of one of the obtuse-angled columns from IBM La Gaude and of one of the dramatic "tree" columns used in the library at Saint John's University (see p. 172). The catalogue featured essays by Wolf

Von Eckhardt and Richard Stein; a serious reflective assessment of Breuer's work by Huxtable, generated by the exhibition, was published in the *New York Times*.[72] The exhibition traveled under the auspices of the American Federation of Arts, opening at the Museum of Science and Industry in Chicago on December 12, 1973. In the fall of 1974, essentially the same exhibition was on view at the Centre de création industrielle at the Louvre, and then it went to the Bauhaus-Archiv Museum in Berlin.[73] Impressive as this display of a lifetime of achievement in modern architecture and design may have been, and as interesting as that achievement was to the critics and the press, the anticipated practical results for the firm were not realized. No new business came in because of it, and many visitors to the exhibition assumed that its purpose was to honor the memory of a major architect no longer living.[74]

Almost a decade later, in the final year of his life, Breuer was given another one-man show, this time at the Museum of Modern Art, the American institution that probably had meant the most to him historically, professionally, and personally. In terms of prestige, the MoMA exhibition could not have been more important, for, in the words of Christopher Wilk, who curated the show and wrote the catalogue, "it was the third in a series of five exhibitions devoted to twentieth century designers whose work has had a profound effect on design in our time. The Marcel Breuer exhibition was preceded by those on Charles Eames (1973) and Ludwig Mies van der Rohe (1977) and will be followed by ones on Alvar Aalto and Le Corbusier."[75] The exhibition was entitled "Marcel Breuer Furniture and Interiors," and although it did indeed put Breuer on a par with Mies, Aalto, and Le Corbusier, the associative prestige obviously accrued more to his furniture and interior designs than to his buildings. In fact, years had passed since the architecture of Breuer, and even that of Gropius, had been considered in the same league as that of Mies, Aalto, and Le Corbusier. By 1985, Winfried Nerdinger, without detracting from Gropius's immense importance as an educator and as founder of the Bauhaus, in a critical study of his work as architect, designer, and planner, was to put Gropius in a new and certainly diminished perspective.[76]

Less than three weeks before the opening of the exhibition at the Museum of Modern Art, on July 1, 1981, Marcel Breuer died. "The last modernist,"[77] and surely the most productive one, he had never wavered in his belief in and perpetuation of the modern movement. His resolute commitment has been justified by the current renewal of interest in modernist buildings—preserving or remaking them—and in their architects.

Forecasting the epitaph to his extraordinary career in architecture, as a younger man Breuer had put it plainly: "Modern architecture is not a style, it is an attitude. The designer frees himself from precedent and starts fresh. He analyzes the functional and structural needs of a building, and considers the social implications of the assignment. The result is usually simple in line, striking in effect."[78]

1   Robert Gatje to Eric Boissonas, December 5, 1963, Correspondence, AAA.

2   On this subject in general, see Carol Herselle Krinsky, *Contemporary Native American Architecture: Cultural Regeneration and Creativity* (New York: Oxford University Press, 1996).

3   *Architectural Record*, March 1965, 135.

4   *Architectural Record*, December 1968, 99.

5   Frederick Koeper, *American Architecture*, vol. 2, *1860–1976* (Cambridge, Mass.: MIT Press, 1990), 410.

6   "An Interview with Marcel Breuer," *Connection, Visual Arts at Harvard*, Fall 1966, 19. I am grateful to President Frances D. Fergusson of Vassar College for telling me about this interview and providing me with a copy.

7   Tician Papachristou, conversation with author. All quotations from Papachristou in this chapter are from this conversation.

8   Editorial, *Architectural Forum*, July–August 1968, 112; Lawrence O. Houstoun, Jr., "Evaluation: Housing the Department of Urban Development," *Journal of the American Institute of Architects*, April 1977, 54.

9   Marcel Breuer, draft of comments at the presentation of the Whitney Museum project, November 1963, 2, Speeches and Writings, AAA.

10 *Engineering News-Record*, September 28, 1967, 11.

11 "Neighborhood," *Avenue*, December 1992, 34.

12 Herbert Muschamp, "Remodeling New York for the Bourgeoisie," *New York Times*, September 24, 1995.

13 Quoted in Calvin Tomkins, "Modern vs. Postmodern," *New Yorker*, February 17, 1986, 66.

14 George S. Lewis, conversation with author.

15 For the history of Breuer's memorial to Franklin Delano Roosevelt, and for sources of information in this paragraph, see Isabelle Hyman, "Marcel Breuer and the Franklin Delano Roosevelt Memorial," *Journal of the Society of Architectural Historians* 54 (1995): 446–58.

16 Constance L. Breuer, Robert Gatje, Herbert Beckhard, and others, conversations with author. All quotations from Gatje in this chapter are from this conversation.

17 Breuer refers to a favorable 1959 review by Julian Huxley sent to him by Ise Gropius, but without citing the source (Breuer to Ise Gropius, February 13, 1959, UNESCO file, AAA).

18 G. E. Kidder Smith, *The New Architecture of Europe* (Cleveland: World, 1961), 78.

19 Lewis Mumford, "Unesco House: Out, Damned Cliché!" and "Unesco House: The Hidden Treasure," in *The Highway and the City* (New York: Harcourt, Brace & World, 1963), 67–78, 79–87.

20 Mumford, "Hidden Treasure," 85.

21 Mumford, "Out, Damned Cliché!" 70

22 Mumford, "Out, Damned Cliché!" and "Hidden Treasure," 73, 79.

23 Ibid., 73, 82.

24 Mumford, "Hidden Treasure," 82.

25 Ibid.; Klaus Herdeg, *The Decorated Diagram: Harvard Architecture and the Failure of the Bauhaus Legacy* (Cambridge, Mass.: MIT Press, 1983), 6–11.

26 Memorandum, August 7, 1962, Roberto Collection, Series 1, box 4, "New York University Buildings," New York University Archives, Elmer Holmes Bobst Library.

27 New York University News Bureau, press release, n.d. [ca. March 17, 1964], Roberto Collection, Series 1, box 4, "New York University Buildings," New York University Archives, Elmer Holmes Bobst Library.

28 Ada Louise Huxtable, "Building's Case History," *New York Times*, August 9, 1963.

29 Elliott Willensky and Norval White, *AIA Guide to New York City*, 3d ed. (San Diego, Calif.: Harcourt Brace Jovanovich, 1988), 521.

30 Houstoun, "Evaluation," 55, 56.

31 Marcel Breuer, interview for *Schokbeton* [trade publication of Schokbeton Products], October 1973, 4.

32 A. M. McIntyre to Breuer, August 17, 1953, SUL 41.

33 Breuer, interview for *Schokbeton*, 4.

34 Breuer to Abbot Baldwin Dworschak, November 20, 1956, SUL 98.

35 Hamilton Smith, conversation with author.

36 Breuer, interview for *Schokbeton*, 4. "Baroque" was a term used by Breuer and Gropius to mean something historical, premodern.

37 Quoted in Winthrop Sargeant, "Profile of Marcel Breuer" (manuscript draft, prepared for the *New Yorker*, ca. 1971–72).

38 William W. Landsberg to author, November 1, 1994.

39 Hamilton Smith, memorandum, August 27, 1974, SUL 87.

40 Marcel Breuer, interview with Shirley Reiff Howarth, November 21, 1977, in "Marcel Breuer: On Religious Architecture," *Art Journal* 38 (1979): 260.

41 Ada Louise Huxtable, "Cold Comfort: The New French Towns," *New York Times Magazine*, November 19, 1978, 164–69.

42 Breuer, interview for *Schokbeton*, 3–4. Breuer's ideas expressed in this paragraph come from this interview.

43 Breuer to Allen Tate, September 13, 1966, Correspondence, AAA.

44 Rufus Stillman to Breuer, March 12, 1963, SUL 79.

45 Information supplied by Robert Gatje, who was associate architect on the project.

46 Press release, February 23, 1967, Photos, "Portraits of Marcel Breuer," AAA.

47 Hyman, "Marcel Breuer and the Roosevelt Memorial," 455.

48 Breuer, interview with Howarth, 260.

49 Breuer to Herbert Bayer, April 1, 1980. I am grateful to Joella Bayer for copies of the Bayer-Breuer correspondence of these years.

50 Breuer to Reverend Louis B. laPres, December 5, 1966, Correspondence, AAA.

51 Breuer to William Staehelin, April 9, 1969, Correspondence, AAA.

52 Making his point by way of dramatic overstatement, postmodernist architectural historian Charles A. Jencks dated the death of modernism to the dynamiting on July 15, 1972, of the failed Pruitt-Igoo housing development (1952–55) in St. Louis, equating it with the demise of the social and aesthetic ideals for housing established by CIAM (*The Language of Post-Modern Architecture*, 4th ed. [London: Academy Editions, 1987], 9). Stanley Abercrombie composed an obituary for postmodernism (1972–86), calling it "a minor, short-lived style" (*Interior Design*, December 1986, 145). Joseph Giovannini wrote that "post-modernism, which to a large extent was nurtured in professional publications, is being abandoned by those publications" ("Design Notebook," *New York Times*, March 12, 1987).

53 Udo Kultermann, *Architecture in the Seventies* (New York: Architectural Book, 1980), 1.

54 Breuer to William Staehelin, January 1, 1975, Correspondence, AAA.

55 Breuer to Herbert Bayer, June 28, 1975. Letter made available by Joella Bayer through Constance L. Breuer.

56 On this subject in the 1960s and 1970s, see Kultermann, *Architecture in the Seventies*, passim.

57 Quoted in "Marcel Breuer Asked to Evaluate Hotel Plan," *Kabul Times*, August 3, 1972, 3.

58 Breuer-Harvard University Marshal correspondence, April 23 and May 19, 1970, Correspondence, AAA.

59 Breuer to A. Elzas, September 26, 1974, Correspondence, AAA.

60 Breuer to Luxembourg Bank official, July 17, 1974, Correspondence, AAA.

61 Breuer to a friend, July 17, 1974, Correspondence, AAA.

62 Breuer to Beat von Segesser, September 17, 1974, Correspondence, AAA.

63 Breuer to Beat Jordi, March 9, 1976, Correspondence, AAA.

64 Quoted in Sargeant, "Profile of Marcel Breuer."

65 Breuer to Beat Jordi and to Jacques Koerfer, March 1976, Correspondence, AAA.

66 Breuer to the partners in Marcel Breuer and Associates, March 2, 1976, Correspondence, AAA.

67 Breuer to Mario Jossa, March 4, 1976, Correspondence, AAA.

68 Partners to Breuer, March 3, 1976, Correspondence, AAA.

69 Breuer to Eric Boissonnas, March 4, 1976, Correspondence, AAA.

70 Breuer to Peter Blake, April 13, 1976, Correspondence, AAA.

71 Philip Herrera, "Breuer: The Compleat Designer," *Time*, December 4, 1972, 96–97.

72 *Marcel Breuer: An Exhibition Organized by the Metropolitan Museum of Art* (New York: Metropolitan Museum of Art, 1972); Ada Louise Huxtable, "Illuminating Show of Breuer's Work," *New York Times*, November 30, 1972.

73 Renate Scheffler, ed., *Marcel Breuer: Ausstellung im Bauhaus-Archiv, Berlin-Charlottenburg* [exhibition catalogue] (Berlin: Bauhaus-Archiv, 1975).

74 Gatje, conversation with author.

75 Christopher Wilk, *Marcel Breuer: Furniture and Interiors* (New York: Museum of Modern Art, 1981), 7.

76 Winfried Nerdinger, *Walter Gropius: The Architect Walter Gropius: Drawings, Prints, and Photographs from Busch-Reisinger Museum, Harvard University Art Museums, Cambridge/Mass., and from Bauhaus-Archiv Berlin* [exhibition catalogue] (Berlin: Mann Verlag, 1985); see also Marcel Franciscono, review of *Walter Gropius: Der Mensch und sein Werk*, by Reginald R. Isaacs, *Journal of the Society of Architectural Historians* 46 (1987): 432–33.

77 As Breuer was called in *Newsweek*, August 17, 1981, 70.

78 Breuer, lecture at the Walker Art Center, Minneapolis, Minnesota, June 1959, Speeches and Writings, AAA.

Church of St. Francis de Sales, Muskegon, Michigan. 1964–66

Saint John's University Library, Collegeville, Minnesota. 1964–66

Whitney Museum of American Art, New York. 1964–66

Kent School, Girls' Chapel, Kent, Connecticut. 1967 (not built). Rendering

New York University, Technology Building II, University Heights, New York. 1967–70. Rendering

Soriano House, Greenwich, Connecticut. 1971–73

Saier House, Glanville, France. 1972–73

Atlanta Central Public Library, Atlanta, Georgia. 1977–80

OPPOSITE
Mundipharma, Headquarters and Manufacturing Plant, Limburg, Germany. 1973–75

Scarlet. Silk tapestry. 1974

PART 2

WORKS (BUILT AND NOT BUILT)

For built works, the dates represent the period of construction. When known, the date of Breuer's initial connection with the work appears in the summary. Works that were not built are those for which a record exists—correspondence with the potential client, a contract, a program description, a sketch, drawing, or model, and their dates represent Breuer's involvement with the project. Following each summary, archival sources and a selected bibliography are given. Credits for partnerships, collaborations, associations, and consultations are based on Breuer office records.

1a. West facade

INSTITUTIONAL
MUSEUMS

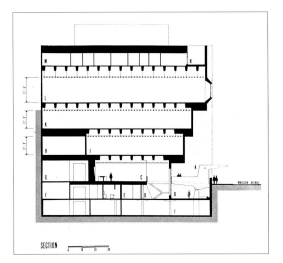

1b. Section

1
Whitney Museum of American Art,
New York, New York, 1964–66

MARCEL BREUER AND HAMILTON P. SMITH, ARCHITECTS

MICHAEL H. IRVING, CONSULTING ARCHITECT

In July 1963, Breuer agreed to design a new building for the Whitney Museum of American Art, a replacement almost twice the size of its former building, which had been sold to the Museum of Modern Art. His casual pen-and-ink sketch for the west facade, with its irregular projecting window, appeared on the reverse of a note of November 7 from Louis Kahn.[1] A presentation of the design to the clients took place on November 12.

The cubo-projective and terraced profile of the building—an ingenious way to provide large gallery floors on a small footprint—went back to 1920s Europe, to Breuer's first awareness of modern architecture in the cubic arrangements of the Adolf Loos buildings he saw in Vienna in 1920 and to his own design for the Elberfeld hospital (1929), with its overhanging cantilevers. Frank Lloyd Wright's nearby Guggenheim Museum also must have been in Breuer's mind when he designed a top-heavy tapering form fronted by a moat. The cornerstone ceremony took place on October 20, 1964; Breuer was in Europe and was represented in New York by Hamilton Smith. The new museum, Breuer's only building in Manhattan, opened on September 27, 1966 (see p. 173).

1c. Lobby

Lower than many of its near neighbors, the Whitney is a bold, beetle-browed, Cyclopean building with three progressively extended overhangs above the base. It reaches its height not by rising from grade but by sinking below it, carving out space for a double-story sculpture court. Because of the drop, the building's height does not cut off light to structures to the east and west. The museum's modest scale was one way that Breuer respected site and context; another was the privacy given both to the Whitney's visitors and to its residential neighbors by including only a few windows. Not needed for light or ventilation, the seven windows of varied size and seemingly random location still give the comfort of orientation and awareness of the outside by framing urban vistas.

The treatment of the corner is one of Breuer's most humane achievements. Without compromising the abstract language of his design, he solved the dilemma of building on a narrow Manhattan cross street by opening the corner with the triadic sequence of projections instead of closing it with a full wall. Separated from adjacent buildings to the south and east by thin concrete slabs, the building is linked to the south slab by a windowed stair recessed from the facade plane.

Inside, the impression of a huge volume of expansive space in the lobby is repeated in the immense size of the passenger elevator, which was originally painted bright, primary blue ("Breuer blue"). The floor area needed was six or seven times greater than the site, leading Breuer to design galleries on five levels, which produced a net gallery area of almost 30,000 square feet. The gallery height of 12 feet, 9 inches (in the top gallery, 17 feet, 6 inches) accommodated the largest paintings of that period. Uninterrupted by piers or beams, galleries are covered by a precast-concrete grid ceiling suspended from the structure and holding movable lighting strips as well as tracks for floor-to-ceiling partitions. Offices and a conference room on the two top floors, hidden from the street by a slope at the top of the facade, were arranged around a library and opened through glass walls to adjacent terraces with high parapets.

Alluding metaphorically to a moat spanned by a covered bridge (perhaps to the American vernacular covered bridge), Breuer set back the glass-walled facade of the entrance lobby so that it is reached after crossing over the sunken sculpture court. An earlier version of the facade preserved in a rendering did not include the canopy at the entrance to this bridge. The moat and bridge are concrete, as are the bearing walls. Upper facade and flanks are sheathed with granite, a material Breuer considered "durable and serene," in a shade of gray that is a restraining factor in the visual impact of the building on the neighborhood.

The individualistic thick-framed windows on the west and north give the building its most notable detail, their near-whimsey described by Breuer as "a contrast to the strength of the main building lines."[2] They illustrate his allegiance to the trapezoid shape, and they have been copied in buildings in locations as distant as Albuquerque, New Mexico, and Melbourne, Australia.[3]

ARCHIVAL: **SUL 55, Drawings; AAA Contract, Correspondence, Photos, Project Record Book; City of New York Landmarks Preservation Commission, Records.**

BIBLIOGRAPHIC: *Architectural Forum*, January 1964, 90–93, and September 1966, 80–85; *Architectural Record*, January 1964, 13; *Progressive Architecture*, January 1964, 49, and October 1966, 238–41; *L'architettura*, July 1964, 190; *Deutsche Bauzeitung*, June 1965, 461–63; *Industrial Design*, September 1966, 58–65; *Interiors*, October 1966, 98–107; *L'Architecture d'aujourd'hui*, December 1966, 8–10; *L'Oeil*, February 1967, 20–25; *Design* (Bombay), July 1967, 105–11; *Architecture, formes et fonctions* 13 (1967): 14–17; *Process: Architecture*, no. 32, 60–65; Gatje, *Marcel Breuer*, 196–200; Stoller, *Whitney Museum of American Art.*

2
Cleveland Museum of Art, Education Wing,
Cleveland, Ohio, 1968–70

MARCEL BREUER AND HAMILTON P. SMITH, ARCHITECTS

The success of the Whitney Museum of American Art brought Breuer the commission to design a new wing, somewhat larger than the New York City building, for the Cleveland Museum of Art. On March 9, 1967, he contracted "to construct an education wing as an addition to the existing museum," and by April he received his registration to practice in Ohio. Construction began in August 1968 and was completed by December 15, 1970. The new museum opened to the public on February 1, 1971.

Existing on the site was the classical limestone Cleveland Museum of Art building of 1896 as well as an irregular-U-shaped wing added to the original fabric by Cleveland architect Paul Ruth in 1958. Between 1958 and 1967, the museum's collection increased not only in the number of objects but also, characteristic of the era, in the size of paintings. Space was needed for new galleries and for the growing education department, a representative development in museums in the 1960s in an effort to answer the cultural needs of larger and broader populations. The new wing would provide special exhibition galleries (with movable partitions and without intrusive columns) on two levels, a music department, an auditorium, two lecture halls, and classrooms. Lobby, roof terrace, and sunken garden were to be new public spaces. Ceilings in the galleries were composed of modular units with tracks for panels and lighting in a system like that at the Whitney. And, like the Whitney, the Cleveland Museum was given a monumental passenger elevator that corresponded to the expansive spaces of the interior.

The facade of the nineteenth-century museum was untouched, but the visible limestone portions of the 1958 wing were wrapped in the striped granite veneer of the Breuer building so that old and new were visually and physically consolidated. More sensitive to contextual considerations than he is given credit for, Breuer specified limestone for exterior paving and stairs so that color and finish would conform to the limestone walls on the east side of the old building. Placed in close parallel alignment with the north flank of the old wing, Breuer's building matched itself to existing floor levels and furnished effective points of communication.

The principal entrance is a dramatic 115-foot cantilevered concrete canopy, purposely visible as a direction signifier from the parking areas a discreet distance away; the bilevel exhibition spaces open to the lobby on the ground floor and, on the second floor, to the older galleries, with the two levels and the two buildings joined by an open stair. To free the ground-floor gallery of intrusive columns, the ceiling structure supports its own weight.

Prefabricated panels of grainy split-face granite bonded to concrete account for the light- and dark-gray sheathing of the exterior walls. The museum's striped skin is one of Breuer's most striking inventions, a highly personal interpretation of the sun-and-shadow effects that were an important feature of modernist surfaces and a sophisticated embellishment of the flat windowless projecting and receding blocks that shape the building. It also reflects Breuer's known admiration for the great medieval cathedral at Orvieto, and for the patterned brick architecture of early modern Germany.[4]

ARCHIVAL: **SUL 76, 90–96; AAA Photos; Cleveland Museum of Art Archives.**
BIBLIOGRAPHIC: *Progressive Architecture*, March 1968, 47–48; *Architectural Forum*, March 1971, 7, and September 1971, 20–25; *L'architettura*, January 1972, 604–5; *Process: Architecture*, no. 32, 74–77.

2. View along the north facade

3
Heckscher Museum, Expansion,
Huntington, Long Island, New York,
1973–77 (NOT BUILT)

MARCEL BREUER AND HAMILTON P. SMITH, ARCHITECTS

A project to expand the small, suburban Heckscher Museum came into the office toward the end of Breuer's incumbency and terminated after his retirement in 1976. A contract dated July 16, 1973, was signed by Hamilton Smith for Marcel Breuer and Associates "to construct a new wing to be connected to the existing museum." Design development progressed into 1977 through several interim agreements during which the town of Huntington replaced the museum's board of trustees. Eventually, the project was halted because of lack of funds. Application had been made for a federal public-works grant, without success.

Renderings and plans record an elegant two-story building of hard-edged blocks with a glazed facade folded around an open terrace, reached by a bridge across a sculpture garden.

ARCHIVAL: **SUL Drawings; AAA Contract, Photos.**

4
Museum for the Nordrhein–Westfalen Collection, Competition,
Düsseldorf, Germany, 1974–75 (NOT BUILT)

MARCEL BREUER, ARCHITECT

Late in 1974, Breuer was invited to participate in a competition for a museum to house the Nordrhein-Westfalen Collection in Düsseldorf. He submitted a model; the competition was judged in December 1975, but he did not win. In 1986, at the time of the controversy over the expansion of the Whitney Museum of American Art, the director of the Kunstsammlung Nordrhein-Westfalen, Werner Schmalenbach, wrote to the Landmarks Preservation Commission of New York that "the Whitney Museum in New York is one of the great museums in the United States. . . . This building was the reason why I invited Marcel Breuer to participate in the competition for the new building of our museum in Düsseldorf." [5]

ARCHIVAL: **SUL Drawings; AAA Correspondence.**

3. Rendering of the entrance and sculpture garden

5. Entrance facade

5
Grosse Pointe Public Library,
Grosse Pointe, Michigan, 1951–52

MARCEL BREUER, ARCHITECT

The building was originally designated the Ferry-Sales Central Library in Grosse Pointe, since it was made possible by gifts from Dexter M. Ferry, Jr., and Murray W. Sales, "two local citizens who visualized Grosse Pointe's lack of adequate public library facilities."[1] The commission came to Breuer through his former student at Harvard, Ferry's son, W. Hawkins Ferry.[2] A model was presented to the Board of Education on May 14, 1951, and the groundbreaking ceremony took place in September; the building was dedicated on January 25, 1953. During construction, in the summer of 1952, Breuer received the UNESCO commission, and while he was in Paris much of the work in Grosse Pointe was overseen by William Landsberg.

As the site of the two-story building was shared by the athletic field of an adjacent high school, guidelines for Breuer suggested that the new library "not conflict" with the school's traditional architecture. After Breuer presented the preliminary design, he was told that the library professionals "feel that your plan is superior to anything thus far developed by the Detroit Library system."[3] The result is a well-designed, unassuming suburban building that respects its context and fulfills its mission. The Breuer office was commissioned also to purchase and design the interior furnishings; in the 1990s, a unique Breuer-designed teak boomerang desk elevated on low brick piers was still in use at the entrance to the main reading room.

The structural frame and the floor and roof slabs are of reinforced concrete. Exterior walls with red-brick veneer and white window trim complement the traditional "colonial" image of most of the neighborhood architecture, institutional and residential. The off-axis main approach is a stone-paved terrace furnished with bush-hammered concrete benches and defined by low concrete-capped walls (reminiscent of those in Frank Lloyd Wright's early houses) that extend along the adjacent lawn.

Breuer wanted the concrete walls bordering the terrace steps to be bush-hammered "to create a patina of criss-cross marks that smoothed and refined the surface, exposed the aggregate and rounded the sharp corners so that the concrete was acceptable to the touch, and the intrinsic aesthetic qualities of the material were realized," remembered Landsberg.[4] As local contractors had no experience with bush-hammering, and as Breuer especially liked the bush-hammering of the fireplace in his contemporaneous Caesar Cottage, in Lakeville, Connecticut, a sample was requested from the Connecticut contractor.

The large and luminous main reading room has one wall almost fully glazed, compartmentalized by three full pilasters making four large bays, each subdivided by mullions into four lights over three in a typical Breuer rhythm of 1, 3, 4. Exterior side elevations on the first level have narrow window slits in the brick wall. The second floor opens to a sun-shaded balcony on the west.

Supplementary expenses were necessary to improve ventilation after the library was in operation. Air-conditioning as an afterthought required inserting a mechanicals room on the second floor, cutting off a passage from one side of the building to the other that was part of the original design.

ARCHIVAL: SUL 36–38, Drawings; AAA Correspondence, Photos; Grosse Pointe Public Library Archives.
BIBLIOGRAPHIC: *Architectural Record*, December 1952, 158–59.

Hunter College Library, 1957–60. See no. 15.

6. Rendering of the entrance facade

6
Institute for Advanced Study, Library,
Princeton, New Jersey, 1959 (NOT BUILT)

MARCEL BREUER, ARCHITECT

Housing units by Breuer built in 1955–56 for members of the Institute for Advanced Study led to a proposal in 1959 for a new library, but the project did not go forward. In her book on Wallace K. Harrison, Victoria Newhouse recounts that "in 1949 the possibility arose of building a new library [at the Institute for Advanced Study] for history, social science and mathematics. But partly because the project was opposed by the mathematics department, the building committee did not approach an architect about the project until 1959. First a proposal by Marcel Breuer and then one by Kenneth Stone Kassler were rejected."[5]

The rendering shows a Breuer "shoebox" format, with clerestory windows above an unarticulated floating facade plane bisected by an inserted stair. Side entrances are in pierced screens placed at a shallow distance from the terminal bays to form a corridor. Breuer appropriated this device from his contemporaneous Hunter College library. The facade terminated short of the end wall screens, creating a rhythmic irregularity to offset the symmetry of the design.

ARCHIVAL: AAA Photos.

Saint John's University, Library, 1964–66. See no. 43.

7. Entrance facade

7
Clarksburg Harrison Public Library,
Clarksburg, West Virginia, 1974–75

MARCEL BREUER AND HAMILTON P. SMITH, ARCHITECTS

A contract for a new central branch of the city and county public-library system was awarded to Breuer on January 10, 1973; groundbreaking took place in the spring of 1974, and construction was completed in 1975. In a demonstration of civic pride through architecture, a two-line banner headline on the first page of the *Clarksburg Exponent* of January 11, 1973, carried the news, "Marcel Breuer, World-Famous Architect, to Design New Library Building Here." The article went on to report that "a Marcel Breuer building will be a 'first' in the Appalachian area . . . an enduring edifice for which Clarksburg will be famous."

A modest budget was possible because the building needed only basic materials and standard construction techniques (brick and cement-block walls, dry-wall partitions, and suspended acoustic ceilings). "Clarksburg is a brick-built town; the old library is preserved on the same site. Brick was chosen therefore as the exterior material for the new building," wrote Hamilton Smith on December 22, 1976.[6]

Composed with the heavy, dense massing characteristic of Breuer's work in the 1960s and 1970s, the library is a stark two-story box with a wide and deep off-center penetration that creates a glazed entrance wall with main reading-room window above. The two levels are connected by a large open stairway lighted by skylights. The exterior is a commanding display of closed and open volumes, flat planes, lateral overhangs, and asymmetries. Enclosed garden-courtyards on each flank serve as outdoor reading rooms. About this, Smith wrote on February 21, 1975, that "[in our buildings] the exterior space often becomes an extension of the interior, particularly when a wall element [and materials such as brick] continue from inside out. This approach will be noticed on the Library, we believe, and partly for this reason we were pleased that the Board had the wisdom to retain the garden walls in the face of [a] budget problem."[7]

ARCHIVAL: **SUL 76, 110–12, Drawings.**

8
Atlanta Central Public Library,
Atlanta, Georgia, 1977–80

MARCEL BREUER AND HAMILTON P. SMITH, ARCHITECTS

STEVENS AND WILKINSON, ASSOCIATE ARCHITECTS

Atlanta Central Public Library, located at One Margaret Mitchell Square, was the main branch of the Atlanta public-library system and one of the last buildings that Breuer worked on before his retirement (see p. 179). Although the design concept dates to 1971, there was no contract until 1976 because of disagreements between the library administration and the city government with regard to a bond referendum needed to raise funds for the construction and to other controversial issues. Construction finally was begun in October 1977 and was completed in May 1980.

The idea to seek an internationally famous architect for the new library was promoted by its board of directors and by the library's director, Carlton Rochell, who was particularly enthusiastic about Breuer's Whitney Museum of American Art. Rochell and members of the board requested interviews with three architects in New York and visited two (Breuer and Paul Rudolph).

The Breuer office received a 275-page program for the new building based on a capacity of 1,000 users and 1 million volumes. A model built from the Breuer design was considered by the board to be a highly successful interpretation of the program. The library was designed with eight stories above grade and two below (for future growth). The three levels are joined by a monumental staircase. The structural system is steel frame and concrete slabs, with the exterior wall sheathed in precast-concrete panels bush-hammered for texture. The architects were called on to justify the selection of precast concrete instead of natural stone for the exterior;[8] they pointed out that in addition to the impact on the construction budget, precast-concrete panels

could be given the special shapes called for by the design—for example, the recessed windows with splayed reveals. The panels could be cast in L-shape, and therefore "turn the corner" (not possible in natural stone), and could be cast large enough for the 15-foot floor-to-floor vertical dimension. Natural-stone panels would have been prohibitively weighty, requiring a masonry back-up wall on which to hang and thereby doubling the load supported by the steel frame. The southwest entrance facade is cantilevered above a terraced plaza-forecourt with an area intended for sculpture—a space recessed below grade and defined by steps on three sides. The glass wall fronting the forecourt offered a comprehensive view into the library from outside.

One of the best works of Breuer's late career, the Atlanta building is a departure from his standard library "box." Instead, he reinvented the stepped profile, grand massing, few windows and "severe, hard-edged, geometric volumes," as Hamilton Smith described them, of the Whitney Museum.[9]

ARCHIVAL: **SUL 59–61, 126–29, Drawings, Sketches; AAA Photos.**
BIBLIOGRAPHIC: *Architectural Record*, March 1981, 83–87; *Journal of the American Institute of Architects*, mid-May 1981, 192–97; *Process: Architecture*, no. 32, 70–73.

8a. Southwest corner

8b.
Central stair

9a. Sketch by Breuer

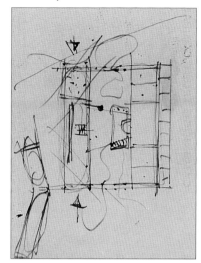

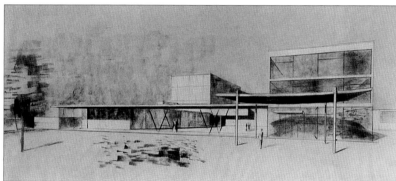

9b. Rendering

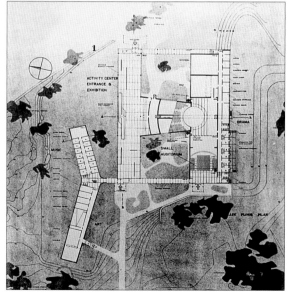

9c. Plan

9

Wheaton College, Art Center, Competition,
Norton, Massachusetts, 1938   (NOT BUILT)

WALTER GROPIUS AND MARCEL BREUER, ARCHITECTS

In June 1938, 243 architects and firms entered a competition sponsored by the Museum of Modern Art and *Architectural Forum* for an art center at Wheaton College. The program called for a large auditorium and a smaller theater, a library, lecture rooms, studios, gallery space, and practice rooms. Four outstanding architects (or partnerships) had been invited to participate: Gropius and Breuer, William Lescaze, Richard Neutra, and Lyndon and Smith. First prize was awarded to Richard Bennett and Caleb Hornbostel for a design that was "greatly admired for its skillful use of the site."[1] Gropius and Breuer were second.[2] About Gropius and Breuer's design, one of the jurors, Walter Curt Behrendt, said that "I cannot recommend that Wheaton College be put in the position of repeating errors of the Bauhaus, but rather she take a [design] which displays to me a youthful understanding of all the principles of modern architecture and a feeling for New England."[3]

Recognizable as Breuer's invention by its reflection of his Garden City of the Future (1936) and by an autograph sketch at Syracuse, the Wheaton College complex was an ingeniously organized design wherein classrooms were housed in a narrow "boomerang" connected by a glazed passage to a tall block with auditorium and library. The block was joined to an exhibition gallery wing by the trapezoidal mass of the theater. The gallery unit was fronted by a transparent wall that, together with slender posts supporting a curved canopy at the entrance, contributed exceptional lightness and elegance to the design.

ARCHIVAL: **SUL 16, 42, 50; AAA Photos;** see Nerdinger, *Walter Gropius*, 196–97, 269, and *Walter Gropius Archive* 3:69–71.
BIBLIOGRAPHIC: *Architectural Forum*, August 1938, 148–49; *Pencil Points*, September 1938, 551–65; Blake, *Marcel Breuer*, 70–73; Wright, "Architecture of Walter Gropius," 41–42; Breuer, *Sun and Shadow*, 179; McCormick, "Wheaton College Competition for an Art Center," in *Modernism in America*, ed. Kornwulf, 23–67; Nerdinger, *Walter Gropius*, 196–97, 269, and *Walter Gropius Archive* 3:69–71; Driller, "Frühwerk," 358–59.

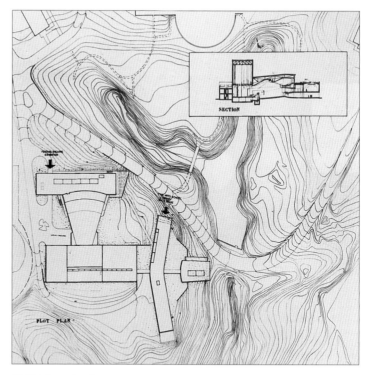

10. Site plan and section

10

College of William and Mary, Festival Theater and Fine Arts Center, Competition,
Williamsburg, Virginia, 1938–39 (NOT BUILT)

WALTER GROPIUS AND MARCEL BREUER, ARCHITECTS

A few months after the competition for the Wheaton College Art Center, Gropius and Breuer were invited to compete for another theater/fine arts center on a college campus, this time at the College of William and Mary in Williamsburg, Virginia. A full account, summarized here, is given by James D. Kornwolf, who describes it as part of an effort by the American National Theatre and Academy (ANTA) to establish national festival theaters in various regions of the country and "to reinvigorate the legitimate theatre in the United States."[4] The competition was the brainchild of A. Conger Goodyear, president of the board of trustees of the Museum of Modern Art and of ANTA. Williamsburg (in the process of its colonial restoration) was selected because of the strong program in theater and fine arts at the College of William and Mary and because it was the location of the first theater built in the United States, in the early eighteenth century.

Four architects or architectural firms in addition to Gropius and Breuer accepted an invitation to compete: Stone and Goodwin, Michael Hare, Harrison and Fouilhoux, and Richard Neutra; Frank Lloyd Wright had declined. An official announcement of the competition was published in the November 1, 1938, issue of *Architectural Record*,

and 128 designs were submitted anonymously. Prizes and honorable mentions were awarded in February 1939: first prize went to Eero Saarinen in collaboration with Ralph Rapson and Frederick James; Gropius and Breuer received no citation. The project dissolved within a year, however, because it failed to generate financial support.

The Gropius and Breuer plan was a variation of the Wheaton College design. The theater component had three stepped interlocking elements: entrance lobby and exhibition gallery, joined to a taller trapezoidal auditorium with balcony, backed by the high box for the stage that rose from the area for theater administration. This ensemble was linked by an elevated bridge to the slender bent rectangle of the fine arts center, with its drafting rooms, lecture rooms, and studios, and beyond that to the library building.

In November 1939, there was an exhibition in the Department of Architecture at Harvard's Graduate School of Design of prize drawings from the competition circulated by the Museum of Modern Art.[5] The failure of Gropius and Breuer to win either a prize or a mention must have been an embarrassment to the architects and to the GSD.

ARCHIVAL: **AAA Photos; see Nerdinger,** *Walter Gropius Archive* **3:125–28.**
BIBLIOGRAPHIC: **Kornwolf, "College of William and Mary,"** in *Modernism in America*, ed. Kornwolf, 125–75; Nerdinger, *Walter Gropius*, 270, and *Walter Gropius Archive* **3:125–28; Driller, "Frühwerk," 360.**

11. Rendering

11

Black Mountain College, Lake Eden Campus,
Black Mountain, North Carolina, 1939–40 (NOT BUILT)

WALTER GROPIUS AND MARCEL BREUER, ARCHITECTS

The history of this small, innovative undergraduate college near Asheville, North Carolina, radical in its philosophy of teaching and learning, and with an emphasis on the arts, is recounted in Mary Emma Harris's *Arts at Black Mountain College*. The isolated location of the college far from research facilities, the experimental character of its curriculum, and a continual lack of funds contributed to the problem of recruiting faculty. But because its opening in the fall of 1933 coincided with the beginning of the exodus of intellectuals and artists from Germany, Black Mountain College developed a faculty of brilliant refugee artists led by Josef Albers, who went there to teach in the school's first year. Immediately after the closing of the Dessau Bauhaus in the summer of 1933, Philip Johnson had proposed that Albers join Black Mountain as Professor of Art. The college continued to maintain strong Bauhaus ties: Anni Albers set up a weaving workshop there on the Bauhaus model, and Josef Albers brought in his former Bauhaus student Alexander (Xanti) Schawinsky, who taught drawing, painting, and typography; supervised student photography; and gave seminars in architecture.

In January 1940, Gropius and Breuer were commissioned to design buildings for a new campus. Worried about the future of its original location, the college in June 1937 had purchased almost 700 acres of property at nearby Lake Eden and began planning for the development of a new educational environment.[6] In lectures and seminars illustrated with sketches based on Gropius's Dessau Bauhaus building, Schawinsky promoted the idea of Gropius as designer for the new buildings. Breuer visited for three days in April 1939, and followed up with a report written on May 11;[7] drawings were made in September;[8] Gropius visited the campus in December. As part of a fund-raising effort, the Gropius and Breuer model and plans were exhibited at the Museum of Modern Art on January 9, 1940, when Albers and Gropius spoke about the college's educational philosophy and building needs. A photograph of Gropius and Breuer with their model appeared in the *New York Herald Tribune* on January 10.

It was the impact of the war in Europe, according to Harris, that forced the college to give up the Gropius-Breuer plans.[9] President Franklin Roosevelt's address to Congress on May 16, 1940, requesting more than $1 billion to develop American defenses, led the college to expect that it would be impossible to raise money and equally impossible to obtain building materials in wartime.[10] It was decided, therefore, to construct a campus with simpler structures that could be built by faculty and students under the direction of an architect and a builder. Harris writes that "in the summer of 1940 A. Lawrence Kocher, an architect who had been a friend of the college from the beginning, was asked to make new plans. Why the college did not turn to Gropius and Breuer for simpler plans is unclear, though Kocher's willingness to join the faculty as resident architect was probably a deciding factor."[11]

In Gropius and Breuer's design for the Lake Eden Campus, a concentrated group of tallish buildings (known as Study, Lobby, and Auditorium) was chosen as the best system. Connected by covered walkways, the buildings were sited around the southern shore of the lake for sunlight and view. They were set down at irregular angles and levels following the shoreline and grouped in what the architects called a "free composition, avoiding any rigid axis or rectangular relations to each other."[12] The emphasis was to be on flexibility of organization, reflecting the college's avoidance of rigid organization in its philosophy of education. The main building (Study) was narrow, four stories tall, and bent at a wide angle, its upper floors cantilevered in two directions. It was supported on two rows of pilotis and projected over the lake; one row of pilotis stood in the water (a dramatic device that Breuer would apply to his East River apartment project in New York in 1946). For a panoramic view, the wall of its general meeting room was to be a single piece of curved glass. The roof, which doubled as a sun terrace, had a Le Corbusier–inspired free-standing parabolic wall for wind protection and sun reflection. The thin pilotis made possible a clear vista toward the lake from the land. Steel-frame structures with walls of painted brick or fieldstone would be, in the opinion of the architects, the most economical solution for that region. An infirmary and two-room faculty apartments, some with a balcony, were included in the program. Students were to have individual studies and share sleeping space; faculty studies were to be interspersed with those for students.

Gropius was closely involved in the development of the Black Mountain project because of Albers, the Museum of Modern Art, and the experimental nature of the school and its ties to the Bauhaus. As far as the design is concerned, the correspondence files and the reports that issued from the architects' office, as well as the shapes of the buildings, make clear that it was Breuer's design. Sophisticated, dramatic, and probably impractically expensive to construct, Black Mountain (like Wheaton) would have made been a major contribution to modern architecture in America had it been realized.

ARCHIVAL: **SUL 29, 30, Drawings, Sketches; AAA Photos; see Nerdinger,** *Walter Gropius*, **271, and** *Walter Gropius Archive* **3:121–24.**
BIBLIOGRAPHIC: **Blake,** *Marcel Breuer*, **74; Wright, "Architecture of Walter Gropius," 44–45; Nerdinger,** *Walter Gropius*, **198, 271, and** *Walter Gropius Archive* **3:121–24; Harris,** *Arts at Black Mountain College*; **Driller, "Frühwerk," 356–58.**

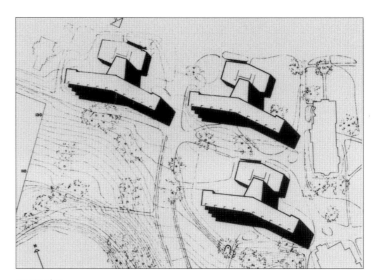

12. Site plan

12
Smith College, Dormitories, Competition,
Northampton, Massachusetts, 1945 (NOT BUILT)

MARCEL BREUER, ARCHITECT

In 1945, Breuer won $100 and Honorable Mention for his design for three identical four-story buildings, submitted to the Smith College Dormitories Competition. In January 1946, the drawings were exhibited at the Museum of Modern Art and in 1947 in Williamstown, Massachusetts. Space for living, dining, recreation, entertainment, study, storage, and other aspects of undergraduate life were provided by the three-part organization of each building—two large units and a smaller link. The design was based on signature Breuer shapes, many having originated in Garden City of the Future: a tall, narrow, and slightly bent Y, the trapezoidal stem of which became a smaller, lower connecting wedge nested into a polygonal unit.

ARCHIVAL: **SUL 51; AAA Photos.**
BIBLIOGRAPHIC: *Nuestra arquitectura*, **November 1947, 179–80; Blake,** *Marcel Breuer*, **83; Driller, "Frühwerk," 348.**

13. West elevation

13
Vassar College, Ferry Cooperative Dormitory (Ferry House),
Poughkeepsie, New York, 1950–51

MARCEL BREUER, ARCHITECT

Breuer signed a contract with Vassar College in February 1950 "to erect a cooperative dormitory for 25 students." Construction began in July and was substantially complete by December. Dedicated on October 5, 1951, the building was the gift of Dexter M. Ferry, Jr., of Detroit, whose family had a long association with Vassar and with modern architecture. His sister, Queene Ferry Coonley (Vassar, class of 1896), in 1908 had commissioned one of Frank Lloyd Wright's most celebrated early houses, the Coonley House in Riverside, Illinois. Ferry's son, W. Hawkins Ferry, was a student at the Graduate School of Design at Harvard from 1937 to 1939, when Gropius and Breuer were teaching there, and was a strong supporter of their work. In 1949, Breuer built the first of two Baltimore houses for Ferry's daughter, Edith Ferry Hooper (Vassar, class of 1932), and, on her recommendation, was commissioned to design the Bryn Mawr School for Girls (1971–72) in Baltimore. For Dexter Ferry, Breuer also built the Grosse Pointe Public Library (1951–52).

Ferry House was the first significant architectural addition to the campus since the 1930s and marked Vassar's entry, in a visual sense, into the twentieth century. Breuer's bright, airy, flat-roofed building took shape behind the dark-red brick massings of James Renwick's Second Empire Main Building (1861–65) as a largely unwelcome alien. It was inevitable that a proposal for a modern building on a traditional college campus in 1950 would create debate, as it did among the Vassar trustees.[13] Breuer's recent success with his exhibition house at the Museum of Modern Art (1948–49), however, and the presence on the MoMA house committee (headed by Philip Johnson) of Mrs. John D. Rockefeller III, trustee of Vassar and MoMA, were important supports in his favor. The project finally was approved, but the site was changed from a prominent location at the heart of the campus to a marginal area near the outbuildings that serviced the college.

Few architects at that moment were in a better position than Breuer to design a modern building that was modest in materials and size (he referred to it as "an oversized house not an undersized dormitory"[14]), with the special program of Ferry House, whereby resident students would save money by doing their own housekeeping and management. In the context of a college for women in the 1950s, its program was seen also as preparation for the inevitable domestic duties facing the students in the future.

Despite its size, the dormitory made a powerful impact with its purposeful noncontextualism. Breuer did not intend that it relate to the architectural history of the campus; to the contrary, he dramatized its uniqueness. Exterior brick was painted white; transparency and bright colors were set against the dense massing, dark brick, and small windows of the traditional dormitories.

Since the early 1940s, Breuer had experimented with binuclear designs. The Ferry House format was a cubic block for the public rooms and a long box for the dormitory, the two joined by a smaller narrow strip (entrance) and separated by level. At ground level were a kitchen, dining room, and living room, which could be united by way of a sliding partition. A stair with cantilevered treads, "floating" independently without anchorage by rails or foundations, led to the dormitory wing, elevated on steel pilotis, with its lounge and entry to a roof sundeck. A roof deck had been a common feature in modern villa architecture in Europe, introduced by Le Corbusier, and it appeared in Breuer's earliest architectural projects. Sited above the entrance link and reached from the dormitory corridor, it was an especially appealing feature for the students. A pipe-supported, corrugated asbestos-cement *brise-soleil* enriched the wall plane of the dormitory and created patterns of sun and shade on its surfaces. The low free-standing exterior boundary walls were visual metaphors for hedges, and they functioned as benches.

Beyond its role in Vassar's history, Ferry House became a premier example of modern architecture in the United States. It earned a place in the Museum of Modern Art's 1952 exhibition "Built in the USA: Post-War Architecture," was featured in illustrated articles in the international architectural press, and was the centerpiece of an essay by William H. Jordy. The building deteriorated after the mid-1960s and was restored, with changes, in the 1990s.

ARCHIVAL: **SUL 16, 17, 35, 39, Drawings; AAA Contract, Photos.**
BIBLIOGRAPHIC: *Architectural Record*, **January 1952, 127–34;** *Progressive Architecture*, **July 1955, 130–31; Hitchcock and Drexler, eds.,** *Built in USA*, **50–51; Breuer,** *Sun and Shadow*, **180; Jordy, "The Domestication of Modern: Marcel Breuer's Ferry Cooperative Dormitory at Vassar College," in** *American Buildings and Their Architects*, **165–219.**

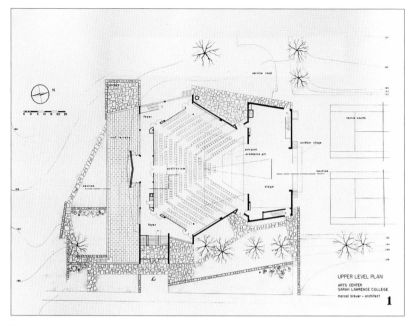

14a. Plan

14
Sarah Lawrence College, Art Center,
Bronxville, New York, 1951–52

MARCEL BREUER, ARCHITECT

An agreement between Breuer and Harold Taylor, president of Sarah Lawrence College, for an art center with theater, lounge, studio workshops, offices, and kitchen was dated June 27, 1951; construction was completed in 1952. Although it was the largest of Breuer's built works up to this time, the materials and external format suggested not an institutional but a residential building, appropriate to the small size and suburban location of the college.

In the original format, a multilevel series of walled terraces linked by steps led to interconnected structures that housed the studio workshops, facilities for the college community, and, above all, a hexagonal theater seating 500. It was Breuer's first opportunity to construct an experimental theater, and he used some of the ideas that he had developed in his design for the theater in Kharkov in 1930. Audience participation was invited; the flexibility of the system (removable seats, wall partitions that opened and closed, an orchestra pit that could be raised) suited the theater to outdoor spectacles as well as indoor events such as college dances. In a Constructivist manner, Breuer formed the boundary walls (brick, terra-cotta flue tiles, fieldstone) into rectangles that elided and intersected.

The college was satisfied with its art center because in 1955, Taylor came back to Breuer with a new proposal for a dormitory probably inspired by the work at Vassar, but nothing came of this.

ARCHIVAL: **SUL 49, Drawings; AAA Contract, Correspondence, Photos.**
BIBLIOGRAPHIC: *Architectural Forum*, December 1952, 134–39; *L'Architecture d'aujourd'hui*, December 1953, 66–71; *Arts & Architecture*, February 1953, 22–23; Breuer, *Sun and Shadow*, 173–75.

14b. View from the west

15b. Classroom and administration building, southwest facade

15a. Model

15
Hunter College Library, Classroom, and Administration Buildings,
Bronx, New York, 1957–60

MARCEL BREUER, ARCHITECT **ROBERT F. GATJE,** ASSOCIATE
EDUARDO CATALANO, CONSULTING ARCHITECT

Breuer's first permanent buildings in New York City were designed for the Bronx campus of Hunter College (now Lehman College). The commission came through Hunter administrators who admired Breuer's work at Saint John's Abbey. The agreement of July 21, 1955, with the City of New York Board of Higher Education called for two buildings: a new library and a classroom and administration building. The latter was completed by October 1959. Mayor Robert F. Wagner of New York delivered the address at the dedication ceremony. The library was completed by June 1960.

The three-story classroom and administration building was designed as a square (178 x 178 x 40 feet) around a square landscaped courtyard. Solid masonry supported concrete slabs on a base of fieldstone; a fieldstone base was also used for the library. Interiors were shaded across narrow corridors by pierced sunscreens of 1-foot lengths of square terra-cotta flue tiles with rounded corners.

The library building, with its hyperbolic-paraboloid roof, was one of Breuer's most acclaimed structural accomplishments (see p. 148). Hyperbolic-paraboloid roofs had been used in South America, but were rare in the United States, especially on the scale used at Hunter. The roof, 120 feet wide and 180 feet long, was formed by three pairs of thin (3.5-inch) reinforced-concrete shell sections bracing each other, each one 60 feet square, shaped as an inverted umbrella and supported by a central column of concrete. Alternating wavy stripes of light- and dark-gray roofing produced a striking bird's-eye view. The white-painted underside of each umbrella was articulated by ribs made by gaps left between the plywood forms used for the concrete. Because only six columns were needed to support the light roof, the space beneath was open and unobstructed. Strips of lighting grid were hung below the ceiling surface and created an "open architecture" of transparency and light.

A binuclear composition, Hunter's two boxlike buildings were linked by a cruciform lobby reached by an elevated ramp leading from a small trapezoidal plaza framed by low stone walls.

Challenged on the issue of contextualism at Hunter, Breuer claimed to have creatively interpreted for the new buildings the colors and materials of the nearby conventional collegiate Gothic buildings of the existing campus:

The process of architectural design needs flexibility and understanding. For instance, on the Hunter College project we have not used the red brick of the surrounding buildings. Instead, we have been quite content to use flue tiles for the sun protection screens which happen to be similar in color. Also, after a decision to use stone for part of the facade, we have used, but in a pattern, the same limestone as is used for the stone trim of the neighboring buildings.[15]

Three years after the buildings were completed, Ada Louise Huxtable, writing in the *New York Times* about the commission given to Breuer for a new headquarters for the Housing and Home Finance Agency (later HUD) in Washington, D.C., commended him for having set a higher standard for public buildings with Hunter. She called Hunter a "superior civic-minded design," something "novel, daring, and unlike anything the city has built before or since."[16]

In the summer and fall of 1957, the Hunter College model was included in a United States government exhibition in Berlin, "America Builds," designed by Peter Blake, about the American building industry.

ARCHIVAL: **SUL 137, Drawings; AAA Contract, Correspondence, Photos, Project Record Book.**
BIBLIOGRAPHIC: *Progressive Architecture*, May 1957, 112–15, and April 1960, 178–87; *Civil Engineering*, February 1958, 97; *New Yorker*, February 13, 1960, 24; *L'Architecture d'aujourd'hui*, September 1960, 90–93; Jones, ed., *Marcel Breuer*, 116–21; Gatje, *Marcel Breuer*, 61–67.

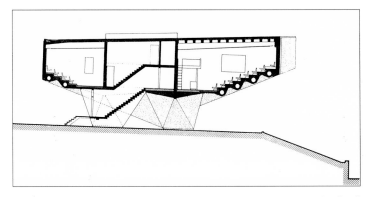

16a. Section, Begrisch Hall

16
New York University Buildings Complex,
University Heights, New York, New York, 1959–70

MARCEL BREUER AND ASSOCIATES, ARCHITECTS

Residence Hall, 1959–61
Student Center, 1959–61

MARCEL BREUER, ARCHITECT

ROBERT F. GATJE, ASSOCIATE

Begrisch Hall, 1959–61
Technology I, 1959–61
Technology II, 1967–70

MARCEL BREUER, ARCHITECT

HAMILTON P. SMITH, ASSOCIATE

A complex of buildings—laboratories, lecture hall, student center, and residence hall, set within terraced gardens and flying walkways—was the first part of a comprehensive plan for the expansion of New York University's School of Engineering and Science on its "uptown" campus. Breuer's NYU gave to one of New York's dramatic riverside locations a commanding and powerful group of modernist structures not intimidated by the noble Classicism of Stanford White's historic colonnaded Hall of Fame and dome-crowned Gould Library, with which they shared the site. The design process was under way by October 1956.

Breuer's plan, which responded to the steep slope and limited size of the site, was ingenious: a bridge connected the elevated lecture hall (Begrisch Hall) to the second floor of the laboratory building (Technology I); the kitchen and dining room in the student center were on the same underground level, but because of the natural grade the dining room had windows overlooking the view; roof terraces above the kitchen and dining room were on the same level as the student cen-

16b. Aerial view from the northwest

ter lounge; and the middle level of the seven-story residence hall was reached from the lounge by two covered bridges, eliminating the need for elevators.

Technology Building I, begun in 1959 and completed in June 1961 for the Departments of Physics, Electrical Engineering, and Mathematics, was a reinforced-concrete-frame structure with floor and roof slabs; brick veneer on the exterior separated strips of windows. Soaring above the entrance on the east was one of Breuer's dramatic sculptured canopies. The reinforced-concrete-and-brick bent rectangle of the residence hall was set on tapered piers at the base of the hillside; a glazed volume separated it from the concrete mass of its fire-stair tower.

Begrisch Hall, with two auditoriums, was built in the same years as Technology I, the residence hall, and the student center; it was dedicated on June 3, 1961 (see p. 155). The dramatic cantilevered hulk (which Breuer would reinterpret at Flaine) had a Russian antecedent in Konstantin Melnikov's Workers' Club (1927–28) in Moscow, a land-

mark of Russian modern architecture of which Breuer was aware. The concrete mass of the building rose from the support of two cantilevered side-wall trusses. The formboard imprint on the concrete surfaces of Begrisch Hall was an integral part of the design and reflected the affection that Breuer had for vertical cypress siding in his first years in practice in America. Indeed, at the NYU complex, he brought together many of his favorite devices, including the boomerang and trapezoid shapes, the pierced wall, and the monumental entrance canopy.

Technology Building II (see p. 175), a graduate-student and research facility for applied sciences, had been forecast with the comprehensive plan of 1956 and underwent several design revisions. Construction began in February 1967 and was completed in September 1970. Designed as an eight-story wing for laboratories and offices and a three-story wing for classrooms, joined by a service-core tower with elevator, the building conformed to Breuer's institutional mode of this period, with its wall of precast units above a row of concrete trees.

For the last phase of the comprehensive plan, the Breuer office on June 27, 1969, offered "our services in connection with the contemplated construction of three new buildings on the University Heights Campus of New York University." But the university did not contract with Breuer for the new work, and in the early 1970s the ambitious program for expansion dissolved with the financial decline of New York University and the sale of its uptown campus in 1973 to the City of New York; today it is Bronx Community College/CUNY.

ARCHIVAL: **SUL 140, Drawings; AAA Correspondence, Photos; New York University Archives.**
BIBLIOGRAPHIC: ***Architectural Record***, September 1959, 186–88, and April 1962, 139–43; *Architettura*, July 1962, 182–83; *Aujourd'hui*, February 1962, 86–89; *L'Architecture d'aujourd'hui*, April 1963, 24–25; Jones, ed., *Marcel Breuer*, 64–71; Papachristou, *Marcel Breuer*, 110, 112; Gatje, *Marcel Breuer*, 76–81, 201–2.

17. Aerial perspective

16c. West facade, Begrisch Hall

17
Cardinal Stritch College, Tri-Arts Center,
Milwaukee, Wisconsin, 1965–66 (NOT BUILT)

MARCEL BREUER, ARCHITECT

BRIELMAIER, SHEVER AND SHEVER, ASSOCIATED ARCHITECTS

There is little information about this project in the Breuer archives; the commission came to him on the basis of his successes at other Catholic institutions. A contract with Sister Mary Acquin, president of Cardinal Stritch College, was dated June 11, 1965. As at Wheaton College in 1938 and Sarah Lawrence College in 1952, this program called for an arts center at an undergraduate college. Predictably, Breuer recycled his layout for Wheaton. A rendering and a series of presentation drawings prepared in April 1966 reveal an ambitious design for an interconnected three-part structure, the centerpiece of which was a large theater. A slender gallery with two curved walls preceded by a concrete canopy and reached by way of a landscaped patio served as the entrance. It opened on the north to a pavilion containing facilities for art students. On the south, it led to the circular lobby, beyond which lay the vast trapezoid of the theater, which rose above the roofs of the other structures and was surrounded by a landscaped terrace. Beyond the terrace on the east and west were classrooms and practice studios for the music students.

This arts center is one of Breuer's most "Egyptian" designs. Suggesting in appearance a Nile Valley temple complex, it evolved at the time Breuer was thinking and writing about relations between modern buildings and the architecture of ancient Egypt.[17]

ARCHIVAL: **SUL Drawings; AAA Contract, Photos.**

18
University of Mary, Annunciation Priory of the Sisters of St. Benedict,
Bismarck, North Dakota, 1967–68

MARCEL BREUER, ARCHITECT

HAMILTON P. SMITH AND TICIAN PAPACHRISTOU, ASSOCIATES

University of Mary is an integral part of the Priory of the Annunciation; in the 1960s, the prioress of the convent was also the president of University of Mary, which is located a short distance from the convent. On September 1, 1965, Breuer agreed to design a four-building complex, consisting of a residence hall; a college hall for the administration, with chapel; a science hall with laboratories and classrooms; and a lecture hall. Construction began in April 1967 and was complete by September 1968.

The flat-roofed buildings are long and low; their precast-concrete window units are combined with walls of richly worked stone and terra-cotta flue tiles. The distinctive concrete V-trusses that Breuer used at the convent are also used at the university to support the roof slab of the outdoor corridor that runs between buildings.

ARCHIVAL: **SUL 137, Drawings, Sketches; AAA Photos, Project Record Book; Priory Archives.**
BIBLIOGRAPHIC: Papachristou, *Marcel Breuer,* **100–109.**

19
University of Massachusetts, Murray Lincoln Campus Center and Garage,
Amherst, Massachusetts, 1967–70

MARCEL BREUER AND HERBERT BECKHARD, ARCHITECTS

The design for a ten-story campus center at the University of Massachusetts in Amherst was approved by the trustees in November 1965, part of an ambitious architectural expansion of the campus that was characteristic of many academic institutions in the 1960s. Construction began on September 1, 1967, and was completed in 1970.

Lack of space required several facilities to be subterranean. Areas for conferences and meetings, cafeteria, bookstore, and other services were placed beneath the building and its stair-framed elevated terrace. Entrances to the below-ground levels were via Breuer "igloos" formed with one right and one oblique angle. The tower had guest rooms and apartments on the first through fifth floors, administrative offices on the sixth and seventh, and restaurants on the eighth and ninth. The building was formed as a thick slab with the uppermost two stories cantilevered, and stair towers, beveled at the bases, added to the flanks. The south facade overlooked and was reflected in the campus pond.

In appearance, the building belongs to a type of brooding, assertive concrete structure designed by Breuer in the mid- to late 1960s that explored the possibilities of concrete. These works are rich in the contrast of textures and scale and are characterized by heavy volumes and complex rhythmic variations.

The program included a six-level subterranean garage and walkway to the campus center, with the ground-level roof serving as a paved plaza for pedestrian traffic.

ARCHIVAL: **SUL 62–65, 72, Drawings; AAA Project Record Book.**
BIBLIOGRAPHIC: *Architectural Record*, May 1966, 174–75; Papachristou, *Marcel Breuer*, 119; *Process: Architecture*, no. 32, 78–83.

19. View from the southeast

20
Yale University, Becton Engineering and Applied Science Center,
New Haven, Connecticut, 1967–70

MARCEL BREUER AND HAMILTON P. SMITH, ARCHITECTS

Correspondence between Breuer and Kingman Brewster, Jr., president of Yale, about a laboratory building for the Department of Engineering and Applied Science, began in January 1964. On March 25, 1966, Breuer agreed to construct such a building on Prospect Street, bordered by Trumbell and Grove Streets and Hillhouse Avenue, an area where a complex of several science halls already existed. The working drawings were completed in January 1967, but when a question about context arose the architect was flexible: asked by Yale to review the design, Edward Larrabee Barnes went back to Breuer and recalls his willingness ("why not?") to revise his original concept by lowering Becton Center two stories in response to the height of nearby buildings.[18]

For Becton Center, Breuer designed a four-lane laboratory–office system he had proposed in 1960 for an unexecuted project at Brookhaven National Laboratory—office, pedestrian corridor, laboratory, service corridor—where the laboratory would borrow its light from windowed offices across a glass-walled corridor. Partitioned office spaces are standardized and modular, with two windows and high ceilings that expand each modest unit. Supporting elements are located below grade. The long west facade (offices) is windowed, but the east (laboratory services corridor) is not; short walls on the north and south are massed into volumetric blocks that enclose service features (staircase). On the east, the building opens to a broad paved terrace; on the west, the street side, it is lifted above a five-bayed loggia by the muscular, faceted tree-pilotis that Breuer favored for institutional buildings. The exterior of Becton Center resembles other Breuer precast-unit facades of the mid-1960s, but the detailing, density, and textural variations (bush-hammered, form-boarded, smooth) of the concrete give this building exceptional vitality and a powerful visual impact that is often deadened in photographs.

ARCHIVAL: **SUL 139, Drawings; AAA Correspondence, Photos, Project Record Book.**
BIBLIOGRAPHIC: *Progressive Architecture*, December 1965, 37; *Architectural Record*, April 1966, 184–85; Papachristou, *Marcel Breuer*, 161.

20. West facade

21. Elevation drawing

garage. The planning strategy here, as at Becton Center at Yale, was adapted from Breuer's Brookhaven project, allowing windowless laboratories to borrow light from windowed offices across a glass-walled corridor; one end of each wing was also windowed. Laboratory and research spaces were free of structural interruption.

The exterior fabric was to be architectural concrete, both precast and poured-in-place, and brick where the walls were related to the brick-paved plaza. The precast panels were typical of what Breuer was designing for institutional facades in the 1960s. Strongly three dimensional, they were load-bearing and provided sun control for the windows; their hollowed vertical channels served as mechanical-supply chases, while the interiors of their underwindow planes accommodated air-supply units.

ARCHIVAL: **SUL 149, Drawings, Photos.**

21
Harvard University, Biology and Chemistry Building,
Cambridge, Massachusetts, 1969 (NOT BUILT)

MARCEL BREUER AND ROBERT F. GATJE, ARCHITECTS

On May 6, 1969, Breuer agreed "to construct a Biology-Chemistry building on the campus of Harvard University." Older laboratories and other buildings on the site were to be demolished to provide about 60,000 square feet for the new construction, which Harvard hoped would "give an architectural lift to the life science quadrangle."[19] The program called for research, teaching, and laboratory space for the Departments of Biology, Molecular Biology, Chemistry, and Biochemistry, and "good communicating paths" for the scientists.

A bi-winged building—one block for Biology, and the other for Chemistry, connected through a multilevel bridge and basement tunnels—was designed with one of the seven-story blocks set on the ground, and the other elevated on eight quadrangular pilotis. To best utilize the site, the structures were placed as close as possible to the northern and eastern boundaries, freeing space for an ample brick-paved plaza and outdoor dining terrace above an underground parking

22
University of Virginia, Physics Building,
Charlottesville, Virginia, 1971–72 (NOT BUILT)

MARCEL BREUER AND HERBERT BECKHARD, ARCHITECTS

RAWLINGS, WILSON, AND FRABER, ASSOCIATE ARCHITECTS

A contract dated September 1971 was signed by the University of Virginia and Marcel Breuer and Associates for a new physics building budgeted at $5 million. It was to contain 110,750 square feet of gross area "for graduate level instruction and study in Physics." A building was designed that in profile replicated Breuer's Armstrong Rubber Company, in West Haven, Connecticut, completed the previous year. The presentation drawings were prepared in January 1972, but by June a letter to the Breuer office from the associate architects carried the news that the project had met with infinite delay.

ARCHIVAL: **AAA Contract, Photos.**

23. View of the complex

23
State University of New York (SUNY) at Buffalo, Faculty of Engineering and Applied Science Buildings Complex,
Amherst, New York, 1975–78

MARCEL BREUER AND ROBERT F. GATJE, ARCHITECTS

The Breuer office was part of a design group first assembled in the 1960s to devise a long-range master plan to develop 160 acres of the campus of SUNY Buffalo. Work on Breuer's portion—a complex of buildings for the Departments of Industrial, Chemical, Electrical, Mechanical, and Civil Engineering, plus a School of Library Science— was under way by 1975. After Breuer retired in 1976, Robert Gatje supervised the remaining construction, completed in 1978.

Buffalo's formidable winter weather was taken into account, so the design called for an interconnection among the buildings by way of corridors and bridges at the second rather than the ground level. One view, therefore, within the otherwise formulaic composition is particularly arresting: by the joining of a tower structure to a low-rise across the road by means of an elevated bridge, one of modernism's most heroic images—Gropius's Dessau Bauhaus (1926), with the bridge linking the workshops to the administrative building—consciously or unconsciously was revived.

ARCHIVAL: **SUL 71, 73, Drawings.**
BIBLIOGRAPHIC: **Gatje,** *Marcel Breuer*, **234–37.**

24
Litchfield High School,
Litchfield, Connecticut, 1954–56

25
Torrington High School,
Torrington, Connecticut, 1955–57 (NOT BUILT)

MARCEL BREUER AND O'CONNOR & KILHAM, ARCHITECTS

HERBERT BECKHARD, ASSOCIATE

In the rapidly expanding suburban culture of the 1950s, several schools in and around Litchfield, Connecticut, were commissioned to Breuer through his connection to the Rufus Stillmans and the Torin Corporation.[1] Correspondence about a high school for Litchfield was initiated in 1951–52. By 1953, Breuer had an approved design; construction began in 1954 and was completed in 1956. Programmed for about 700 students, it was an example of the sprawling, open-plan, low-lying structure that was the suburban ideal of the period and a departure from traditional closed and blocky school buildings. Light, airy, and easily connected to the outdoors, Litchfield High School was designed as a Y, enclosing and surrounded by lawns and shrubs. Laboratories, classrooms, and administrative offices were in the arms of the Y. Joined to the main body by a glazed corridor on the northeast was the shop building; a music building was appended on the southeast and a gymnasium on the southwest. The lyrical contour of the gymnasium facade (see p. 46) is one of Breuer's most stunning images; as already noted, its source is Gropius's redesigned Machine Hall from the 1914 Werkbund Exhibition in Cologne, to which Breuer added a characteristic rhythmic lilt, reminiscent of the sinuous lines of his Isokon plywood furniture.

In July 1956, Breuer made an agreement (amended in 1957) with the city of Torrington to build a new high school for 1,800 students. There has been some confusion between these two high school projects because the city of Torrington is described in the documents as "a municipal corporation located in Litchfield County." Torrington High School was never constructed although it was designed, and the drawings and a rendering reveal another low, spread-out complex of buildings based on nested trapezoids with a gymnasium that is a variation on the Litchfield scheme.

ARCHIVAL: **SUL 34; AAA Contract, Correspondence, Photos.**
BIBLIOGRAPHIC: *Progressive Architecture,* August 1958, 108–14; Jones, ed.,
Marcel Breuer 1921–1961, 1962, 176–77.

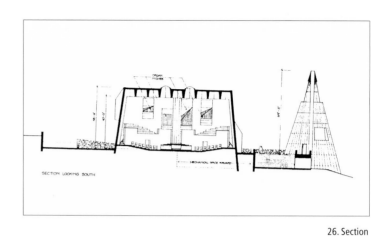

26. Section

26
Kent School, Girls' Chapel,
Kent, Connecticut, 1967 (NOT BUILT)

MARCEL BREUER AND ROBERT F. GATJE, ARCHITECTS

On January 16, 1967, Breuer contracted with the Kent School Corporation for a chapel for its newly established Girls' School. Kent had been an all-male institution and was constructing a nearby campus for its expanded student population. Robert Gatje recalls that bell ringing was an important tradition at Kent Boys' School, and it was the intention of the administration to make it important also at the Girls' School. The design for a new chapel, therefore, was to include a campanile (see p. 174).

The campanile, with its ring of eight bells, was a monumental free-standing structure sited across a wall-enclosed terrace from the chapel. Its height (about 70 feet) and isolation emphasized its importance in the program. Breuer had already designed two bell towers—at Saint John's Abbey in Collegeville, Minnesota, and the Priory of the Annunciation in Bismarck, North Dakota—and this was to be the third in the group of remarkable concrete structures inspired by the combination of engineering and geometry. It was designed as a vertical hyperbolic-paraboloid shell, its rotating body leading the visitor to encircle it and comprehend its full sculptural character. The massing was lightened by two large openings, one housing the bells and the other for the ringers.

Working once again in the Egyptian mode he adopted for smaller religious structures in the 1960s, Breuer designed the chapel as an almost windowless, heavy, ground-based block with four huge faceted projections for organ niches on the south and for a large window on the east. The material was to be rough-textured architectural concrete, exposed on the interior, where it would contrast with a waxed red-brick floor. The interior space was spanned by beams intersecting above the center to form coffers that framed lightwells.

A building of powerful expression, the Kent School chapel is allied stylistically with the Whitney Museum of American Art, completed a year earlier. It would have been an exceptional modernist landmark in New England, but the project was abandoned when the administration decided, as explained in a letter to Breuer, to "spend the money on people not buildings."

ARCHIVAL: **SUL 149, Drawings; AAA Photos.**

BIBLIOGRAPHIC: **Papachristou,** *Marcel Breuer,* **168–69; Gatje,** *Marcel Breuer,* **215.**

27. Rendering of the main plaza and library

27
Campus High School,
Roxbury, Boston, Massachusetts, 1967–68

MARCEL BREUER AND TICIAN PAPACHRISTOU, ARCHITECTS

The plan for a school for 5,000 pupils was at the core of an ambitious, but only partially realized, urban-renewal project intended to replace a slum with new residential, commercial, and industrial buildings (see no. 116). An experiment in education, the high school was to be cast in the role of a university/campus type of institution, large in size and richly endowed with faculty, equipment, and facilities to encourage students to spend time there. Its theater and other amenities were expected to attract visitors from other parts of the city, as college campuses do.

The Breuer office first produced in 1967 two designs, one a sixteen-story tower divided into four "sub-schools" with below-ground connections to outlying facilities, such as the gymnasium. The alternative plan called for four individual four-story Ys with bridges connecting the classroom and athletic facilities. About a year later, a school complex of gymnasium, classrooms, and a colonnaded library about half the size and capacity of the low-rise version was designed and eventually built. The structure was essentially prefabricated and easily assembled, made of precast concrete formed into individual panels that could be lifted into place with a crane. However, physically and ideologically, the project ended on a low note: there were doubts midway through the project about the progressive educational ideals on which the program was founded, and within a year after the school began to operate, much of it was ruined through acts of vandalism.

ARCHIVAL: **SUL 161, Drawings; AAA Photos.**

BIBLIOGRAPHIC: **Papachristou,** *Marcel Breuer,* **196–97;** *Process: Architecture,* **no. 32, 82–85.**

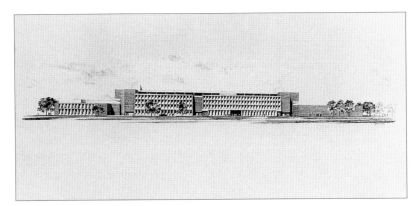

28. Rendering

28
West Queens High School,
Long Island City, New York, New York,
1969–70 (NOT BUILT)

MARCEL BREUER AND HERBERT BECKHARD, ARCHITECTS

Sixty-eight drawings for this project for a large high school close to Manhattan are with the Breuer Papers at Syracuse University. Portions of the facade have closed and uninflected surfaces with the distinctive striping that resembles Breuer's wing for the Cleveland Museum of Art, under construction at this time. The contrast between these passages and the longer stretches of inset precast windows, together with the projecting and receding volumes, gives this design its character. The mixture of taller and lower volumes, asymmetrical but balanced units, open and closed masses, and flat and rough texture creates variety and visual interest in the elevation of a modest institutional structure that is one of Breuer's strongest projects of the late 1960s.

ARCHIVAL: **SUL Drawings; AAA Photos.**

29
Oglala Community High School
(Pine Ridge High School),
Pine Ridge, South Dakota, 1973–75 (NOT BUILT)

MARCEL BREUER AND HERBERT BECKHARD, ARCHITECTS

Breuer and the Department of the Interior, Bureau of Indian Affairs, reached an agreement in October 1973 for a school complex for 500 students, with staff housing, to be known as the Oglala Community High School, on the Pine Ridge Indian Reservation in southwestern South Dakota. Comprising 2,786,540 acres, in the 1970s Pine Ridge was the second largest Native American reservation in the United States and the home of the Oglala branch of the Sioux (Oglala Lakota). A notation among the project papers in the Breuer office files describes it as "as poor as America gets." Most of the students who were to attend the school lived on the reservation in small villages, rural clusters, or isolated dwellings. The new school was to have been part of the federal government's initiative for encouraging tribal autonomy and improving life on the reservation, which included centralizing the school system.

Although programmed as a "special facilities" high school for grades 9 through 12, the school would have been open to all members of the community who wanted an education. It was founded on newer educational strategies by which students were not grouped according to age or grade level but by ability and interests. Conventional classroom space was replaced by large open plans that accommodated small cells of instructional activity around "learning resource centers" that held books and audiovisual materials. The gymnasium and swimming-pool structures were considered especially important features.

The project was developed in the Breuer office from September 1973 to July 1974 with information received from the South Dakota State Department of Public Instruction. The estimated preliminary budget costs were based on figures for constructing and furnishing a school building of 87,300 square feet. Taken into consideration (and added to construction cost projections) was the absence of building

29. Rendering

contractors near the reservation and of local skilled workers in the mechanical trades, so that living quarters for an imported workforce were needed.

On September 23, 1975, the office forwarded drawings, specifications, and a final cost estimate for the complete project to the Bureau of Indian Affairs in Albuquerque, New Mexico. The rendering reveals a series of structures reminiscent of pueblo-mastaba shapes—closed, with canted sides and flat roofs. The taller gymnasium building is linked by a covered walkway to a lower group of classroom centers, with precast-concrete window elements providing powerful sculptural projections. In this design, Breuer successfully amalgamated within a modern framework—and consistent with the building's context—images of Native American vernacular forms and East Coast American progressive educational open-school plans.

ARCHIVAL: **SUL Drawings; AAA Contract, Photos.**

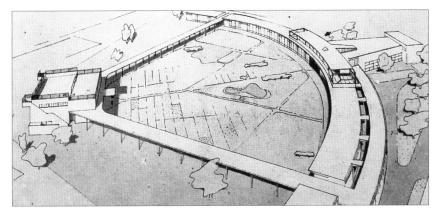

30. Aerial perspective

30
Elementary School for 480 Children, Competition,
London, England, 1936 (NOT BUILT)

MARCEL BREUER AND F. R. S. YORKE, ARCHITECTS

Breuer's first school design was an entry by Breuer & Yorke in 1936 for a "schools competition" promoted by the *London News Chronicle* that called for "a large senior mixed elementary school for 480 children, in classes of 30, in an urban district." The Breuer & Yorke proposal did not win or place, but it was illustrated as one of the "other schemes submitted" in the March 25, 1937, issue of the *Architects' Journal*. Drawings do not survive among the partnership materials in the Prints and Drawings Collection of the RIBA, but photographs showing elevations, a perspective view, an aerial view, and a plan are with the Breuer papers in the Archives of American Art.

An architectural expression of new philosophical thought and social policies regarding education in England, the project was a modern displacement of the multistory hierarchical-block format of traditional school buildings. A classroom building—low, almost fully glazed, and shaped as a wide arc—interlocked with a two-story wedge-shaped hall and was connected by splayed covered walkways to a tiered-block gymnasium. The penetration of large amounts of light and air anticipated the open plan of suburban schools of the 1950s, even though the competition description called for the building to be sited in an urban precinct. Circulation was via ramps and upper and lower walkways. Following new directions in the planning of schools, the architects designed a building with easy direct access to the outside and large classrooms that served multiple functions through lightweight movable furniture that could be formed into changing groups. The ramps and grand curve of the main building mass anticipate some of Breuer's large-scale institutional architecture of the 1950s and 1960s, such as the UNESCO Headquarters and IBM La Gaude.

ARCHIVAL: **AAA Photos.**
BIBLIOGRAPHIC: *Architects' Journal*, March 25, 1937, 537; Driller, "Frühwerk," 355–56.

31
Northfield Elementary School,
Litchfield, Connecticut, 1953

MARCEL BREUER AND O'CONNOR & KILHAM, ARCHITECTS

Northfield Elementary School, one in a group of schools that Breuer designed in the 1950s in and around Litchfield, Connecticut, was set in a rural landscape. A small-scale, low-budget institution with only five classrooms, it was formed as a single-story block. It featured such Breuer devices as a pergola as part of the facade and a brick wall perpendicular to the main mass projecting beyond the roofline. The building became the Montessori School of northwestern Connecticut.

ARCHIVAL: **SUL Drawings; AAA Photos.**
BIBLIOGRAPHIC: **Breuer,** *Sun and Shadow,* **176.**

31. Model

32
Bantam Elementary School,
Bantam, Connecticut, 1954–56

MARCEL BREUER AND O'CONNOR & KILHAM, ARCHITECTS

HERBERT BECKHARD, ASSOCIATE

Another of the institutional buildings in the Litchfield, Connecticut, area designed by Breuer was an elementary school for the village of Bantam. Here, he used one of his most adaptable binuclear designs, wherein two boxes—one a square (for a multipurpose school–community space), and the other a rectangle (for classrooms and kindergarten)—were joined off-axis by a pergola-fronted linking element made up of a glass-walled entrance lobby, teachers' offices, and "health room." Low, spread out, light in color, with easy access to the outdoors, and set in the countryside, the building conformed to visual ideals of 1950s modernism and to educational ideals of postwar America, where formal differences between residential and institutional architecture were minimized. The bearing walls were concrete block; the roof was supported by wooden beams. After it ceased being used as a school, the building became the Geographical Area 18 Court and Post Office. It retained most of its original features, including the reticulated mullion design that Breuer liked for large glazed surfaces at this period.

ARCHIVAL: **SUL Drawings; AAA Photos.**
BIBLIOGRAPHIC: *Progressive Architecture,* **January 1954, 95, and February 1957, 118–21; Breuer,** *Sun and Shadow,* **177.**

32. Pergola at the main entrance

33
Connecticut Junior Republic,
Litchfield, Connecticut, 1955

MARCEL BREUER AND THOMAS C. BABBITT, ARCHITECTS

Founded in the late nineteenth century as a social experiment, the Junior Republic was a self-governing community ("village") for adolescents ("citizens") who needed guidance and direction. It was modeled on the ideals and organization of the government, in miniature. One of the earliest of the Junior Republic villages was established in Litchfield, Connecticut. Rufus Stillman was president of the board of trustees of the Connecticut Junior Republic in 1955 when Breuer was given the commission to build a new complex of buildings. With inexpensive materials, Breuer interpreted the institution, appropriately, in the idiom of his current residential architecture. The long, low structure was nested within lateral walls of brick and beneath an overhanging flat roof, with one dividing brick wall extending well beyond the roofline. Almost fifty years later, the school is still serving its original function.

ARCHIVAL: **SUL Drawings; AAA Photos.**

33. Rendering

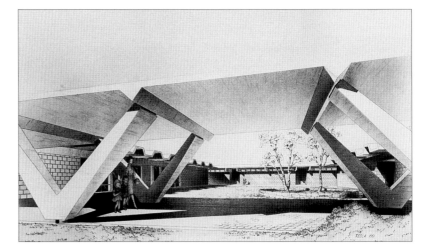

34. Rendering of walkway trusses

34
Whitby School,
Greenwich, Connecticut, 1959–60 (NOT BUILT)

MARCEL BREUER, ARCHITECT **ROBERT F. GATJE,** ASSOCIATE

On July 20, 1959, Breuer entered into an agreement with the secretary-treasurer of the Whitby School, a small Montessori School in Greenwich, Connecticut, to build, furnish, and decorate an elementary school. The job came to him because the director of the school admired Saint John's Abbey. The idea was to make a small start and allow the school to grow. Sited around a courtyard were to be classroom and administrative pavilions of brick, glass, and concrete approached through a covered walkway. The pavilions were low, boxy structures with folded plate and long-span concrete roofs in an unusual trough format that enlivened the upper profiles. The roof of the walkway was supported by the dramatic V-shaped supports favored by Breuer at this period and used, for example, at the Priory of the Annunciation and its University of Mary in Bismarck, North Dakota. Working drawings were completed on February 23, 1960, and the project was put out for bid in March. It was canceled because of high costs and ended in arbitration.

ARCHIVAL: **SUL Drawings; AAA Contract, Photos, Project Record Book.**
BIBLIOGRAPHIC: **Gatje,** *Marcel Breuer,* **91–92.**

35
State School for the Mentally Retarded,
Hempstead, Long Island, New York,
1969–71 (NOT BUILT)

MARCEL BREUER AND TICIAN PAPACHRISTOU, ARCHITECTS

An agreement was reached on March 3, 1969, between Marcel Breuer and Associates and the Health and Mental Hygiene Facilities Improvement Corporation, Albany, New York, for "the comprehensive planning, complete design and construction of a new state school for the mentally retarded." The proposal was filed as number D35281 on April 15, 1969, under the auspices of the New York State Department of Mental Hygiene; the new facility, for approximately 500 children and young adults, was to be located at Mitchell Field in Hempstead, New York, on Long Island. Working drawings were completed and bids were taken, but the project was not built because of changes in the philosophy of care for the mentally retarded and because of the reduction of funding for state projects. Renderings reveal a complex of interconnected cross-shaped, light-filled buildings on a large, square landscaped site. Approaches were via ramps, terraces, and covered walkways; the predominant material was to be precast concrete offset by split-face block masonry.

ARCHIVAL: **SUL Drawings; AAA Contracts; Photos.**
BIBLIOGRAPHIC: **Papachristou,** *Marcel Breuer,* **205.**

36
Greenwich Village Public School 3,
New York, New York, 1971–72 (NOT BUILT)

MARCEL BREUER, ARCHITECT

From December 1971 through February 1972, Marcel Breuer and Associates worked on a project for the New York City Board of Education to convert an existing five-story junior high school in Greenwich Village into an experimental primary school, known as the Meiser Charette School, that would be organized according to new educational programs. The existing spaces were to be modernized by the removal of partition walls and the renovation of old systems. A schematic plan of the ground floor filed with the Breuer Papers at Syracuse University shows spaces provided for preschool children, community functions, meeting rooms, and offices.

ARCHIVAL: **SUL 12, Drawings.**

35. Rendering

37. Entrance canopy and administration-gym wing

37

Bryn Mawr Lower School and Elementary School (Bryn Mawr School for Girls of Baltimore City), Baltimore, Maryland, 1971–72

MARCEL BREUER AND HAMILTON P. SMITH, ARCHITECTS

Breuer agreed on July 30, 1970, to design "on the present school campus [Bryn Mawr School for Girls] classrooms and related facilities for younger students to be known as the Lower School." Construction began in the summer of 1971 and was completed before November 1972. The job came to the Breuer office through Edith Ferry Hooper, dedicated Breuer client and chairman of the building committee. The program called for a new 22,500-square-foot school for 220 girls from kindergarten through grade 5 and about 26 faculty members. On a spacious site bordering a woodland, three units—administration and gymnasium wing, classroom wing for grades 2 to 5, and smaller classroom wing for kindergarten and grade 1—were arranged in an L-shape

with entrances opening from a covered walkway. The complex was preceded by a narthex supported by four deep piers. The philosophy of education followed at the school called for open classrooms and free-flowing spaces without partitions or traditional enclosures; they were organized around a central skylighted space. Projecting and receding volumes replaced conventional flat peripheral walls and enriched the play of interior space; split-face concrete block gave texture to the exterior walls. Beyond the buildings were play areas, athletic fields, and parking spaces. The suburban setting was similar to that of many Breuer houses, and the project was conceived by the architects as houselike in scale and design (the units were described as "classroom houses").

ARCHIVAL: **SUL 82–84, 137, 160, Drawings; AAA Photos.**

38. Perspective sketch

38
Hospital for 1,100 Beds, Competition,
Elberfeld, Germany, 1928–29 (NOT BUILT)

MARCEL BREUER, WITH THE ASSISTANCE OF GUSTAV HASSENPFLUG

Discussing modern materials in his chapter in the book *Circle*, Breuer used as an example the combination of glass and steel with sound- and heat-insulating materials, such as cork, that he proposed in this project for a large hospital complex at Elberfeld (see p. 68). He also cited the project in his study of tall buildings in *Die Form*.

The units in the Elberfeld complex, including a segregated structure for infectious diseases, ranged in height from three to twelve stories and were set within a landscaped park on sloping terrain. Patients' rooms gave on to deep balconies; in good weather, the sickbed could be rolled outside through wide casement windows. The setback terraces were formed by stepped recesses that offered light and a view and kept shadows from falling on the lower stories. An intricate support system organized for the projecting levels was devised of column and beam, and suggested the structural underpinnings of large sports stadiums. Circulation within the buildings was by way of elevator banks linked by a bridgelike pedestrian corridor. In structure, design, and size, the stepped high-rise hospital was more ambitious than any project Breuer had designed up to this point.

ARCHIVAL: **AAA Photos; BHA Photos.**
BIBLIOGRAPHIC: **Breuer, "Beiträge zur Frage des Hochhauses,"** *Die Form* **5 (1930): 113–17, and "Architecture and Material," in** *Circle*, **ed. Martin, Nicholson, and Gabo, 193–202; Blake,** *Marcel Breuer*, **39–41; Jones, ed.,** *Marcel Breuer*, **238; Grohn,** *Gustav Hassenpflug*, **34; Driller, "Frühwerk," 349–51.**

39
Sanatorium for 45 Beds,
Essen, Germany, 1930 (NOT BUILT)

MARCEL BREUER, ARCHITECT

A "klinik" in Essen is listed by Breuer in some of the inventories he compiled of his work,[1] but there is no information about such a project. Joachim Driller suggests that it might be synonymous with a sanatorium project in Dortmund mentioned in correspondence between Breuer and Sigfried Giedion. Possibly relevant to the existence of such a project is the fact that Breuer was in Essen in 1930 when he was installing his tubular-steel furniture in a lecture hall in the Folkwang Museum.[2]

ARCHIVAL: **SUL 50; AAA Correspondence.**
BIBLIOGRAPHIC: **Driller, "Frühwerk," 351, 355.**

40
Jewish Hospital for 220 Beds, Competition,
Zagreb, Yugoslavia, 1930 (NOT BUILT)

MARCEL BREUER, WITH THE ASSISTANCE OF GUSTAV HASSENPFLUG

Still another hospital proposal around 1930 appears in Breuer's work lists. Magdalena Droste says that Gustav Hassenpflug assisted Breuer in this competition entry, as he had with the Elberfeld Hospital project.[3] Three large annotated drawings in the Bauhaus-Archiv[4] were studied closely by Joachim Driller, who published them for the first time and who points out that this hospital design, like that of the Dortmund "klinik," is mentioned in correspondence between Breuer and Sigfried Giedion.[5] He notes the similarity of the stepped form of the building to that of the Elberfeld hospital and describes a many-windowed T-shaped structure where the upper two floors of the three-story (with roof terrace) principal wing—a long box—were set back. A glass-walled lobby fronted this wing (administrative offices, laboratories, and director's apartment); patients' and nurses' rooms were on the upper floors. An exterior cantilevered stair led from the first upper floor to the garden. The smaller wing (operating rooms and nurses' rooms) was perpendicular to the main body and was elevated on pilotis.

ARCHIVAL: **BHA Drawings (Inv. 1881/1–3).**
BIBLIOGRAPHIC: **Driller, "Frühwerk," 351–54.**

41
Sanatorium for 80 Beds,
Dortmund, Germany, ca. 1930–32 (NOT BUILT)

MARCEL BREUER, ARCHITECT

In his work inventories, Breuer listed an eighty-bed sanatorium in Dortmund.[6] It has been given attention only by Joachim Driller, who says that it was "a completely finished design mentioned in the correspondence between Giedion and Breuer." Driller believes that it may be the same project as the Essen sanatorium. Since the two cities are not far from each other in the Nordrhein region, Breuer indeed may have confused them when, in 1956, he made an inventory of his work for Giulio Carlo Argan.[7]

ARCHIVAL: **SUL 15, 50.**
BIBLIOGRAPHIC: **Driller, "Frühwerk," 355.**

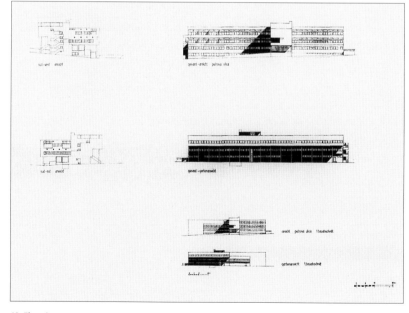

40. Elevations

42. Model

42

Long Beach Hospital, Nurses' Residence,
Long Beach, Long Island, New York, 1945 (NOT BUILT)

MARCEL BREUER, IN ASSOCIATION WITH SERGE CHERMAYEFF

On January 3, 1945, Breuer agreed to plan a residence for nurses, interns, and office personnel at Long Beach Hospital. In an appeal to the War Production Board, made in 1944, not to defer the project to the end of the war, the client made the case that without any other hospital in the immediate vicinity, Long Beach Hospital served not only the civilian population, but officers and enlisted men and women and their families from the naval station at nearby Lido. Budgeted at $50,000 (based on 40 cents per cubic foot of building volume), the new residence was a project of the "utmost economy." Its program called for twenty to twenty-four single rooms with one bath for every two rooms, separate room and bath for supervisor and housekeeper, and double rooms and separate entrance for other personnel. On January 20, Breuer presented a model and five drawings to the building committee. With minor changes, his design was approved and he was given the go-ahead for working drawings and specifications. Because at this time Breuer was licensed in Massachusetts and Pennsylvania but not in New York, he formed an association for the project with Serge Chermayeff so that Chermayeff's name would appear on the drawings. On March 8, however, Breuer was requested to "stop all work as we have been advised you are not licensed to operate in the State of New York,"[8] apparently an excuse designed to mask a commitment on the part of hospital officials to another architect before Breuer entered the picture. The project was halted, and a contractual dispute ensued. It was settled so that Breuer was paid a fee, but his drawings and specifications were turned over to the hospital.

The design is known from photographs of the model. Breuer revived the design, with variations, five years later for the Ferry Cooperative Dormitory at Vassar College. The similarity in requirements—rooms for twenty-four nurses and a supervisor at Long Beach and rooms for twenty-five college girls and a faculty resident at Vassar—may have suggested the reuse. One unit elevated on pilotis above a flagstone terrace contained the private rooms, while another, perpendicular and interlocking at ground level, was for public and communal spaces. A sheltered terrace on the roof of the lower wing was reached by a door in the dormitory wing.

ARCHIVAL: SUL 26, Drawings; AAA Photos.
BIBLIOGRAPHIC: Driller, "Frühwerk," 348.

Convent of the Sisters of Divine Providence, Infirmary, 1975–76. See no. 50.

43
Saint John's Abbey and University Complex,
Collegeville, Minnesota, 1954–68

MARCEL BREUER AND ASSOCIATES, ARCHITECTS

TRAYNOR AND HERMANSON, ASSOCIATED ARCHITECTS

Monastery Wing, 1954–55
Residence Hall I, 1957–59
Church and Campanile, 1958–61

MARCEL BREUER, ARCHITECT

HAMILTON P. SMITH, ASSOCIATE

Library, 1964–66
Science Building, 1964–66
Residence Hall II, 1965–67

MARCEL BREUER AND HAMILTON P. SMITH, ARCHITECTS

Campus Center (Student Union and Swimming Pavilion), 1966

DESIGNED, BUT NOT BUILT, BY BREUER

Institute for Ecumenical and Cultural Research, 1967–68

MARCEL BREUER AND ROBERT F. GATJE, ARCHITECTS

Hill Monastic Manuscript Library, Bush Center, 1974

HAMILTON P. SMITH, ARCHITECT

43a. Sanctuary

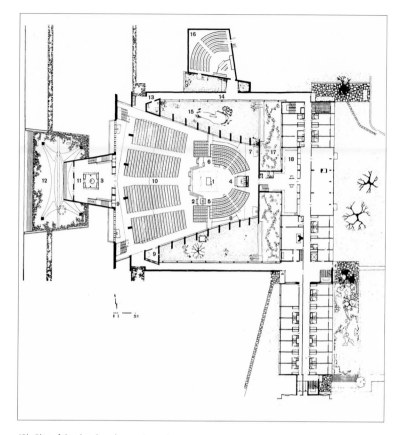

43b. Plan of the church and monastery wing

Breuer visited Saint John's Abbey for the first time on April 17, 1953, one of twelve internationally famous modern architects who had received a letter from Abbot Baldwin Dworschak inquiring about their interest in designing a new monastery. "We feel that the modern architect with his orientation toward functionalism and honest use of materials is uniquely qualified to produce a Catholic work," the abbot wrote.[1] Pietro Belluschi, Breuer, Walter Gropius, Richard Neutra, and Eero Saarinen were among the recipients of the letter in the United States.

The "Comprehensive 100-Year Plan" devised in 1953 for the abbey and for Saint John's University (a liberal arts college operated by Saint John's Abbey) was one of the most gratifying commissions of Breuer's career, as it gave him responsibility for the design, construction, landscaping, materials, colors, interiors, works of art, church furniture (altars, communion tables, and so on), and more. With Hamilton Smith—first as principal associate and then as partner—Breuer's work for Saint John's continued for two decades.

43c. Monastery wing

43d. Library facade

Work on the Comprehensive Plan began in May 1953; the first structure was to be the monastery wing. Construction was started on May 20, 1954, and by the fall of 1955 the building was occupied. The three-story rectangular box had bedroom-studies for retired and infirm priests, dormitories for clerics, recreation rooms, visitors' quarters, a reception room, and a private chapel for the abbot. The planning was based on a module of 12 (individual priests' rooms at 12 feet, and clerics' dormitories at 24 feet). On the exterior, the south facade, which faces a lake, had balconies and sun shades. "Members of the community living in the new building are very much pleased with it and its vari-

ous features including those about which we expressed some doubt when Mr. Breuer first proposed them," wrote the abbot to Smith on June 16, 1956.[2]

A preliminary design for the church—with its campanile, baptistery and font, chapter house, crypt, cloisters, and link to the monastery wing—was set down in 1953. Revisions and a new design were presented to the community in May 1957; construction began in June 1958, and the building was consecrated on August 24, 1961 (see p. 142).

The huge transeptless concrete church, formed as a trapezoid (178 feet wide at the front and 84 feet at the rear), was built to accommodate 1,700 people and comprises a "nave," balcony, and deep choir with a horseshoe of stalls enfolding the central altar, above which is suspended a perforated (for light fixtures) baldachin. Breuer specified amber glass for the lantern above the baldachin to provide the interior with a golden glow. The rear balcony is cantilevered from huge apertured piers; the main body of the church is free of supports that would obstruct visibility and inhibit community. As the structure narrows and lowers toward the altar, the sloping web walls form a series of Vs of decreasing height. They, and the accordian-fold trusses and longitudinal beams of the ceiling, evoke memories of the piers and rib vaults of traditional church architecture.

The most spectacular image in the Saint John's complex is the 112-foot-high campanile, which houses the five bells transferred from the old church; it is essentially a free-standing stabile in the Calder tradition (see pp. 36, 141). A slender trapezoidal slab cantilevered vertically from an arched support of parabolic cross-vaults, in turn cantilevered from subterranean foundations, it fronts the north facade and rises above the atrium baptistery. Breuer referred to it as a bell banner, seeing in the shape of its upper portion the banners carried in ecclesiastical processions. Because the north-facing church facade would receive no direct sun, it was the wish of the community to have some kind of "panel" to deflect the sun's rays from the south to the interior of the church. The banner was that reflecting panel, and the tracery screen of the north facade, made of 540 cast-in-place concrete hexagons, each framing a stained-glass panel, was the light transmitter. The hexagonal format was a reworking of an earlier (and more satisfactory) design in which large concrete-framed rectangles of glass were arranged in a Mondrianesque composition.

The stained glass—what Breuer called "the most important [artistic] element of the church"—led to an aesthetic crisis during construction. Breuer proposed that Josef Albers design the glass, but there was unexpected resistance to the suggestion, a concern that an abstract composition such as Albers would surely design might lack spiritual content. Art consultant Frank Kacmarcik worked hard to mediate, but

43e. Campanile and church, with a view of the folded wall

the committee voted 7 to 5 against. By rejecting one of the most important abstract artists of the twentieth century, the community lost the opportunity to make Saint John's a celebrated example of modern stained-glass art. Breuer managed, however, to have Albers design the small stained-glass window in the abbot's private chapel in the monastery wing.

Whitney S. Stoddard proposed that the notion of a campanile wall with perforations for bells came from Breuer's travels in the Greek Islands in 1931 and 1932;[3] Spanish colonial mission churches with bells exposed to the sky were meaningful, too, to Breuer. This is borne out by a note in his handwriting on the reverse of a photograph of San José, Laguna Pueblo, New Mexico, kept among his photographs of Saint John's: "adobe wall with bells reminiscent to concrete banner of St. John's church."

A major change in the design of the base of the campanile, documented by many sketches from Breuer's hand, was the result of his work on the UNESCO Headquarters and his constant view of the Eiffel Tower. Reflecting the élan of the Paris landmark, the bell slab was made to rest on tall, smooth-curved arches instead of on a pair of upward-tapering legs, closed in on the sides and framing a rectilinear space. The campanile rises over the atrium-baptistery, a glass-walled area sited at the entrance to the church to signify the importance of baptism as the first sacrament.

The design and program for a new library existed by 1960. The building, to accommodate about 600 users, was begun in 1964 and was dedicated in May 1966 (see p. 172). It was planned as a two-level structure with basement, the levels connected by an open central stair. The interior is highly dramatic, in contrast to the exterior, which is little more than a plain box, purposely unprepossessing so as not to compete with the church building across the open plaza. The exterior walls are sheathed in large slabs of gray granite separated by concrete pilasters—structural elements that produce lateral bracing. Inside, private space is provided by partitioning the large library tables into study compartments.

The structural material of the library is reinforced concrete. The roof and ceiling of the upper floor are supported by the branches that rise from two large column clusters (structural trees that are also utility cores) on 27-foot centers, freeing the space visually and physically. This is in the tradition of great library structures, such as those of Henri Labrouste in the nineteenth century, that become tents of soaring space and light. The concrete "trees" were basically inspired by the work of Pier Luigi Nervi, but whereas Nervi's treelike columnar forms celebrate slenderness, lightness, elegance, and linearity, Breuer worked in a heavier manner with denser, squatter, more muscular members and a more sculptural result.

Smith designed an annex in 1974—the Hill Monastic Manuscript Library, Bush Center—established for the study of manuscripts and documents on microfilm. It is a two-level complex at the level of the basement and lower floor of the main library, to which it has direct access.

ARCHIVAL: SUL 70, 97–109, 112–18, Drawings, Sketches; AAA Correspondence, Photos; Saint John's Abbey Archives.

BIBLIOGRAPHIC: *Arts & Architecture*, June 1954, 14–15, and February 1962, 18–20; *Architectural Forum*, July 1954, 148–55; December 1956, 107–9; November 1961, 131–37; December 1963, 72–73; and May 1968, 40–57; *Liturgical Arts*, May 1956, 60–61; *Design Quarterly* 53 (1961): 1–31; *L'Architecture d'aujourd'hui*, February 1962, 40–47; *Architectural Record*, November 1961, 131–42, and February 1964, 124–25; *Domus*, June 1962, 3–8; Breuer, *Sun and Shadow*, 191–95; Stoddard, *Adventure in Architecture*; Jones, ed., *Marcel Breuer*, 36–47; Jordy, "The Domestication of Modern: Marcel Breuer's Ferry Cooperative Dormitory at Vassar College," in *American Buildings and Their Architects*, 216–19; Howarth, *Concrete and the Cross*; *Process: Architecture*, no. 32, 66–69, 100–104; Gatje, *Marcel Breuer*, passim.

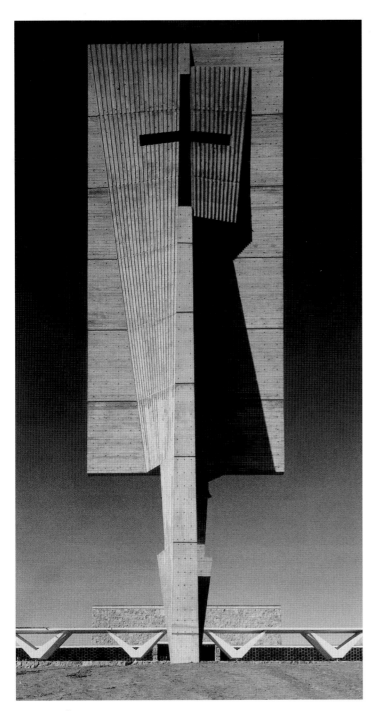

44a. Campanile

44
Annunciation Priory of the Sisters of St. Benedict,
Bismarck, North Dakota, 1956–63

Phase I, 1958–59
Phase II, 1961–63

MARCEL BREUER, ARCHITECT **HAMILTON P. SMITH,** ASSOCIATE

TRAYNOR AND HERMANSON, ASSOCIATED ARCHITECTS

A priory for the Benedictine Sisters of the Annunciation was founded in 1947 in temporary quarters in Bismarck, North Dakota. By 1954, needing to expand, the Sisters decided to build a large new priory seven miles south of the city on an isolated hilly site overlooking the Missouri River valley. They approached Breuer because of his work at Saint John's Abbey. Responding to a letter from the prioress five years after the work was finished, Breuer wrote on May 23, 1968: "[You have] something very remarkable not primarily on account of the architecture, but [because] you went to the trouble to choose your architects from New York and you left them enough freedom—aside from your very exact guidance—to find an expression for your requirements according to their best judgement."[4]

The project was to be long range, built in stages because of the limited budget. Planning began in the Breuer office in September 1954; a design for Phase I (classroom and dormitory wing, community facilities wing) was ready by December 1955; construction was started in May 1958 and completed in October 1959.

Breuer and Traynor and Hermanson, "architects associated," agreed on March 11, 1960, to build Phase II, the permanent convent (convent wing, chapel, bell tower). Breuer would also design or select all furnishings and design headstones for the Sisters' cemetery. Construction of Phase II began on April 10, 1961, and was completed in July 1963. The small temporary chapel (gold leaf on mosaic tile, a red baldachin, and concealed skylight) that served from 1959 to 1963 was so highly regarded by the community that it was kept as part of the permanent complex.

Breuer designed an integrated four-wing ensemble (convent, chapel, community dining hall, and classrooms) around three large open courtyards separated by walkways and arranged to conform to patterns of circulation prescribed by the ritual life of the order. The success of this and his other monastic work can be attributed to his fanatical attention to the uses of the space and to his perception that the institutions were also homes. Two two-story enclosed passageways running east-west, one cloistered and the other a wide thoroughfare screened by terra-cotta tiles, connect the four wings. A third passage, on the south, open and with dramatic V-shaped concrete roof supports

resting on fieldstone, is a canopied entrance loggia. The main doors are of translucent glass that appears black, a creative invention for a modern convent—not closed, but visually impenetrable.

The roof system of the chapel is that of half-hyperbolic-paraboloid concrete shells, textured by formboards and joined at their high edges along the long axis of the building. Sheathed with copper outside and whitewashed on the inside, they are carried on four exterior buttresses, freeing the interior space of obstructions. Breuer's interest in hyperbolic-paraboloid construction, which began in the mid-1950s with the roof of the Hunter College library, was at its height in the early and mid-1960s, when he used it in planning such ecclesiastical projects as the Kent School Girls' Chapel, Olgiata Parish Church, and the church of St. Francis de Sales. Cantilevered from the cloistered passageway to the chapel is a small greenhouse niche for altar flowers. A projecting window anticipates the windows at the Whitney Museum of American Art.

The low-lying ensemble of the priory is dominated by an extraordinary free-standing campanile of textured concrete, 100 feet high, on axis with the chapel (see p. 157). It alone is worth a journey to the convent. The geometry of the campanile—straight lines connecting points along the base with points along a line rotated 90 degrees at the top to create warped surfaces—is expressed in the contrast of vertical ribbed surfaces with those of smoother horizontal bands, all made by the wooden formboards used for the concrete work. Hamilton Smith wrote that the "formboard imprints were not random but carefully controlled, their patterns designed by the architect."[5]

Phase III of the convent project was the construction of the nearby University of Mary (see no. 18).

ARCHIVAL: **SUL Drawings; AAA Correspondence, Photos, Project Record Book; Priory of the Annunciation Archives.**

BIBLIOGRAPHIC: *Architectural Record*, April 1956, 181–86; January 1961, 105–9; and December 1963, 95–102; *Deutsche Bauzeitung*, June 1961, 426–29, and March 1966, 188; *L'Architecture d'aujourd'hui*, June 1961, 80–82, and September 1965, 74–75; *Liturgical Arts*, February 1964, 50–59; *Arts & Architecture*, November 1964, 16–19; Papachristou, *Marcel Breuer*, 92–99; *Process: Architecture*, no. 32, 90–93.

45
Westchester Reform Temple,
Scarsdale, New York, 1957–59

WILLIAM W. LANDSBERG, ARCHITECT

MARCEL BREUER, DESIGN CONSULTANT

William W. Landsberg said of this project: "I was the architect of record and Breuer was the consultant, but he had complete charge of the design. Our understanding was that he would do the design and I would do everything else. Breuer came up with the Star of David design: the hexagon in the center was the main seating area, and one of the points was the bema."[6] The temple was dedicated in September 1959, and Breuer delivered an address on the occasion.

ARCHIVAL: **AAA Photos.**

46
Temple B'nai Jeshurun,
Short Hills, New Jersey, 1961 (NOT BUILT)

MARCEL BREUER, ARCHITECT

HERBERT BECKHARD, ASSOCIATE

The contract of January 12, 1961, called for a large suburban temple with the capacity to seat 3,000, a smaller chapel, social facilities with a kitchen, and an adjacent school with approximately twenty-seven classrooms. Breuer was also to furnish and decorate all the spaces and to design the landscaping. The program was fully developed through presentation drawings, a rendering, and a model, but the bids came in too high over the budget and the project was abandoned.

Buildings and courtyards were arranged with the square, 70-foot-high synagogue flanked on one side by a three-story school (originally sketched by Breuer to repeat the shape of the temple) and on the other by a small hexagonal chapel and a larger two-story social hall. The school was formed as a long, narrow rectangle with double-loaded central corridors for classrooms and offices. A long stone-walled walkway linked the buildings and was intersected by a projecting mini-building that was the entrance and main lobby of the temple, whose structure was described by Papachristou as "formed by [thirty-six] folded concrete arches rising from the square plan to join radially at the center of the roof."

The ambitious program lacked an inventive strategy for organizing the separate elements. Breuer repeated themes from previous work—the folded wall, the hexagon, the mural stonework of suburban residences—but neither they nor the individual structures were integrated into a coherent composition.

ACHIVAL: **SUL Drawings, Sketches; AAA Contract, Correspondence, Photos.**
BIBLIOGRAPHIC: ***Architectural Record,*** March 1962, 127–31; Jones, ed., *Marcel Breuer,* 98–99; Papachristou, *Marcel Breuer,* 238.

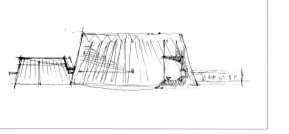

46a. Sketch by Breuer

47
St. Luke's Church,
Fairport, New York, 1964 (NOT BUILT)

MARCEL BREUER AND HERBERT BECKHARD, ARCHITECTS

Presentation drawings and a model were made in 1964 for a new St. Luke's, an Episcopal church in Fairport, New York, near Rochester, the only Protestant church among Breuer's ecclesiastical commissions. It was planned for a sloping site; the sections and elevations of the upper sanctuary (with auxiliary building below) illustrate Breuer's mastaba building type, a low compact structure with a flat roof and canted sides. Walls were mostly unpierced, except for a large stained-glass window and a smaller window on the west, both projecting from the wall. Additional light entered from six lightwells in the ceiling. The entrance to the church was through a deep narthex protruding from the windowless facade.

ARCHIVAL: **SUL Drawings, Sketches; AAA Photos.**
BIBLIOGRAPHIC: ***Architectural Record,*** April 1966, 178–79.

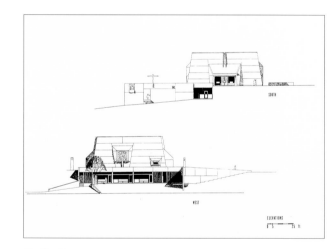

47. Elevations

46b. Rendering

48a. Sanctuary

48
Church and Rectory of St. Francis de Sales,
Muskegon, Michigan, 1964–66

MARCEL BREUER AND HERBERT BECKHARD, ARCHITECTS

The referral to Breuer for a church and rectory just outside Muskegon, Michigan, in the area of Norton Shores came from Frank Kacmarcik, who had been arts consultant at Saint John's Abbey. Working drawings were completed on November 1, 1963; groundbreaking took place on May 20, 1964; and the first mass in the new building was celebrated on December 18, 1966 (see p. 171). St. Francis de Sales is Breuer's most dramatic and Expressionistic building inside and out, a triumph of concrete technology. As they rise, the warped, windowless side walls (light enters through roof skylights) revolve and twist into self-supporting hyperbolic paraboloids. The concrete ribs of the interior altar wall are modern equivalents of the lines that energized the great Gothic churches of Europe. The maximum clear height of the interior is 85 feet; the wide space at the rear narrows toward the altar; a free-standing balcony reached by stairs is supported by and cantilevered from four wedge-shaped columns.

Breuer spoke about the church with Shirley Reiff Howarth, director of the Hackley Art Museum in Muskegon, in an interview that was published in *Art Journal* in 1979.[7] (Howarth had curated an exhibition about Breuer's religious architecture, "Marcel Breuer: Concrete and the Cross," in 1978.) He explained that the concrete hyperbolic paraboloids were used to enclose the space and were not (as at the library at Hunter College) the structural system. The trapezoidal facade wall, preceded by a narthex with baptistery, tilts back against the paraboloids and forms another of Breuer's Egyptoid pylons of this period, a close relative of facades designed for three unexecuted projects: St. Luke's Church, Kent School Girls' Chapel, and Olgiata Parish Church. A projecting enclosure for the bells and a chapel for the Blessed Sacrament that protrudes from the wall of the sanctuary on the west ally this building with Breuer's contemporaneous work at the Whitney Museum of American Art. The exterior is architectural concrete textured with formboard patterns. Herbert Beckhard, in his own practice after Breuer's death, made additions to the building.

ARCHIVAL: **SUL 138, Drawings; AAA Photos, Project Record Book.**
BIBLIOGRAPHIC: *Architectural Record*, March 1962, 132–36, and November 1967, 130–37; *Liturgical Arts*, May 1962, 110–11, and February 1965, 52–53; *L'Architecture d'aujourd'hui*, June 1963, 16–18; *Journal of the American Institute of Architects*, April 1968, 69, and May 1973, 32–33; *Art Journal* 38 (1979): 257–60; Papachristou, *Marcel Breuer*, 134–43; *Process: Architecture*, no. 32, 94–99.

48b. Southeast end of the church

Kent School, Girls' Chapel, 1967 (not built). See no. 26.

49
Olgiata Parish Church (Chiesa parocchiale delle Sante Rufina e Seconda, Olgiata Romana),
near Rome, Italy, 1968–70 (NOT BUILT)

MARCEL BREUER, ARCHITECT

MARIO JOSSA, ASSOCIATE

November 12, 1968, is the date of a letter of agreement between Breuer and Società Generale Immobiliare, the largest developer and construction company in Italy at the time, for "a church in Rome." The commission came through architect Mario Jossa, who headed the Breuer office in Paris and whose uncle was the Vatican's Apostolic Delegate in Washington, D.C.[8] Olgiata was a prosperous residential community in the Roman countryside developed by Immobiliare. The first design, for which drawings and a model were prepared, was based on the hyperbolic paraboloid. It links this church with the group of religious structures Breuer was designing in the 1960s at a moment when he was particularly interested in hyperbolic-paraboloid construction and Egyptian imagery. The lateral walls of the sanctuary twist up to meet a tilted, closed facade of Roman travertine with sloping pylonic sides. This proposal was abandoned because of substantial changes in the program and was replaced by the definitive second design, also carried to full working-drawing stage, in which the walls of the exterior were transformed into a "stepped H-P" and the entrance and sanctuary were reoriented. Sited on the rise of a slope leading to a brook were the church and, across a stepped terrace, a two-part administration building. The lateral walls of the church formed a series of shallow projections rising and expanding from the low truncated triangle of the entrance to the tall skylighted sanctuary, the exterior upper wall of which served also as campanile. The project, not built because Immobiliare underwent financial difficulties during the 1970s, would have been one of Breuer's most brilliant formal and structural compositions.

ARCHIVAL: **SUL 66; Drawings (Mario Jossa).**
BIBLIOGRAPHIC: **Papachristou,** *Marcel Breuer*, **198–99.**

49a. Second design, church roof plan and administration building plan

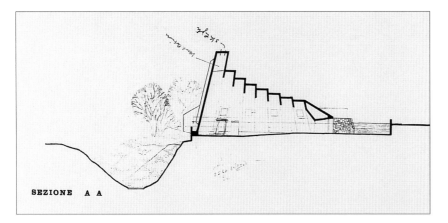

49b. Second design, section

50a. Chapel and cloistered courtyard

50
Convent of the Sisters of Divine Providence,
Baldegg, Switzerland, 1968–72

Infirmary, 1975–76

MARCEL BREUER, ROBERT F. GATJE, AND MARIO JOSSA, ARCHITECTS

BEAT A. H. JORDI, ASSOCIATED ARCHITECT

BEAT VON SEGESSER, ASSOCIATED ARCHITECT (COORDINATION, SWITZERLAND)

The project for a new motherhouse for the Sisters of Divine Providence in Baldegg, near Lucerne, who live according to the Franciscan Rule, began with an architectural competition. "We prefer a simple, clear, uncompromising architecture in which the Franciscan spirit is expressed; it must therefore be modern architecture through which the character of the house will be realized," wrote the Sisters in one of the competition programs.[9]

The selection by an outside jury of a design by a Swiss architect was rejected by the Sisters; the same fate was met by the design chosen in a second (1967) competition, also by a Swiss architect. Breuer

entered the picture when it was proposed, as the solution to an awkward dilemma, that a "foreign" (non-Swiss) architect be consulted. Breuer met with the Sisters in the fall of 1967, and the project came to contract on September 20. He had the Priory of the Annunciation and his extensive work at Saint John's Abbey as recommendations. Building of the motherhouse was begun in 1968 and was finished in 1972. It was followed by the construction of an adjacent infirmary and old-age home. The completed convent is an imposing structure of concrete and rough fieldstone with windows deeply recessed within the faceted precast-concrete modular framework, designed in Breuer's rigid, hard-edged additive style of the late 1960s.

The half-hour-by-half-hour program formulated by the Sisters determined the layout of the buildings and the patterns of circulation. The result was a Siamese-E plan, whereby the structured conventual life of chapel, residence, study, work, dining, and recreation was coordinated with the architectural environment. Lateral wings framed four cloistered courtyards; the chapel—the heart of the complex—and the dining space formed the central back-to-back projections of the E, joined to the wings by corridors.

Breuer was guided by rules of clausura and by requirements that the individual Sister be undisturbed by the outside world and have a view into the landscape. The cloisters were to be visible from the Sisters' rooms, but no visitor would see into or enter them; silence was crucial. An early layout was reversed north to south so that the chapel—an innovative design with projecting window panels and a double-fold corner—would face south, to the woods, and traffic would approach from only the north.[10]

Breuer brought a set of preliminary drawings to Baldegg from New York in May 1968. They included a sketch for a geometrically bold bell tower, like the one in Bismarck, North Dakota, but the Sisters in Switzerland preferred the framework to contain a cross instead of bells. They found the proposed seating system for the chapel—benches at right angles—"too distracting" and favored a faceted-curve format instead. For ease of cleaning, they wanted casement rather than the sliding windows specified in the design.

Two requests—for a sloping roof and exterior rolling blinds—were sticking points in the early planning, but the architects prevailed. About the sloping-roof proposal, Robert Gatje wrote to the supervising architect that "this may well prove to be an insurmountable architectural obstacle to Mr. Breuer's conception of the project."[11] On the proposal for rolling blinds for the windows, Gatje wrote on September 5, 1968, that "we have reviewed this matter thoroughly with Mr. Breuer. He is well aware of the strong Swiss tradition in favor of devices such

as this, and we have used them elsewhere. However, his conclusion, based primarily on aesthetic grounds, is that their use in this type of facade would destroy the architectural effect and he cannot accept them. Mr. Breuer feels very strongly about this point."[12]

Drawings for the infirmary and old-age home were sent to Baldegg in November 1974. The north facade of the convent and the south facade of the infirmary were to overlap as little as possible to preserve views from the windows of each. For architectural harmony, the cornice height and floor levels of the infirmary, designed as a wide-angled U with interior court, would correspond to those of the convent. The infirmary project was carried out by the Bern office of Swiss architect Beat Jordi, who had worked for Breuer in New York, in coordination with the offices in New York and Paris. Jordi was in private practice and was associate architect for the convent. During 1975 and 1976, his sketches and drawings would travel to New York and be returned to Bern with Breuer's detailed comments and revisions. In February 1976, Breuer interrupted a visit to Paris about Baldegg to return to New York because of his health; within a few weeks, he retired from practice. In a letter to Jordi, he expressed his intention of "carrying the Baldegg job to the end."[13]

ARCHIVAL: **SUL 138, 147, 148, 160, Drawings, Sketches; AAA Correspondence, Photos**.
BIBLIOGRAPHIC: *Architecture Plus*, April 1973, 64–69; *Werk*, April 1973, 432–39; Papachristou, *Marcel Breuer*, 194–95; Gatje, *Marcel Breuer*, 218–21.

50b. Preliminary sketch

51a. Overall view

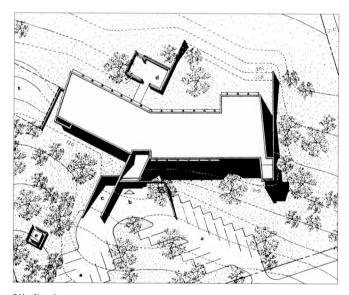

51b. Site plan

51
American Press Institute Conference Center,
Reston, Virginia, 1972–74

MARCEL BREUER AND HAMILTON P. SMITH, ARCHITECTS

Since its founding in 1946, the American Press Institute (API), an organization that conducts seminars about newspaper publishing, was quartered at Columbia University. A new API building, for which Breuer received the commission, was to be located in Reston, Virginia. In November 1971, drawings were prepared. Construction was started a year later, and in October 1974 the completed new building—with twice the space in which the institute had operated—was dedicated. Sited on 4 acres of wooded terrain that inclines toward a small lake, the two-story building is set out in the wide-angled, elongated boomerang shape with off-center extrusions long favored by Breuer for its efficiency in smaller buildings. It is another version of binuclearity—a separation of zones by the bend of the building without relinquishing the continuity needed for interaction. Administrative offices and services were on the ground floor; on the upper level was the seminar space. Steel and reinforced formboard-textured concrete are the structural materials, together with the load-bearing deeply recessed precast-concrete window panels that run the full length of the southwest elevation and along one portion of the northeast. Recessed window bays create shaded depths separated by rhythmically alternating sharp-edged piers, in the excessively repetitive manner Breuer succumbed to at this period for the economy of prefabrication. The Breuer office was unhappy with the appearance of the first panels and highly critical of the technology used at the plant where they were fabricated, demanding an improvement, which it eventually got.

The building transcends the aesthetic infelicity of the cookie-cutter panels because it sits close to the ground and the run-on effect is interrupted on the northeast by projecting masses that give sculptural force to the interlocking forms. Austere, knife-edged, tapered walls resembling those in Breuer's Roosevelt Memorial project define the entrance area. In 1974, Breuer designed a tapestry that was installed in the principal entrance space. It was one of many designs for rugs and tapestries that Breuer produced over a period of thirty years; they often reflected the ground plans of his buildings (see p. 180).

ARCHIVAL: **SUL 86–89; AAA photos.**
BIBLIOGRAPHIC: *Process: Architecture,* **no. 32, 86–89.**

GOVERNMENTAL AND CIVIC

52

War Memorial (Cambridge Honor Roll),
Cambridge, Massachusetts, 1944–45 (NOT BUILT)

MARCEL BREUER AND LAWRENCE B. ANDERSON, ARCHITECTS

A collaborative effort was launched in 1944 by Harvard, MIT, local veterans' organizations, and the Cambridge War Memorial Committee to place an architecturally distinguished war monument on Cambridge Common. Harvard's Breuer and MIT's Lawrence Anderson were the "architects in association," with Anderson principally responsible for the landscaping.[1] On a flagstone-paved plaza 70 feet square at the southern tip of the common, traversed by the park's main walkway, would be erected a memorial carrying the names of about 15,000 Second World War servicemen and -women from Cambridge.

By March 1945, preliminary drawings, working drawings, specifications, and models had been made for a minimal composition of light and glass. Thick slabs of untempered plate-glass slabs 7 feet high and 6 feet wide, with no frame or visible support, were cantilevered from underground concrete foundations and lifted above the plaza. The glass was a Pittsburgh Plate Glass Company product named Herculite, described by Breuer as "specially treated, practically unbreakable and many times the strength of granite."[2] Transferred to both sides of the translucent glass by a photographic process and then baked into the surface were the names of the honored, running the full width of the slabs at eye level. A translucent strip of light gray film was also baked into the glass on each reverse side to facilitate the reading of names.

Beneath concrete benches bordering the plaza were concealed lighting tubes that illuminated the textured flagstone of the pavement and the surface of the glass slabs. Breuer emphasized the contrast of materials—the translucency, "immateriality," and precision of the glass and the lettering; the rough surface of the flagstone; the density of the concrete. "As the glass slabs are practically shadowless," he said, "the plaza at night will appear like an illuminated floating square."[3] Breuer's sketches preserved at Syracuse University document several experimental designs that he made before settling on the rectilinear arrangement that, in plan and elevation, bears the imprint of the geometry of Mies van der Rohe's Barcelona pavilion (1929).

Philip Johnson, then head of the Department of Architecture at the Museum of Modern Art, was enthusiastic about the design and wrote to Breuer, suggesting a replica for an exhibition of war memorials planned for the garden of the museum in the spring of 1946.[4] The exhibition never materialized, but in the September 1945 issue of *Art News*, Johnson praised the design in an article on war memorials.

The monument was scheduled for construction during the summer of 1945, but the single bid received in June was higher than the civic budget of $25,000. Breuer made revisions to reduce the cost, but the lowest bid was still $4,000 too high. Although it was not a substantial amount, the City Council postponed the project. When nothing had been done by September 1946 (it was considered too unorthodox), local newspapers began to pick up the story and complain. In July 1948, Anderson made a final effort to collect architects' fees and then turned the matter over to a lawyer. In December, the city of Cambridge gave Breuer and Anderson about half the original fee.

ARCHIVAL: **SUL 15, 39, 41–43, Drawings; AAA Photos.**
BIBLIOGRAPHIC: **Philip C. Johnson, "War Memorials: What Aesthetic Price Glory?"** *Art News*, September 1945, 9–25; Blake, *Marcel Breuer*, 84–85; Breuer, *Sun and Shadow*, 34; Jones, ed., *Marcel Breuer*, 250; Driller, "Frühwerk," 376–77.

52a. Sketch by Breuer

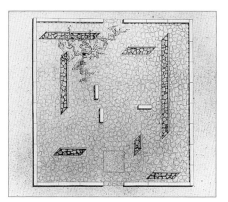

52b. Rendered plan

53
Airport Terminal Buildings,
Fairbanks and Anchorage, Alaska, 1949–53

MARCEL BREUER, CONSULTING ARCHITECT

The United States government sponsored a project under the auspices of the Department of Commerce for international airport terminal buildings in Fairbanks and Anchorage, Alaska, for which Breuer was consulting architect with particular responsibility for the design and materials of the interior public areas. The referral came from Harry A. Morris, who had been Breuer's student at Harvard. A Washington, D.C., engineering firm, Thomas P. Bourne Associates, had requested Morris as chief architect for the project, and on May 2, 1949, Morris wrote to Breuer that "I was asked to suggest a consultant of such reputation that all parties concerned would realize that the services which the firm proposes to render would be undeniably top quality."[5] The job was bid in 1951; as described in *Progressive Architecture*, the terminal in Anchorage was built as a series of uniform bays of light steel with curtain walls of insulated metal panels. In May 1953 it was nearing completion in Anchorage, and Breuer received final payment for his participation.

ARCHIVAL: **SUL 10, 28;** AAA Photos.
BIBLIOGRAPHIC: *Progressive Architecture*, May 1953, 15–16; Driller, "Frühwerk," 373.

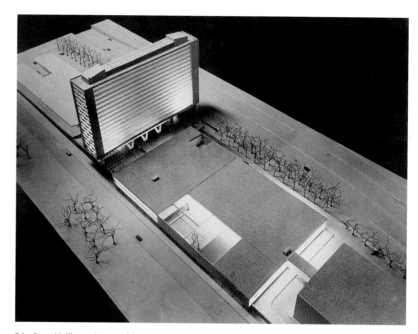

54a. Porte Maillot project, model

54
UNESCO, Headquarters,
Paris, France, 1952–58

MARCEL BREUER AND BERNARD ZEHRFUSS, ARCHITECTS

PIER LUIGI NERVI, STRUCTURAL ENGINEER

Porte Maillot, 1952

A site of 7.5 acres next to the Ecole Militaire, Jacques-Anges Gabriel's eighteenth-century masterpiece, was provided by the French government for a headquarters for the United Nations Educational, Scientific and Cultural Organization (UNESCO).[6] When a design by French architect Eugène Beaudouin was rejected by a UNESCO advisory committee, in 1952 new architects were appointed and a new location was found adjacent to Porte Maillot. The architects were now a two-part international design team consisting of "The Three" and their advisory panel of "The Five." Breuer, architect Bernard Zehrfuss of France, and structural engineer Pier Luigi Nervi of Italy were The Three (BNZ). Eero Saarinen was named consultant to The Three. The Five were Le Corbusier (France), Lucio Costa (Brazil), Sven Markelius (Sweden), Ernesto Rogers (Italy), and, as chairman, Walter Gropius (United States). Breuer operated from New York and Nervi from Rome; both made frequent trips to Paris. Zehrfuss was in control of the BNZ office at 9 rue Arsène-Houssaye.

The BNZ design submitted on September 19, 1952, required a vote by the General Assembly for acceptance. Three buildings united by bridges and corridors were set out in a line: a seventeen-story concrete-and-glass-slab Secretariat; a two-story Conference Building; and, for UNESCO's biannual plenary sessions, an auditorium with outdoor amphitheater. The proportions of the slab emphasized its width. The glass surfaces were bordered by a concrete framework and articulated by a pattern of windows and sun breaks. A wide parabolic shell covering the main lobby was the result of Nervi's creative concrete engineering. The Secretariat and Conference Building were joined across a patio by a bridge supported by V's.

Criticism, aesthetic and urbanistic, arose immediately.[7] The appearance and height of the Secretariat were deplored. The choice of so conspicuous a site—on the main axis of Paris—was denounced. Even before it reached the General Assembly, the design was rejected by the Paris building committee. In a *New York Times* article with a Paris dateline of November 1, 1952, it was reported that civic authorities "today turned down plans for a seventeen story 'sandwich-shaped' United Nations 'skyscraper' because it would interfere with the view of the Arc de Triomphe." It was said that it "looked like a Notre Dame built of radiators." Negative reaction in France, moreover, to the appearance of the recently completed United Nations Secretariat in New York City also fueled antagonism to the design for Paris.

The polemic is not hard to understand in Paris of the early 1950s, when proposals for modern buildings and for tall buildings were doomed to fail. As late as 1975, Paul Goldberger, then architecture critic of the *New York Times* and writing about modern architecture in Paris, observed that new or innovative building—anything that disturbed the city's unified urban texture established by the scale and materials of older structures and the Beaux-Arts tradition—was destined to be regarded with hostility and skepticism.[8] "France's unfortunate architectural atavism" was the way the country's attitude toward modern architecture was described by G. E. Kidder Smith in 1961.[9]

Despite efforts of The Three to save it, the UNESCO design of 1952 was to have no future.

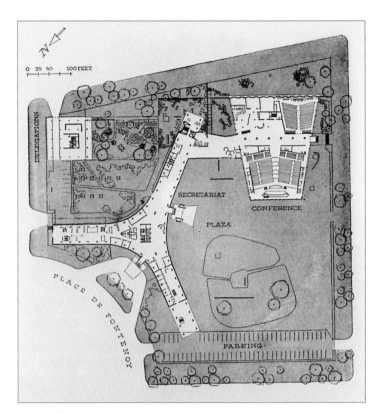

54b. Plan, Place de Fontenoy

Place de Fontenoy, 1955–58

After the failure of BNZ's UNESCO I, the government requested a new design, reappointed the members of The Five and offered a change of site—back to the original location near the Ecole Militaire. When it came before the General Assembly on July 1, 1953, the revised project was accepted. Painting and sculpture were to be an integral part of the architectural plan, and letters between Breuer and Gropius in 1954 reveal their concern about politics and the selection of artists. Construction began in February 1955. The question of a garden was settled in the winter of 1957 with a commission to Isamu Noguchi (see p. 32). The November 3, 1958, meeting of the General Assembly marked the official opening of the new UNESCO.

On the northeast corner of the site stands the building for permanent delegations: a block with glazed facades enframed by concrete, four stories over a narrower one-story concrete base—in essence, an elegant fragment of failed UNESCO I. The Y-shaped, glass-walled Secretariat is lifted on seventy-two powerful, tilted concrete pilotis that show Breuer at his sculptural best (see p. 134). Oval in section at the base, they rise and fan into faceted triangles to form a corridor at ground level. Nervi's concrete canopies lift above the entrances on the north and south.

54c. Aerial view, Place de Fontenoy

On the Place de Fontenoy side, the building's curve completed Gabriel's semicircle behind the Ecole Militaire. A low, slightly bent rectangular block links the trapezoidal Conference Building to the Secretariat at midsection. The east and west walls of the Conference Building are of folded concrete, with a surface that bears the textures of the wooden formboards and contrasts with the smooth travertine and granite of the longer sides; it is covered with a ribbed "butterfly" copper roof (see p. 133). Regarded by Lewis Mumford as "the one structure of great architectural distinction in the group of three,"[10] it was attributed by him to Nervi. Much of its quality does come from the brilliance of the engineering of the thin concrete shell and from the workmanship that produced the crisp folded walls, but the overall plan and design are clearly Breuer's—not simply the shape and spatial constructs, but details such as the Mondrianesque window wall of the entrance facade.

In 1958, serious problems arose in connection with the glass walls and windows of the Secretariat. On learning of breakage in the sliding glass panels, Breuer wrote to Pierre Marcel in the BNZ office on April 7, 1958, that "your letter was a surprise indeed and a rather frightening one." But by September, the even more troubling problem of extreme heat inside the offices had begun to escalate. A decision made in 1952 not to install air-conditioning had been a crucial mistake. There were more than 1,000 windows in the Secretariat, yet Breuer had believed that the heat of the sun could be controlled by sun shades and vertical screens of solar glass shielding the south and east facades. (These filters contributed to what Kidder Smith described as the "welter of facade elements."[11]) Breuer had failed to make the leap from detailing small houses and institutions—in both Europe and postwar America before air-conditioning was considered essential—to considering the requirements for this, his first large building and its huge office workforce. The heat problem was documented in the nine-page *Rapport sur la protection contre la chaleur des bureaux du Palais de l'UNESCO*, released on March 26, 1959, and Breuer's copy in the Archives of American Art has his very defensive comments in the margins. By late December 1960, a letter from Gropius to Breuer referred to negative

54d. View of the complex

articles on UNESCO by Mumford and John Burchard, particularly their comments about unbearable heat in the offices. In his reply, Breuer admitted that it was serious, but concluded that the problem was with the materials:

[A] stone or brick building with partitions of the same material and with plastered walls and ceilings and with solid slab floors will be a much cooler building than one with thin, movable, steel or composition partitions, with acoustic ceilings and with hollow or light slab floors covered with linoleum . . . when these materials started to be used, one used air conditioning with them. . . . [T]he Unesco secretariat building was the first large structure using unfavorable materials for interior partitions and finishes but not having air conditioning.

After the headquarters was completed, it (and its works of art) received some favorable reviews, but most of the important critical appraisals, particularly Mumford's (about the Secretariat, not the Conference Building, which he liked), were caustic: *Le Monde*, for example, railed that "this new aggrandizement of Unesco demanded the destruction of 83 trees on the Place de Fontenoy. The future will decide the worth of this functional architecture denuded of aesthetics and sensitivity."[12]

For Breuer, UNESCO may have been the validation of modernism in a historic city, but Mumford regarded it as "once-modern modernism," already stale.[13] The systems and structure were becoming outdated, and the forms had been in Breuer's repertoire since Garden City of the Future (1936), which was noted by Mumford: "These forms were admirable as experiments; now automatically repeated they are no longer experiments. They were conceived in terms of function and now they are reduced to tricks of decoration."[14]

The BNZ office was closed by November 30, 1958. In the draft of a letter from the architects to the Director General, Breuer concluded by saying: "It seems that, in [the] case of this project, a great opportunity has not been entirely missed and we feel as we always felt, grateful for the opportunity."[15]

54f. Main hall, Secretariat

POSTSCRIPT

In August 1960, UNESCO, needing more office space, drafted a contract with BNZ for a fourth building and an underground garage. On April 14, 1961, Breuer sent Nervi and Zehrfuss two schematic sketches for a typical floor plan with modular offices and a cross section with floor elevations. He suggested that "the ground floor should be as transparent as possible with as few columns as possible so that the visual effect of the open piazza is maintained." Throughout the summer, Breuer developed the design in detail, conferring with Nervi and Zehrfuss on points of structure and materials. But the project did not materialize, and eventually there was a falling out between Zehrfuss and his partners. Zehrfuss in 1965 built an underground portion "without any collaboration or agreement concerning a collaboration, neither with Nervi nor with myself," as Breuer put it.

ARCHIVAL: SUL 139, Drawings; AAA UNESCO files, Contract, Correspondence, Photos.
BIBLIOGRAPHIC: *Architectural Forum*, August 1952, 132–35; October 1952, 150–57;
June 1953, 105–13; and December 1958, 80–88; *Architects' Journal*, November 6, 1952,
555–62; *Techniques et architecture*, November 1952, 8–13; *Architectural Record*,
December 1952, 11–14; July 1953, 10–11; April 1955, 217–24; February 1958, 165–69;
November 1958, 14–15; and May 1960, 145–56; *Arts & Architecture*, February 1953,
21–22; December 1953, 17–19; and February 1958, 12–13; *Progressive Architecture*,
March 1958, 65–69; August 1960, 124–29; and March 1962, 71–73; *New Yorker*,
October 11, 1958, 188–90; *L'Architecture d'aujourd'hui*, January 1959, 1–36; *Architectural Design*, February 1959, 57–70; Mumford, "Unesco House: Out, Damned Cliché!"
and "Unesco House: The Hidden Treasure," in *Highway and the City*, 67–87; Breuer, *Sun
and Shadow*, 196–205; Jones, ed., *Marcel Breuer*, 78–97; Gatje, *Marcel Breuer*, passim.

54g. Fire stair, Secretariat

55. South facade

55
United States Embassy,
The Hague, the Netherlands, 1956–59

MARCEL BREUER, ARCHITECT

Breuer's United States Embassy in The Hague originated in a government initiative to display American modern architecture abroad (see p. 133). The four-story building, fitted out with rich materials on the interior, is formed as an L on the corner of the Lange Voorhout and the Korte Voorhout, folded around a garden-courtyard with the two wings connected by an inset transparent-glass block. Across a terrace to the northwest and behind the Lange Voorhout wing is a lower trapezoidal auditorium building that bears the same formal relationship to the taller structure as does the Conference Building to the Secretariat at UNESCO Headquarters. The facades of both wings are faced with limestone and polished granite in a pattern of trapezoids framed top and bottom by two rows of rectangular blocks. The lower part of the double trapezoid (critics read them as "coffins") forms the inset window; a monumental two-story opening enframes the impressive, deeply inset glass-walled entrance of each wing.

The dense building mass, relieved by only texture and restricted areas of glass, is characteristic of much of Breuer's work of the mid-1950s. Residents of The Hague referred to the embassy as *steenklomp* (lump of stone), and—the eternal burden of modern buildings in historic cities—it was scorned because of its seeming disregard for its urban context. In her studies of the State Department's program, Jane C. Loeffler documents the critical reaction (some even before it was built) to Breuer's building, not only because of its "absence of association" to Dutch vernacular and historical architecture and its lack of "reference to de Stijl or any other elements of modern art associated with that region," but also because (and probably most painful to Breuer, even though aimed at the State Department) in parts of the Dutch press he "was seen as a European rather than an American artist."[16]

ARCHIVAL: **SUL 50, Drawings; AAA Photos.**

BIBLIOGRAPHIC: *Architectural Record,* December 1956, 171–76, and January 1960, 123–29; *L'Architecture d'aujourd'hui,* February 1960, 61–63; *Deutsche Bauzeitung,* June 1960, 304–9; Loeffler, "The Architecture of Diplomacy: Heyday of the United States Embassy-Building Program 1954–1960," *Journal of the Society of Architectural Historians* 49 (1990): 251–78; Jones, ed., *Marcel Breuer,* 166–9; Loeffler, *Architecture of Diplomacy,* esp. 212–17.

56
Department of Housing and Urban Development (HUD), Headquarters,
Washington, D.C., 1965–68

MARCEL BREUER, NOLEN-SWINBURNE AND ASSOCIATES,

AND HERBERT BECKHARD, ARCHITECTS

In August 1963, a joint architectural venture was undertaken by Marcel Breuer and Associates and Nolen-Swinburne and Associates. The client was the government's General Services Administration (GSA); the building was the headquarters for about 5,000 employees of the Housing and Home Finance Agency (HHFA), which became the Department of Housing and Urban Development (HUD) after government housing agencies were centralized in 1963. Construction began on July 20, 1965, and was completed in August 1968.

A structure of ten stories with mechanicals penthouse, the HUD building provided 700,000 square feet of office space and other facilities. Shaped as a long-bodied double-Y drawn in from the corners of the site, the building is oriented to the street on one curved side and to a small landscaped garden on the other. The design can be compared with that of Breuer's IBM La Gaude, which also meets the ground by way of faceted tree columns that carry the structural walls. Unlike its counterpart in France, however, the HUD building is ungainly, with a heavy superstructure and columns that appear to taper too quickly to a small base. Exterior walls are made of interlocking load-bearing precast-concrete panels (12 tons each), into which are set windows framed with black aluminum. A granite-faced projecting stair tower terminates each of the four wings. The structure is organized by an internal

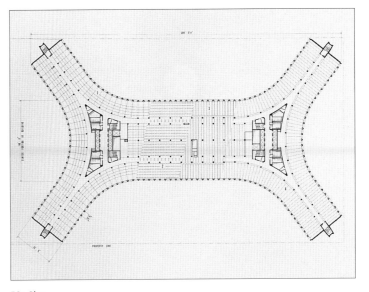

56a. Plan

system of square, cast-in-place concrete columns supporting beams and a load-bearing precast outer skin. Offices and double-loaded corridors were configured from 30-x-20-foot bays, but the work areas seem cramped and narrow today. Two service cores (elevator shafts, stairs, and so on), one at each end of the central space, anchor the building. The ground floor is set back behind the tree columns, which form an arcade 15 feet deep around the building. This "pedestrian area" beneath the massive concrete structure is low, dark, and inhospitable and suggests an above-ground basement where no one wishes to linger.

In 1995, the Commission of Fine Arts of Washington, D.C., approved a proposal for the redesign and renovation of the plazas adjacent to the building.[17]

ARCHIVAL: **SUL 74, Drawings; AAA Contract, Correspondence, Photos, Project Record Book.**

BIBLIOGRAPHIC: *Progressive Architecture*, March 1965, 190, 192; *Architectural Record*, March 1965, 135–39, and December 1968, 99–106; *L'architettura*, August 1965, 256–57; *L'Architecture d'aujourd'hui*, September 1965, 44; *Architectural Forum*, October 1968, 32; *Journal of the American Institute of Architects*, April 1977, 53–57; Papachristou, *Marcel Breuer*, 72–80; *Process: Architecture*, no. 32, 32–35; Gatje, *Marcel Breuer*, 142.

56b. View from the northeast

57. Model

57
Central Park Stables and Police
Precinct House, Competition,
New York, New York, 1966–67 (NOT BUILT)

MARCEL BREUER AND ASSOCIATES, ARCHITECTS

Marcel Breuer and Associates was one of five firms invited to participate in a competition announced by the New York City Parks
Department "intended as an effort to raise the aesthetic quality of civic
architecture," according to Robert A. M. Stern, Thomas Mellins, and
David Fishman in *New York 1960*.[18] The plan was to construct, on an
8-acre site south of the Eighty-sixth Street transverse through Central
Park, a station house for the Twenty-second Precinct and a combined
stable–riding ring for the public and the mounted police. The riding
ring would also accommodate polo-playing Squadron A of the
National Guard. Other participating architects were Edward Larrabee
Barnes, Kelly and Gruzen, Philip Johnson, and Whittlesey, Conklin &
Rossant. The prize, in addition to the commission, was $100,000 con-
tributed by Urban America, Inc., a nonprofit organization dedicated to
improving the quality of American cities.[19] One reason given for the
selection of the winning design by Kelly and Gruzen (I. M. Pei was the
architect), announced in February 1967, was that compared with the
other proposals it was simply less visible inside the park.[20]

For this project, Breuer put together a design that combined the
folded wall he had used at Saint John's Abbey and UNESCO Headquarters with features of the high school gymnasiums he had designed
for Litchfield and Torrington in the mid-1950s, brought up to date with
splayed angles and tapering terminal piers.

Parks Department documents relating to the project are filed in
the New York City Municipal Archives;[21] the competition was extensively covered in the press at the time, and *New York 1960* has full biblio-
graphical references for published sources. The project was abandoned under pressure from civic groups working to preserve Central
Park and prevent further encroachment.

ARCHIVAL: **AAA Photos; New York City Municipal Archives.**
BIBLIOGRAPHIC: **Stern, Mellins, and Fishman, *New York 1960*, 788 and notes.**

58a. Rendering of interior view

58
Franklin Delano Roosevelt Memorial,
Washington, D.C., 1966–67 (NOT BUILT)

MARCEL BREUER AND HERBERT BECKHARD, ARCHITECTS

First prize for a Franklin Delano Roosevelt memorial design was awarded to the architectural firm of Pedersen and Tilney in a competition held in 1960. Its abstract format was controversial, however, and it did not receive the approval, required by Congress, of the Commission of Fine Arts. Despite revisions, a temporary halt to the initiative for a monument was brought about by differences of opinion regarding the revised version and by the disapproval of it by the Roosevelt family. In 1966, deciding to select an architect instead of sponsoring another competition, the FDR Memorial Commission reviewed the work of several prominent architects and chose Breuer. On December 20, 1966, he presented his design to the commission.

The site was 6 acres in West Potomac Park, just off one of the lobes of the Tidal Basin in the District of Columbia's memorial area. With respect to the nearby monuments to Presidents Washington, Jefferson, and Lincoln, the Roosevelt memorial was required to take "a less dominant form" and to be "harmonious as to location, design, and land use." Breuer planned an open plaza on which seven stone triangles appeared to revolve in a pinwheel arrangement around a monumental granite block at the center, propelled by a force contained with-

in an invisible circular frame. At their highest point, the triangles rose 60 feet. Reached from fan-shaped corridors of space between the spokes, the 32-foot cube floated in the center of the plaza and bore on one of its sides an image of Roosevelt in low relief, transferred from a photographic enlargement to the surface of the stone through a newly developed stonecutting technology. Recordings of Roosevelt's voice in excerpts from his most celebrated speeches would be heard at intervals from hidden loudspeakers in areas around the portrait.

The Commission of Fine Arts met on January 25, 1967;[22] on the following day, Breuer was to make his presentation. The minutes of the on-the-record portions of the discussion among the commission members reveal that although their first reactions were tentative and cautious, it soon became clear that the design appealed to none of them. There was uncertainty about whether to consider the granite triangles as sculpture or architecture, and the sharp-edged tapering forms were severely criticized. Aline Saarinen regarded the proposal as an example of "pop art sculpture" made of "mechanical and electronic tricks . . . the concept of a canned voice is abhorrent." While the government had supported architectural modernism for many of its institutions, a heroic memorial structure was more problematic, particularly when the person memorialized was still in the living memory of much of the nation.

The most perceptive and accurate criticism of Breuer's design was leveled against it by Theodore Roszak, who understood it as "dated." The Breuer proposal *was* anachronistic, a revival of obsolete Bauhaus modes that Roszak recognized when he went on to say about it that

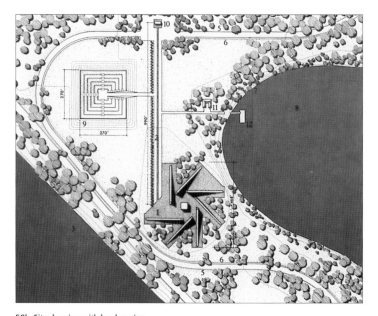

58b. Site drawing with landscaping

58c. Rendering of approach view

"this might have been all right for the Cabinet of Doctor Caligari but I don't think it has much to do with today." The meeting ended with a clear mandate for rejection of the design, but the commission reconvened the next day for Breuer's presentation. He described his proposal as the combination of a memorial and a parklike place for a leisurely walk; he explained how the forms appeared to "grow out the ground" and how it fit into the axial composition of Washington. On the controversial matter of Roosevelt's voice recordings, he recounted how impressed he had been by the president's radio speeches soon after he had emigrated to the United States. The voice and the portrait on the central cube were substitutes for the conventional statue or bust of the deceased in traditional monuments.

"Listening to Breuer's point of view I . . . am not so strongly against it as I was earlier," said Hideo Sasaki. "I keep wondering if anyone else did it, would it get any better." That question also "terrified" Saarinen. But Gordon Bunshaft, not an admirer of Breuer's architecture in general or of this project in particular, brought the discussion back to its original hard line: "What you're all talking about is that Breuer is a very nice man [who] made a very nice presentation . . . and I'd hate to see this thing built just because Breuer is a nice guy. I'd rather see nothing built." These comments tilted the balance again, and criticism of Breuer's memorial design was resumed. Beneath the debate lay the initial disappointment of all the commission members with the design, one of the principal reasons for which was summed up by William Walton: "We think this is way out of date." Breuer's memorial proposal was unanimously rejected. It was reconsidered in 1969, but its rejection was reaffirmed.

ARCHIVAL: **SUL Drawings; AAA Correspondence, Photos; Commission of Fine Arts Archives; National Capital Planning Commission Archives.**
BIBLIOGRAPHIC: *Architectural Record*, July 1966, 36; January 1967, 33; and March 1967, 35; *Architecture and Engineering News*, January 1967, 4; *Progressive Architecture*, July 1966, 101, and January 1967, 35; *Journal of the American Institute of Architects*, July 1966, 8; *Architectural Forum*, January–February 1967, 124; Hyman, "Marcel Breuer and the Franklin Delano Roosevelt Memorial," *Journal of the Society of Architectural Historians* 54 (1995): 446–58; Gatje, *Marcel Breuer*, 227–29.

58d. Oskar Schlemmer. Stage design for Grabbe's "Don Juan und Faust." 1925

58e. Herbert Bayer. Berlin Rundfunk Exhibition. 1936. Model

59
Grand Coulee Dam, Columbia Basin Project,
Grand Coulee, Washington, 1972–78

Third Power Plant and Forebay Dam, 1972–75
Visitor Arrival Center, 1976–78

MARCEL BREUER AND HAMILTON P. SMITH, ARCHITECTS

Breuer's proposal was submitted to the Bureau of Reclamation in
Washington, D.C., on February 12, 1968, and the contract for the
"architectural design of Grand Coulee Third Power Plant and Forebay
Dam" was awarded on February 21; the power plant went into operation in August 1975 (see p. 159). He designed an 1,170-foot-long

addition to the original Grand Coulee Dam, the mammoth power-
producing concrete dam that bridges the Columbia River and services
one of the world's largest hydroelectric systems. According to the
Pacific Northwest Region Bureau of Reclamation's project data book,
as of 1983 Grand Coulee Dam was the largest concrete structure ever
built. The Breuer extension, the third power plant in the complex and
the retainer for a newly excavated forebay, is a stepped monolith of
reinforced concrete, comprising a sloping dam that rises 550 feet
above bedrock and is broad enough at the top to support a two-lane
highway; curved penstocks that carry water from the forebay to turbines in the power plant; and a power plant that is essentially a gigantic

59b. Perspective rendering of the power plant interior

59c. Visitor Arrival Center, interior

machine hall housing the generating units for the dam's power facility, its concrete walls folded for increased strength and rigidity. These trusslike walls had to support cranes capable of lifting enormous loads (275 tons) of generator components. Along the exterior facade from the top of the dam to the top of the power plant runs an inclined glass-enclosed elevator for visitors; an observation balcony is cantilevered 36 feet from the power-plant wall.

The power-plant interior—wide and high, framed by massive corrugated walls—is one of Breuer's most monumental conceptions, dwarfing everyone and everything. Even he referred to its scale as "truly Egyptian." Giant power generators are installed in circular beds beneath the black-terrazzo surface of the floor and are closed by circular covers.

The appearance of Breuer's addition was considered so satisfactory by the Bureau of Reclamation that it wanted to bring the older portions of the dam into conformity with the new design. Breuer was asked to "proceed with the development of an architectural design concept for modifying the exterior appearance of the existing Grand Coulee Powerplant facilities."[23] The government impetus for what would have been an extraordinary image of American concrete design in the service of engineering—the world's largest concrete structure formatted in the Breuer manner—was, however, deflected and the project was never realized.

In April 1972, Breuer again entered into an agreement with the Bureau of Reclamation, this time for the design of the Grand Coulee Visitor Arrival Center. A model was made depicting a two-level structure, elevated and shaped as a pair of tip-touching diamonds intersecting a square, fronted by a wide stepped plaza. But funds for this project were cut back, and in 1974 it had to be redesigned in a reduced version. Far less inventive than the original plan, the new design was set out in compact circular format. Made of precast-concrete panels, the exterior smooth above with hooded windows below, it belongs to the formulaic sharp-edged Breuer constructs of the mid-1970s. But its chunky spaceship image serves as a metaphor of protection against the aggressive forces of nature, a preparation for the containment so dramatically illustrated by the great dam to which it introduces the visitor.

ARCHIVAL: **SUL 71, Drawings; AAA Contract, Photos. Archives, Bureau of Reclamation, Grand Coulee Project Office.**

BIBLIOGRAPHIC: ***Progressive Architecture**, December 1968, 45; *Architecture Plus*, May–June 1974, 126; *Architectural Record*, December 1978, 126–27; Papachristou, *Marcel Breuer*, 54–57; *Process: Architecture*, no. 32, 50–54.*

60
Department of Health, Education and Welfare (HEW), Headquarters (Hubert H. Humphrey Federal Building),
Washington, D.C., 1972–76

MARCEL BREUER AND HERBERT BECKHARD, AND

NOLEN-SWINBURNE AND ASSOCIATES, ARCHITECTS

As in the case of the headquarters for the Department of Housing and Urban Development, the headquarters for the Department of Health and Human Services (DHHS, formerly Health, Education and Welfare [HEW]) was designed by Marcel Breuer and Associates for the General Services Administration (GSA) as a joint venture with the architectural firm of Nolen-Swinburne and Associates. Marcel Breuer and Associates were the designing architects, and they "had the last word with respect to aesthetic matters whereas Nolen and Swinburne had the last word with respect to technical matters."[24]

The building, named in 1977 to honor former Vice President Hubert H. Humphrey, is located on the Mall on Independence Avenue and was designed to accommodate about 3,000 workers. The undertaking is described in Breuer office correspondence as "a long drawn out affair." The design process began in 1967 and 1968, and construction was started in May 1972; the building was completed below the established budget and was occupied in September 1976; the dedication ceremony took place on November 1, 1977.

One of Breuer's most powerfully sculptural and rhythmically articulated buildings, this precast-concrete-and-steel structure had 890,000 square feet of space on seven above-ground floors, a mechanicals penthouse, and three underground parking levels. Because a freeway tunnel and a sewer ran beneath the site, shafts to vent exhaust fumes from the tunnel were required, and a low-frequency rumble from tunnel fans had to be neutralized. Since much of the underground area, therefore, was occupied by ducts, mechanical space, and sewer lines, only a few points remained at which to place load-bearing columns. The innovative structural system designed to meet these challenges consisted of large, widely spaced columns that rose from basement to penthouse, where they supported bridgelike trusses—the distinctive sloping roofline represents the triangular ends of the trusses. A secondary system of vertical hangers was suspended from the trusses, and from these were "hung" the six office floors. Three elevator service cores provided additional structural stability, and into each corner of the almost square building a massive stair shaft was inserted. A wide, stepped plaza was created by the deep setback of the glass-enclosed lobby space.

The facade is textured by a variety of surfaces, by exposed granite aggregates, and by thin horizontal ribs. Rhythmic variations come from the short and long stresses of the vertical fins, some straight, others canted. Recessed window units—doubles alternating with singles—are also receptacles for mechanical systems and structural-steel members.

ARCHIVAL: SUL 56, 73, 74, 120–25, Drawings; AAA Correspondence, Photos.
BIBLIOGRAPHIC: *Architectural Record*, December 1967, 120–23; *Contract Interiors*, July 1978, 82–83; Papachristou, *Marcel Breuer*, 132–33; *Process: Architecture*, no. 32, 40–43.

Oglala Community High School (Pine Ridge High School), 1973–75 (not built). See no. 29.

61
Australian Embassy,
Paris, France, 1973–75

HARRY SEIDLER, ARCHITECT

MARCEL BREUER, CONSULTING ARCHITECT

PIER LUIGI NERVI, CONSULTING ENGINEER

MARIO JOSSA, ASSOCIATE

When an agreement was signed in 1973 between Harry Seidler and Associates and the Commonwealth of Australia for an Australian Chancery and staff apartment building in Paris, Seidler said that "it was natural for me to ask Breuer's Paris office to be our 'architecte d'opération' —it meant re-establishing a working relationship with him after many years."[25] The project also united Breuer and Pier Luigi Nervi in Paris two decades after their collaboration on the UNESCO Headquarters. On October 22, 1973, Breuer wrote to Seidler on his Paris office letterhead that "your suggestion to associate me and my office with your Australian Embassy project is very much appreciated."[26]

The details of Breuer's participation were worked out in his correspondence with Seidler and in Seidler's correspondence with the Australian government. By December 1973, Breuer had sent Seidler drawings—designs for the stepped format of the end walls of the Chancery, and for modular elements of the precast facades—about which Seidler wrote that "we are able to incorporate virtually everything into the model and final drawings."[27] On January 9, 1974, Seidler sent Breuer the final presentation drawings and photographs of the model, saying that "we are certainly happy with the scheme." The groundbreaking ceremony took place on January 6, 1975.

ARCHIVAL: SUL 138; AAA Correspondence.
BIBLIOGRAPHIC: *Bauen und Wohnen*, September 1975, 373–76; *L'Architecture d'aujourd'hui*, May–June 1976, xxiii; *Modern Design*, November 1978, 42–47; *Domus*, November 1978, 20–27; Kenneth Frampton and Philip Drew, *Harry Seidler: Four Decades of Architecture* (London: Thames and Hudson, 1992).

COMMERCIAL AND INDUSTRIAL
OFFICE BUILDINGS

62. Aerial view

62
Van Leer Office Building,
Amstelveen, the Netherlands, 1957–58

MARCEL BREUER, ARCHITECT

A world-headquarters office building with adjacent canteen was commissioned to Breuer by Van Leer Vatenfabrieken, a prominent Dutch oil-drum company located in Amstelveen, near Amsterdam. Breuer's frequent travel to Holland for the construction of his United States Embassy in The Hague was convenient for the Van Leer undertaking. The project went through three design stages, and on October 4, 1957, the client recorded in a memo that "the van Leer organization herewith recognizes their obligation to build project #3 . . . according to the design and instructions of Marcel Breuer."[1] The building is an ingenious composition of wide-span Siamese-Ys (office wings) joined at the stems above a recessed base, connected by a long spur to an independent structure (canteen) formed by a pair of intersecting trapezoids. A decade later, the angled Ys would be changed to curves at IBM La Gaude, but as a basic format the double Y in any variation served Breuer well for winged office-building design since 1936.

The steel-frame, glass, and concrete two-story building is fronted by a tall, deep, off-center entrance preceded by a canopied stair spanning a garden moat (see p. 145). The Y-stems are covered by a folded concrete roof; the canteen, beneath a similar roof, is reached from the first office level by a long glazed corridor. Upper levels of the office wings are connected by a suspended bridge. A light-filled, weightless structure, Van Leer was a departure from the closed structures more typical of Breuer's work even in the 1950s and is one of his few glass-curtain-wall designs. Evenly spaced symmetrical bays terminating in end walls of travertine contribute to a classically poised composition that owes much of its linear transparency and equilibrium to Miesian precedents.

Projecting solar-glass sun filters protected the south facades, but there was no provision for mechanical cooling—not unusual in the north of Europe in the 1950s, even for modern buildings with a lot of glass—and Van Leer employees suffered. Without thick masonry walls, sun control as an aspect of building design proved to be a failed modernist ideal by mid-century. In 1964, Breuer was informed by Oscar van Leer that "the most unsatisfactory ventilation and climatological conditions exist in our building."[2] The company planned extensive improvements and told him that it would solicit "advice and suggestions how this can be accomplished with a minimum degree of detriment to the architectural features of our office building."[3]

ARCHIVAL: **SUL 138, Breuer travel file, Drawings; AAA Correspondence, Photos, Project Record Book.**

BIBLIOGRAPHIC: *Progressive Architecture*, April 1959, 89; *Architectural Record*, August 1959, 125–34; *Arts & Architecture*, November 1959, 18–20; *L'Architecture d'aujourd'hui*, October 1959, 92–95; *Journal of the American Institute of Architects*, November 1960, 96–97; *Baumeister*, May 1961, 393–99; Jones, ed., *Marcel Breuer*, 132–40.

63
One Charles Center,
Baltimore, Maryland, 1960 (NOT BUILT)

MARCEL BREUER, ARCHITECT

HAMILTON P. SMITH, ASSOCIATE

Breuer's One Charles Center tower was one of six competitive designs submitted in March 1960 for a project for downtown Baltimore sponsored by the Baltimore Urban Renewal and Housing Agency. Thomas Karsten, for whom Breuer had built a house in 1956, was a member of the developers' syndicate submitting the Breuer design; Mies van der Rohe was the designer for a rival developer from Chicago. All six proposals were illustrated in the April 1960 issue of *Architectural Forum*. Breuer's tower had twenty-two floors of offices and two retail levels rising from a terraced plaza. The structure was concrete floor and roof slabs and an exterior bearing wall of poured-in-place architectural concrete framed by limestone sheathing. A 5-foot, 6-inch module produced a minimum two-window, 11-foot office that could be modified according to need.

Although Breuer prided himself on providing flexibility of space and economy of structure, the external appearance of the building depicted in the rendering is that of a lifeless slab with an unrelieved sameness of pattern on all sides, reminiscent of the "radiator grill" image for which UNESCO I had been so sharply criticized. The best passages were the inventive tree columns supporting and appearing to lift the building at the corners from the lower terrace on the west—forceful sculptural forms that Breuer used successfully for dramatic effect and structural function in this and other works of this decade. Although One Charles Center was beautifully lifted, what was lifted was banal.

The design was not accepted. Breuer liked the model of this building, and in April 1965 asked that it be sent to the National Institute of Arts and Letters for a show of works by new members.

ARCHIVAL: **SUL Drawings; AAA Correspondence, Photos.**

BIBLIOGRAPHIC: *Architectural Forum*, April 1960, 7–9; *Arts & Architecture*, March 1961, 16–17; Jones, ed., *Marcel Breuer*, 74–77.

63. Rendering

64
New England Merchants'
Bank Building, Competition,
Boston, Massachusetts, 1964 (NOT BUILT)

MARCEL BREUER AND HERBERT BECKHARD, ARCHITECTS

In December 1964, Breuer submitted drawings in a competition for a forty-two-story office tower for the New England Merchants' Bank, to be located near the new city hall in downtown Boston. One of several descendants of Breuer's generic open-plan tower type of the 1960s, the bank tower was almost twice as tall as its One Charles Center prototype. At base and crown, patterned bands fronted the mechanical zones, and the facades were composed of tiers of load-bearing precast-concrete panels.

ARCHIVAL: **SUL Drawings; AAA Photos.**
BIBLIOGRAPHIC: **Papachristou,** *Marcel Breuer,* **111.**

64. Rendering

65
175 Park Avenue (Grand Central Tower),
New York, New York, 1967–69 (NOT BUILT)

MARCEL BREUER AND HERBERT BECKHARD, ARCHITECTS

The New York City Landmarks Preservation Commission (LPC) designated Grand Central Terminal as a landmark in 1967. There could be no alteration to the exterior (the interior was not protected) without the approval of the LPC. The decision was opposed by Grand Central's owner, Penn Central Railroad Group, on the grounds that it restricted development opportunities for the site, a prime location (with almost 2 million usable square feet of air rights), at a time when there was a shortage of office space in New York. For Breuer, the project began with a telephone call on November 9, 1967, from consultants to the British builder-developer Union General Properties (UGP), which wanted a design for an office tower that would be "a companion" to the fifty-nine-story Pan Am Building (now Met Life, completed in 1963) and would meet the approval of the LPC. In February 1968, Breuer's appointment as architect was announced in the *New York Times.*

To appease the preservationists, Penn Central pledged to restore to its original grandeur the great public space of the pedestrian concourse of the terminal, victim of decades of commercial intrusion. But the equally grand waiting room would be eliminated to provide space for structural trusses, for offices in the mechanical area just above, and for two new stories with an intermediate mezzanine.

Breuer's first design was for a fifty-five-story slab of cast stone and granite to float above the terminal, preserving the Beaux-Arts facade; there was talk of a heliport on the roof (see p. 152). The structure was to be steel frame, supported on massive steel trusses cantilevered in four directions from the central elevator core. Drawings and renderings for Project I were intended as only promotional diagrams, with facade elements still to be designed. Even so, they reveal the weaknesses of Breuer's towers—the boxy shape and repetition of small rectangular units without relief on the vast facades. The LPC rejected Project I, calling it an "aesthetic joke," according to Paul Goldberger in the *New York Times* of September 16, 1990. Breuer then proposed a new design in two versions (the variations were in the tower-to-ground supports) as Project IIa (vertical legs) and Project IIb (sloping legs). Still optimistic, on December 9, 1968, he cabled his New York office from Paris that "I'm sure we can win with second project."

The position of the Breuer office on the landmarking issue reflected a predictable modernist approach in its claim that "in some cases landmarks will have to be removed by the pressures of the 'living city.'" In Project II, therefore, the significant change was to eliminate the inharmonious union of the floating tower above the Beaux-Arts facade; instead, the tower's formal integrity from top to bottom was retained by moving it south on the site and lodging it in place of the historic facade. The building height above the Forty-second Street level and the distance from the Pan Am Building were increased; the square footage of rentable office space and the number of office floors were increased, as were the number of elevators and escalators; commercial space was reduced. At the south facade, the loads were transferred below by means of a monumental truss supported by massive sloping columns that reached to the edge of the roadway-bridge.

The designs for Projects IIa and IIb were rejected, as their predecessor had been, by the LPC, on August 26, 1969. The response to the design still resonates more than a quarter century later: Ada Louise Huxtable remembered it in the *New York Times* of November 26, 1994, as "a gargantuan tower of aggressive vulgarity."

Penn Central filed suit to overturn the LPC's action, claiming that it constituted an unconstitutional taking of its property for public use without just compensation. For ten years, the case was before the courts. Ultimately, the United States Supreme Court in 1978 ruled 6 to 3 in favor of the LPC in what Jerold S. Kayden characterized in *Preservation News* of October 1988 as the "high noon" of the "most famous legal showdown of the historic preservation movement."

ARCHIVAL: **SUL Drawings; AAA Correspondence, Photos, Project File.**
BIBLIOGRAPHIC: *Progressive Architecture*, April 1968, 52; August 1968, 46, 48; and July 1969, 27; *Architectural Forum*, July 1968, 10, 72–73, 112, and May 1969, 16–18; *Architectural Record*, July 1968, 36, and October 1969, 37; New Yorker, June 29, 1968, 23; *Art in America*, September 1968, 42–43; *Progressive Architecture*, July 1969, 27; Papachristou, *Marcel Breuer*, 186–89; Gatje, *Marcel Breuer*, passim.

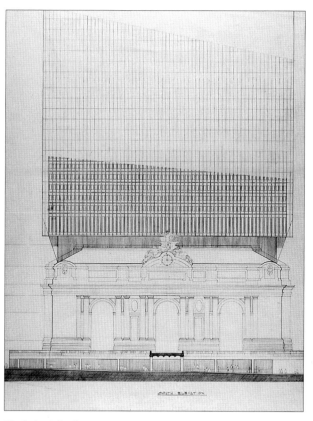

65a. Project I, detail

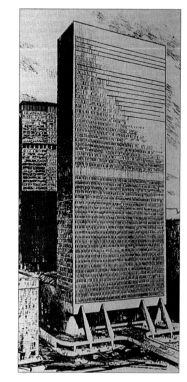

65b. Project IIa   65c. Project IIb

66
Bristol Center (Harrison State Development Corporation) Office Building,
Syracuse, New York, 1968–71 (NOT BUILT)

MARCEL BREUER AND HERBERT BECKHARD, ARCHITECTS

On November 1, 1968, Breuer entered into contract for an urban-redevelopment project in Syracuse, New York, seat of the Onondaga County government and an important banking and insurance center in upstate New York. It was understood that Marcel Breuer and Associates would be architects for all the buildings and all the site work once the developers had a commitment for the full project. Schematic designs, dated March 5, 1969, were prepared for phase I (an office building of approximately 120,000 square feet).

By March 1970, additional financial partners had joined the venture, and by mid-June new requirements were worked out for the office building: more commercial space at the ground-floor level and a new module for more efficient office space. Half the space would be occupied by a single tenant (Bristol-Meyers), and the remaining half would be sublet; eventually, the primary tenant would occupy the entire building. By June 1971, the project expanded further so that the site would include two motion-picture theaters, a hotel, and a parking structure. But, as an example of the fragility of many redevelopment ventures of the late 1960s and early 1970s, on July 5, 1971, the project was halted. Architects and the developers reached a financial settlement six months later.

The rendering of the final design for the office building depicts an elevated fourteen-story structure above a setback ground-level base for shops; corner pilotis; and an exceptional pair of concrete "trees" of prismatic form. Despite the usual tall-building formulas by which Breuer was trapped in the late 1960s, this building, because of its pleasing proportions and the imaginative shape of the twin trees, is a departure from the monotony and inertness of the others.

66. Rendering

ARCHIVAL: **SUL Drawings; AAA Contract, Photos, Project File.**
BIBLIOGRAPHIC: **Papachristou,** *Marcel Breuer,* **193.**

67
Cleveland Trust Company, Headquarters,
Cleveland, Ohio, 1969–71

MARCEL BREUER AND HAMILTON P. SMITH, ARCHITECTS

Breuer's office tower, originally designed for the Cleveland Trust Company, rises behind the nineteenth-century bank, a classical domed rotunda by George B. Post. Breuer was suggested for this work in January 1967 by Sherman Lee, director of the Cleveland Museum of Art, for whom he had designed a new wing for the museum. The original program called for a two-tower, two-phase construction, with both towers—one large, and the other smaller and obliquely set into it—enfolding Post's rotunda. Only phase I (phase II had been scheduled for 1975) was carried out. It produced an irregular footprint, with one corner of the squarish plan sliced away with a long diagonal. Lifted above black granite pilotis that screen a loggia leading to the lobby are twenty-five stories of office space articulated by cast-stone window units, deep-set and with rounded corners, separated at regular intervals by strips of black granite and framed at the base and crown by broad granite bands. The unaccented repetition of units of textured cast stone (produced by exposing the aggregate) and sleek black-granite strips is visually stultifying, and the fine details are too small to make a coherent impression from the ground. The tower reflects the unrealized and disparaged Project II for 175 Park Avenue (1968–69), as success with tower types continued to elude Breuer.

ARCHIVAL: **SUL 75, Drawings; AAA Correspondence, Photos.**
BIBLIOGRAPHIC: *Architectural Record*, March 1973, 124–26; Papachristou, *Marcel Breuer*, 202–3.

67. View of the new tower next to the nineteenth-century bank

68
Sixty State Street,
Boston, Massachusetts, 1969–71 (NOT BUILT)

MARCEL BREUER AND HERBERT BECKHARD, ARCHITECTS

Early in 1969, a large site was assembled in Boston by Cabot, Cabot & Forbes Company, on which it planned to build an office tower of 1.5 to 2 million square feet. The contract with Breuer, signed on July 10, 1969, called for a "quality" building. Cast once again in Breuer's 1960s tower mode, and perhaps closest in appearance to the headquarters of the Cleveland Trust Company, it was a tower with setbacks, rising above an elevated four-story pavilion, with too much uninflected window-unit surface. In June 1971, the project was suspended, and Marcel Breuer and Associates were ordered to stop work, allegedly because too expensive a building had been designed. The contract with Breuer was terminated by the client, which in October 1971 first approached Pietro Belluschi to take over the commission and then retained Emery Roth & Sons. On December 21, 1972, a settlement was reached between Breuer and the client.

ARCHIVAL: **SUL Drawings; AAA Contract, Correspondence, Photos.**

69
Southern New England Telephone Company, Traffic Service Position Systems Building,
Torrington, Connecticut, 1973–74

MARCEL BREUER AND HAMILTON P. SMITH, ARCHITECTS

Breuer agreed to build a traffic service positions building for Southern New England Telephone Company in December 1972. Drawings were soon completed for a modest (13,000-square-foot) structure on a wooded site adjacent to the Torin Corporation, from which it leased the land; construction was finished in 1974.

The building was designed to hold operating equipment, executive offices, a conference room, employee desks, and a training area. A low, almost square block with open courtyard, residential in mood and setting, it is one of Breuer's most successful late works. On each facade, he varied the rhythms, intervals, materials, and details. Closed on much of the exterior by its bearing walls of split-face block and punctuated by deep-set precast-concrete window units, the building on the interior opens through glass walls to a landscaped courtyard with pools and benches.

ARCHIVAL: **AAA Contract, Photos.**

70
European Investment Bank,
Luxembourg, 1973–74 (NOT BUILT)

MARCEL BREUER, CONSULTANT

In 1973, Breuer agreed to act as design consultant for a new headquarters building for the European Investment Bank in Luxembourg. The bank then appointed, "with the support and agreement of the consultant," Denys Lasdun & Partners, London, as architect. Among the Breuer Papers at Syracuse University are a ground plan and section dated October 5, 1973, for a narrow eleven-story structure of boomerang shape raised above a run of branched tree columns. Illness made it necessary for Breuer to give up his work for the bank in 1974.

ARCHIVAL: **SUL Drawings; AAA Contract, Photos, Project File.**
BIBLIOGRAPHIC: **Gatje,** *Marcel Breuer,* **272.**

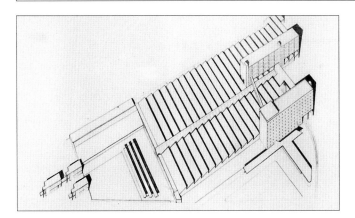

71. Isometric drawing

71
H. Fuld and Company
Telephone Factory, Competition,
Frankfurt, Germany, 1929 (NOT BUILT)

MARCEL BREUER, WITH THE ASSISTANCE OF GUSTAV HASSENPFLUG[1]

Breuer entered a competition sponsored by the H. Fuld telephone and telegraph factory. Joachim Driller noted that the design was one of ten bought by the company[2] (phrases such as "sold project" [*ankauf*] appear on some of Breuer's work lists and photographs[3]). Breuer stated in autobiographical accounts that his design was ranked third (of the ten). Driller reported the jury's criticisms (Ernst May and Walter Gropius were among the jurors) and Gropius's strong effort, to no avail, to get Breuer involved in the realization of the project along with the winner, a local Frankfurt architect.[4] Breuer envisioned an ambitious four-structure complex with two long, low warehouse sheds covered by sawtoothed roofs and adjacent to railroad tracks. Next to and above the sheds were two tallish blocks, one for production and the other for administration, linked by a covered walkway. Thin columns along the full extent of one of the high buildings and at the end facade of the other allowed light to reach the lower sheds, which were in their shadow. South of the factory building, Breuer sited a large, open canteen and, beyond it, housing blocks for the workers. This factory was one of the projects that Breuer selected for discussion in his article in *Die Form*, making a case for the economies of its plan and the social-welfare benefits it offered to workers.

ARCHIVAL: **SUL 39; AAA Photos; Driller, "Frühwerk," 370–72.**
BIBLIOGRAPHIC: **Breuer, "Beiträge zur Frage des Hochhauses," *Die Form* 5 (1930): 113–17; Blake, *Marcel Breuer*, 39, 42; Jones, ed., *Marcel Breuer*, 241; Driller, "Frühwerk," 370–72.**

FACTORIES

72
O. E. McIntyre, Inc.,
Westbury, Long Island, New York, 1954

MARCEL BREUER AND WILLIAM W. LANDSBERG, ARCHITECTS

This plant and office for a mail-order company employing 750 people was one of Breuer's most sophisticated small industrial buildings. Like his factories for the Torin Company, the first of which preceded this project by a year, the McIntyre plant was conceived as a simple boxlike structure with an open-plan, light-filled work space. Three large areas for direct-mail processes and a small area for offices to one side were enveloped by glass walls divided by mullions. Metal braces supporting exterior sunbreaks were formed with the lyrical curves that Breuer had invented for his Isokon plywood furniture. As he did in some of his residences, notably the contemporaneous Neumann House in Croton-on-Hudson, New York, Breuer enlivened the walls in the production areas by painting them bright red, electric blue, and yellow to contrast with nearby grays and whites. Outside, a dining terrace for employees was furnished with umbrellas, chairs, and tables and was surrounded by trees that had been preserved during construction.

A long marquee decorated with a bright red soffit and braced by colonnettes ran perpendicular to the main facade to signify the entrance. This device was reused and monumentalized as the entrance canopy at Breuer's wing for the Cleveland Museum of Art almost fifteen years later.

ARCHIVAL: **SUL Drawings; AAA Photos, Project File.**
Bibliographic: *Architectural Record*, February 1955, 157–60; *Architectural Forum*, March 1972, 50; Breuer, *Sun and Shadow*, 125, 182.

72. Entrance facade

Torin Corporation Buildings and Projects, 1952–76

Breuer's work for Torrington Manufacturing Company (the name was changed to Torin Corporation in 1969) raised small-scale industrial architecture in postwar America to a new aesthetic level. A manufacturer of air-moving equipment (fans and impellers), Torin had its corporate headquarters and a manufacturing and technical division in Torrington, Connecticut, where by 1963 the company owned 60 acres. Breuer's longtime connection to the company began in 1950 through Rufus Stillman, who was then vice president and later chairman of the board. Rufus and Leslie Stillman's enthusiasm for Breuer's architecture led to three Stillman Houses, two Gagarin Houses, the Caesar Cottage, the Becton Center at Yale University, several schools in the vicinity of Litchfield, Connecticut, and nine buildings for Torin. A tenth Torin project, the Still River Division, was built by MBA after Breuer's retirement. Stillman documented the history of the Torin buildings through 1971 and his client-architect relationship with Breuer in an article in the March 1972 issue of Architectural Forum. The company eventually was sold, and all the buildings in the original complex in Connecticut and elsewhere were changed and/or adapted for other uses.

73. Rear facade

73
Torin Corporation,
Oakville, Ontario, Canada, 1952–53

MARCEL BREUER, ARCHITECT

The earliest of Breuer's Torin structures was for the company's Canadian Division, commissioned in 1952 when Rufus Stillman invited him to design a 12,000-square-foot manufacturing plant with 80 percent factory space and 20 percent office space. The building was completed in July 1953. It was Breuer's first opportunity to design an industrial building. With it, he established his basic Torin model and corporate image—a long shedlike building with flat roof, the interior workplace a mostly unpartitioned space with the capability for extensive expansion (it was eventually enlarged to 40,000 square feet). The front facade was divided into six bays by projecting posts that carried the roof; a strip of windows protected by solar-glass sunshades stretched along the wall plane at midpoint. The rear facade was one of Breuer's most original and pictorial inventions, with its window wall set above a white-brick base, enframed by projecting roof and flanks, and divided by mullions that created the image of an intricate tapestry weave. To the side of the entrance, a low wall of perforated brick carrying the company name in bold letters hid the parking field and extended the long line of the building. Breuer's use of white-painted brick as the exterior skin, enhanced by bright red and blue paint at the entrance, made the building appear to be a work of abstract sculpture set down in a flat field.

"It seems one of the finest, simplest pieces of architecture I have ever seen. I would like to live in it," an admirer wrote to Breuer in 1955 after seeing the building for the first time and perceiving in its open plan, scale, materials, and details correspondences to the residential architecture that constituted the bulk of Breuer's practice in these years.

ARCHIVAL: **SUL Drawings; AAA Correspondence, Photos.**

BIBLIOGRAPHIC: *Architectural Forum*, March 1972, 46–51; *L'Architecture d'aujourd'hui*, December 1956–January 1957, 36–37; Breuer, *Sun and Shadow*, 115, 122–23, 186–87; Jones, ed., *Marcel Breuer*, 154–55.

74
Torin Corporation,
Van Nuys, California, 1955–56

MARCEL BREUER, ARCHITECT

CRAIG ELLWOOD, SUPERVISING ARCHITECT

The 50,000-square-foot Torin (Western Division) plant in an industrial area next to both a railroad and the airport in Van Nuys, California, was the second work by Breuer for his industrial client. A two-story rectangular block of modular metal-frame construction on a concrete base, the building was twice as wide as deep with eighteen bays on the east and west facades and nine bays on the north and south. Potential for 100 percent expansion to the east and west was integral to the planning. The interior was a large open worpshed; a strip of offices with lower ceilings ran along the north end. Outside, on the west, within a precinct defined by masonry walls of differing heights, lengths, and patterns of perforation, was a parking area and a terrace with tables and benches covered by a double wooden pergola. The California sun piercing the slats of the pergola made a pleasing pattern of stripes on the terrace pavement. These civilities represented Breuer's efforts to meet the personal needs of workers in an industrial environment. Still devoted to sun-control devices, Breuer used detachable solar-glass sun filters on the exterior facades. On the long sides, the bays were constructed of glass and continuous corrugated aluminum; they could be removed one by one, since they were fastened to the frame by studs that spanned the columns. In 1984, the building was sold. The new owners discovered that the self-supporting framework was "remarkably well constructed" and that the roof and outer skin could be separated from the structure.[5] Instead of being destroyed, the frame was picked up, installed in a different location, and given a new skin and roof. "Everyone involved in this commented on how well the building had been engineered: it was made to be earthquakeproof and to resist direct impact from an airplane because of its location next to the airport," the chief engineer recalled.

ARCHIVAL: **SUL Drawings; AAA Correspondence, Photos.**

BIBLIOGRAPHIC: *Journal of the American Institute of Architects*, December 1960, 65; *Architectural Forum*, March 1972, 46–51; John Peter, *Aluminum in Modern Architecture* (Louisville, Ky.: Reynolds Metal Company, 1960), 40–41; Jones, ed., *Marcel Breuer*, 156–57.

74. Wall with detachable sun filters

75
Torin Corporation,
Rochester, Indiana, 1960–68

MARCEL BREUER, ARCHITECT

ROBERT F. GATJE, ASSOCIATE

An informal contract for Breuer's third Torin commission was signed in early 1959, and construction of the first stage was begun on April 1, 1960. Erected in three stages, the steel-frame and concrete-block structure was completed in 1968. The Torin (Indiana Division) plant was one of Breuer's most classical buildings in terms of balance and proportion, even with the off-center entrance portico and each facade composed in a different expressive mode. The entrance facade was indebted in its clarity of structure and modular format to Mies van der Rohe's Crown Hall at IIT, completed in 1956. Breuer's building was defined by bays framed by black-painted steel that indicated the structure. The window sun shades were texturally enriched by projecting hexagonal steel grates.

ARCHIVAL: **SUL 74, 75, 150, Drawings; AAA Photos, Project File, Project Record Book.**
BIBLIOGRAPHIC: *Architectural Forum*, **March 1972, 48.**

75. Facade detail

76. Rendering

76
Torin Corporation, Machine Division Factory,
Torrington, Connecticut, 1963

MARCEL BREUER AND ROBERT F. GATJE, ARCHITECTS

The construction of a factory to produce strip- and wire-forming machinery began in March 1963 and was completed in September. The 71,250-square-foot complex for 250 employees was designed as a two-box structure with a smaller, lower office and laboratory wing joined to a larger and taller factory unit that needed the doubled height for its operations. While at the same time in Nivelles, Belgium, Breuer was building for Torin a precast-concrete structure with a three-dimensional surface, in Torrington, Connecticut, the company's Machine Division was rising as a basic steel-frame box with inexpensive porcelain-enameled aluminum siding. For the interior of the office wing in Torrington, he used the same system of movable wood partitions and wood lighting grid that he designed for Nivelles.

Of all the buildings designed by Breuer for the Torin Corporation, this was the most utilitarian and commonplace in format, although it gained some character by the contrast of its white fluted siding against the darkness of the surrounding woods.

ARCHIVAL: **SUL Drawings; AAA Photos, Project Record Book.**
BIBLIOGRAPHIC: *Architectural Record*, **December 1963, 126–27;** *Architectural Forum*, **March 1972, 50–51; Papachristou,** *Marcel Breuer*, **62.**

77. Entrance facade

77
Torin Corporation,
Nivelles, Belgium, 1963–64

MARCEL BREUER AND HAMILTON P. SMITH, ARCHITECTS

ANDRE AND JEAN POLAK, ARCHITECTS ("COORDINATORS," BRUSSELS, BELGIUM)

Serving as the international headquarters of Torin, the Belgian Division plant in Nivelles, south of Brussels, was begun in the summer of 1963. In addition to the manufacturing area were offices with laboratory space above, a cafeteria, a loading dock, and an employees' bicycle shed.

In the few years since he had planned Torin's factory in Rochester, Indiana, Breuer had become increasingly interested in the construction efficiency and sculptural effects of precast-concrete panels and their fabrication by the Dutch Schokbeton method, which produced a dense concrete of excellent quality.[6] At Nivelles, in conformity with his standard modular design for Torin plants, Breuer once again produced a low, flat-roofed box with an off-center canopied entrance on the main facade. This time, however, the structure was enclosed on each side by deep precast-concrete panels, 5 feet wide and 20 feet high, with a slightly mottled surface, prefabricated in Holland by Schokbeton and transported to the job site. Breuer formulated the panels in three varia-

tions: a taller hooded window unit for the manufacturing area, the window framed with a right-angled C and a blind field with projecting spine in relief above; a lower hooded window with the same frame and same superimposed relief field for the offices; and a full-height blind niche for the terminal bays. The vertical spines stiffened the panels structurally, and the projecting window hoods were intended to serve as protection against sun and rain. Major structural members, such as girders with a 40-foot span in the manufacturing zone, were also made of precast prestressed concrete, fabricated like the exterior wall panels by Schokbeton and shipped to Nivelles. An important building in terms of Breuer's dedication to concrete construction in the 1960s, Nivelles, with its precast panels, started him down a road that would lead to the repetitive, formulaic buildings that, in an aesthetic sense, marred the production of his later years. The sharp-edged projecting forms lacked the rugged force that concrete could express when used by Le Corbusier or the lyrical grace when mastered by Pier Luigi Nervi. Still, in 1963, Breuer's panels, with their relief patterns and rich chiaroscuro, bestowed considerable architectural dignity on a utilitarian industrial building.

ARCHIVAL: **SUL 74, 150, Drawings; AAA Photos.**

BIBLIOGRAPHIC: *Architectural Record*, January 1965, 151–56; *Arts & Architecture*, December 1965, 10–11; *L'architettura*, December 1965, 530–31; *Architectural Forum*, March 1972, 49; Papachristou, *Marcel Breuer*, 52–53.

78
Torin Corporation, Administration Building,
Torrington, Connecticut, 1966

MARCEL BREUER AND HERBERT BECKHARD, ARCHITECTS

Set into a hill on the wooded landscape of the Torin campus in Torrington, Connecticut, near the Machine Division factory, the brick and concrete Administration Building was a 15,000-square-foot bilevel structure for the company's corporate offices and electronic-data-processing equipment. Construction was in process during the spring of 1966. The brick-framed entrance on the upper level led to a lobby and reception area, from which opened executive offices, a conference room, general office space, and a stair to the lower level, where the computers were housed. Not deviating from his Torin *typus*, Breuer shaped the building as a box, three times as long as deep (8 bays x 24), with the main entrance off-center and a free-standing low brick wall to the side. Maintaining his preference for concrete and for cladding with precast units, he enclosed the building with window panels, "each weighing 16 tons—the panels function as sunshades above and as housing for the fan coil units below," Rufus Stillman reported.[7] The length of the building worked against the effectiveness of Breuer's individual-panel format, subordinating it to an assembly-line repetition. The rear elevation was a more interesting composition of window panels and rhythmically arranged brick walls. On the lower level, narrow brick piers and square panels of glass were framed by a pair of triangular retaining walls of brick (translated into black granite for the contemporaneous Roosevelt memorial project). Often at his best in detailing corner solutions, Breuer brought together the long and short facades as independent projecting elements bordered in brick, and accented the union with extended brick walls below.

The company's corporate symbol, a large concrete T that stood a short distance from the building, was an independent architectural sculpture cast in a form similar to that of the window panels.

ARCHIVAL: **SUL 74, Drawings; AAA Correspondence, Photos.**
BIBLIOGRAPHIC: *Architectural Record*, April 1966, 186, and February 1967, 131–36; *Architectural Forum*, March 1972, 50; Papachristou, *Marcel Breuer*, 58–61.

78. Rendering of the west elevation

79
Torin Corporation,
Swindon, England, 1965–66

MARCEL BREUER AND ROBERT F. GATJE, ARCHITECTS

FRISHMAN SPYER ASSOCIATES, SUPERVISING ARCHITECTS

The plant for the British Division of Torin was built on a 7-acre site in an industrial park in Swindon, Wiltshire, known as the Greenbridge Industrial Estate, providing space for offices, a laboratory, and a reverberant sound room. On July 29, 1964, Rufus Stillman wrote to Breuer that "we will be building some 40,000 square feet of factory and office in England starting the spring of 1965. This building will pretty much follow the program of our Brussels building modified to meet economic building methods in England. . . . We will use the Brussels plan as a program base."[8] By September 21, Breuer was requesting information from Robert Gatje in the Paris office about firms in England that specialized in prefabricated concrete, especially "exterior precast panels ready for glazing without metal window frames; columns, girders, and beams in precast post-stressed concrete; roof panels. We want to vary the actual profiling of the outside wall panels without changing their dimensions, details or window sizes."[9] Although the intention of both Stillman and Breuer was to repeat the successful prefabricated-concrete construction and attractive appearance of Nivelles, costs in England made such a plan impossible. Instead, the program of the Machine Division in Connecticut became the model. The Swindon plant, therefore, was a box sheathed in white aluminum siding with black brick at the canopied entrance; doors and windows were framed with brick and outlined with natural aluminum; concrete was used for bases and retaining walls. The structural steel and "roof furniture" were painted bright red-orange. The combination of white, red, and black aesthetically enhanced this industrial building, although in *Buildings of England*, Nikolas Pevsner writes: "The Torrington factory . . . [is] a neat steel-framed building but nothing very remarkable to look at."[10] The project was plagued by construction problems.

ARCHIVAL: **SUL 74, 149, 150, Drawings; AAA Photos, Project File.**
BIBLIOGRAPHIC: *Architectural Review*, July 1967, 22–23; *Deutsche Bauzeitung*, September 1968, 1387–88; *Architectural Forum*, March, 1972, 49; Gatje, *Marcel Breuer*, 151–52.

80
Torin Corporation, Technical Center,
Torrington, Connecticut, 1971

MARCEL BREUER AND HERBERT BECKHARD, ARCHITECTS

Located on the Torin campus between the Administration Building and the Machine Division, Torin Tech Center was built in 1971. Here Breuer broke with his Torin formula and replaced the box format with a U-shaped structure approached from a sunken paved terrace, producing the most original and aesthetically successful of the company's buildings. It was planned to house all the technical functions of the company along with laboratory and research facilities in one large open space with subsidiary blocks for utilities at one end and reception at the other. Materials on the exterior were split-concrete block, deeply recessed precast-concrete window units with diagonal terminals, and floor-to-ceiling walls of glass. The precast concrete of the window units was suppressed in favor of the split concrete of the facing, and the result was more satisfactory than in the Torin buildings where the precast was overwhelming.

ARCHIVAL: **SUL Drawings; AAA Photos, Project File.**
BIBLIOGRAPHIC: *Architectural Forum*, March 1972, 50.

81
Torin Corporation,
Penrith, Australia, 1976

MARCEL BREUER AND HERBERT BECKHARD, ARCHITECTS

HARRY SEIDLER AND ASSOCIATES, ASSOCIATE ARCHITECTS

The Torin factory in Penrith, Australia, was designed by Breuer and his partner Herbert Beckhard in association with Harry Seidler, based in Australia. A powerful work of almost windowless cuboid forms of rough-textured stone and concrete, the Penrith factory is "Egyptian" in its bold geometries and dense massing and in its composition as a long rectangle fronted by a pair of truncated mastabas.

ARCHIVAL: **SUL 74, Drawings; AAA Photos, Project File.**
BIBLIOGRAPHIC: *Architectural Record*, August 1977, 108–9.

81. North facade

80. Northwest side

New York University, Technology Building I, 1959–61.
See no. 16.

LABORATORIES AND RESEARCH FACILITIES

82
Brookhaven National Laboratory, Chemistry Building,
Upton, Long Island, New York, 1960 (NOT BUILT)

MARCEL BREUER, ARCHITECT

ROBERT F. GATJE, ASSOCIATE

Brookhaven National Laboratory was a research institution run for the United States Atomic Energy Commission by Associated Universities, a consortium of nine universities, on the site of a former United States Army camp on Long Island. The project called for a new building for the Department of Chemistry. Members of the department hoped to break with precedent by selecting the architect themselves, at least for the preparation of a preliminary master plan, instead of the choice coming from the General Services Administration (GSA) in Washington, D.C. After interviewing several architects, including Ludwig Mies van der Rohe and I. M. Pei, the building committee selected Breuer. According to Robert Gatje, Richard Dodson, chairman of the department, "was interested in the way science could be influenced by the architecture of the space within which the scientists worked."[1] Between May and December 1960, a diagrammed master plan (not a building design) was worked out in discussions with Dodson, who proposed an unconventional laboratory layout: directly across from the lab proper, and separated from it by a corridor, would be the scientist's office with a window on one side and a glass wall on the other. In this way, "light could be borrowed across the corridor from the office." On its other side, the lab would be flanked by a utility corridor where pipes, ducts, and electricity brought in from a central chase would be run and where repair and other technical work could take place. The space sequence would be windowed office, glass-walled corridor for pedestrian traffic, laboratory, utility corridor for access to services, windowed office. Although this became a standard way to design labs, it was new, if not unique, for the time, according to Gatje. The GSA, however, insisted on its own selection process for the architect, and Breuer did not build the new Chemistry Building for Brookhaven. His design for the lab, however, was used in the building that was erected.

ARCHIVAL: **SUL Drawings; AAA Project Record Book.**
BIBLIOGRAPHIC: **Gatje,** *Marcel Breuer,* **92–94.**

83
IBM Research Center,
La Gaude, France, 1960–62

First Expansion, 1968–70
Second Expansion, 1976–78

MARCEL BREUER AND ROBERT F. GATJE, ARCHITECTS

RICHARD AND MICHEL LAUGIER, SUPERVISING ARCHITECTS (NICE, FRANCE)

Needing to expand its Paris research and development laboratories, IBM erected a new laboratory and office building on a dramatic site near the Côte d'Azur. The referral to Breuer came from Eliot Noyes, who was an adviser to IBM. Construction began in July 1960 and was completed in 1962. As he did for his smaller industrial client, the Torin Corporation, Breuer planned a modular building for IBM that then became its standard laboratory–office type and company-identifying image. IBM wanted a low building instead of a tower, believing that efficiency of circulation was aided by avoiding passenger elevators. The format became a concrete-frame two-story double-Y lifted by pilotis shaped as powerful abstract caryatids. Executive and research offices were on the first floor, along with an auditorium, a kitchen, a cafeteria, and a dining terrace for employees; on the second floor was the laboratory space. To construct the work in a minimum amount of time, massive prefabrication was necessary. Some elements—the concrete deck slabs and the pilotis—were cast on site. Prefabrication prevailed on the interior also, where there were few permanent elements (staircase walls and washrooms) and where demountable wood partitions separated offices and labs. Since by practice and tradition outside offices were considered essential in France, Breuer's double-Y—more accurately in this case an elongated X—was especially suited to this project because it made it possible for all offices and labs to be windowed and to have views of the landscape.

According to Robert Gatje, whose article in the February 1963 issue of *Progressive Architecture* provides essential information and background for the building, the steep, irregular terrain required variations in the shaft height (from 13 to 24 feet) of the poured-in-place pilotis. Their massive proportions were determined not only by the weight of the structure, but also by added loads from heavy equipment in the labs. Despite the load, the number of interior columns was kept to a minimum so that most of the space had a clear span of about 40 feet

83. Aerial view

from one exterior wall to the other. Wedge-shaped segments in the acoustic tile of the suspended ceilings negotiated the curves of the plan.

Breuer's preference in this period for cladding with precast-concrete panels determined the sculptural character of the IBM exterior—vast curving stretches of deeply nested windows above slanted bases—and expressed its modular systems. Windows on the narrow ends of the Ys were screened with terra-cotta flue tile, a material favored by Breuer since the 1950s.

The original program called for occupancy for 600 people; the 12-by-12-foot office was designed for two engineers. Already in 1964 more space was needed, but it was not until August 1967 that discussions took place about a program and design for an expansion of 60,000 square feet.

First Expansion

MARCEL BREUER AND ROBERT F. GATJE, ARCHITECTS

Plans for the expansion were in work in Breuer's Paris office by January 1968, with Mario Jossa as partner-in-charge; the building was completed in 1970. It was understood by architect and client that the expansion would preserve both the exceptional site and the appearance of the original building: "I would like to express here again our feeling as architects that putting the new buildings with their back against the hillside is the best way to underplay the two expansion wings of considerable volume and to maintain the significance of the present building," Breuer wrote to IBM on September 1, 1967.[2] The rectangular block of the first expansion, consequently, was sited so that it was partially sunk into the terrain of the terrace of the original building and was adjacent to its ramp, distracting as little as possible from the main structure (connected to it with an elevator tower). Offices in the expansion were 8 feet by 10 feet, each accommodating one engineer instead of the shared arrangement in the first building. That the window panels were narrower than those in the original was a worry for the client, which feared that the fins might obstruct the views.

In 1968, the IBM complex was declared a national monument; in 1976, it was awarded the Grande Médaille d'or as an "outstanding example of contemporary architecture in France."

The construction of a second expansion, joined directly to the original building and externally similar in appearance, was overseen by MBA from 1976 to 1978 after Breuer's retirement.

ARCHIVAL: SUL 38, 66, Drawings; AAA Correspondence, Photos, Project Record Book.
BIBLIOGRAPHIC: *Architectural Forum*, March 1961, 98–99; *Progressive Architecture*, February 1963, 132–37; *L'architettura*, May 1963, 42–43; *L'Architecture d'aujourd'hui*, February 1963, 18–25, and December 1963, 44; *Fortune*, February 1963, 92–93; *L'Oeil*, March 1963, 44–49; *Japan Architect*, March 1963, 12–22; *Die Bauwelt*, April 1963, 432–36; *Techniques et architecture*, May 1963, 162–65; *Revue de l'Union internationale des architectes*, October 1963, 32–35; *Architectural Record,* May 1979, 128–29; *Process: Architecture* 32 (1982): 48–49; Papachristou, *Marcel Breuer*, 24–33; Gatje, *Marcel Breuer*, passim.

84a. Administration wing, bridge, and laboratory

84
Sarget-Ambrine, Headquarters and Pharmaceutical Laboratories,
Merignac, France, 1965–67

MARCEL BREUER AND ROBERT F. GATJE, ARCHITECTS

Expansion (Sarget II), 1970–72

MARCEL BREUER, ROBERT F. GATJE, AND MARIO JOSSA, ARCHITECTS

The commission came to the Paris office through architect Jack Freidin, who recommended Breuer to his client Mortimer Sackler, of the family of American pharmaceutical magnates; the Sacklers had purchased a French affiliate and were seeking an architect experienced with construction in France. One of several descendants of Breuer's headquarters for the Department of Housing and Urban Development, the curved administration building was typical of the period, with its row of eight poured-in-place faceted pilotis beneath a run of twenty-three identical precast panels. Completed in 1967 and dedicated on July 1, 1968, the complex was expanded for the first time between 1970 and 1972. A second expansion was undertaken by MBA after Breuer's retirement.

This corporate headquarters and pharmaceutical plant was located on a picturesque site with old trees and a stream north of the highway connecting Bordeaux with its airport at Merignac. The administrative facilities, in one wing, were connected by enclosed bridges and covered walkways to the laboratories and the manufacturing and storage facilities, in the other. Breuer's sketch and the finished ground plan best describe one of his most interesting designs. The laboratory wing was contained within the large rectangular manufacturing and

storage structure and was fronted and joined by a bridge to the smaller, curved administration wing, which had stair projections at each end. As the curved structure was not axially aligned with its rectangular neighbor, its off-center position gave the composition a dynamic tension. The bridge between them (a borrowing of Walter Gropius's second- and third-floor bridge between the administration and workshop wings of the Dessau Bauhaus) ran at an oblique angle so that the full ensemble resembled a swinging pendulum at the base of a clock. Breuer's first sketches were for a more static design, with the bridge unit in a straight line and the administration wing oriented to the west rather than the east. The three-story arc was raised on pilotis, with elevator lobby and conference hall on the ground level. From the first upper level, a bridge led directly to the two-story manufacturing wing; a double-loaded central corridor on each of the upper two levels served the private offices and other facilities. Exterior materials were prefabricated and poured-in-place concrete, local masonry, and black anodized aluminum for the window frames.

ARCHIVAL: **SUL 138, 150, 151, Drawings, Sketches; AAA Photos.**
BIBLIOGRAPHIC: *Techniques et architecture*, October 1967, 76–78; Papachristou, *Marcel Breuer*, 190–92; Gatje, *Marcel Breuer*, 56–59.

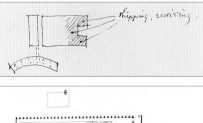

84b. Sketch by Breuer

84c. Plan

**New York University, Technology Building II, 1967–70.
See no. 16.**

**Yale University, Becton Engineering and Applied Science
Center, 1967–70. See no. 20.**

85
Armstrong Rubber Company, Headquarters,
West Haven, Connecticut, 1968–70

MARCEL BREUER AND ROBERT F. GATJE, ARCHITECTS

The building is located in the Long Wharf development area outside New Haven, Connecticut, on what had been unstable, low-lying land, filled in and developed by the city. Now a grassy plain, the site is close to the Connecticut Turnpike. When Armstrong Rubber Company, later Pirelli Armstrong Tire Company, asked to buy the land from the city, reform Mayor Richard Lee, whose goals for New Haven included rebuilding the city with significant architecture, agreed on condition that a notable architect design the building. He suggested Breuer. That Breuer's fee was lower than that of other famous architects who were being considered by the company management, and that his building for the Department of Housing and Urban Development had been brought in on time and under budget, were important factors in the decision to hire him.[3] Construction began in March 1968 and was completed in August 1970. Two facilities were needed: one for research and development laboratories for the manufacture of automobile and airplane tires, and the other for corporate headquarters administration. Because of the building's location at an important intersection of interstate roadways, the mayor wanted a tall structure that would be a dramatic gateway to the city. Breuer proposed, therefore, that instead of two buildings side by side, the facilities be brought together as a

tower, the office unit hung above the research block with a wide stretch of empty space in between. He took his old binuclear H-form and turned it on end.

The building is a concrete-and-steel-frame structure built on pilings sheathed in precast and poured-in-place architectural concrete, light in color and deeply modeled for maximum chiaroscuro (see p. 157). The ground-based two-story block is the research and development tier; administrative offices are in the narrower four-story mass above, hung from a series of story-high trusses. The two end trusses are supported by concrete piers. The entire building (200,000 square feet) was planned on a 6-by-6-foot module. According to Robert Gatje, the original design called for one additional story atop the administration building, eliminated for reasons of economy. The "hole" between the upper and lower elements had the potential to be filled with two additional floors, and a drawing was made showing that configuration. The vertical center of the side facades are steel trusses covered with a concrete skin that act as bridge abutments from which the upper unit is hung, unsupported from below. Admiration was expressed by company executives for the architects' grasp of the program and for the efficiency of the coordinated paths of communication. The building was, moreover, completed on time and was "only 2% over budget—our fault not his," they said.[4]

In its unusual and arresting format, the Pirelli Armstrong building is scaled to the highway that fronts it. It is, indeed, the dramatic gateway to New Haven that Lee envisioned. But the inventiveness of the contour and the creative definition of the side facades are compromised by the weaknesses that the building shares with much of Breuer's dehumanized corporate architecture of the late 1960s in his effort to be cost-efficient—mechanical repetitions of small bays with few accents, and an absence of muscle tone and textural variation in the stiff and weighty concrete. Even with its shortcomings, it remains one of the best of his works at this time and in this genre.

ARCHIVAL: **SUL 75, Drawings; AAA Photos, Project Record Book.**
BIBLIOGRAPHIC: **Papachristou,** *Marcel Breuer*, **158–60; Gatje,** *Marcel Breuer*, **109–14.**

Harvard University, Biology and Chemistry Building, 1969 (not built). See no. 21.

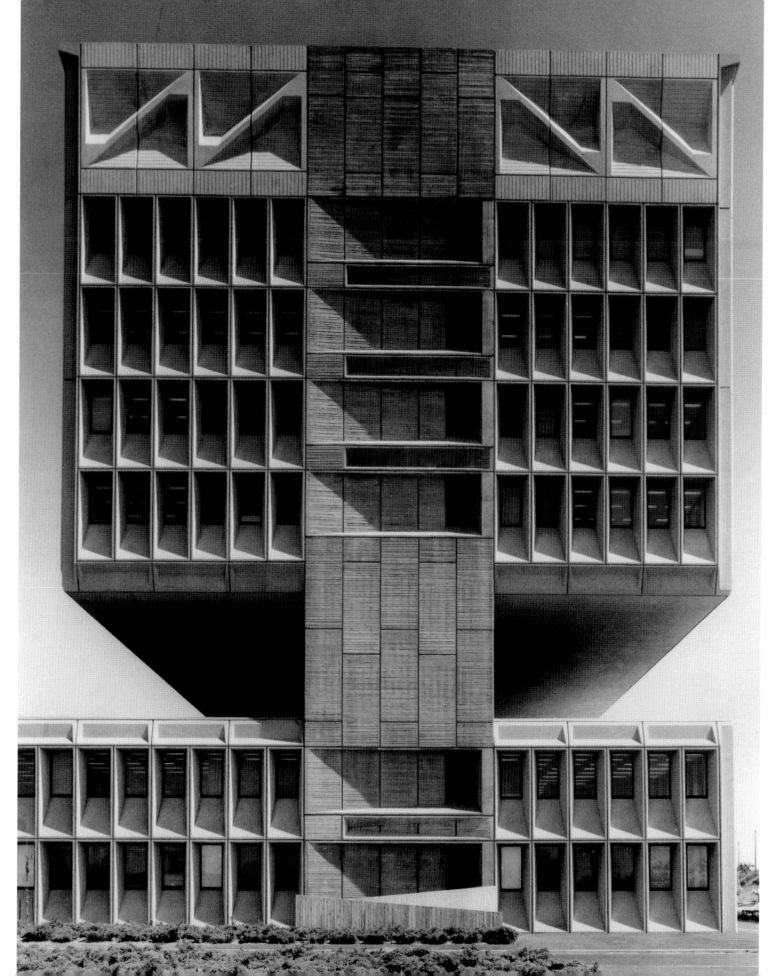

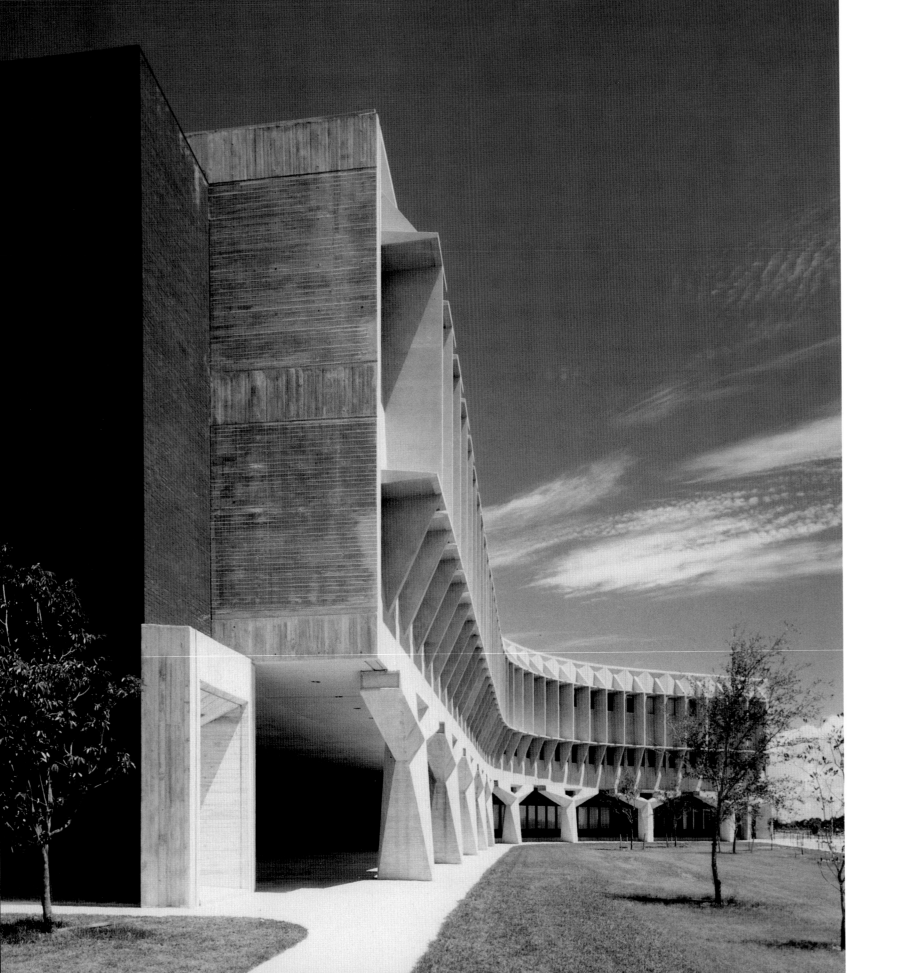

86
IBM Administrative, Laboratory, and Manufacturing Facility,
Boca Raton, Florida, 1968–72

Phases I and II, 1968–70
Phase III, 1970–72

MARCEL BREUER AND ROBERT F. GATJE, ARCHITECTS

The commission for a new facility with over 2,000 employees for the Southeast Division of IBM, on a 500-acre site near Boca Raton, Florida, was given to Breuer because of the success of IBM La Gaude. Construction (of Phases I and II of the master plan) began on November 7, 1968, and was completed on August 1, 1970 (see p. 176). The contract for Phase III was dated November 1969, and the buildings were completed in 1972. Phases I and II of the complex included units for manufacturing and warehousing, but the core elements were a pair of concrete administrative and laboratory wings based on Breuer's curved double-Ys at La Gaude. In Boca Raton, the facades have two levels of additive window panels lifted above faceted concrete trees. The layout conformed to Breuer's interest in less structure and greater floor area, and the 60-foot span of the wings across their depth was divided into successive spans of 12-foot offices, 6-foot corridor, 24-foot laboratories, 6-foot corridor, and 12-foot offices. The placement of the curving double-Ys in the overall plan illustrates the effect of urban images of Paris on Breuer—in this instance, the configuration of buildings (including his own UNESCO Headquarters) around the open Place de Fontenoy.

ARCHIVAL: **SUL 67–69, 130–37, 157–60, 166–71; AAA Correspondence, Photos, Project Record Book.**
BIBLIOGRAPHIC: *Architectural Record*, February 1971, 113–18; *L'architettura*, September 1971, 326–27; *Process: Architecture* 32 (1982): 45–47; Papachristou, *Marcel Breuer*, 200–201; Gatje, *Marcel Breuer*, 245–46.

87
Mundipharma, Headquarters and Manufacturing Plant,
Limburg, Germany, 1973–75

MARCEL BREUER AND ROBERT F. GATJE, ARCHITECTS

Mundipharma was the second European plant built by the Breuer office for the Sackler pharmaceutical empire, the first being the headquarters and laboratory facilities for Sarget-Ambrine, although the design was largely determined by the client (see p. 178). Robert Gatje recalls that Mortimer Sackler purchased a German company around the time of the exhibition "Marcel Breuer at the Metropolitan Museum of Art" (November 1972–January 1973). At the exhibition, he admired photographs of Saint John's Abbey Church and requested that the design of his new building in Germany be based on the folded-plate concrete-wall format that Breuer had used at the abbey and at UNESCO Headquarters. He also proposed that the lower level be "buried" below ground with only clerestory windows visible.[5]

Mundipharma was designed and detailed in the New York office; its construction was overseen by the Paris office. On January 23, 1973, Gatje presented a facade sketch that was approved by the client. Low-slung and graceful, with good proportions and a suave interior arrangement of space, Mundipharma is one of the best precast structures to come out of the Breuer office in the 1970s. The folded-wall system was effectively carried out, and the building was lightened by "floating" above the clerestoried base.

ARCHIVAL: **SUL Drawings; AAA Contract, Photos.**
BIBLIOGRAPHIC: **Gatje,** *Marcel Breuer*, **264–66.**

University of Virginia, Physics Building, 1971–72 (not built). See no. 22.

State University of New York at Buffalo, Faculty of Engineering and Applied Science Buildings Complex, 1975–78. See no. 23.

OPPOSITE
86. Arcade

Throughout his career, Breuer renovated, furnished, designed, and redesigned numerous stores, both interiors and facades, and showrooms in Europe and the United States—among them the Matzinger and Wohnbedarf stores in Switzerland,[1] S. S. Kettenladen stores in Berlin, Motley's Fashion Studio in London, an Eastern Airlines ticket office in Boston, and showrooms for Scarves by Vera fashion design in New York and Los Angeles. These works belong more appropriately with studies of Breuer's furniture and interiors, and several are illustrated and discussed in Christopher Wilk's Marcel Breuer: Furniture and Interiors.

STORES

89. Rendering of the facade

88
Almy, Bigelow & Washburn,
Salem, Massachusetts, 1944–45 (NOT BUILT)

MARCEL BREUER, ARCHITECT

In November 1944, Breuer was asked for "architectural services" in connection with the design for a new Almy, Bigelow & Washburn department store to replace the existing store on the same site. He prepared preliminary plans to explore layout possibilities and to anticipate construction expenses and the financing for a new store against the alternative of remodeling the existing building. The general cost estimate, given by the contractor in February 1945, was $300,000, and the decision was not to go ahead with a new building.

ARCHIVAL: **SUL 29, Drawings.**
BIBLIOGRAPHIC: **Driller, "Frühwerk," 375.**

89
Abraham & Straus, Exterior,
Hempstead, Long Island, New York, 1951–52

MARCEL BREUER, CONSULTING ARCHITECT

Breuer was named "Consulting Architect for Exterior Design" for a large new suburban branch of Abraham & Straus, the famous Brooklyn department store, in September 1950. The location was Hempstead, Long Island, at the time an important center of business and politics.[2] The Breuer office—William Landsberg was chief draftsman on the job—produced elevations, perspectives, and exterior design details in the summer of 1951; the new store opened on February 28, 1952. It was a flat-roofed, two-story-and-basement building of brick and stone exterior; the foundations and supporting concrete columns allowed for the future addition of two floors. Except for display windows, the exterior was unfenestrated to protect the merchandise from damaging exposure to sunlight. Attempting to achieve some sense of "intimacy," despite what he called a "monumental approach" to the design ("large, continuous components"),[3] Breuer used some of the same materials and colors for the external finish of this suburban department store as in his suburban houses of the period—textured white-painted brick and rubble stone that through differences of color and texture made "an aesthetic effect."[4] He varied the surface by alternating areas of plain and textured brick, bearing in mind the planned two-story addition, which he foresaw as one story plain and the other textured. He articulated the main facade with a recessed entrance fronted by a pair of columns from ground to roof. On the upper level were five flagpoles, one above each window. Unconstitutionally (but understandably for this era in American politics), the Hempstead building inspector approved this feature on the condition that "only American flags can be displayed on these poles."[5] Despite an optimistic beginning and the commissioning of the exterior to the well-known architect, cost concerns, a predetermined structure, and constrictive local ordinances helped produce a building that resembled not much more than a basic warehouse. The store served the community for four decades, but on June 19, 1992, the *New York Times* reported: "A & S in Hempstead Closing after 40 Years," a victim of the city's decline. The article was illustrated with a current photograph taken from the same viewpoint as the rendering of Breuer's facade of 1950. The broad horizontal expanse was still there, but Breuer's distinctive 1950s "look" and the materials he chose had been replaced.

ARCHIVAL: **SUL 41, Drawings; AAA Photos.**

BIBLIOGRAPHIC: *Architectural Forum*, May 1952, 127–31; Driller, "Frühwerk," 375.

90a. Department-store corner, with sculpture by Naum Gabo

90
De Bijenkorf Department Store Complex,
Rotterdam, the Netherlands

Department Store, Office Annex, Movie Theater, and Construction Field Office, 1955–57

MARCEL BREUER AND A. ELZAS, ARCHITECTS

DANIEL SCHWARTZMAN, CONSULTANT

Parking Garage, 1970–74

MARCEL BREUER AND ROBERT F. GATJE, ARCHITECTS

Planning for De Bijenkorf (beehive) department store began in New York in the Breuer office in 1953, with Dutch architect A. Elzas handling the European side of the project. A model was shipped to Rotterdam in August 1954; construction was started in the winter of 1955; a construction field office was shaped to harmonize with the symbolic hexagons of the store facade (see p. 30). Opening ceremonies took place on March 19, 1957; on May 21, Naum Gabo's 85-foot-high, free-standing construction was unveiled by the burgomaster of Rotterdam. The ensemble belongs to the postwar rebuilding of Rotterdam after the nearly total obliteration of the historic and commercial center of the city by German bombs on May 14, 1940.[6] Rotterdam's main business thoroughfare, Coolsingel, was straightened and widened as part of the new plan. Instead of rebuilding and incorporating into the new urban scheme the nearby and severely damaged original De Bijenkorf (1929–30), built by Willem Dudok and celebrated for its brickwork and ribbon-windowed modernism, it was decided to build a completely new Bijenkorf store on Coolsingel. Breuer designed a five-story smooth-surfaced square building with an adjoining office annex to the north. To balance the projecting mass of Hotel Astoria, a structure that survived the bombing but now extended beyond the newly established building line of Coolsingel, the city planners wished to interrupt the run of Breuer's planar facade with a projecting end bay. The idea was unacceptable to De Bijenkorf's owners and to Breuer, who suggested instead a large piece of sculpture that would produce the same effect. In January 1954, Breuer asked Gabo, whom he had known since the 1930s in London,[7] to create a monumental outdoor construction, the sculptor's largest public commission. Gabo's first design was for a sculpture affixed to the facade, brilliantly suggestive of the vibrating wings of a hovering bee at the entrance to a hive. It was rejected by Rotterdam's city planners because it did not produce a projection forceful enough along the street line.[8] In January 1956, Gabo's redesigned model for a free-standing construction made of prestressed concrete, steel ribs, stainless steel, bronze wire, and marble was accepted.

The Bijenkorf interior conforms to ideals of department-store architecture, with its huge open selling floors interrupted only by faceted columns that support the reinforced-concrete slab structure. On the exterior, display windows are inset beneath flat planes of facades clad in travertine. On the Coolsingel side, the travertine is cut into hexagons, not only an image of the honeycomb interior of the beehive from which the store takes its name, but also one of Breuer's favorite shapes. As early as 1938, he wrote that the stores in his Garden City of the Future (1936) were "like the interior of honeycombs," claiming that the hexagon inspired efficient planning by providing the greatest amount of space while still adjacent to another space, an arrangement that could not be accomplished with a circle.[9] The travertine of the flanking facades of the Rotterdam store is not shaped as hexagons, but as rectangles (a change of design sharply criticized by Lewis Mumford in an important study of the building[10]). Widely spaced narrow slits as tall as the hexagons and the rectangles they pierce, and three large horizontal cuts, are the only window openings in the upper stories. Mumford praised the steel and glass curtain wall of the annex:

At the rear of this four-square structure, facing north, the architect Marcel Breuer has produced one of the best office-building facades I have seen anywhere. By using a sort of valance of opaque glass in the upper part of the windows, he has achieved a maximum of useful light with a minimum of glare. . . . Breuer has made a step in the right direction to rescue modern buildings from the dust-collecting Venetian blind and the icicle-collecting brise-soleil, or external sun screen.[11]

Reinventing the format of his curvilinear Ariston Club (1947) and its original source—the recreation building in Garden City of the Future—Breuer designed the construction field office as an elevated tri-hexagon pinwheel supported by a steel column with ribs and reached by a stair. Intended as a temporary structure, it proved so

pleasing in shape and so cheerful in its primary colors that after the store was completed it was not demolished, but became a children's museum. The Cineac movie theater adjacent to De Bijenkorf demonstrated Breuer's skill with theater interiors. In 1970 Breuer renewed his connection to De Bijenkorf by undertaking the design of a large parking garage next to the store, the construction of which was carried out by a Dutch firm. When it was completed in the summer of 1974, Breuer was ill. On July 17, he wrote to the Bijenkorf people that he "could not undertake a trip to Europe. . . . I am very sorry about that [and] at the moment have to be satisfied knowing that you have a positive opinion about [the building]."[12]

ARCHIVAL: **SUL 49, 138, Drawings; AAA Correspondence, Photos.**
BIBLIOGRAPHIC: *Architectural Forum*, September 1957, 132–35; *Architectural Record*, November 1957, 167–75; *Zodiac*, no. 1 (1957): 145–58; *Die Bauwelt*, April 1958: 340–43; *Nuestra arquitectura*, May 1958, 17–23; *Bauen und Wohnen*, August 1958, 257–62; Mumford, "A Walk Through Rotterdam," in *Highway and the City*, 31–40.

90b. Office annex, north elevation

91. Model

91
New Haven Railroad, Passenger Station,
New London, Connecticut, 1955 (NOT BUILT)

MARCEL BREUER, ARCHITECT

EDUARDO CATALANO, CONSULTANT

It was probably Florence Knoll who, around 1954 or 1955, brought Breuer to the attention of Patrick B. McGinnis, for a short time president of the New Haven Railroad. During his tenure, McGinnis initiated an architecture and design project and called on Breuer, Eero Saarinen, and Minoru Yamasaki to improve the appearance of New Haven Railroad trains and passenger stations. Little of McGinnis's ambitious scheme could be executed before he left the New Haven to become president of the Boston & Maine Railroad. Yamasaki, Leinweber & Associates completed a vaulted passenger-ramp shelter in New Haven, Connecticut; Breuer's plan for the New London station was never carried out. What Breuer envisioned—it was the period when he was thinking about uses for the hyperbolic paraboloid—was realized in his almost contemporaneous library for Hunter College. For the New London project, as at Hunter, Breuer designed a series of inverted umbrellas—thin concrete-shell sections supported by a slender central column. Four units braced one another and formed the covering shelter for passengers on the outdoor platform as well as the roof of the glass-walled station building with good visibility to the tracks. Waves of dark and light stripes, made of roofing material in alternating shades of gray, produced a striking design on the roof surface. Across the track at the parking lot (for 1,600 cars), a smaller unit of similar construction marked the entrance to a below-grade passenger tunnel. A streamlined overpass–pedestrian ramp, with the elliptical curve favored by Breuer, replaced the grade-level crossing.

ARCHIVAL: **SUL Drawings; AAA Photos.**
BIBLIOGRAPHIC: *Industrial Design*, February 1956, 52–70; *L'Architecture d'aujourd'hui*, March 1956, 46–47; *Architectural Forum*, June 1956, 107–12; Jones, ed., *Marcel Breuer*, 142–45.

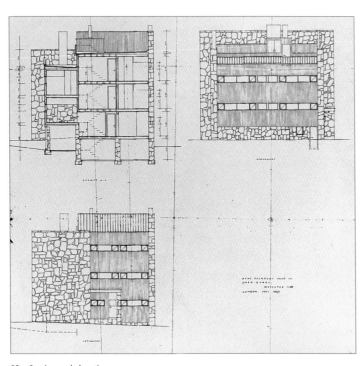

92a. Section and elevations

92b. Model

RECREATIONAL
RESORTS, CLUBS, AND HOTELS

92
Hans Falkner Ski Lodge,
Ober-Gurgl, Austria, 1937–38 (NOT BUILT)

MARCEL BREUER, ARCHITECT

Sketched on a hotel advertisement for the 1936–37 season in Ober-Gurgl, Breuer's favorite ski resort in the Austrian Tyrol, is a rectangle with compass points indicating the site of a new modern ski lodge that Hans Falkner, head of the Ober-Gurgl ski school, asked him to build.[1] Although small in size, in terms of structural invention it was one of Breuer's most far-reaching projects. He designed it in London in the summer of 1937 and worked on it in Cambridge, Massachusetts, after arriving at Harvard in the fall. At first, problems about availability and type of materials held the project back. Then the design—a daring modern intruder among the peak-roofed cabins and mountain crags of the classic Tyrolean village—was disapproved by the local authorities. In any event, had construction begun as planned in the spring of 1938, it would have collided with the Austrian Anschluss.

Ground plans and elevations with German text, executed in brown ink on heavy paper by an anonymous draftsman in July 1937, were brought by Breuer to the United States and are now at Syracuse University Library. A crude model of cork, plywood, and paper was made by Breuer's Harvard students, under his supervision, at the request of *Architectural Record* as the project was prepared for publication in the September 1938 issue of the magazine.

The limited funds at Falkner's disposal and the location of Ober-Gurgl—6,300 feet above sea level with no road after 4,800 feet, reached only by horse-drawn sled in winter and by wagon at other times—inspired Breuer to base his design not on heavy steel, concrete, and glass, which were difficult to transport and thus expensive, but on local stone and light wood. "It presented an opportunity that proved that modern forms are not dependent on steel, glass, concrete or cantilevered balconies, a chance to show that modern architecture is founded on a mentality, an approach to planning, not on a certain technique," he said.[2] Windowless stone bearing walls, solid from foundation to roof, carried all loads and abutted and projected beyond the plane of walls of wood pierced with two levels of ribbon windows. Breuer had already used projecting, solid stone bearing walls in the Gane Pavilion a year earlier. The window walls of light wood carried only their own weight, as the floor-to-ceiling load was borne by the stone walls and the interior walls. The structure of the wood walls was defined by a truss format that gave them a rigidity that Breuer compared with that of reinforced concrete. No lintels were needed above the long strips of windows because they were framed by the stiff wood construct. Breuer planned the wood strips of the exterior sheathing to run vertically, but Falkner asked him to make the cladding horizontal because it was "more Tyrolean." The terraces on the flat roof were intended for sunning, with separate areas for men and women made private by screens of vertical wood slats and opaque glass. Bathrooms (four for twenty guests) and the drying rooms (for clothes) were grouped in the center of the building and were ventilated through a common internal shaft. The one-, two-, and three-bed guestrooms were arranged around a central stair core.

With its stepped roof-decks above a three-story cubic volume, Breuer's ski hotel bore an unmistakable visual parallel to his Constructivist cabinetwork of around 1924. The trussing system he invented for its wood-wall construction made it easy for him to adapt to American wood-framing techniques when he began to build with Walter Gropius in New England. He used that system for the structure of many of his early residential works in the New World, notably the Hagerty, Fischer, Chamberlain, and Weizenblatt Houses.

ARCHIVAL: **SUL 5, 6, 9, 18, 42, Drawings; AAA Correspondence, Photos.**
BIBLIOGRAPHIC: *Architectural Record*, September 1938, 57–59; Blake, *Marcel Breuer*, 56; Breuer, *Sun and Shadow*, 29; Driller, "Frühwerk," 345–48, and *Breuer Houses*, 98–101, 259.

93. Entrance side

93
Ariston Club,
Mar del Plata, Argentina, 1947–48

MARCEL BREUER, WITH EDUARDO CATALANO AND FRANCISCO COIRE, ARCHITECTS

During a stay in Argentina in 1947 to teach and consult, Breuer worked on the development of the beach resort Mar del Plata with Eduardo Catalano, Francisco Coire, and other architects in the "Buenos Aires Group." He designed the Ariston Club for dining and dancing, and returned to the United States while Catalano oversaw the construction. On October 20, 1947, Catalano wrote that the building authorities had accepted the drawings and construction had begun. The club opened in February 1948 to great success: "People come every day and evening to have some drinks and congas . . . everybody is 'deeply enchanted' about the design and it has become the 'different' place to enjoy life," wrote Catalano on March 11.[3] Nicknamed "the Cloverleaf," the club was designed as two floating biomorphic slabs of poured concrete supported by pilotis, joined by modular windows, and anchored by a core with a cantilevered reinforced-concrete stair. During construction, a number of elements were changed, and the completed building departed from Breuer's original conception. The stair was altered in form and material, and a glass-walled kitchen was relocated from the upper floor to ground level. This allowed the upper floor to function as "a complete cloverleaf for cocktails and dance, with the bar in one of the leaves," Catalano reported.[4] With the kitchen now working by way of a dumbwaiter, Breuer wrote to Catalano, wondering "how much sense the service stair still makes."[5] Originally the building was fronted by a "mobile" in the form of a sign designed by Catalano with the club name, but the sign was destroyed by heavy winds and was replaced by lettering applied to the surface of the building. In 1949, when submitting photographs for publication, Breuer asked that they be retouched to remove the lettering, which was, he said, "applied quite differently from the instructions, and I think it looks very bad and spoils the building."[6] The source of Breuer's design was his elevated, softly curved biomorph in Garden City of the Future of ten years earlier; within another ten years, it would be transformed into the hexagonal cloverleaf of the De Bijenkorf construction field office in Rotterdam.

ARCHIVAL: **SUL 39; AAA Photos.**
BIBLIOGRAPHIC: *Architectural Record*, October 1948, 136–39; Blake, *Marcel Breuer*, 98–99; Driller, "Frühwerk," 374.

94. Model

94
Recreational Apartments,
Tanaguarena, Caracas, Venezuela, 1958 (NOT BUILT)

MARCEL BREUER AND JULIO VOLANTE, ARCHITECTS

HERBERT BECKHARD, ASSOCIATE

With his associate Herbert Beckhard, and in collaboration with
Venezuelan architect Julio Volante of TECSA, Breuer planned a large
recreational seaside cooperative-apartment complex at Tanaguarena,
near Caracas, in 1958. Preliminary drawings are dated March 6, 1958.
The narrow twenty-story apartment slab was intended for 600 families
and was joined to a building with recreational facilities in accord with
beach-club life—pool, cabanas, marina, restaurants, bars, and
lounges. The design of the tall building was borrowed from the undu-
lating river facade of Alvar Aalto's MIT senior dormitory (1948) in
Cambridge, Massachusetts. Aalto designed the serpentine format
to allow all the rooms a view of the river; in Breuer's project in
Tanaguarena, it was to provide a wide vista of the sea. The projection—
from deeply inset apertures for sun protection—of the pierced wall
balconies gave some texture to the facades. Breuer returned here to Le
Corbusier's apartment-house prototype (Unité d'habitation) of balconied slab on pilotis, but with a banal 1950s swing made by the sleek
S-curve that was a response to a South American predilection for
sinuous shapes.

ARCHIVAL: **SUL Drawings, AAA Photos.**
BIBLIOGRAPHIC: ***Arts & Architecture***, October 1960, 16–18; Jones, ed., *Marcel Breuer*,
130–31; Papachristou, *Marcel Breuer*, 237.

95. View of a bunkhouse from the lake

95
Halvorson Fishing Camp,
Dryberry Lake Island, Toronto, Ontario, Canada, 1960

MARCEL BREUER, ARCHITECT

HAMILTON P. SMITH, ASSOCIATE

Minnesota businessman Roy Halvorson, father of June Alworth Starkey, for whom Breuer built a house in Duluth, Minnesota, wanted to develop a rocky Canadian island as a rugged fishing resort for his employees, most of whom were Finnish or of Finnish background. In January 1959, he asked Breuer to design a master plan and individual buildings that would be constructed to stand the weight of heavy accumulations of snow. He had in mind a main lodge with dining area for thirty-six people, a kitchen, and a lounge; six individual cabins or bunkhouses, each with sleeping facilities for six and a minimal kitchen; a "Finnish bath"

(sauna); and a sheltered boathouse. Breuer received a surveyor's report of the site in January 1960. There is no record of when his plans were transmitted to Halvorson, but construction—without Breuer office supervision—was under way during July and August. Materials were transported by tug and barge. Breuer expressed doubts that the process would bring about a true Breuer product without serious compromises, but he went ahead with it. At least one bunkhouse with an adjacent service building was erected. On a remote Canadian island, therefore, stood a roughly constructed Breuer box on stilts—its glass window wall recessed within the sheltering roof and flanks so there is shade and a continuous balcony—joined by a deck and roof beam to a smaller elevated boxlike structure (the service building) to the rear. It is not known if the full project as conceived was built.

ARCHIVAL: **SUL 152,** Drawings; AAA Photos.

96. Hôtel Le Flaine, view from the southwest

Affiliates of the ambitious project included the Société d'études de participation et de développement (SEPAD) as promoter, the Bureau d'études et de réalisations urbains (BERU) as economic-planning consultant, and an independent planner of ski runs, Emile Allais. Although principally a ski town, Flaine attracted year-round tourism and became a prosperous venture.

Breuer opened an office in Paris principally for overseeing the Flaine project, with Gatje as the resident partner beginning in 1964. Phase I of Flaine was completed by December 1968; the winter of 1969 was the first year that the resort was in use. A later phase of the project, which included the Hôtel Résidence at Fédération (the plaza in the center of town) and the chapel, dates to 1974 to 1976. The construction of the chapel in 1974 was a worry for Breuer, who was concerned about the thinness of the slate on the walls and roof and about the watertightness of the slate roofing: "We never built a slate roof before and the whole matter rests with the expert knowledge and assurance of the specialist for slate, which I always considered to be the most characteristic and common roofing material in France."[7] Flaine gave Breuer his first opportunity to realize the construction of a complete town. He laid out the buildings and designed the patterns of the modular units with which they were built. Although in method and material, in the load-bearing faceted concrete panels of the facades, and in the urbanist theories on which the planning was based, the buildings belong to their time, in form and spirit they hark back to the huge elevated and balconied apartment blocks and dramatic cantilevers of the modern movement of late-1920s Germany and Russia that in 1970 appeared retrograde.

ARCHIVAL: SUL 138, 147–49, Drawings, Paris Office Files; AAA Correspondence, Photos. BIBLIOGRAPHIC: *Architectural Record*, March 1962, 121–36; April 1966, 180–83; and August 1969, 101–7; *L'Architecture d'aujourd'hui*, December 1962, 60–61, and June 1966, 32–33; *L'Oeil*, February 1969, 18–23; *Interiors*, June 1971, 94–101; Jones, ed., *Marcel Breuer*, 30–35; Papachristou, *Marcel Breuer*, 63–71; *Process: Architecture*, no. 32, 55–59; Gatje, *Marcel Breuer*, passim.

96
Flaine,
near Chamonix, France, 1961–76

Phase I, 1961–68
Phase II, 1974–76

MARCEL BREUER AND ROBERT F. GATJE, ARCHITECTS

BUREAU D'ETUDES ET DE REALISATIONS URBAINS, CONSULTANTS

An agreement was drawn up in New York on January 25, 1960, between Breuer and French developer Eric Boissonnas, his friend and neighbor in New Canaan, Connecticut, to build a resort town in the mountain valley of Flaine, an almost inaccessible location with difficult terrain near Chamonix (see p. 170). The project had been launched before Breuer entered the picture, and the decision had been made to use prefabricated-concrete modular parts. Inventive methods were devised to overcome problems of construction and access; engineering finally provided vehicular approach to the town, allowing the first stages of construction to begin in February 1961. Originally assisted in New York by Herbert Beckhard, Breuer went to Paris in May with a master plan and a program for construction. After the master-plan phase, Beckhard began working on the church of St. Francis de Sales, and Robert Gatje became the partner-in-charge for Flaine. The plan was for a resort town for a maximum population of about 6,000, with hotels, condominium-apartment buildings, row houses (tall and low buildings), chalets, a town hall and post office, a social hall and cinema, an interdenominational chapel, a firehouse, a school, shops, a skating rink, ski lifts and ski jump, a covered swimming pool, facilities for ice hockey and tennis, a funicular, parking areas, and workers' quarters.

97
Resort Town,
near Bordeaux, France, 1971 (NOT BUILT)

MARCEL BREUER AND ROBERT F. GATJE, ARCHITECTS

Breuer agreed on February 22, 1971, to design a resort town in France on the Atlantic coast between Biarritz and Bordeaux, part of an effort by the French government to develop about 5,000 acres in the area for tourism and recreation, particularly for workers' vacations. The land was divided into twelve study parcels to explore possibilities for development; the Breuer office was given "Aquitaine Project Number 8," representing about 500 to 600 acres to house 50,000 people. In his interview with Winthrop Sargeant for the *New Yorker* at the time he was working on this project, Breuer described the terrain as resembling that of Cape Cod. Behind the projected community was a pine forest planted by Napoleon; stretching in front were sand dunes and a long beach. Breuer developed a scheme that placed settlements both on the sea and on artificially created inland waterways where there would be sailing and bathing. In addition to family housing, in small-scale buildings, he wanted artists' studios and workshops as well as theaters, galleries, and a hotel complex with shopping and recreational facilities. Everything in the community was to be in walking distance; cars would be left in a large parking area.

The project was submitted and accepted; the development was to be under the direction of an interministerial council for the Aquitaine region that protected varied special interests—the coastline, the environment, the forests, and so on. But the financing of the project evaporated as a result of political scandals, and, according to Robert Gatje, "all the drawings were put on the shelf."[8]

ARCHIVAL: **SUL Drawings; AAA Contract.**

98
Hotels,
Kabul and Bāmiān, Afghanistan, 1972–74 (NOT BUILT)

MARCEL BREUER AND ASSOCIATES, IN ASSOCIATION WITH

WALTER BRUNE + PARTNER, ARCHITECTS

As part of an effort to develop tourism in Afghanistan, Breuer was invited to examine proposals for new hotels in Kabul and Bāmiān that had been prepared for the tourism department of the World Bank. Stimulated by the challenge of introducing modern architecture to a developing country, he and Robert Gatje visited Afghanistan in July 1972.[9] In October 1973, Breuer made an agreement with the government of the Republic of Afghanistan to provide a design for the hotels; the German architects Walter Brune + Partner, of Düsseldorf, would handle the working drawings and supervise the construction. Aware of the jarring contrast that would result from inserting modern buildings into the vernacular context of the country's architecture, Breuer said that the new structures should be "an expression in sympathy with the mud-brick culture . . . you must express the culture but something entirely new must come out of it." This is consistent, forty years later, with his view of the relationship of modernism to indigenous architecture expressed in his talk delivered in Zürich in 1934 that became his published essay "Where Do We Stand?" A sketch of the design development stage of the hotel in Kabul, made in June 1974, reveals a weighty mass of additive blocks raised on thin slabs, with window panels faceted in familiar precast patterns. It appears to lack the contextual "sympathy" that Breuer claimed was needed for architectural development in Afghanistan.

ARCHIVAL: **SUL Drawings; AAA Contract, Correspondence, Photos.**
BIBLIOGRAPHIC: **Gatje,** *Marcel Breuer,* **passim.**

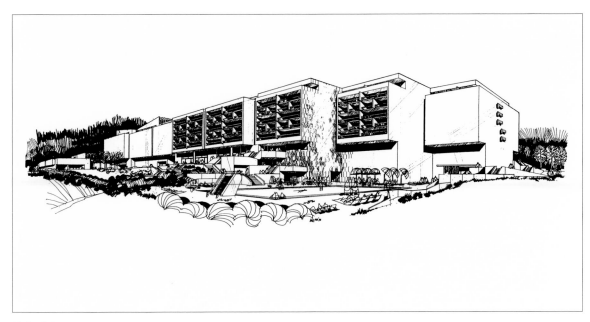

99. Rendering

99
Hotel and Lift Station,
Mount Touchal, Teheran, Iran, 1975 (NOT BUILT)

MARCEL BREUER AND ROBERT F. GATJE, ARCHITECTS

On October 4, 1975, Breuer agreed to produce a conceptual study for a luxury hotel and lift station in Iran located on the Valenjak plateau on Mount Touchal, in the Alborz range. The Breuer office produced a large scale model, perspective views, diagrammatic plans and sections, and a rendering. With a series of projecting and receding blocks of medium height and deeply inset balconied rooms, the projected hotel had four stories and a penthouse terrace lifted on a high base above a pool and stepped plaza—framed by exotic "orientalizing" curvilinear contours—for shops and other facilities. A powerful concrete structure in Breuer's late "muscular" style, the hotel depended on significant self-borrowing—from the projecting volumes of the Whitney Museum of American Art, for example—and on older formulas for multiple-family dwellings that ultimately harked back to European projects of the late 1920s, specifically Mies van der Rohe's buildings in the Weissenhof housing project (1927) in Stuttgart, which continued to affect Breuer's work.

ARCHIVAL: **AAA Contract, Photos.**
BIBLIOGRAPHIC: *Progressive Architecture*, October 1976, 58–59.

THEATERS

100. Perspective drawing and plan

For theaters by Breuer that were part of larger complexes, such as art centers, see Institutional: Colleges and Universities (Wheaton, Black Mountain, College of William and Mary, Sarah Lawrence, Cardinal Stritch). Breuer also designed auditoriums and theaters for museums (Cleveland Museum of Art), department stores (De Bijenkorf), public buildings (UNESCO), and the United States Embassy in The Hague.

100
Ukrainian State Theater, Competition,
Kharkov, Soviet Union, 1930–31 (NOT BUILT)

MARCEL BREUER, WITH THE ASSISTANCE OF GUSTAV HASSENPFLUG

Breuer, with Gustav Hassenpflug's assistance, was among the nearly 100 foreign entrants in an international design competition sponsored in 1930 by the Soviet Union for a new 4,000-seat theater in Kharkov, Ukraine (see p. 68). The ambitious project was Breuer's first theater design, but he had been readied for the challenge by stage production and performance at the Bauhaus (where in 1925 and 1926 he had designed the auditorium seats), by his association with modern theater producer Erwin Piscator (for whom he had designed an apartment in Berlin in 1927), and by his familiarity with the ideas of Piscator and Walter Gropius about Total Theater and audience interaction.

It was expected that the new theater in Kharkov would be revolutionary in concept, based on high technology, and flexible in function, serving as a multiperformance arena for civic, political, and athletic events as well as for theater and opera. Breuer's notes, which describe his design, were published in the architectural periodical *Die Bauwelt* in 1931:

The tendency in the development of the theater lies in the active cooperation of the audience. The auditorium must therefore be designed to give the audience the greatest possible freedom of movement so that it can easily get on stage or the actor can go into the auditorium—so the auditorium is a field of action itself that is visible and audible to each onlooker. . . . The "active theater" requires a new arrangement of seats. The individual swivel folding seats are not arranged in rows parallel to the stage but rather along the length. So next to each seat there is a free passage for the greatest freedom of movement and activity of onlookers. Each one can sit or leave his seat, without his neighbor having to get up. . . . The scenery should be able to be changed without noticeable breaks. So one must divide the area of the stage from the place where the scenes are built up or taken down to prevent mutual disturbances. The design solves this via side stages that can be raised and lowered. . . . The finished scenes are brought up to the stage level and are pushed to the front of the stage, so the montage occurs during the scene without disturbing the play. . . . The orchestra pit can be brought up to the height of the stage. In the conventional arrangement of seats, the last ones are over 60 m. away from the stage, but the limit of good sound and visibility is 40–45 m. So the seating arrangement is hardly appropriate for a theater of 40.[1]

Breuer designed a large steel-and-concrete trapezoidal auditorium elevated on a stepped terrace and covered by a sliding roof. Supported by exposed lateral trusses, the roof could be moved back for open-air performances. The entrance facade, curved and glazed, was preceded by a projecting terrace-canopy on pilotis in the center and a long pedestrian ramp at the side. A massing of boxy volumes at the stage end of the sloping theater housed the side stages and backstage machinery. Suspended from the auditorium ceiling was a lighting grid. The seats, each independent from its neighbors and supported by a single metal post, were arranged along the length of the fan-shaped auditorium and made it simple for spectators to move about. Joachim Driller cites an article in the *Baugilde* of 1931 criticizing Breuer's design, where it was pointed out that the distance of the last rows from the stage was beyond "the limits of good visual and auditory reception."[2]

First prize (Gropius won eighth prize) was awarded to Aleksandr and Viktor Vesnin, Constructivist architects and theater designers, but the project was never realized.

ARCHIVAL: **SUL Photos; AAA Photos.**
BIBLIOGRAPHIC: **Breuer, "Theater von Charkow," *Die Bauwelt*, August 13, 1931, 27–29; *Nuestra arquitectura*, September 1947, 14–15; Blake, *Marcel Breuer*, 40, 43; Argan, *Marcel Breuer*, 75–76; Jones, ed., *Marcel Breuer*, 241; Driller, "Frühwerk," 361–62, with additional bibliography.**

101
London Theatre Studio,
London, England, 1936–37

MARCEL BREUER AND F. R. S. YORKE, ARCHITECTS

In 1936, the London Theatre Studio (L.T.S.), a newly founded theater group that was a "training ground for young actors, directors and designers" in London,[3] moved into an old Methodist chapel in Islington. The group was closely connected to Motley, theater costume and fashion designers whose boutique on Garrick Street had been designed by Breuer. Using the space of the chapel, and on the foundations of an adjacent structure left incomplete, Breuer designed and built a new theater (stage and auditorium) for annual "programmes" produced by L.T.S. students for the public.[4] He also built the dressing rooms, rehearsal rooms, workshops, and offices and designed all the furniture.[5] The theater space was given extra height by the removal of the existing floor. Acoustic wallboard over studs, and plastered-over compressed wood were used in place of expensive soundproofing. Although it was a partnership project, the design was Breuer's, with F. R. S. Yorke contributing technical advice.[6] Breuer later described the work in a letter of January 29, 1941, as "the stage of a theatre school with 120 seats and with no more equipment than a number of reflectors and a portable switchboard [for lighting]. Behind the stage was the workshop where the students themselves manufactured the sets."[7] The whole enterprise was reminiscent of Bauhaus theater projects.

Drawings for the project, dated July 1936, are in the Prints and Drawings Collection of RIBA. Construction took place during 1936 and 1937. With a limited budget, Breuer produced a minimal and polished arrangement of audience seats, elevated rear lighting gallery, and stage with curving proscenium.

ARCHIVAL: **SUL 8, 9; RIBA Drawings Collection.**
BIBLIOGRAPHIC: ***Architects' Journal*, July 29 1937, 186–88; December 16, 1937, 995–96; and January 13, 1938, 99; Mills, "F. R. S. Yorke"; Driller, "Frühwerk," 362; Michael Mullin, *Design by Motley* (Newark: University of Delaware Press, 1996), 39, 58–61.**

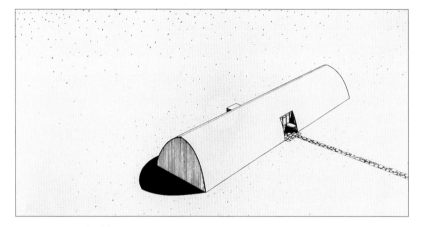

102a. Perspective sketch

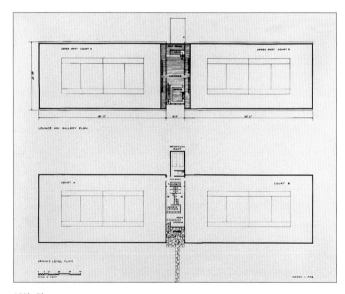

102b. Plans

102
Tandem Tennis Courts and Club,
New York, New York (?), 1946 (NOT BUILT)

MARCEL BREUER AND CHARLES BURCHARD, ARCHITECTS

Charles Burchard was Breuer's student, then one of "the boys" who worked in his Cambridge office, and later a faculty colleague at Harvard. In the 1940s, Breuer and Burchard were "architects in association" for several projects, one of them the design for a tandem tennis courts–sports club for Sherman M. Fairchild, entrepreneur, inventor, and head of Fairchild Engine and Airplane Corporation. Burchard met Fairchild in 1942: "We talked about some ideas of using laminated wood counterbalanced arches in factory construction, and [sun control] synchronized with heating and lighting systems," Burchard wrote to Breuer. "What it all came to is that [he] is paying me to make some studies. I haven't come very far with it yet but something may come out of it."[1] One thing that came out of it was the tennis-club design in 1946. Plans and perspective drawings were developed for preliminary cost estimates. The tandem clay courts, separated by an 18-foot passageway into which club facilities (on two levels) were inserted, were framed by a series of "three point laminated wood arches (sixty-one arches per court), fixed just above grade to a reinforced concrete wall which is continuous all around the structure."[2] At ground level, the club portion of the building held locker rooms and bathrooms; above were offices, a lounge, and spectator galleries.

A perspective drawing dated March 1, 1946, shows a flagstone terrace and a glazed and paneled front wall with cantilevered canopy excavated deeply into the long, curved plane of the pointed-arch building. Well organized in layout and "Quonset hut" in shape, the tennis club would have been an original and out-of-the-ordinary realization of the program. It is not known where the club was to be located or why it was not built. Since it was Burchard who discussed the laminated-wood arch technology with Fairchild, it is likely that much (possibly all) of the design was his.

ARCHIVAL: **SUL Drawings, 41, 42.**
BIBLIOGRAPHIC: **Driller, "Frühwerk," 373.**

103
Sports Complex,
Flushing Meadows–Corona,
New York, 1967–68 (NOT BUILT)

South Complex Buildings and "Spines"

MARCEL BREUER AND HERBERT BECKHARD, ARCHITECTS

North Complex

KENZO TANGE & URTEC, ARCHITECTS AND URBANISTS

Central Mall

LAWRENCE HALPRIN & ASSOCIATES, LANDSCAPE ARCHITECTS

Master Plan and Program

LAWRENCE HALPRIN & ASSOCIATES, WITH THE CONSULTATION OF MARCEL BREUER

AND HERBERT BECKHARD AND OF KENZO TANGE & URTEC

The project was sponsored by the Recreational and Cultural Affairs Administration of the Department of Parks of the City of New York. Its purpose was the redevelopment as a sports park of the former World's Fair grounds in Flushing Meadows–Corona Park in Queens. Thomas P. F. Hoving, parks commissioner under newly elected Mayor John V. Lindsay, put together a joint enterprise in 1966, inviting as a team (but with separate contracts) Marcel Breuer and Associates, Kenzo Tange & Urtec, and Lawrence Halprin. (Hoving's successor, August Heckscher, explained that the project had been assigned to private firms because "it is beyond the scope of our limited architectural and engineering forces."[3]) Breuer entered into contract with the city on September 8, 1967.

Tange's buildings were for performing arts—theaters, workshops, library and listening rooms, and the like. Halprin designed a landscaped mall. Breuer's portion of the complex consisted of "spines" that framed Halprin's mall and that were linked to Tange's buildings and an outdoor stadium on the north, and two large structures that made up the southern portion of the site: an arena for basketball and track in one, and indoor and outdoor pools for water sports in the other. The "spines," crowned with roof terraces and pergolas, were for shops, restaurants, and changing rooms. The spread of Breuer's low buildings contrasted with the compact volumes of Tange's mixed-height ensemble, shaped as a right-angled S. Although the structural technology of Breuer's buildings was inventive—"The precast roof of each building is hanging on cables suspended from a large folded concrete frame"[4]—in appearance they were consistent

with his massive, hard-edged concrete work of the 1960s, dependent for formal definition on a reworking of the diagonals, trapezoids, and faceted surfaces that he favored. Compared with the fresh arrangement of quadratic masses of Tange's neighboring buildings, the Breuer project appeared dated.

The bureaucratic and financial complexities involved with working for the city on this ambitious project proved insurmountable, and the park was never realized. Bitterness, disillusionment, and disappointment, recorded in the correspondence, were experienced by all participants: "our poor project," Breuer wrote to Tange on June 24, 1968.[5] For the Breuer office, the investment of time and effort was, according to Robert Gatje, "a financial disaster," and the hope of providing a recreational facility for the city was crushed.

ARCHIVAL: **AAA Contract, Photos.**

BIBLIOGRAPHIC: *Architectural Record,* August 1967, 109–11; *L'Architecture d'aujourd'hui,* April–May 1972, LIX; Papachristou, *Marcel Breuer,* 177–81; Stern, Mellins, and Fishman, *New York 1960,* 1055–57.

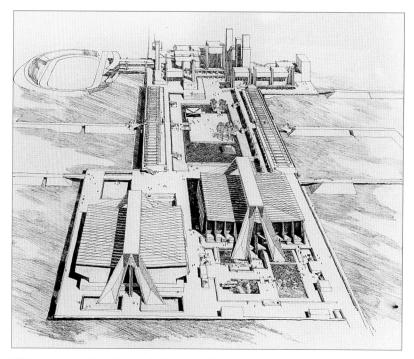

103. Perspective drawing of the complex from the south

GAGFAH, Berlin, Germany, 1928

Some of Breuer's work lists include the entry "GAGFAH, Berlin 1928" under the rubric "Exhibition Buildings."[1] *Although no documents support this hypothesis, it may be that soon after settling in Berlin in 1928, he found work in connection with the temporary exhibition hall erected for GAGFAH, an acronym for Gemein-nützige Aktien Gesellschaft für Angestellten Heimstätten (Cooperative Corporation for Employees' Homesteads), the developers of a conventional housing settlement in Fischtalgrund in the southwestern section of the city. More likely, Walter Gropius gave Breuer some responsibility for the temporary pavilion that he and László Moholy-Nagy were designing in the same year for Allgemeine Hauserbau A. G. (AHAG, General Housing Construction Company), of which Gropius's friend Adolf Sommerfeld was general director, located also in Fischtalgrund next to the GAGFAH hall, and that Breuer confused the names.*

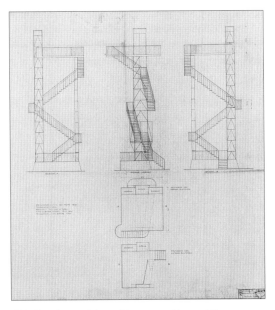

104a. Elevations, and plans of the upper and lower platforms

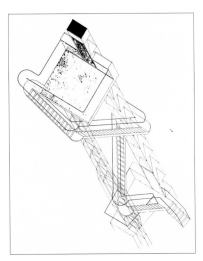

104b. Axonometric drawing

104
Sun Tower or Sun Platform [Exhibition Structure?], 1929 (NOT BUILT)

MARCEL BREUER, ARCHITECT

Along with the many working drawings from Breuer's Berlin practice (1928–33), now at Syracuse University, is a plan and an elevation for a mysterious cranelike "sun tower." The structure had been known from photographs of the drawings at the Archives of American Art in a folder labeled "Mr. Breuer cannot identify." (In his later years, Breuer also failed to recognize a photograph of a drawing of his theater project for Kharkov [1930].) Still, the verso of the tower photos carries the stamp "Marcel Breuer architekt, Berlin w. 35 Potsdamerstrasse 121c," the stamp of a Berlin photographer, the words *Sonnen-Turn* in Breuer's handwriting, the date "27.IV.29," and the abbreviated signature "Hs" for Breuer's assistant Gustav Hassenpflug.

A series of vertical and horizontal intersections below a balustraded platform are connected by stairs with curving rails. The openwork structure and the diagonal of the stair associate the object to Russian technological images of the 1920s and to construction cranes and transmission towers, such as Naum Gabo's Project for a Radio Station (1919–20), El Lissitzky's Lenin Tribune (1920), and, most saliently, the open metal forms of Vladimir Tatlin's model of his Monument to the Third International (1919–20). It should be noted that in 1920, Breuer's first year at the Bauhaus, sketches for towers were exercises carried out by Johannes Itten's students and that Itten himself sketched towers in various formats, the model for one of which—the spiral Turm des Feuers—was built in Weimar.[2]

ARCHIVAL: **SUL Drawings; AAA Photos.**

105
House for a Sportsman, Building Exhibition,
Berlin, Germany, 1931 (NOT BUILT)

MARCEL BREUER, WITH THE ASSISTANCE OF GUSTAV HASSENPFLUG

Plans, elevations, and model interiors for a "Haus für einen Sportsmann," a combined residence and health-and-fitness studio designed for a gymnastics teacher, were displayed at the Berlin Bauausstellung of 1931 (Internationale Ausstellung für Stadtbau und Wohnungswesen) as part of an independent exhibit about modern living, "Die Wohnung Unserer Zeit," of which Mies van der Rohe was director.[3] A flat-roofed rectangle almost twice as long as deep and elevated on a four-step podium, the house opened to a large outdoor training and workout terrace covered on the long side by a deep overhanging roof that was supported by slender steel columns and pierced by three lightwells. Marked by a projecting canopy, the entrance was sited on the southeast corner of the shorter side. With the roof carried by colonettes, walls were relieved of their supporting function. They were glass, and they slid back to unite interior and training terrace into one expansive space. Aside from the permanent enclosures of kitchen and bathroom, the interior was an open space with some alcoves for sleeping, studying, and dining, organized by modular storage walls and movable folding partitions that gave flexibility and variation of function. In design and structure, the one-story open-plan building was indebted to Mies's Barcelona pavilion (1929). In Joachim Driller's view, its spatial disposition was taken from Le Corbusier's Weissenhof House II.[4] Architecture as a means of promoting good modern living by way of calisthenics and physical fitness was recognized in the title of an article about the exhibition, "Wohnraum und Biologie," in the July 2, 1931, issue of *Innendekoration*, although, as Magdalena Droste and Manfred Ludewig observe, at the time the concept of a house for a sportsman was "utterly unrealistic in view of the world-wide economic crisis."[5] Christopher Wilk, who gives the fullest description of the house and its furnishings, notes that Breuer had designed a small apartment for a gymnastics teacher in Berlin a year earlier, and suggests that the theme of a House for a Sportsman was chosen because of ideas that Breuer had been unable to carry out in that limited commission.[6] Together with the House for a Sportsman, Breuer exhibited a small (70-square-meter, or 753-square-foot) model apartment as a prototype for minimum living in a multifamily building. Wilk published a full-page illustration of the living room, demonstrating that the apartment (open space divided by partitions) is most interesting in the way it allows for, in his words, "the multipurpose use of standardized furniture types."[7]

ARCHIVAL: **SUL Drawings; AAA Photos.**

BIBLIOGRAPHIC: *Moderne Bauformen*, August 1931, 377–79; *Innendekoration*, July 2, 1931, 258–61; *Rassegna di architettura*, September 15, 1931, 342–55; Breuer, "Architecture and Material," in *Circle*, ed. Martin, Nicholson, and Gabo, 195; Hitchcock, "Marcel Breuer and the American Tradition," 9; Blake, *Marcel Breuer*, 35; Jones, ed., *Marcel Breuer*, 241; Wilk, *Marcel Breuer*, 96–103; Driller, *Breuer Houses*, 54–56, 259.

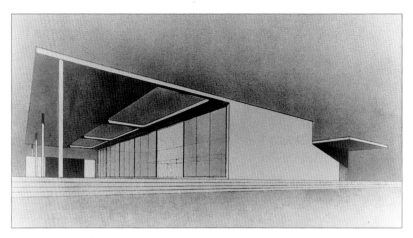

105a. Perspective rendering showing the terrace

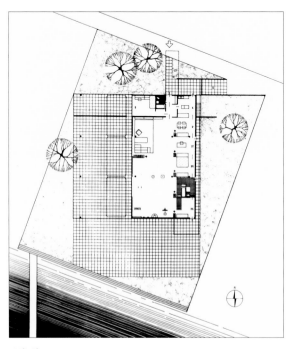

105b. Plan

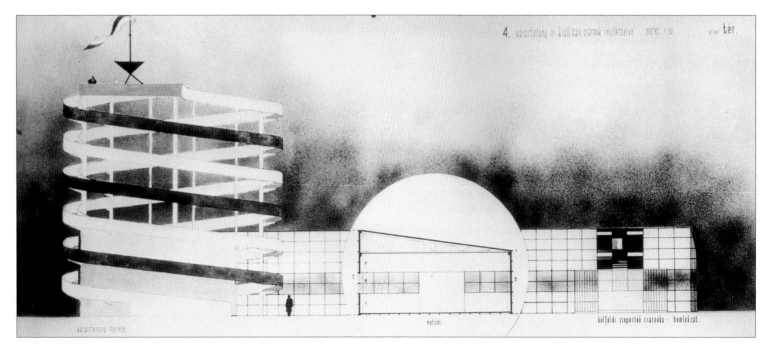

106. Rendered section

106
Spring Trade Fair, Competition,
Budapest, Hungary, 1934–35

MARCEL BREUER, JOZSEF FISCHER, AND FARKAS MOLNAR, ARCHITECTS

Collaborating with his friends (and partners in a casual joint practice in Budapest), Hungarian architects Jozsef Fischer and Farkas Molnár, Breuer entered a competition for temporary buildings for a trade fair to be held in Budapest in the spring of 1935. An assemblage of ramps, towers, and pavilions, the fair buildings were sited around a permanent, conventionally styled exhibition hall in a park. The design was awarded first prize. Joachim Driller interviewed Fischer in the 1980s and records that he said that the design was mostly Breuer's.[8] There has been confusion in the historical record about whether the project was carried out. A site plan and two views were included in the exhibition of Breuer's work at Harvard in 1938. Henry-Russell Hitchcock, who was in constant communication with Breuer while working on the text of his catalogue for the exhibition, referred to it as an "executed scheme" and wrote that Molnár and Fischer "were responsible for the execution."[9] Yet labels affixed to photos in Breuer's files read: "The design, *though unbuilt* [emphasis added], received first prize."[10] Driller's interview with Fischer now sets the record straight: according to Fischer, because members of the controlling conservative Hungarian architectural circles (including the builder) were outraged by the mod-

ernist design, they manipulated cost estimates for construction to the high end, and consequently only two small pavilions from the full ensemble were erected.[11] The paramount image was that of a tower of dynamic continuum composed of a pair of intertwining spiral ramps that were supported by columns that led to and from an observation platform at the top. Adjacent to the tower was a series of glass-fronted flat-roofed modular pavilions ornamented with colorful banners. An exuberant and sparkling composition of free forms, often curving, and of modernist structure and materials that created a luminous transparency, the Spring Trade Fair buildings symbolized a brief, light-hearted moment in modern architecture before the politics of war halted its progress.

ARCHIVAL: **AAA Photos.**

BIBLIOGRAPHIC: *Casabella*, March 1935, 38–41; Hitchcock, "Marcel Breuer and the American Tradition," 12; Blake, *Marcel Breuer*, 55; Breuer, *Sun and Shadow*, 28; Jones, ed., *Marcel Breuer*, 239; Driller, "Frühwerk," 363–64.

107
Gane's Pavilion,
Bristol, England, 1936

MARCEL BREUER AND F. R. S. YORKE, ARCHITECTS

Gane's Pavilion was a temporary four-room house of stone, glass, and wood designed by Breuer while in partnership with F. R. S. Yorke to display, at the Royal Agricultural Show in Bristol in July 1936, modern furniture manufactured by P. E. Gane (see p. 86). An inscription on the drawing sheet indicates that the plan, elevation, and furniture table in the Prints and Drawings Collection in the RIBA were based on a "consultation [with client?] of 27 April 1936." The contour of the one-story open-plan building formed a trapezoid, with the living-room wall following a shallow curve. Working among English modernists appears to have generated Expressionist elements in Breuer's designs, furniture as well as architecture, but the curved wall at the Gane Pavilion has been associated with the shape of the entry level of Le Corbusier's Pavillon Suisse (1931).[12] Breuer defended his wall by claiming for it no source other than his own aesthetic preference, and his wish to demonstrate that modern architecture had more to it than right-angled geometry.

Full-length sliding glass panels in the dining room, living room, and bedroom opened to a terrace and garden. A portion of that terrace was roofed with a pergola, the edge of which, creating a pleasing tension, rested on only a part of the supporting pier. Traditional rubble stone was put into the service of modern shapes: piers and exterior walls were creased sharply at the edges as though formed of concrete;

the natural irregularities of the edges of the large rocks were tamed with machine precision into geometries, while the texture and outlines of the smaller stones kept their random nature. A free-standing garden wall designed as a wind screen was a dynamic Constructivist extension into space, a device that Breuer used here for the first time and would exploit in later residential architecture.

The building was brought to the attention of the American public in 1937 at the exhibition of English modern architecture at the Museum of Modern Art. In Henry-Russell Hitchcock's catalogue, the illustrations were arranged alphabetically by architect, so they began with an exterior, a plan, and an interior of Breuer's Gane Pavilion. In his essay, Hitchcock pointed to the modern format of the stonework as an illustration of a British preference for traditional materials in contrast to a modernist partiality for cement and stucco surfaces that weather poorly and soon become dirty.[13]

ARCHIVAL: **AAA Photos; RIBA Drawings Collection.**

BIBLIOGRAPHIC: *Architects' Journal*, August 20, 1936, 241–42; *Architectural Review*, August 1936, 69–70; *Architectural Record*, May 1937, 40–41; Hitchcock and Bauer, *Modern Architecture in England*, 44–45; Hitchcock, "Marcel Breuer and the American Tradition," 15; Yorke, *The Modern House in England*, 50–51; Blake, *Marcel Breuer*, 58–59; Jones, ed., *Marcel Breuer*, 14; Wilk, *Marcel Breuer*, 142–43; Driller, *Breuer Houses*, 84–89, 260.

107b. South facade

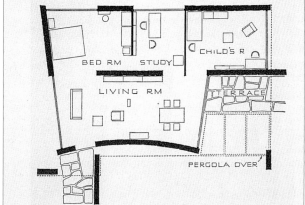

107a. Plan

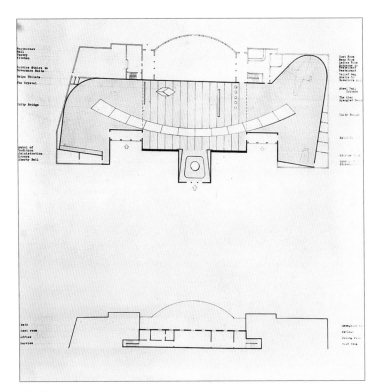

108. Plans

108
Pennsylvania State Exhibition, World's Fair,
New York, New York, 1939

WALTER GROPIUS AND MARCEL BREUER, ARCHITECTS

During the summer of 1938, Walter Gropius and Breuer were appointed architects-in-chief of the Pennsylvania State Exhibition at the New York World's Fair of 1939. The exhibition was to be housed in the Pennsylvania State Pavilion, a building designed by architects other than Gropius and Breuer to replicate Independence Hall in Philadelphia.

Gropius and Breuer's specifications are dated February 6, 1939; work was completed in the spring. Herbert Bayer and Xanti Schawinsky collaborated with the partners on the planning and design of the displays, reconstituting the collaborative team of Gropius, Breuer, and Bayer at the "section allemande" of the Deutsche Werkbund exhibition in Paris in 1930. Disappointment about the project arose within the modernist community on several counts and was expressed in a letter to Gropius from George Howe (who, with William Lescaze, had designed the touchstone modernist Philadelphia Savings Fund Society Building in 1931): the pavilion was historicizing instead of modern; there was a disjunction between the traditional exterior and the modern interior; and no Pennsylvania architect was on the design team for the interior.[14] According to David H. Wright, the partners

were unable to "retain architectural control of the interior, as the execution was largely out of their hands and the money for the project was in a constant state of flux."[15] Robert A. M. Stern, Gregory Gilmartin, and Thomas Mellins point out, moreover, that the pavilions of the twenty-three states and Puerto Rico that composed the fair's "Court of States" were purposeful reconstructions of each state's architectural heritage and "represented a reaction to the increasing dominance of European-inspired Modernism as well as a reflection of increased patriotic sentiment in the face of an unstable and threatening international situation."[16] They consider Gropius and Breuer's exhibition space as "one of the Fair's most strikingly Modernist interiors as well as one of its most exquisite rooms."

Pennsylvania's natural resources and contribution to American democracy were the organizing themes. The wide entrance to the large glass-paved rectangular Hall of Democracy was framed by walls of anthracite and approached through a steel-walled atrium. The hall was the center of a symmetrical complex of three connecting rooms, with the curved-wall Hall of Progress on one side and the Hall of Tradition on the other. Along the walls, exhibits were displayed in cases and were viewed from a curving aluminum ramp-bridge that traversed the three rooms and was suspended from the ceiling with steel cables. The furniture in the exhibition was designed by Breuer and manufactured for him in New York City by Schmieg and Kotzian. There are no documents for the individual design contributions of the partners, but the lyrical curves of the lateral halls and the wide arc of the pedestrian bridge speak clearly for Breuer and are reflections of his English work with F. R. S. Yorke carried out in the years just before the World's Fair. They reflect, too, the contours of his Isokon furniture designs of the same years. Steel cables for support was also a preferred Breuer device, used in his residential architecture for cantilevered decks and terraces and for ramps as early as the Harnischmacher House (1932) and through the 1940s and 1950s.

ARCHIVAL: **AAA Photos;** see Nerdinger, *Walter Gropius Archive* 3:86–120.
BIBLIOGRAPHIC: *Architectural Forum*, June 1939, 405, 410; Wright, "The Architecture of Walter Gropius," 44; Nerdinger, *Walter Gropius*, 200–201, and *Walter Gropius Archive* 3:86–120; Driller, "Frühwerk," 368–70; Stern, Gilmartin, and Mellins, *New York 1930*, 742.

109
House in the Museum Garden, Museum of Modern Art,
New York, New York, 1948–49

MARCEL BREUER, ARCHITECT

To explore the problem of good design and the small postwar house, in 1948 the Museum of Modern Art initiated a program to exhibit in its garden custom-built model houses by well-known modern architects.[17] Specifications for Breuer's unprefabricated exhibition house were drafted on August 19, 1948; the house was opened to the public on April 14, 1949, and remained on view until October 30 (see pp. 120, 123). On the ground floor were a combined living-dining room with

pass-through to kitchen, two bedrooms, a playroom with separate entrance, a bath, a utility room with adjacent service yard, outside terraces defined by bench-height stone walls, and a garage. Above the garage and reached by both an interior and an exterior stair with independent entrance was the "parents' bedroom" (closed to the living room below by only a curtain), a bathroom, and a sun terrace—spaces made possible by the upward slope of the roof. Breuer chose sailboat rope held in place by riggings of stainless-steel cable as rails for the upstairs balcony and the stair.

The furnishings of the house forecast the consumerism of postwar American culture. Visitors were as fascinated by the modern housewares, linens, and window shades as by the architecture, and

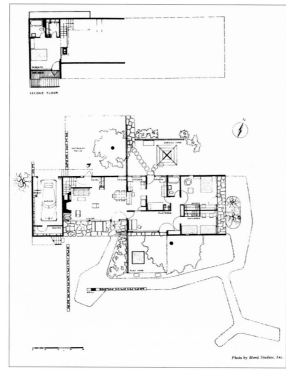

109b. Plan

109c. House photographed in 1990

almost as many pages in the *Museum of Modern Art Bulletin* were given to the listing of suppliers and manufacturers as to the photographs and text about the house. Breuer designed a popular radio-television-phonograph and, with prescience, wrote to the product-design manager at Philco that "I have given these television matters a good deal of study because I feel that this is a new field which needs design consideration . . . television must be considered in the planning and furnishing of a house."[18]

Clad with unpainted vertical cypress boarding, the three-bedroom house was covered by Breuer's "inverted pitch" (butterfly) roof without gutters and drains at the edges, a format with which he had been experimenting since 1945 and had adapted from Le Corbusier's Errazuris House (1930) in Chile. The roof was designed to overhang the windows, shading the interior and part of the exterior terrace adjacent to the living room. The house went through several design stages, particularly with regard to the relation of the garage to the master bedroom. George Lewis, who worked on the plans at Breuer's East Eighty-eighth Street office, recalled that the automobile space was originally placed next to the entrance patio on the north, with the bedroom adjacent to the living room at ground-floor level on the west, until Breuer slid the garage over to the south and elevated the bedroom above it.[19]

Although Breuer said of the house that "special consideration is given to the children," it was thought by some that the separation of children's space and parents' space might represent a "misguided ideal of family life" and that a flagstone floor was an ideal surface for neither children nor the housewife on her feet in the kitchen.[20] Still, well timed to correspond to the growing American obsession with suburban family life, Breuer's unpretentious and refreshingly "modern" house, with its flowing space and flexible zones of activity, drew large crowds and appealed to a following enthusiastic enough to generate the construction of numerous editions. It gave Breuer new recognition and visibility, and it contravened a popular idea of modern architecture as cold, white, and cubic.

In January 1950, the house was purchased and relocated on scenic wooded terrain outside New York City in Westchester County, where it remains in excellent condition.

ARCHIVAL: **SUL 1, 3, 22, 23, 50, 51; AAA Photos.**

BIBLIOGRAPHIC: **"The House in the Museum Garden, Marcel Breuer, Architect,"** *Museum of Modern Art Bulletin* 16 (1949); *New Yorker*, March 5, 1949, 22–23, and June 25, 1949, 72–76; *Architectural Record*, May 1949, 10; *Architects' Journal*, June 2, 1949, 499–502; Blake, *Marcel Breuer*, 110–14; Jones, ed., *Marcel Breuer*, 214–16; Droste and Ludewig, *Marcel Breuer Design*, 32–34; Stern, Mellins, and Fishman, *New York 1960*, 474–76; Driller, *Breuer Houses*, 180–89, 263.

110
Interama (State of Florida Inter-American Center Authority Terminal Building), Miami International Airport,
Miami, Florida, 1965–67 (NOT BUILT)

MARCEL BREUER AND HERBERT BECKHARD, ARCHITECTS

This was an unrealistically ambitious project to construct a permanent exposition center called Interama on a 1,700-acre tract between Miami and Miami Beach, Florida, to promote inter-American trade and culture. It was the brainchild of Irving E. Muskat, chairman of the Inter-American Center Authority, an agency of the state of Florida. Interama would be made up of four "communities" that represented participating countries. National houses, a ceremonial plaza, an exhibition area, auditoriums, a conference building, information centers, and student housing were to be part of the plan. The project, with the collaboration of "six of the world's most prominent architects"—Marcel Breuer, Louis I. Kahn, Paul Rudolph, José Luis Sert, Edward Durrell Stone, and Harry M. Weese—was announced to the public in February 1967. Groundbreaking was scheduled for the spring and completion for 1968. A contract between the Inter-American Center Authority and Marcel Breuer and Associates "to erect . . . Community C" was dated March 29, 1965. Community C represented Argentina, Brazil, Paraguay, and Uruguay. A letter of February 10, 1967, to Breuer stated that "the Executive Committee of the Inter-American Center Authority . . . approved your design development submission. You are, therefore, authorized to proceed with the preparation of the working drawings."[21]

For Community C, Breuer designed a dramatic ensemble. Within a walled precinct along the water's edge he set buildings, terraces, and ramps dominated by the massive forms of an exhibition hall, a conference building, and a theater with canted flanks and tiered steps that suggested the Mayan architecture he knew from his travels to Mexico. The small, low, boxlike student houses, reached by bridges, and the U-shaped complex of national houses, were variations on his one- and two-story housing schemes.

The project deteriorated rapidly: on March 17, 1968, project architect-in-chief Robert Bradford Browne wrote to Breuer that "hopes for Interama's success grow dimmer every day. I am sincerely sorry that you and the others who worked so hard have to watch it all go down the drain."[22] A week later, Muskat wrote that it was "most unfortunate . . . [and] you should not be penalized for Florida's failures."[23]

ARCHIVAL: **SUL Drawings; AAA Contract, Correspondence, Photos.**
BIBLIOGRAPHIC: ***New York Times*, February 25, 1967, 31; *Architectural Record*, March 1967, 40–41.**

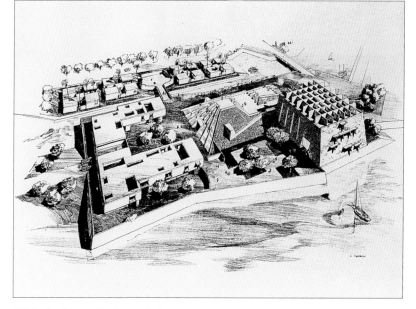

110. Rendered perspective, Community C

URBANISM AND URBAN PLANNING

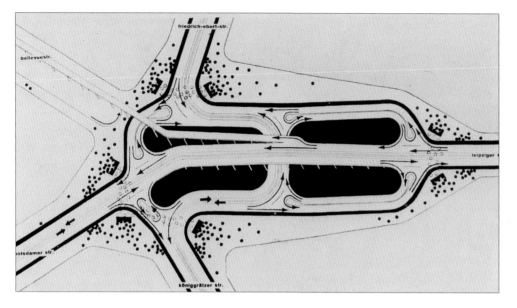

111. Plan

111
Potsdamer Platz,
Berlin, Germany, 1928–29 (NOT BUILT)

MARCEL BREUER, ARCHITECT

Plans to modernize parts of Berlin in the late 1920s by reorganizing patterns of vehicular and pedestrian traffic led to Breuer's proposal for redesigning Potsdamer Platz by adapting a sleek, curving, cloverleaf pattern of "non-crossing traffic." He devised a multilevel circulation system with pedestrian crossings and access to subways below street level. For vehicles, roads would be elevated on piers above the street surface in a cloverleaf pattern that changed the direction of traffic without intersection, an idea that is now a fixture for efficient highway-traffic patterns.

To surround Potsdamer Platz, Breuer, a believer in normalized structures and an admirer of continuous uniform terraces (such as those in eighteenth-century Bath), designed an uninterrupted wall of standardized multilevel structures, curving at the corners to follow the shape of the roads. Ramps leading into and out of garages in the buildings were joined to the roads.

ARCHIVAL: **AAA Photos.**
BIBLIOGRAPHIC: **Hitchcock, "Marcel Breuer and the American Tradition," 9;** *Nuestra arquitectura,* September 1947, 4–5; Blake, *Marcel Breuer,* 38; Jones, ed., *Marcel Breuer,* 237.

112
Garden City of the Future, Model,
London, England, 1936

MARCEL BREUER AND F. R. S. YORKE, ARCHITECTS

Garden City (also called Civic Center) of the Future was a large demonstration model, 9.5 by 5.5 feet, commissioned to Breuer & Yorke by the British Cement and Concrete Association (see pp. 76, 84). It was displayed at the London Building Exhibition of 1936, held in Olympia, the famous nineteenth-century exhibition building in Hammersmith. In a letter written in 1942, Breuer wrote that "I designed it during my partnership with F. R. S. Yorke in London in 1936."[1]

He referred to it as a "Utopian" scheme. Guided by Le Corbusier's urbanism, it represented the central portion of a "new seaside town in England where the residential and business sections meet."[2] The water lay to the south; the residential west was adjacent to open countryside and had clusters of multistoried and balconied apartment blocks carried on columns and separated by zones of greenery; a school with playing fields was on the north; and the traffic center was formed as a cloverleaf that reflected Breuer's experiments with the replanning of Berlin's Potsdamer Platz. Pedestrian paths were separated from vehicular traffic; trains ran below-ground. The centralized shopping complex between the residential and commercial sections was a large, elevated quadrangular structure with pedestrian ramps and underground roadways. Its individual shops—probably hexagonal (to make the most of the space) because Breuer described them as arranged "like the cells of a honeycomb"[3]—faced an interior court. Facades were defined by stepped cantilevers supported by trusslike buttresses, such as those Breuer had proposed for his hospital project for Elberfeld, Germany. Near the shopping center were restaurants, a theater resembling that designed for Kharkov, Ukraine, and a café in the polymorphic shape that Breuer transformed into the Ariston Club at Mar del Plata, Argentina. Office buildings at the eastern edge of the town were formed as multilevel double-Ys, a fruitful invention that was to become a signature format for Breuer's commercial and institutional buildings, especially in the 1960s, and that may have had its source in the shape of Hans Poelzig's unexecuted project, designed in 1929, for a library building for the Reichstag.[4]

For its dependence on concrete construction, and as the carrier of a large number of Breuer's past and future architectural motifs, Garden City of the Future was the most fruitful planning project of his career.

ARCHIVAL: **SUL 18, 53; AAA Photos; RIBA Drawings Collection.**
BIBLIOGRAPHIC: *Architects' Journal*, March 1936, 470, 477–82; *Architectural Review*, April 1936, 168; Hitchcock, "Marcel Breuer and the American Tradition," 14–15; *Nuestra arquitectura*, September 1947, 48–51; Yorke and Gibberd, *The Modern Flat*, 193–98; Blake, *Marcel Breuer*, 59–60.

113
South Boston Redevelopment Plan,
Boston, Massachusetts, 1943 (NOT BUILT)

MARCEL BREUER, ARCHITECT

This was a study for a planning project in South Boston involving the clearance of a 24-acre slum area—an example of the misguided massive destruction for renewal that was typical of the period—to make room for 1,000 to 2,000 families. Breuer designed a grand series of pentagonal "communities" composed of integrated buildings, gardens, facilities, and services in a centralized redevelopment mode that was more humanized than the modernist standby of "tower in the park." Each complex included apartment blocks forming the pentagonal frame, one-story shops with parking fields, a community garden, and a three-story school in the center ("the heart") of the community piazza. The school gymnasium and auditorium were used as community centers. Although housing and urban-development theory and practice changed drastically during the years Breuer was in practice, this design from the early 1940s was a resourceful and community-based solution for slum clearance, as each pentagon functioned as its own residential and commercial neighborhood and community.

ARCHIVAL: **SUL 46; AAA Photos.**
BIBLIOGRAPHIC: *Pencil Points*, June 1944, 70.

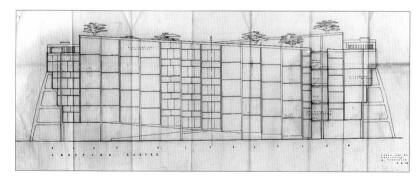

112. Shopping center, section

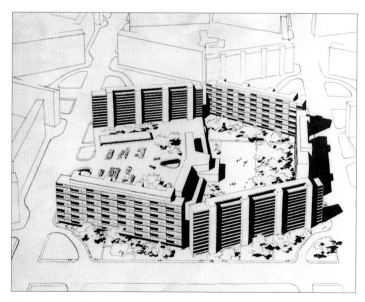

113. Aerial perspective

114. Rendering

114
El Recreo Urban Center,
Caracas, Venezuela, 1959 (NOT BUILT)

MARCEL BREUER, ERNESTO FUENMAYOR NAVA, AND MANUEL SAYAGO, ARCHITECTS

HERBERT BECKHARD, ASSOCIATE

An ambitious multistructure urban-planning project for downtown Caracas, Venezuela, El Recreo was initiated by Venezuelan architects Ernesto Fuenmayor Nava and Manuel Sayago, who invited Breuer to collaborate. A letter from Breuer to them, written on October 4, 1959, served as a "working agreement" whereby the project was to be credited equally to "we three architects" and Herbert Beckhard as associate. Beckhard moved from New York to Caracas to oversee the project. Following the publication of the project in *Architectural Record*, the credits became the subject of a completely justifiable complaint on the part of the Venezuelan architects.[5] El Recreo Urban Center was an eclectic ensemble of buildings situated around four office towers raised on columns, with the north facades fully fenestrated and the narrow ends of the slabs unarticulated. Organized around a wide pedestrian piazza served by ramps, the towers had at their base subsidiary buildings for commerce and recreation: a pair of trapezoidal structures of folded-plate construction and a series of covered markets with barrel-vaulted roofs.

ARCHIVAL: **SUL Drawings; AAA Contract, Correspondence, Photos.**
BIBLIOGRAPHIC: *L'Architecture d'aujourd'hui,* February–March 1960, 76–80; *Architectural Record,* June 1960, 183–86; *Arts & Architecture,* October 1960, 14–18; *Architectural Design,* September 1960, 369–70; Jones, ed., *Marcel Breuer,* 112–15.

Flaine, Phase I, 1961–68. See no. 96.

115
ZUP de Bayonne,
Bayonne, France, 1966–73

MARCEL BREUER AND ROBERT F. GATJE, ARCHITECTS

To keep urban expansion organized and under control, the French government in 1952 established its Zone à urbaniser par priorité (ZUP) program, so named because of its priority over other types of new housing and development projects. In this case, the project was a low-income satellite town for 15,000 in a wooded area of 332 acres close to Bayonne, near the border with Spain. It was brought to Breuer's attention in 1963 by Max Stern of Paris, a colleague of Breuer and Robert Gatje through his role in the planning of Flaine and head of the Bureau d'études et réalisations urbaines (BERU), economic planners who established the program for the Bayonne site. Breuer began preliminary work on the master plan during 1963 and 1964; ZUP de Bayonne was in construction through 1973. The master plan set out a town of 3,000 family units with civic and cultural facilities at its core, fourteen-story slabs with floor-through duplex apartments sited along its sinuous perimeter, groups of four-story residential walk-ups forming a network of courtyards, and rows of one-and-a-half-story houses. The complex but space-saving "skip-stop apartment scheme" (skip-floor corridors and through-floor duplex apartments), used for organizing the disposition of apartments in the slab towers, is described in detail in the August 1969 issue of *Architectural Record.* The format of lower buildings massed in front of taller ones was a carryover from Breuer's unexecuted housing projects of the late 1920s. Variations in the height of buildings and the animation of facades were intended to avoid monotony in a self-contained town integrating residential, civic, cultural, and commercial life.

ZUP de Bayonne was a determined effort to move away from traditional French urban architecture. Apartment towers symbolized modern living, and open spaces and plazas were an alternative to the corridor-like streets common in French cities. Concrete—textured and smooth surfaced—was the structural material: poured-in-place floor slabs and pilotis contrasted with load-bearing window walls of smooth precast panels with deep-set windows. Breuer diversified the patterns of window openings in the towers, but, small in scale, the variations tended to be visually lost. For the lower buildings, he modulated the plasticity of the surfaces by recessing and projecting the planes that defined the window areas. Among the most exhilarating shapes in Breuer's architectural repertoire were the municipal water towers planned, but not built, for ZUP de Bayonne (see p. 160). They were reminiscent of some of the visionary designs in the General Motors Futurama exhibit at the 1939 New York World's Fair, and reflected the powerfully expressive geometries of Etienne-Louis Boulée and Claude-Nicolas Ledoux.

115. View of the plaza, looking north

While the overall planning emanated from the Breuer office (chief architects of the project), and while the majority of buildings were designed by Breuer, over the course of time additional structures that became part of the new town (principally apartment towers and school buildings) were the work of local architects. They were in Breuer's name, but often did not meet his approval. He became concerned about visible architectural features such as exterior walls, roofs, and balcony railings that were not rigorously detailed in the working drawings of other architects. To one of the architects, Gatje wrote: "As you must be aware it may be a little hard for Lajkó to accept tile roofs at the center of the ZUP and I think you should be prepared to defend your choice."[6] By 1972, the original "proud vision" of the designers was, according to Gatje, "in danger of being frittered away piece by piece," with many of the later buildings ignoring the master plan and disappointing Breuer with regard to architectural concept, materials, and siting.[7]

For the working-class population of ZUP de Bayonne, the modern amenities in the new town were an improvement over conditions of crowded inner cities. But the settlement of the town took place during a period of theoretical and practical revisionism in urban renewal. The open center and peripheral towers of Breuer's ZUP de Bayonne were soon to be discredited by new planning ideologies.

ARCHIVAL: **SUL 138, Paris Office File; AAA Contract, Correspondence, Photos.**
BIBLIOGRAPHIC: *Architectural Record*, **April 1966, 172–77, and August 1969, 101–12;** *L'architettura*, **February 1970, 676–77; Papachristou,** *Marcel Breuer*, **82–91; Gatje,** *Marcel Breuer*, **passim.**

116
Madison Park Urban Renewal,
Roxbury, Boston, Massachusetts, 1967–68 (NOT BUILT)

MARCEL BREUER AND TICIAN PAPACHRISTOU, ARCHITECTS

Breuer contracted in 1967 for a large urban-renewal project in the Roxbury section of Boston, Massachusetts, that would include apartment houses, an office building, an industrial building, and, at the heart of the complex, a high school with athletic facilities for a student body of 5,000. Alternative design possibilities were developed.[8] Only part of the project saw the light—in 1976 to 1978, a version of the high school, Madison Park High School (Roxbury Campus High School; see no. 27), was built.

ARCHIVAL: **SUL 161.**
BIBLIOGRAPHIC: **Papachristou,** *Marcel Breuer*, **196–97.**

Resort Town, near Bordeaux, France, 1971 (not built). See no. 97.

RESIDENTIAL
MULTIPLE-FAMILY HOUSING

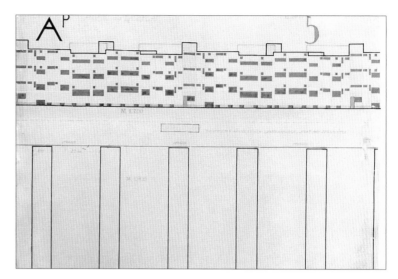

117a. Elevation and plan

117
Apartment House, Project,
Weimar, Germany, 1923 (NOT BUILT)

MARCEL BREUER, BAUHAUS

Published by Cranston Jones and Breuer in *Marcel Breuer: Buildings and Projects*, the drawing for a "skipped-level" apartment-house facade is described as "Breuer's first architectural design." Joachim Driller observes that its two-dimensional geometry resembles the abstractions of Josef Albers and contemporary Bauhaus weaving-workshop designs for fabrics or carpets. Variations in the size and placement of windows, and the small air-circulation vents, demonstrate Breuer's early interest in complex patterns of dark and light made by window and wall. The "skipped level" or "skip-stop" interior plan for multiple dwellings, which he used through the 1960s, is expressed here: a corridor (or elevator landing) at skipped levels gives access to interlocked duplex apartments, those with either double-height living rooms or two levels of rooms whose arrangement is reversed one floor above and one floor below. A typical apartment plan shows the children's room separated from the master bedroom by the living room and kitchen.

ARCHIVAL: **BHA Photos (Inv. F9261-2).**
BIBLIOGRAPHIC: **Jones, ed.,** *Marcel Breuer,* **233; Driller,** *Breuer Houses,* **259.**

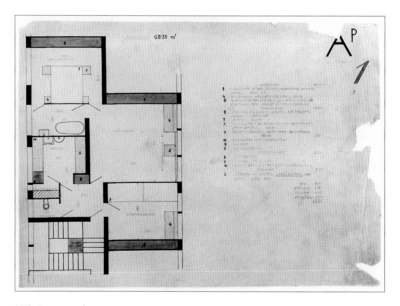

117b. Apartment plan

118
Apartment House, Model,
1923–24 (NOT BUILT)

MARCEL BREUER, BAUHAUS

A model of a mid-rise working-class dwelling with small apartments (*Wohnhochhaus*) was prepared in 1923 as an entry for a 1924 competition sponsored by the architectural periodical *Bauwelt* in a search for a new housing type (see p. 52). One hundred fifty-eight designs were submitted to a panel of judges that included Ludwig Mies van der Rohe.[1] Captions in Breuer's handwriting on photographs of the model describe it as a "project for a multi-story duplex apartment house with continuous terrace gardens 1923," but he dated it elsewhere as 1924. Seven stories of duplex apartments open to terraces stretching along the rear facade. The concept of a "tall" apartment slab probably originated at the Weimar Bauhaus in the independent architecture study group organized by Breuer and Georg Muche in 1923.[2] A coexistent drawing by Muche for a fifteen-story dwelling depicts a building different in character and materials from Breuer's, and not shaped as a narrow slab.

By limiting the depth of each apartment to two rooms, as in row houses, Breuer created the narrow slab profile. He gave to these apartments the aspect of an individual residence with amenities usually associated with houses, not apartments—greenery, access to the outdoors, and sunlight (as both front and rear were open to natural illumination, the interior spaces were bright). The terraces offered open-air living and a small space for recreational gardening. In designing this slab format, Breuer is credited by Bauhaus historian Hans Wingler with creating "an entirely new type of building which years later became commonly accepted as an integral component of modern apartment architecture."[3] The format had not appeared in low-income housing experiments in 1920s Germany before Breuer's model, according to Ronald Wiedenhoeft.[4] But the notion of mid-rise (six- or seven-story) apartment blocks and stacked duplex apartments had its origin in the urban designs of Le Corbusier, such as the Ville Contemporaine (1922); from Le Corbusier's Maison Citrohan 2 of the same year came the ideas of raising a building on pilotis, double-story living rooms, and full-height windows. As Breuer's design was realized in the dimensions of a scale model, it related naturally to his furniture experiments of 1922 to 1924. The slab format is an analogue to his large wall cabinets; the continuous terraces are transformations of bookcase shelves with vertical dividers.[5]

When the Bauhaus-Archiv was planning a Breuer exhibition in 1974 (based on the Metropolitan Museum of Art show of 1972), Wingler asked Breuer for material about the model of 1923–24 in the hope of using it to build a new model. Replying, Breuer wrote: "I have absolutely no drawing or other data in existence for the Wohnhochhaus. There is only the one poor photo of the rather poor model, and I believe your so positive idea for a new model has to be abandoned."[6]

ARCHIVAL: AAA Correspondence, Photos; BHA Photos.
BIBLIOGRAPHIC: Jones, ed., *Marcel Breuer*, 233; Wingler, *Bauhaus*, 388–89; Wiedenhoeft, *Berlin's Housing Revolution*, 166–70; Driller, "Frühwerk," 308–9.

118. Model

119. Perspective drawing

119
Apartment-House Complex, Competition, Spandau-Haselhorst,
Berlin, Germany, 1928 (NOT BUILT)

MARCEL BREUER, WITH THE ASSISTANCE OF GUSTAV HASSENPFLUG

For a government competition for a large experimental workers' housing settlement on a 450,000-square-meter (4.8-million-square-foot) site in the Spandau-Haselhorst section of Berlin, Breuer and Gustav Hassenpflug submitted a perspective drawing and site scheme with descriptive text. Sponsored by the Reichsforschungsgesellschaft für Wirtschaftlichkeit im Bau-und Wohnungswesen (RFG, National Research Institute for Efficiency in Housing Construction), founded in 1927, the competition was the brainchild of Martin Wagner. Serving also as a competition judge, Wagner at the time was building director of Greater Berlin and one of the most enlightened policy makers and proponents of the social benefits of economically planned urban housing. (Later he became Breuer's colleague at Harvard, brought there by Walter Gropius.) The RFG favored and promoted the parallel-row system of uniform apartment blocks (*reine Zeilenbebauung*) for large-scale housing settlements, with the narrow end of the block to the street and its traffic, and the wide facades oriented north-south for light and supposed serenity. RFG guidelines indicated a preference for low- and medium-rise rather than high-rise buildings. In Breuer's design, three long rows of tall (eighteen-story) slabs two rooms deep have between them rows of single-family, two-story houses with individual gardens. The whole ensemble is set within a park dotted with playgrounds and promenades, and it reflects urban-housing ideals formulated by Le Corbusier. The height was determined by the capability of the elevator; the distance between the rows of tall structures was equal to the height of the buildings. Self-contained community amenities such as child-care facilities, restaurants, laundries, and garages were installed in the lower two stories of the tall buildings.

ARCHIVAL: **AAA Photos; BHA Drawings, Photos.**
BIBLIOGRAPHIC: **Breuer, "Beiträge zur Frage des Hochhauses,"** *Die Form 5* (1930): **113–17; Blake,** *Marcel Breuer,* **39; Jones, ed.,** *Marcel Breuer,* **238; Wiedenhoeft,** *Berlin's Housing Revolution,* **121–23, 166, 169–70; Nerdinger,** *Walter Gropius,* **116–18.**

120
Apartment Hotel,
1928–30 (NOT BUILT)

MARCEL BREUER, WITH THE ASSISTANCE OF GUSTAV HASSENPFLUG

An example of the interest that urban apartment blocks with central-ized services held for architects in the late 1920s is this proposal for a residential hotel in a landscaped park. The building rose eleven stories above a two-tiered base and was sheathed with a glass curtain wall. The apartment layouts represented four variations on the small-apart-ment theme,[7] with one of the rooms serving double function as living room and bedroom. A tiled roof terrace covered by awninged bays was used for leisure activity. Breuer described the project in 1938 when he sent photographs to the Mulvane Art Museum, Washburn College, in Topeka, Kansas, for an exhibition of modern domestic architecture and housing sponsored by the United States Housing Authority. Expressing his continuing efforts to design for flexibility of function, he wrote: "A kind of boarding house, or hotel . . . the apartments can be combined with each other, giving always between a two-room apartment, one room, which can be added to one of the apartments as needed. The apartments themselves contain two units, which are at the same time bedroom and living room, separated and connected by the kitchen, bath, and entrance part."[8] A model of the building and a typi-cal furnished apartment that might have been installed within were on display from May to July 1930 in an international exhibition in Paris at the Grand Palais as part of the contribution of the Deutsche Werkbund to the exhibition.[9]

ARCHIVAL: **SUL 15; AAA Photos.**
BIBLIOGRAPHIC: **Giedion,** *Walter Gropius*, **50–51; Jones, ed.,** *Marcel Breuer*, **239; Driller, "Frühwerk," 344.**

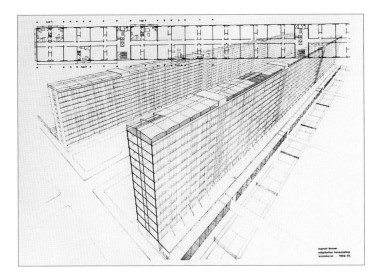

120. Perspective drawing and plan

121
Apartment House, Project for Paul and Marianne Harnischmacher,
Wiesbaden, Germany, 1934 (NOT BUILT)

MARCEL BREUER, ARCHITECT

Knowledge of this project comes from letters between Breuer and Marianne Harnischmacher in September and October 1934.[10] As a real-estate venture, the Harnischmachers wanted to build a small apartment house with four duplex apartments on property that they owned not far from their house designed by Breuer in 1932. Marianne Harnischmacher sent Breuer her rough sketch of a right-angled arrangement, about which he pointed out that the tenants would see into one anothers' windows. He sketched several alternatives ("I think one should give each tenant the private feeling of an entire villa [each with its own entrance]") and proposed cost-saving construction strategies. He envisioned apartments with a two-story living room and full window wall, similar to that in the weekend house on the Danube he had designed a few months earlier. The example of Le Corbusier houses, with, as Reyner Banham discerned, their source in Parisian artists' studio-houses,[11] was probably behind the design concept for this project. Breuer mentioned the possible disadvantage of the need for more heating because of the large space, "although in Geneva two-story living spaces were rented for the first time in Corbusier's apart-ment house."

Since Breuer was not residing or practicing in Germany in 1934 but commuting between Budapest and Zürich, the idea of a collabora-tion on the apartment house with Gustav Hassenpflug, recently returned to Germany after three years in the Soviet Union, was consid-ered but rejected by Breuer and the clients. The project stalled, and Breuer wrote to Ise Gropius on Christmas Day 1934 that "Harnisch-macher is also silent. One doesn't know whether he didn't like my sketches or whether he is having difficulties."[12] Politics probably played a role, as Ise replied on January 19, 1935, asking, "What have you heard from Harnischmacher? We had news from D. Cocker that there is a general prohibition in the region of Suddeutschland and there is nothing that can be done there at the moment."[13]

ARCHIVAL: **AAA Correspondence.**
BIBLIOGRAPHIC: **Driller,** *Breuer Houses*, **260.**

122
Doldertal Apartment Houses,
Zürich, Switzerland, 1935–36

ALFRED & EMIL ROTH AND MARCEL BREUER, ARCHITECTS

Breuer collaborated with Swiss cousins Alfred and Emil Roth on a pair of privately financed small apartment buildings set amid independent villas on a hillside in the Zürich suburb of Doldertal. A comprehensive history of the Doldertal houses, based on interviews with Alfred Roth and on material in the Sigfried Giedion Archives, was first presented by Joachim Driller in his dissertation in 1990 and then augmented in 1996 by Artur Rüegg in an exhibition in Zürich and in the accompanying catalogue. Additional material is with the Breuer Papers at Syracuse University and in Driller's *Breuer Houses.*

Alfred Roth, trained as an architect and a mechanical engineer, had worked with Le Corbusier; Emil Roth was one of the group of young Swiss architects who in 1932 had built the Neubuhl *Siedlung* in Zürich, a celebrated example of interwar Swiss modernism. The client was Sigfried Giedion, architectural historian, supporter of modern architecture, and secretary-general of CIAM, who owned the property and, with his wife, Carola Giedion-Weicker, lived in a nearby villa.

Sited obliquely one behind the other on the hillside, the steel-frame-and-curtain-wall Doldertal apartment buildings have two stories above pilotis and a third-story penthouse. The original disposition of the space in each house was described by Breuer in 1938 as a five-room and a one-room apartment on the first floor, a six-room apartment on the second floor, and a three-room and a two-room penthouse studio. Each apartment had direct access to a terrace except for the one-room apartment, which opened to the garden.[14] The buildings were surrounded by trees and shrubs, so living in the apartments, with their terraces and many windows, approximated life in private villas. At ground level, each block had an inset glass-walled entrance hall with staircase, a covered carport, storerooms, and a laundry room. The houses were built between April 1935 and January 1936, when Breuer was residing in England, but he had first joined the project in the summer of 1933 from Budapest soon after the Roths had submitted their proposal for a complex of three buildings to the Zürich building authorities. Because the length of each block exceeded the zoning limit, this proposal was rejected. (Aware that modern apartment blocks in a neighborhood of conservative villas would be considered intrusive and alien, the Roths had designed low [two-story] but long buildings.)

Giedion must have had misgivings about the Roths' ability to succeed with their design, since he independently contacted Breuer in Budapest and sent him the Roths' proposal. Breuer, who admired the design, made some suggestions—to use steel-skeleton construction, to make the bedrooms multifunctional, to provide a terrace for each apartment—and was careful to warn Giedion that he wanted "to avoid personal complications at all costs, especially since I find the Roth project really good in its essential points."[15] Giedion negotiated a satisfactory collaborative arrangement among the three architects, and from the fall of 1933 through the winter of 1934 correspondence flowed between Breuer in Budapest and the Roths in Zürich with revisions and adjustments. In this renewed effort to receive authorization, a design consisting again of three two-story buildings, each with a setback penthouse and sited obliquely to the street, was proposed to the authorities in January 1934. "It contained all the main elements of the final project," Roth later said of this design.[16] Still, anticipating an objection to this version, too, because of the novelty of the setback roof structure, the architects prepared a third design, with the buildings parallel to the street and without penthouses. However, in the spring of 1934, the authorities approved the second design, classifying it as "an exception" to established regulations and "an experiment."[17] Finally, two of the three buildings from the second project, each shorter in length than the originals, were built.

Preparing for the construction, which was to start at the end of March 1935, Alfred Roth had written to Breuer on December 24, 1934, that "Giedion is totally in agreement that we two should settle the relationship with you between us, so that there will be no professional danger to you in our country whatsoever." As a Hungarian national living in England, Breuer had to confront problems relating to the

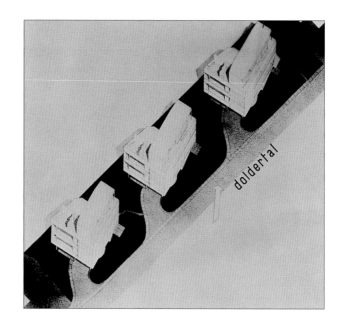

122a. First proposal, isometric site plan

122b. View from the southeast

practice of architecture in Switzerland. Relations between the Roths and Breuer, and among the client and his three architects, were harmonious throughout the construction process, which was completed in January 1936. But tensions about money arose in April, and a particularly acrimonious situation between Breuer and the Roths developed in the fall of 1936 when the project began to be published and photographs and plans exhibited. Credits were inaccurate; the names either were not given equal weight or were not cited in the order agreed on by the architects (in Hungarian publications, for example, Breuer's name was to appear first). On one occasion, Breuer's name was omitted altogether.[18] The issue even was taken up by the Hungarian delegation at the CIRPAC Congress in La Sarraz, Switzerland, in September 1936. Giedion became fed up with the hostilities and, in an effort to put an end to "this tiresome conflict," wrote to Alfred Roth in a tone of exasperation, pointing out that in publications "the names were mentioned three different ways for one and the same mutual work. . . . If in every publication your three names had very simply been given in accordance with the facts, this unpleasant conflict would never have arisen."[19] He goes on: "So I ask you please . . . not to undertake to try to prove, as you did in your letter to Breuer, your contribution to the work on a percentage basis. . . . If all future publications say Alfred and Emil Roth and Marcel Breuer everyone will be satisfied." Responding to a request from Carola Giedion-Weicker in 1976 for historical remembrances about Doldertal, Breuer wrote: "I hope, CW, that this letter is the last chapter of the Doldtertal controversy."[20]

The structure is steel frame with reinforced-concrete floors. Outside walls, non-weight-bearing and structurally independent of the floors, were made of brick finished with stucco after it was decided not to use concrete for the outer shell. Foundations for the pilotis are cross-tied to each other by reinforced-concrete beams. The setback walls of the penthouse were wood framed for lightness, faced externally with panels of asbestos cement and internally with plywood. The staircase is structurally free of the body of the building. More than half a century later, the Doldertal apartment buildings continue to be a brilliant success structurally, functionally, and aesthetically. They were restored between 1993 and 1996.

ARCHIVAL: **SUL 6–8, 10, Drawings; AAA Correspondence, Photos.**
BIBLIOGRAPHIC: *Architectural Record*, October 1936, 252, 287–94; *Architectural Review*, February 1937, 56–59; *L'Architecture d'aujourd'hui*, February 1937, 52; *Nuestra arquitectura*, November 1947, 150–62; Yorke and Gibberd, *The Modern Flat*, 66–69; Blake, *Marcel Breuer*, 49, 52–54; Roth, ed., *The New Architecture*, 47–60; von Moos, Alfred Roth, 88–92; Driller, "Frühwerk," 309–34, and *Breuer Houses*, 66–82, 259–60; Rüegg, *Die Doldertalhäuser*.

123
Aluminum City Terrace,
New Kensington, Pennsylvania, 1941–42

WALTER GROPIUS AND MARCEL BREUER, ARCHITECTS

Near the town of New Kensington in Westmoreland County, Pennsylvania, in 1941 and 1942, Walter Gropius and Breuer built a housing complex sponsored by the Federal Works Agency (FWA) originally intended for the defense workers in the Alcoa aluminum factories (see p. 110). This region of Pennsylvania was the site of "the most intensive concentration of defense housing in the United States" during the wartime years,[21] and Aluminum City Terrace was the first housing project executed in the United States by the emigré architects. The Alcoa plant moved its operations away from New Kensington, however, so potential tenants for the new houses were no longer migrant defense workers but the local population. The commission came from the chief of defense housing in Washington, D.C. Breuer had visited him in April 1941 in an aggressive effort to bring to the agency's attention the Gropius-Breuer practice; private building had almost come to a halt by 1941, and new construction was exclusively for the government. In May, Gropius and Breuer were awarded the New Kensington contract with a limit of $3,500 per housing unit. The FWA gave them twelve days to produce preliminary drawings, perspectives, and a model, and then eighteen days more to complete working drawings and specifications. For 250 families, the architects designed one-, two-, and three-bedroom simplex and duplex units with living room, dining space, kitchen, utility room, heating room, and entrance hall with stair for the duplexes. Each unit had a balcony, an independent terrace with a garden opening from the living room, and a projecting tool shed that served also as a separating element between units (its origin was in J. J. P. Oud's kitchen court and laundry space at the Weissenhofsiedlung, the experimental housing settlement built in Stuttgart in 1927). For the professional architectural press, "unusual details" at New Kensington were sunshades, hoods over entrance doors, and ramps leading from entrance path to door,[22] but they had been common features of housing projects, built and unbuilt, by Gropius and by Breuer in Germany in the late 1920s.

In August 1941, Gropius and Breuer severed their partnership,[23] but work on the project continued. By June 1942, the first units were occupied, and by September the project was complete except for the landscaping, which had been commissioned to an independent landscape architect. From the $28,000 allotted to landscaping costs, $21,000 was cut, so the first photographs revealed the bare shale and clay ground without topsoil and plantings. The completed project was regarded as a failure in the community and was criticized in the

Pittsburgh and local press. Part of the acrimony it generated was the result of a political argument between an incumbent pro-public-housing mayor and his opponent, who used New Kensington as the target of attacks on each other. In June 1943, Breuer, disturbed by negative reactions, visited New Kensington to talk to the people living there because "after all that is what counts."[24] He was hurt to discover that the community center was to be enlarged by other architects (Sorber and Hoone of Greensburgh, Pennsylvania).[25] Although criticized locally, the design was admired by the United States Housing Authority, one of whose officers wrote to Breuer that "I have been extolling the virtues of this unit plan to several members of our organization."[26] B. J. Hovde, director of the Pittsburgh office of the FWA, told Breuer that "the New Kensington Defense Housing project is recognized in housing circles as one of the most interesting projects yet produced"[27] and that "I am still a great admirer of the New Kensington project which you and Dr. Gropius designed. It has been a great disappointment, however, to note the tardiness with which the project has been rented and the hostility of the local community to this type of architecture. . . . [I]t is obvious that a good deal of education will be necessary before modern architecture will be easily accepted."[28]

Gropius and Breuer's project consisted of one- and two-story, flat-roofed terrace housing arranged in long blocks on hilly wooded terrain, sited in casual rather than in the rigid patterns that had been favored in post–First World War German *Siedlungen*; a few twin (two-family only) units were set against steep slopes that inclined more than 30 degrees. The informality of the arrangement of the blocks—what Breuer called "an ungeometric setting of free rhythm"—was dictated by the difficult and uneven site and became one of the features most admired by professionals. Eero Saarinen, for example, at that period closely involved in the theory and practice of defense housing, including his own project in Center Line, Michigan, for 476 defense worker families, praised the placement of housing blocks at New Kensington for giving "a pleasant variety of endless vistas and views."[29] The principal entrance side (north) of the units was faced with sand-colored brick veneer; the rear (south) was of cedar covered by colorless preserver. At ground level, the siding was laid horizontally; on the upper story, vertically. The brick veneer and adjacent siding patterns were an inventive contrast of texture and material, but the aesthetics of an unpainted wood surface were little appreciated. This became a sore point when the wood, which had been too green to paint at the time of construction, weathered badly and within two years was unsightly. To capitalize on sunlight and view, the south-facing windows were designed to be large, horizontal, without mullioned compartments, and protected from the summer sun by a louvered overhang—a sophisticated sun-control feature that neither the management nor the tenants under-

stood: they complained that rainwater dripped through the slats. Tenants were critical, too, of the orientation of the units, since the south facades, considered the "back" and faced with wood, not brick, had terraces, gardens, and large windows but were alongside the road, whereas the brick (the "better" and more valued side because brick is more expensive than wood) faced away from the road; thus a visitor would approach not by way of the primary but via the secondary entrance.

Structure and design at New Kensington were driven by low-cost directives. Partially prefabricated wood-frame construction was used; most of the doors, windows, and mill sections of simple design were standardized and delivered to the building site already cut. For the south window openings, the wood-frame structure was trussed (the method Breuer proposed for his Ober-Gurgl ski hotel) so that costly steel supports above the wide spans were not needed.[30] On the sharply sloping sites, the twin units were constructed on lally columns of heights that varied according to the irregularity of the slope to save the expense of site-grading and foundation work and to use the difficult inclines. As late as 1951, a director of the National Capitol Housing Authority in Washington, D.C., commenting to Breuer on his design, noted that it had certain features "novel to our experience in public housing," and as illustrations cited the exposed columns supporting the houses and the open-plan living room–kitchen–dining room.[31] Misinterpreting the drawings, the builders, unable to imagine rooms where the walls did not meet the ceiling and where a view was allowed from kitchen into living room (to watch the children), carried the wall studs between kitchen and living room to the ceiling.[32] By 1949, the notion of children's activity under observation from the kitchen became one of the extolled advantages of Breuer's exhibition house at

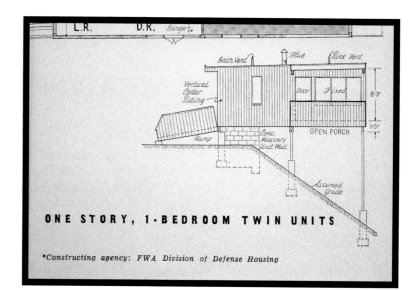

123a. Side elevation

123b. One-story unit with balcony

the Museum of Modern Art. But for the perplexed workers in New Kensington, the low wall between their rooms made them seem like "barnyard stalls."

Half a century later, Aluminum City Terrace has become a thriving cooperative. Although altered, the units are still immediately recognizable as those of the Gropius-Breuer design. The louvers were replaced, and the houses, in the words of Franklin Toker, "were radically Americanized" by turning what had been the rear into the front entrance with a garden, since suburban Americans like having "lawns" at the front.[33] Not understood or even considered desirable by the tenants in 1941 and 1942 were amenities that had been developed by the architects in Europe for private modern villas for upper-middle-class clients.

ARCHIVAL: SUL 18, 44–46, 52; AAA Photos; see Nerdinger, *Walter Gropius*, 275, and Walter Gropius Archive, 3:314–47.

BIBLIOGRAPHIC: *Architectural Forum*, October 1941, 218–20, and July 1944, 65–76; *Architectural Review*, September 1944, 72–76; *Task* 5 (1944): 28–35; *Nuestra arquitectura*, November 1947, 145–49; Eero Saarinen, "Architecture and Defense Housing," in *Four Papers on Housing Design*, Publication no. N165 (Chicago: National Association of Housing and Redevelopment Officials, September 1942), 5–8; Blake, *Marcel Breuer*, 78–79; Breuer, *Sun and Shadow*, 166–67; Sarah Allaback, "Aluminum City Terrace," in *Historic American Engineering Record*, HAER no. PA-302 (Department of Defense Legacy Resource Management Program and Historic American Buildings Survey/Historic American Engineering Record, Washington, D.C., 1994, photocopy).

124
Defense Housing,
Wethersfield, Connecticut, 1942 (NOT BUILT)

MARCEL BREUER, ARCHITECT

An agreement between Breuer and the United States Housing Authority was proposed in January 1942 for the design of a defense-housing project in Wethersfield, Connecticut, under the auspices of the Federal Works Agency (FWA). The project called for sixty-five dwelling units in thirty-three buildings of frame construction at an estimated cost of $4,879 per unit. B. J. Hovde, director of the Pittsburgh office of the FWA and an admirer of Gropius and Breuer's Aluminum City Terrace in New Kensington, Pennsylvania, sent a telegram to Sumner Wiley, a director in the United States Housing Authority in Washington: "Wish to congratulate you on choice of Marcel Breuer architect Wethersfield Project Hartford Connecticut. Breuer's outstanding work with Gropius on New Kensington Defense Housing Project amply justified choice of that firm."[34] Breuer intended to use prefabricated construction at Wethersfield and, in an undated letter, wrote to the FWA requesting copies of its publication Standards for Demountable Houses.[35] Joachim Driller says that he presented reworked designs of his prefabricated Yankee Portables of the same year as the basic housing type for Wethersfield. Breuer alerted Richard Stein and Charles Burchard, two of his favorite Harvard architects, to stand by and he made a few rough ground-plan sketches for unit layouts, one page of which survives at Syracuse University. The agreement was never entered into, however, and by March 1942 the project had been abandoned, probably for lack of appropriations.

ARCHIVAL: **SUL 7, 15, 16, 18 (unit plan sketches filed with the Aluminum City Terrace material).**
BIBLIOGRAPHIC: **Driller, "Frühwerk," 184.**

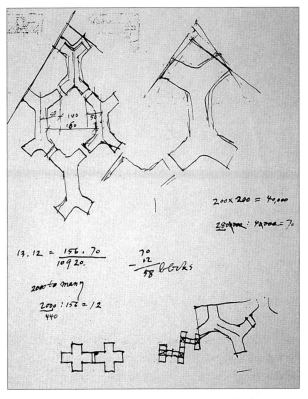

125. Sketches by Breuer

125
"Stuyvesant Six: A Redevelopment Proposal,"
New York, New York 1944 (NOT BUILT)

MARCEL BREUER, ARCHITECT

Urban redevelopment financed with private capital—specifically, Stuyvesant Town in New York, sponsored by the Metropolitan Life Insurance Company—and its relation to the architectural profession was the subject of an article by Breuer in the June 1944 issue of Pencil Points, in which he, one of a number of architects critical of the Stuyvesant Town design approved in 1943 by the New York City Planning Commission, published an alternative proposal called Stuyvesant Six.[36] The Stuyvesant Town project to house 24,000 tenants in thirty-five thirteen-story towers was announced by Mayor Fiorello H. La Guardia on April 19, 1943. Called by the New York Times a "suburb in the city" (although more than half the apartments had only one bedroom and were not for families), the community of moderate-rent apartment buildings would rise on a slum-cleared landscaped site of 72 acres in Manhattan near the East River after the Second World War. As early as November 1943, Breuer wrote to Frederick H. Ecker, chairman of the board of the Metropolitan Life Insurance Company, requesting an appointment to discuss the project.[37] Breuer was intensely interested in the implications of Stuyvesant Town for large-scale postwar urban planning. Not only as a teacher of students of architecture but also as a private practitioner, he wished to ally himself with revised plans and issues that might evolve from the New York project and with future housing developments. He spent much of 1943 and 1944 developing his Stuyvesant Six proposal, altering the configuration of the apartments, the shape of the buildings, and the placement of the towers on the site. He consulted his old friend and Harvard colleague Martin Wagner, former chief of Berlin city planning, about computing costs and rents.[38] Breuer calculated that his plan would increase the monthly rental revenue and reduce ground coverage. Not called into question was the tower-in-the-park concept, on which the social and economic ideology of early modern housing was based. It was also the design philosophy on which much of New York City housing was to be based because of its espousal by Robert Moses, then chairman of the mayor's committee on slum clearance. Despite challenges such as Breuer's, the Stuyvesant Town project as approved by the Planning Commission was completed in 1947. It was, however, the end of middle-class urban housing of this kind. Not geared to families and with few apartments of more than one and two bedrooms, it was displaced by the phenomenal development during the 1950s of the single-family house in the suburbs, in which Breuer himself played a significant role. Stuyvesant Town and its European modernist predecessors were discredited, furthermore, for their towered isolation from a neighborhood context after housing policies underwent a seismic shift following the revisionist viewpoint put forward by Jane Jacobs in *The Death and Life of Great American Cities*.

ARCHIVAL: **SUL 18, 42, Sketches; AAA Photos.**

BIBLIOGRAPHIC: **Breuer, "Stuyvesant Six: A Redevelopment Study,"** *Pencil Points*, **June 1944, 66–70, 102, 118;** *Task* **1–6 (1941–45); Plunz,** *A History of Housing in New York City.*

126
Apartment House, Project for Bert Geller,
Lawrence, Long Island, New York, 1945 (NOT BUILT)

MARCEL BREUER, ARCHITECT

Bert Geller, Breuer's client for the renowned binuclear residence of 1945 in Lawrence, Long Island, was interested in developing a small suburban apartment house as a real-estate venture to meet housing needs after the end of the Second World War. In October 1945, Breuer provided Geller with the planning data for a forty-five-unit apartment building, with eighteen two-bedroom and twenty-seven one-bedroom apartments with garages, back yards, and side yards, "as required by the local code."[39] Although the code permitted fifty-six apartments, Breuer proposed forty-five because the smaller number would "allow a nice green area between the wings, good winter sun for living and bedrooms, and privacy for the windows." The estimated total investment was $336,000. Nothing came of the project.

ARCHIVAL: **SUL 43.**

127
Apartment House,
New York, New York, 1946 (NOT BUILT)

MARCEL BREUER, ARCHITECT

While experimenting with plans for apartment-house development during the mid-1940s, Breuer recognized the real-estate potential of Manhattan's Sutton Place. (He had also correctly identified Gramercy Park, Washington Square, Seventy-ninth Street and the Hudson River, and Englewood Cliffs, New Jersey, as especially promising and scenic sites.) He attempted to persuade Edgar J. Kaufmann, Jr., son of the Pittsburgh department-store magnate, to invest in a privileged apartment-house development on Sutton Place, between Fifty-fourth and Fifty-fifth Streets adjacent to the East River. Kaufmann objected to the "doorman swankiness" of the area and in January 1946 wrote to Breuer that "I believe it is a job for insurance companies, banks, or regular apartment realty people rather than private investors."[40]

Breuer's apartment-house project for Sutton Place South was a forward-looking solution for a multiple-family dwelling in an urban setting, combining a residence with a tennis, swimming, and boating club above a busy roadway. The design exists in several versions, but the concept was that of a U-shaped structure, its three light-filled wings of unequal size folded around a wide landscaped court (see p. 28). The building was lifted above East River Drive on pilotis that rested on walls of stone along the river's edge. A stair linked the court level with a boat dock below, and the north wing of the structure was extended eastward above the water, its pilotis sustained by a wall built into the riverbed. (In another version, these pilotis stand on faceted concrete piles.)[41] On the roof were sundecks and tennis courts.

Circulation inside the building was arranged in Breuer's preferred "skip-stop" mode, where a corridor at every third level gave access to the apartments (each with a terrace or balcony) above and below.

ARCHIVAL: **SUL 43, 53, Drawings; AAA Photos.**
BIBLIOGRAPHIC: **Blake,** *Marcel Breuer,* **82.**

128
Duplex-Apartment Complex,
Englewood Cliffs, New Jersey, 1946 (NOT BUILT)

MARCEL BREUER, ARCHITECT

To solve the postwar problem of housing for returning veterans, in 1946 the Federal Housing Administration (FHA) encouraged the construction of rental apartments by private industry with private capital utilizing FHA mortgage insurance. In this connection, Breuer tried to raise money to purchase a 13-acre tract of land in Englewood Cliffs, New Jersey, close to Manhattan and with a view of the Hudson River, and then to finance the construction of a 500-unit apartment complex with its own community facilities designed to attract families with children. The estimates of costs and revenues that he sent to the United States Housing Authority in Washington, D.C., and the apartment layouts he submitted to the FHA were rejected.

ARCHIVAL: **SUL 43.**

129
Baltimore Garden Apartments,
Baltimore, Maryland, 1954 (NOT BUILT)

MARCEL BREUER, ARCHITECT

Preliminary presentation drawings were made in April 1954 for a private development project in Baltimore, Maryland, for a garden-apartment complex. The design was based on a proposal for eighty apartments arranged in six apartment blocks three stories high, with a combination of one- and two-bedroom simplexes, two- and three-bedroom duplexes, and studio (economy) apartments. Revisions were suggested at a meeting in the summer of 1954 among the developers, the building authorities, regional representatives of the Federal Housing Administration (FHA), and an insurance company: to increase the number of apartments; to decrease the length of the blocks; to reduce the square footage of some of the apartments; to eliminate the common stair for duplex and studio, providing a separate stair for each; and to eliminate two-bedroom duplexes.

In a letter of July 1, 1954, to the developers, Breuer provided solutions to all the proposed revisions. Even though this project was one of his most economical, tightly planned, and, in terms of living-space arrangements, ingeniously laid out multifamily complexes, it did not have a future.

ARCHIVAL: **SUL Drawings.**

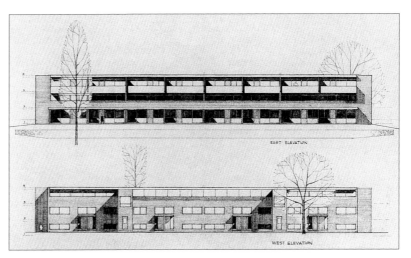

129. Elevations

130
Institute for Advanced Study, Members' Housing,
Princeton, New Jersey, 1956

MARCEL BREUER, ARCHITECT

ROBERT F. GATJE, ASSOCIATE

On July 11, 1955, Breuer contracted with the Institute for Advanced Study to erect "a project for members' housing." He had been recommended to Robert Oppenheimer, then heading the institute, by designer Florence Knoll, who at about the same time recommended him to Patrick McGinness for various New Haven Railroad designs.

One- and two-story building blocks and semidetached houses comprised 107 open-plan apartments of mixed size in five variations, from one-room bachelor apartments to two- and three-bedroom units with studies. They were enhanced by agreeable features that Breuer was able to squeeze out of the limited budget, such as sunshades, flagstone terraces, free-standing fireplaces, built-in kitchen cabinets, balconies, and carports. Perforated walls of concrete between units contributed to privacy. Much of the planning that had gone into Breuer's unexecuted Baltimore Garden Apartments reappeared in this complex, enriched by the special features. Basic planning ideals common to both projects are traceable to Aluminum City Terrace (1941–42). Varied in length and profile, the blocks in Princeton were sited as an unrigid assemblage of mixed sizes and shapes around informal courts and no-traffic areas. The B unit entrance facade was animated by bays of unarticulated surface and glass planes alternating with cantilevered balconies. In the 1990s, the original flat roofs of the blocks were changed to peaked roofs, along with other insensitive and inappropriate modifications of the original appearance.

ARCHIVAL: **SUL 49, Drawings; AAA Contract, Photos.**
BIBLIOGRAPHIC: *Architectural Record*, March 1958, 156–64; *L'Architecture d'aujourd'hui*, June 1958, 88–89; *Bauen und Wohnen*, April 1960, 129–32; Breuer, *Sun and Shadow*, 166–67; Jones, ed., *Marcel Breuer*, 150–53; Gatje, *Marcel Breuer*, 59–61.

131
Fairview Heights Apartments,
Ithaca, New York, 1963–64

MARCEL BREUER AND HAMILTON P. SMITH, ARCHITECTS

Breuer's work at Saint John's Abbey was admired by the Schickel family—private developers, architects, and engineers—who selected him as the architect for a housing project they sponsored in Ithaca, New York, primarily for the faculty and staff of Ithaca College and Cornell University. Construction began on June 3, 1963, and was completed in July 1964. A housing project insured by the Federal Housing Administration (FHA) with 150 residential units, a playground, carports, and landscaping, Fairview Heights is a complex made up of a seven-story block (for singles and couples) lifted on canted concrete legs and set among two-story row houses (for families with children). The inclined site had to be leveled to conform to FHA and local construction codes and zoning ordinances for multiple dwellings; the playground was carved out of the natural slope that remained below the artificially leveled portion. In projects of limited design scope and with construction economies such as this one, Breuer often introduced quality materials and subtle enlivening features. On the exterior of the long facades, the bearing walls are of color-contrasted brick-face and concrete, with projecting concrete sunbreaks for plasticity, texture, and chiaroscuro. The concrete-and-brick-face sections of the end walls are set out in rhythmic patterns, coordinated with a floor-to-floor alternation of wide and narrow window lights. On the upper floor of the row houses, the frames of the brick panels intersect the upper and lower concrete plinths, producing, in combination with projecting fin walls, a three-dimensional Constructivist composition. Still dependent in appearance on post–First World War housing experiments in Germany, the row-house portion of the project, with the small above-door concrete canopies on the entrance side and the sheltered unit-separating terraces on the garden side, can be compared with Gropius and Breuer's housing prototype of Aluminum City Terrace, a 1940s expression of 1920s housing ideals. When he first saw Fairview Heights in the 1970s, a Cornell University faculty member who had grown up in Germany remarked that he felt he "was back in Europe."[42]

ARCHIVAL: **SUL Drawings; AAA Contract, Photos, Project Record Book.**
BIBLIOGRAPHIC: *Progressive Architecture*, September 1964, 96–97; *Architectural Record*, December 1964, 143–48; *Interiors*, December 1964, 49–53; *Industrial Design*, February 1965, 32–37.

131. Seven-story block, general view

130. Entrance side, two-story B unit

Breuer's houses are now documented and definitively studied, with questions of attribution addressed in the case of partnership projects, by Joachim Driller in Breuer Houses, the English-language edition of his Marcel Breuer: Die Wohnhäuser, 1923–1973.

132
Single-Family Dwelling Type 3, Bauhaus Housing Settlement,
1923 (NOT BUILT)

MARCEL BREUER, BAUHAUS

While still a student, Breuer planned one of several variations (Type 3) on single-family house types for Walter Gropius's experimental Bauhaus housing settlement (Bauhaussiedlung) in the am Horn region of Weimar, a project of 1922 that was never realized.[1] Variations were also designed by Adolf Meyer and Farkas Molnár. Type 3, with three rooms and a kitchen, was the smallest of the houses. Above the flat roof of the L-shaped, two-bedroom body of the house rose the double-height clerestoried living-room block. As Breuer's first published architectural designs, the floor plan and isometric drawing appeared in Gropius and Moholy-Nagy's Ein Versuchshaus des Bauhauses in 1925.

ARCHIVAL: **AAA Photos.**
BIBLIOGRAPHIC: **Walter Gropius and László Moholy-Nagy, eds., *Ein Versuchshaus des Bauhauses*, Bauhausbücher 3 (Munich: Langen, 1925); Mezei, "Ungarische Architekten am Bauhaus," in *Wechsel Wirkungen*, ed. Gassner, 357; Driller, *Breuer Houses*, 259.**

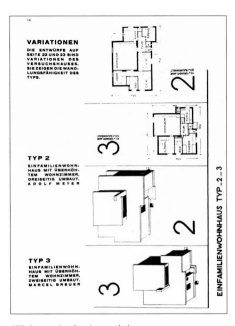

132. Perspective drawings and plans

RESIDENTIAL
SINGLE-FAMILY HOUSES, 1920s

133
Small Metal House (Kleinmetallhaus), 1925–26 Type,
1925–26 (NOT BUILT)

MARCEL BREUER, BAUHAUS

Experimenting with metal prefabrication for single-family dwellings, in 1925–26 Breuer designed a house that could be constructed in three weeks (see p. 27). A bilevel box, it had on the first floor a double-height living space and kitchen, and two bedrooms separated by a bathroom on the L-shaped mezzanine. The bedrooms opened to the upper part of the living space by means of movable walls of opaque glass. The levels were joined by a stair along the windowed living-room wall that ascended to a terrace. To form the terrace, protected by a canopy, the roof was framed at one end by metal railings. Windows appeared on only the long (front) side; the short sides, in order to be joined as row-house units, were windowless. The structural system of the house—a light metal modular frame onto which infill panels of wall, window, and door were mounted—was developed from standardized industrial prototypes. Breuer was indebted to Le Corbusier's experiments at Maison Citrohan for the double-story living rooms and blank side walls. His use of prefabrication and of metal as a material for residential architecture was the outgrowth of his position as teacher at the Dessau Bauhaus at this time, when the cabinetmaking and metal workshops were combined and, together, were his domain. Joachim Driller points out that the atmosphere at the Bauhaus when the small metal house was invented was rife with acrimony and rivalry about who first originated the idea of metal for house construction. Breuer expected his small metal house to be realized; while those by others were, his was not.[2]

ARCHIVAL: **AAA Drawing, Photos.**
BIBLIOGRAPHIC: **Breuer, "Das Kleinmetallhaus Typ 1926," *Offset-Buch und Werbekunst* 7 (1926): 371–74; Walter Gropius, *Internationale Architektur: Auswahl der besten neuzeitlichen Architekturwerke*, Bauhausbücher 1, 2nd ed. (Munich: Langen, 1927); Hitchcock, "Marcel Breuer and the American Tradition," 7–8; Blake, *Marcel Breuer*, 24, 26; Jones, ed., *Marcel Breuer*, 235; Driller, *Breuer Houses*, 46–51, 259.**

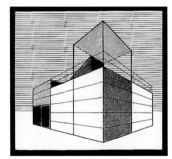

133. Perspective drawing

134
Small Metal House (Kleinmetallhaus), 1927 Type,
1927 (NOT BUILT)

MARCEL BREUER, BAUHAUS

An unsigned drawing of floor plans and house forms in the Bauhaus-Archiv in Berlin has been linked to Breuer because it represents six variations (A–F) on his small metal house 1926 Type.

ARCHIVAL: **BHA Drawing (Inv. 1881).**
BIBLIOGRAPHIC: ***Sammlungs-Katalog, Bauhaus Archiv-Museum*** (Berlin: Mann Verlag, 1981), 189; Mezei, "Ungarische Architekten am Bauhaus," in *Wechsel Wirkungen*, ed. Gassner, 362; Driller, *Breuer Houses*, 10, 259.

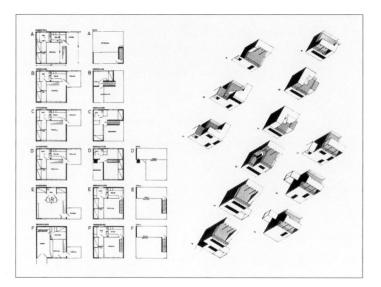

134. Plans and axonometric drawings

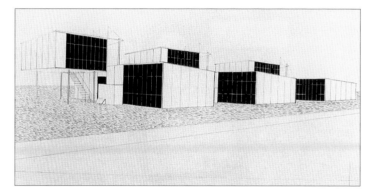

135. Perspective drawing

135
BAMBOS Houses, Types 1, 2, and 3,
1927 (NOT BUILT)

MARCEL BREUER, BAUHAUS

When the Bauhaus moved to Dessau, the city government commissioned Walter Gropius to build not only the school facilities but also dwellings for the masters.[3] In a pine grove a few hundred feet from the school, three semidetached duplexes for six masters (László Moholy-Nagy, Lyonel Feininger, Georg Muche, Oskar Schlemmer, Wassily Kandinsky, and Paul Klee) and a detached house for Walter and Ise Gropius—all planned in the Gropius office—were built in 1925 and 1926. Resentful, the young masters sought housing for themselves. Gropius raised the money, and in 1927 Breuer designed elevations and ground plans for prefabricated metal row houses mostly for faculty members now identified as Breuer, Josef Albers, Hannes Meyer, Herbert Bayer, Otto Meyer-Ottens (Gropius's overseer of construction at that time), and Joost Schmidt (hence BAMBOS).[4] The structure was to be a steel-skeleton frame with modular panels of asbestos-cement for walls and partitions. Variations (Types 2 and 3) were played on the basic theme of BAMBOS Type 1—an independent two-story dwelling derived from Breuer's small metal houses of 1926 and 1927. BAMBOS 1 had a south-facing living room at ground level, a study or workroom opening to a terrace, a kitchen, and auxiliary spaces. On the upper level were two bedrooms (or multipurpose rooms) separated by a bathroom; above the living room was a roof terrace. The configuration and number of rooms varied for BAMBOS 2 and 3. As in the case of his small metal house, Breuer had expectations that the BAMBOS project would be carried out, and, once again, he was disappointed when for financial and political reasons it was abandoned.[5]

ARCHIVAL: **AAA Photos.**
BIBLIOGRAPHIC: Blake, *Marcel Breuer*, 26; Jones, ed., *Marcel Breuer*, 236; Driller, *Breuer Houses*, 52–53, 259.

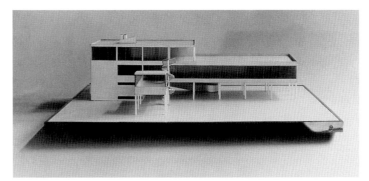

136. Model

136
Schneider House,
Wiesbaden, Germany, 1929 (NOT BUILT)

MARCEL BREUER, ARCHITECT

In the exhibition of Breuer's work at Harvard in 1938, two photographs (nos. 12 and 13) were described in the unillustrated catalogue as "1929: Schneider Residence, Wiesbaden; photo of model, south view and north view," but there is no record of a Schneider House in Wiesbaden in any inventory of Breuer's work.

Almost twenty years later, in *Sun and Shadow*, Breuer included an illustration of a house model identified as "Design for a House in Maehrisch-Ostrau" of 1928, and repeated it in *Marcel Breuer*, edited by Cranston Jones. "Melder House in Maehrisch-Ostrau" (then in Czechoslovakia, near the Oder River and close to the Polish border) appears in Breuer's chronological work lists (for example, one sent to Giulio Carlo Argan in 1956 for the monograph on Breuer he was preparing[6]). The two projects have been confused but now can be correctly identified by comparing a photograph of a drawing in the Archives of American Art labeled "Melder House" and a recently discovered drawing (see no. 139) of 1930 from Breuer's Berlin studio labeled "Haus M" and to see that they are the same.

The Schneider house model shows two intersecting volumes—one ground-based, tall and boxy, and the other a long rectangle elevated on pilotis—that were reached by an entrance pavilion with a roof terrace set perpendicular to the body of the house. An exterior spiral stair linked the ground and the pavilion roof terrace. Breuer described the structure as concrete frame.

ARCHIVAL: **AAA Photos, Correspondence.**
BIBLIOGRAPHIC: **Hitchcock, "Marcel Breuer and the American Tradition," catalogue following p. 18; Breuer, *Sun and Shadow*, 23; Jones, ed., *Marcel Breuer*, 238; Driller, "Frühwerk," 185, and *Breuer Houses*, 259.**

137
Weekend House, Types I and II,
1929 (NOT BUILT)

MARCEL BREUER, ARCHITECT

Drawings donated to the Syracuse University Library in 1999 by Constance L. Breuer include a project for a simple weekend house (one-story, wood frame above a cement base, exterior walls of smooth stucco, and interior walls of plywood) in two variations. The floor plan and elevation are dated February 7, 1929. In both versions, the interior space is divisible into two sections (four beds) by a curtain or movable partition; off the main space are a kitchen, bathroom, closet, and, opening from the outside, a storage room. In the larger Type II, the storage room and closet are side by side. In both versions, the roof is flat but inclined 10 degrees at each side. Floor-to-ceiling glass, compartmentalized into twelve panes (three tiers of four), make up the living-room wall.

ARCHIVAL: **SUL Drawings nos. 71, 72 (CLB donation, 1999).**

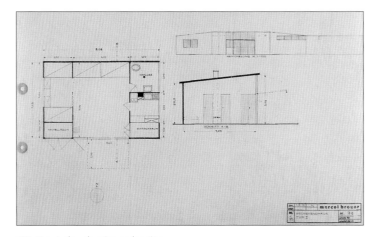

137a. Type I, plan, elevation, and section

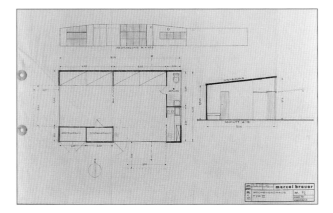

137b. Type II, plan, elevation, and section

138
Dwelling (Wohnhaus) I and II,
1929 (NOT BUILT)

MARCEL BREUER, ARCHITECT

Villas of substantial size, Wohnhaus I (drawings dated March 2, 1929) and Wohnhaus II (drawings dated February 22, 1929) join the Schneider House of the same year and Haus M of 1930 as important examples of early residential projects by Breuer because they predate the Harnischmacher House (1932). They are, moreover, unusual and without precedent in Breuer's work, but could not have been designed without Breuer's knowledge of the architectural experiments at the Weissenhofsiedlung of 1927. Wohnhaus I is a complex three-story long box with oblique angles and streamlined curves, fronted by paved terraces on three levels and abutted at the second level by another box with extended terrace and exterior stair; the roofline is piano-shaped in profile. Wohnhaus II differs from Wohnhaus I in form and layout. Set on an L-shaped terrace, the first-floor block contains a living-dining room, library, stair hall, kitchen, and bathroom, while the bedroom level above has a large roof terrace. The most unusual feature of the design is the sloping glass-paned wall above the stair hall, forming one side of the terrace.

ARCHIVAL: **SUL Drawings nos. 81, 82 (CLB donation, 1999).**

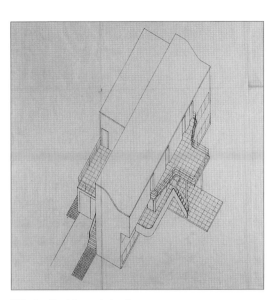

138a. Dwelling I, isometric drawing

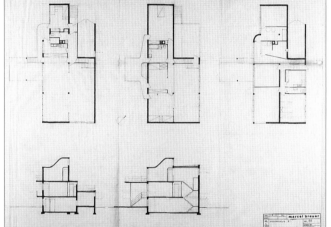

138b. Dwelling I, plans and sections

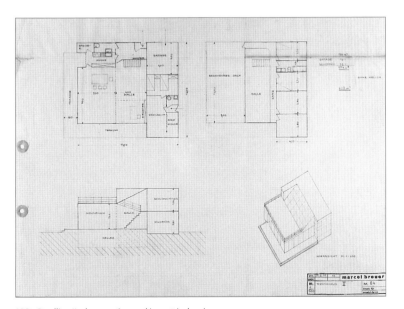

138c. Dwelling II, plans, section, and isometric drawing

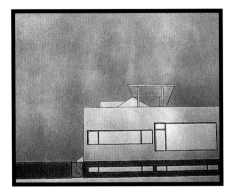

139a. Elevation

139
Haus M (Melder House),
Maehrisch-Ostrau, Czechoslovakia,1930 (NOT BUILT)

MARCEL BREUER, ARCHITECT

A sheet dated September 9, 1930, with a plan and elevations for a house identified only as "Haus M" comes from Breuer's Berlin office. Important as an illustration of his experiments with houses before the Harnischmacher House (1932), Haus M is a square block with an upper-story setback for a large terrace. On the first floor is a room for plants and a study; the upper floor has two bedrooms, a guest room, a bath, and a terrace. Elevations reveal a complex fenestration system.

ARCHIVAL: **SUL Drawing no. 384 (CLB donation, 1999).**

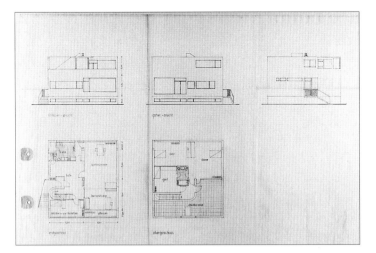

139b. Plans and elevations

SINGLE-FAMILY HOUSES, 1930s (EUROPE)

140
Harnischmacher House I,
Wiesbaden, Germany, 1932

MARCEL BREUER, ARCHITECT

A trilevel steel-skeleton structure with extruded porches, and as radically different from neighboring houses as Gerrit Rietveld's Schroeder House (1924) in Utrecht had been, the house for Paul and Marianne Harnischmacher was Breuer's first constructed building and his homage to Le Corbusier's villa architecture (see p. 72). It was destroyed in the Second World War, but had been published in important journals soon after its completion in 1932. Breuer's own descriptive summary of the house and its structure is with his papers at Syracuse University.[1] It was prepared in his Zürich studio at 66 Seefeldstrasse and records the construction dates as July 20 to December 20, 1932, and the cost as 35,000 Reichmarks.

The house was sited on a steep slope, its full height visible from only the garden side (south), where the two upper stories were lifted above a setback ground floor by bush-hammered concrete pilotis. The upper stories and garden were reached from outside by two stairways parallel to the south facade. From the north, or street, side, the appearance of the house was that of a closed concrete mass, the entrance signaled by a projecting canopy. To the west of the entrance, a trapezoidal driveway led to the garage. Open air, a view, and a garden were priorities in the planning. The house was set, therefore, as far as possible into the northeast corner of the site, allowing a large area for the garden and having almost no windows on the north and the east.

On the first floor, the dining room extended to a rail-framed porch cantilevered to the south, the roof of which served as the floor of a balcony-terrace for the second story. The cantilever originally sheltered a boccie court at ground level, later closed in by the Harnischmachers with glass walls. A second porch, projecting to the west and also framed with slender metal rails, opened from the mid-level study.

The composition of the Harnischmacher House was of Constructivist complexity, with extensions in different directions, interplay of right angles and diagonals, split levels, interpenetrating open and closed volumes, and varying textures and materials. Henry-Russell Hitchcock saw the influences of Le Corbusier and J. J. P. Oud in the urbanity of the design, which he claimed was "definitely not of the school of Gropius but of a quite independent architectural personality who has evidently studied and profited from French and Dutch modern as much as from German."[2] Joachim Driller disagrees with this interpretation, regarding the house as a prime example of what he charac-

140. Garden side

terizes as Breuer's Bauhaus-based "additive, spatial box" manner of construction, derived from furniture design: the Harnischmacher House is "a large piece of furniture [*Grossmobel*]."[3]

In 1954, Breuer designed a second house for the Harnischmachers on property they owned next to the original site. On the remaining foundations of Harnischmacher House I and cellar, a new house was built by different owners after the Second World War with no relation to the appearance of Breuer's building.

ARCHIVAL: **SUL 10, 17; AAA Correspondence, Photos; BHA Photos.**
BIBLIOGRAPHIC: *Architectural Record*, May 1934, 426–29; *Werk*, July 1934, 197–201; *Architectural Review*, July 1935, 13–14; *L'Architecture d'aujourd'hui*, January 1935, 55–57; Hitchcock, "Marcel Breuer and the American Tradition," 11; Blake, *Marcel Breuer*, 44–47; Jones, ed., *Marcel Breuer*, 242; Breuer, *Sun and Shadow*, 26–27, 66–67; Wilk, *Furniture and Interiors*, 109–12; Droste and Ludewig, *Marcel Breuer Design*, 25; Driller, *Breuer Houses*, 22–34, 58–65, 260.

141
Wolf House,
Burgkunstadt, Germany, 1933 (NOT BUILT)

MARCEL BREUER, ARCHITECT

In August 1933, Walter Gropius, in Berlin, received a letter from Albin Wolf, a lawyer in Burgkunstadt, a small town in the Main River valley, describing a building site on which he hoped to build ("I must exercise extreme economy") a single-family house of five or six rooms.[4] Gropius recommended Breuer for the job: "Like many others today, he currently has very little employment because of the economic situation and would for this reason be prepared to undertake [the project]. . . . We are dealing here with a stroke of luck, which I urgently recommend you to take advantage of."[5] On September 10, Breuer sent Wolf a proposal for "the course of execution" and for the terms of agreement.[6] How far the project progressed beyond this, if at all, is not known, although it is likely that Breuer sketched a plan or an elevation if he had already made the calculations. The project demonstrates Gropius's continuing efforts to advance Breuer's career.

ARCHIVAL: **AAA Correspondence, with sketches.**
BIBLIOGRAPHIC: **Driller, "Frühwerk," 191.**

142
Weekend House on the Danube,
Budapest, Hungary, 1933–34 (NOT BUILT)

MARCEL BREUER, ARCHITECT

In late 1933 and 1934, Breuer was in practice in Budapest with Farkas Molnár and Jozsef Fischer. During the summer of 1934, he and Herbert Bayer took a kayak trip down the Danube,[7] and in a postcard to Alfred Roth written in September 1934, Breuer said that "I have a house to build here, small but on the Danube and therefore on columns."[8] Joachim Driller notes that during this time a reference to a small house Breuer was supposed to build in Budapest appears in correspondence between Walter Gropius and Sigfried Giedion.[9]

Nothing was known of this project before a photograph of drawings for a two-story house turned up in some of the material in the possession of Constance L. Breuer.[10] It reveals a perspective view, three ground plans (first and second floors and the colonnaded support structure), and a cross section from the south. On the verso is inscribed, but not in Breuer's handwriting, "weekend house Budapest 1933." The trapezoidal ground plan and curving glazed facade were small-scale reworkings of Breuer's design for the theater in Kharkov (1931) and forecast the main body of his house (1939) in Lincoln, Massachusetts, while the double-height living room was a later version of the small metal house, 1926 Type. Elevated on nine columns with a space for parking beneath, the house was entered by means of an exterior stair from ground to cantilevered balcony. On the open-plan first floor, one bedroom was separated from the living-dining space by a curving fixed partition, and a stair ran along the north wall. Above was one bedroom, a bathroom, and a balcony. The windowless bent wall (to make a right angle at the southeast) of the south facade, the straight front of the cantilevered porch against part of the first-floor curve, and the oblique angle of the balustraded upper-floor north balcony are idiosyncratic elements and impart a complexity and ambitiousness characteristic of Breuer's early work not only in architecture, but also in furniture. The location on the Danube and the river views must have determined the expansive glazing of the facade and the relatively large size of the first- and second-floor balconies.

ARCHIVAL: **Photo (CLB).**
BIBLIOGRAPHIC: **Driller, *Breuer Houses,* 259–60.**

143
Rose House (Shangri-La),
Lee-on-Solent, Hampshire, England, 1936–37

MARCEL BREUER AND F. R. S. YORKE, ARCHITECTS

Following his debut with the Harnischmacher House (1932), Breuer had to wait for four years and endure the dislocations of exile before he had another opportunity to build a private residence. In 1936 and 1937, after settling in London, with his English partner he built two. If the second, the Macnabb House, was primarily Breuer's design, at the Rose House, F. R. S. Yorke's contribution, at least to the plan, was greater. The clients, Mr. and Mrs. Hugh Rose, specifically requested that the plan be the same as Yorke's Torilla (1934–35), a house in Nast Hyde, Hertfordshire, designed before he and Breuer entered into partnership (but with additions by Yorke and Breuer in 1936). Drawings for Shangri-La are dated July 1936. There was a double-height living room with balcony, a "sleeping terrace" that was an extension of the bedroom, a swimming pool, a butler's quarters, and kennels. Driller's interview with draftsman T. Randall Evans indicates little or no involvement by Breuer in this house. Yet some of the detailing and materials reflect his presence: a handrail of copper tubing, reinforced-concrete walls against horizontal wood boarding painted white and tinted with rose, soffits of pale blue, and an exterior cantilevered stair outside the main bedroom leading from sleeping terrace to pool.

ARCHIVAL: **SUL 8, 10; RIBA Drawings Collection.**
BIBLIOGRAPHIC: ***Architects' Journal,*** January 6, 1938, 8–16; ***Architectural Review,*** January 1939, 33–34; Gould, ***Modern Houses in Britain,*** 32; Mills, "F. R. S. Yorke," 31–33; Driller, "Frühwerk," 116–19, 194–201; Powers, ***In the Line of Development,*** 8; Driller, ***Breuer Houses,*** 260.

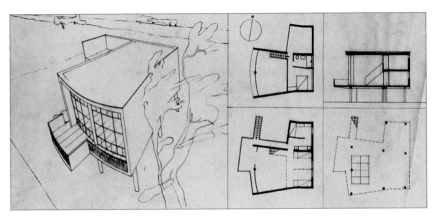

142. Perspective drawing, plans, and section

144

Macnabb House (Sea Lane House),
Angmering-on-Sea, Sussex, England, 1937

MARCEL BREUER AND F. R. S. YORKE, ARCHITECTS

The large seaside house at Angmering-on-Sea had a two-story wing with an open-plan living room, dining room, and a large, S-curved terrace, and an adjacent six-bedroom wing with a reinforced-concrete floor slab elevated on oval columns, also of reinforced concrete (see p. 86). In his study of modern houses in Britain, Jeremy Gould claimed that the Macnabb House demonstrated "one of the few functionally justified uses of pilotis in England allowing the maximum area of the small garden to be used" and making views of the sea possible from the bedrooms.[11] (One questions, however, a garden area sited beneath a mass of concrete and deprived of direct sunlight.)

The house was designed for James Macnabb in 1936; drawings are dated October and November; an agreement between owner and builder is dated February 4, 1937, indicating the approximate beginning date of construction.[12]

F. R. S. Yorke included the Macnabb House in the revised and enlarged second edition of *The Modern House in England*. It was thought by Henry-Russell Hitchcock to be more the work of Yorke than Breuer,[13] but the house has been studied with great attention by Joachim Driller, who also interviewed T. Randall Evans, draftsman in the Breuer & Yorke office when the house was built. Driller reports that according to Evans, Sea Lane House "is entirely Breuer's work."[14] Driller analyzed the drawings and isolated four planning stages; he identified the contributions—those of Breuer dominating—of each of the partners. In the absence of the war-destroyed Harnischmacher House I (1932), Driller regards the Macnabb House as the "missing link" between Breuer's European and American work.[15]

ARCHIVAL: **SUL 8, 10, 39, 42; AAA Photos; RIBA Drawings Collection.**

BIBLIOGRAPHIC: *Architects' Journal*, January 6, 1938, 8–16; *Architectural Review*, January 1939, 29–31; Hitchcock, "Marcel Breuer and the American Tradition," 15; Yorke, *The Modern House in England*, 88–89; Gould, *Modern Houses in Britain*, 20; Mills, "F. R. S. Yorke," 31–33; William J. R. Curtis, *Modern Architecture Since 1900*, 3d ed., rev. and expanded (Upper Saddle River, N.J.: Prentice-Hall, 1996), 335; Driller, *Breuer Houses*, 90–97, 260.

145

Two Houses for Masters, Eton College,
Willowbrook, Buckinghamshire, England, 1938

MARCEL BREUER AND F. R. S. YORKE, ARCHITECTS

It is generally agreed that F. R. S. Yorke received the assignment and started the design for two-story twin houses on adjoining sites for masters at Eton College around 1935, before his partnership with Breuer. Three undated drawings in the Prints and Drawings Collection at RIBA, however, are signed by both architects. The buildings were completed after Breuer left England for the United States. Even with a modest budget, the program provided many rooms, and a paved terrace covered by a wooden pergola reached from the living room through a tall sliding window. Lining the upstairs corridor with closets instead of placing them in the bedrooms is a Breuer design device.[16] Joachim Driller has identified two planning stages—the elimination or reduction of some features in the second stage was an effort to reduce costs—and attributes to Breuer's intervention the bringing of the houses to a more coherent conclusion than was evident in the earlier stage.[17]

ARCHIVAL: **SUL 8; RIBA Drawings Collection.**

BIBLIOGRAPHIC: *Architectural Review*, January 1939, 32–33; *Architect and Building News*, February 3, 1939, 168–69; Yorke, *The Modern House in England*, 54–55; Gould, *Modern Houses in Britain*, 32; Mills, "F. R. S. Yorke," 33; Driller, *Breuer Houses*, 260.

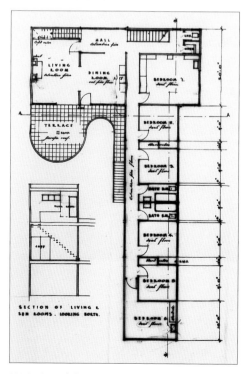

144. Section and plan

SINGLE-FAMILY HOUSES, 1937–41 (GROPIUS-BREUER PARTNERSHIP)

146. Garden facade, with sunshade

146
Gropius House,
Lincoln, Massachusetts, 1937–38

WALTER GROPIUS AND MARCEL BREUER, ARCHITECTS

The Gropius House, the first one built in the Woods End colony in Lincoln, Massachusetts, sponsored by Helen Storrow,[1] has been widely published and long extolled as a modern classic. Restored in 1988 for its fiftieth birthday, it is in the care of the Society for the Preservation of New England Antiquities and is open to the public.

Joachim Driller identified in the Gropius Archive in Cambridge, Massachusetts, a sketch for an L-shaped ground plan that may represent Gropius's initial layout of the house, later changed (possibly by Breuer) to a block format.[2] Breuer returned to Europe during November and December 1937 and was away when the house was designed. Leonard Currie, working in the Gropius-Breuer office at the time, remembers that after Breuer came back he understandably (as Gropius was both client and architect) "kept away from it." But he says that one element—the garden facade sunshade—was Breuer's contribution.[3] Driller came to the same conclusion through his analysis of the design history of the house.[4] The exterior vertical cladding also points to an intervention by Breuer. Of attempts to recognize Breuer's hand in the house, Driller's is the most convincing, with references to the past work and design strategies of each of the architects. That Breuer was, in general, loathe to raise sensitive and contestable authorship issues about joint projects explains his silence about any role in this historic building.

ARCHIVAL: See Nerdinger, *Walter Gropius*, 194, and *Walter Gropius Archive* 3:33–68.
BIBLIOGRAPHIC: Nerdinger, *Walter Gropius*, 194, and *Walter Gropius Archive* 3:33–68; Driller, "Frühwerk," 125–59, 201–5, and *Breuer Houses*, 104–17, 260.

147b. View from the sea wall

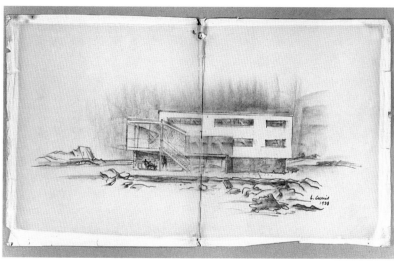

147a. Sketch of Breuer's design by Leonard Currie

147
Hagerty House,
Cohasset, Massachusetts, 1938

WALTER GROPIUS AND MARCEL BREUER, ARCHITECTS

The job began with an enthusiastic letter to Gropius from John Hagerty,[5] who had been won over to modern architecture as a Harvard undergraduate (class of 1932) and heard Gropius speak at the Architectural Club in Boston soon after his arrival in the United States. At first, Hagerty wanted a summer house for his mother, Josephine Hagerty (she became the official client) and his two brothers. The family soon decided, however, that it should be a full-time residence. The program called for a five-bedroom house with a three-car garage on an oceanfront site on Atlantic Avenue in Cohasset, Massachusetts, remembered by Leonard Currie as "limited and strange—rather bare and bleak as the house was on the beach and the high seas swept up to and under it."[6] Although fervent and optimistic about the project at the start, the Hagertys are revealed in the correspondence as naive about modern architecture in general and, as many clients were, about processes and costs involved in building a house. Telling Gropius in his initial letter that "this is my first venture in building," Hagerty, imagining a modest program and a small budget, envisioned hollow tile and cement as the structural materials and suggested as builder a contracting company "that builds filling stations—I imagine they'd be the most inexpensive."[7]

The drawings were made by Currie; a model was built, and construction of the house began in May 1938 and was completed by December, escaping catastrophe when the historic hurricane of 1938 passed west of Boston on September 21 (see p. 104). The house became one of the classic modern houses of 1930s America, but the relations between client and architects, and the construction process, during which many revisions were made, were a disaster. The undertaking ended with a nineteen-page accusation against the architects by Josephine Hagerty, a nineteen-page defense by Breuer, and a letter to Gropius and Breuer from Josephine Hagerty's lawyers. In 1949, John Hagerty wrote a retrospective article for *Interior Design and Decoration* that in intent was humorous and self-mocking, but in effect excoriated the design, the materials, the construction, modern architecture ("I began to wonder if modern architecture were a subversive foreign plot"), and the (unnamed) architects.[8] He also explained that the family had decided to sell but had a change of mind and made major revisions, so that "[we now have] a weather-proof, ship shape *naturalized American* home [emphasis added]."

Built of steel and wood frame, the Hagerty House is a three-level box with two residential stories above a tall fieldstone foundation that on one side contained garage and service spaces, and on the other a setback outdoor terrace of concrete. Above the foundation, the house is abutted on the south by a projecting porch with open terrace above, irregular in shape and supported by lally columns. A light, openwork stair with no stringers and no risers connects the porch to the rocky beach and runs parallel to the long south facade. Two of the garden walls were to be of glass brick until a revision in the design called for stone. The stone came from the site, its natural roughness brought under control in a manner that recalls Breuer's stonework strategy at the Gane Pavilion two years earlier. Galvanized pipe, nautical by analogy, was used for the railings on porch and terrace and for the exterior stair.

On the question of authorship of the design, there is ambiguity. In his article, Hagerty appears to say that the general format had been set by Gropius, and then Breuer entered the picture: "About this time the architect was joined by an associate who had a mind of his own and merely mumbled and smiled when objections came up."[9] Still, all the drawings at Syracuse University carry the legend "Hagerty House, Cohasset, Massachusetts, Breuer." The same identifying device is found on the drawings made in 1938 for the Margolius House,[10] indicating that when Breuer wanted to be certain that design credit accrued to him he saw to it that his name, in addition to the partnership stamp, appeared on the drawings. Also, on the verso of a photograph used in a local newspaper on July 29, 1938, now in the Archives of American Art, there is the following inscription: "modernistic house now under construction in Cohasset. Arch. Marcel Breuer, Harv. Sch. of Arch." It was Breuer, furthermore, who kept the original drawings in his possession.

Currie, recalling the project in 1995, wrote that "I am quite defensive about the Hagerty House. I thought Lajkó's design was brilliant in spite of some differences during construction with John Hagerty and his mother."[11] Currie's recollections are particularly relevant because he still had his original "quick litho-crayon" sketches. When he referred to "Lajkó's design," he meant a change devised by Breuer from what had been Gropius's first formulation, whereby a projecting stair tower adjacent to the garage and containing the entrance and upper spaces was eliminated and its function coalesced into the volume of the garage block. The result is a more coherent composition,

Corbusian rather than Cubistic, relating to the long facade of the Harnischmacher House (1932) and its source in the villa at Garches. In a sketch by Currie of the near-final appearance of the house, the porch has one and not two levels, the wall plane immediately to the east is glazed, and the ground-level terrace is framed by projecting stone. Although Gropius probably introduced a first concept to the Hagertys, the final design was Breuer's.

Breuer had been in the United States for only three months when the job came into the office; construction began nine months later. It was his first experience with building processes in America apart from his marginal involvement with the Gropius House (in construction at the same time), and it became his first post-Europe house. Many design features and details were new to the contractors. It was the first time that plate-glass manufacturers in Boston had to make and install glass panels and sliding doors of that size and format, and the first time that doors of *glass* had to be bolted against the force of the Atlantic winds. At the same time, Gropius and Breuer had no idea about the fierce weather that Atlantic coast houses had to be protected against in terms of material and design. The clients complained, apparently with justification, about the constant problem of the wind, with fixtures and glass panels rattling in their frames and doors blowing open. Unable to see anything but the sky when seated in the dining room or the second-floor study, they also complained justifiably about the height of the windows above the floor.

After remaining unoccupied for two years, the Hagerty House was sold in 1960. The new owners intended to bring it back to the original (Breuer sent them blueprints of the working drawings),[12] and were happy to find in it nine of the original Breuer chairs.

ARCHIVAL: **SUL 6, 15, 18, 25; AAA Correspondence, Photos; Drawings (Leonard Currie); HUL (GSD) Vertical File for specifications; see Nerdinger,** *Walter Gropius Archive* **3:78–85.**

BIBLIOGRAPHIC: *Architectural Review,* **November 1939, 189–90;** *Architectural Forum,* **December 1939, 455–59, and April 1940, 295–303; John Hagerty, "From the Rock Ribb'd Shores,"** *Interior Design and Decoration,* **August 1949, 54–61; Ford and Ford,** *Modern House in America,* **44–45; Blake,** *Marcel Breuer,* **63–64; Jones, ed.,** *Marcel Breuer,* **245; Nerdinger,** *Walter Gropius,* **270, and** *Walter Gropius Archive* **3:78–85; Driller,** *Breuer Houses,* **118–23, 260.**

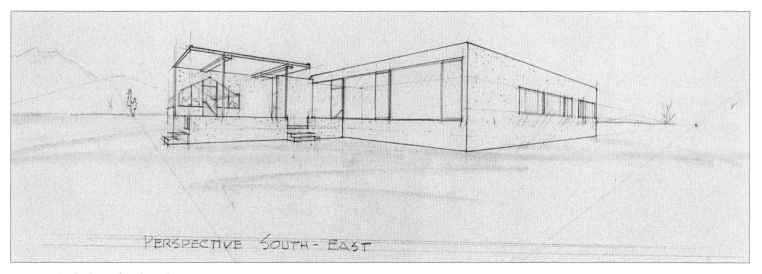

148. Perspective sketch, view from the southeast

148
Margolius House,
Palm Springs, California, 1938–39 (NOT BUILT)

WALTER GROPIUS AND MARCEL BREUER, ARCHITECTS

In the summer of 1938, Breuer was asked by Hilde Margolius if he would design "a small modern home in Palm Springs, California [where] the restrictions call for a one story house, modern Spanish exterior."[13] The "restrictions" referred to the Spanish Colonial image desired by Las Palmas Estates, the development community in which the house was to be built. "I would be delighted to do it," he responded, "and I would especially like to do a one story house. . . . I only hope that the idea of a 'Spanish exterior' isn't taken too seriously by you. I much prefer a plan independent of any style except my own feeling about modern aesthetic. A one story modern house with good relations to the garden, possibly with a patio, would look quite naturally rather Spanish even if it is not designed in the Spanish style."[14] By the end of August, there was a signed agreement and Breuer sketched a ground plan and worked out preliminary dimensions (see p. 110). Although the house was modest in size, program, and budget, he provided long stretches of open interior space, diagonal sight lines, a sliding skylight, movable partitions, and, in response to the benevolent environment of the southern California desert, a roof deck.

It was to Breuer that the invitation to design the house was directed. He consulted Gropius about the terms of agreement with the supervising architect, but once the project was launched the responsibility for its design and execution was completely in his hands. Perspective sketches have "Margolius Residence Breuer" penciled in the corner; questions for Breuer and his answers and notes are written over many sheets of drawings. All the correspondence flows exclusively among Breuer, the client, and John Porter Clark, a Palm Springs architect possibly recommended by Richard Neutra,[15] who was to supervise the construction.

Perspective sketches and working drawings were executed and signed by Leonard Currie. In November 1938, Breuer sent the clients scale drawings and perspective sketches; working drawings and specifications followed. On paper at least, the project developed steadily, but within six months, as the consequence of a personal crisis in the lives of David and Hilde Margolius, the project was aborted.[16]

Breuer designed a longitudinal structure with the major axis stretching north-south inside the principal living block, from which two asymmetrical wings were extended. Living spaces and a patio made up the main block; the south arm had a terrace-loggia, greenhouse, and workshop with a roof sleeping deck; in the north wing were the laundry with walled drying yard, servants' space, and garage. The main portal (a clear-glass door set into a glass curtain) was located in a corner, nested within an alcove and reached by a ramp. The entrance led to a granite-paved heated patio, roofed with a sliding glass skylight. Breuer's interpretation of this patio as a transitional courtyard between public path and living space is one of the ways in which he showed regard for the original injunction to design a "Spanish" house. By calling for traditional accessories of courtyard architecture found in Latin countries—plants, water, paving stone, light, and open air—he suggested simultaneously a reception atrium, an indoor garden, and an initial architectural encounter with the house.

The south wing was an elevated terrace reached by steps from the garden and bordered by a parapet wall with four steel-pipe columns painted white and partly sheltered by the roof they supported. The device of a terrace overspread by a projecting roof sustained by colonettes in a single-story house originated in the House for a Sportsman (1931) and within a decade would evolve into the great pierced cantilever above the dining-room terrace of the Robinson House (1947–48). To merge or separate the living and dining areas, Breuer contrived a floor-to-ceiling revolving partition of painted plywood, slightly curved, that may have been a unique design feature in American houses of the period, but came out of his experience with modern interiors in Europe of the late 1920s and early 1930s. They included the House for a Sportsman, where he divided such a space with a folding partition; the monumental curved wall of ebony veneer designed by Mies to define the space for dining in the Tugendhat House; and the houses that Berthold Lubetkin built in 1936 at Whipsnade in which the dining space was defined by a parabolic screen. Lubetkin's source, as well as everyone else's, was probably the curved screen wall of the dining room in Le Corbusier's villa at Garches.

Possibly the most alluring features of the Margolius House plan were to be found in the south-terrace complex, for which Breuer designed a workshop and a greenhouse, the glazed facade of which he brought forward to articulate the west wall so the verdant interior of the greenhouse would be part of the terrace. Next to the greenhouse was a workshop lighted by a glazed clerestory; above the shop and reached by an external stair was the roof deck. When the bids came in too high, Breuer redesigned the project, eliminating everything in the south wing except the colonnaded terrace, and protected the now-exposed west with a vertical grill of cypress. He relocated the roof deck above the kitchen.

The structure was to be wood frame above a concrete foundation, and the specifications called for surfaces to be finished outside and inside with white stucco. A small idiosyncratic detail conforms to the requirement for a Spanish look: he shaped the exterior margins and corners not as sharply bent right angles, but as slightly softened, barely rounded edges that send out faint resonances of "adobe" construction. That his solution was successful and that the house would have been unique, but acceptable in Las Palmas Estates, is documented by Clark's letter of December 5, 1938: "I have submitted your excellent design for the Margolius House and obtained approval from the architectural jury. . . . I am very happy to have the plans passed by a conservative jury in a tract consisting solely of traditional houses."[17]

ARCHIVAL: **SUL 5, 26, 29, Drawings.**

BIBLIOGRAPHIC: **Hyman, "A Marcel Breuer House Project of 1938–1939,"** *Syracuse University Library Associates Courier* 27 (1992): 55–84; Driller, *Breuer Houses*, 260–61.

149a. View from the southwest

149
Breuer House,
Lincoln, Massachusetts, 1939

WALTER GROPIUS AND MARCEL BREUER, ARCHITECTS

"Mrs. Storrow was kind enough to offer me the opportunity of build-ing a house for myself in Lincoln with the same conditions under which you built the one for Gropius," Breuer wrote to Helen Storrow's lawyer on November 15, 1938.[18] He began the sketches in the same month; working drawings and finished plans were made by "the [Harvard] boys" in the office—principally Eliot Noyes and Robert Woods Kennedy, who oversaw the construction. In December, Breuer sent Storrow preliminary plans, elevations, and perspectives for what he called his "studio-house." A contract with the builder—Custance Brothers, of Lexington, Massachusetts—was dated February 21, 1939; work began immediately, and Breuer moved in around June 22 (see pp.

92, 104). He was very satisfied with the work and on November 17, 1939, wrote to Howard Custance: "My house in Lincoln which you built gives me a great deal of pleasure. . . . I only hope to be in a posi-tion in the future to have you as my builder many times."[19] By January 1940, various problems had set in, however: the fixed glass window panels let in rainwater, and there was trouble with the heating system. A variance was applied for and granted for the erection of the "one-car garage" with storage space. A Breuer invention, the garage or carport was a trapezoid with walls that did not reach the ground so that "the snow would blow in and blow out again"—a design feature he would reuse in later houses.

The total cost of the house was $11,364.10, and the value of the land was $2,500. Until July 1940, Breuer paid $93 a month rent without a lease, based on 10 percent of Storrow's expenses for construction, landscaping, fees, and such. On July 15, 1940, Storrow's lawyer sent Breuer a three-year lease at an annual rental of $1,128 with an option to purchase for $13,850.

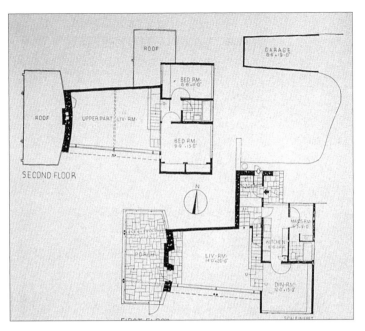

149b. Plans

"The house I have planned for myself has quite a large living room, two bedrooms [separated by a bathroom], kitchen, dining room, a room for storage and heating, and the porch. It has about 30,000 cubic feet," Breuer wrote to Storrow soon after he began the rough sketches; he described it as "simple."[20] The porch, which was "large enough for a ping-pong table," was on the west; to the east was the two-story wing with the bedrooms and bath; the kitchen was to the north, with the dining room–studio to the south. "The large window of the studio is protected from the summer sun by the cantilever part of the roof," he wrote. It was the first time he would be living in a semi-rural setting, and he wanted the white, wood-frame house "to be placed as much to the west as possible so that the porch is very near (or amidst) the trees." He did not intend the porch to be used in the winter, when "the door to it is covered up so as to make an uninterrupted wall around the fireplace."

The living room–study was high-ceilinged, formed on a trapezoidal ground plan like that of the Gane Pavilion and raised above the level of the dining room (prefiguring the split-level planning of the 1940s). After 1940, a stupendous mobile by Alexander Calder, a wedding gift from the artist to the Breuers, hung from the ceiling. Stairs led from the living room to the mezzanine bedrooms above, one of which opened directly to the living room. The fireplace wall curved (as it did at Gane's) and was made of fieldstone; all the rooms had Breuer-designed built-in plywood casework. Two sets of paired columns of wood were anchored in the low stone wall of the screened porch and supported the porch roof beams; another pair of columns stood in front of the south-facing window of the living room to support the cantilevered roof.

From the beginning, Breuer envisioned an additional wing, recognizing the space limitations of his "bachelor house." To the person who owned the house in 1967, Breuer wrote: "Originally I planned the house with a later addition. The one-car carport should have been replaced with a two-car carport and on top of this structure there was a good size bedroom and bathroom projected. Access to this room was by means of a stair rising from the inside of the present entrance to the right of the entrance door."[21] Breuer married Constance Crocker Leighton in March 1940; in August, Custance Brothers submitted to him a cost estimate for building an addition to "your house in Lincoln according to plans submitted by you."[22] Financially pressed at this time, Breuer did not proceed with the expansion—nor did he eventually buy his house from Storrow, as the other renters on Woods End Road did, a decision he later regretted.[23]

ARCHIVAL: SUL 6–9, 18, 41, 47; AAA Correspondence, Photos; BHA Photos; see Nerdinger, *Walter Gropius Archive* 3:72–77.

BIBLIOGRAPHIC: *Architectural Forum*, July 1939, 455–59, and December 1939, 455–59; *Nuestra arquitectura*, November 1947, 169–73; *L'Architecture d'aujourd'hui*, July 1948, 10–11; Ford and Ford, *Modern House in America*, 46–48; Blake, *Marcel Breuer*, 66–68; Jones, ed., *Marcel Breuer*, 254; Breuer, *Sun and Shadow*, 84, 129, 135; Nerdinger, *Walter Gropius*, 194, and *Walter Gropius Archive* 3:72–77; Driller, *Breuer Houses*, 124–30, 261.

150
Ford House,
Lincoln, Massachusetts, 1939

WALTER GROPIUS AND MARCEL BREUER, ARCHITECTS

The third Gropius-Breuer house in Lincoln, Massachusetts, was built for Harvard professor James Ford and Katherine Morrow Ford: a tall shallow box with a stair tower and a massive stone chimney tower (for two fireplaces) added to the narrow end, which forms the living-room wall on the first floor and the study wall on the second. Comprising two stories and a basement, the house is wood frame on a foundation of concrete blocks. A glass-walled dining room projects from the main block to the south—the entrance side—onto a walled flagstone terrace overhung by an open-slatted canopy. Extending from the block on the north is the stair tower, which on the second floor opened to a corridor linking two bedrooms and a study. A sunscreen of redwood boards set into brackets runs the full length of the second story, shading the windows of bedroom and study. Even though the Ford House has an affinity to the Hagerty House, and Driller sees evidence of Breuer's methods of composition, Breuer claimed not to have participated in its design.

ARCHIVAL: SUL 15; AAA Photos; see Nerdinger, *Walter Gropius Archive* 3:269–87.
BIBLIOGRAPHIC: *House Beautiful*, December 1939, 41–43; *Architectural Record*, March 1940, 108–11; Hitchcock and Drexler, eds., *Built in USA*, 38–39; Ford and Ford, *Modern House in America*, 49–51; Blake, *Marcel Breuer*, 65; Nerdinger, *Walter Gropius*, 271, and *Walter Gropius Archive* 3:269–87; Driller, "Frühwerk," 169–71, 217, and *Breuer Houses*, 261.

151
Fischer House and Studio,
New Hope, Pennsylvania, 1939

Guest Cottage, 1946–47

WALTER GROPIUS AND MARCEL BREUER, ARCHITECTS

The Fischers knew Breuer at the Bauhaus, where Margrit (Grit) was a sculptor and Edward L., one of the few Americans there, was a graphic artist. Fischer took a leave of absence from his job in the Berlin office of an American advertising agency to study at the school.[24] When the couple were planning their New Hope, Pennsylvania, house in 1938 and 1939, Fischer was working in New York. They visited and admired the Hagerty House and Breuer's house in Lincoln. The clients refused to allow photographs or publication of their house, or unknown visitors to see it. This angered Breuer, who, following some unpleasant exchanges, wrote to Fischer that "I certainly hope you will leave me the

right to publish my work according to my judgement"[25] and then again, exasperated, "we will forget about the photographing of your house altogether."[26] The clients held firm, refusing to permit *Architectural Record* to publish an article, and, consequently, before the publication of Joachim Driller's *Breuer Houses* the Fischer House was rarely mentioned in Breuer literature.

Preliminary sketches were prepared in February 1939, followed in March by revisions, working drawings, and specifications. Drawings by Eliot Noyes for a studio were made in April and revised in June. Gropius and Breuer received their registration to practice architecture in Pennsylvania on August 4, 1939; the house was completed in October or November. Gropius had little to do with it.

A two-story house of wood-frame construction with vertical sheathing and some stone wall slabs, it is built on a cement-block foundation. The upper story—a long rectangular block—is cantilevered above a shorter and wider block, and is supported by stone slabs and slender columns to form the entrance on the narrow side and create a roof terrace on the long flank. An independent wood-frame sculpture studio was built about 20 feet from the house, but was connected to it visually with a free-standing wall.

The Fischers were demanding clients; angry letters flew between them and Breuer during the course of design and construction. The house, nevertheless, proved to be one of the finest of the early works and the clients were satisfied; a guest cottage, which Driller has recognized as a mirror image of the Martine House, was completed around March 1947. Breuer was practicing in New York City by this time, and Harry Seidler, working in the New York office, made the drawings for the cottage.

ARCHIVAL: SUL 6, 15, 16, 18, 31, 42, 54, Drawings; AAA Correspondence.
BIBLIOGRAPHIC: Blake, *Marcel Breuer*, 63; Driller, "Frühwerk," 239–43, 254, and *Breuer Houses*, 261, 262–63.

151. View from the south

152
Frank House,
Pittsburgh, Pennsylvania, 1939–40

WALTER GROPIUS AND MARCEL BREUER, ARCHITECTS

The clients were Robert J. Frank, an engineer who oversaw all aspects of the design and construction, and his wife, Cecelia K. Frank; they were close friends of the Kaufmann department-store family, for whom Frank Lloyd Wright had just built Fallingwater. Clearly the Frank House was commissioned as something of a counterpart to Fallingwater, with the Franks choosing Gropius (probably at the suggestion of Edgar Kaufmann, Jr.) because he was the premier European modernist in America and therefore an appropriate "analogue" to the American Wright. In this way, they would not appear to be imitating their friends at Bear Run, Pennsylvania. That Gropius and Breuer understood this motivation is obvious in parallels between the two residences in terms of spaciousness, comfort, and luxury to a degree that neither of the architects, in their work jointly or independently, had experienced before.

Working drawings were prepared in April 1939; construction was begun in September, and the house was completed (under the supervision of a local architectural firm) in the summer of 1940. David H. Wright, in his thesis on Gropius, stated that "this enormous house was designed primarily by Breuer."[27] Gropius, who read the thesis, did not contradict the assignment of credit, but he claimed as his contribution Wright's observation that "one device in the stone facing is particularly interesting: over the steel frame the stone is half as thick as are the panels between, thus subtly expressing the structure and at the same time relieving the smooth surface."[28] However, the working arrangement of the two partners on this job was recalled by Leonard Currie, who did the drawings and remembers that it was primarily Gropius's design.[29] The boxy nature of the house—a long rectangle on a sloping site—is relieved by the curved staircase wall of glass brick that Currie remembers as Breuer's contribution. The luxurious requirements of the program were numerous: full air-conditioning well before it became a staple of residential architecture; an elevator; a children's dining room; nine bathrooms; plentiful subsidiary spaces for recreation and service; a multitude of rooms for living, sleeping, studying, and entertaining on a grand scale; and landscaped gardens with pools, terraces, pergolas, and trellises.

The interior decoration was Breuer's responsibility entirely. Specifications for furniture and accessories—more extensive and elaborate than anything Breuer was ever to do—were set out in a thirteen-page typed document. Christopher Wilk says that "virtually all the objects in the house—chairs and tables, wall units, and lighting fixtures, even a small radio and piano—were specially designed for the commission."[30] Breuer enlisted Anni Albers to design some of the fabrics; Edgar J. Kaufmann, Jr., arranged for many fabrics and accessories to be supplied by the Kaufmann Department Store and for the manufacture of Breuer's furniture designs.

The house has received relatively little attention in the history of American modern residential architecture, even in studies of Gropius-Breuer architecture, because from the beginning the clients were hypersensitive about privacy. It had, furthermore, an unhappy association for the architects with regard to student opinion at Harvard, where the house was singled out for its glamour and its luxurious excesses and used as an example of the betrayal of the professed principles of economy and social idealism—especially with regard to housing—of European modernism.[31]

The Frank House was published, with many of Ezra Stoller's photographs and a plan, as "A House in Pittsburgh, Pa.," in the March 1941 issue of *Architectural Forum*, where it was described as the "largest residence ever built in the International Style." Breuer objected to the article: "They used intentionally the term 'International Style' which was never used by us, and which I am quite certain, is misleading. It is misleading as 'international' and it is misleading as 'style' and I would appreciate it very much if you would call our architecture simply 'modern' or 'contemporary.' These are not very definite terms but we have no better ones."[32]

In *Pittsburgh: An Urban Portrait*, Franklin Toker understands the Frank House in the tradition of the great nineteenth-century American mansions built in that area of the city by the great steel millionaires: "It functions in exactly the same mode as the old mansions on Woodland, particularly the Mellon House, with its indoor swimming pool, vestibule, salon, servants' quarters, and even a porte-cochere."[33] Toker also recounts that in controlling the construction of his house, engineer Frank "insisted that the house be welded—almost all previous steel buildings had been riveted—out of consideration for the tranquility of his neighbors."

In 1961, the clients, wishing to have an addition to the house, wrote to Gropius, who wrote to Breuer, but each claimed that he had no time to undertake it.

ARCHIVAL: **SUL 9, 18, 33; AAA Correspondence, Photos; see Nerdinger,** *Walter Gropius Archive* **3:131–268.**

BIBLIOGRAPHIC: *Architectural Forum*, March 1941, 160–70; Blake, *Marcel Breuer*, 74–75; Wilk, *Furniture and Interiors*, 151–56; Nerdinger, *Walter Gropius*, 272–73, and *Walter Gropius Archive* 3:131–268; Toker, *Pittsburgh*, 256–57; Driller, *Breuer Houses*, 132–37, 261.

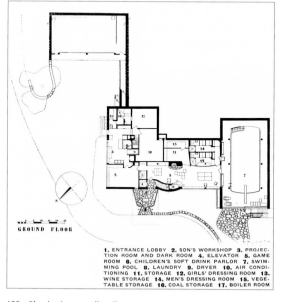

GROUND FLOOR

1. ENTRANCE LOBBY 2. SON'S WORKSHOP 3. PROJECTION ROOM AND DARK ROOM 4. ELEVATOR 5. GAME ROOM 6. CHILDREN'S SOFT DRINK PARLOR 7. SWIMMING POOL 8. LAUNDRY 9. DRYER 10. AIR CONDITIONING 11. STORAGE 12. GIRLS' DRESSING ROOM 13. WINE STORAGE 14. MEN'S DRESSING ROOM 15. VEGETABLE STORAGE 16. COAL STORAGE 17. BOILER ROOM

152a. Plan (staircase wall at 6)

152b. Staircase wall at night

153a. West side

153
Chamberlain Cottage,
Wayland, Massachusetts, 1940–41

WALTER GROPIUS AND MARCEL BREUER, ARCHITECTS

Mr. and Mrs. Henry G. Chamberlain of Cambridge, Massachusetts, liked Breuer's house in Lincoln and, honoring their request, he incorporated some of its features into the year-round weekend retreat that he designed for them on 20 acres of wooded land in Wayland, Massachusetts, not far from Lincoln (see p. 28). "We finally decided that we would try to raise another thousand dollars for a porch similar to yours," Mrs. Chamberlain wrote to Breuer.[34] Their appreciation of the Lincoln house is what brought the job directly to Breuer; the correspondence makes clear that the responsibility for the house from design to completion of construction was his. The contract was dated November 12, 1940, and construction began almost immediately. The program called for a small, inexpensive, and informal "camp"; the Chamberlains called it their "shoestring house," and it is referred to more often as a cottage than as a house. They requested a combined living and dining space that could also accommodate a sleep-in guest, a bedroom, shelves for 500 to 1,000 books, a desk, and storage space for a 16-foot boat. The contour of the boat, stored in the basement, is drawn on the ground plan like a Pharaonic ship in its own sepulchral chamber. The basement was reached from the outside by a door in the stone foundation wall flanked by extending stone walls. The flat roof was intended as a sun-bathing terrace.

One of Breuer's most successful and admired designs—its profile view, in the opinion of this author and others, a source for Mies van der Rohe's Farnsworth House (1949–51) in Plano, Illinois[35]—the Chamberlain Cottage became an instant success in the judgment of the knowledgeable public and for the clients. It was completed in March 1941, and on April 24, Mrs. Chamberlain wrote to Breuer that "we like the house more and more as we continue to use it. We are however pestered by sightseers. Twenty-nine strangers came on Easter Sunday from Harvard entirely disrupting our egg hunt and Easter celebration."[36]

A flat-roofed, single-story, box-like wooden structure cantilevered beyond a low foundation wall of stone and abutted by the perpendicular off-center volume of a large screened porch to the north, the Chamberlain Cottage was organized around a free-standing stone fireplace (appearing for the first time in Breuer's work) in the main living section. The kitchen, with its built-in cabinets, opens to the living room on one side and, on the other, to the porch. Elevated above the ground, but linked to it by a ramp, the porch was articulated on its sides by the twin columns of Breuer's Lincoln house used here, as there, to support the roof beams. On the south facade, opposite the porch, the principal entrance was reached by way of a short diagonal stair and parapet of distinctive profile added to the house block. The stair, built without foundation, is hung on the cantilevered landing joists.

While the house was praised for its appearance and good planning, it was the ingenuity of its structure—based on Breuer's invention for the construction of his ski lodge in Ober-Gurgl and adapted for American wood-frame construction—that brought it special acclaim. Breuer described it in a letter to F. R. S. Yorke in March 1943:

The traditional American frame construction is considered in this, as in most of my others, as having truss-like walls, which can be cantilevered or built over large openings without beams. Very similar to reinforced concrete walls. On this principle the west end of this cottage is cantilevered 8 feet over the foundation without heavy beams—only by means of the slab-like stiffness of the walls.[37]

Not fully certain that the engineering would be successful, Breuer asked the builder to make an exact measurement between a fixed point on the ground and the bottom of the west wall before and after the removal of the temporary supports: "What I would like now is to find out whether the cantilevered part has bent down at all and how much."[38]

Breuer's notion of approximating reinforced concrete in wood, where the walls become rigid slabs (instead of covered frames) and act as trusses, was applied also to the designing of wide openings for windows without increasing the weight and size of the lintels or without using metal or brick. He used it, too, for the construction of the suspended stair, which he described to Yorke as "built without foundation, hanging on the cantilevered landing joists and the parapet wall, made of three layers of cross-wise boarding."[39] The walls were strengthened by diagonally placed wood boarding—Douglas Fir was the material for both interior and exterior finish. As a harmonious contrast to the wood of the walls and the stone of the fireplace, the ceiling was of plywood panels painted white.

By the spring of 1941, troubles with a leaky roof had set in, but because they loved the house the Chamberlains complained good-naturedly. The plywood ceiling had begun to disintegrate before December 1941; Breuer and the builder attributed it to the absorption of moisture by the insulation material (rockwool): "The insulation technique of frame construction is a fairly new one, and it may be that we still have to collect experiences in order to avoid any risk."[40] The solution was to provide the space between the roof joints with outside ventilation. (Breuer would be plagued by drainage problems connected to flat-roof construction so often that finally, in the late 1950s, declaring to Herbert Beckhard, "No more flat roofs," he began to pitch the roofs slightly.[41])

ARCHIVAL: **SUL 6, 9, 15, 18, 21, 23, 33, 42, 45, 50, 54, Sketches; AAA Photos; see Nerdinger, *Walter Gropius Archive* 3:668–70.**

BIBLIOGRAPHIC: ***Architectural Forum**, November 1942, 76–77; *House & Garden*, June 1945, 62; *L'Architecture d'aujourd'hui*, July 1948, 6–7; Hitchcock and Drexler, eds., *Built in USA*, 36–37; Yorke, *Modern House*, 2d ed., 108–9; Blake, *Marcel Breuer*, 71–72, 76–77; Jones, ed., *Marcel Breuer*, 246; Nerdinger, *Walter Gropius*, 272, and *Walter Gropius Archive* 3:668–70; Driller, *Breuer Houses*, 138–43, 261.*

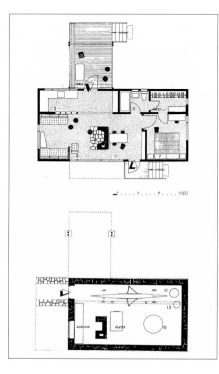

153b. Plans

154
Weizenblatt House,
Asheville, North Carolina, 1940–41

WALTER GROPIUS AND MARCEL BREUER, ARCHITECTS

For a wooded site in Asheville, North Carolina, Dr. Sprinza Weizenblatt commissioned a duplex residence made up of two apartments, each with a separate entrance; she planned to occupy the upper floor and rent the lower one. The proximity of Asheville to Black Mountain College may have led her to Gropius and Breuer, who were planning the new Black Mountain campus at this time. Construction was under way by November 1940, and the house was completed by May 1941. As in the Chamberlain House, the wood-frame construction system—windowed walls of wood "hung" between stone walls—had its source in the system that Breuer had developed for the resort in Ober-Gurgl. (Referring to the construction of the Weizenblatt House in February 1945, Breuer wrote: "I gave Konrad [Wachsmann] a model photo of a ski hotel in Obergurgl showing the same principle of construction."[42]) It was also the preponderance of stone wall slabs in the composition that allied this design to the Tyrolean prototype. There were, however, some supporting members of steel in the house. For each of the apartments, the program called for two bedrooms, a combined living room and dining room, a study, a maid's room, and a terrace (below) and balcony (above). Access to the apartments was by way of an independent stair tower outside the edge of the main volume, but connected to it by an open louvered wall.

The supervising architect was Anthony Lord, of Asheville. In Cambridge, Gropius looked at and initialed some of the correspondence, but appears to have had little to do with the design or construction. In the post-partnership agreement between Gropius and Breuer, the Weizenblatt House was to be known as Breuer's.

Unusual in appearance because of the requirement for two full apartments with the same layout vertically stacked, the house is a version of some of the tall-box white villas designed by Le Corbusier in the 1920s, at Weissenhof and elsewhere, but here translated into the American vernacular materials of fieldstone and redwood and rotated to form intersecting volumes. The roof extended beyond the surface of the facade, and the glass of the living-room windows turned the corner— "like a shop window," in Breuer's words.[43] Natural-color redwood was used for exterior siding and on the interior for some ceilings (others were painted white), but the principal exterior material is gray stone. After the house was in use, a marked temperature difference in the upper and lower stories distressed the client. The upper apartment was uncomfortably warm; corrective attempts were made by ventilating the

154. Side view

roof with grilles set into the ceiling of the closets. The client was unhappy, too, about the way sound traveled between the apartments.

The house is not well known in the Gropius-Breuer canon because it was not often published. It is in good condition today.[44] Breuer claimed not to have been satisfied with the way it was photographed in several campaigns. Yet photos by Elliott Lyman Fisher in the Breuer archives are as good as those of many other Breuer houses, and the Weizenblatt House appeared as the cover illustration of the special Breuer issue of *Nuestra arquitectura*. One suspects either that he was disappointed with the house or that the client was so unhappy that Breuer was embarrassed. He did, however, include it in his *Sun and Shadow* to make a point about the combination of stone and wood.

ARCHIVAL: **SUL 7, 15, 18, 42, 47, Drawings; AAA Photos.**
BIBLIOGRAPHIC: **Breuer, *Sun and Shadow*, 88; Driller, "Frühwerk," 336–41, and *Breuer Houses*, 261.**

155
Abele House,
Framingham, Massachusetts, 1940–41

WALTER GROPIUS AND MARCEL BREUER, ARCHITECTS

Gropius and Breuer's houses in Lincoln, Massachusetts, attracted many visitors and brought new clients. One such client was Dr. Virgil Abele of Framingham, Massachusetts, for whom the Gropius-Breuer office designed and built a residence in 1940 and 1941, and who requested a duplication of the off-angle entrance of the Gropius House. Working drawings were prepared in October 1940 and revised in the spring of 1941; it was one of the joint projects that were incomplete at the time of the severance of the partnership. In his letter to Breuer about credits, Gropius refers to the Abele House as "entirely by me."[45] The house bears the stamp of Gropius and has no obvious idiosyncratic Breuer devices.

That there may have been a conflict, perhaps even a competition between the architects about this work is now known from a Breuer ground plan sketch at Syracuse University. On the sheet he wrote: "designed Sunday 11 aug. 40. discussed with Gropius 12th. 28,656 cbf [cubic feet] against Gropius 37. He reduces his project, cuts greenhouse to get 32,000 cbf. Lyman and Currie find G[ropius] plan and perspective Tuesday night the 13th. Then G. shows to the Doctor Monday the 19th." The house was published in *Architectural Forum* in June 1943 with only Gropius's name.

ARCHIVAL: **SUL Sketches (CLB donation, 1995); see Nerdinger, *Walter Gropius Archive* 3: 290–313.**
BIBLIOGRAPHIC: ***Architectural Forum*, June 1943, 77–79; Nerdinger, *Walter Gropius*, 274; Driller, *Breuer Houses*, 261.**

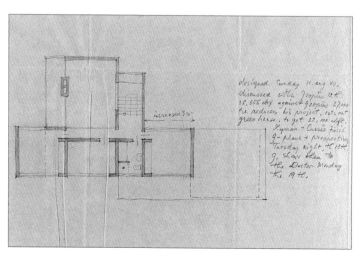

155. Sketch with inscription by Breuer

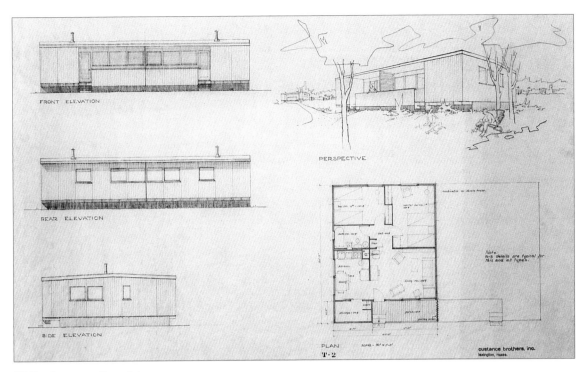

156. Elevations, perspective, and plan

156
Yankee Portables,
1942 (NOT BUILT)

MARCEL BREUER, ARCHITECT

Continuing to experiment with the prefabrication systems that he had explored in Germany in the late 1920s, and inspired by United States leadership in mass-production, Breuer hoped to formulate an "American" minimum house based on industrial processes that had their origins in Henry Ford's assembly lines. In 1942, he designed a prefabricated "de-mountable" unit, adaptable and expandable, that could be produced singly or in quantity, with which he hoped to secure government approval for defense housing (see p. 107). The search for a name (revealing Breuer's fascination with New England Yankee traditions) led to joking wordplay preserved in his notes, moving from "Nomadic Nest," "Custance [the builder] Collapsible Castle," and "Yankee Yanks Down Homes" to "Yankee Portable Houses" and, finally, "Yankee Portables." Edward Larrabee Barnes, George S. Lewis, and Charles Burchard worked on the project; eleven drawings survive at Syracuse University, some by Barnes and Lewis. One-story, wood-frame, flat-roofed bungalow-type structures with porches, erected on a concrete pile foundation, Yankee Portables could have one, two, or three bedrooms. They were detailed with interior plywood finishes and Breuer-invented horizontal sliding windows with screens. Their principal structural element was an elastic wall joint that allowed ample tolerance for the prefabricated parts. Breuer worked out an arrangement with the wood-milling company headed by Jay Roy Lewis (father of George S. Lewis) to manufacture the prefabricated parts and with Custance Brothers, building contractors, to assemble them. Custance Brothers submitted the designs, specifications, and estimates to the National Housing Agency in Washington, D.C.: "We certainly hope it will be possible to consider us for some of your pending projects."[1] No contract was forthcoming, but, according to Joachim Driller, when Breuer soon received an offer from the National Housing Agency for defense workers' housing in Wethersfield, Connecticut, he submitted designs for reworked Yankee Portables, replacing the flat roofs with a butterfly roof.

ARCHIVAL: SUL 7, 15, 18, 42, 47, Drawings, Photos.
BIBLIOGRAPHIC: Blake, *Marcel Breuer*, 80; Breuer, *Sun and Shadow*, 169; Jones, ed., *Marcel Breuer*, 246; Driller, *Breuer Houses*, 261–62.

157. Structural model

157
Plas-2-Point House,
1943 (NOT BUILT)

MARCEL BREUER, ARCHITECT

In response to projected housing needs in the postwar period, Breuer developed this economical prefabricated two-bedroom unit to be used singly or in blocks of one-story row houses (see p. 113). He named it Plas-2-Point for its plastic-coated plywood material, which was exceptionally light in weight, and two-point support system, and based its structure on the trussing system of an airplane wing. Secured to the ground on two foundation blocks so that full foundations and grading work would not be necessary, the house consisted of prefabricated roof and floor trusses cantilevered from central girders. Supporting posts tied the girders together and carried the roof load. Plywood panels were used for roof, ceiling, floor, and non-load-bearing walls, giving the structure its rigidity.[2]

A small model was made in July 1943 by Breuer's students at Harvard. Because Monsanto plastic products would be specified in construction, the project was featured in an illustrated advertisement by Monsanto in the October–November 1943 issue of its magazine to promote "postwar plastics," with a statement by Breuer. Within a few years, however, Breuer became deeply discouraged about the future of architect-designed prefabrication. His was a prophetic insight; indeed, as Reyner Banham made clear, when compared with "commercial prefabricators who don't bother with architecture," the concept of prefabricated houses designed by architects was a miserable failure in twentieth-century modernism.[3]

ARCHIVAL: SUL 47, Sketches; AAA Photos.
BIBLIOGRAPHIC: Breuer, "Designing to Live in a Post-War House," *Monsanto Magazine*, October–November 1943, 22–24, 35; *Nuestra arquitectura*, November 1947, 142–44; Blake, *Marcel Breuer*, 80–81; Breuer, *Sun and Shadow*, 168; Jones, ed., *Marcel Breuer*, 248; Driller, *Breuer Houses*, 262.

Experimental Small Houses, 1943–46

In response to competitions and other initiatives sponsored by journals and manufacturers of building products to prepare for postwar housing demands, Breuer made a number of experimental studies from 1943 to 1946 for functional, cost-efficient homes that he believed could be "heated, protected, insulated, mechanized, and erected on a scale far more developed than in pre-war times."[4] Often binuclear in organization, these projects became the foundation of his postwar suburban residential architecture. The year 1946 was still a time of austerity for private building, with materials not yet back on the market and severe government restrictions limiting the amount of enclosed living space. By 1947, plywood was obtainable in abundance, and the production of it and other building materials was rapidly overcoming most of the shortages.

158
California Arts & Architecture / Pepperill Manufacturing Company House, Competition,
1943–44 (NOT BUILT)

MARCEL BREUER, ARCHITECT

In 1943, Breuer entered his design for a $5,000 to $6,000 postwar binuclear house in a competition sponsored by the journal *California Arts & Architecture*. Although it did not win, the design was published in the December 1943 issue accompanied by an essay by Breuer in which he wrote that the design was "not for a minimum shelter but for a rather high standard of living."[5] In 1944, he submitted the design and essay to the Pepperill Manufacturing Company of Boston, which was seeking housing for its employees. Pepperill rejected the "very beautiful" house, however, because "after giving a good deal of thought to the matter, our Editorial Board feels that our employees would not be sufficiently advanced to appreciate such an unusual style."[6] An H-plan house, its two zones (one elevated) were covered by a butterfly roof and were joined by an entrance hall that led to both the interior and a patio stretching between the wings so plants and flowers would be visible from the entrance. "One [zone] is for common living. . . . [T]he second in a separate wing is for concentration, work, and sleeping," Breuer wrote.[7] Bedrooms were designed to be used also as studies; none of the rooms had common party walls. A terrace to the south was intended for leisure games and outdoor dining; windows and glass walls allowed wide views.

ARCHIVAL: **SUL 7, 18, Photos; AAA Correspondence, Photos.**
BIBLIOGRAPHIC: **Breuer, "Design for Postwar Living: Project for a Worker's House,"** *California Arts & Architecture*, **December 1943, 24–25;** *L'Architecture d'aujourd'hui*, **July 1948, 17; Blake,** *Marcel Breuer*, **86–88; Jones, ed.,** *Marcel Breuer*, **258; Driller,** *Breuer Houses*, **262.**

159
Postwar House for *Ladies' Home Journal,*
1944–45 (NOT BUILT)

MARCEL BREUER, ARCHITECT

Breuer received a letter in December 1944 from the associate editor of the *Ladies' Home Journal* who, some years earlier, had seen his house in Lincoln, Massachusetts.[8] Breuer was asked if he would be interested in "submitting an idea" for a series that the popular magazine was running for "practical solutions to better and lower-cost living" in the postwar era. The series was directed "to families earning $2,000–$3,000 a year." If the preliminary design was accepted, Breuer would be asked for working drawings for an inch-scale model and would then receive a fee of $1,000. He designed a two-zone, 1,200-square-foot structure estimated at $4,000 to $6,000 that could be used for single, twin, or row houses. One zone had a 30-foot combination study, living room, and dining area divided by a free-standing fireplace, with a view to the garden through glass walls; adjacent to a porch (optional) for outdoor dining was the kitchen. With enough space for a desk, the bedrooms served also as studies (Breuer called them "bed-living rooms"). A cantilevered louver strip of roof provided sun protection for the horizontal sliding windows. There were several options for what he called "the extreme simplicity of construction": prefabricated on a 3-foot, 4-inch module with stressed-plywood walls; locally produced out of semi-prefabricated parts; or built in traditional frame construction with wood or plywood sheeting inside and out.

Breuer submitted his design on February 7, 1945, and accompanied it with a three-page descriptive essay.[9] They were not published in the series.

ARCHIVAL: **SUL 51, Drawings; AAA Photos.**
BIBLIOGRAPHIC: **Blake,** *Marcel Breuer,* **107; Driller,** *Breuer Houses,* **262.**

160
Pencil Points / Pittsburgh Plate Glass Company House, Competition,
1945 (NOT BUILT)

MARCEL BREUER, ARCHITECT

This small, efficiently organized two-level house of about 1,400 square feet with basement, submitted for a competition ("nom-de-guerre UTYA-IPG") sponsored by *Pencil Points* and the Pittsburgh Plate Glass Company, was one of Breuer's most far-reaching designs. (It became the most direct precursor of his own first residence in New Canaan, Connecticut.) Levitated and Janus-faced, it had one facade cantilevered over pilotis and held by tension cables and turnbuckles, while the other was fully glazed at ground level and shaded with a slatted gray aluminum sunshade. In the free space beneath the pilotis was the carport. On the ground floor were a living-dining room, with large stone fireplace and sliding glass doors to the outside, and a kitchen adjacent to an enclosed drying yard. The upper floor had a large outdoor deck reached through a louvered glass door. The emphasis on glass surfaces and transparency was related to the partial sponsorship of the competition by Pittsburgh Plate Glass. The intended location was New England.

ARCHIVAL: **AAA Photos.**
BIBLIOGRAPHIC: **Blake,** *Marcel Breuer,* **95; Driller,** *Breuer Houses,* **262.**

161. Rendering

161
Binuclear House,
Miami, Florida, 1945 (NOT BUILT)

MARCEL BREUER, ARCHITECT

A model, a rendering, and plan and elevation drawings, dated October 6, 1945, were made for a binuclear house with a square two-level bedroom wing set off-axis to a larger single-story, boxlike living wing. The wings were linked by a stone-and-glass entrance recessed beyond a pergola. The long west facade of the living wing served as a poolside outdoor porch and was defined by a deep, projecting roof supported by eight pilotis and perforated above the three bays to the north and the one to the south. An exterior stair along the south flank led to a protected roof deck. The house was designed specifically for recreation and outdoor living appropriate for its Florida setting, and it had a number of features that had already turned up in Breuer's work when the outdoors were taken into account—for example, in the House for a Sportsman. The indebtedness of the abstract composition of this and other binuclears to architectonic Constructivist works of the mid-1920s is clear. Breuer used the design for his 1947 Lawnhurst House project.

ARCHIVAL: **SUL Drawings; AAA Photos.**
BIBLIOGRAPHIC: *Architectural Record*, April 1946, 82–85; Blake, 87; Driller, *Breuer Houses*, 262.

162
Veterans' House A,
1945 (NOT BUILT)

MARCEL BREUER, ARCHITECT

Small and affordable, Veterans' House A for returning servicemen was a two-story double house with a butterfly roof set within terraces and gardens. The two "wedges" were united by an appended covered porch on the ground floor, flanked at each end of the south facade by a garage. The open-plan living and dining space and kitchen were on the ground floor in an L-shaped configuration; bedrooms, bath, and storage were above, reached by the interior stair.

ARCHIVAL: **AAA Photos.**
BIBLIOGRAPHIC: *L'Architecture d'aujourd'hui*, July 1948, 8; Blake, *Marcel Breuer*, 109; Driller, *Breuer Houses*, 262.

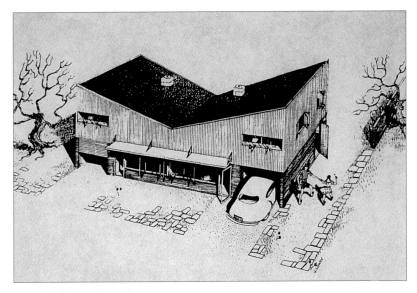

162. Rendered perspective

163
Veterans' House B,
1945 (NOT BUILT)

MARCEL BREUER, ARCHITECT

Basic, functional Veterans' House B could be a single or double house or one unit in a row-house series. It was formed as a raised square, supported at one end on pilotis. The second-story living and dining space, kitchen, two bedrooms, and bath were reached by a stair that ran parallel to the north facade and leveled off to become a porch-deck. From the living room, the deck was reached through floor-to-ceiling casement windows. Ribbon windows shielded by awnings defined the south (sun-receiving) facade. The ground floor adjacent to the garden contained the garage and a room for storage (or another bedroom).

ARCHIVAL: **AAA Photos.**

BIBLIOGRAPHIC: *L'Architecture d'aujourd'hui,* **July 1948, 9; Blake, 109; Driller,** *Breuer Houses,* **262.**

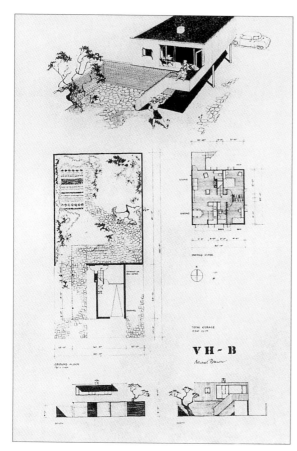

163. Perspective, plans, and elevations

164
"A Realistic House in Georgia": Competition Sponsored by *Progressive Architecture/* Rich's Department Store,
Atlanta, Georgia, 1945(?) (NOT BUILT)

MARCEL BREUER, ARCHITECT

Breuer submitted this undated competition design anonymously (it was identified as "Pecs"). A one-story, binuclear house of about 1,350 square feet, it was composed with two rectangular volumes, elided rather than aligned as parallels, so that the link (a stone-paved screened porch) connected with one element at midpoint and with the other at the end. The east elevation had two diagonal roofs, one slightly lower than the other; the north elevation—with entrance door and sun louver above the windows—was a flat-roofed rectangle. A screened porch and pergola led to a terrace.

ARCHIVAL: **AAA Photos.**

165
Chicagoland Prize Homes, Competition,
1946 (NOT BUILT)

MARCEL BREUER, ARCHITECT

A symmetrical H-plan binuclear dwelling of 1,642 square feet was designed by Breuer for an unidentified Chicago-based competition in 1946. The two wings—one a bedroom-study wing, and the other a living wing—were connected by a ramped corridor that on one side opened to a partly covered patio.

ARCHIVAL: **SUL 51; AAA Photos.**

BIBLIOGRAPHIC: **Driller, "Frühwerk," 220.**

166. South facade

166
Geller House I,
Lawrence, Long Island, New York, 1945

MARCEL BREUER, ARCHITECT

In November 1944, Breuer met with Mr. and Mrs. Bertram (Bert) Geller, who set out their program for a spacious family house in Lawrence, Long Island, for which Breuer would also design the furnishings. They wanted a large living-dining room, a kitchen with dining space, a master bedroom, two bedrooms for three children, a children's play area, an additional bedroom, a screened porch, a utility-laundry room, a maid's room and bath, and a separate two-car garage with guest quarters.

Planning was begun immediately; by December, Breuer had started the sketches (see p. 115). Despite a wait for materials because of wartime shortages and priorities, the house was near completion in September 1945 (at more than twice the original cost estimate), and Breuer was looking for a landscaper. He designed a binuclear butterfly-roof house, combining a square and a long narrow volume arranged slightly off-axis with a bridging element that was entrance on one side and

porch on the other. Low, free-standing stone walls of varied lengths parallel and perpendicular to the architectural massings defined the boundaries and separated the house from its surroundings. The lifted roofs provided expansive interior space. Vertical cedar siding and field-stone were the primary materials; a complex pattern of rectangular and trapezoidal windows and glazed walls articulated the facades.

As an early postwar modern house in a New York City suburb, startling at the time among the nearby traditional houses, Geller House I received a great deal of attention. It was the winning design in a competition sponsored by *Progressive Architecture*, and in *House & Garden* it was called "tomorrow's house today." Breuer built a second house for the Gellers in 1968–69.

ARCHIVAL: **SUL 13, 14, 43, Drawings.**

BIBLIOGRAPHIC: *House & Garden*, January 1947, 61–67, and February 1947, 56–59; *Progressive Architecture*, February, 1947, 51–66, and June 1947, 57; *Architectural Review*, October 1947, 115–17; *L'Architecture d'aujourd'hui*, July 1948, 18–24; Blake, *Marcel Breuer*, 88–90; Jones, ed., *Marcel Breuer*, 225–27; Diller, *Breuer Houses*, 144–51, 262.

167. South facade

Smaller than and very different from the Geller House, the Tompkins House, located close to the water in Hewlett Harbor on Long Island, belonged to a houseform category that Breuer named his "offset" type. It was a two-story, flat-roofed cantilevered structure, with an exterior stucco finish painted in bright colors. The greater part of the roof area of the first level was the sun deck for the second-floor bedrooms; the second floor extended toward the north to form the roof of a carport. The silhouette, ground-based in one direction and cantilevered in the other, resembled the elided rectangles of Constructivist art.

ARCHIVAL: **SUL 17, 18, 31, Drawings; AAA Photos, Correspondence.**
BIBLIOGRAPHIC: *House & Garden*, August 1947, 60–65; *Architectural Record*, September 1947, 66–73; *Architectural Review*, October 1947, 117–18; *L'Architecture d'aujourd'hui*, July 1948, 14–16; Blake, *Marcel Breuer*, 96–97; Jones, ed., *Marcel Breuer*, 228–29; Diller, *Breuer Houses*, 262.

167
Tompkins House,
Hewlett Harbor, Long Island, New York, 1945–46

MARCEL BREUER, ARCHITECT

In the spring of 1945, while he was still at Harvard and at work on the Geller House, Breuer agreed to build a house for Gilbert Tompkins, an artists' agent who was probably introduced to him by Edward L. Fischer. A model and preliminary drawings were presented to the client early in May. So soon after the war, with continuing shortages of materials, priority for private building was needed from the Federal Housing Authority (FHA), and it was granted to Tompkins in July. Because Breuer was not yet licensed to practice in New York, he designated himself as "architectural consultant." In November, however, he found it necessary to write to Tompkins that "I do not expect to receive my New York license [for] two or three months, consequently I fear I must resign herewith as your consultant architect."[10] (It is not clear how he was able to carry out the Geller House if he was not licensed in New York.) Breuer's associate in Cambridge, Massachusetts, Charles Burchard, who was licensed, became the official architect "for the completion" of the job.[11] It was an expedient subterfuge, and there is no question about the source of the design.

168
Maas House,
Lattingtown, Long Island, New York, 1945–47 (NOT BUILT)

MARCEL BREUER, ARCHITECT

A house project for Walter Maas, president of Dorland, Paris, came to Breuer in October 1945 through Herbert Bayer. (In Germany, Bayer had been director of art and design for Dorland, a major international advertising agency.) In a situation similar to the contemporaneous commission for the Tompkins House, Breuer, because he was not yet licensed to practice in New York, suggested that Maas commission Charles Burchard, who acted as a front man in these situations: "You may feel assured that all architectural services will be performed by him in the same spirit as though executed by me."[12] A preliminary design met with the client's approval, but in April 1946 the project ran into difficulties due to postwar construction restrictions and the need for priorities for the acquisition of building materials to be authorized by the Federal Housing Authority. The house was redesigned as a smaller structure to meet the requirements of the government's emergency housing program, but in the end the project was postponed indefinitely.

ARCHIVAL: **SUL 26, Drawings.**
BIBLIOGRAPHIC: Driller, "Frühwerk," 289–92, and *Breuer Houses*, 262.

169
Bandler House,
Cambridge, Massachusetts, 1946 (NOT BUILT)

MARCEL BREUER, ARCHITECT

Breuer reached an agreement on February 19, 1946, with Dr. and Mrs. Bernard Bandler to extensively remodel an existing house in Cambridge, Massachusetts. In May, he left Cambridge to start his private practice in New York City and arranged for the construction of the Bandler House with a firm of Boston builders. After returning to Cambridge and meeting with the client on June 8, however, Breuer realized that it would be "extremely difficult if not virtually impossible" to develop the design and supervise the work from New York.[13] He left blueprints of his drawings with the Bandlers, gave them a list of local architects to consider, and withdrew as architect.

ARCHIVAL: **SUL 29, Drawings.**

170
Martine House,
Stamford, Connecticut, 1946–47 (NOT BUILT)

MARCEL BREUER, ARCHITECT

Both Layng Martine and Breuer were searching in the New Canaan, Connecticut, area for property in September 1946. By constructing two houses near each other simultaneously, they believed, there would a saving on costs. Breuer found land in New Canaan, but Martine bought property in North Stamford instead. Martine then decided not to proceed with a house, but preliminary drawings and a model had already been made. The client complained that the design "did not much resemble what we had expected from our conversations."[14] He felt that it was suited to a flat site and not a hilltop, that the view was ignored, that the ramp was in the wrong place, and that the north was exposed to the coldest wind. Photographs of the model indicate that Martine may have had a point—the composition indeed appears unrelated to the terrain. It was a two-story long house with a wide run of windows on the upper story shaded by a sunbreak cantilevered beyond the inset fieldstone ground-floor base. A steep exterior ramp led to an appended terrace—the whole ramp–terrace unit unintegrated with the body of the house. The criticisms created a strained relationship, and Martine wrote that "we now feel that our ideas and yours do not sufficiently coincide to make for a very satisfying client-architect relationship." What seemed like an optimistic venture a year earlier ended awkwardly. Breuer did not discard the idea of the economy of putting up two houses in tandem, however, and he did so in 1947 with his first house in New Canaan and the Mills House.

ARCHIVAL: **SUL 31, Drawings; AAA Photos.**
BIBLIOGRAPHIC: **Driller,** *Breuer Houses,* **262.**

171. Perspective sketch

171
Lawnhurst House,
Greenburgh, New York, 1947 (NOT BUILT)

MARCEL BREUER, ARCHITECT

In January 1947, Breuer sketched a long box house of 1,200 square feet, with the potential for expansion, for Richard Lawnhurst. It was to be of wood-frame construction covered by a butterfly roof, with a pergola and terrace on one side. The design was based on Breuer's experimental study of 1945 for a house in Miami, Florida. The specifications, dated March 27, became the basis for the specifications (prepared in April) for Breuer's first house in New Canaan, Connecticut. Because Lawnhurst was concerned about costs, Breuer replaced the design with a second and more modest scheme in September, but it was not acceptable to the client. There is no record of a Lawnhurst House beyond this point, and no photographs of an executed work.

ARCHIVAL: **SUL 30, Drawings.**
BIBLIOGRAPHIC: **Driller, *Breuer Houses*, 263.**

172
Mills House,
New Canaan, Connecticut, 1947–48

MARCEL BREUER, ARCHITECT

The client was Edward E. Mills, who worked for the publisher Longmans, Green. The Mills House and Breuer's own house were constructed simultaneously on adjacent property in New Canaan, Connecticut, by the same local builder in an effort to reduce expenses. The drawings, too, had been made at the same time so they could be estimated together. By May 7, 1947, Breuer had sent Mills a perspective and floor plan. The house is a simple H-form, the two blocks joined by an entrance unit preceded by an uncovered terrace that is protected by a low stone wall. At the front, the roofline is extended with a sunbreak of wood strips. Although there were problems during construction with heating pipes beneath the concrete floor, the house was built quickly and was occupied early in 1948. There are drawings at Syracuse University, dated 1951, for an addition. The house has since been destroyed.

ARCHIVAL: **SUL 12, Drawings; AAA Photos.**
BIBLIOGRAPHIC: **Driller, *Breuer Houses*, 263.**

173
Breuer House–New Canaan I,
New Canaan, Connecticut, 1947–48

MARCEL BREUER, ARCHITECT

Breuer took title in May 1947 to a property of almost 7 acres on Sunset Hill Road in New Canaan, Connecticut, adjacent to that of his client Edward Mills. Specifications were adapted in April from those prepared for the Lawnhurst House. When Breuer left in August for three months in South America, the construction of his house was overseen by Eliot Noyes and Harry Seidler. Most of the drawings were made by Seidler, who wrote to Breuer on August 5: "Please don't worry about the house. We will do our best to see it through."[15] "Floated" above a concrete pedestal that was recessed on all sides and contained a workshop, storage area, children's playroom, bedroom, and bath was a continuous long-box wood-frame structure, 20 by 74 feet, sheathed in vertical and diagonal siding (see p. 125). Breuer believed that stud framing could function as a truss to create floating cantilevers if it was reinforced with diagonal siding to carry some of the load. This idea is countered by Edward R. Ford, who, in his postmodern study of the house in *The Details of Modern Architecture*, interprets the diagonal siding as not structurally effective but "applied to the true structure of the studs and sheathing." In his view, it is therefore an "ironic" element since "what appears on the exterior of the building is in effect ornament."[16] An open porch off the upper-level living room (north) was dramatically cantilevered over the slightly inclined grounds. At the south end was a cantilevered master bedroom. To further increase support for the porch and the projecting sunshade suspended above it without using steel or concrete or heavy framing members in the structure, Breuer called for marine cables and turnbuckles to "hang" the projecting elements from the walls of the house.

Breuer had been worried, justifiably, about "the eccentric weight" of the cantilevered porch, and recognized it as a risky experiment: "If it doesn't stand up we will have to set some supports under the porch," he wrote to Noyes on September 2.[17] Serious problems developed with the stresses on the marine hardware during construction (Breuer had erred in specifying the cable strength and fittings, and they had to be changed). By September 12, Noyes told him that "your porch is now hanging by the cables and looks very exciting to all of us";[18] two weeks later, Seidler wrote that "all the temporary supports are out and quite

truly it looks really unbelievable."[19] But the optimism did not hold, and by October temporary posts had been put back under the house. Breuer later had to design a permanent short stone wall on the northeast corner for security. The open-plan interior arrangement of aligned living spaces with few partitions ensured light and expansiveness. "What I value most of [Frank Lloyd Wright's] achievements," Breuer later would say, "is his sense of interior space. It is a liberated space."[20] He explained the design of his house in functionalist and economic terms in a letter of June 22, 1948, to Ada Louise Huxtable, at that time assistant curator in the Department of Architecture at the Museum of Modern Art:

The main living functions are on one level . . . this level is elevated over the natural ground. The lower portion of the house . . . is reduced as much as possible—less foundation, less concrete work, less insulation, less expense wherever you are connected with the terrain. This is the main reason for the cantilevered type of construction, which is large in the upper main level in relation to the small lower base level. Most of the furniture was built-in—the only movable pieces were beds, sofas, dining table and chairs.[21]

Porch and ground were joined by what was to become a distinctive Breuer signature of an open cantilevered metal stair with wooden treads. Breuer sold the house in 1950. In 1986, Herbert Beckhard was commissioned to renovate and expand it.

ARCHIVAL: **SUL 2, 12, 17, 31, 39, 41, 43, 44, 50, Drawings; AAA Correspondence, Photos, Writings and Speeches file.**
BIBLIOGRAPHIC: *Architectural Record,* October 1948, 92–99; *Architectural Review,* January 1949, 10–14; Blake, *Marcel Breuer,* 100–106; Breuer, *Sun and Shadow,* 72–73, 94, 103, 107, 138; Argan, *Marcel Breuer,* 88–89; Jones, ed., *Marcel Breuer,* 222–24; Wilk, *Furniture and Interiors,* 168–73; Masello, *Architecture Without Rules,* 22–29; Driller, *Breuer Houses,* 170–79, 263.

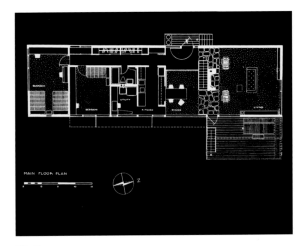

173. Plan

174a. View from the north

174
Robinson House,
Williamstown, Massachusetts, 1947–48

MARCEL BREUER, ARCHITECT

In October 1946, Breuer designed a residence for Preston and Helen Robinson in Williamstown, Massachusetts, on a spectacular site overlooking the Berkshires (see pp. 22, 29). Like the Gellers, the Robinsons wanted an architect-designed modern house and had a well-thought-through program. They discovered Breuer by researching the architecture publications of the period, their method described in an often quoted letter from Helen Robinson to Katherine Morrow Ford, writer for *House & Garden*, coauthor of *The Modern House in America*,[22] and owner of one of the Gropius-Breuer houses in Lincoln, Massachusetts. "We went to the Library," Robinson wrote, "to gain some insight into how the various architects solved their various problems."[23] The Robinsons "threw out" Frank Lloyd Wright, the Californians, and "the Youngsters," but they liked Breuer's work, finding in it "strong evidence of an evolutionary process going on." And, indeed, the 4,800-square-foot house that Breuer built for the Robinsons remains one of his most beautiful and most anthologized works. The client-architect relationship was harmonious from the outset, and Breuer provided the Robinsons with all the features their program required. Preliminary plans were worked out by December 1946. While Breuer was in South America in the summer and fall of 1947, the work was supervised by Harry Seidler and Eliot Noyes; the house was finished in November 1948.

As he had done for the Gellers, Breuer used his binuclear H-plan, with each wing a different shape, but in the Robinson House the rectangular wing was the sleeping and privacy zone, while the mostly stone-floored square unit was used for living and entertaining. The wings were linked by an element that served as entry hall and were roofed with the reverse diagonals of the butterfly format. For winter weather, the roof design was probably a mistake; the subsequent owners (but not the Robinsons) claimed that it could not hold the weight of the snow.[24]

Like the Geller House, the Robinson House rests on the ground. But the site in Williamstown slopes gently, and Breuer expressed the change in level with an interior stone ramp—somewhat unfriendly in the angle and length of its incline—that leads from entry hall to living room. One of the earliest of Breuer's rugged stone fireplaces, often compared with works of sculpture, dominates the living room.

The salient feature of the house is a cantilevered canopy—a triangular wooden truss—pierced with a rectangular opening (to protect from excessive heat and high-velocity winds) that lifts over the stone-paved east terrace, giving the building its defining profile and framing the view of the mountains from the glass-walled living room. It can be traced back in Breuer's work to the House for a Sportsman (1931). With low retaining walls of fieldstone extending from the house into the landscape, he completed the composition of straight lines and diagonals projecting from a quadratic core.

The Robinsons lived in the house until 1975.

ARCHIVAL: **SUL 17, 39, 41, Drawings; AAA Photos.**
BIBLIOGRAPHIC: *Architectural Record*, February 1949, 84–93; *House & Garden*, February 1949, 40–47, 107–9; Blake, *Marcel Breuer*, 91–94; Breuer, *Sun and Shadow*, 50–51, 112; Argan, *Marcel Breuer*, 86–87; Jones, ed., *Marcel Breuer*, 218–21; Rowe, "Neo-Classicism and Modern Architecture," in *Mathematics of the Ideal Villa and Other Essays*, 119–38; Driller, *Breuer Houses*, 152–69, 263.

174b. East terrace

175. View from the south

175
Kniffin House,
New Canaan, Connecticut, 1947–48

MARCEL BREUER AND ELIOT NOYES, ARCHITECTS

The Kniffin House, begun in December 1947 and completed and occupied in October 1948, was one of the few residences designed by Breuer that came in below the estimated cost. The clients were admirers of Breuer's first house in New Canaan and requested a number of its features: they "would like the house to open up on entering so that you see through living room–dining room to outside (as in your house); overhead spot for lighting—as in your house," wrote Eliot Noyes in his notes on the original program.[25] The house was shaped as a T; the two-story wing—for master and guest rooms opening from a tall living room on the west—included a balcony and an exterior stair, as in the Museum of Modern Art exhibition house; at ground level on the east was the zone for children and servants. Partitions between the children's bedrooms were extended beyond the facade to become external vertical louvers for sun control, their ends flush with the projecting roof fascia board. The house has been destroyed.

ARCHIVAL: **SUL 11, 40, Drawings; AAA Photos.**
BIBLIOGRAPHIC: *Architectural Record*, September 1953, 159–63; *L'Architecture d'aujourd'hui*, December 1953, 72–74; Breuer, *Sun and Shadow*, 160–61; Driller, *Breuer Houses*, 263.

176
Scott House,
Dennis, Massachusetts, 1947–48

Addition, 1958–59

MARCEL BREUER, ARCHITECT

Conversations with the client, New York City lawyer Stuart N. Scott, about a vacation house on Cape Cod began in the spring of 1947 and were followed by a planning process complicated by Breuer's absence from his office that summer during his South American teaching sojourn. Working drawings were ready by the middle of December, and the house was completed in 1948. The program called for a tripartite residence to be built on a sharp incline: (1) a one-story main house (insulated and heated for year-round use) with a living-dining room, three bedrooms, and a partially covered terrace facing the water; (2) a servant's room and bath for summer use only, a drying yard for laundry, tool storage, and a covered parking area for two cars; and (3) a "dormitory" for four beds with bathrooms and dressing rooms, without heat and for summer use only, and with a covered terrace. The servant's area and the dormitory were to be separate from the main house. The arrangement was realized in a composition of two parallel and separate blocks with the service and dormitory functions in one of the blocks divided by a partition wall. An addition was completed in 1959.

ARCHIVAL: **SUL 24, 31, 32, 154, Drawings; AAA Photos.**
BIBLIOGRAPHIC: Driller, *Breuer Houses*, 263.

177
Thompson House,
Ligonier, Pennsylvania, 1947–49

MARCEL BREUER, ARCHITECT

The contract between Breuer and Mrs. Arthur W. Thompson for a large, luxurious house was dated January 31, 1947. In March, the client received a preliminary plan and a model, and she told Breuer it was not what she had expected: "I realized I had not made it clear to you that I wanted to use 18th century English furniture which I have collected."[26] This unusual response from a Breuer client, obviously not fully committed to modernism, is explained by the fact that she was the mother of Rolland (Rollo) Thompson, an architect who had been a student at the Graduate School of Design and was working as a draftsman at the Breuer office. Mrs. Thompson made many requests for changes during the planning process that Breuer was willing to go along with: eliminating built-ins and shelves in deference to her wish for "plain walls" (painted plaster and natural wood instead of stone) against which to place her furniture, flat roofs that varied in height, and raised hearths at fireplaces. But he saw that it was necessary to draw the line and establish some control early and wrote that "I am afraid I will have to base the design on my own standards of judgement and I am asking you now for this confidence."[27] On April 3, he was undoubtedly pleased to report that "I am very happy that you liked the plans I presented, and that you gave me the go-ahead for the working drawings."[28] Some of the drawings (more than 200 survive) were made by Rolland Thompson; others, by William Landsberg and Harry Seidler. As the site was exceptionally beautiful, landscaping and terracing were important features of the design—one of Breuer's best with regard to relations between house and setting. Special (luxury) features included three heated ponds—one outside the master bedroom to be deeper than the others to permit water lilies to grow—a wine cellar, and a separate guest wing. Comparable in cost, size, and luxury to the Frank House of seven years earlier, the Thompson House illustrates Breuer's design language as it evolved into its postwar expression. Stone was the principal exterior material, in accordance with the wishes of the client, and unusually long, low independent stone walls defined the terraces and the enclosures, stretching along the property and thus reflecting the layout of the house. Breuer was locked in battle with the client and her landscape architect as they tried to "soften" ("demodernize") the walls with plantings, thereby reducing the compositional role they played in the design.

ARCHIVAL: **SUL 19–21, 39, Drawings; AAA Photos.**
BIBLIOGRAPHIC: *L'Architecture d'aujourd'hui,* September 1952, 8–9; Breuer, *Sun and Shadow,* 88, 92, 96–97, 101; Driller, *Breuer Houses,* 263.

177. West facade

178
Sandor House,
Mamaroneck, New York, 1948 (NOT BUILT)

MARCEL BREUER, ARCHITECT

A contract with George Sandor for a house in Mamaroneck, New York, was drawn up on February 4, 1948. Breuer did some preliminary work during February, but the client was unable to sell his old house and the project was abandoned.

ARCHIVAL: **SUL 31.**
BIBLIOGRAPHIC: **Driller, "Frühwerk," 227.**

180. View of cottage and studio

179
Kepes Cottage,
Wellfleet, Massachusetts, 1948–49

180
Breuer Cottage,
Wellfleet, Massachusetts, 1948–49

MARCEL BREUER, ARCHITECT

Studio Addition to Breuer Cottage, 1961–62

MARCEL BREUER AND HERBERT BECKHARD, ARCHITECTS

In July and August 1948, Breuer planned a vacation cottage for his close friends, the Gyorgy Kepeses, on Long Pond in Wellfleet on Cape Cod. Kepes, a Hungarian artist-designer and one of Breuer's chess partners, was Professor of Visual Design at the School of Architecture and Planning at MIT. Before emigrating to Cambridge, Massachusetts, he had known Breuer in Berlin in 1930 and in London in 1934 to 1937. The Breuers, too, had "fallen in love with" Wellfleet, having rented houses there for several summers.[29] When on August 20, 1948, Breuer sent drawings and specifications for the Kepes Cottage to Ernest Rose, a Wellfleet builder, he wrote: "I am going around with the idea of building exactly the same house for myself at Williams Pond, but I have not definitely decided yet."[30] (Breuer had the idea, not carried out, for developing a community of five to seven houses sited far apart on 20 acres of a pine-forested peninsula not far from the ocean and surrounded by four ponds, referred to in the archival material as the

"Wellfleet Development" or "Wellfleet Settlement.") The design and working drawings were prepared under Breuer's supervision by Wilhelm Viggo von Moltke. By September, the decision had been made, and Breuer commissioned Rose "to do the building work for my summer house #2 at Williams Pond."[31] The design (which generated a third Wellfleet cottage, for the Howard Wises, in 1963) was based on Breuer's long-house type, one room deep, raised above the ground on pilotis and on a solid pier made of cement block below the living-room fireplace, and fenestrated with screened sliding windows in hardwood tracks. It was the builder who suggested cement blocks instead of bricks below the floor on the fireplace base. "This would give a wall 8″ thick which would be better as your height is quite great," he wrote, and Breuer agreed. The exterior tongue-and-groove boarding ran vertically; the same cedar was used for the flooring throughout the interior. From the long face of the rectangle, a screened porch with parapet, supported by trusses anchored to the footing by means of galvanized angles, projected forward, beyond the overhanging sunscreen. A screened terrace extended from the opposite long facade.

In 1961, Breuer with Herbert Beckhard added a full wing joined to the main house by way of the entrance breezeway. With a studio, bathroom, fireplace, and porch it functioned as an independent dwelling.

ARCHIVAL: SUL 27, 31, 32, Drawings; AAA (NYC) Correspondence: Letters Roll 1211 (Kepes Papers).

BIBLIOGRAPHIC: *Interiors*, July 1946, 60–65; *Architectural Record*, November 1966, 134–36; Blake, *Marcel Breuer*, 100; Jones, ed., *Marcel Breuer*, 249; Masello, *Architecture Without Rules*, 76–77; Driller, *Breuer Houses*, 262.

181
Hooper House I,
Baltimore, Maryland, 1949

MARCEL BREUER, ARCHITECT

Arthur U. and Edith Ferry Hooper[32] wished to append a modern three-bedroom annex to their traditional stone house and to remodel the existing residence (see p. 131). Early in October 1948, Breuer went to Baltimore to meet the Hoopers for the first time. From this friendship, he would go on to do a second house for them; the Grosse Pointe Public Library, whose benefactor was Edith Hooper's father, Dexter Ferry; Ferry Cooperative Dormitory at Vassar College; and the Bryn Mawr School for Girls.

The contract was signed in October, and Edith Hooper visited the Geller House on November 15. She wrote to Breuer that she felt "confident that you can somehow make a harmonious whole out of our present stone pile and our addition" and expressed concern about the design factors involved in joining the irregular roof of the old residence to the new building.[33] The annex—a two-level long box with stone as its dominant material to harmonize with the old structure—was photographed for *House & Garden* by Breuer's friend André Kertész.

ARCHIVAL: **SUL 77, Drawings.**
BIBLIOGRAPHIC: ***House & Garden,** April 1951, 96–103; Driller, **Breuer Houses**, 264.*

182
Rand House,
Harrison, New York, 1949

MARCEL BREUER, ARCHITECT

The clients were Paul and Ann Rand. Paul Rand was a well-known graphic and industrial designer, later to become Professor of Graphic Design at Yale. At first, the Rand House was to be located in Woodstock, New York; working drawings were prepared, but this project was abandoned. On June 6, 1949, a contract was signed for a house to be built in Harrison, New York, instead. By August, Paul Rand wanted drastic changes that unnerved the builder: "He has got to stop being frantic about the building. . . . I suggest the next time Mr. Rand makes a change we charge him $10,000 for it and use the money to endow a home for prematurely aged architects and builders." A week later, Breuer withdrew as architect. It was a gentlemanly parting of the ways and probably inevitable since both client and architect were artists. On August 24, Breuer wrote to Paul Rand:

We both feel that you would like to make your decisions as to changes, interior arrangements, and completion of your house yourself, without having to cope with my own points. Though I regret not being able to finish the house and refer to it as my work, I recognize only too well your own creative drives. . . . You have no obligation whatsoever as to photographing or publishing the house. Should you, however, decide to do so, I would like to be informed of this and such publication should only be done with my approval. The house probably will be labelled "In consultation with Marcel Breuer, architect."[34]

Two years after the house was completed, the Rands decided to sell it and build in western Connecticut. Ann Rand wrote to Breuer: "We may want to publish the house in various magazines . . . and as we agreed, we want to decide how the house should be credited. Paul suggests, in accord with what you and I discussed before, that we say Marcel Breuer, Architect in collaboration with Paul Rand, Designer. Please let us know if this is agreeable."[35] The house appears on Breuer's list of his works.[36]

ARCHIVAL: **SUL 31, 52, Drawings; CLB Correspondence.**
BIBLIOGRAPHIC: **Driller, *Breuer Houses*, 264.**

House in the Museum Garden, Museum of Modern Art, New York, 1948–49. See no. 109.

184
Potter House,
Cape Elizabeth, Maine, 1949–50

MARCEL BREUER, ARCHITECT

Breuer was pleased to be building a house in Maine, although there was concern about procuring materials; the client warned Breuer that "there is no local source for cypress siding or for modern hardware."[2] A model was built; the design underwent several revisions; the house was completed in March 1950. No photographs exist, but the drawings—for a two-zoned butterfly-roof house cantilevered above pilotis—are at Syracuse University. The construction went smoothly, more or less, and the clients were content with the house, but tensions over costs and complaints about the heating system and roof leaks soured their relations with Breuer. Breuer kept apart the files for this house and for others that had similar problems, and rarely, if ever, included these buildings in registers of his work.

ARCHIVAL: **SUL 28, Drawings.**
BIBLIOGRAPHIC: **Driller, *Breuer Houses*, 264.**

183. Rendered perspective

183
Herrick House,
Canajoharie, New York, 1949–50

MARCEL BREUER, ARCHITECT

The clients came to Breuer because of the "thrill we experienced when we first saw the Kniffin House."[1] Completed in March 1950, the Herrick House was another case where relations between client and architect deteriorated by the end of the job.

The drawings in Syracuse show a wood-frame long box with an unusual sunbreak extension above the south facade. A canopy above the entrance connected the house to a free-standing carport.

ARCHIVAL: **SUL 24, Drawings.**
BIBLIOGRAPHIC: **Driller, *Breuer Houses*, 264.**

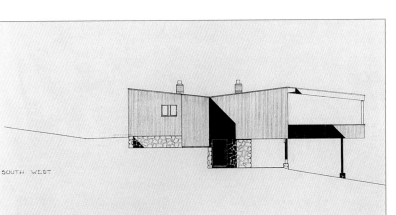

184. Southwest elevation

185
Tilley House,
Middletown, Red Bank, New Jersey, 1949–50

MARCEL BREUER, ARCHITECT

The Tilley House was a near-replica of Breuer's exhibition house at the Museum of Modern Art . In September 1949, Breuer gave the clients the specifications of the exhibition house, with addenda, and they thanked him "for the small variations you introduced."[3] His office supervised the construction, and the house—a three-bedroom version of the prototype—was completed by June 1950.

ARCHIVAL: **SUL 31, 32, Drawings.**
BIBLIOGRAPHIC: **Driller,** *Breuer Houses,* **264.**

187. Facade with full-height glass panels, balcony, and stair

186
Marshad House,
Croton-on-Hudson, New York, 1950

MARCEL BREUER, ARCHITECT

Breuer contracted with the Marshads on October 4, 1949, for a house in a development called Harmon Park Community, and by March 1950 construction was under way. Because this was one of the houses about which there was a disagreement between Breuer and the client, it was not included in the Breuer canon before Joachim Driller's study of the houses. There are no photographs, but the working drawings (for a "simple, one-box house," as Driller describes it) are at Syracuse University.

ARCHIVAL: **SUL 34, Drawings.**
BIBLIOGRAPHIC: **Driller,** *Breuer Houses,* **264.**

187
Smith House,
Aspen, Colorado, 1950

MARCEL BREUER, ARCHITECT

The contract of November 7, 1949, called for a house to be completed no later than October 1, 1950. That Breuer was asked to design a house so far from his New York base is explained by the presence in Aspen, Colorado, of his friend Herbert Bayer, who was design consultant for Walter Paepcke's Container Corporation of America from 1946 to 1956. (Paepcke, for whom Breuer would design a house in Aspen in 1959), was responsible for developing Aspen into a prominent resort and cultural center.) By May 1950, difficulties arose with the client, who was overseeing the construction, and Breuer wrote him several sharp-toned letters of rebuke.[4] Despite continued discord, construction progressed through the summer, and the house was occupied by December. A final dispute was brought before the American Arbitration Association. Breuer was awarded full settlement of his claim, but he considered the job "a disappointment—also a financial one—for practically everybody who was connected with it."[5] The house is recorded in drawings and correspondence at Syracuse University and in progress snapshots at the Archives of American Art: a wood-frame-and-concrete-slab long box (upper story) that bridges and overhangs a bisected, stone-veneered pedestal (lower story). On the "view" side one of the two central floor-to-ceiling glass panels opens to a balcony with stair.

ARCHIVAL: **SUL 23–25, Drawings; AAA Contract, Correspondence.**
BIBLIOGRAPHIC: **Driller,** *Breuer Houses,* **264.**

188
Lauck House,
Princeton, New Jersey, 1950

MARCEL BREUER, ARCHITECT

Construction of the Tilley House, the replica of the house in the MoMA garden, in Red Bank, New Jersey, led to the commission for the Lauck House in nearby Princeton. The clients wanted "not only a Breuer house but, in particular, the Modern Museum House you are building in Red Bank and elsewhere."[6] They told Breuer, however, that

one of the usual considerations that a client has for selecting an architect is the building of a house that will be personal and exclusively his. In this instance, the house in question has already been built more than once . . . under these circumstances, we do feel that it is proper for us to have an understanding with you that a duplication of this house or one based on its general design shall not be built within a radius of 10 miles from Nassau Hall, Princeton, New Jersey.

"I am perfectly in accord" was Breuer's reply.[7]

ARCHIVAL: **SUL 11, 12, Drawings.**
BIBLIOGRAPHIC: **Driller, *Breuer Houses*, 265.**

189
Foote House,
Chappaqua, New York, 1950

MARCEL BREUER, ARCHITECT

Another of the replicas of the MoMA exhibition house, its construction overseen by a supervising contractor with Breuer serving as consultant, the Foote House was built in 1950.

ARCHIVAL: **SUL 28; AAA Correspondence.**
BIBLIOGRAPHIC: **Driller, *Breuer Houses*, 264.**

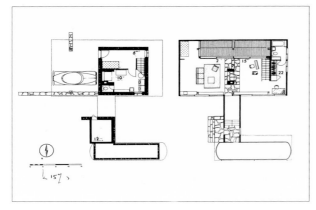

190a. Plans

190
Wolfson Trailer House,
Pleasant Valley, New York, 1950

MARCEL BREUER, ARCHITECT

This was an unusual commission because Manhattan resident Sidney Wolfson, who had been using a trailer as a country "studio" since 1946, wanted to keep the trailer and annex it to a new building. (Trailers were used in the immediate postwar period to fill the gap created by the scarcity of housing.) Breuer coordinated his visits to Pleasant Valley, New York, with those to nearby Vassar College in Poughkeepsie, where his Ferry Cooperative Dormitory was in progress. The specifications called for a wood-frame structure clad with vertical cypress. Informal sketches by Breuer are at Syracuse University. Through a narrow corridor, Breuer connected the metal trailer (elevated so it rested on a stone wall) to the simple box of the new house, which was cantilevered from a stone base. Broad stone steps led to the entrance terrace, adjacent to the corridor. The interior space was a symmetrical open plan with a studio, living room, and nested porch covered by a roof pierced by a pair of rectangular openings.

ARCHIVAL: **SUL 2, 12, Drawings; AAA Contract, Correspondence, Photos.**
BIBLIOGRAPHIC: ***House & Home*, January 1952, 120–23; *L'Architecture d'aujourd'hui*, September 1952, 12–13; Breuer, *Sun and Shadow*, 36; Jones, ed., *Marcel Breuer*, 192; Papachristou, *Marcel Breuer*, 222; Driller, *Breuer Houses*, 264.**

190b. Trailer and house

191
Clark House,
Orange, Connecticut, 1950–51

MARCEL BREUER, ARCHITECT

Breuer began sketches in 1949 for what he described as "a rather large residence" on a 10-acre site.[8] After several reworkings of the design, the house was completed in December 1951. Since a modern house was still a novelty in that region, it received streams of visitors during and after construction. A two-story, six-bedroom, four-bathroom house of 6,000 square feet, including garage, the Clark House was arranged on two levels to conform to the hilly site. In keeping with the organization he preferred when there was sufficient space and budget, Breuer separated by level the children's wing from the adults' quarters. The structure was concrete slab and steel. Typologically, the house belongs to a dominant Breuer mode of the early 1950s: a long, low rectangle with a skin of fieldstone, cypress, and glass; fieldstone walls extending into the landscape; floor-to-ceiling glass walls; flat roof; and alternating closed and open volumes on the facades. Driller's analysis of this house comparing it to one by Louis Kahn is of particular interest.

ARCHIVAL: **SUL 13, Drawings; AAA Contract, Correspondence, Photos.**
BIBLIOGRAPHIC: ***House and Home***, May 1952, 105; ***L'Architecture d'aujourd'hui***, September 1952, 14–16; ***World's Contemporary Architecture, U.S.A. II*** (Tokyo: Kaigai Bunka Chuokyoku, 1953); Breuer, ***Sun and Shadow***, 33, 37, 85, 113; Jones, ed., ***Marcel Breuer***, 193–95; Papachristou, ***Marcel Breuer***, 222; Driller, ***Breuer Houses***, 264–65.

192
Englund House,
Pleasantville, New York, 1950–51

MARCEL BREUER, ARCHITECT

The association of Breuer and the client began around 1949, and this ill-fated house (partly destroyed in a storm soon after completion) was designed in the spring of 1950 and finished in the fall of 1951. The client wrote a bitter and highly critical letter about Breuer personally and professionally in January 1952 when Breuer presented his final bill; the dispute went to arbitration. There are no photographs in the Breuer files, but the drawings reveal a compact two-story wood-frame house above a stone-faced base, the second story cantilevered to the rear above pilotis.

ARCHIVAL: **SUL 27, 28, Drawings.**
BIBLIOGRAPHIC: ***Process: Architecture***, no. 32, 15; Driller, "Frühwerk," 245–47, 477–79, and ***Breuer Houses***, 265.

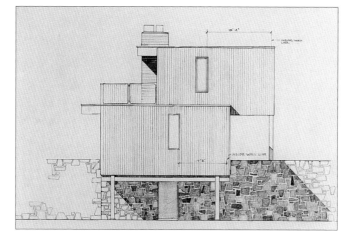

192. West elevation

191. West facade

193a. East facade

193b. View from the living area to the porch

Often published and much admired, Stillman House I was one of Breuer's most successful postwar houses and one of the most important commissions of his career in terms of his friendship with the clients and the work it generated within the Stillmans' network of business, family, and friends. The Stillmans sold their house in 1964 to an architect, lived in two more houses that Breuer built for them, bought back Stillman I, and, in the 1990s, were living in it with few changes from the original.

ARCHIVAL: **SUL 34, 49, Drawings; AAA Photos.**

BIBLIOGRAPHIC: *House and Home*, May 1952, 108–9; *L'Architecture d'aujourd'hui*, September 1952, 2–4 and cover; *World's Contemporary Architecture, U.S.A. II* (Tokyo: Kaigai Bunka Chuokyoku, 1953); Breuer, *Sun and Shadow*, 70, 146–48, 150–53; Argan, *Marcel Breuer*, 93; Jones, ed., *Marcel Breuer*, 210–13; Papachristou, *Marcel Breuer*, 223; Driller, *Breuer Houses*, 265.

193
Stillman House I,
Litchfield, Connecticut, 1950–51

MARCEL BREUER, ARCHITECT

Although it was Breuer's exhibition house at MoMA that attracted Rufus and Leslie Stillman to his work, the house he designed for them in 1950 was not one of the clones. It was to be built in Litchfield, Connecticut, a farming community in the hills of northwestern Connecticut, rich with eighteenth- and nineteenth-century houses. Drawings were prepared in August 1950; Breuer inspected the job on October 29, 1950, and wrote that "I was very pleased to see the house and the excellent workmanship it shows."[9] In 1951, a garage and studio were added. The house was designed as a two-level rectangular box with extruded porches—the long-house type. On the upper level, an open plan united kitchen, dining area, and living room as one efficient large space. A brick fireplace and slate hearth, fronting the stair to the lower level, separated living and dining areas. A hallway from the entrance led past the kitchen to the master bedroom suite, and the living room opened to a deep outdoor porch. An overhanging flat roof shaded the large frameless glass windows on the facade away from the entrance and toward the view. Bedrooms and baths for children and guests were on the lower level. The structural system was wood frame, steel, and concrete. On the exterior, the vertical siding was cypress. A canopy suspended above the entrance was held by stainless-steel marine rigging and supported by piers. On a brick wall at one end of the swimming pool was a mural by Alexander Calder.

194
McComb House,
Poughkeepsie, New York, 1950–54

MARCEL BREUER, ARCHITECT

The client became aware of Breuer's architecture after seeing an article in *House and Home*. An agreement was made on June 30, 1950, for an ambitious house, but Peter McComb requested an arrangement that would allow him to do much of the work himself. He expanded the program, impractically, with the result that his own labor was increased far more than anticipated. Because Breuer was working nearby at both Vassar College and the Wolfson Trailer House, he was able to participate to some extent during the construction process. But he had little patience with the project, since it was built in bits and pieces, generated arguments between client and builder, and involved much amateur work. He strongly advised against the client's idea for a sliding door between dining room and kitchen, for example: "For this kind of use the sliding type is most inconvenient and difficult, as you can well imagine if you think of trying to open and close it with both hands full," wrote William Landsberg to McComb.[10]

ARCHIVAL: **SUL 40; AAA Contract.**

BIBLIOGRAPHIC: **Driller,** *Breuer Houses*, **265.**

195. Carport and house

196. Entrance facade

195
Hanson House,
Lloyd Harbor, Huntington, Long Island, New York, 1951

MARCEL BREUER, ARCHITECT

A contract between Breuer and John Wellmer Hanson, an admirer of the exhibition house at MoMA, was dated December 18, 1950; specifications were developed from those for the Marshad House. The Hanson House was a classic Breuer single-story residence, its units organized beneath the profile of a butterfly roof; materials were vertical cypress siding, glass, and stone. The long box of the living unit was joined to the open carport by a narrow entrance hall. A low stone wall defined the broad trapezoidal terrace that fronted the living quarters. Sometime before 1966 the house was expanded, but not by Breuer.

ARCHIVAL: **SUL 34; AAA Contract, Photos.**
BIBLIOGRAPHIC: *Architectural Record*, September 1953, 164–66; Jones, ed., *Marcel Breuer*, 217; Papachristou, *Marcel Breuer*, 222; Driller, *Breuer Houses*, 265.

196
Pack House,
Scarsdale, New York, 1951

MARCEL BREUER, ARCHITECT

Commissioned in January 1950, the Pack House is a fine example of Breuer's brick-faced residences of the 1950s: an L-shaped concrete-and-wood-frame structure with an outer skin of whitewashed brick veneer, and interior walls of natural-finish plywood above flagstone flooring with radiant heat. Outside were long, low fieldstone walls and pierced slab walls of whitewashed brick. The correspondence reveals that it was a house that gave Breuer special satisfaction.

ARCHIVAL: **SUL 27, 28, Drawings; AAA Contract, Correspondence, Photos.**
BIBLIOGRAPHIC: **Breuer, *Sun and Shadow*, 98–99; Argan, *Marcel Breuer*, 94; Driller, *Breuer Houses*, 265.**

197
Witalis House,
King's Point, Long Island, New York, 1951

MARCEL BREUER, ARCHITECT

Breuer planned a house in 1948 for advertising executive Edmond V. Witalis; the project went forward with numerous interruptions and revisions. It was completed in 1951, but there were difficulties about contractual terms among owner, builder, and architect. Breuer reluctantly brought the matter to the American Arbitration Association in late 1951 or early 1952. By July 1952, however, Breuer and Witalis had settled privately, and their correspondence remained "friendly."

Freehand sketches by Breuer and working drawings are at Syracuse University. Breuer sketched in 1948 and 1949 a pitched-roof two-level long house entered by a free-hanging stair. The upper floor and its deep cantilevered balcony were clad in vertical siding above a fieldstone pedestal base. In the final version, done in 1950, the house had a flat roof and a base of painted concrete block.

ARCHIVAL: **SUL 29, Drawings, Sketches.**
BIBLIOGRAPHIC: **Driller,** *Breuer Houses,* **264.**

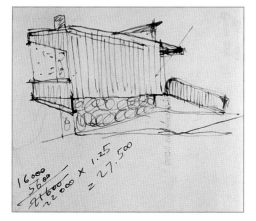

197a. Sketch by Breuer

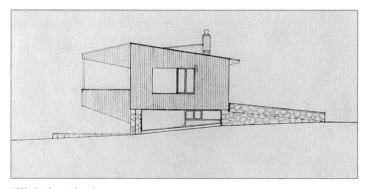

197b. Southeast elevation

198
Breuer House–New Canaan II,
New Canaan, Connecticut, 1951

MARCEL BREUER, ARCHITECT

Breuer sold his first house in New Canaan, Connecticut, and he and his family moved out on April 13, 1951. His new house, also in New Canaan, was in construction at this time. A wood-frame box clad in stone and glass, it was open to a square courtyard at the center of the stony entrance facade and, through glass walls, to a rectangular terrace with view at the rear. It was a one-story house with an open-plan living room and dining room divided by a partition, and a master bedroom (with a large sliding glass window to the garden) separated from the other private spaces by the entrance area and a corridor. The glass walls in the living and dining room were almost 7 feet tall, allowing exceptional transparency and light. The dominant compositional feature of the exterior was the geometry of the stone walls, free-standing and intersecting.

The house was sold in 1976; it was later renovated and expanded for the new owners in several campaigns by Herbert Beckhard.

ARCHIVAL: **SUL 40, 41, Drawings, Sketch; AAA Correspondence, Photos.**
BIBLIOGRAPHIC: *House and Home,* May 1952, 103–4; *L'Architecture d'aujourd'hui,* September 1952, 4–7; *Bauen und Wohnen,* December 1956, 409–13; Breuer, *Sun and Shadow,* 65, 162–63; Jones, ed., *Marcel Breuer,* 196–99; Papachristou, *Marcel Breuer,* 222; Masello, *Architecture Without Rules,* 30–37; Driller, *Breuer Houses,* 265.

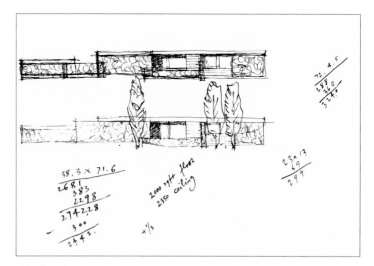

198a. Sketch by Breuer

198b. Entrance facade

199
George Robinson House,
Redding Ridge, Connecticut, 1952 (NOT BUILT)

MARCEL BREUER, ARCHITECT

Because it was for a client with the same surname, a preliminary plan of 1952 for a house for George Robinson is filed in the Breuer archives with the material for the Preston Robinson House (1947–48) in Williamstown, Massachusetts. There is no other information about it.

ARCHIVAL: **SUL 17.**
BIBLIOGRAPHIC: **Driller,** *Breuer Houses,* **265.**

200. South facade

200
Caesar Cottage,
Lakeville, Connecticut, 1952

MARCEL BREUER, ARCHITECT

A house for Harry I. Caesar, a relative of Rufus and Leslie Stillman, was built in 1952 (see p. 30). A modest weekend wood-frame "cottage" perched above a small base, it was situated on a wooded lakefront with near neighbors on both flanks. Consequently, Breuer designed it for privacy above all. He gave it a squarish format, with lateral walls of cypress vertically and diagonally set (acting as structural bracing) and affixed to projected beams that became extended blinders on the entrance facade. The blinders closed off the view to the sides and directed attention instead to the lake in one direction and the woods in the other. The entrance door was off-axis in the plane between the two extended walls, which enframed the windowed south facade toward the woods.

The smaller lower level of random fieldstone resembled the base of a sculpture and contained space for storage and heating. On this base rested the much larger upper level, supported by lally columns and cantilevered above a truss to the edge of the water. A balcony, opening from the dining room and projecting beyond the fully glazed north wall, which illuminated the interior, suggested a ship's deck. The entrance to the upper level and its living quarters was by way of a wooden ramp with taut cables, also purposely appropriating marine imagery. When he used the device of cable and ramp at Aluminum City Terrace, in New Kensington, Pennsylvania, in 1941 Breuer himself made the analogy in a letter of May 12, 1944, to *Architectural Forum:* "Gangplanks similar to those on boats are used for connection between entrance path and door." The living-room fireplace was a massive and frequently photographed sculpture of bush-hammered concrete. Robert Gatje recalls that Breuer kept the model of the Caesar Cottage on his desk for years, regarding it as one of his best designs.[11]

ARCHIVAL: **SUL Drawings; AAA Correspondence, Photos.**
BIBLIOGRAPHIC: *L'Architecture d'aujourd'hui,* September 1952, 10–11; Hitchcock and Drexler, eds., *Built in USA,* 52; Breuer, *Sun and Shadow,* 43, 44–45, 144; Jones, ed., *Marcel Breuer,* 200–203; Papachristou, *Marcel Breuer,* 224; Droste and Ludewig, *Marcel Breuer Design,* 146–47; Driller, *Breuer Houses,* 265.

201
Levy House,
Princeton, New Jersey, 1952–53

Addition, 1956

MARCEL BREUER, ARCHITECT

The Levys' art collection was an important factor in their program for an "informal" house. Light, wall space, and "provision for rearrangement" of the works of art were priorities. An agreement with Breuer was made in July 1952, and the house was completed in 1953. He designed a two-level long house with the upper bedroom wing cantilevered beyond the lower and supported by columns. The master bedroom and adjoining study were at one end, sheltered in a cove formed by the overhanging roof and side walls; the second bedroom was within the block at its other end. Breuer worked out a third bedroom addition in the spring of 1956.

ARCHIVAL: **SUL 40, Drawings; AAA Photos.**
BIBLIOGRAPHIC: **Driller,** *Breuer Houses*, **264.**

202
Tibby House,
Port Washington, Long Island, New York,
1952–53 (NOT BUILT)

MARCEL BREUER, ARCHITECT

The Tibby House was to be a version of the exhibition house at MoMA. Preliminary drawings were made in November and December 1952 for a 2,500-square-foot house, the upper level formed from the space beneath the lifted roof. More compartmentalized than open plan, the house project required a circulation pattern more complex than that of other Breuer houses of the type, probably because of an ambitious program and the client's wish to incorporate many separate functions. When in March 1953 it became clear that the costs would be too high, the project had to be abandoned, to the mutual regret of client and architect. To Tibby, Breuer wrote: "I hate to lose you as clients . . . together we could have built a good house."[12]

ARCHIVAL: **SUL 28, Drawings.**
BIBLIOGRAPHIC: **Driller,** *Breuer Houses*, **265–66.**

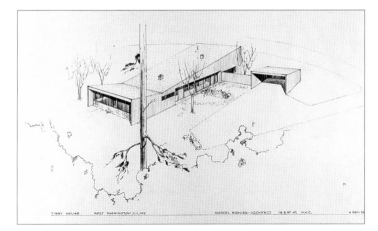

202. Rendered perspective

203
Crall House, Gates Mills, Ohio,
1953 (NOT BUILT)

MARCEL BREUER, ARCHITECT

One "pre-preliminary" perspective drawing at Syracuse University dated September 25, 1953, records a singular Breuer house design that he appears not to have repeated. In plan, the two-story house is arranged as a large symmetrical H with a perpendicular wing projecting from the link. In elevation, it is an odd assortment of heterogeneous features, including a peaked roof (which must have been the client's demand), and a full unshaded terrace that is the roof of the projecting wing.

ARCHIVAL: **SUL Drawing; AAA Correspondence.**
BIBLIOGRAPHIC: **Driller,** *Breuer Houses*, **266.**

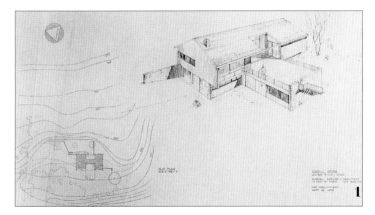

203. Pre-preliminary site plan and perspective

204
Aufricht House, Addition,
Mamaroneck, New York, 1953

MARCEL BREUER, ARCHITECT

Two drawings at Syracuse University, dated June 5 and 9, 1953, represent Breuer's design for an addition to the existing Westchester County house of Dr. Gustave Aufricht.

ARCHIVAL: **SUL Drawings; AAA Contract, Correspondence.**

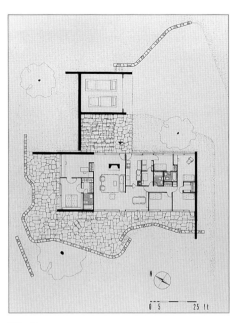

205a. Plan

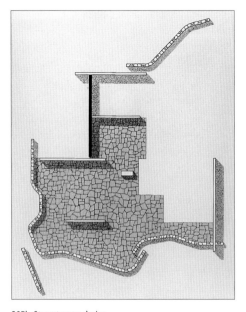

205b. Stone terrace design

205
Neumann House,
Croton-on-Hudson, New York, 1953–54

Pool House, 1973

MARCEL BREUER, ARCHITECT

For Vera and George Neumann, Breuer made several showrooms for their house-furnishing and fashion-design business, Scarves by Vera,[13] and for their residence produced one of his finest houses. It was designed as a unified rectangular block connected across a paved patio to a carport and framed on the south and the west by wide paved terraces. The Neumann family situation gave Breuer his program, for the house had to be arranged as though it were "two apartments," one for the Neumanns and the other for children and grandparents; in between was the "common area."

Writing to L'*Architecture d'aujourd'hui* in 1954, Breuer said that

the main aesthetic notion of this building is the contrast between the free curving stone retaining walls and the colored slab walls. The slab-like walls of the house alternate in color [and materials]: painted concrete block walls, glass walls, and natural stone walls. The retaining wall of the terrace and the driveway follow the free contours of the land, of the desirable width needed for the terrace, and sometimes missing and sometimes enclosing the existing trees, but always considering them.[14]

The exterior appearance of the Neumann House was a brilliant interplay of color, form, and materials, with the concrete-block walls painted bright red and Breuer blue, in sharp contrast to the colors of the natural surroundings. The terrace precinct was outlined by a retaining wall of a lyrical design reminiscent of Breuer's sinuous plywood frames for his Isokon furniture of two decades earlier.

A pool house to the rear of the residence was designed in 1972 and constructed in 1973. An outdoor pool had been built in 1954; it does not appear on published plans, since it was a late decision and was built after the house was completed.

ARCHIVAL: **SUL 153, Drawings; AAA Correspondence.**
BIBLIOGRAPHIC: *House and Home*, March 1955, 107–11; *Interiors*, June 1956, 109–10; Breuer, *Sun and Shadow*, 46–47, 86, 90–91, 130, 145; Jones, ed., *Marcel Breuer*, 158–61; Papachristou, *Marcel Breuer*, 222; Driller, *Breuer Houses*, 266.

206. Entrance facade

206
Snower House,
Kansas City, Kansas, 1953–54

MARCEL BREUER, ARCHITECT

There is scant information in the Breuer archives about the Snower House, but there are drawings, transparencies, and a copy of the 1953 contract for the Kansas City, Kansas, residence. Robert Gatje worked on it soon after joining the Breuer office and made an inspection visit during construction. He recalled that the house was sited on a corner lot in a developing residential community where there were restrictive covenants about shapes and materials that tended to preclude modern houses.[15] Since the client wanted a Breuer house, he and the architect successfully interpreted the rules to meet the restrictions but still produce a modern house.[16] It was a flat-roofed long box with diagonal wood cladding cantilevered from a concrete base.

ARCHIVAL: **SUL Drawings; AAA Contract, Photos.**
BIBLIOGRAPHIC: **Driller,** *Breuer Houses*, **266; Gatje,** *Marcel Breuer*, **52.**

207
Edgar Stillman, Jr., Cottage,
Wellfleet, Massachusetts, 1953–54

MARCEL BREUER, ARCHITECT

Mary and Edgar Stillman, Jr., of New York City and Middlebury, Connecticut, relatives of Rufus and Leslie Stillman, agreed on August 13, 1953, to build a summer cottage in Wellfleet, Massachusetts, on almost 5 acres of land at water's edge (see p. 31). Breuer forwarded plans, a preliminary design, elevations, and perspective drawings for a wood-frame house above concrete piers, with cedar siding and sliding walls of glass. Oriented and elevated to take advantage of an open field and a grand view of Cape Cod Bay, the Stillman Cottage shows Breuer at his best with a modest program, simple materials, and an ideal location. Another of his long boxes with an in-line arrangement of interior spaces broadened on both long facades with porches or decks, the cottage was organized with the living room–dining room and the screened and open porches at one end, and the bedrooms, bath, and study at the other. An overhanging roof offered shade, and floor-to-ceiling screens and glazing opened the public rooms to air and light.

ARCHIVAL: **SUL 79, Drawings; AAA Contract, Correspondence, Photos.**
BIBLIOGRAPHIC: **Breuer,** *Sun and Shadow*, **156–57; Jones, ed.,** *Marcel Breuer*, **173.**

208. View from the south

208
Grieco House,
Andover, Massachusetts, 1954

MARCEL BREUER, ARCHITECT

When Vito Grieco saw the Clark House in Orange, Connecticut, he wanted to have a Breuer house, although smaller, and wrote to the architect on January 22, 1954, describing the location and the program. He told Breuer that he especially admired the two-wing system—one for living, and the other for sleeping—at the Clark House. Conversations between client and architect resulted in a house of 2,000 square feet that was quickly and efficiently constructed.

Breuer designed a two-level, binuclear L-shaped structure with the stair hall as the link. The south facade was pierced by a long ribbon of windows, and a highly distinctive sunbreak grill adapted from Breuer's contemporaneous McIntyre plant—deep and long and affixed to vertical supports with taut cable—was set against the volume of the house. Its verticals extended above the roofline and below the cantilevered volume of the house in an irregular rhythm. The grill also served as a sculptural element to contrast with the flatness of the windowed facade.

ARCHIVAL: **SUL 152, Drawings; AAA Contract, Correspondence, Photos.**
BIBLIOGRAPHIC: *Architectural Record*, November 1955, 164–67; Breuer, *Sun and Shadow*, 154–55; Jones, ed., *Marcel Breuer*, 190–91; Papachristou, *Marcel Breuer*, 224; Driller, *Breuer Houses*, 266.

209
Harnischmacher House II,
Wiesbaden, Germany, 1953–54

MARCEL BREUER, ARCHITECT

In December 1953, Paul and Marianne Harnischmacher decided to build a second house close to the site of their historic house of 1932, which was destroyed in the Second World War. Working drawings, made in metric and adapted in part from current Breuer houses, were prepared in February 1954 in the New York office and were sent to Wilhelm Neuser, the local architect in Wiesbaden who was to oversee construction. "The drawings are a mixture of American and German building techniques," Breuer explained, "[and] are only meant to give Mr. Neuser an idea of what we have in mind and to work out details."[17] "The whole roof construction, including most of the beams, is of wood. I believe this would be the simplest solution, though it is somewhat 'American,'" he continued. For the large American kitchen they wanted, the clients were sent photographs and drawings of kitchen details from Breuer House–New Canaan II, Stillman House I, and the Clark House. With rosy memories of the first experience, Breuer wrote to them on March 24, 1954, that "I hope the work will go as smoothly as with our first house and that you will be as satisfied with the house itself as I am with the idea of having a second Harnischmacher House."[18]

By designing Harnischmacher House II in conformity with his suburban style of the 1950s, particularly that of the long-box format, Breuer was now exporting American postwar modernism to Germany, whereas he had originally imported the Franco-German modernism of Harnischmacher I to America. Since he was often in Paris at work on

209. Paul Harnischmacher in the garden of his house

the UNESCO complex during the planning stages of Harnischmacher House II, much of his communication with the clients was routed in a three-way arrangement, whereby the drawings were sent to him in Paris from New York and then sent on to Wiesbaden after he had checked them. Construction began in April 1954, and the Harnischmachers were living in the house by November. Following the wishes of the client, stone was used generously outside and inside and was contrasted with stucco surfaces—those of the wall areas beneath the windows on the outside and the full walls of the interior. A south-facing pergola and garden terrace in front of the large windows of the master bedroom, study, living room, and dining room were defined by granite piers set on a stone parapet and supporting the pergola beams.

In August 1955, Harnischmacher House II was awarded a prize by a group of German architects; it was also the only private residence in Wiesbaden to receive a plaquette from the city marking its award-winning status. "It makes me more than happy that the house of the Harnischmachers finds recognition in Wiesbaden," wrote Breuer on December 19, 1955.[19]

For its owners, the building was an enormous success; Breuer was moved when he learned that Paul Harnishmacher, in failing health in the spring of 1956, found the house so salutary that it served "as if it were a sanatorium."[20]

ARCHIVAL: **SUL 152, Drawings; AAA Photos.**
BIBLIOGRAPHIC: **Breuer, *Sun and Shadow*, 61; Driller, *Breuer Houses*, 190–95, 266.**

210
Starkey House (Alworth House),
Duluth, Minnesota, 1954–55

MARCEL BREUER, ARCHITECT

HERBERT BECKHARD AND ROBERT F. GATJE, ASSOCIATES

A contract between Breuer and June Halvorson Alworth for a house in Duluth, Minnesota, was drawn up in July 1954. (After Alworth was widowed and then married to Robert J. Starkey, the Alworth House was known as the Starkey House.) A luxurious, expansive residence sited on the shore of Lake Superior, its good press coverage reinforced the image of Breuer as a reigning modernist residential architect in America of the 1950s whose work took root as far away from his European origins as Minnesota. The house was featured in the October 22, 1956, issue of *Time* with four illustrations in color, a perspective cutaway, and a photo of Breuer.

One of Breuer's decentralized compositions, the Starkey House is a tri-nuclear arrangement of three boxes: a living and dining pavilion, a wing for sleeping and children, and a garage and storage area. The arrangement of the volumes on sloping terrain allied it with Mies van der Rohe's Tugendhat House (1928–30), whose low, closed entrance mass at the top of the slope hides the main, view-oriented block. In Brno, the building was set into the side of the hill, whereas in Duluth it was cantilevered over the slope, supported on wood columns slightly elevated on metal rods. The proximity of the lake inspired Breuer once again to put into play the marine imagery he particularly favored at the time by using taut wire, a suspended gangplank bridge, and ship-rail bannisters.

Structurally ingenious, the living–dining room pavilion was suspended from a pair of massive laminated-wood beams placed above the roof, allowing, as reported in *Time*, "an uncluttered expanse of ceiling from wall to wall." A paved area with outdoor fireplace beneath the cantilever, defined by fieldstone walls, provided additional outdoor living space.

ARCHIVAL: **SUL Drawings; AAA Correspondence, Photos.**
BIBLIOGRAPHIC: ***Time*, October 22, 1956, 90–93; *Architectural Record*, January 1957, 156–60; *L'architettura*, June 1957, 104–5; *Bauen und Wohnen*, December 1957, 411–15; *Domus*, March 1958, 1–3; Jones, ed., *Marcel Breuer*, 163–65; Papachristou, *Marcel Breuer*, 231; Masello, *Architecture Without Rules*, 38–43; Driller, *Breuer Houses*, 196–201, 266.**

210. Lakefront side

211
Karsten House,
Owings Mill, Maryland, 1955–56

MARCEL BREUER, ARCHITECT

Construction of a house for Baltimore lawyer Thomas L. Karsten was completed in 1956. Similar to the Clark House and other Breuer residences of the mid-1950s, the Karsten House was long and low, with a flat, overhanging roof and open and closed volumes created by contrasting natural fieldstone walls with floor-to-ceiling glazed entrances between terrace and interior.

ARCHIVAL: **SUL 35, 38, 39, Drawings; AAA Contract, Correspondence.**
BIBLIOGRAPHIC: **Driller,** *Breuer Houses***, 266.**

212
Laaff House,
Andover, Massachusetts, 1955–57

MARCEL BREUER, ARCHITECT

HERBERT BECKHARD, ASSOCIATE

On January 21, 1955, Breuer's secretary wrote to him in Paris that "Mr. Laaff telephoned from Lawrence, Mass. They've seen the Grieco House and wondered if you would do a house for them." Within a few months, Breuer met the clients and worked out the program and design. The Laaff House exemplifies Breuer's fieldstone houses of the 1950s in its side-by-side combination of stone in its natural state, stone painted white, and glass. It is composed in essentially the same overall format as the contemporaneous Gagarin House I—a long rectangle (but on only one level and enclosing a set-back entry court) with a smaller square abutted. Light entered the main living spaces through not only the large glass walls but also a clerestoried strip in the upper part of the wall above the fireplace.

ARCHIVAL: **SUL Drawings; AAA Correspondence, Photos.**
BIBLIOGRAPHIC: *Architectural Record*, **January 1960, 136–38, and May 1960, 128–31;** *Arts & Architecture*, **July 1960, 18–19; Jones, ed.,** *Marcel Breuer*, **170–72; Papachristou,** *Marcel Breuer*, **231; Masello,** *Architecture Without Rules*, **56–61; Driller,** *Breuer Houses*, **266.**

213. View of the dining and living areas

213
Gagarin House I,
Litchfield, Connecticut, 1956–57

MARCEL BREUER, ARCHITECT

HERBERT BECKHARD, ASSOCIATE

Gagarin House I was one of Breuer's most glamorous and photogenic houses of the 1950s, with a terrazzo dance floor on the roof, terraces, and a swimming pool (see p. 33). The commission came through Rufus Stillman. A drawing showing roof deck and covered terraces is at Syracuse University, along with several quick ground-plan sketches by Breuer. Construction took place during 1956 and 1957; the structure is steel-frame and reinforced-concrete slab. A long box abutted by a shorter perpendicular extension with a master-bedroom suite and private patio, the house is arranged on two levels connected by a series of steps.

A children's wing with five bedrooms and a playroom constituted the lower level. An unusual angled entrance was a departure from the strict rectilinearity used by Breuer in similar formats.

ARCHIVAL: SUL 143–45, Drawings; AAA Contract, Correspondence, Photos, Project Record Book.
BIBLIOGRAPHIC: *Architectural Record*, October 1957, 211–16; *Domus*, March 1958, 4–6; *Bauen und Wohnen*, March 1958, 87–89; *Deutsche Bauzeitung*, June 1958, 252–54; Jones, ed., *Marcel Breuer*, 146–48; Papachristou, *Marcel Breuer*, 230; Masello, *Architecture Without Rules*, 44–49; Driller, *Breuer Houses*, 266.

214
Staehelin House,
Feldmeilen, Switzerland, 1957–58

MARCEL BREUER, ARCHITECT

HERBERT BECKHARD, ASSOCIATE

EBERHARD EIDENBENZ, ASSOCIATE (SWITZERLAND)

A sense of the capacity of the Staehelin House (see pp. 34, 136), a luxurious, spacious residence for art collectors on a dramatic site near Zürich, is conveyed by a letter from client William R. Staehelin to Breuer in 1965: "Dear Lajkó, Yesterday sixty people have lunched on one table in our living room. It was a great success."[21] The Staehelins' principal residence was in Zürich; the house in Feldmeilen, on a sloping wooded field overlooking the Zürichsee, was to be a nearby retreat. They discovered Breuer by looking through books about modern houses. He and Richard Neutra were invited to visit, and the selection turned largely on a personal impression of the two men.[22] A program was submitted by the Staehelins on July 31, 1956; working drawings were begun in April 1957, and construction was completed in 1958. A sprawling composition with exterior walls and overhanging rooflines arranged as overlapping and eliding Constructivist planes, the house is laid out as four linked, forward-projecting boxes, separated from the garage by a long, naturally lighted corridor that hides the entrance and, along with the stone walls, ensures a sense of privacy and inwardness. A change in levels from entrance to living room is bridged by ramps.

On the upper floor, the master suite and guest room open to a large roof deck. Quarters for the children on the ground floor are apart from the public rooms and have their own entrance and garden. This organization, appearing often in Breuer houses, is European rather than American in inspiration, and has its source in the Haus am Horn (1923) in Weimar erected for the Bauhaus Ausstellung, where the children's room had its own door to the outside.[23] A special feature of the main section of the Staehelin House is an interior garden court adjacent to the glass-walled dining room; a third inner garden is located outside Staehelin's studio. The structure is steel frame with a system of reinforced-concrete slabs, bearing walls, and interior columns.

Among the most appreciative of Breuer's clients, the Staehelins felt that he had changed their lives.[24] His house encouraged them to live a kind of life they found to be "congenial—aesthetically and intellectually—and spiritually uplifting."[25] "We daily bless the day when we first met," Staehelin wrote to Breuer after living in the house for eight years.[26]

ARCHIVAL: 74, SUL 154, 155; AAA Photos, Project Record Book.
BIBLIOGRAPHIC: *L'Architecture d'aujourd'hui*, November 1959, 4–5; *Bauen und Wohnen*, December 1959, 418–23; *Deutsche Bauzeitung*, January 1960, 8–13; *Architectural Record*, January 1960, 132–35; *L'Oeil*, December 1960, 100–105; *Arts & Architecture*, January 1961, 14–15; *Interiors*, August 1962, 80–85; *Abitare*, December 1962, 2–20; Jones, ed., *Marcel Breuer*, 124–29; Papachristou, *Marcel Breuer*, 233; Masello, *Architecture Without Rules*, 50–55; Driller, *Breuer Houses*, 202–9, 266.

215
Krieger House,
Bethesda, Maryland, 1957–58

MARCEL BREUER, ARCHITECT

Breuer was first in touch with Seymour Krieger in 1956; the 4,300-square-foot house was completed in 1958. A steel-frame structure, the Krieger House is compact in format, with the children's zone and parents' zone separated by the main living spaces, in a customary Breuer arrangement. Included in the design were paved terraces and rubble-stone retaining walls that extended into the eastern portion of the property.

ARCHIVAL: **SUL 177, Drawings; AAA Contract, Photos, Project Record Book.**
BIBLIOGRAPHIC: **Driller,** *Breuer Houses,* **266.**

216
Hooper House II,
Baltimore, Maryland, 1957–59

MARCEL BREUER, ARCHITECT

HERBERT BECKHARD, ASSOCIATE

Long associated with philanthropist and art collector Edith Ferry Hooper and her family, Breuer, in January 1956, was commissioned to design a new seven-bedroom, 7,000-square-foot house on lakefront property in Baltimore adjoining the city's bird sanctuary (see p. 35). Construction was completed in early 1959. The house is on two levels, the lower set into the hill. The upper west facade, defined by a rugged fieldstone wall, is pierced by the entry. The main living spaces, all with direct access to the outdoors, are also on the upper level and are arranged in binuclear fashion, with the entrance gallery (leading to an inner atrium) as the joining/separating element: the living-dining room and kitchen are on one side; the bedrooms, children's playroom, guest room, and maid's room are on the other. The entrance gallery has a 5-foot-wide sliding glass door at each end through which the atrium and lake could be seen. The lower level—for stables, caretaker's apartment, and other auxiliary functions—projected to the west, touching the upper level at only one corner.

The house was restored in 1993 by Jonathan S. Foster.

ARCHIVAL: **SUL 76–78.**
BIBLIOGRAPHIC: *Architectural Record,* **May 1961, 70–73;** *Deutsche Bauzeitung,* **November 1961, 849–52;** *House Beautiful,* **April 1993, 112–17; Jones, ed.,** *Marcel Breuer,* **72–73; Masello,** *Architecture Without Rules,* **62–67; Driller,** *Breuer Houses,* **210–15, 266.**

217
Paepcke Vacation House,
Aspen, Colorado, 1959 (NOT BUILT)

MARCEL BREUER, ARCHITECT

HERBERT BECKHARD, ASSOCIATE

Breuer designed a weekend and vacation house of exceptional individuality in Aspen, Colorado, for prominent industrialist Walter Paepcke, developer of Aspen and president of Container Corporation of America, for whom Herbert Bayer worked as design consultant. A 6-foot-high stone wall enclosed the house precinct on all sides, providing a private outdoor terrace, entrance court, and carport. The house was structured with a sweeping barrel vault of reinforced concrete 13 feet high at the apex and painted white, beneath which the rooms were set within a rectangular framework. The commanding spatial feature of the interior was a large living-dining room with a "conversation pit" in front of the fireplace at the western end. This core was framed by an L-shaped corridor of bedrooms, baths, and kitchen. In 1969, Breuer reused the house design, with modifications, for Geller House II.

ARCHIVAL: **SUL 55, Drawings; AAA Photos.**
BIBLIOGRAPHIC: *Architectural Record,* **January 1960, 130–31; Jones, ed.,** *Marcel Breuer,* **105; Masello,** *Architecture Without Rules,* **62–67; Driller,** *Breuer Houses,* **267.**

217. Rendering

218. Preliminary perspective sketch

218
Ustinov House,
Montreux, Switzerland, 1959–60 (NOT BUILT)

MARCEL BREUER, ARCHITECT

ROBERT F. GATJE, ASSOCIATE

In September 1959, Breuer agreed to design a house in Montreux, Switzerland, for actor, playwright, and stage director Peter Ustinov. Ustinov came to Breuer through William R. Staehelin, whose grand house in Feldmeilen, near Zürich, Breuer had completed the previous year. Swiss architect Eberhard Eidenbenz was to act as supervising architect, as he had for the Staehelin House. Between September 1959 and April 1960, Breuer met a number of times with the Ustinovs to work out the program. Working drawings were begun in January 1960, but by June, when the job was bid, relations between client and architect regarding the project had deteriorated. Breuer's design proved far more expensive to build than the clients wished; at the same time, the correspondence reveals that the clients' requests for changes and additions were not always practical. After arguments and disagreements, both parties retained lawyers.

The design had an interesting afterlife, however. A daring and dramatic reinterpretation of Breuer's binuclear format beneath a double-hyperbolic-paraboloid concrete-shell roof, it was difficult and expensive to construct and required highly experienced contractors and craftsmen. An attempt in 1968 to build a house based on this design for José Soriano in Greenwich, Connecticut, was given up and replaced with a less radical structure of stone and wood. Finally in 1972, the "Ustinov House" was successfully built as the Saier House, near Deauville, France, where it looked and functioned as Breuer had intended.

ARCHIVAL: **SUL 155, Drawings; AAA Contract, Photos.**
BIBLIOGRAPHIC: **Papachristou,** *Marcel Breuer,* **238; Driller,** *Breuer Houses,* **267.**

SINGLE-FAMILY HOUSES, 1960s

219. Beachfront (east) elevation

219
McMullen Beach House,
Mantoloking, New Jersey, 1960

MARCEL BREUER, ARCHITECT

HERBERT BECKHARD, ASSOCIATE

Correspondence and construction records for the McMullen Beach House appear to be lost, but the drawings are at Syracuse University. One of Breuer's most striking residential structures, the McMullen House is an unclichéd example of the beach-house genre, defined by contrasts of light and dark wood, closed and open volumes, earthbound and elevated masses (see p. 169). In a two-story cube lifted from the ground and supported by double beams and wood columns are the main living areas; at ground level is a smaller glazed cube with entrance. For privacy, the north and south elevations are closed, except for small sliding windows. On the fully glazed ocean side, a partially fixed sunscreen covers the upper portion of the recessed living-room facade, which is fronted by a deck. The deck projecting from the dining room is covered by a skeleton pergola corresponding to the lines of the railing. The full expanse of the west facade has a fixed louvered sunscreen.

If there is any late Breuer building that could be interpreted as a restatement of his Bauhaus furniture experiments, it is the McMullen House. The deck railing and pergola on the east facade are a version of the frame of the de Stijl–inspired wooden armchair of 1922, with its transparency and intersecting blunt-edged structural members projecting into space. The body of the house, too, was developed as though it were a massive cabinet with grill front.

ARCHIVAL: **SUL Drawings; AAA Photos.**
BIBLIOGRAPHIC: *Architectural Record*, November 1961, 150–52; *Deutsche Bauzeitschrift*, April 1962, 521–22; *L'Architecture d'aujourd'hui*, September 1962, 71; Jones, ed., *Marcel Breuer*, 100–103; Masello, *Architecture Without Rules*, 68–73; Driller, *Breuer Houses*, 266–67.

220
Kacmarcik House,
St. Paul, Minnesota, 1961

MARCEL BREUER, ARCHITECT

For Brother Frank Kacmarcik—artist, designer, liturgical-art consultant, and later a member of the community of monks at Saint John's Abbey—Breuer designed a house in 1961. Kacmarcik wished to work out many of the details himself, with the assistance of the contractor, and to oversee the construction. In September 1961, working drawings were sent from the Breuer office to Kacmarcik, along with copies of a design for the kitchen, which was to be reworked by Kacmarcik from another (unspecified) Breuer house. Sometime later, the Breuer office sent drawings for lighting layouts. A sheet of elevations at Syracuse University shows a projecting flat roof above a closed, compact rectangular box sheathed in brick and relieved by glazing at the entry and on the northwest and southwest faces.

ARCHIVAL: **SUL 104, Drawings.**

221
Van der Wal House,
Amsterdam, the Netherlands, 1962–63 (NOT BUILT)

MARCEL BREUER AND HAMILTON P. SMITH, ARCHITECTS

For Dutch businessman and art collector Gerrit Van der Wal, a friend from the time that Breuer was working on the De Bijenkorf department store in Rotterdam, Breuer designed in 1962 a two-story, three-bedroom residence in Amsterdam adjacent to a canal. Preliminary sketches depict a closed, compact, massive structure, sharp-edged and angular, rectangular in layout with the rooms axially aligned. An important consideration in the program was the accommodation of the Van der Wal art collection, mostly sculpture. "I tried to give the house as much continuous solid wall surface as possible as a background for sculpture and painting," Breuer wrote.[1] "I thought of building the house in rough concrete; the effect would be similar to that of the large assembly hall of Unesco," he added.

An entrance gallery on the north led to the dining room and kitchen area past a door-height partition; a few steps down was the living room, also separated by a partition from two studies; beyond was the south terrace. The south wall of the living room and study was glazed above a wide stone sill "for sculpture or for sitting or sunning," with sliding glass panels leading to the roofless, low-walled outside terrace. In a letter to Breuer of March 13, 1963, the clients expressed their worries about light and their concern that the overhangs of balcony and roof would make the house gloomy in Amsterdam's cloudy climate.[2] In any event, after trying from 1963 to 1966 without success to get building permission from city authorities, in 1966 the Van der Wals bought a house built in 1937 in the neighboring town of Amstelveen, and Breuer's design was never executed.

ARCHIVAL: **SUL 155, Drawings; AAA Correspondence, Photos.**
BIBLIOGRAPHIC: *Architectural Record,* **November 1966, 130–31;** Papachristou, *Marcel Breuer,* **81;** Driller, *Breuer Houses,* **216–23, 267.**

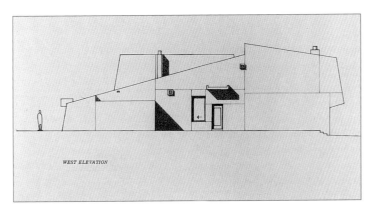

WEST ELEVATION

221. West elevation

222
Wise House,
Wellfleet, Massachusetts, 1963

Addition, 1972

MARCEL BREUER AND HERBERT BECKHARD, ARCHITECTS

Breuer's vacation house on Williams Pond in Wellfleet, Massachusetts, on Cape Cod, built in 1948 and enlarged in 1961–62, was admired by New York City art gallery owners Mr. and Mrs. Howard Wise. In September 1962, Breuer agreed to build for the Wises a duplicate of his house, "with the whole plan reversed so that it is a mirror image of the floor plan of my house." It was constructed in 1963; in 1972, the clients wished to expand the breezeway connection between the main house and the studio with the addition of a lower deck extended to the west so that they could have an outdoor room. The foundations were planned so that the cedar decking could accommodate scrub pines growing through it.

ARCHIVAL: **SUL 155, Contract, Drawings, Photos.**
BIBLIOGRAPHIC: *Architectural Record,* **November 1966, 134–36;** Masello, *Architecture Without Rules,* **74–79;** Driller, *Breuer Houses,* **262.**

223. View from the east

223
Koerfer House,
Moscia, Switzerland, 1963–66

MARCEL BREUER AND HERBERT BECKHARD, ARCHITECTS

Breuer received an inquiry in January 1963 from Jacques Koerfer of Bern, an industrialist and important collector of twentieth-century art, about constructing a "modern, comfortable and homely house" for family vacations in the Swiss canton of Tessin. The property, 13,000 square meters (140,000 square feet), was situated in Moscia on a steep hillside with a magnificent view of Lake Maggiore. Breuer jotted down questions on the back of the letter: "How does he come to me? How old are the children? What is his profession?" He suggested that Koerfer look at the Staehelin House because it, too, was a large residence for an art collector. On February 4, 1963, he and Koerfer entered into an agreement, and the first sketches, made in March, depict a house covered by a hyperbolic-paraboloid roof, an idea rejected by the client. By 1966, construction was essentially complete for a grand house inserted into the hillside, fronted by tiers of powerful granite walls and paced by terraces that are linked by stairs with cantilevered treads. The structure is based on the concrete flat-slab system, and the basic materials are reinforced concrete, granite, and glass. Formed as a flat-roofed concrete-framed glazed cube, the house rises through three levels and is wrapped by two strata of wide granite-paved terraces supported by square columns. The exposed concrete of the exterior walls, columns, and ceiling portions were bush-hammered as they emerged from the formboards, exposing the aggregate and texturing the surfaces.

The main living spaces are on the second floor; the smaller third floor—the roof-terrace level—has the children's suites and guest quarters; at ground level are the entry, servant's room, garage, and facilities. The levels are interconnected through strategically placed interior and exterior stairs.

Like that of the Robinson House of twenty years earlier, the design of the Koerfer House—its terraces and glass walls—was determined by the dramatic view and the movement of the sun. The terrace outside the glass-walled entry is overhung and shaded by the living-room terrace, with its square perforations that allow trees to grow through them, while the penthouse terrace is exposed to full light. A skylighted pool house, sketched in 1965, was built against a nearly vertical rock wall to the north of the site.

ARCHIVAL: **SUL 74, 80, 81, Drawings; AAA Correspondence, Photos.**
BIBLIOGRAPHIC: *Architectural Record*, **November 1966, 132–33;** *Werk*, **September 1967, 556–60;** *Architectural Forum*, **December 1969, 52–59;** *Journal of the American Institute of Architects*, **May 1972, 39;** *L'Oeil*, **November 1974, 22–27;** Papachristou, *Marcel Breuer*, **148–57;** *Global Architecture*, **no. 43;** *Global Architecture Detail*, **no. 7;** Masello, *Architecture Without Rules*, **94–101;** Driller, *Breuer Houses*, **224–35, 267.**

224
De Gunzberg Chalets,
Megève, France, 1964 (NOT BUILT)

MARCEL BREUER, ARCHITECT

Breuer and Baron Alain de Gunzburg of Paris corresponded in January 1964 about plans for a compound of three or four chalets in Megève, a winter resort in Haute-Savoie. De Gunzburg sent Breuer a survey of the property and zoning regulations for the region.[3] In return, Breuer sent him a copy of his terms of agreement with Jacques Koerfer for the house then in construction in Switzerland.[4] An unsigned contract dated February 18, 1964, specifying fees and the engagement of a supervising architect is with Breuer's papers in the Archives of American Art. Breuer made preliminary plans, but by September the project had been given up, and he wrote de Gunzberg, saying that "the various plans about Megève are being returned to you."[5]

ARCHIVAL: **SUL 152.**

225
Stillman House II,
Litchfield, Connecticut, 1965

MARCEL BREUER AND HERBERT BECKHARD, ARCHITECTS

During 1963 and 1964, Breuer designed a new and larger house in Litchfield, Connecticut, for Rufus and Leslie Stillman, whose first Breuer house was built in 1950. Breuer's own ground-plan sketch on graph paper for a building of approximately 3,000 square feet, including garage, is at Syracuse University. In construction during the summer of 1965, the house was completed in December. Wanting a significant change from the format of Stillman House I, the clients asked for a "U-shaped building in order to have a sun trap and windbreak with a southeast exposure."[6] They also wanted a change in materials and a new aesthetic ("We want masonry—great big thick walls with holes and window seats"), conforming to the aesthetic shift in Breuer's residential work in the early 1960s toward heavy masses and an Expressionist handling of concrete. Breuer gave special attention to the specifications for the concrete work—type of cement, formboard impressions, pouring procedure—written in a manner usually associated with large institutional buildings rather than residences. The living room, dining room, and kitchen is one unpartitioned area, forming the link in a U-shaped layout, with a wing on the west for the children and one on the east for the parents. Fronting the living room

is a vast terrace that is framed and protected by rugged stone walls. Windows are large sliding glass panels. On the exterior east flank of the house is a monumental 50-foot retaining wall, 4 feet above the grade of the driveway and diminishing toward the east. The thick-walled residence, with its exterior finish of textured white stucco, is locked into a massive fieldstone wall. From these materials, textures, and colors, in combination with the symmetrical ground plan and balanced elevation, emerges Breuer's most classical, most Mediterranean house.

ARCHIVAL: **SUL 79, Drawings, Sketch; AAA Contract, Photos.**
BIBLIOGRAPHIC: *Architectural Record*, November 1966, 126–29; *House & Garden*, May 1967, 132–33; *Progressive Architecture*, July 1967, 128–29; Papachristou, *Marcel Breuer*, 164–67; Masello, *Architecture Without Rules*, 88–92; Driller, *Breuer Houses*, 267.

225. South facade

226a. View from the south

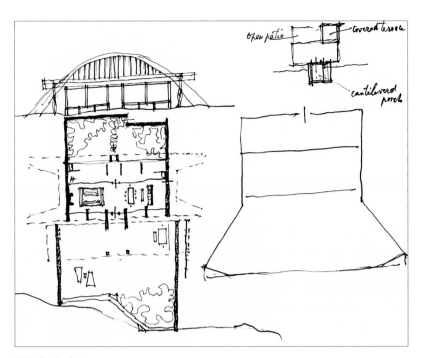

226b. Sketches by Breuer

a relatively large one in a highly developed area of Long Island, neighboring houses on the east and west were within view; consequently, the house was planned without windows on those elevations. The entrance, on the north, is across a broad terrace that is the width of the house; the south facade is fully glazed, but subdivided by an independent two-story sunscreen made of deep concrete compartments in a geometric pattern intended to diminish summer heat and light and illustrating Breuer's continued belief in sun control through architectural devices.

Breuer's awareness of Le Corbusier's expressive use of concrete, possibly the vaults in the Maisons Jaoul (1956) in Neuilly-sur-Seine, as well as early Corbusier experiments with open-plan duplex systems and their interpenetrating parallel spaces, lies behind some of the features of the design of the Paepcke Vacation House and its transformation into Geller House II.

ARCHIVAL: **SUL 74, 141, 142; AAA Photos.**

BIBLIOGRAPHIC: *House & Garden*, February 1970, 68–73; *Architectural Record*, July 1970, 115–18; Papachristou, *Marcel Breuer*, 170–73; Masello, *Architecture Without Rules*, 108–16; Driller, *Breuer Houses*, 267.

226
Geller House II,
Lawrence, Long Island, New York, 1968–69

MARCEL BREUER AND HERBERT BECKHARD, ARCHITECTS

For Mr. and Mrs. Bert Geller, his first house clients as an independent practitioner in the United States and for whom he built a landmark suburban house in 1945, Breuer designed a second and completely different residence two decades later. On March 15, 1967, he and the Gellers contracted for the new house, which was built during 1968 and 1969. In a dramatic case of adaptive reuse of an earlier design, with the Gellers' consent, Breuer based the house on his unexecuted 1959 project for the Paepcke Vacation House in Aspen, Colorado. A textured-concrete-and-stucco structure, square in shape and roofed with a tautly curved parabolic concrete vault, Geller House II suggests a sophisticated Quonset hut. Made of "Gacoflex elastomeric liquid roofing," the vault was separated from the side walls by a compressible material so it could expand and contract with thermal changes without affecting the rest of the structure. As one of Breuer's best expressions of voluminous space, the interior of Geller House II is an open-plan duplex: the spaciousness of the first level (three bedrooms, living-dining room, and kitchen) was expanded by its extension (to 16 feet, 6 inches) into the upper level studio and by its connection to the exterior landscape through the huge glass wall of the south facade. Although the site was

227
Soriano House,
Greenwich, Connecticut, 1971–73

MARCEL BREUER AND TICIAN PAPACHRISTOU, ARCHITECTS

In this commission for José M. Soriano, Breuer was able to adapt the plans for his unrealized Ustinov House in Montreux. A first contract was signed on February 15, 1968. The original working drawings and specifications were used as the basis for the new proposal, but as concrete construction of this type for residential architecture was exceptionally expensive on both continents, and as the bids came in too high, as they had in Switzerland, a new agreement was made in October 1970 for design changes that would reduce costs. Although the layout would remain the same, the structural materials would be wood and stone instead of reinforced concrete. A sloping wood-frame roof over the core of the house would be substituted for a hyperbolic-paraboloid roof; some spaces, such as the master bedroom and the terrace area, would be reduced in size; and a reflecting pool would be eliminated. New working drawings and specifications were prepared; construction began in April 1971, and the revised building—made of warm sand-colored stone combined with glass and white-painted wood—was completed in 1973 (see p. 177).

The plan was another version of Breuer's binuclear H, where two rectangular volumes, each with two levels, are joined by a narrow entry bridge and covered by sloping roofs. Tapered retaining walls of thick stone extended from house to grounds. The house has been destroyed.

ARCHIVAL: **SUL 74, Drawings; AAA Contract, Photos.**
BIBLIOGRAPHIC: **Papachristou,** *Marcel Breuer*, **182–83 (before design revision); Driller,** *Breuer Houses*, **267.**

228
Saier House,
Glanville, France, 1972–73

MARCEL BREUER AND MARIO JOSSA, ARCHITECTS

An agreement between Louis Saier of Neuilly-sur-Seine and Breuer for a "maison particulière à Glanville (Calvados)," to be the responsibility of Breuer's Paris office, was dated May 9, 1972; construction was completed in 1973 (see p. 177). The history of the design goes back, as did the first design of the Soriano House, to 1959 and the unrealized project for the Ustinov House in Montreux, a striking concrete-and-glass reinvention by Breuer of his 1940s butterfly theme, whereby the pavilion core of the house was roofed with a pair of hyperbolic-paraboloid shells. A project that had reached the working drawings and bidding stage before being filed away because, among other reasons, the concrete structure was too expensive to build, the design of the Ustinov House reappeared in 1968 when Breuer used it for a first concept for the Soriano House, later replaced by a more affordable wood-and-stone house.

Robert Gatje recounted that a photographic enlargement of a rendering of the Ustinov House used as a backdrop display in a showroom of Breuer furniture in Paris in 1972 attracted the attention of Saier, who, even after learning the discouraging history of previous efforts, was not deterred in his determination to build it.[1] The New York office assembled the working drawings of the original Ustinov House, which had been measured in meters, and sent them to Paris, where they were adapted for the program and the site of the Saier House.[2] The living room–dining room core of the house was covered by a partially pre-stressed double-hyperbolic-paraboloid shell supported by triangular concrete buttresses, the three lowered corners of the roof shells anchored to the buttresses by bronze connecting elements, cross-shaped in plan. According to Gatje, the New York office paid close attention to the structural engineering during construction; at the end of the job, it was the opinion of the office that the house had been "beautifully built" with "exquisite" concrete work.[3]

A dramatic two-level, two-unit house set at the top of a rise, the upper level of living room, dining room, and kitchen in the main house opens to the landscape through walls of glass divided into irregular fields; bedrooms are on the lower level. Across the pool terrace is a subsidiary residence wing, with a garage, three bedrooms, and a private garden. Above the living room–dining room wing, the concrete roof soars from the center into pointed, sharp-edged canopies. The contours, including those of the exterior walls, are tapered and pointed, shapes that had long played an important role in Breuer's dynamic "diagonalizing" work. Here they are emphasized by the concrete instead of by wood, stone, or brick.

ARCHIVAL: **SUL 74, 147, 149, Drawings; AAA Contract, Photos.**

BIBLIOGRAPHIC: *L'Oeil*, May 1975, 68–73; *Architectural Record*, August 1977, 105–7; Driller, *Breuer Houses*, 236–40, 267.

230. Approach from the south

230
Stillman House III,
Litchfield, Connecticut, 1973–74

MARCEL BREUER AND TICIAN PAPACHRISTOU, ARCHITECTS

Rufus Stillman approached Breuer a third time to design a house in Litchfield, Connecticut, that he and his family would occupy; an agreement with a contractor was signed on March 26, 1973. For a client as familiar as Stillman was with Breuer's repertoire of forms and ideas and his process of design, a residence like this could be the result of only a sophisticated and highly personal dialogue between client and architect. In Stillman House III, Breuer put into play once again a format that since the 1940s had been one of his most successful and adaptable—two well-organized rectangular units, one longer than the other, separated and linked by a narrow bridge that united the parts through an axial alignment. The smaller, earthbound rectangle is a one-story guest wing with two bedrooms; the bridging precinct, marked out by thick stone walls, is the site of a large terrace and the entry to both wings. A screened porch, cantilevered to the south above a slope and toward the view, projects beyond the lower level (carport, workshop, and wine cellar) of the post-supported, hovering residential wing; it is perpendicular to the main flow of space between living-dining room and bedroom suite. Open, efficient, compact, and unpretentious, Stillman House III is a distillation of Breuer house modes in concept and in details. What distinguishes it from earlier exemplars is the unusual combination of thick, rugged whitewashed stone walls and the wood cladding, stained dark with white trim, of the residential wing.

229
Gagarin House II,
Litchfield, Connecticut, 1973–74

MARCEL BREUER AND TICIAN PAPACHRISTOU, ARCHITECTS

Construction of Gagarin House II began in June 1973; the house was completed the following year. Built on the same road as Breuer's Gagarin House I (1956), this smaller two-level building was a reworking of any number of Breuer binuclear houses, which, thirty-five years after the earliest experiments with an exciting new concept in residential architecture, had become formulaic. The house is distinguished, however, by the design and craftsmanship of the stone walls that form the base of the upper level and that define the terraces on the north and south, and by the choice of construction materials, "atypically sturdy for residential work," in the words of Stanley Abercrombie.[4] Steel beams are used for the roof spans, reinforced concrete for the main floor slab, and masonry for the exterior walls.[5]

ARCHIVAL: **SUL 143–45, Drawings; AAA Contract, Photos.**

BIBLIOGRAPHIC: *Global Architecture*, no. 43; Driller, *Breuer Houses*, 267.

ARCHIVAL: **SUL Drawings; AAA Contract, Photos.**

BIBLIOGRAPHIC: *Global Architecture*, no. 43; *Global Architecture Detail*, no. 5; *Process: Architecture*, no. 32, 29–31; Driller, *Breuer Houses*, 242–47, 267.

MUSEUMS (pp. 182–85)

1   Louis Kahn to Breuer, November 7, 1963, Correspondence, AAA.

2   Comments (draft), presentation of project, November 12, 1962, Speeches and Writings, AAA.

3   The Whitney window appears as an alien element on the top (twenty-fourth) floor of the Board of Works tower in Melbourne, Australia (Architecture Plus, May–June 1974, 128), by Perrott Lyon Timlock Kesa & Associates, Architects, and on the facade of George Clayton Pearl's Breueresque Presbyterian Hospital in Albuquerque, New Mexico.

4   See p. 21, n. 31, in this volume.

5   Werner Schmalenbach to Gene Norman, chairman, Landmarks Preservation Commission, New York, December 11, 1986, City of New York Landmarks Preservation Commission, Records.

LIBRARIES (pp. 186–90)

1   Friends of the Grosse Pointe Public Library, press release, May 31, 1951, SUL 37.

2   On the Ferry family, see p. 95 in this volume.

3   Kenneth L. Moore to Breuer, April 21, 1951, SUL 37.

4   William W. Landsberg, conversation with author.

5   Victoria Newhouse, *Wallace K. Harrison, Architect* (New York: Rizzoli, 1989), 181.

6   SUL 76.

7   SUL 76.

8   SUL 129.

9   Hamilton Smith to Ella Gaines Yates, October 5, 1979, SUL 129.

COLLEGES AND UNIVERSITIES (pp. 191–205)

1   Thomas J. McCormick, "Wheaton College Competition for an Art Center," in *Modernism in America, 1937–1941: A Catalogue and Exhibition of Four Architectural Competitions*, ed. James D. Kornwolf (Williamsburg, Va.: College of William and Mary, 1985), 31.

2   Ibid.

3   Quoted in ibid.

4   James D. Kornwolf, "College of William and Mary: Competition for a Festival Theatre and Fine Arts Center, November 1938–February 1939," in *Modernism in America*, ed. Kornwolf, 129.

5   "Harvard Annual Reports, Harvard Report 1939–40," in *Official Register of Harvard University*, April 10, 1941 (Cambridge, Mass.: By the University, 1941), 271.

6   Mary Emma Harris, *The Arts at Black Mountain College* (Cambridge, Mass.: MIT Press, 1987), 56.

7   SUL 29.

8   Breuer to Josef Albers, September 19, 1939, SUL 29.

9   Harris, *Arts at Black Mountain College*, 56.

10   Ibid.

11   Ibid., 60.

12   Project description, SUL 29

13   Sarah Gibson Blanding to Breuer, October 24, 1949, SUL 35.

14   Marcel Breuer, draft of project description, February 3, 1950, SUL 35.

15   Breuer to Charles M. Willard, Jr., May 22, 1957, Correspondence, AAA.

16   Ada Louise Huxtable, "Building's Case History," *New York Times*, August 9, 1963.

17   See p. 16 in this volume.

18   Edward Larrabee Barnes, conversation with author.

19   Project description, SUL 149.

HIGH SCHOOLS (pp. 206–9)

1   See pp. 128, 146 n. 33, and 259 in this volume.

HOSPITALS AND SANATORIUMS (pp. 215–17)

1   List of works, Breuer to Giulio Carlo Argan, February 1, 1956, Correspondence, AAA.

2   Magdalena Droste and Manfred Ludewig, *Marcel Breuer Design* (Cologne: Taschen, 1992), 23.

3   Ibid., 25.

4   I am grateful to Magdalena Droste, formerly of the Bauhaus-Archiv in Berlin, who brought these drawings to my attention.

5   Joachim Driller, "Marcel Breuer: Das architektonische Frühwerk bis 1950" (Phil. diss., Albert-Ludwigs-Universität, Freiburg, 1990), 352, nn. 3, 5.

6   List of works, April 25, 1938, included with the application submitted by Gropius and Breuer, Associated Architects, for the competition for Goucher College.

7   Breuer to Argan, February 1, 1956.

8   Superintendent, Long Beach Hospital, to Breuer, SUL 26.

RELIGIOUS INSTITUTIONS (pp. 218–30)

1   Quoted in Whitney S. Stoddard, *Adventure in Architecture: Building the New Saint John's* (New York: Longmans, Green, 1958), 23–24.

2   Abbot Baldwin Dworschak to Hamilton P. Smith, June 16, 1956, SUL 108.

3   Stoddard, *Adventure in Architecture*, 98.

4   Breuer to Mother M. Edane, May 23, 1968, Priory of the Annunciation Archives.

5   Architect's Report, SUL 137.

6   William W. Landsberg, conversation with author.

7   Shirley Reiff Howarth, "Marcel Breuer: On Religious Architecture," *Art Journal* 38 (1979): 257–60.

8   I am grateful to Mario Jossa for furnishing much of this information.

9   Convent of the Sisters of Divine Providence Archives.

10   SUL 160.

11   SUL 147.

12   Ibid.

13   Breuer to Beat Jordi, March 9, 1976, Correspondence, AAA.

GOVERNMENTAL AND CIVIC (pp. 232–49)

1   In 1945, architect Lawrence B. Anderson was professor in the Department of Architecture at MIT; he became chairman in 1947, and from 1965 to 1972 was dean of the School of Architecture and Planning. He died in 1994.

2   Breuer to Eduardo Catalano, July 22, 1947, SUL 39.

3   Marcel Breuer, "Notes to accompany preliminary drawings and model for the Cambridge War Memorial," March 26, 1945, SUL 41.

4   Philip Johnson to Breuer, October 2, 1945, SUL 15.

5   Harry A. Morris to Breuer, May 2, 1949, SUL 28.

6   Unless otherwise indicated, material pertaining to this summary of UNESCO I and II is taken from the UNESCO file, AAA. Translations are by the author.

7   *Time*, May 25, 1953, 70.

8   Paul Goldberger, "New Architecture in Paris—The Worst in the World?" *International Herald Tribune*, July 19–20, 1975.

9   G. E. Kidder Smith, *The New Architecture of Europe* (Cleveland: World, 1961), 75, 78.

10   Lewis Mumford, "Unesco House: The Hidden Treasure," in *The Highway and the City* (New York: Harcourt, Brace & World, 1963), 79.

11   Kidder Smith, *New Architecture of Europe*, 83.

12   Quoted in "Letter from Paris," *New Yorker*, October 11, 1958, 190.

13   Lewis Mumford, "Unesco House: Out, Damned Cliché!" in *Highway and the City*, 76.

14   Ibid., 73.

15   Breuer to Luther Evans, November 7, 1958, UNESCO file, AAA.

16   Jane C. Loeffler, "The Architecture of Diplomacy: Heyday of the United States Embassy-Building Program, 1954–1960," *Journal of the Society of Architectural Historians* 49 (1990): 267, and *The Architecture of Diplomacy: Building America's Embassies* (New York: Princeton Architectural Press, 1998), 217; see also Ada Louis Huxtable, "Sharp Debate: What Should an Embassy Be?" *New York Times Magazine*, September 18, 1960.

17   The Commission of Fine Arts was established in 1910 as an advisory body to the government regarding the aesthetics of public works of art in Washington, D.C.

18   Robert A. M. Stern, Thomas Mellins, and David Fishman, *New York 1960: Architecture and Urbanism Between the Second World War and the Bicentennial* (New York: Monacelli Press, 1995), 778.

19   Ibid.

20   Ibid.

21   I am grateful to Henry J. Stern, Commissioner, City of New York Parks and Recreation, for this and other information about the competition.

22   All material and quotations pertaining to the meetings on January 25 and 26, 1967, are taken from the Minutes of the Commission of Fine Arts, January 1, 1967–March 31, 1967. I am grateful to Sue A. Kohler, historian of the commission, for making them available to me, and for her book, *The Commission of Fine Arts: A Brief History, 1910–1976, With Additions, 1977–1984* (Washington, D.C.: Government Printing Office, 1985).

23   Chief engineer, Bureau of Reclamation, to Marcel Breuer and Associates, April 15, 1970, Grand Coulee file, AAA.

24   Herbert Beckhard, text of deposition, October 15, 1976, SUL 123.

25   Quoted in Kenneth Frampton and Philip Drew, *Harry Seidler: Four Decades of Architecture* (London: Thames and Hudson, 1992), 157.

26   Breuer to Harry Seidler, October 22, 1973, filed with Australian Embassy contract, AAA.

27   Harry Seidler to Breuer, December 18, 1973, Correspondence, AAA.

OFFICE BUILDINGS (pp. 250–57)

1   Correspondence, AAA.

2   Oscar van Leer to Breuer, April 29, 1964, Breuer travel file, SUL.

3   Ibid.

FACTORIES (pp. 258–65)

1   According to Joachim Driller, the Berlin engineer F. Samueli was part of the team ("Marcel Breuer: Das architektonische Frühwerk bis 1950 [Phil. diss., Albert-Ludwigs-Universität, Freiburg, 1990], 370).

2   Ibid., 372.

3   For example, the one dated May 28, 1943, SUL 50.

4   Driller, "Frühwerk," 372.

5   Efrom Feder, engineering manager of the Torin Engineered Blowers Division of Fasco Industries, kindly recalled the circumstances in a telephone conversation with the author.

6   In the conventional method in use at the time, after the concrete was poured into a form, a vibrator attached to a cable was inserted and moved around to force the concrete into every cavity. To ensure this result, the concrete was poured into the form as a wettish slurry with less ultimate strength than if a dry concrete were used. With this type of concrete, the coarse aggregate often was segregated from the fine, and it settled at the bottom of the form, leaving crevices in the outer skin. In the Schokbeton method, a very stiff, drier concrete was used; it was poured into forms on a "shock table" that heaved with repeated rhythmic "shocks" that moved the concrete into all the crannies and produced a denser and better quality finished concrete product.

7   *Architectural Forum*, March 1972, 50.

8   Rufus Stillman to Breuer, July 29, 1964, SUL 150.

9   Breuer to Robert Gatje, September 21, 1964, SUL 149.

10   Nikolas Pevsner, *Buildings of England*, 2nd ed., rev. (Harmondsworth: Penguin Books, 1975), 516.

LABORATORIES AND RESEARCH FACILITIES (pp. 266–73)

1   Robert Gatje, conversation with author.

2   Breuer to IBM, September 1, 1967, SUL 66.

3   From a recording made on the occasion of the tenth anniversary of the building. I am grateful to Constance L. Breuer for making the tape available to me.

4   Ibid.

5   Gatje, conversation with author.

STORES (pp. 274–76)

1   Credits for the design of the facade of the Wohnbedarf store (1932–33) in Zürich are given as M. Breuer and Robert Winkler; for the facade of Wohnbedarf in Basel of the same year, the credits read M. Breuer and Eduard Schoni.

2   Another Abraham & Straus store for which Breuer would do a design was planned in the fall of 1950 for Princeton, New Jersey, but the project never was launched (SUL 41).

3   Breuer to Abraham & Straus, January 7, 1951, SUL 41.

4   Ibid.

5   Project engineer to Abraham & Straus, May 21, 1951, SUL 41.

6   Lewis Mumford, "A Walk Through Rotterdam," in *The Highway and the City* (New York: Harcourt, Brace & World, 1963), 31.

7   Isabelle Hyman, "The Marcel Breuer Papers and Michael Ventris," *Syracuse University Library Associates Courier* 24 (1989): 7–9.

8   For the history of Gabo's sculpture for De Bijenkorf, see Colin C. Sanderson, comp., and Christina Lodder, ed., "Catalogue Raisonné of the Constructions and Sculptures of Naum Gabo," in *Naum Gabo: Sixty Years of Constructivism*, ed. Steven A. Nash and Jorn Merkert (Munich: Prestel-Verlag, 1985), 243.

9   Clipping, "Designer Here Plans Stores Like Interior of Honeycomb," *Boston* [illegible], July 19, 1938, SUL 49.

10   Mumford, "The Cave, the City, and the Flower," in *Highway and the City*, 39, 47.

11   Ibid., 39–40.

12   Breuer to De Bijenkorf, July 17, 1974, Correspondence, AAA.

RESORTS, CLUBS, AND HOTELS (pp. 278–85)

1   SUL 5.

2   Marcel Breuer, memorandum on Ober-Gurgl, August 12, 1938, for publication in *Architectural Record*, September 1938, SUL 18.

3   Eduardo Catalano to Breuer, March 11, 1949, SUL 39.

4   Eduardo Catalano to Breuer, February 15, 1948, SUL 39.

5   Breuer to Eduardo Catalano, March 29, 1948, SUL 39.

6   Breuer to editor of *L'Architecture d'aujourd'hui*, September 8, 1949, SUL 51.

7   Breuer to Eric Boissonnas, November 7, 1974, Correspondence, AAA.

8   Robert Gatje, conversation with author.

9   A full account of the background for this project is in Robert Gatje, memorandum, June 29, 1972, Correspondence, AAA.

THEATERS (pp. 286–87)

1   Marcel Breuer, "Theater von Charkow," *Die Bauwelt*, August 13, 1931, 27–29.

2   Joachim Driller, "Marcel Breuer: Das architektonische Frühwerk bis 1950" (Phil. diss., Albert-Ludwigs-Universität, Freiburg, 1990), 361.

3   Michael Mullin, *Design by Motley* (Newark: University of Delaware Press, 1996), 58–61.

4   Ibid., 61.

5   Ibid.; see also *Architects' Journal*, July 29, 1937, 186–88.

6   Phyllida Mills, "F. R. S. Yorke: The English Tradition" (Third-year diss., Cambridge University, 1988), annotated bibliography.

7   Breuer to H. Herrey-Zweigenthal, January 29, 1941, SUL 9.

SPORTS FACILITIES (pp. 288–89)

1   Charles Burchard to Breuer, February 2, 1942, SUL 16. In 1946, Breuer and Burchard thought about forming a partnership in Cambridge as Marcel Breuer, Charles Burchard, Architects, Industrial Consultants, the draft contract for which is in SUL 41. They never formalized the arrangement, although they carried out several projects in association.

2   Charles Burchard, report, SUL 42.

3   August Heckscher, memorandum, September 8, 1967, Contracts, AAA.

4   Tician Papachristou, *Marcel Breuer: New Buildings and Projects, 1960–70* (New York: Praeger, 1970), 177.

5   Breuer to Kenzo Tange, June 24, 1968, Correspondence, AAA.

EXHIBITION STRUCTURES (pp. 290–97)

1   Marcel Breuer, "Biography," January 10, 1940, SUL 50.
2   *Das frühe Bauhaus und Johannes Itten* (Berlin: Bauhaus-Archiv, 1994), 73–81.
3   Previously unknown working drawings for the House for a Sportsman as well as for others designed for the Berlin Bauausstellung of 1931 (a booth for the cork industry to display cork products, for example) were donated in 1999 by Constance L. Breuer to SUL.
4   Joachim Driller, "Marcel Breuer: Das architektonische Frühwerk bis 1950" (Phil. diss., Albert-Ludwigs-Universität, Freiburg, 1990), 186.
5   Magdalena Droste and Manfred Ludewig, *Marcel Breuer Design* (Cologne: Taschen, 1992), 24.
6   Christopher Wilk, *Marcel Breuer: Furniture and Interiors* (New York: Museum of Modern Art, 1981), 99.
7   Ibid., 105.
8   Driller, "Frühwerk," 363.
9   Henry-Russell Hitchcock, "Marcel Breuer and the American Tradition in Architecture" [essay and exhibition catalogue, Harvard University, Graduate School of Design, June–September 1938] (GSD, Cambridge, Mass., 1938, Mimeographed), 12, HUAL.
10 Photos, AAA.
11 Driller, "Frühwerk," 363–64.
12 John Meunier, review of *The Decorated Diagram*, by Klaus Herdeg, *Architectural Education* 38 (1985 [1986]): 31.
13 Henry-Russell Hitchcock and Catherine K. Bauer, *Modern Architecture in England* (New York: Museum of Modern Art, 1937), 35.
14 Winfried Nerdinger, *Walter Gropius: The Architect Walter Gropius: Drawings, Prints, and Photographs from Busch-Reisinger Museum, Harvard University Art Museums, Cambridge, Mass., and from Bauhaus-Archiv Berlin* [exhibition catalogue] (Berlin: Mann Verlag, 1985), 200.
15 David H. Wright, "The Architecture of Walter Gropius" (Thesis for Honors, Harvard College, 1950), 44.
16 Robert A. M. Stern, Gregory Gilmartin, and Thomas Mellins, *New York 1930: Architecture and Urbanism Between the Two World Wars* (New York: Rizzoli, 1987), 742.
17 Museum of Modern Art, interim report, May 12, 1948, Henry-Russell Hitchcock Archive, Department of Fine Arts, New York University. I am grateful to Mosette Broderick for making this document available to me.
18 Breuer to product-design manager, Philco, May 11, 1949, SUL 22.
19 George Lewis, conversation with author.
20 "American Gift," *New Yorker*, March 5, 1949, 26.
21 Inter-American Center Authority to Breuer, February 10, 1967, Correspondence, AAA.
22 Robert B. Browne to Breuer, March 17, 1968, Correspondence, AAA.
23 Irving Muskat to Breuer, March 25, 1968, Correspondence, AAA.

URBANISM AND URBAN PLANNING (pp. 298–301)

1   Breuer to Marian Becker, Cincinnati Modern Art Society, October 8, 1942, SUL 15.
2   Marcel Breuer, statements in page fragment from an unidentified Boston newspaper, 1938, SUL 53.
3   Ibid.
4   See p. 85 in this volume.
5   *Architectural Record*, June 1960, 183, where the credits appeared as Marcel Breuer, Architect, Herbert Beckhard, Associate, Fuenmayor and Sayago, Associated Architects.
6   Robert Gatje to architect, October 27, 1969, Correspondence, AAA.
7   Robert Gatje, conversation with author.
8   They are illustrated in Tician Papachristou, *Marcel Breuer: New Buildings and Projects, 1960–70* (New York: Praeger, 1970), 196–97.

MULTIPLE-FAMILY HOUSING (pp. 302–15)

1   *Die Bauwelt*, April 3, 1924, 263–64.
2   See p. 51 in this volume.
3   Hans M. Wingler, *Bauhaus* (Cambridge, Mass.: MIT Press, 1986), 388.
4   Ronald Wiedenhoeft, *Berlin's Housing Revolution: German Reform in the 1920s* (Ann Arbor, Mich.: UMI Research Press, 1985), 166. Driller raises the question about whether the priority should be given to Ludwig Hilbersheimer ("Marcel Breuer: Das architektonische Frühwerk bis 1950" [Phil. diss., Albert-Ludwigs-Universität, Freiburg, 1990], 308), and, on this, see Wiedenhoeft, *Berlin's Housing Revolution*, 170–72.
5   Christopher Wilk, *Marcel Breuer: Furniture and Interiors* (New York: Museum of Modern Art, 1981), figs. 12, 17, 19.
6   Breuer to Hans Wingler, September 24, 1974, Correspondence, AAA.
7   Cranston Jones points out that the apartment plans were similar to those of the BAMBOS houses (*Marcel Breuer: Buildings and Projects, 1921–1961* [New York: Praeger, 1962], 239).
8   Breuer to Catherine Bauer, United States Housing Authority, December 20, 1938, SUL 15.
9   See p. 68 in this volume.
10 Marianne Harnischmacher to Breuer, September 25, 1934, and Breuer to Marianne Harnischmacher, October 21, 1934, Correspondence, AAA.
11 Reyner Banham, "Ateliers d'Artistes: Paris Studio Houses and the Modern Movement," *Architectural Review*, August 1956, 75–83.
12 Breuer to Ise Gropius, December 25, 1934, Correspondence, AAA.
13 Ise Gropius to Breuer, January 19, 1935, Correspondence, AAA.
14 Breuer to Wallace S. Baldinger, director, Mulvane Art Museum, December 20, 1938, SUL 15.
15 Breuer to Sigfried Giedion, August 22, 1933, SUL 7.
16 Quoted in Stanislaus von Moos, Introduction to *Alfred Roth: Architect of Continuity* (Zürich: Waser Verlag, 1985), 88.
17 Ibid.
18 It had been agreed that in all publications and exhibitions of the project, except in Hungarian publications and exhibitions, the Roths' names would appear first in the credits. In Hungarian publications, Breuer's name would appear ahead of the Roths. On October 3, 1936, a letter was sent to Breuer in London from Switzerland regarding an exhibition (the Swiss Pavilion at the Milan Triennial) in which the Dolderthal buildings were featured, explaining that "the text of the inscription which properly contains your name as collaborator was given to me by Mr. Alfred Roth. Through the error of an official your name was forgotten and three weeks ago was changed. I have no knowledge of a protest or indignation shown by visitors" (SUL 7).
19 Sigfried Giedion to Alfred Roth, October 3, 1936, SUL 7.
20 Breuer to Carola Giedion-Weicker, April 5, 1976, Correspondence, AAA.
21 Frank L. Palmer, Allegheny County Housing Authority, to *Building and Real Estate Journal*, August 28, 1941, SUL 18.
22 *Architectural Forum* to Walter Gropius, August 29, 1941, SUL 18.
23 See pp. 108–9 in this volume.
24 Breuer to B. J. Hovde, July 21, 1943, SUL 45.
25 Report, July 14, 1943, SUL 45.
26 Harold S. Myers to Breuer, July 3, 1941, SUL 45.
27 B. J. Hovde to Breuer, November 29, 1941, SUL 45.
28 B. J. Hovde to Breuer, July 7, 1943, SUL 45.
29 Eero Saarinen was addressing a conference of the National Association of Housing Officials in January 1942. His remarks were published as "Architecture and Defense Housing," in *Four Papers on Housing Design*, Publication no. N165 (Chicago: National Association of Housing and Redevelopment Officials, September 1942), 5–8.
30 See p. 88 in this volume.
31 Earl von Storch to Breuer, February 7, 1951, SUL 52.

32 "Please observe the section on drawing No. A5 which shows the height of this partition wall as 4′10″, Breuer wrote to D. D. Meredith on October 23, 1941 (SUL 45). And to the Technical Review Section Chief at the FWA, on November 24, 1941, he wrote: "The partition wall between the kitchen and the living room was kept at 4′10″ so that whoever was working in the kitchen (usually the housewife) could supervise the living room and entrance at the same time, simply by looking over it. This is an advantage in taking care of small children, or when conducting a conversation with other members of the family who are sitting in the living room" (SUL 45). However, it did create another problem in that the back of the refrigerator projected above the partition wall, an oversight that Breuer remedied with the unfortunate suggestion to cover the back with a piece of painted plywood.

33 Franklin Toker, *Pittsburgh: An Urban Portrait* (University Park: Pennsylvania State University Press, 1986), 311.

34 B. J. Hovde, telegram to Sumner Wiley, January 29, 1942, SUL 15.

35 Breuer to Federal Works Agency, n.d., SUL 15.

36 The history of the Stuyvesant Town project is summarized in Robert A. M. Stern, Thomas Mellins, and David Fishman, *New York 1960: Architecture and Urbanism Between the Second World War and the Bicentennial* (New York: Monacelli Press, 1995), 279–84.

37 A copy of Breuer's letter of November 5, 1943, to Frederick H. Ecker does not survive, but Ecker's reply of November 9 and the data sheet are in SUL 42.

38 Breuer to Martin Wagner, December 29, 1943, and January 1, 1944, SUL 42.

39 Breuer to Bert Geller, October 19, 1945, SUL 43.

40 Edgar J. Kaufmann, Jr., to Breuer, n.d. [January 1946], SUL 43.

41 Peter Blake, *Marcel Breuer: Architect and Designer* (New York: Museum of Modern Art, 1949), fig. 149.

42 Conversation with author.

HOUSES 1920s (pp. 316–319)

1 See p. 45 in this volume.

2 Joachim Driller, *Breuer Houses*, trans. Mark Cole and Jeremy Verrinder (London: Phaidon Press, 2000), 46.

3 Reginald R. Isaacs, *Gropius: An Illustrated Biography of the Creator of the Bauhaus* (London: Little, Brown, 1991), 120.

4 Through an unpublished letter written by Oskar Schlemmer in the Bauhaus-Archiv, Magdalena Droste and Joachim Driller have identified these names as those from which the acronym was derived. This is a correction of information from captions on photographs from Breuer's office, now in the Archives of American Art, where the names appear as Bayer, Albers, Muche, Breuer, Otte, and Schmidt (Magdalena Droste and Manfred Ludewig, *Marcel Breuer Design* [Cologne: Taschen, 1992], 21, n. 31; Cranston Jones, ed., *Marcel Breuer: Buildings and Projects, 1921–1961* [New York: Praeger, 1962], 236; Driller, *Breuer Houses*, 53.

5 Driller, *Breuer Houses*, 52.

6 Belva Barnes [draftsman in Breuer's office] to Giulio Carlo Argan, February 1, 1956, Correspondence, AAA.

HOUSES 1930s (pp. 320–23)

1 Marcel Breuer, memorandum, n.d. [probably ca. 1934], SUL 10.

2 Henry-Russell Hitchcock, "Marcel Breuer and the American Tradition in Architecture" [essay and exhibition catalogue, Harvard University, Graduate School of Design, June–September 1938] (GSD, Cambridge, Mass., 1938, mimeographed), 11, HUAL.

3 Joachim Driller, "Marcel Breuer: Das architektonische Frühwerk bis 1950" (Phil. diss., Albert-Ludwigs-Universität, Freiburg, 1990), 48.

4 Albin Wolf to Walter Gropius, August 29, 1933, Correspondence, AAA.

5 Walter Gropius to Albin Wolf, August 31, 1933, Correspondence, AAA; see also pp. 72–73 in this volume.

6 Breuer to Albin Wolf, September 7, 1933, Correspondence, AAA. The site-plan sketch and Breuer's calculations of dimensions and space requirements for the house are in AAA.

7 Arthur A. Cohen, *Herbert Bayer: The Complete Work* (Cambridge, Mass.: MIT Press, 1984), 32.

8 Quoted in Joachim Driller, *Breuer Houses*, trans. Mark Cole and Jeremy Verrinder (London: Phaidon Press, 2000), 259–60.

9 Ibid., 259.

10 I am grateful to Constance L. Breuer for making the photograph available to me.

11 Jeremy Gould, *Modern Houses in Britain, 1919–1939* (London: Society of Architectural Historians of Great Britain, 1977), 20.

12 Preliminary designs, elevation and ground plan, working drawings, and contracts are in the Prints and Drawings Collection of RIBA.

13 Hitchcock, "Marcel Breuer and the American Tradition," 15.

14 Driller, *Breuer Houses*, 97; see also Alan Powers, *In the Line of Development: FRS Yorke, E Rosenberg and CS Mardall to YRM, 1930–1992* [exhibition catalogue] (London: RIBA Heinz Gallery, 1992), 17.

15 Driller, *Breuer Houses*, 97.

16 See p. 124 in this volume.

17 Driller, "Frühwerk," 192–94.

HOUSES 1937–41, GROPIUS-BREUER PARTNERSHIP (pp. 324–37)

1 See p. 105 in this volume, and Winfried Nerdinger, *Busch-Reisinger Museum: The Walter Gropius Archive* (New York: Garland, 1990), 3:443–48.

2 Joachim Driller, *Breuer Houses*, trans. Mark Cole and Jeremy Verrinder (London: Phaidon Press, 2000), 106.

3 Leonard Currie to author, April 24, 1995.

4 Driller, *Breuer Houses*, 104–17.

5 John Hagerty to Walter Gropius, October 23, 1937, SUL 25.

6 Currie to author, April 24, 1995.

7 Hagerty to Gropius, October 23, 1937.

8 John Hagerty, "From the Rock Ribb'd Shores," *Interior Design and Decoration*, August 1949, 56.

9 Ibid., 55.

10 Isabelle Hyman, "A Marcel Breuer House Project of 1938–1939," *Syracuse University Library Associates Courier* 27 (1992): 61.

11 Currie to author, April 24, 1995.

12 Breuer to Elaine Harkness, August 18, 1960, Correspondence, AAA.

13 Hilde Margolius to Breuer, August 10, 1938, SUL 26.

14 Breuer to Hilde Margolius, August 11, 1938, SUL 26.

15 Hyman, "Marcel Breuer House Project," 60.

16 Preserved at Syracuse University are thirty-three drawings and sketches along with the specifications and correspondence from which the project can be reconstructed.

17 John Porter Clark to Breuer, December 5, 1938, SUL 26.

18 Breuer to David H. Howie, November 15, 1938, SUL 8.

19 Breuer to Howard Custance, November 17, 1939, SUL 8.

20 Breuer's description of his house in Lincoln is from letters to Helen Storrow, December 12, 1938, SUL 8, and Arthur McK. Stires, *House and Garden*, February 16, 1940, SUL 18.

21 Breuer to Phillips Ketchum, Jr., June 26, 1967, Correspondence, AAA.

22 Howard Custance to Breuer, August 8, 1940, SUL 8.

23 Constance L. Breuer, conversation with author.

24 Howard Dearstyne, *Inside the Bauhaus*, ed. David Spaeth (New York: Rizzoli, 1986), 29.

25 Breuer to Edward Fischer, February 27, 1940, SUL 16.

26 Breuer to Edward Fischer, May 31, 1940, SUL 16.

27 David H. Wright, "The Architecture of Walter Gropius" (Thesis for Honors, Harvard College, 1950), 45.

28 Quoted in ibid.

29 Leonard Currie to author, July 28, 1991.

30 Christopher Wilk, *Marcel Breuer: Furniture and Interiors* (New York: Museum of Modern Art, 1981), 151. Files for the furnishings, kept with the Breuer papers at Syracuse University, are profuse.

31 *An Opinion on Architecture* (Cambridge, Mass., 1941), 14–15.

32 Breuer to M. A. Clegg, March 27, 1941, SUL 18.

33 Franklin Toker, *Pittsburgh: An Urban Portrait* (University Park: Pennsylvania State University Press, 1986), 256–57.

34 Mrs. H. G. Chamberlain to Breuer, November 10, 1940, SUL 24.

35 Driller cites Wolf Tegethoff, a Mies scholar, as one in "Marcel Breuer: Das architektonische Frühwerk bis 1950," (Phil. diss., Albert-Ludwigs-Universität, 1990), 251.

36 Mrs. H. G. Chamberlain to Breuer, April 24, 1941, SUL 54.

37 Breuer to F. R. S. Yorke, March 8, 1943, SUL 45.

38 Breuer to Stanley I. Phalen, February 10, 1941, SUL 33.

39 Breuer to Yorke, March 8, 1943.

40 Breuer to Mrs. H. G. Chamberlain, December 3, 1941, SUL 33.

41 Herbert Beckhard, conversation with author.

42 Breuer to H. Herrey, Architect, February 19, 1945, SUL 18.

43 Breuer to Anthony Lord, October 22, 1940, SUL 47.

44 I am grateful to my colleague Professor Carol Herselle Krinsky for a firsthand report about the house.

45 Walter Gropius to Breuer, October 11, 1948, Walter Gropius Papers (Breuer Letters), HL.

HOUSES 1940s (pp. 338–55)

1 Howard Custance to National Housing Agency, March 25, 1942, SUL 7.

2 See p. 112 in this volume.

3 Reyner Banham, review of *The Dream of the Factory-Made House*, by Gilbert Herbert, *Design Book Review* 8 (1986): 18–20.

4 Marcel Breuer, "Design for Postwar Living: Project for a Worker's House," *California Arts & Architecture*, December 1943, 24.

5 Ibid.

6 Agnes Bourneuf to Breuer, April 7, 1944, SUL 7.

7 Breuer, "Design for Postwar Living," 24.

8 Richard Pratt to Breuer, December 6, 1944, SUL 51.

9 Marcel Breuer, "Post-War House for the *Ladies Home Journal*," SUL 51.

10 Breuer to Gilbert Tompkins, November 13, 1945, SUL 18.

11 Charles Burchard to Gilbert Tompkins, November 29, 1945, SUL 18.

12 Breuer to Walter S. Maas, November 19, 1945, SUL 26.

13 Breuer to Bernard Bandler, June 10, 1946, SUL 29.

14 Layng Martine to Breuer, August 21, 1947, SUL 31.

15 Harry Seidler to Breuer, August 5, 1947, SUL 39.

16 Edward R. Ford, *The Details of Modern Architecture* (Cambridge, Mass.: MIT Press, 1990), 315.

17 Breuer to Eliot Noyes, September 2, 1947, SUL 39.

18 Eliot Noyes to Breuer, September 12, 1947, SUL 39.

19 Harry Seidler to Breuer, September 24, 1947, SUL 39.

20 Marcel Breuer, in *Architectural Forum*, June 1959, 238. The April and June issues were memorials to Frank Lloyd Wright.

21 Breuer to Ada Louise Huxtable, June 22, 1948, SUL 43.

22 James Ford and Katherine Morrow Ford, *The Modern House in America* (New York: Architectural Book, 1945).

23 Helen F. Robinson to Katherine Morrow Ford, November 30, 1948, SUL 17.

24 Conversation with author.

25 Eliot Noyes, Kniffin House program, n.d., SUL 11.

26 Mrs. A. W. Thompson to Breuer, n.d. [early March 1947], SUL 21.

27 Breuer to Mrs. A. W. Thompson, March 12, 1947, SUL 21.

28 Breuer to Mrs. A. W. Thompson, April 3, 1947, SUL 21.

29 Constance L. Breuer, conversation with author.

30 Breuer to Ernest Rose, August 20, 1948, SUL 32.

31 Breuer to Ernest Rose, September 27, 1948, SUL 32.

32 See p. 195 in this volume.

33 Edith Hooper to Breuer, November 15, 1948, SUL 39.

34 Breuer to Paul Rand, August 24, 1949, SUL 31.

35 Ann Rand to Breuer, October 12, 1951, CLB.

36 Breuer, list of works, 1956, AAA.

HOUSES 1950s (pp. 355–73)

1 Alvin R. Tilley to Breuer, June 19, 1950, SUL 32.

2 Arnold Potter to Breuer, February 2, 1949, SUL 28.

3 Newton J. Herrick, Jr., to Breuer, November 15, 1949, SUL 24.

4 See p. 138 in this volume.

5 Breuer to Benjamin L. Spivak, September 17, 1951, SUL 24.

6 Gerold M. Lauck to Breuer, January 11, 1950, SUL 11.

7 Breuer to Gerold Lauck, January 12, 1950, SUL 11.

8 Breuer to Daniels Construction Company, March 24, 1950, SUL 13.

9 Breuer to Rufus Stillman, October 29, 1950, SUL 34.

10 William Landsberg to Peter K. McComb, April 3, 1951, SUL 40.

11 Robert Gatje, conversation with author.

12 Breuer to Jack Tibby, April 24, 1953, SUL 28.

13 See, for example, Marcel Breuer, *Marcel Breuer: Sun and Shadow: The Philosophy of an Architect*, ed. Peter Blake (New York: Dodd, Mead, 1955), 137.

14 Breuer to *L'Architecture d'aujourd'hui*, December 7, 1954, Correspondence, AAA.

15 Gatje, conversation with author.

16 Ibid.

17 Breuer to Mr. and Mrs. Paul Harnischmacher, February 10, 1954, SUL 152.

18 Breuer to Mr. and Mrs. Paul Harnischmacher, March 24, 1954, SUL 152.

19 Breuer to Wiesbaden Stadtbaurat Simon, December 19, 1955, SUL 152.

20 Breuer to Marianne Harnischmacher, May 7, 1956, SUL 152.

21 William Staehelin to Breuer, May 25, 1965, Correspondence, AAA.

22 It was not the first time that Breuer's personality appealed to a client over that of Neutra; it also happened at the time of the architect selection process at Saint John's Abbey.

23 Hans M. Wingler, *Bauhaus* (Cambridge, Mass.: MIT Press, 1986), 67.

24 Staehelins, conversation with author.

25 Ibid.

26 William Staehelin to Breuer, July 29, 1964, Correspondence, AAA.

HOUSES 1960s (pp. 374–79)

1 Breuer to G. Van der Wal, December 29, 1962, SUL 155.

2 G. Van der Wal to Breuer, March 13, 1963, SUL 155.

3 Alain de Gunzburg to Breuer, January 3, 1964, SUL 152.

4 Breuer to Alain de Gunzburg, January 6, 1964, SUL 152.

5 Breuer to Alain de Gunzburg, September 16, 1964, SUL 152.

6 Client's program, n.d., SUL 79.

HOUSES 1970s (pp. 380–81)

1 Robert Gatje, conversation with author.

2 Robert Gatje to Paris office, June 26, 1972, SUL 147.

3 Gatje, conversation with author.

4 Stanley Abercrombie, "Three Houses by Marcel Breuer," in *GA (Global Architecture)*, no. 43 (Tokyo: Edita, 1977), unpag.

5 Ibid.

Chronology of Work

Works that were built are in **boldface**; the dates represent the period of construction, and the number in the right-hand column is the project number used in Part II.

EUROPE

1920–28: Bauhaus, Weimar and Dessau

1928–35: Berlin, Zürich, and Budapest (Independent Architect)

1935–37: London (Partnership with F. R. S. Yorke)

UNITED STATES

1937–41: Cambridge, Massachusetts (Gropius-Breuer Partnership)

1942–46: Cambridge, Massachusetts (Independent Architect)

1946–55: New York, New York (Marcel Breuer, Architect)

1956–76: New York, New York (Marcel Breuer and Associates, Architects)

Locations of Built Work

Some buildings Breuer designed have been destroyed, moved, renamed, put to new uses, or are lost to record. This is a register of the original locations of Breuer's built work (not including temporary exhibition structures).

NORTH AMERICA

UNITED STATES

CALIFORNIA
Van Nuys
Torin Corporation (Western Division) (moved)

COLORADO
Aspen
Smith House

CONNECTICUT
Bantam
Bantam Elementary School
Greenwich
Soriano House (destroyed)
Lakeville
Caesar Cottage
Litchfield
Connecticut Junior Republic
Gagarin House I
Gagarin House II
Litchfield High School
Northfield Elementary School
Stillman House I
Stillman House II
Stillman House III
New Canaan
Breuer House–
    New Canaan I
Breuer House–
    New Canaan II
Kniffin House
    (destroyed)
Mills House
    (destroyed)
New Haven
Yale University, Becton
    Engineering and Applied
    Science Center
Orange
Clark House
Torrington
Southern New England
    Telephone Company
Torin Corporation
    (Administration Building)
Torin Corporation (Machine
    Division Factory)
Torin Corporation
    (Technical Center)

Dennis
Scott House
Framingham
Abele House
Lincoln
Breuer House
Ford House
Gropius House
Roxbury
Campus High School
Wayland
Chamberlain Cottage
Wellfleet
Breuer Cottage
Edgar Stillman, Jr., Cottage
Kepes Cottage
Wise House
Williamstown
Robinson House

MICHIGAN
Grosse Pointe
Grosse Pointe Public Library
Muskegon
Church and Rectory of
    St. Francis de Sales

MINNESOTA
Collegeville
Saint John's Abbey
    and University
Duluth
Starkey (Alworth) House
St. Paul
Kacmarcik House

NEW JERSEY
Mantoloking
McMullen Beach House
Princeton
Institute for Advanced
    Study, Members' Housing
Lauck House
Levy House
Red Bank
Tilley House

NEW YORK
Amherst
State University of New York
    at Buffalo, Faculty of
    Engineering and Applied
    Science Buildings Complex
Bronxville
Sarah Lawrence College,
    Art Center
Canajoharie
Herrick House
Chappaqua
Foote House

West Haven
Armstrong Rubber Company

DISTRICT OF COLUMBIA
Department of Health,
    Education and Welfare
    (HEW) (Hubert H.
    Humphrey Federal
    Building)
Department of Housing and
    Urban Development (HUD)

FLORIDA
Boca Raton
IBM Administrative,
    Laboratory, and Manu-
    facturing Facility

GEORGIA
Atlanta
Atlanta Central
    Public Library

INDIANA
Rochester
Torin Corporation
    (Indiana Division)

KANSAS
Kansas City
Snower House

MAINE
Cape Elizabeth
Potter House

MARYLAND
Baltimore
Bryn Mawr Lower School
    and Elementary School
Hooper House I
Hooper House II
Bethesda
Krieger House
Owings Mill
Karsten House

MASSACHUSETTS
Amherst
University of Massachusetts,
    Murray Lincoln Campus
    Center and Garage
Andover
Grieco House
Laaff House
Cohasset
Hagerty House

Croton-on-Hudson
Marshad House
Neumann House
Harrison
Rand House
Hempstead
Abraham & Straus
Hewlett Harbor
Tompkins House
Huntington
Hanson House
Ithaca
Fairview Heights
    Apartments
King's Point
Witalis House
Lawrence
Geller House I
Geller House II
New York
Hunter College, Library,
    Classroom, and
    Administration Buildings
    (Bronx Campus)
New York University Buildings
    Complex (University
    Heights Campus)
Whitney Museum of
    American Art
Pleasant Valley
Wolfson Trailer House
Pleasantville
Englund House
Poughkeepsie
McComb House
Vassar College, Ferry
    Cooperative Dormitory
Scarsdale
Pack House
Westchester Reform Temple
Westbury
O. E. McIntyre, Inc.
Westchester County
House in the Museum
    Garden (moved from the
    Museum of Modern Art)

NORTH CAROLINA
Asheville
Weizenblatt House

NORTH DAKOTA
Bismarck
Annunciation Priory of the
    Sisters of St. Benedict;
    University of Mary

OHIO
Cleveland
Cleveland Museum of
    Art, Education Wing

Cleveland Trust Company
    Headquarters

PENNSYLVANIA
Ligonier
Thompson House
New Hope
Fischer House
New Kensington
Aluminum City Terrace
Pittsburgh
Frank House

VIRGINIA
Reston
American Press Institute
    Conference Center

WASHINGTON
Grand Coulee
Grand Coulee Dam, Third
    Power Plant and Forebay
    Dam; Visitor Arrival Center

WEST VIRGINIA
Clarksburg
Clarksburg Harrison
    Public Library

CANADA

ONTARIO
**Dryberry Lake Island,
Toronto**
Halvorson Fishing Camp
Oakville
Torin Corporation
    (Canadian Division)

EUROPE

BELGIUM
Nivelles
Torin Corporation
    (Belgian Division)

ENGLAND
Angmering-on-Sea
Macnabb House
    (Sea Lane House)
Lee-on-Solent
Rose House (Shangri-La)
London
London Theatre Studio
Swindon
Torin Corporation
    (British Division)
Willowbrook
Houses for Masters,
    Eton College

FRANCE
Bayonne
ZUP de Bayonne
Flaine
Resort Town
Glanville (Calvados)
Saier House
La Gaude
IBM Research Center
Merignac (Bordeaux)
Sarget-Ambrine Head-
    quarters and Pharma-
    ceutical Laboratories
Paris
UNESCO Headquarters

GERMANY
Limburg
Mundipharma Head-
    quarters and Manufac-
    turing Plant
Wiesbaden
Harnischmacher House I
    (destroyed)
Harnischmacher House II

THE NETHERLANDS
Amstelveen
Van Leer Office Building
Rotterdam
De Bijenkorf Department
    Store Complex
The Hague
United States Embassy

SWITZERLAND
Baldegg (near Lucerne)
Convent of the Sisters of
    Divine Providence
Feldmeilen (near Zürich)
Staehelin House
Moscia (Tessin)
Koerfer House
Zürich
Doldertal Apartment
    Houses

AUSTRALIA

NEW SOUTH WALES
Penrith
Torin Corporation

SOUTH AMERICA

ARGENTINA
Mar del Plata
Ariston Club

Selected Bibliography

Selected bibliographies for individual works appear with the entries in Part II.

"Airy Architecture." *New Yorker*, February 13, 1960, 24.

Albrecht, Donald, ed. *World War II and the American Dream: How Wartime Buildup Changed a Nation* [exhibition catalogue]. Cambridge, Mass.: MIT Press, 1995.

Anderson, David Christian. *Architecture as a Means for Social Change in Germany, 1918–1933*. Ann Arbor, Mich.: University Microfilms, 1973.

Argan, Giulio Carlo. *Marcel Breuer: Disegno industriale e architettura*. Milan: Görlich, 1957.

Banham, Reyner. *The Architecture of the Well-Tempered Environment*. London: Architectural Press, 1984.

Bayer, Herbert, Walter Gropius, and Ise Gropius, eds. *Bauhaus 1919–1928* [exhibition catalogue]. New York: Museum of Modern Art, 1938, 1975.

Benton, Charlotte. *A Different World: Emigré Architects in Britain, 1928–1958*. London: RIBA Heinz Gallery, 1995.

Blake, Peter. *Marcel Breuer: Architect and Designer*. New York: Museum of Modern Art, 1949.

———. "The Selective Eye of Marcel Breuer." *House Beautiful*, March 1967, 153–58.

———. *Architecture for the New World: The Work of Harry Seidler*. New York: Wittenborn, 1973.

———. *Form Follows Fiasco: Why Modern Architecture Hasn't Worked*. Boston: Little, Brown, 1977.

———. *No Place Like Utopia: Modern Architecture and the Company We Kept*. New York: Knopf, 1993.

Breuer, Marcel. "Form Funktion." *Junge Menschen: Monatshefte für Politik, Kunst, Literatur und Leben*, November 1924, 191. [Reprinted as "On the Reorganization of the Bauhaus." In *Marcel Breuer: Buildings and Projects, 1921–1961*, edited by Cranston Jones, 261–62. New York: Praeger, 1962.]

———. "Das Kleinmetallhaus Typ 1926." *Offset-Buch und Werbekunst* 7 (1926): 371–74.

———. "Metallmöbel und moderne Räumlichkeit." *Das neue Frankfurt*, January 1928, 11.

———. "Beiträge zur Frage des Hochhauses." *Die Form* 5 (1930): 113–17. [Reprinted in *"Die Form": Stimme des Deutschen Werkbundes, 1925–1934*, edited by Felix Schwarz and Frank Gloor, 163–67. Gütersloh: Mohn, 1969.]

———. "Die Werkbundausstellung in Paris 1930." *Zentralblatt der Bauverwaltung*, July 9, 1930, 477.

———. "Das Innere des Hauses." *Die Bauwelt*, May 7, 1931, 615–16.

———. "Theater von Charkow." *Die Bauwelt*, August 13, 1931, 27–29.

———. "Where Do We Stand?" *Architectural Review*, April 1935, 133–36. [Reprinted in *Casabella*, March 1935, 2–7; *Werk*, December 1935, 426–27; *Nuestra arquitectura*, September 1947; and Peter Blake, *Marcel Breuer: Architect and Designer*. New York: Museum of Modern Art, 1949, 119–22.]

———. "Architecture and Material." In *Circle: International Survey of Constructive Art*, edited by J. L. Martin, Ben Nicholson, and N. Gabo, 193–202. London: Faber and Faber, 1937.

———. "Photograph of Rockefeller Center." *Architects' Journal*, December 9, 1937, 942.

———. "Marcel Breuer and Moholy-Nagy Leave for America: An Artist's Impression." *Architects' Journal*, January 13, 1938, 38.

———. "Tell Me, What Is Modern Architecture?" *House & Garden*, April 1940, 47. [Reprinted in *GSD News*, Harvard University Graduate School of Design, Fall 1995, 32.]

———. "Design for Postwar Living: Project for a Worker's House." *California Arts & Architecture*, December 1943, 24–25.

———. "Stuyvesant Six: A Redevelopment Study." *Pencil Points*, June 1944, 68–70, 102, 118.

———. "Autobiography." Handwritten notes ("biographical data") for a professional autobiography, n.d. [ca. 1947]. SUL 39.

———. "What Is Happening to Modern Architecture?" Statement presented at symposium, Museum of Modern Art, New York, February 11, 1948. [Published in *Museum of Modern Art Bulletin* 15 (1948): 15, and *Arts & Architecture*, May 1948, 31.]

———. "Aspects of the Art of Paul Klee." *Museum of Modern Art Bulletin* 27 (1950): 3–5.

———. *Marcel Breuer: Sun and Shadow: The Philosophy of an Architect*. Edited by Peter Blake. New York: Dodd, Mead, 1955.

———. "Les Buts de l'architecture." *Architecture, formes et fonctions* 9 (1962–63): 6–29.

———. *Matter and Intrinsic Form* [second annual Reed and Barton Design Lecture, presented at the University of Michigan, Ann Arbor, March 6, 1963]. Taunton, Mass: Reed and Barton, 1963.

———. "The Contemporary Aspect of Pharaonic Architecture." Preface to *Living Architecture: Egyptian*, by Jean Louis de Cenival. New York: Grosset & Dunlap, 1964.

———. "Genesis of Design." In *The Man-Made Object*, edited by Gyorgy Kepes, 120–25. New York: Braziller, 1966.

———. "An Interview with Marcel Breuer." *Connection, Visual Arts at Harvard*, Fall 1966, 16–20.

———. "Forms and Functions." *Architecture, formes et fonctions* 13 (1967): 14–17.

———. Interview with Winthrop Sargeant, ca. 1971–72, for "Profile of Marcel Breuer." Manuscript, prepared for *New Yorker*. Courtesy Jane Sargeant.

———. Interview with Istvan Gardos, n.d. [1972 or 1973]. Transcription in German. Marcel Breuer Papers, Archives of American Art, Smithsonian Institution, Washington, D.C.

———. Interview for *Schokbeton*, October 1973.

———. Interview for *Les Archives du XXième siècle*, March 30 and 31, 1974. Transcription in French. Marcel Breuer Papers, Archives of American Art, Smithsonian Institution, Washington, D.C.

———. Interview with Shirley Reiff Howarth, "Marcel Breuer: On Religious Architecture." *Art Journal* 38 (1979): 257–60.

Buddenseig, Tilmann, ed. *Berlin 1900–1933: Architecture and Design* [exhibition catalogue]. Berlin: Mann Verlag, 1987.

Christ-Janer, Albert, and Mary Mix Foley. *Modern Church Architecture: A Guide to the Form and Spirit of 20th Century Religious Buildings*. New York: McGraw-Hill, 1962.

Clem, Adam Eli. "The City in Miniature: From Chair to Building in the Work of Marcel Breuer." Art history thesis, Vassar College, 1993.

Coe, Peter, and Malcolm Reading. *Lubetkin and Tecton: Architecture and Social Commitment*. London: Arts Council of Great Britain, 1981.

Cohen, Arthur A. *Herbert Bayer: The Complete Work*. Cambridge, Mass.: MIT Press, 1984.

Cook, John W., and Heinrich Klotz. *Conversations with Architects*. New York: Praeger, 1973.

Cormier, Leslie Humm. "The Woods End Colony: An Architects' Refuge in America." M.A. thesis, Brown University, 1983.

———. "Walter Gropius, Emigré Architect: Works and Refuge, England and America in the 30s." Ph.D. diss., Brown University, 1986.

———. "Walter Gropius, Emigré Architect: The Persistence of Typeforms." *Arris, Journal of the Southeast Chapter of the Society of Architectural Historians* 4 (1993): 19–31.

Dearstyne, Howard. *Inside the Bauhaus*. Edited by David Spaeth. New York: Rizzoli, 1986.

Doumato, Lamia. *Marcel L. Breuer: Architect and Designer*. Monticello, Ill.: Vance Bibliographies, 1979.

Driller, Joachim. "Marcel Breuer: Das architektonische Frühwerk bis 1950." Phil. diss., Albert-Ludwigs-Universität, Freiburg, 1990.

———. *Marcel Breuer: Die Wohnhäuser, 1923–1973*. Stuttgart: Deutsche Verlags Anstalt, 1998.

———. *Breuer Houses*. Translated by Mark Cole and Jeremy Verrinder. London: Phaidon Press, 2000.

Droste, Magdalena. *Bauhaus 1919–1933*. Cologne: Taschen, 1990.

Droste, Magdalena, and Manfred Ludewig. *Marcel Breuer Design*. Cologne: Taschen, 1992.

Dunster, David. *Key Buildings of the Twentieth Century*. Vol. 1, *Houses, 1900–1944*. New York: Rizzoli, 1985.

"The Faceted, Molded Facade: Depth, Sun and Shadow [with statement by Breuer]." *Architectural Record*, April 1966, 171–86.

Ford, Edward R. *The Details of Modern Architecture*. Cambridge, Mass.: MIT Press, 1990.

Ford, James, and Katherine Morrow Ford. *The Modern House in America*. New York: Architectural Book Publishing Co., 1945.

Forgács, Eva. *The Bauhaus Idea and Bauhaus Politics*. Translated by John Batki. Budapest: Central European University Press, 1995.

Frampton, Kenneth. *Studies in Tectonic Culture: The Poetics of Construction in Nineteenth and Twentieth Century Architecture*. Cambridge, Mass.: MIT Press, 1995.

Franciscono, Marcel. *Walter Gropius and the Creation of the Bauhaus in Weimar*. Urbana: University of Illinois Press, 1971.

Das Frühe Bauhaus und Johannes Itten [exhibition catalogue]. Stuttgart: Hatje, 1994.

Gassner, Hubertus, ed. *Wechsel Wirkungen: Ungarische Avantgarde in der Weimarer Republik* [exhibition catalogue]. Marburg: Jonas Verlag, 1986.

Gatje, Robert F. *Marcel Breuer: A Memoir*. New York: Monacelli Press, 2000.

Giedion, Sigfried. "El arquitecto Marcel Breuer." *Arquitectura*, March 1932, 82–90.

———. *Walter Gropius: Work and Teamwork*. New York: Reinhold, 1954.

———. *Space, Time and Architecture*. 5th ed. Cambridge, Mass.: Harvard University Press, 1967.

Gould, Jeremy. *Modern Houses in Britain, 1919–1939*. London: Society of Architectural Historians of Great Britain, 1977.

"Great Teachers: Marcel Breuer." "A Teacher and Mentor" (Edward Larrabee Barnes and Harry Seidler interviewed by William Saunders); Philip Johnson, "An Artist in Architecture." *GSD News*, Harvard University Graduate School of Design, Fall 1995, 26–33.

Grohn, Christian. *Gustav Hassenpflug: Architektur, Design, Lehre, 1907–1977.* Düsseldorf: Manzona, 1985.

Gropius, Ise. Diaries. English translation. Microfilm 2393, Archives of American Art, Smithsonian Institution, Washington, D.C.

Gropius, Walter. *The New Architecture and the Bauhaus.* Translated by Morton Shand. 1935. Reprint. Cambridge, Mass: MIT Press, 1965.

Harmon, Robert B. *The Architecture of Marcel Lajos Breuer: A Selected Bibliography.* Monticello, Ill.: Vance Bibliographies, 1980.

Harris, Mary Emma. *The Arts at Black Mountain College* [exhibition catalogue]. Cambridge, Mass.: MIT Press, 1987.

Herbert, Gilbert. *The Dream of the Factory-Made House: Walter Gropius and Konrad Wachsmann.* Cambridge, Mass: MIT Press, 1986.

Herdeg, Klaus. *The Decorated Diagram: Harvard Architecture and the Failure of the Bauhaus Legacy.* Cambridge, Mass.: MIT Press, 1983.

Hines, Thomas S. *Richard Neutra and the Search for Modern Architecture.* New York: Oxford University Press, 1982.

Hitchcock, Henry-Russell. "Marcel Breuer and the American Tradition in Architecture" [essay and exhibition catalogue, Harvard University, Graduate School of Design, June–September 1938]. GSD, Cambridge, Mass., 1938. Mimeographed.

Hitchcock, Henry-Russell, and Catherine K. Bauer. *Modern Architecture in England* [exhibition catalogue]. New York: Museum of Modern Art, 1937.

Hitchcock, Henry-Russell, and Arthur Drexler, eds. *Built in USA: Post-War Architecture* [exhibition catalogue]. New York: Museum of Modern Art, 1952.

Hochman, Elaine S. *Bauhaus: Crucible of Modernism.* New York: Fromm International, 1997.

"The House in the Museum Garden, Marcel Breuer, Architect." *Museum of Modern Art Bulletin* 16 (1949).

Howarth, Shirley Reiff. *Marcel Breuer: Concrete and the Cross.* Muskegon, Mich.: Hackley Art Museum, 1978.

Huxtable, Ada Louise. *Kicked a Building Lately?* Berkeley: University of California Press, 1976.

Hyman, Isabelle. "The Marcel Breuer Papers and Michael Ventris: A Biographical Note." *Syracuse University Library Associates Courier* 24 (1989): 3–12.

———. "A Marcel Breuer House Project of 1938–1939." *Syracuse University Library Associates Courier* 27 (1992): 55–84.

———. "Marcel Breuer and the Franklin Delano Roosevelt Memorial." *Journal of the Society of Architectural Historians* 54 (1995): 2–14.

Isaacs, Reginald R. *Walter Gropius: Der Mensch und sein Werk.* 2 vols. Berlin: Mann Verlag, 1983, 1984.

———. *Gropius: An Illustrated Biography of the Creator of the Bauhaus.* London: Little, Brown, 1991.

Itten, Johannes. *Design and Form: The Basic Course at the Bauhaus.* Translated by John Maass. New York: Reinhold, 1964.

Izzo, Alberto, and Camillo Gubitozzi. *Marcel Breuer: Architettura, 1921–1980.* Florence: Centro Di, 1981.

Jackson, Anthony. "The Politics of Architecture: English Architecture, 1929–1951." *Journal of the Society of Architectural Historians* 24 (1965): 97–107.

———. *The Politics of Architecture: A History of Modern Architecture in Britain.* London: Architectural Press, 1970.

Jacobus, John. *Twentieth Century Architecture: The Middle Years, 1940–65.* New York: Praeger, 1966.

Jarzombek, Mark. "'Good-Life Modernism' and Beyond." *Cornell Journal of Architecture,* Fall 1990, 76–93.

Johansen, John. "Remembering Marcel Breuer." Taped interview with Constance L. Breuer, December 2, 1985. Transcription by Isabelle Hyman. Marcel Breuer Papers, Archives of American Art, Smithsonian Institution, Washington, D.C.

Jones, Cranston. "Marcel Breuer: The Bauhaus Continued." In *Architecture Today and Tomorrow,* 92–101. New York: McGraw-Hill, 1961.

———, ed. *Form Givers at Mid-Century* [exhibition catalogue]. New York, 1959.

———, ed. *Marcel Breuer: Buildings and Projects, 1921–1961.* New York: Praeger, 1962.

Jordy, William H. "The International Style in the 1930s." In "Modern Architecture Symposium (MAS 1964): The Decade 1929–1939." *Journal of the Society of Architectural Historians* 24 (1965): 10–14.

———. "The Aftermath of the Bauhaus in America: Gropius, Mies, and Breuer." In *The Intellectual Migration: Europe and America, 1930–1960,* edited by Donald Fleming and Bernard Bailyn, 485–543. Cambridge, Mass.: Harvard University Press, 1969.

———. "The Domestication of Modern: Ferry Cooperative Dormitory at Vassar College." In *American Buildings and Their Architects: The Impact of European Modernism in the Mid-Twentieth Century,* 165–219. Garden City, N.Y.: Doubleday, 1972.

Kentgens-Craig, Margret. *The Bauhaus and America: First Contacts, 1919–1936.* Cambridge, Mass.: MIT Press, 1999.

Kepes, Gyorgy. "Remembering Marcel Breuer." Taped interview with Constance L. Breuer, August 29, 1983. Transcription by Isabelle Hyman. Marcel Breuer Papers, Archives of American Art, Smithsonian Institution, Washington, D.C.

Kidder Smith, G. E. *The New Architecture of Europe.* Cleveland: World, 1961.

Kirsch, Karin. *The Weissenhofsiedlung: Experimental Housing for the Deutscher Werkbund.* 1927. Reprint. New York: Rizzoli, 1989.

Koeper, Frederick. *American Architecture.* Vol. 2, 1860–1976. Cambridge, Mass.: MIT Press, 1990.

Kornwolf, James D. "College of William and Mary Competition for a Festival Theatre and Fine Arts Center." In *Modernism in America, 1937–1941: A Catalogue and Exhibition of Four Architectural Competitions,* edited by James D. Kornwolf, 125–75. Williamsburg, Va.: College of William and Mary, 1985.

———. "Goucher College Competition for a Campus Development Plan and Library." In *Modernism in America, 1937–1941: A Catalogue and Exhibition of Four Architectural Competitions,* edited by James D. Kornwolf, 69–123. Williamsburg, Va.: College of William and Mary, 1985.

Kuh, Katharine. "Remembering Marcel Breuer." Taped interview with Constance L. Breuer, August 3, 1983. Transcription by Isabelle Hyman. Marcel Breuer Papers, Archives of American Art, Smithsonian Institution, Washington, D.C.

Kutschke, Christine. "Bauhausbauten der Dessauer Zeit: Ein Beitrag zu ihrer Dokumentation und Wertung." Diss., Hochschule für Architektur und Bauwesen, Weimar, 1981.

Lane, Barbara Miller. *Architecture and Politics in Germany, 1918–1945.* Cambridge, Mass.: Harvard University Press, 1968.

Loeffler, Jane C. "The Architecture of Diplomacy: Heyday of the United States Embassy-Building Program, 1954–1960." *Journal of the Society of Architectural Historians* 49 (1990): 251–78.

———. *The Architecture of Diplomacy: Building America's Embassies.* New York: Princeton Architectural Press, 1998.

"Marcel Breuer, Teacher and Architect." *House and Home,* May 1952, 102–15.

"Marcel Breuer: The Buildings of St. John's Abbey, Collegeville, Minnesota." *Design Quarterly* 53 (1961): 1–31.

"Marcel Breuer: American Houses," *2G: International Architecture Review* 17. Barcelona: Gustavo Gili, 2001.

"Marcel Breuer." In *Architects on Architecture: New Directions in America,* compiled by Paul Heyer, 264–67. New York: Walker, 1966.

Marcel Breuer: An Exhibition Organized by the Metropolitan Museum of Art [exhibition catalogue]. Foreword by Wolf von Eckhardt. Statement by Richard G. Stein. New York: Metropolitan Museum of Art, 1972.

"Marcel Breuer: Koerfer House (with Herbert Beckhard), Moscia, Tessin, Switzerland, 1963–67; Stillman House III (with Tician Papachristou), Litchfield, Connecticut, 1972–74; Gagarin House II (with Tician Papachristou), Litchfield, Connecticut, 1973–74." Edited and photographed by Yukio Futagawa. Text by Stanley Abercrombie. *GA (Global Architecture),* no. 43. Tokyo: Edita, 1977.

"Marcel Breuer: Koerfer House (with Herbert Beckhard), Moscia, Tessin, Switzerland, 1963–67; Stillman House III (with Tician Papachristou), Litchfield, Connecticut, 1972–74; Gagarin House II (with Tician Papachristou), Litchfield, Connecticut, 1973–74." Edited and photographed by Yukio Futagawa. Text by Stanley Abercrombie. *GA (Global Architecture) Detail,* no. 5. Tokyo: Edita, 1977.

Masello, David. *Architecture Without Rules: The Houses of Marcel Breuer and Herbert Beckhard.* New York: Norton, 1993.

"MBA: The Legacy of Marcel Breuer." *Process: Architecture,* no. 32. Tokyo: Process Architecture, 1982.

McCormick, Thomas J. "Wheaton College Competition for an Art Center." In *Modernism in America, 1937–1941: A Catalogue and Exhibition of Four Architectural Competitions,* edited by James D. Kornwolf, 23–67. Williamsburg, Va.: College of William and Mary, 1985.

Mezei, Otto. "Ungarische Architekten am Bauhaus." In *Wechsel Wirkungen: Ungarische Avantgarde in der Weimarer Republik,* edited by Hubertus Gassner, 339–87 [exhibition catalogue, Neue Galerie, Kassel, and Museum Bochum]. Marburg: Jonas Verlag, 1986.

Mills, Phyllida. "F.R.S. Yorke: The English Tradition." Third-year diss., Cambridge University, 1988.

Muller, Hannah B. "Bibliography." In *Marcel Breuer: Architect and Designer*, by Peter Blake, 123–26. New York: Museum of Modern Art, 1949.

Mumford, Lewis. *The Highway and the City*. New York: Harcourt, Brace & World, 1963.

Nash, Steven A., and Jörn Merkert, eds. *Naum Gabo: Sixty Years of Constructivism*. Munich: Prestel, 1985.

Naylor, Gillian. *The Bauhaus Reassessed*. New York: Dutton, 1985.

Nerdinger, Winfried. *Walter Gropius: The Architect Walter Gropius: Drawings, Prints, and Photographs from Busch-Reisinger Museum, Harvard University Art Museums, Cambridge, Mass., and from Bauhaus-Archiv Berlin* [exhibition catalogue]. Berlin: Mann Verlag, 1985.

———. *Busch-Reisinger Museum: The Walter Gropius Archive*. 3 vols. New York: Garland, 1990.

"Neue Bauten von Marcel Breuer." *Bauen und Wohnen*, September 1975, 361–68.

Neumann, Eckhard, ed. *Bauhaus and Bauhaus People*. New York: Van Nostrand Reinhold, 1970.

Newhouse, Victoria. *Wallace K. Harrison, Architect*. New York: Rizzoli, 1989.

Ockman, Joan, ed., with Edward Eigen. *Architecture Culture, 1943–68*. New York: Rizzoli, 1993.

"Oeuvres de Marcel Breuer, présentation de Pierre Gueguén." *Aujourd'hui*, September 1957, 48–75.

"Oeuvres récentes de Marcel Breuer, architecte." *L'Architecture d'aujourd'hui*, July 1948, 3–26.

Papachristou, Tician. *Marcel Breuer: New Buildings and Projects, 1960–70*. New York: Praeger, 1970.

Pearlman, Jill. "Joseph Hudnut's Other Modernism at the 'Harvard Bauhaus.'" *Journal of the Society of Architectural Historians* 56 (1997): 452–77.

Plunz, Richard. *A History of Housing in New York City: Dwelling Type and Social Change in the American Metropolis*. New York: Columbia University Press, 1990.

Pommer, Richard. "The Flat Roof: A Modernist Controversy in Germany." *Art Journal* 43 (1983): 158–69.

Pommer, Richard, and Christian F. Otto. *Weissenhof 1927 and the Modern Movement in Architecture*. Chicago: University of Chicago Press, 1991.

Portoghesi, Paolo. "Marcel Breuer." *Zodiac* 8 (1961): 54–57.

Powers, Alan. *In the Line of Development: FRS Yorke, E Rosenberg and CS Mardall to YRM, 1930–1992* [exhibition catalogue]. London: RIBA Heinz Gallery, 1992.

"Recent Work of Marcel Breuer." *Architectural Record*, January 1960, 125–38.

Richter, Annemarie. "Ein Wohnhaus, eingerichtet von Marcel Breuer." *Die Bauwelt*, August 21, 1981, 1380–81.

Roth, Alfred, ed. *The New Architecture*. 4th ed. Zürich: Girsberger, 1948.

Rowe, Colin. *The Mathematics of the Ideal Villa and Other Essays*. 4th ed. Cambridge, Mass.: MIT Press, 1985.

Rüegg, Arthur. *Die Doldertalhäuser, 1932–1936: Ein Hauptwerk des Neuen Bauens in Zürich: Zwei Mehrfamilienhäuser von Alfred & Emil Roth und Marcel Breuer* [exhibition catalogue]. Zürich, 1996.

Saint, Andrew. "The Battle of the Bauhaus." In *The Image of the Architect*, 115–37. New Haven, Conn: Yale University Press, 1983.

Sandler, Irving, and Amy Newman, eds. *Defining Modern Art: Selected Writings by Alfred Barr, Jr*. New York: Abrams, 1986.

Scheffler, Renate, ed. *Marcel Breuer: Ausstellung im Bauhaus-Archiv, Berlin-Charlottenburg* [exhibition catalogue]. Berlin: Bauhaus-Archiv, 1975.

Schlemmer, Tut, ed. *The Letters and Diaries of Oskar Schlemmer*. Translated by Krishna Winston. Evanston, Ill.: Northwestern University Press, 1990.

Scully, Vincent, Jr. "Doldrums in the Suburbs." In "Modern Architecture Symposium (MAS 1964): The Decade 1929–1939." *Journal of the Society of Architectural Historians* 24 (1965): 36–46. [Reprinted in *Perspecta 9/10: The Yale Architectural Journal* (1965): 281–90.]

———. *Modern Architecture*. Rev. ed. New York: Braziller, 1974.

———. *American Architecture and Urbanism*. New rev. ed. New York: Holt, 1988.

Seidler, Harry. "Remembering Marcel Breuer." Taped interview with Constance L. Breuer, January 2, 1985. Transcription by Isabelle Hyman. Marcel Breuer Papers, Archives of American Art, Smithsonian Institution, Washington, D.C.

———. "Marcel Breuer." In *Contemporary Architects*, 126–28. 2d ed. Chicago: St. James Press, 1987.

Smith, Elizabeth A. T., ed. *Blueprints for Modern Living: History and Legacy of the Case Study Houses*. Cambridge, Mass.: MIT Press, 1989.

Stern, Robert A. M., Gregory Gilmartin, and Thomas Mellins. *New York 1930: Architecture and Urbanism Between the Two World Wars*. New York: Rizzoli, 1987.

Stern, Robert A. M., Thomas Mellins, and David Fishman. *New York 1960: Architecture and Urbanism Between the Second World War and the Bicentennial*. New York: Monacelli Press, 1995.

Stillman, Rufus. "One Client's Point of View." In *Marcel Breuer: Sun and Shadow: The Philosophy of an Architect*, edited by Peter Blake, 147–48. New York: Dodd, Mead, 1955.

———. "A Client and His Architect." *Architectural Forum*, March 1972, 46–51.

Stoddard, Whitney S. *Adventure in Architecture: Building the New Saint John's*. New York: Longmans, Green, 1958.

Stoller, Ezra. *Whitney Museum of American Art*. Photographs by Ezra Stoller; new photography by Jeff Goldberg. Introduction by K. Michael Hays. New York: Princeton Architectural Press, 2000.

Toker, Franklin. *Pittsburgh: An Urban Portrait*: University Park: Pennsylvania State University Press, 1986.

"Trabajos de Marcel Breuer" [special double issue]. *Nuestra arquitectura*, September–November 1947.

"Travaux récents de Marcel Breuer." *L'Architecture d'aujourd'hui*, September 1952, 1–15.

UNESCO Headquarters in Paris. Preface by Luther H. Evans. Introduction by Françoise Choay. Photographs by Lucien Hervé. Stuttgart: Hatje, 1958.

von Moos, Stanislaus. *Alfred Roth: Architect of Continuity*. Zürich: Waser Verlag, 1985.

"Walter Gropius y Marcel Breuer, Arqs." *Nuestra arquitectura*, December 1946.

Whitford, Frank. *Bauhaus*. London: Thames and Hudson, 1986.

Wiedenhoeft, Ronald. *Berlin's Housing Revolution, German Reform in the 1920s*. Ann Arbor, Mich.: UMI Research Press, 1985.

Wilk, Christopher. *Marcel Breuer: Furniture and Interiors*. New York: Museum of Modern Art, 1981.

Wingler, Hans M. *Bauhaus*. Cambridge, Mass.: MIT Press, 1986.

Wright, David H. "The Architecture of Walter Gropius." Thesis for Honors, Harvard College, 1950.

Yorke, F. R. S. *The Modern House*. 4th ed. London: Architectural Press, [1934] 1943.

———. *The Modern House in England*. 2d ed., rev. London: Architectural Press, [1937] 1945.

Yorke, F. R. S., and E. F. Gibberd. *The Modern Flat*. 2d ed. London: Architectural Press, 1948.

Yorke, F. R. S., with Penelope Whiting. *The New Small House*. 3d ed., enlarged. London: Architectural Press, [1953] 1954.

Index

Page numbers in *italics* refer to illustrations.

Photograph Credits